THE PUZZLE OF LATIN AMERICAN ECONOMIC DEVELOPMENT

FOURTH EDITION

Patrice Franko

Colby College

ROWMAN & LITTLEFIELD

Lanham • Boulder • New York • London

Executive Editor: Susan McEachern
Editorial Assistant: Katelyn Turner
Senior Marketing Manager: Kim Lyons

Credits and acknowledgments for material borrowed from other sources, and reproduced with permission, appear on the appropriate page within the text.

Published by Rowman & Littlefield
An imprint of The Rowman & Littlefield Publishing Group, Inc.
4501 Forbes Boulevard, Suite 200, Lanham, Maryland 20706
www.rowman.com

Unit A, Whitacre Mews, 26–34 Stannary Street, London SE11 4AB, United Kingdom

British Library Cataloguing in Publication Information Available

Library of Congress Cataloging-in-Publication Data
Names: Franko, Patrice M., 1958– author.
Title: The puzzle of Latin American economic development / Patrice Franko, Colby College.
Description: Fourth Edition. | Lanham : Rowman & Littlefield Publishing Group, Inc., [2019] |
   Revised edition of the author's The puzzle of Latin American economic development,
   c2007. | Includes bibliographical references and index.
Identifiers: LCCN 2018017882 (print) | LCCN 2018019319 (ebook) | ISBN 9781442212183
   (ebook) | ISBN 9781442212169 (cloth : alk. paper) | ISBN 9781442212176 (pbk. : alk. paper)
Subjects: LCSH: Latin America—Economic conditions—1982– | Latin America—Economic
   policy.
Classification: LCC HC125 (ebook) | LCC HC125 .F682 2018 (print) | DDC 338.98—dc23
LC record available at https://lccn.loc.gov/2018017882

♾™ The paper used in this publication meets the minimum requirements of American
National Standard for Information Sciences—Permanence of Paper for Printed Library
Materials, ANSI/NISO Z39.48-1992.

Printed in the United States of America

CONTENTS

Tables, Figures, and Boxes

Tables

Boxes

PREFACE

This book explores the puzzle of economic development in Latin America. Despite a similar starting point in the late 1800s, why didn't Latin America continue to grow at the pace of North America? How can we understand the economic path it took? What are the contemporary opportunities and constraints? This is not a general textbook on development, but it tries to provide tools from development, trade, and finance for students to evaluate policy outcomes in Latin America. Without ignoring the historical antecedents, the central task of the text is an analysis of contemporary problems in Latin America. It is essentially the story of the character and contradictions of the new economic model in Latin America.

The text begins with the conceptual and historical foundations of development in Latin America. After briefly raising questions about the meaning of development and issues on the Latin America economic agenda, Chapters 1 and 2 set a broad historical context with a focus on inputs and outputs to characterize the period leading up to World War II. The question of primary product exports as an engine for growth is a central theme. Chapter 3 takes up import substitution industrialization, providing a theoretical and applied context for state-led development policy in the region. The debt crisis and macroeconomic stabilization attempts are treated in Chapters 4 and 5. Questions of credibility and confidence return as constraints on flexible adjustment in the 1990s.

The challenge of the first part of the text was compressing into five chapters readings that at one time constituted the bulk of a course on Latin American development. Beloved material is missing. But if a course on Latin America is to be one semester, we no longer have the luxury of spending two weeks on dependency theory and then another two unraveling structuralism and import substitution industrialization. Whereas I used to spend nearly a month debating the debt problem and hyperinflation, if we do so now there is less room for capital markets, trade integration, social policy, and the environment. Yet students need to understand the historical antecedents to appreciate the difficulties of contemporary policy. This book provides the background in a condensed approach, then moves on to the neoliberal model and contemporary challenges.

The second part of *The Puzzle of Latin American Economic Development* tackles the contemporary challenges of development in a globalized economy. After discussing new capital flows to the region in Chapter 6, we debate interventions by states to reduce vulnerability. In Chapter 7, after a review of trends in trade liberalization, the opportunities and obstacles to integration are discussed. Chapter 8 looks at the way in which globalization and marketization have affected competitiveness of industry and associated input markets for labor and technology, while Chapter 9 takes up the contemporary challenges of agriculture. The unifying theme of these chapters is the optimal degree of policy intervention in the face of opportunities and constraints presented by globalization of finance and production.

The final group of chapters addresses the social and environmental challenges that the region faces. After analysis of the problem of persistent poverty and inequality in the region in Chapter 10, Chapters 11 and 12 grapple with the problem and promise of health reform and education. Chapter 13 on the environment in Latin America reinforces the environmental dimension that has run through the text. Social, gender, and environmental issues pervade the text because they are intimately connected with problems of stabilization, liberalization, and competitiveness in the global arena. The chapters on poverty, education, health, and the environment focus the student on these issues not as the effects of other policies but as profound challenges that must be addressed for Latin America to meet the goals of sustainable, equitable development. This fourth edition attempts to capture the dynamic changes and challenges in a region confronting deep internal divides and stiff global competition. As social and environmental deficits have dominated the political agenda, heterogeneous patterns of economic policy responses have emerged. Students are asked to evaluate these changes in light of the historical pendulum swing of policies in the region.

This book is written for students with varying economics competencies. My students often ask whether they should take this course before or after taking trade, finance, and development. My experience is that the benefits accrue either way. If a student has strong theoretical tools, their depth of understanding of the problem of development in Latin America is more nuanced. However, engaging the difficult choices facing Latin American economic policymakers provides an applied context to acquire conceptual tools to solve the puzzle of strong, sustainable, and equitable growth in the region. For many students, the luxury of how to sequence economics courses is a moot point. They come to a course on the economics of Latin America after realizing, through a study-abroad program or through interdisciplinary course work, that an understanding of economic trends in the region is critical to a comprehension of contemporary politics and society. This may be their only course in Latin American economic development. This book therefore has no prerequisites other than an introductory sequence of economic principles. Throughout the text terms are explained, and box presentations provide illustrations and real-world examples. Words in bold type are defined in the glossary at the end of the book. This is designed to minimize the distraction to the better-equipped student eager to cut to the heart of the development issue.

Unlike many of the fine edited collections that provide a rich array of reading material, this text presents the fundamentals alongside the issues. An instructor may want to use a supplementary book, create a personalized reader from some of the terrific pieces cited in the endnotes of each chapter, or supplement readings with case studies. Writing this book has been a gratifying and humbling experience. There is so much engaging work on the problem of economic development in Latin America from which to draw. The explosion of papers on the Internet has made the fourth edition particularly challenging. It was, of course, always daunting to condense a thoughtful, provocative, and well-researched article or book into a two- or three-line summary. Notes have been left in throughout the text to indicate to even the beginning student that the theory of economic development in Latin America is the product of a mosaic of ideas and policies. The more advanced student should aggressively track down these readings, which provide the nuanced texture of the debate in the field that a single text could never hope to convey. My thanks to all upon whose work I liberally drew, and my apologies for any errors or omissions. I look forward to hearing from readers of this book to clarify pieces that I may have misrepresented or to point out works that I neglected to consult.

This book is the legacy of years of teaching bright and engaged students in my course on contemporary economic policy in Latin America at Colby College in Waterville, Maine. My students pushed me with their insightful questions (some of which I hope are answered herein) and motivated me with their enthusiasm for understanding Latin American economic development. My research assistants over the past years have been active collaborators in this book effort. Justin Ackerman, Leonardo Aguilar da Costa, Jeana Flahive, Katie Gagne, Erwin Godoy, Luisa Godoy, Justin Harvey, Mariah Hudnut, Meg Knight, Louise Langhoff-Roos Bigger, Jill Macaferri, Joanna Meronk, Gillian Morejon, Josh Schneider, Melanie Scott, Jacqueline Smith, and Mary Beth Thomson became data sleuths and Internet wizards; each has left an indelible imprint on the text. Former students now with professional lives of their own in the field— David Edelstein, Marina Netto Grande Campos, M. Holly Peirce, and Kristin Saucier—were valuable sources of information. Courtney Fry made substantial contributions to the revisions of the chapters on health, education, and poverty. Key contributors to the fourth edition include BriAnne Illich, Tara Brian, Jackie Boekelman, Julia Endicott, Alexa Busser, Laura Maloney, Hillary Sapanski, and Mari Zeta Valladolid; I don't think I would have pulled this off without the last push from RAs Kaiya Adam, Ella Jackson, Paula Jaramillo, and Chasity McFadden. I also have a debt to the students and faculty in the Georgia Tech Executive Masters Program in Logistics (EMIL) for providing the incentive (and inputs) to think more clearly about microeconomic foundations in Latin America. I am very grateful for all of my students' hard work and dedication. Of course, any mistakes are mine alone.

Each addition of this text has been shepherded by my wonderful and patient— and after twenty years now dear friend—Susan McEachern. Her assistants Rebeccah Schumaker and Katelyn Turner were incredibly kind and supportive in addressing my problems—even when my overflowing plate became their problem. I appreciate the efficient (and patient) work of Ramanan Sundararajan's Team at Integra Software Services.Pvt.Ltd. for the fast production turn-around. My stepchildren and their spouses, Dana and Erik Anderson and Josh and Eden Maisel, inspire me by their own commitments to teaching and policy work—and I love the enthusiasm of our five grandsons Conrad, Weber, Gus, Tyler, and Leo. My greatest debt of gratitude is to my husband, Sandy Maisel, who continues to believe in me; I am lucky to share both an academic and personal journey with such an amazing partner.

I dedicate this book to my mother—for all the times I cut short phone calls or disappeared into the writing black hole. She and my late father gave me (and my four siblings) the gift of education; she continues to provide the unconditional support that every person needs to access the valued life described by Amartya Sen.

ABBREVIATIONS

ADR	American depository receipts
ALBA	Bolivarian alternative of the Americas
ALMPs	active labor market policies
BECC	Border Environment Cooperation Commission
BEFIEX	Special Fiscal Benefits for Exports
BEMs	big emerging markets
BNDE	Brazil's State National Development Bank
BOP	Bottom of the Pyramid
CACM	Central American Common Market
CAFTA	Central American Free Trade Agreement
CAN	Community of Andean Nations
CCT	Conditional Cash Transfer
CD	Certificate of Deposit
CDM	Clean Development Mechanism
CEC	Commission for Environmental Cooperation
CELAC	Community of Latin American and Caribbean States
CERs	Certified Emissions Reductions
CET	common external tariff
CORFO	Corporacion de Fomento de la Produccion
CSR	corporate social responsibility
DRIFs	Demand-Driven Rural Investment Funds
ECLA	UN Economic Commission for Latin America
ECLAC	UN Economic Commission for Latin America and the Caribbean
EFA	Education for All
ESF	emergency social fund
EU	European Union
FDI	foreign direct investment
FIESP	Federation of Industries of São Paulo
FTA	free trade area
GCI	Global Competitiveness Index
GDP	gross domestic product
GEF	Global Environmental Facility
GERs	gross enrollment ratios
GMOs	genetically modified organisms
GNI	gross national income
GNP	gross national product
GVC	global value chain
HDI	Human Development Index
HFA	Health for All
HIPC	highly indebted poor country

HOI	human opportunity index
IADB	Inter-American Development Bank
ICTs	information and communications technologies
IFC	International Finance Corporation
ILO	International Labor Organization
IMF	International Monetary Fund
IMIP	Institute Materno-Infantil de Pernambuco
ISE	Index of Sustainable Enterprise
ISI	import substitution industrialization
ITIN	individual taxpayer identification number
LAC	Latin America and Caribbean
LACFTA	Latin American and Caribbean Free Trade Agreement
LIBOR	London Interbank Offer Rate
LPI	logistics performance index
MAC	marginal abatement cost
MBIs	market-based initiatives
MDGs	millennium development goals
MDI	Mesoamerican Development Institute
Mercosur	South American Common Market
MIT	middle income trap
MNCs	multinational corporations
MOH	Ministry of Health
MPI	Multidimensional Poverty Index
MSD	marginal social damage
NAFTA	North American Free Trade Agreement
NAFTA-TAA	NAFTA Transitional Adjustment Assistance
NCDs	noncommunicable diseases
NGO	nongovernmental organization
NTAEs	nontraditional agricultural exports
OAS	Organization of American States
ODA	official development assistance
OECD	Organization for Economic Cooperation and Development
PA	Pacific alliance
PAHO	Pan American Health Organization
PES	payments for environmental services
PHC	primary health care
PPP	purchasing power parity
PPPs	public private partnerships
PRGF	Poverty Reduction and Growth Facility
PRSPs	poverty-reduction strategy papers
PTAs	preferential trade agreements
R&D	research and development
ROSCAs	rotating savings and credit associations
S&D	special and differential
SEC	Security and Exchange Commission
SOEs	state-owned enterprises

SDGs	sustainable development goals
TFP	total factor productivity
TNCs	transnational corporations
UNCTAD	UN Conference on Trade and Development
URV	real unit of value
USAID	US Agency for International Development
USDA	US Department of Agriculture
USTR	US trade representative
WHO	World Health Organization
WTO	World Trade Organization

North and South America

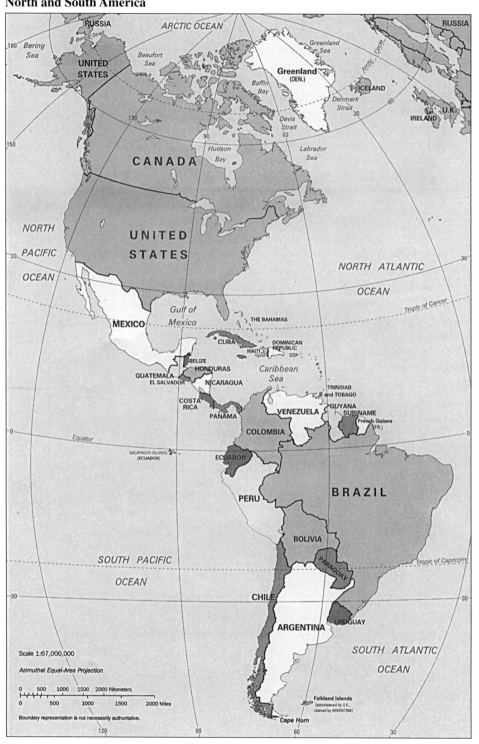

South America

Central America and the Caribbean

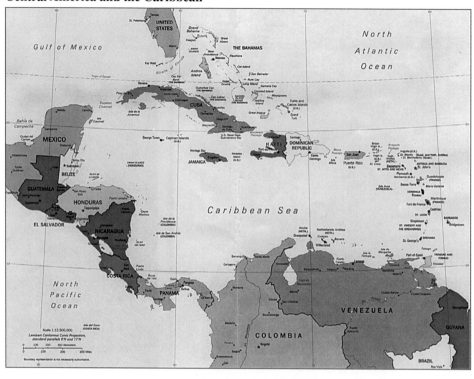

CHAPTER ONE

DEVELOPMENT IN LATIN AMERICA

Conceptualizing Economic Change in the Region

Latin America contains cities of splendor . . . *(iStock/UlrikeStein)*

. . . and pockets of poverty. *(Courtesy of David Mangurian and the Inter-American Development Bank)*

Latin Americans live in a complex economic system, simultaneously inhabiting the frontiers of finance and technology while also appearing hopelessly mired in a vicious circle of poverty. Consider the following stories.

Carlos Slim Helu is the richest man in Latin America and one of the wealthiest men in the world. Primarily invested in telephone industry, Carlos Slim's family runs Mexico's and the region's largest cellular phone company (América Movil), as well as the powerful Mexican Telmex communications conglomerate.[1] Said to have a Midas touch for selecting business acquisitions, he moved beyond the Mexican fixed line and mobile market to consolidate his telecom empire by snapping up companies throughout the region.[2] Slim has featured on the *Forbes* billionaires list since 1991; in 2017 with a net worth of US$54.5 billion he was Latin America's richest man and the sixth wealthiest on the globe.[3] Slim's greatest asset is diversification. His investment group Grupo Carso is a Mexican conglomerate that today ranges from North America to Tierra del Fuego; this company has three main divisions—industrial, retail, and infrastructure and construction—and includes a number of subsidiary companies such as the Sanborns retail chain, Sears' Mexican subsidiary, and Cigatam, the second-largest cigarette maker in the country.[4]

Although he made his money in markets, Carlos Slim has become a vocal critic of free trade as a development strategy for the region, arguing that the Mexicans have nothing to show for it and that the state must be a major investor in education and infrastructure.[5] Said to have one of Latin America's largest collections of Rodin sculptures, he is also the founder of Foundation of the

Historic Center of Mexico City, dedicated to restoring colonial buildings in Mexico City's historic city center.[6] Additionally, as part of his philanthropic work, he heads the Latin America Development Fund project. His Carlos Slim foundation has an endowment of US$3.5 billion that is dedicated to strengthening national identity and social integration through family-based values, the creation of better job opportunities, education, sports, hospitals, and promotion of the arts. Bill Clinton highlighted his philanthropy in noting that in Mexico "he has personally supported more than 165,000 young people in attending university, paid for numerous surgeries, provided equipment for rural schools and covered surety bonds for 50,000 people who were entitled to their freedom but could not afford."[7]

Brazilian soccer superstar Ronaldo reached the apex of soccer fame, becoming one of the highest-paid players in soccer history—and arguably one of the best footballers ever. After battling knee injuries for two-and-a-half years, his remarkable comeback led Brazil to its fifth World Cup title. The retired striker for the Spanish team Real Madrid signed deals with Nike and the Italian milk company Parmalat, as well as Brazil's number-one beer maker, Brahma, earning an estimated US$200–250 million in salary and endorsements. Born in a poor *favela*, or slum, in Rio de Janeiro, Ronaldo had to quit soccer as a young boy because he didn't have the bus fare. Sixteen of Ronaldo's relatives lived at the home where he grew up, and he slept on the sofa with his older brother. The home was simply furnished—with a freezer and a television as the only appliances. Ronaldo's appointment as a UNDP Goodwill Ambassador has, along with fellow player Zinédine Zidane, helped raise more than US$4 million to help eliminate poverty worldwide.[8]

Peruvians sign on to the Internet. *(Courtesy of David Mangurian and the Inter-American Development Bank)*

Indigenous populations are under threat throughout the region. In Peru, Amadeo García García is the last remaining member of his tribe to communicate in Taushiro. His fellow tribesmen were decimated by disease brought by contact. Hunter-gatherers and fisher people forced from the land, Amadeo's children, now city-dwellers, worry about their father's steady state of intoxication as he mourns the loss of his community.[9] In a little more than Amadeo's lifetime, at least thirty-seven languages have disappeared in Peru alone. In Nicaragua, both the Mayagna people and the native plants of Bosawas may last only two more decades. Due to the deforestation pressures from cattle and logging along with incursions of new roads with nonindigenous settlers, forest areas to support fruit harvesting and hunting have shrunk. Antonia Gámez, a sixty-six-year-old Mayagna chief, laments the loss of young tribal members leaving the forest in search of work—and fears the limited resources to support remaining populations. More than thirty thousand members of the Mayagna indigenous community are in danger of disappearing, despite efforts in the capital city of Managua to guarantee the rights of those living in this world heritage site.[10]

A small-scale farmer, Ricardo Sanhueza, lives less than 150 miles north of Santiago, Chile, in Petorca, a town struggling with water scarcity. Rural dwellers always had abundant access to water—until water rights were privatized in the 1980 Chilean constitution. With pressures from agriculture, the mining industry, and sanitation, traditional communities face off against mining corporations, agribusinesses, and forestry companies for access. These trade-offs will only be heightened by climate change. The dried dirt and stone of the Petorca River and the water trucks that arrive to hydrate the seventy thousand residents are sad symbols of the clash of markets and culture as casualties of development. Resident Monica Flores's memories of childhood play and community rituals have changed with the loss of water rights for the community.[11]

Karla was stabbed twice at fourteen when she refused to join a Honduran gang. The next day she left, silently slipping away without goodbyes to family or friends. As one of 58,000 youths who migrated from Central America in 2015 to escape violence, she walked endlessly through jagged conditions into Mexico. She was sexually assaulted by her guide—and then detained by Mexican authorities for two days before being deported and returned to a protective shelter in Tegucigalpa. As an internally displaced minor, she is hardly safe and likely to be locked into a life of poverty.[12]

Judith Yanira Viera, from El Salvador, is eighteen years old. For more than a year she worked in the Taiwanese-owned Mandarin International *maquiladora* factory in the San Marcos Free Trade Zone where she made shirts for the Gap, Eddie Bauer, and JCPenney. From Monday to Thursday her shift went from seven in the morning until nine at night. On Fridays she would work straight through the night, 7 a.m. through 4 a.m. She and her coworkers would sleep overnight on the factory floor. The following day, they would work from 7 a.m. until 5 p.m. Despite these very long hours, the most she ever earned was 750 *colones*, about US$43 per month.

Economically, Latin Americans range from the very wealthy Carlos Slim to the desperately poor Judith Yanira Viera. Resources available to create working lives may be the tobacco plant or the complex strands of the Internet. International markets—for clothing, fruit, or sports—may propel some to relative affluence, but there are always the masses left behind in Ronaldo's *favela*. Economic life in Latin America is multilayered, from traditional rural life to dirty assembly factories to ultramodern skyscrapers in cosmopolitan cities. Latin American economic **development** is a puzzle. This text invites you to make some sense of this complex problem. Questions that we will explore in trying to unravel this puzzle include the following:

- How do so many fragments of different levels of economic life join to form a coherent whole?
- With a far wider income range than industrial countries, with available technologies running from a simple shovel to a sophisticated financial machine, what kind of macroeconomic policies can address the complex microeconomic structure of Latin America?
- How does this multilayered economy interface with the world market?
- How have the pressures of globalization and the international market transformed the varied lives of Latin Americans?

As an introduction to the puzzle of Latin American economic development, this book attempts to clarify the complexity of economic life in Latin America. We will try to understand the potential that Carlos Slim has been able to tap, as well as the constraints keeping many farmers and factory workers in poverty.

A Conceptual Map: What Is Economic Development?

To understand the multilayered economic home of Karla and Carlos Slim, we first need to contextualize it within a theory of economic development. The objectives of this chapter are to explore briefly the meaning of development and to highlight selected characteristics of economic policy and performance in Latin America. In an ideal world, readers of this text would have taken courses in economic development, international trade, and international finance before embarking on a study of Latin American economics. However, many students come to understand the economic importance of Latin America late in their academic careers and simply don't have the time (or may even lack the interest,) to backtrack through this important theoretical framework. The economic component may be only a small part of your broader interest in the region. For you, this section raises some of the questions that would be grappled with over a longer period of time in a course on development theory. Students with a background in development theory are invited to draw on that broader conceptual framework and apply it to the case of Latin America to answer fundamental questions of this book: How can we understand the process of economic development in the Latin American region? How can we reconcile the different lives of Ronaldo and the Garcías within a single economic system?

Characteristics of Development

What characteristics do we normally associate with developed and less-developed countries? Try ranking the United States, Mexico, Brazil, Ecuador, Canada, and France on the following measures:

- Which countries have the highest rates of urbanization?
- Which countries have the highest per capita rates of **growth**?
- Which countries have the highest per capita carbon dioxide emissions?

The answers might surprise you. In Brazil, 90.6 percent of the population lives in urban areas; this is followed by 85.8 percent in France, 81.8 percent in the United States, 81.1 percent in Canada, 79.2 percent in Mexico, and 67.5 percent in Ecuador. Average growth of per capita gross domestic product (GDP) in 2015 ranged from 1.8 percent in the United States, 1.1 percent in Mexico, 0.9 percent in France, and 0.1 percent in Canada to include negative growth rates of 1.3 and 4.6 percent in Ecuador and Brazil, respectively. The United States has the dubious honor of leading the list of per capita carbon dioxide emissions at 16.3 metric tons in 2015, followed by Canada at 13.5, France at 5.0, Mexico at 3.9, Ecuador at 2.8, and Brazil at 2.5.

This short exercise raises a few questions. What do we mean by a developed (versus an underdeveloped) country? Are countries neatly classifiable? What is the diversity of economic experience within Latin America itself? How can we begin to think about a development strategy with relatively divergent conditions? You might want to open the most recent *World Development Report* or log onto the World Bank homepage at www.worldbank.org to look at some of the other data within the Latin America region and comparisons between Latin America and the rest of the world.

Table 1.1 summarizes some of these statistics. You may be surprised at the diversity you find. The per capita income in Chile, the wealthiest of Latin American countries, is more than seven times that of its Andean neighbor Bolivia, one of the poorest. Along with Uruguay, its poverty rate, measured by the international standard of US$3.20 a day, is quite low at 3.1 percent. Its national poverty line (like the United States, countries have national references) is higher at 11.7 percent, a rate much lower than the average of national poverty lines around 30 percent. Like Brazil, Mexico, and Guatemala, Chile's Gini coefficient (a measure of inequality) is very high at 47.7. Inflation is all over the map—ranging from 0.6 percent in Costa Rica to a virtually unmeasurable (and officially unreported) 500 percent plus in Venezuela. Both wealthier and poorer countries export minerals, hydrocarbons, beef, bananas, and soy—along with higher-technology autos, aircraft, and medical equipment. Large countries such as Brazil and Mexico have complex economies; others like Panama have smaller trading zones. Our text will investigate the historical and contemporary aspects of this diverse region, trying to make some sense of its complicated economic landscape. You are encouraged to go to the UN regional portal CEPALSTAT (http://estadisticas.cepal.org/cepalstat) or to the World Bank's trove of numbers (http://data.worldbank.org) to explore more variables that present the complexity of the region.

Clean, potable water is a step forward for the community, but its collection is part of the double duty of work that women perform in the developing world. *(Courtesy of the Inter-American Development Bank)*

Table 1.1. Basic Economic Indicators for Latin America

Country Name	GDP per Capita (constant 2010 US$)		GINI	Poverty Headcount Ratio at US$3.20/day (2011 PPP*) (% of population)		Poverty (% at National Lines)	Inflation (%)	Major Exports
	Around 1990	2016 or Closest	2016 or Closest	Around 1990	2016 or Closest	2016 or Closest	2016	
Argentina	6,173.68	10,153.99	42.7	4.4	—	—	42.8	Soya beans, maize, vegetable oil residues, trucks, cars
Bolivia	1,323.78	2,457.62	45.8	—	12.9	38.6	3.5	Hydrocarbons, zinc, silver, platinum, vegetable oil residues
Brazil	8,391.19	10,826.27	51.3	36.3	9.3	8.7	6.7	Soya beans, iron ore and concentrates, crude petroleum, poultry, raw sugar, aircraft
Chile	5,851.48	15,019.63	47.7	16.3	3.1	11.7	4.1	Copper, fish, sulfate wood pulp
Colombia	4,152.19	7,525.86	51.1	21.0	13.1	27.8	5.8	Petroleum, coal, coffee, cut flowers
Costa Rica	4,847.60	9,714.10	48.2	21.8	4.2	21.7	0.6	Medical instruments and orthopedics, bananas, tropical fruits
Cuba	4,394.02	6,444.98	—	—	—	—	4.5	Medicaments, cigars and cheroots, crustacea and mollusks
Dominican Republic	2,784.58	6,909.13	44.9	60.2	6.9	32.4	1.6	Cigars, bananas, jewelry, clothing, scrap metals, beverages
Ecuador	3,675.45	5,191.10	46.5	—	11.8	23.3	2.4	Petroleum, bananas, crustacea and mollusks, fish, flowers
El Salvador	2,083.98	3,802.86	40.8	32.5	9.8	34.9	-0.9	Knitted garments, plastic, raw sugar

Country								Main exports
Guatemala	2,131.08	3,100.21	48.7	56.2	25.3	59.3	4.2	Raw sugar, bananas, coffee, knitted garments
Guyana	1,521.97	3,783.54	—	60.4	—	—	0.8	Sugar, bauxite, rice, gold
Honduras	1,587.46	2,137.81	50.1	58.3	34.8	63.8	2.9	Coffee, insulated wire and cable, crustacea and mollusks, palm oil, bananas
Mexico	7,044.82	9,707.91	48.2	25.2	11.8	53.2	2.8	Cars, trucks and parts, crude petroleum, statistical machines
Nicaragua	1,164.19	1,946.37	46.6	56.6	13.8	29.6	3.1	Insulated wire and cable, knitted undergarments, meat of bovine animals, coffee, knitted outer garments
Panama	3,801.02	10,982.37	51.0	34.4	7.0	23.0	1.0	Bananas, fish, crustacea and mollusks, sawlogs and veneer logs, meat and fish meal
Paraguay	2,634.00	3,925.56	48.0	—	7.4	26.6	3.8	Electric energy, Soya beans, meat, vegetable and soya oil residues
Peru	2,880.89	6,089.40	44.3	—	9.3	21.8	3.6	Ores and concentrates of copper, zinc, and lead, refined copper, meat and fish meal
Suriname	6,314.87	8,108.24	—	—	—	—	52.4	Alumina, gold, crude oil, lumber, shrimp and fish, rice, bananas
Uruguay	6,903.53	14,010.00	41.7	2.3	1.4	9.7	9.9	Meat, soya beans, logs, dairy, rice
Venezuela, RB	11,383.36	13,708.98	42.5	14.7	—	33.1		Crude petroleum, methyl alcohol, iron ore and concentrates, sponge iron or steel, nitrogenous fertilizers

Source: Data from World Development Indicators database.
*PPP Purchasing Power Parity dollars are adjusted for inflation.

What do we mean by development? When we think about the challenges of development and underdevelopment in Latin America, what do we really mean? Are cellphones and toilets the goal of development? How does "promoting development" translate into something concrete for the policymaker to target? US president Harry S. Truman, in his inauguration speech in January 1949, envisioned a bold new program, based on "the concepts of democratic fair-dealing," to make the "benefits of our scientific and industrial progress available for the improvement and growth of underdeveloped areas."[13] Although the word "underdeveloped" had been introduced in 1942 by Wilfred Benson, a member of the secretariat of the International Labour Organization, development economists such as Paul Rosenstein-Rodan spoke of "economically backward areas," and Arthur Lewis characterized the emerging challenge as the gap between rich and poor countries throughout the 1940s.[14] Truman popularized the term "underdevelopment" but did not clearly define it. Since Truman, the goal of development has been to undo the hardships of underdevelopment—without a clear statement of the positive objective. What does it mean to be developed? With the advent of the Cold War, the world was divided into industrial market economies, the communist or "second" world, and finally the rest of the globe or the "third" world. These nations were once again the residual—what was left over when the rest of the counting was done. Since the collapse of the Berlin Wall, the second world has euphemistically been referred to as "transitional economies or emerging markets." What exactly are they transitioning toward? What is a usable definition of the goal of "development"?

In common language, development describes a process in which the potential of an organism is released to achieve its mature form. Dictionary definitions point to growth or expansion to bring about a more advanced state. When we think of the development of a tree or an animal, we have a clear idea of the appearance of the mature, advanced form. In economics we find ourselves in a bit of trouble. We can measure degrees of industrialization or access to a wider array of consumer products, but things become murky when we try to associate the terms "modern," "mature," and "developed" with societies having well-articulated economic infrastructures. Given the long list of ills associated with modern society, we should be clear in our understanding that more sophisticated production techniques and a wider range of electronic toys do not necessarily imply a better or happier society. In addition, we don't know which members of society have access to the gains of economic growth. More industrialization—particularly with the associated environmental costs—does not necessarily mean an increase in the well-being of citizens.

How then should we think about development? Is a developed country simply the opposite of a poor country? Is a developing country a rich country in the making? Box 1.1 presents the thoughts of development economists and practitioners on defining the term. Generally, they find it easier to agree on what constitutes the alleviation of poverty and meeting the basic needs of a population than on what represents the achievement of wealth or the satisfaction of material wants. This text looks at development as a process of meeting the basic human needs of the population, enhancing options for the allocation of economic resources both today and in the future and increasing the choices citizens have in their daily lives. It pays particular attention to how much is produced and for whom, and it

Lack of access to adequate housing leaves millions in misery. *(Courtesy of David Mangurian and the Inter-American Development Bank)*

addresses the environmental sustainability of production for future generations. One measure to promote progress on development was the adoption of the millennium development goals or MDGs. These goals were adopted at the United Nations Millennium Summit in 2000 and broadly sought to reduce global poverty by 2015 as well as improve health and educational outcomes among the world's least advantaged people. Latin America was the only region to achieve the first of the MDGs, halving extreme poverty from 12 to 6 percent. An extraordinary 72 million people escaped poverty and 50 million joined the middle class. The majority of countries have access to safe drinking water—but no country has met the goal of maternal health. The development agenda, however, is not complete.

BOX 1.1.   DEVELOPMENT, UNDERDEVELOPMENT, AND GROWTH: AN EVOLUTION OF DEFINITIONS

WEBSTER'S DICTIONARY

"The act, process, or result of developing; the state of being developed; a gradual unfolding by which something is developed, a gradual advance or growth through progressive changes."

W. ARTHUR LEWIS (1954)

"The central fact of economic development is rapid capital accumulation, including knowledge and skills with capital."[a]

CELSO FURTADO (1964)

"Economic development, being fundamentally a process of incorporating and diffusing new techniques, implies changes of a structural nature in both the systems of production and distribution of income. The way in which these changes take place depends, to a large extent, on the degree of flexibility of the institutional framework within which the economy operates."[b]

P. BAUER AND B. YAMEY (1967)

"The widening of the range of alternatives open to people as consumers and producers."[c]

B. HIGGINS (1968)

"A discernible rise in total and in per capita income, widely diffused throughout occupational and income groups, continuing for at least two generations and becoming cumulative."[d]

THEOTONIO DOS SANTOS (1968)

"Development means advancement towards a certain well-defined general objective which corresponds to the specific condition of man and society or can be found in the most advanced societies of the modern world. The model is variously known as modern society, mass society and so on."[e]

DENIS GOULET (1971)

"Underdevelopment is shocking: the squalor, disease, unnecessary deaths, and hopelessness of it all! No man understands if underdevelopment remains for him a mere

continued

statistic reflecting low income, poor housing, premature mortality, or underdevelopment. The most empathetic observer can speak objectively about underdevelopment only after undergoing, personally or vicariously, the 'shock of underdevelopment.'"[f]

DUDLEY SEERS (1972)

"The questions to ask about a country's development are therefore: what has been happening to poverty? What has been happening to unemployment? What has been happening to inequality? If all three of these have declined from high levels, then beyond doubt this has been a period of development for the country concerned."[g]

CHARLES K. WILBER (1973)

"Development itself is simply a means to the human ascent."[h]

SIMON KUZNETS (1973)

"A country's economic growth may be defined as a long-term rise in capacity to supply increasingly diverse economic goods to its population, this growing capacity based on advancing technology and the institutional and ideological adjustments that it demands."[i]

JAMES J. LAMB (1973)

"If there is to be a possibility of choosing a human path so that all human beings may become the active subjects of their own history, it must begin at the level of new analysis. Development should be a struggle to create criteria, goals, and means for self-liberation from misery, inequity, and dependency in all forms. Crucially, it should be the process a people choose which heals them from historical trauma, and enables them to achieve a newness on their own terms."[j]

PAUL STREETEN (1979)

"A basic-needs approach to development starts with the objective of providing the opportunities for the full physical, mental, and social development of the human personality and then derives ways of achieving this objective."[k]

PETER J. A. HENRIOT (1981)

"'Underdevelopment' is seen as the flip side of the coin of 'development.' It refers to the process whereby a country, characterized by subsistence agriculture and domestic production, progressively becomes integrated as a dependency into the world market through patterns of trade and/or investment."[l]

ORTHODOX PARADIGM (1980s)

"The view of the historical process contained in the orthodox paradigm is clear from this characterization: it is one in which developing societies move toward ever greater availability of goods and services for their citizens."[m]

WORLD COMMISSION ON ENVIRONMENT AND DEVELOPMENT (1987)

"Humanity has the ability to make development sustainable—to ensure that it meets the needs of the present without compromising the ability of future generations to meet their own needs. . . . [S]ustainable development is not a fixed state of harmony, but rather a process of change in which the exploitation of resources, the directions of investment, the

continued

continued

orientation of technological development, and institutional change are made consistent with future as well as present needs."[n]

GERALD M. MEIER (1995)

"Although requiring careful interpretation, perhaps the definition that would now gain widest approval is one that defines economic development as the process whereby the real per capita income of a country increases over a long period of time—subject to the stipulations that the number of people below an 'absolute poverty line' does not increase, and that the distribution of income does not become more unequal."[o]

AMARTYA SEN (1998)

"It is not hard to see why the concept of development is so essential in general. Economic problems do, of course, involve logistics issues, and a lot of it is undoubtedly 'engineering' of one kind or another. On the other hand, the success of all this has to be judged ultimately in terms of what it does to lives of human beings. The enhancement of living conditions must clearly be an essential—if not the essential—object of the entire economic exercise and that enhancement is an integral part of the concept of development."[p]

JOSEPH E. STIGLITZ (1998)

"It used to be that development was seen as simply increasing GDP. Today we have a broader set of objectives, including democratic development, egalitarian development, sustainable development, and higher living standards."[q]

NANCY BIRDSALL (2005)

"Global inequality poses enormous challenges for managing and civilizing globalization so that it works for the developing world. Monetary inequality matters to people. Moreover, in developing countries, where markets and politics are by definition far-from-perfect, inequality is likely to be destructive, reducing prospects for growth, poverty reduction, and good government. Globalization is too often asymmetric, i.e. benefiting the rich more than the poor, both within and across countries. The world is not 'flat,' as *New York Times* columnist Thomas Friedman has suggested. Rather, what appears to be a level playing field to people on the surface is actually a field of craters in which other people are stuck—and hard to see."[r]

---

a. W. Arthur Lewis, "Economic Development with Unlimited Supplies of Labour," *Manchester School* 22(2) (1954). Reprinted in A. N. Agarwala and S. P. Singh, eds., *The Economics of Underdevelopment* (New York: Oxford University Press, 1963).

b. Celso Furtado, *Development and Underdevelopment*, trans. Ricardo W. de Aguiar and Eric Charles Drysdale (Berkeley: University of California Press, 1965), 47. Originally published as *Dialectica do desenvolvimento, Rio de Janeiro* (Berkeley: University of California Press, 1964).

c. Peter Bauer and Basil Yamey, *The Economics of Underdeveloped Countries* (New York: Cambridge University Press, 1967), 151.

d. Benjamin Higgins, *Economic Development: Problems, Principles, and Policies* (New York: Norton, 1968), 148.

e. Theotônio Dos Santos, "La crisis de la teoría del desarollo y las relaciones de dependencia en América Latina," *Boletin de CESO* 3 (1968). This article appeared in English as "The Crisis of

continued

Development Theory and the Problem of Dependence in Latin America" in *Underdevelopment and Development*, ed. H. Bernstein (Harmondsworth, UK: Penguin, 1973).

f. Denis Goulet, *The Cruel Choice: A New Concept in the Theory of Development* (New York: Atheneum, 1971), 23.

g. Dudley Seers, "What Are We Trying to Measure?" *Journal of Development Studies* (April 1972).

h. Charles K. Wilber, *The Political Economy of Development and Underdevelopment* (New York: Random House, 1973), 355.

i. Simon Kuznets, "Modern Economic Growth: Findings and Reflections," *American Economic Review* 63(3) (June 1973): 247.

j. Kenneth P. Jameson and Charles K. Wilber, *Directions in Economic Development* (Notre Dame, IN: University of Notre Dame Press, 1979), 38. Originally in James J. Lamb, "The Third World and the Development Debate," *IDOC-North America* (January–February 1973): 20.

k. Paul Streeten, "A Basic Needs Approach to Economic Development," in Jameson and Wilber, *Directions*, 73.

l. Peter J. Henriot, "Development Alternatives: Problems, Strategies, Values," in *The Political Economy of Development and Underdevelopment*, 2nd ed., ed. Charles K. Wilber (New York: Random House, 1979), 11.

m. Jameson and Wilber, *Directions*, 7.

n. World Commission on Environment and Development, *Our Common Future* (Oxford: Oxford University Press, 1987), 8–9.

o. Gerald M. Meier, *Leading Issues in Economic Development*, 6th ed. (Oxford: Oxford University Press, 1995), 7.

p. Amartya Sen, "The Concept of Development," in *Handbook of Development Economics*, Vol. 1 (Amsterdam: North-Holland, 1988).

q. Boris Pleskovic and Joseph E. Stiglitz, eds., *Annual World Bank Conference on Development Economics, 1997* (Washington, DC: World Bank, 1998), 19.

r. Nancy Birdsall, President, Center for Global Development, email correspondence, November 2005, based on concepts in her 2005 Annual WIDER Lecture *Rising Inequality in the New Global Economy* at the United Nations University's World Institute for Development Economics Helsinki, October 2005.

Global Comparisons

Although Latin America performs better than many of the poorest countries in the world, much work remains to be done to bring the ability to choose a valued life to the majority of its citizens. We can see in box 1.2 that, with the exception of maternal health, the region made strong progress in achieving the millennium development goals. With a dramatic shift in the income pyramid that pulled the poor upward into the middle class, other quality of life indicators were also improved (table 1.2).

The international focus has now shifted to the **sustainable development** goals (SDGs), an agenda agreed to by 193 heads of state to guide policy toward the year 2030. They address aspects of multidimensional well-being and promote resilience in socio-economic systems. The achievement of the SDGs in Latin America will foster the continued transformation of the region's economic pyramid, promoting social protection through the lifecycle. For the poor, the SDGs create benchmarks in health, housing, and basic services and encourage financial

BOX 1.2. THE MILLENNIUM DEVELOPMENT GOALS REPORT, 2015 LATIN AMERICA

GOAL 1: ERADICATE EXTREME HUNGER AND POVERTY

Reaching the target of halving the extreme poverty rate, with the proportion of people living on less than US$1.25 a day falling from 13 percent in 1990 to 4 percent in 2015. However, disparities remain large among the two subregions. The extreme poverty rate in the Caribbean decreased from 33 to 22 percent between 1990 and 2015, and from 12 to 4 percent in Latin America.

The region has also reached the hunger reduction target. The proportion of under-nourished people in the total population has decreased from 15 percent in 1990–1992 to 6 percent in 2014–2016. However, in 2014–2016, the prevalence of undernourishment in Latin America is estimated to be less than 5 percent, while in the Caribbean it is 20 percent.

GOAL 2: ACHIEVE UNIVERSAL PRIMARY EDUCATION

Impressive strides in expanding access to primary education, with the adjusted net enrol-ment rate growing from 87 percent in 1990 to 94 percent in 2015. The region has also achieved parity in primary education between boys and girls.

GOAL 3: PROMOTE GENDER EQUALITY AND EMPOWER WOMEN

The MDG Report 2015 finds that the region has the highest representation of women in parliaments (27 percent in 2015) among all developing regions and an even higher than average share compared to developed regions. The proportion of seats held by women in single or lower houses of national parliament increased from 15 percent in 2000 to 27 percent in 2015, higher than the average share of 26 percent in devel-oped regions in 2015. Women in Latin America and the Caribbean participate in paid employment nearly as much as men, with women holding forty-five out of every one hundred wage-earning jobs in the non-agricultural sector in 2015, the highest among all developing regions.

GOAL 4: REDUCE CHILD MORTALITY

The region reached the target of a two-thirds reduction in the under-five mortality rate with a reduction in its under-five mortality rate by 69 percent between 1990 and 2015. The mortality rate for children under five dropped from 54 deaths per 1,000 live births in 1990 to 17 in 2015.

GOAL 5: IMPROVE MATERNAL HEALTH

Maternal mortality remains high in the region. 2013 data indicate that there were 190 maternal deaths per 100,000 live births in the Caribbean compared to 77 in Latin America.

The proportion of pregnant women in the region with access to at least four antenatal care visits increased from 75 percent in 1990 to 97 percent, making it one of the highest among all developing regions.

The region has made slow progress towards reducing adolescent childbearing, with a high adolescent birth rate of 73 births per 1,000 girls in 2015.

GOAL 6: COMBAT HIV/AIDS, MALARIA AND OTHER DISEASES

Although the Caribbean is the region with the sharpest decline in the number of people newly infected with HIV, with the new infections dropping by 56 percent between 2000 and 2015,

continued

Latin America exhibited a slow decline in the number of new infections. For those living with HIV, 44 percent receive antiretrovirals, the highest rate among developing regions.

GOAL 7: ENSURE ENVIRONMENTAL SUSTAINABILITY

The region is also very close to reaching the target of halving the number of people without basic sanitation. The proportion of the population using an improved sanitation facility increased from 67 to 83 percent between 1990 and 2015.

GOAL 8: DEVELOP A GLOBAL PARTNERSHIP FOR DEVELOPMENT

(Largely for Developed Countries)

Source: www.un.org/millenniumgoals/bkgd.shtml

inclusion. For those in the vulnerable and middle classes, SDGs aim to protect past regional achievements, particularly by addressing precarious informal and low-productivity jobs through improvements in labor quality. The SDGs recognize the importance of developing strong cognitive and socio-emotional skills at an early age, coordinating the labor market with education and training throughout the lifecycle. They encourage sustainability of economic and environmental systems, deepening capacities of the care economy from infancy through the end of life. Citizen participation with an aim of creating social cohesion will require intersectoral coordination among ministries to shepherd a development transition that exits poverty and opens a set of citizenship rights without exclusion based on factors of income, gender, ethnic, racial, or sexual identity. This text will help you understanding the obstacles and opportunities in the journey toward these new development horizons.[15]

Growth versus Development

From the definitions in box 1.1, we can see that most economists agree: development is far more than economic growth. It is useful, however, to clarify the difference between the two terms. Joseph Schumpeter distinguishes growth as a process of gradual change, with all quantities—such as wealth, savings, and population—increasing slowly and continuously; development is characterized as rapidly propelled by innovations.[16] Robert Lucas defines *growth* as the increase of income proportional to the increase of population and *development* as the process whereby income increases more rapidly than population. In other words, growth does not presuppose technical change; development does.[17] For both Schumpeter and Lucas—economists of very different dispositions—development centrally engages the question of how **technological change** takes place in an economy. A key element in development is the management of technological change or how technology is used to transform the economic structure. This presupposes that technology is in scarce supply and that its use has a price.

Table I.2. Indicators of Standards of Living

	Residential Energy Use per Capita		Human Resources per 10,000 Pop			Personal Computers	Internet Users 2003	Mobile Phones
	Kg Oil Equivalent per Person 2001	% of 2001 US Value	Physicians c. 2001	Nurses c. 2001	Dentists c. 2001	(per 1,000 people)		
Argentina	239.7	27.01	32.1	3.8	9.3	82.0	112	178
Bolivia	75.9	8.55	10.2	12.3	1.3	22.8	32	152
Brazil	116.4	13.12	7.6	3.2	1.2	74.8	82	264
Canada	963	108.51	20.6	5.2	9.5	487.0	513	417
Chile	314.9	35.48	11.5	6.6	4.4	119.3	272	511
Colombia	113.8	12.82	12.7	6.1	7.8	49.3	53	141
Costa Rica	118.9	13.40	11.5	7.1	3.3	197.2	193	111
Cuba	78	8.79	60.4	71.4	4.9	31.8	11	2
Ecuador	105.7	11.91	16.4	5.3	1.7	31.1	46	189
El Salvador	209.3	23.58	12.6	8.1	5.5	25.2	84	176
Guatemala	300.1	33.81	9.5	3.6	1.6	14.4	33	131
Honduras	192	21.63	8.7	3.2	2.2	13.6	25	49
Mexico	172.5	19.44	15.6	10.8	1	82.0	118	291
Nicaragua	232.3	26.17	16.4	1.4	2.9	27.9	17	85
Panama	184.6	20.80	13.8	11.2	2.8	38.3	62	268
Paraguay	239.1	26.94	5.6	2.2	0.8	34.6	20	299
Peru	138	15.55	11.7	8	1.1	43.0	104	106
United States	887.5	100.00	39	8.7	12.4	658.9	551	543
Uruguay	211.5	23.83	20	7.9	5.7	110.1	119	193
Venezuela	147.3	16.60				60.9	60	273

Source: World Resources Institute, Earthtrends online database, www.earthtrends.wri.org, derived from International Energy Agency data, 2004; Population Division of the Department of Economic and Social Affairs of the United Nations Secretariat, 2004; and World Bank, World Development Indicators 2005 (Washington, DC: World Bank, 2005).

In this sense, policy matters very much. Economic development is not simply driven by factor endowments or the quantity of resources but by how land, labor, and capital are combined in new ways to increase productivity and the choices available to a population.

New technologies require new ways of doing things. The leap from feudalism to early capitalism was propelled by technological changes—the introduction of the horse and plow as well as the three-field crop rotation system—that made an agricultural surplus possible. But like the transition into early capitalism, the contemporary process can be politically and socially tumultuous. Development policy can be viewed as the implementation of economic tools when political and social structures as well as economic institutions are rapidly changing. In contrast to the thrust of standard economic theory, where in principle we begin with the *ceteris paribus* condition, or "all else held constant," development policy is harder to carry out consistently due to simultaneous changes in a number of arenas. An economic policymaker in an industrialized country may be able to rely on a bit of automatic pilot under stable conditions; in the developing world, navigation is far more demanding with a variety of new challenges at each turn.

This text chronicles the development journey of Latin America. We begin by trying to understand the attempts of Latin American policymakers to promote growth and development in the region. Chapter 2 focuses on the engine of trade and Latin America's export performance in the late colonial and early independence periods. Chapter 3 looks at a growth strategy widely adopted in the region from roughly the 1950s through the 1980s: import substitution industrialization. We can see through both approaches that the strategies centered largely on the problem of growth and made less progress in the arena of social and environmental change. In Chapters 4 and 5 we discuss two unintended results of the development strategies adopted: high rates of inflation and increased vulnerability to macroeconomic shocks. The policy response to economic disequilibrium was to step back and rely more on markets and less on state intervention in the economy. In more open markets for finance and goods, Chapters 6 and 7 look at implications for international capital flows and trade. How industry and agriculture have fared under a more open, internationalized economic model is taken up in Chapters 8 and 9. Although policies that transformed the structure of Latin American economies from closed to open markets have been largely successful in macroeconomic terms, the rest of our book explores some of the deficits in human and social development hindering sustainable growth.

Basic Human Needs versus Growth as Measures of Development

In addition to thinking about how economies change, we must raise the question of growth: Who benefits from new economic opportunities? Technological change—new combinations of capital and labor to produce a surplus—does not address the general well-being of society. Does the process of economic development help the rich or the poor? A modest goal of development might be for a developed nation to meet the basic human needs of its population. Paul Streeten defines enhancing basic human needs as improving income-earning opportunities for the poor, reforming public services that reach the poor, augmenting the flow of goods and services to meet the needs of all members of the household, and increasing the participation of the poor in the policy-making arena.[18] Streeten goes on to suggest why growth itself is not a good measure of economic development. Rather than generating the predicted theoretical results that growth would trickle down to the poor or that governments would extend benefits through progressive taxation or social services, Streeten argues that growth has been accompanied by increasing **dualism**. That is, when countries grow as measured by annual GDP growth rates, the rich often become richer and the poor more destitute in the process of change. We see the expansion of the modern, capitalist sector alongside a traditional, backward sector—two distinctly different worlds growing side by side. Dualism—the simultaneous existence of modern and traditional economies—complicates the policymaker's task. More importantly, if an economy magnetized by growth neglects the plight of the poor, people without assets are marginalized by the growth process and made even worse off. Those without land, capital, or education, such as the poor peasant in feudal times who lost access to the agricultural commons, can be pushed into the margins of society. Without access to resources, the poor can become poorer. Their attempts to scrape together a subsistence existence often pressure the environment as desperation drives people to use up land or forests or dump open sewage or waste today without thought of tomorrow—for tomorrow holds little promise when they struggle with hunger or sickness. We will see in our concluding chapters that most Latin American economies are shaped by a dichotomy between modern, globalized sectors and low-productivity informal activity.

For development economists such as Michael Todaro, growth must be accompanied by a change in the economic and social rules of the game. Todaro defines development, in addition to raising people's living levels, as "creating conditions conducive to the growth of people's self-esteem through the establishment of social, political, and economic systems and institutions that promote human dignity and respect and increasing people's freedom by enlarging the range of their choice variables."[19] But this is a difficult task. As we will see in Chapters 10 through 12, the social deficit in Latin America must be addressed to promote an equitable and sustainable development policy. As we investigate poverty in Chapter 10, we will analyze ways of measuring human development including the Human Development Index (HDI), which is a composite index comprising three indicators: life expectancy (representing a long and healthy life), educational attainment (representing knowledge), and real inflation-adjusted GDP (representing a decent standard of living). Poverty and the associated social challenges of promoting education and health are discussed in Chapters 11 and 12. Underlying both are the impediments to high productivity with social deficits in health and education.

The United Nations, in its *Human Development Report*, suggests that a human development paradigm incorporates four elements: productivity, **equity**, sustainability, and **empowerment**. People must be enabled to increase their own productivity and participate as fully in the economy as their own talents allow. Gender barriers to achievement must be confronted. Economic growth is therefore a subset of human development models. To encourage fair outcomes, people must have access to equal opportunities. Economic and environmental sustainability is enhanced when all forms of capital—physical, human, and environmental—are replenished to promote access to opportunity, which must be for future generations as well as the present. Finally, development must be by people, not for them. People must participate fully in the decisions and processes that shape their lives for the benefits of genuine development.

Is There a Development Theory?

If the goal is to imitate industrial countries, is the road to a modern economy well marked by stages? Or are there different pathways to modernization? If countries are to progress economically and improve the quality of life for their inhabitants, what is the best way to do it? Is there a theory of economic development that is distinct from the economic theory we apply to our understanding of industrially advanced countries?

These are questions that economists have been grappling with for centuries. Adam Smith in *The Wealth of Nations* puzzled over how nations can best mobilize resources to produce the greatest wealth for their citizens. Box 1.3 highlights some of the conceptual guides that pioneers of development theory have offered in response to these questions. In contemporary times economists have struggled with the problem of understanding why some countries grow and others do not. This text does not assume that countries undergoing rapid economic change will necessarily follow the same pathway to achieve improvements in the quality of life. There may be different strategies to achieve the goal of raising the well-being of their citizens. The new global context for growth that Latin American economies face in the twenty-first century requires a different set of policies from the ones used by the United States and Europe during the Industrial Revolution. Revolutions in information technologies provide opportunities to leapfrog over existing production patters—but also high barriers to entry in production. A country's place in the region, its size, and its natural endowments may also condition its development strategy. Development theory and practice are dynamic, evolving over time.

Challenges for Development Policy in Latin America

Developing countries must contend with a set of economic issues that make economic policy more difficult—and for a student perhaps more interesting—than traditional theory. Throughout this text we will analyze how these issues have been addressed in Latin America from its earliest economic history through contemporary times. It is useful to raise some of these challenges here to help you begin to

Box 1.3.   Pioneers in Economic Development

WALT W. ROSTOW (NEW YORK CITY, 1916–2003)

Walt W. Rostow, an American economic historian, is known for his theory of the stages of economic growth. For Rostow, development was a linear process that began with traditional society, which then moved into the stage of "preconditions for takeoff into self-sustaining growth." The economy would then "take off," follow "the road to maturity," and finally hit "the age of high mass consumption." Rostow believed that the "takeoff" would be caused by an increase in investment, leading manufacturing sectors, and the existence of an institutional framework consistent with expansion.

PAUL ROSENSTEIN-RODAN (AUSTRIA-HUNGARY, 1902–1985)

Development economist Paul Rosenstein-Rodan advanced the concept of balanced growth. He believed that in order to achieve sustained growth, an economy must develop various industries simultaneously, requiring a coordination of investment or a "big push." He was one of the first economists to emphasize market failure and the need for state intervention.

RAGNAR NURSKE (ESTONIA, 1907–1959)

Ragnar Nurske, like Rosenstein-Rodan, advocated balanced growth and further elaborated upon his colleague's work. For Nurske, small market economies were victims of a vicious cycle hindering growth. The small size of the market was responsible for the limited amount of production and income and for the perpetual poverty and stagnation. To break the cycle, an economy needed a "big push" coordinated by a government properly allocating domestic and foreign resources.

ALBERT OTTO HIRSCHMAN (GERMANY, 1915–2012)

Economist Albert O. Hirschman provided a contrary thesis: the idea of unbalanced growth as the principal strategy for development. Building on the concept of development as a state of disequilibrium, Hirschman identified and attacked bottlenecks to growth. Like Nurske and Rosenstein-Rodan, he called for government intervention to achieve sustained growth. Yet Hirschman believed that decision-making and entrepreneurial skills were scarce in underdeveloped economies. Governments should therefore concentrate this scarce resource in a few sectors rather than on the entire economy. Planners and policymakers would need to use "forward and backward linkages" between industries to attack the bottlenecks within an economy.

W. ARTHUR LEWIS (WEST INDIES, 1915–1991)

W. Arthur Lewis, a Nobel Prize winner in economics in 1979, formulated a model in the 1950s known as "economic development with unlimited supplies of labor." Lewis's structure of the economy has a dualistic nature, with divisions into the subsistence sector and the capitalist sector. According to Lewis, underdeveloped economies are characterized by a large subsistence sector with surplus labor and a small capitalist sector, which contributes directly to a low savings rate. Economic growth occurs when there is an increase in the savings rate, which is made possible only when the capitalist sector expands and absorbs the surplus labor from the agricultural sector.

continued

RAÚL PREBISCH (ARGENTINA, 1901–1986)

Raúl Prebisch was an Argentine economist and former chairman of the UN Economic Commission for Latin America (ECLA). Prebisch is well known for the "Prebisch-Singer thesis," which claims that the export of primary products prevalent in developing countries results in a decline of terms of trade—the price of exports compared to the price of imports. There are two important implications of the thesis: first, that a decline in terms of trade results in the transfer of income from the periphery (the developing countries) to the center (the developed countries), and second, the periphery then needs to export more and more to be able to import the same quantities as before. Prebisch's pessimism on terms of trade was used to support import substitution industrialization policies in Latin America.

PAUL ALEXANDER BARAN (UKRAINE, 1910–1964)

Paul Baran is known for his neo-Marxist view of development and for his contributions to the dependency school of thought. Although not completely agreeing with Marx, Baran used Marxist principles to locate the causes of underdevelopment. Countries suffer from low per capita income because the ruling classes fail to productively use the surplus extracted from peasants and wage laborers. Instead, they hold monopoly power over production and the political system. To break this monopoly power and achieve growth, a revolution must take place to replace the dominant classes with one committed to social and economic development.

GUSTAV RANIS (GERMANY, 1929–) AND JOHN FEI (GERMANY, 1923–1996)

Gustav Ranis's early work focused on the economic development of Japan in the post-Meiji period and used it as a successful case of transition to modern growth. From there he began to focus on balanced growth and teamed up with another economist, John Fei, to further develop concepts used by Rostow and Lewis. For both Ranis and Fei, the process of "takeoff," as introduced by Rostow, would occur when the industrial sector absorbed both redundant labor and the disguised unemployed, using Lewis's process of absorption of surplus labor.

IRMA ADELMAN (ROMANIA, 1930–2017)

Irma Adelman is well known for a forty-three-nation cross-country study done with Cynthia T. Morris. The results of the study show an increase in income inequality as poorer nations grow. Both women also provided a quantitative analysis of the effects of social and political factors on economic conditions. Prior to their work, social and political factors had been ignored. Adelman also worked with Sherman Robinson in the areas of policy analysis and economic planning for developing countries and the application of computable general equilibrium models. Her interests included land reform, trends in income distribution and poverty, agriculture development-led industrialization, and the modeling of institutional change.

ANNE KRUEGER (NEW YORK, 1934–)

Anne Krueger's work on foreign trade controls creating windfall gains, known as rent-seeking behavior, and its relationship to corruption in developing countries influenced a new theory in development: the new political economy. Her early work concentrated on international trade and payments theory. Her seminal contributions include arrangements to write down debt in an orderly fashion.

think about the dilemmas of economic policy making in the region. It is important to remember, however, that each of these challenges plays out differently in each country in Latin America; the diversity of experience is probably as great as the set of common problems.

Internal versus External Macroeconomic Balance

Developing countries, in large part because by definition they are capital poor, find themselves reliant on international capital to fuel the growth process. Unlike the United States (which until recently focused little on the domestic economic policy effects of the international sector because they were relatively small), Latin American countries have had to weigh carefully the effects of changes in domestic macropolicy—traditional money supply and fiscal tools—against their effects on the external sector. There is a constant tension between internal and external balance. Lessons from economic history in Latin America will show that a one-sided focus on either the internal or the external sector results in imbalances and the deterioration of the economic plan. Integrating a nation into international capital markets raises important complexities. This may be done in the form of debt (as in the 1890s and 1970s) or through foreign direct investment in the economy, raising questions of multinational presence (such as in the control of the United Fruit Company in Guatemala in the 1950s) or contemporary questions of international labor standards. Countries that orient themselves toward the international export economy—as in Chile through copper or in Ecuador through oil—may have to sacrifice domestic goals to maintain an exchange rate that is compatible with international market conditions. One response to the trade conundrum has been to pursue alternate trade regimes in the form of integration efforts such as the Central American Common Market (CACM) or the South American Common Market (Mercosur). We will be grappling with the need to achieve internal and external balance throughout this text.

Internationalization creates a wide range of opportunities, but it also introduces constraints in domestic policymaking. For entrepreneurs such as Carlos Slim it creates profit, but it may limit the relative well-being of the Garcia family. The entrance of China as a major global presence has created tensions in the region. Countries that specialized in low-wage exports were rapidly undercut by Chinese exports; others were drawn into the providing the Chinese productive machine with commodities, creating a new cycle of the commodity lottery. Although as Kevin Gallagher notes, this creates new opportunities for Latin America, it also generates dislocation for some workers and a new form of dependency on an external partner.[20]

Stability versus Change: The Question of Timing

The process of development involves rapid structural change, yet economic agents like certainty. In traditional economic models we assume perfect information held by all agents. We know that divergence from the assumption of perfect information leads to inefficiencies in the market. How to handle economic agents' need for greater certainty and good information in an environment that is almost by definition (when it is working best) characterized by change is a challenge for policymakers in the developing world. Officials in Latin America must at once be agents of change, flexibly adapting to the dynamic needs of the economic trans-formation while also acting as strict guardians of confidence and stability. The ability to walk this policy tightrope as both motivators and moderators of change often defines policy success. When governments fail to navigate and anchor the economy, they suffer a loss of confidence. Given rapid rates of change, past policy responses have often been volatile and unpredictable, creating uncertainty. Latin American governments have a smaller store of institutional credibility than, for example, the Bank of England or the US Federal Reserve—where the big news might be a 0.25 percent increase in the interest rate and not the freezing of all bank accounts, the 30 percent devaluation of a currency, or the implementation of a currency peg. Confidence-building in economic policy making is a long and slow process—one not easily achieved when the economic waters are rough and choppy. Students of Latin American economic policy always need to ask how the proposed policy is going to affect the confidence and long-run credibility of economic agents.

POLICY FOR WHOM?

Economic policy affects various groups within an economy differently. One of the fundamental challenges facing policymakers in Latin America is the deep divisions that exist in its socioeconomic structure. Latin America is character-ized by high degrees of income inequality. There is a huge gap between the lives of Carlos Slim and Karla. The goal becomes promoting not only growth but some form of equitable growth—quite a tall order. Income inequality intro-duces complications in the measurement of growth. If equality is important, the change in a poor person's income should carry roughly the same weight as that of a rich person. But given inequality, if a rich person earns twenty times more than a poor person, changes in the income of the wealthy receive twenty times the weight of changes in income of the poor in the national growth calculation.[21] If growth is supposed to measure economic performance, even the measures are far from the mark.

In many cases inequality is exacerbated by an ethnic and cultural mosaic of approaches to economic life. Traditional forms of social organization in indigenous communities may clash with the marketization of economic life. Gender also plays a key role in the assessment of policy outcomes. In a society often conditioned by traditional gender roles, policymakers sensitive to the gender divide must ask how accessible terms of credit or access to technology are to the widest range of citizens. Although these problems are not unimportant in policy making in more industrialized countries, the range of difference confronts the policymaker with hard choices. Women in Santiago, for example, may be well-educated, active eco-nomic contributors, whereas their sisters in the Altiplano live a far more traditional life. In assessing policy in Latin America, do not neglect to ask: Policy for whom? Whose needs should policy be designed to meet? Judith Yanira Viera's? Or Carlos Slim's?

PRESENT VERSUS FUTURE VALUE: THE ENVIRONMENTAL DIMENSION

Promoting not only development but also sustainable development—or a strategy that leaves future generations as well-off as the present—may seem unrealistic when more than half of a population lives on the verge of starvation or when inflation eats away at the meager earnings of the working poor. Policymakers in the developing world—like those anywhere—are constrained by political and financial capital. There are only so many things that can be done with limited energy and finances. Daily crises take precedence over long-term planning. This becomes quite evident in the environmental arena. The challenge becomes how not to forfeit future growth while confronting present dilemmas. Even in industrial market economies, characterized by less sensational economic twists and turns, it is hard enough to promote incentives for sustainable use of resources. Imagine the difficulties in a developing country. Enforcement of environmental laws in industrial economies, with stronger institutional and financial resources, is often lax or ineffective. Yet without an environmental sensitivity to the future, policy will not be sustainable over time. Bad choices today have costs tomorrow. Policy to promote rational environmental decision making in Latin America must be carefully crafted—and perhaps supplemented with external capital—for long-term investment in the future. Macro- and microeconomic policies must be assessed through environmental lenses to protect resources for future generations.

THE STATE AND THE MARKET: PROMOTING PARTNERSHIP

Who should be the primary development actor in the region? What should be the relative balance between the state and the market in promoting development in Latin America? These questions have framed much of the policy debate in the region. We will see that the pendulum has swung from a market-led to a state-dominated economy. Social protest in the first years of the twenty-first century by those marginalized by growth has forced a reevaluation of the belief in the return to the market. Whether or not you support a stronger role for the state in economic decision making may be conditioned by your view of the relative sophistication of economic institutions in the region. Irma Adelman and Cynthia Taft Morris, two highly respected development economists, suggest that the crucial factor affecting development is the effectiveness of economic institutions and how economic institutions mediate the way in which gains from growth are distributed.[22] Are the economic institutions—central banks, capital, land and labor markets, redistributive agents, and laws governing property rights—sufficiently strong to promote equitable and sustainable growth without much day-to-day state interference? If independent market institutions or the property code is weak, is policy intervention warranted? Defining where the state can and should supplement the activity of the market is an important element in crafting effective policy for development in Latin America. As Ricardo Hausmann writes, strong institutions are critical to creating the trust for productive collaboration between governments and the private sector.[23] We also pay considerable attention to the role of civil society organizations in helping to navigate the disconnect between unequal market outcomes and rapid growth. These "third sector" actors have become critical in bridging gaps in development.

Three broad schools of thought can be identified with respect to the role of the state in development policy.[24] During the 1950s and 1960s, the success of the socialist model in jump-starting industrialization in the Soviet Union led to a **planning model** that accorded a strong role to the state in promoting development. **Dependency theory** was promoted by economists within Latin America who broadly believed that state intervention was critical to stimulating development. Since markets were viewed as incomplete and unable to send strong and accurate price signals to economic agents, the state was viewed as an essential vehicle to orchestrate the growth process. Without an interventionist state, markets alone would not spontaneously generate growth. State-run activity was seen as necessary in providing infrastructure, such as roads and railways, and public services in education and health. In addition, state activity was encouraged in the direct production of goods and services in which private initiative had failed. The state was also supposed to help to counterbalance the power of domestic and international elites. We will consider the extension of this model to Latin America in Chapter 3 on import substitution industrialization. Today, the potential gains from globalization and international trade, the benefits of entrepreneurship and the profit motive, and the difficulties introduced by problems of accountability and enforcement have created a shift away from the planning model.

The second broad approach falls within the **institutionalist tradition**. Institutionalists accord a strong role to nonmarket institutions. In particular, institutionalists suggest that rather than relying solely on price signals, other forms of organization—judges, chieftains, priests, or community councils—may intervene to settle disputes arising from the conflict over scarce economic resources.[25] Economic problems must therefore be treated within the context of legal, social, and political systems. Economic outcomes were often determined as much by power as by price signals. As the wealthy would be better able to command resources, high degrees of inequality would bias development against the poor. For institutionalists, with a variety of factors influencing outcomes, development does not tend toward equilibrium but may be a bumpy and discontinuous process. As we will see in Chapter 3, the planning model and dependency theorists as well as institutionalist thought informed the position of some of the structuralist thinkers and policymakers in Latin America. **Structuralists**—economists who believed that the particular structure of developing economies warranted a different policy approach—dominated regional policy from the 1940s through the 1970s. Neostructuralists suggest that the modern demands of global red markets require a balancing hand of the state.

A third school of thought in development economics is the **neoclassical tradition**. Linked in part to the **Chicago School** of **orthodox** economic policies, it places the market at the center of the development equation. The orthodox key to development policy is in ensuring that economic agents face accurate price incentives without interference to make the best of all possible economic decisions. State-led activity in infrastructure and public services is seen to have a poor performance record. Well-intended short-term market interventions are viewed as perpetrating unintended long-run misallocations of resources.[26] Strict neoclassical theorists therefore see a minimalist role for the state as a guarantor of rules and property rights and a provider of a limited array of public goods such as defense. The private sector, through the profit motive and Adam Smith's invisible hand, will generate the greatest good for all. Foreign trade and international prices should become the engine for growth. Under the leadership of the late Milton Friedman, the Chicago School was the principal articulator of the Pinochet model in Chile, and it broadly informs the neoliberal policies that dominated development strategies in Latin America in the 1990s.

All development approaches do not necessarily fall into one of these three policy boxes. However, the three tend to define answers to the critical question: Is the market the best of all possible mechanisms to organize economic activity and promote growth, or is state intervention a necessary ingredient to development policy in Latin America? The planner would argue for the hand of the state to guide development policy, the institutionalist would suggest that mechanisms beyond the market are critical in determining economic outcomes, and the subscriber to the Chicago School would staunchly support market-based policies. As we proceed through the puzzle of development in Latin America, you will need to resolve for yourself the most beneficial mix of market, state, and complementary institutions to promote development in the region. As nations navigate the complexities of twenty-first century development in an interconnected global economy, defining when markets work, when interventions are appropriate, and when hybrid approaches may create the conditions for productive and sustainable growth is key.

These five issues—external balance, credibility, distribution, environmental sustainability, and the role of the state—pervade our examination of the backdrop to development policy in the region and our treatment of contemporary issues. In Chapters 2 and 3 we will see how they played out in early development theories in the region. Chapters 4 and 5 address two of the dramatic legacies of imbalances of past mistakes—hyperinflation and debt. Chapter 6 continues the macro-economic story into globalization and financialization of the current period. In Chapter 7 we consider contemporary trade performance, and then we go on to analyze sources of industrial competitiveness as well as the potential of the agricultural sector in Chapters 8 and 9, respectively. We will see the radical macroeconomic changes adopted by the region in the 1990s and evaluate their significant gains for financial stability. But challenges remain. Twenty-first century Latin America continues to lag in productive and sustainable growth. In Chapter 10 we take up the problem of poverty, and in Chapters 11 and 12 we assess educational and health systems in the region. Finally, although we pay attention to the environment throughout this text, in Chapter 13 we look at environmental priorities in Latin America and suggest an agenda for action. In Chapter 14 we conclude with an evaluation of the relative weight of the state and the market in addressing the challenges to a sustainable and equitable development strategy in Latin America.

Key Concepts

Chicago School	empowerment	orthodox
dependency theory	equity	planning model
development	growth	sustainable
dualism	institutionalist tradition	development
		technological change

Chapter Summary

Development: Definitions and Theory

- Development is a word not easily defined in the context of economic advancement. Questions arise as to what kinds of characteristics "developed" countries have or should have.
- A distinction exists between development and economic growth. Development is multidimensional, involving political and social institutional change. Growth focuses on increased output.
- The goals of development extend beyond economic growth. These goals may include meeting basic human needs, increasing economic opportunities for the poor, empowering marginalized groups, and ensuring economic benefits for future generations.
- Economists have not been able to agree on a well-defined theory of development. The development processes for less-developed nations are likely to differ from those followed by industrialized nations. Approaches to development will depend upon the location, size, and natural endowments of each country.
- Three schools of thought for development policy provide policy guides to development strategy: the planning model, the institutionalist tradition, and the neoclassical tradition. Each of these defines a degree to which the state should intervene in the development process and the extent to which the process should be left in the hands of the market.

Challenges in Development Policy in Latin America

Policymakers face five major challenges when designing development policy in Latin America. First, they must establish a delicate balance between the external sector and domestic macropolicy. Second, they must be attentive to the changing nature of the global economic environment as well as preserve confidence and stability within their own economies. Third, to attain equitable growth, they must fashion policies to target different economic, ethnic, and gender groups. Fourth, their policies must balance the allocation of resources between meeting the needs of present as well as future generations. Finally, policymakers are faced with the challenge of deciding the extent to which each state should supplement the activities of its own market to facilitate equitable, sustainable development.

Notes

1. In March 2017 Carlos Slim's América Móvil was given sixty-five days to comply with a competition law passed in 2014. Dolia Estevez, "Billionaire Carlos Slim's America Movil Given 65 Days to Comply with New Antitrust Measures," *Forbes*, March 9, 2017, Forbes.com. On June 21, 2017, the Supreme Court found in favor of América Móvil. Reuters, "Mexico's Supreme Court Rules in Spat Related to Telecom Reform," June 22, 2017, http://telecom.economictimes.indiatimes.com.

2. Dionne Searcey and David Luhnow, "Verizon Pulls Out of Latin America," *Wall Street Journal*, April 4, 2006, A18.

3. "World's Billionaires 2017 Ranking," *Forbes* https://www.forbes.com/billionaires/list/.

4. TK McDonald, "This Is What Carlos Slim's Portfolio Looks Like," April 25, 2016, Investopedia.com.

5. Geri Smith, International—Latin American Cover Story, *BusinessWeek*, February 21, 2000, BusinessWeek.com.

6. "World's Billionaires 2017 Ranking," *Forbes*, www.forbes.com.

7. Carlos Slim Helu Social activity, www.carlosslim.com/responsabilidad_ing.html.

8. United Nations Development Program, "Match Against Poverty," www.undp.org/content/undp/en/home/ourwork/goodwillambassadors/match_against_poverty.html.

9. Nicholas Casey, "Thousands Once Spoke His Language in the Amazon. Now, He's the Only One," *New York Times,* nytmes.com, December 26, 2017.

10. Jose Adan Silva, "Nicaragua's Mayagna People and Their Rainforest Could Vanish," *Inter Press Service, Tierramerica*, January 12, 2018.

11. Marianela Jarroud, "Laissez Faire Water Laws Threaten Family Farming in Chile," *Inter Press Service, Tierramerica*, May 27, 2015.

12. "Children and Families Fleeing Central America Deserve Access to Protection, Not Discrimination and Abuse," Karla's story, Wola VIMEO, www.wola.org.

13. Harry S. Truman, inaugural address, January 20, 1949.

14. W. Arthur Lewis, "Economic Development with Unlimited Supplies of Labor," Manchesster School 22(2) 1954.

15. ECLAC Horizons 2030, http://periododesesiones.cepal.org/36/en/documents/horizons-2030-equality-centre-sustainable-development-summary.

16. Schumpeter (1939), as presented in Paolo Sylos Labini, "The Classical Roots of Development Theory," in *Economic Development: Handbook of Comparative Economic Policies*, eds. Enzo Grilli and Dominick Salvatore (Westport, CT: Greenwood, 1994), 3–26.

17. Lucas (1988), as presented in Sylos Labini, "The Classical Roots of Development Theory," 3.

18. Paul Streeten, "From Growth to Basic Needs," in *Latin America's Economic Development: Institutionalist and Structuralist Perspectives*, eds. James L. Dietz and James H. Street (Boulder, CO: Lynne Rienner, 1987). Originally appeared in *Finance and Development* 16 (September 1979).

19. Michael P. Todaro, *Economic Development*, 5th ed. (White Plains, NY: Longman, 1994), 670.

20. Gerald K. Helleiner, "Toward a New Development Strategy," in *The Legacy of Raúl Prebisch*, ed. Enrique V. Iglesias (Washington, DC: Inter-American Development Bank, 1994), 178.

21. Kevin Gallagher, "Latin America Needs a China Strategy," *Bloomberg*, December 14, 2017.

22. Irma Adelman and Cynthia Taft Morris, "Development History and Its Implications for Development Theory," *World Development* 25(6) (1997): 831–840.

23. Ricardo Hausmann, *The Productivity of Trust*, December 23, 2014, www.project syndicate.org.

24. Karla Hoff, Avishay Braverman, and Joseph Stiglitz, "Introduction," in *The Economics of Rural Organization*, eds. Karla Hoff, Avishay Braverman, and Joseph Stiglitz (New York: Oxford University Press/World Bank, 1993).

25. Ibid.

26. John Martinussen, *Society, State, and Market: A Guide to Competing Theories of Development* (London: Zed, 1997), 260.

HISTORICAL LEGACIES

Patterns of Unequal and Unstable Growth

The legacy of colonial institutions creates obstacles to growth.
(iStock/repistu)

CHAPTER TWO

33

In *One Hundred Years of Solitude*, Colombian novelist Gabriel García Márquez warns us that Latin America recycles its past. To evaluate contemporary policy we must understand the historical legacies of the region. The economic history of Latin America, a continent with diverse national stories and richly textured social histories, is far more complicated and nuanced than this short chapter on historical legacies can ever hope to convey. Here we can only abstract some of the patterns shaping development in the region. Perhaps some of the questions raised in our study of contemporary policy in the region will motivate the serious student of Latin America to revisit the historical pattern of growth at another time.[1] Some questions we will consider include the following:

- What factors shape the growth patterns of countries?
- Why, despite relatively similar starting points, did Latin America fall behind the United States and Canada in terms of growth?
- What are the characteristics of primary product-led growth?
- What were the social forms of economic organization conditioning development patterns?
- What were the environmental implications of the early pattern of development in Latin America?

This chapter assumes the overwhelming challenge of putting contemporary development into a simplified historical framework. It explains how the colonial and early independence periods shaped later development problems by focusing on the inputs and outputs of production. This brief foray is designed to provide a context for policy making today. Like the Buendía family in the García Márquez novel, this chapter highlights the opportunities and the cyclical constraints in the development experience in Latin America.

THE PUZZLE OF COMPARATIVE GROWTH PATTERNS

What early patterns of economic organization in Latin America shaped later growth? Rather than a conventional time line, our discussion is organized around the inputs to development: availability of labor, capital, and technology to promote agricultural and industrial growth at home and abroad. How did available resources constrain and shape development? In table 2.1 we can see that in 1700, per capita gross domestic products (GDPs) in Mexico and the United States were roughly equal. As late as 1850, Argentina and Brazil enjoyed per capita GDPs higher than Canada's. Table 2.2 presents similar results based on a different study; by 2001 GDP per capita in the United States had risen to roughly five times that of Latin nations. In terms of overall GDP, the US economy is more than twice the size of all Latin American economies combined. Why did Latin America stagnate in the twentieth century while the United States and Canada surged ahead?[2]

Table 2.1. Historical per Capita Growth of GDP (in 1985 US$)

	1700	1800	1850	1913	1989
Argentina	NA	NA	874	2,377	3,880
Brazil	NA	738	901	700	4,241
Chile	NA	NA	484	1,685	5,355
Mexico	450	450	317	1,104	3,521
Peru	NA	NA	526	985	3,142
Canada	NA	NA	850	3,560	17,576
United States	490	807	1,394	4,854	18,317
% of US per Capita GDP					
Argentina	NA	NA	62.70	48.97	21.18
Brazil	NA	91.45	64.63	14.42	23.15
Chile	NA	NA	34.72	34.71	29.24
Mexico	91.84	55.76	22.74	22.74	19.22
Peru	NA	NA	37.73	20.29	17.15
Canada	NA	NA	60.98	73.34	95.95
United States	100.00	100.00	100.00	100.00	100.00

Source: Stanley Engerman and Kenneth Sokoloff, *Factor Endowments, Institutions and Differential Paths of Growth among New World Economies: A View from Economic Historians of the United States*, National Bureau of Economic Research Historical Paper No. 66 (Cambridge, MA: National Bureau of Economic Research, 1994).

THINKING ABOUT INPUTS, OUTPUTS, AND ECONOMIC CHANGE

Economic development may be thought of as a process whereby the structure of the economy evolves to adapt to the changing needs of a growing population. Growth of output must outstrip population growth to improve the resources available to people. Population, or labor, constitutes one of the inputs of production. How is it organized and combined with other inputs to produce output? It is useful to think about the fundamentals shaping the structure of an economy. These in turn condition the economy's performance in meeting the requirements of society. Why do economies begin to produce certain goods? How do specializations evolve and change over time? One way to answer this is to consider the inputs available for production and the characteristics of the output market that define product demand. What inputs are available to be made into desired output? What technology is available—and who controls it—to facilitate the process? Whose tastes and desires—local, international, rich, poor—are the target market? Looking at the factors affecting supply and demand will allow us to say something about the structure of an economy and to evaluate how policy was used historically to improve the responsiveness of an economy to the needs of its citizens. Table 2.3 summarizes some of these factors shaping patterns of growth.

Table 2.2.   Historical Population and GDP Data

	1820	1870	1913	1950	2001
Population (million people)					
Total Western Europe	133.0	187.5	261.0	304.9	392.1
Japan	31.0	34.4	51.7	83.8	126.9
Total Asia (excluding Japan)	679.4	730.8	925.7	1,298.6	3,526.6
Africa	74.2	90.5	124.7	227.3	821.1
United States	10.0	40.2	97.6	152.3	285.0
Mexico	6.6	9.2	15.0	28.5	101.9
Argentina	0.5	1.8	7.7	17.2	37.9
Brazil	4.5	9.8	23.7	53.4	177.8
Chile	0.9	1.9	3.5	6.1	15.3
Peru	1.3	2.6	4.3	7.6	27.5
Uruguay	0.1	0.3	1.2	2.2	3.4
Total Latin America	21.7	40.4	80.9	165.9	531.2
World	1,041.8	1,271.9	1,791.1	2,524.3	6,149.0
Per Capita GDP (1990 international Geary Khamis dollars)					
Total Western Europe	1,204	1,960	3,458	4,579	19,256
Japan	669	737	1,387	1,921	20,683
Total Asia (excluding Japan)	577	550	658	634	3,256
Africa	420	500	637	894	1,489
United States	1,257	2,445	5,301	9,561	27,948
Mexico	759	674	1,732	2,365	7,089
Argentina	..	1,311	3,797	4,987	8,137
Brazil	646	713	811	1,672	5,570
Chile	..	..	2,653	3,821	10,001
Peru	..	..	1,037	2,263	2,263
Uruguay	..	2,181	3,310	4,659	4,659
Total Latin America	692	681	1,481	2,506	5,811
World	667	875	1,525	2,111	6,049
GDP (million dollars)					
Total Western Europe	160.1	367.6	902.3	1,396.2	7,550.3
Japan	20.7	25.4	71.7	161.0	2,624.5
Total Asia (excluding Japan)	392.2	401.6	608.7	822.8	11,481.2
Africa	31.2	45.2	79.5	203.1	1,222.6
United States	12.5	98.4	517.4	1,455.9	7,965.8
Mexico	5.0	6.2	25.9	67.4	722.2
Argentina	..	2.4	29.1	85.5	308.5
Brazil	2.9	7.0	19.2	89.3	990.1
Chile	..	..	9.3	23.3	153.3
Peru	..	..	4.5	17.3	99.8
Uruguay	..	0.7	3.9	10.2	25.4
Total Latin America	15.0	27.5	119.9	415.9	3,087.0
World	695.3	1,112.7	2,732.1	5,329.7	37,193.9

Source: The World Economy: Historical Statistics.

Table 2.3.   Factors Shaping Patterns of Growth

Natural resources	Is the country resource abundant?
	Who owns resources?
Land	How is land distributed? Who decides who owns land?
	Are landholdings concentrated or spread out among small stakeholders?
	Are the claims or titles to landholdings clear?
	What is the quality of available land?
Labor resources	How abundant is labor?
	What is the skill level of workers?
Financial capital	Is there a domestic surplus available for reinvestment?
	Do domestic investors find better returns at home or abroad?
	Is growth dependent on an external infusion of funds?
Technology	What is the technological base of the nation?
	Who controls the access to technology?
	Do international patents restrict the free flow of technology?
Policy environment	Is the driving force behind growth the market or the state?
	Is the policy inwardly oriented or open to the international economy?

Source: Patrice Franko.

What factors condition the menu of goods and services that a country produces? Resources, raw materials, and the physical characteristics of land affect production possibilities. Does a country's geographic location matter? Is a country rich in natural resources? Is there a diversity of available resources? Or does the country rely on a limited number of natural commodities? Who owns resources and how they are distributed throughout the population both matter enormously. Asset ownership confers the ability to make a profit on the sale or use of that factor of production. Is the ownership of key resources concentrated in a small, powerful group, or it is evenly spread around the population? Do these assets—land or mines or timber or fish—generate a profit for the owners above and beyond subsistence needs? The development of a group of people with a profit or surplus above and beyond personal subsistence requirements creates an elite class of potential capitalists or investors. These capitalists can then reinvest the surplus to create new growth opportunities—or they can send it out of the country to earn money elsewhere. If this pool of national capital falls short of domestic investment demand, the country finds itself dependent on international sources of funds for growth. The choices that domestic elites make about where to invest their money also shape the available stock of technology employed in the production process. Investments in technological inputs may enhance the productivity of the labor force, or resources may be directed toward producing sophisticated products outside the reach of the common consumer. As we can see, land, capital, and labor—the primary inputs to production—help define the productive structure.

But this structure does not operate in a vacuum. Public policies fashion the productive environment. The legal structure defines property rights and social responsibilities. The policy environment may be shaped by a market philosophy limiting the sphere of government activity, or there may be a demand for the government to address collective needs or redress some of the imbalances created by economic growth. A nation's institutions may continue to be influenced by its colonial past. Furthermore, what a country produces, as well as how and by whom, is conditioned by what the rest of the world is doing. Borders are generally permeable to ideas, goods, services, and prices; countries view productive capabilities relative to the endowments and technological achievements of other nations. Relative advantage matters. A country's position in the international economic order also defines possible pathways to growth. A late-developing country may find that others have already cornered the market in a particular product or process. These supply characteristics of inputs, and production rules, interact with demand. The most efficient producer of an undesired good goes broke. The characteristics of a product—how responsive people are to price changes, the number of substitutes, the frequency and size of purchase—as well as the internal and external market size for a country's tradable goods create the opportunity for profit.

Fundamental supply and demand conditions affect and are affected by macroeconomic variables. Supply constraints or excess demand may give rise to inflation; failure to capture a surplus for reinvestment may result in anemic or slow growth. Attempts to jump-start an economy may simply fuel inflation; policies to manipulate the exchange rate to gain competitive advantage may have unintended domestic effects. The macroeconomic environment therefore shapes the activity of producer and consumer in the market.

How have the supply conditions—land, labor, capital, and technological availability—interacted with the demand factors and the macroeconomic environment to condition historical growth in Latin America? What were the available resources? Who controlled them? What technology was available to the owners of resources? What were the rules of the market? How did demand for products from Latin America affect growth patterns? How and where were profits reinvested? Finding answers to these questions gives us a sense of the historical factors shaping growth in the region.

NATURAL ABUNDANCE: GEOGRAPHY AND THE REWARDS OF THE EXTRACTIVE ECONOMY

Geography was an important determinant in shaping the economic fortune of Latin America. Geography affects long-term growth through health conditions, productivity of land, availability of natural resources, transportation costs, and economies of scale in market size.[3] The diverse physical and human geographies of Latin America—from the peaks of the Andean range to the low, moist floors of the rainforests—create physical barriers to overcome. The geographic diversity of the region has shaped growth patterns. Before the completion of the Panama Canal in 1914, Andean economies were seriously disadvantaged in distance from trade markets; moving a ton of goods from Lima to Bogota cost 52.9 pounds as compared to 2 pounds to Buenos Aires or Montevideo.[4] Trade with port cities promoted an outward focus in a region where overland shipping could be as expensive as sending goods halfway around the world. In Bolivia and Ecuador, for example, costs from the port city to the capital were between four and five times the cost of shipping from England.[5]

Isolation from contact with European settlers may have preserved indigenous cultures but also created obstacles to integration in the global market. Colonizers rejected harsh conditions of the tropical Central American countries and instead invested in institutional development in the more hospitable southern latitudes. Hard-to-control disease vectors, rusting machines, and perennially soggy clothing were not for the weak. Health conditions such as malaria reduced growth by as much as 1 percent.[6] European immigrants flocked to temperate lands, bringing education and market customs.[7] To promote the extraction of rich natural resources, Europeans imposed institutions—sets of rules governing human behavior—that protected their rights to New World wealth.[8] Where resources were abundant, colonial powers placed extractive institutions in elite hands; geographies less generously endowed led to establishing institutions of private property that allows access to broader stakeholders in society to receive returns on investment. Even within countries, geography conditioned the development of settlements and future wealth.[9] Although inhospitable geography should not be seen as fatally consigning countries to poverty, the effects of poor land and frail institutions persist today.

The exploitation of natural resources was at the heart of the colonial period of Latin American development. Latin America was resource rich. Exploration of the region was driven by the Spanish mercantilist search for silver and gold. The New World provided new opportunities for wealth in Europe. Monopoly control over mines and land in the New World was accorded through the *encomienda* system, with a share of the output, or *repartida*, owed in return. Under the encomienda system, rights to land were parceled out by the monarchy, with an associated portion of the profits to be shipped back to Europe. Labor, however, was scarce. In 1503 Queen Isabella of Spain "entrusted" the natives to the landlords, requiring the heads of the estates, or *caciques*, to provide payment, protection, and instruction in the Christian faith in exchange for their services. Indian laborers were also entrapped through debt into purchasing goods from the owner at inflated prices. Extractive activities also laid a toll on the local labor force to bring the silver and gold to Spain. Indigenous peoples were obliged to provide the labor for mining, and Indian populations were decimated by European diseases—smallpox, yellow fever, malaria, and bubonic plague. As indigenous communities were broken up in support of an emerging agricultural sector, the "biological holocaust," as some have called it,[10] claimed the lives of the large majority of the continent's indigenous population.

The Portuguese, given claim to Brazil by the Treaty of Tordesillas in 1494, were initially less driven by the search for precious metals. When the Portuguese arrived, they did not find and conquer the highly organized indigenous civilization of the Incas or the Mayans to lead them to a fabulous pot of silver or gold. Furthermore, with the indigenous population scattered throughout the vast Amazon, labor was a problem. Agriculture took hold before mining. The early importation of African slaves solved labor shortages in the emerging sugar industry. The gold rush began in Minas Gerais, Brazil, in the late 1600s and continued through the middle 1700s, increasing Portuguese interest in the colony. But the relatively early development of Brazilian agriculture exerted a stabilizing influence on the early development pattern. As in the United States, importing slaves relieved the labor constraint in production.

LABOR AND SOCIAL RELATIONS

The exploitation of indigenous labor supplies, the importation of Africans, and European immigration radically changed the racial composition in the region. Around 1900, there were approximately twenty million Latin Americans, a regional population about equal to that of Great Britain and double that of the United States. The small national populations were seen as a constraint on development. Argentina and Brazil were the second and third most popular intercontinental destinations for European immigrants in the late 1800s and early 1900s, but they attracted only 20 percent of the immigration flow, compared to 60 percent for the United States.[11] Four million African slaves were introduced to Brazil from 1531 to 1855.[12] As we can see in table 2.4, limited immigration flows set up different racial patterns in the region. In Spanish America, by 1935 blacks accounted for 13.3 percent of the population and Indians 50.4 percent; in Brazil, African Brazilians made up 35.5 percent of the population, surpassing the Indian population. Interestingly, slavery in Latin America was abolished soon after independence in most Latin American nations, with little of the turmoil that accompanied the transition in the United States. Even in Brazil, where slavery lasted until 1888, racial integration has been far more harmonious than in North America.

Differing racial patterns in Spanish America and Brazil as compared to the United States and Canada had a clear economic dimension. The production of export crops such as sugar and mining activities relied on imported slave labor

Table 2.4. Racial Composition in New World Economies (percentages)

		White	Black	Indian
Spanish America	1570	1.3	2.5	96.3
	1650	6.3	9.3	84.4
	1825	18.0	22.5	59.5
	1935	35.5	13.3	50.4
Brazil	1570	2.4	3.5	94.1
	1650	7.4	13.7	78.9
	1825	23.4	55.6	21.0
	1935	41.0	35.5	23.0
United States and Canada	1570	0.2	0.2	99.6
	1650	12.0	2.2	85.8
	1825	79.6	16.7	3.7
	1935	89.4	8.9	1.4

Source: Stanley Engerman and Kenneth Sokoloff, *Factor Endowments, Institutions and Differential Paths of Growth among New World Economies: A View from Economic Historians of the United States*, National Bureau of Economic Research Historical Paper No. 66 (Cambridge, MA: National Bureau of Economic Research, 1994), Table 3.

and forced Indian labor. Although the southern United States also solved its labor constraint through slavery, 80 percent of the population in the United States and Canada was white in 1825, whereas whites composed only 20 to 25 percent of the population in Spanish America and Brazil. But this small white minority held extraordinary economic power. The white Europeans in Latin America, small in number, were granted property from the monarchies, whereas slaves or manual laborers without assets were the bulk of the population.[13] Income—derived from the ownership of assets—was highly unequal and tied to race from the start in Latin America. Mentally combine the data on per capita GDP in table 2.1 with our information about the small share of the white population. Given that the per capita estimates are an average of the population, imagine how well the white European elite must have lived compared with the rest of the population. Income inequality shaped institutional development in the region. Wealthy elites preferred low tax rates on income and property—resulting in the limited capacity of governments to provide public goods of education and infrastructure. The status quo served vested interests. The Portuguese even prohibited the operation of printing presses in colonial Brazil and stifled the development of a university system.[14]

Despite differences in the emphasis on mining and agricultural activity between Brazil and the rest of the region, early social relations in both the Spanish and the Portuguese colonies tended to be feudal. The traditional authority of the Catholic Church reinforced these social patterns. The *encomienda* system accorded property rights to a small number of landholders, concentrating ownership and crowding the indigenous and mestizo, or those of mixed heritage, onto less-productive land. This system of the *latifundia*, the feudal *hacienda* estates in Spanish Latin America, and the *fazenda* system in Brazil set up a highly unequal socioeconomic system. Furthermore, because internal markets were relatively small, the *latifundia* largely fostered an agricultural sector directed toward Europe. Profits were repatriated, leaving little at home for reinvestment. By 1800 residents in Bourbon, Mexico, paid more taxes than Spaniards in the Metropolis.[15] Powerful elites blocked taxation at the local levels, precluding investment in public schooling at the heart of the North American model. Political opposition to such privilege was weak; by the mid-nineteenth century all Latin American countries retained wealth and literacy requirements to vote.[16] Those eking out a subsistence existence on the *minifundia*, the small parcels of land the peasants farmed, could do little more than feed themselves with their meager earnings. Compared to the United States, greater inequality in wealth, human capital, and political power likely promoted the evolution of weaker internal markets in Latin America.[17] The poor didn't have much money to buy goods. Elites retained positions of political power, blocking forces of economic change.

INDEPENDENCE: POLITICAL CHANGE WITHOUT ECONOMIC TRANSFORMATION

National independence, achieved regionally by 1822 (with the exception of Cuba and Puerto Rico), allowed for a change in rules regarding property rights and trade. However, the violence, lawlessness, and political turmoil of the period of independence reinforced the legitimacy of the *latifundia* as a form of political and economic organization. Lawlessness and revolt were common. People wanted security. The growing pains of nations—the difficulty in raising taxes and providing public services—highlighted the stability of the semifeudal system of social, political, and economic protection that the *coronel*, or the head of the *latifundia*, provided. Accompanied by wars and uncertainty, independence did not deliver conditions for sustained economic growth.[18] The preservation of elite political interests, rather than institutional modernization favoring equal legal rights for citizens, may have had the effect of slowing growth in Latin America as compared to the North.[19] Elites in extractive societies had much to lose from institutional reform and instead preserved their power to extract resource rents.[20] Weak central governments were subordinated to local military and political caudillos. Fiscal deficits emerged, creating a vicious cycle whereby vulnerable governments succumbed to challenges by political elites and civil strife ensued.[21]

The pattern of land tenure was perhaps unnecessarily concentrated. Although we can trace the roots of unequal landholdings to the colonial land tenure system, it is important to point out that after independence, new national governments missed opportunities to redistribute land from conquest, held by the former crowns, or further appropriated from indigenous communities. The lack of change is not surprising. Literacy and wealth requirements limited the vote to the powerful oligarchies.[22] If political elites tied to this system had not been so powerful, fundamental land reforms would have created greater competition in the agricultural sector. With a larger number of small holdings, competitive pressure may have fostered activity in other sectors. Infrastructure, including transportation and energy, was also weak, making it difficult to set up local manufacturing. Thin domestic capital markets made it tough to raise money. In addition, local market demand was too small and product quality was too low for manufacturing to exploit the international sector. Political and economic structures did not help create a climate conducive to institutional change.

Contributing to the desire to maintain a political oligarchy was the fact that people were relatively well-off. By the end of the 1800s, the per capita income in Latin America was US$245, at a time when it reached only US$239 in North America.[23] Unfortunately for national growth, income was concentrated, and reinvestment of profits in entrepreneurial activity was limited. The lack of political change hindered economic transformation. Given the control of the political system by elites, it made little sense to venture into risky investments. The security of the *latifundia* system mitigated against economic risk taking. With political and economic gains consolidated, why embark on an investment likely to fail?

THE GIANT SUCKING SOUND OF SINGLE-COMMODITY EXPORTS

As shown in table 2.5, nations tended to hitch their economic star to a dominant commodity. Coffee, sugar, bananas, and their associated feudal structures of production dominated the export profile. Exports were seen as the engine

Table 2.5.   Single-Commodity Exports as a Percentage of Total Exports

Country	Commodity	% Total Exports, 1938
El Salvador	Coffee	92
Venezuela	Petroleum	92
Cuba	Sugar	78
Panama	Bananas	77
Bolivia	Tin	68
Guatemala	Coffee	66
Honduras	Bananas	64
Colombia	Coffee	61
Dominican Republic	Sugar	60
Chile	Copper	52
Haiti	Coffee	51
Costa Rica	Coffee	49
Nicaragua	Coffee	47
Brazil	Coffee	45

Source: Simon Hanson, *Economic Development in Latin America* (Washington, DC: Inter-American Affairs Press, 1951), 107.

of economic growth. There are winners and losers in the global export game. Despite the similarities in socioeconomic systems, there was a great deal of diversity in economic performance throughout the region, largely connected to the so-called **commodity lottery**.[24] The luck of natural endowment and agricultural advantage—copper and silver in Chile; sugar in Cuba; coffee in Brazil, Colombia, and Costa Rica; cattle in Argentina; bananas from Central America; guano in Peru—defined the winnings in the international export market. International demand had expanded with the opening of the British agricultural market and industrialization in Europe and the United States. In the late 1800s through the early 1900s, a broad consensus for agriculture-led export growth prevailed. This **golden age of primary product exports** in Latin America was facilitated by political stability, expansion of transportation systems encouraging geographic integration, improvements in capital markets promoting capital investment, and secondary industrialization taking place in textiles, food packing, and transportation in support of the agricultural sector. Indeed the period from 1870 to 1913 has been argued to parallel the current era of globalization.[25] Latin America responded to new demands from the industrializing international system by providing raw materials, including key minerals and food.[26] The Latin American economies sampled in figure 2.1 were more strongly export-oriented than those in Europe in 1929. During this period, Central America began the export of bananas, and Brazil entered the rubber boom.

Single-commodity exports, however, were an unstable basis for balanced, sustainable economic growth. Development policy was preoccupied with the needs of the export sector, with little attention to the links with domestic production and demand. In bananas, much of the production was dominated by US multinationals

Figure 2.1.   Merchandise Exports to GDP, 1929

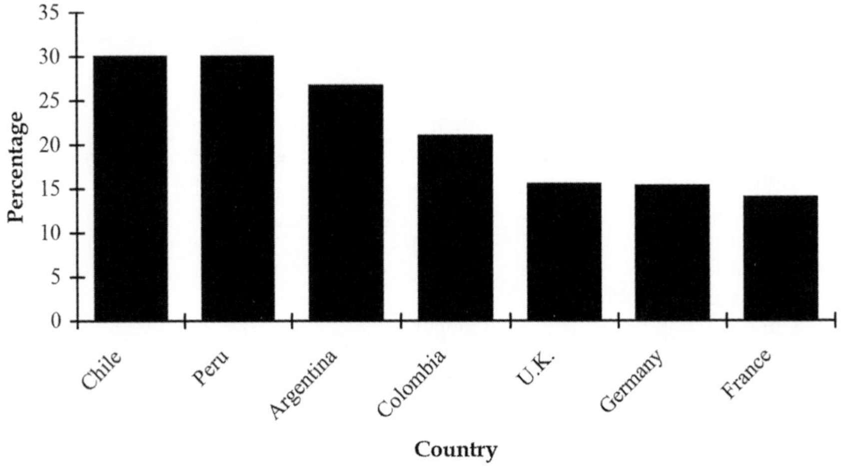

Source: Angus Maddison, "Economic and Social Conditions in Latin America, 1913–1950," in *Long-Term Trends in Latin American Economic Development*, ed. Miguel Urrutia (Washington, D.C.: IADB and John Hopkins University Press, 1991), table 1.13.

functioning as an export **enclave** contributing little to the social development of the country. The powerful United Fruit Company, for example, did not pay a cent of tax to the Costa Rican government, and its workers bought goods imported duty-free in the company store.[27] Central American economies became inextricably linked to an international political economy beyond domestic control. As table 2.6 shows, the

Table 2.6.   Geographic Distribution of Latin American Exports, 1929 (% of total exports)

Country	United States	United Kingdom	France	Germany	Four Country Export Concentration
Cuba	76.6	12.6	2.1	0.8	92.1
Colombia	75.2	4.7	0.5	2.1	82.5
Mexico	60.7	10.3	3.9	7.6	82.5
Brazil	42.2	6.5	11.1	8.8	68.6
Peru	33.3	18.3	1.3	6.1	59.0
Venezuela	28.2	1.9	2.9	4.7	37.7
Chile	25.4	13.3	6.1	8.6	53.4
Uruguay	11.9	23.0	11.9	14.5	61.3
Argentina	9.8	32.3	7.1	10.0	59.2
Average	40.4	13.6	4.2	7.0	65.2

Source: Angus Maddison, "Economic and Social Conditions in Latin America, 1913–1950," in *Long-Term Trends in Latin American Economic Development*, ed. Miguel Urrutia (Washington, DC: IADB and Johns Hopkins University Press, 1991).

problems of single-commodity exports were exacerbated by a high concentration in market destination. Demand for the product was essentially determined abroad. The old saying that when the United States sneezes Latin America gets pneumonia begins to apply in this period.

Placing bets in the commodity casino leaves a country vulnerable to the vagaries of the international market. Commodity wealth—gold, silver, tin, coffee, rubber, sugar, oil—can exert negative effects on the process of development. With strong international demand for a particular product, national resources are sucked into the production or extraction of a single commodity. As international prices boom, so do profits at home. Given comparative advantage, it makes great sense to concentrate production on addressing international demand. Resources move to the hot sector, pressuring input prices throughout the economy. Dubbed the **Dutch disease** because of Holland's experience with natural gas, this produces a distorted pattern of development precariously predicated on the hot commodity. International resources are drawn in, overvaluing the exchange rate. When a commodity is booming, why should investors place their money in a less-lucrative outlet? If tin mining is returning high rates of profit, why invest in a dress factory? Furthermore, if profits from the boom are unequally distributed, a broader multiplier effect of the windfall income in industrial development is even less likely. Investors have monopoly or oligopoly control on the industry, and their continued access to profits or monopoly rents appears assured.

But booms have their busts. When commodity prices in the international market fall, they drag the whole economy down with them—because the commodity has essentially become the economy. For example, in 1920, sugar, a key crop for several Latin American nations, sold at 22.5 cents in May but tumbled to 3.625 cents by the end of that same year.[28] By the end of the decade it reached an all-time low of 1.471 cents—a devastating fall for an economy revolving around "king sugar." Coffee prices dropped 40 percent from 1929 to 1930—a tough shock to national coffers.[29] Another dramatic example was the guano economy in Peru. Between 1840 and 1880, Peru's economy revolved around guano deposits left by birds on the island coasts off Peru, where it barely rains. When substitutes were found for this valued fertilizer, Peru's economy crashed. Because most governmental receipts came from taxes on foreign trade, the effect of a commodity bust was magnified by contractionary fiscal policy.

ENGEL'S LAW AND DECLINING TERMS OF TRADE

In addition to price volatility, concentration in primary product exports is also complicated by the nature of primary product demand. Primary products, particularly agricultural goods, are relatively price and income inelastic. If prices go up for coffee or sugar, as in a boom period, people cut back only slightly on their consumption of these perceived necessities. But on the downslope, with prices falling, people don't buy much more at a lower price. There is a

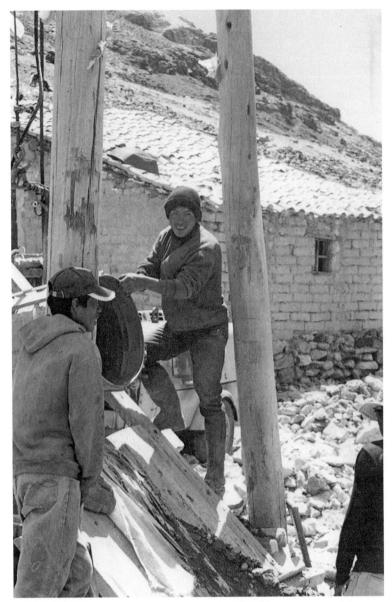

Mining projects such as this one in Bolivia have been a source of export revenues but also introduce questions of export price instability and declining terms of trade. *(Courtesy of Amanda McKown)*

limit to how much coffee or sugar people want. Furthermore, we observe a statistical relationship called **Engel's law**, that shows that as income increases there is a weak increase in the demand for primary products. As world income grows and people become wealthier, the demand for agricultural products does not keep pace, unlike that for most manufactured products. If your country is an agricultural producer, compared to the rest of the world getting richer through manufactured goods, you stagnate. The net result of the **declining terms of trade** is that high rates of growth in the primary product sector may not be enough to act as a catalyst for development. Latin America's terms of trade declined by about 105 from 1880 to 1900 and fell approximately 20 percent more by 1930.[30] **Export pessimism**—the belief that exports would not be the engine of growth—began to characterize the policymaker's mind-set by the early 1920s. In addition to declining terms of trade, the export engine was not strong enough to pull large, low-productivity nontradable sectors.[31] Although the golden age of exports may have acted as a handmaiden to growth, the cycle had turned against Latin America.

THE EFFECTS OF WEAK INDUSTRIAL LINKAGES AND HIGH TARIFF TAXATION

Despite declining terms of trade and export pessimism, primary product export growth is not necessarily a bad thing. Indeed, export growth can provide the opportunity for a country to capture a surplus, reinvest this profit, and reduce dependency on the agricultural product. In Latin America, however, weak links between export industries and the rest of the economy, labor shortages in the manufacturing sector, and foreign competition in industry depressed relative returns. Much export production exhibited characteristics of enclaves isolated from the rest of the economy. Linkages between commodity production and other products were relatively low. For example, coffee did not send signals back down the production chain for much in the way of capital necessary for production (a **backward linkage**), nor did it generate the demand for new industries or products (a **forward linkage**). (The Starbucks coffee bar had yet to be developed!) Cattle ranching is an example of an industry that did contribute to forward linkages in leather processing and the shoe industry, but for the most part, commodity-led industrialization did not stimulate production in other sectors of the economy. In addition, with the notable exception of Argentina, immigration policies limited the labor market, creating shortages in the industrial sector. Ironically, compared to today, high-priced labor in Latin America made manufacturing costly. Domestic markets for financial capital were relatively weak, and foreign investment flowed to areas in which technological or capital constraints restricted entry of local firms. Military conflicts in the newly emerging states drained finances—money most easily acquired by levying import duties. Throughout the region, ad valorem rates reached as high as 40 percent in the late nineteenth century, dampening the positive effect that imported inputs may have had on the economy. By 1865 tariff rates in Latin America were, with the exception of the United States, the highest in the world. Export-led growth was oddly accompanied by import protection used to finance wars.[32]

Dominance of Foreign Capital During the First Wage of Globalization

Investment flows to Latin America postindependence were large and volatile.[33] New government bond issues garnered the attention of London financiers in the 1820s, but most ended in default. By the late 1860s capital flows resumed and dominated large sectors of some economies. Primarily public, loans were used to roll over old debts and finance military spending and railway construction. Brazil was favored for its relative stability, whereas other nations, still rocked by wars, were riskier bets. By the end of 1880, 58 percent of British bonds in the region were in default, cementing in investors' minds the untrustworthiness of sovereign borrowers in Latin America. In the private sector, the British had lucrative interests in railways, sanitation, telegraph companies, banking, shipping, and mining. Private-sector lending grew for the next several decades, largely tied to the trade boom. Inflows were concentrated in Argentina, Mexico, Brazil, Chile, and Uruguay, emerging stars outstripping slow-growing republics in the region. Capital flowed to support infrastructure and industry—widening the gap between rich and poor in the region. Nonetheless, even dynamically growing countries' investors paid dearly for capital flows—returning high profits for risk.

In the first decade of the twentieth century lenders diversified to include North American, French, and German holdings; in this period the ratio of foreign capital to GDP was 2.7, dwarfing Asia at 0.4 and Africa at 1.1. Based on these flows, roughly one-third of the capital stock in the region was supplied by external sources—a significant benefit but one that required market discipline and engendered dependency on constant inflows. Crisis and volatility marked the period as hot money overinflated economies, foreshadowing the stop-and-go nature of debt crises in the 1980s. This epoch of globalization from 1870 to 1914 of open trade and finance, like its parallel a century later, created winners and losers in the region. When foreign capital withdrew in the war years, poorly articulated domestic financial markets were not up to the task of raising and allocating scarce capital. The combination of high levels of foreign investment with commodity export economies tended to generate low returned value to the host economy, depressing possibilities for future growth.[34]

One notable exception to the weakness of domestic capital markets was the case of Brazil. It has been suggested that Brazilian coffee barons were able to underwrite the industrial base of São Paulo while continuing to expand coffee production. It is theorized that this took place because the coffee land was not suitable for agricultural diversification, and *fazendeiros* found themselves in the manufacturing sector in search of new profits.[35] Furthermore, coffee production itself needed so little in the way of reinvestment of surplus that profits were best placed outside the sector.[36] Nonetheless, even under these relatively favorable conditions, development stalled when British financiers fancied more lucrative alternatives.[37]

Table 2.7 illustrates the high rate of foreign investment as a percentage of GDP in the beginning of the century. When foreign capital was withdrawn during World War I, local financial systems were not sufficiently developed to

Table 2.7.   Foreign Investment in Latin America, circa 1913

Creditor	Capital (in millions US$)	Percentage
Great Britain	3,700	43.5
France	1,200	14.1
Germany	900	10.6
United States	1,700	20.0
Others	1,000	11.8

Source: Werner Baer, "Leteinamerica und Westeuropa. Die Wirtschaftsbeziehungen bis zum Ende des Zweiten Weltriegs," in *Lateinamerica-Westeuropa-Vereinigte Staaten Ein atlantisches Dreieck*, eds. W. Grabendorff and R. Roett (Baden-Baden: Nomos, 1985); cited in Walther L. Bernecker and Hans Werner Tobler, eds., *Development and Underdevelopment in America: Contrasts of Economic Growth in North and Latin America in Historical Perspective* (Berlin: Walter de Gruyter, 1993).

intermediate capital needs. Reflecting the importance of external finance and trade, Argentina, for example, did not have a central bank until 1935. Instead, its monetary authority, the Caja de Conversión, was responsible for guaranteeing the external value of the currency, with no domestic lender of last resort in the system.[38] The role of foreign and domestic commercial lenders was also differentiated. Because international bankers dominated short-term, less risky portfolios, domestic institutions were left with longer-term loans to firms and real estate. When foreign banks pulled out, domestic institutions were not able to liquidate their assets quickly enough to respond to the capital shortage, and they could not respond to the needs of the local economy to finance the accumulation of physical capital.[39] International crises created local reverberations as money was withdrawn from Latin America to supplement European war chests.[40] Dependence on foreign capital has decreased over the course of the century, but vulnerability to the whims of the international capital market has remained a constant challenge for policymakers in the region.

THE ENVIRONMENTAL DIMENSION

The environmental costs of an agricultural and extractive economy geared to export markets were substantial. Ecologically sustainable systems of communal agriculture had been practiced in Mesoamerica since at least 1500 BCE. The Spanish Conquest succeeded in its goal of extracting natural riches and also destroyed ancient communal villages and practices.[41] After the mines were stripped, colonists cleared the land for agricultural crops. The introduction of sugar and coffee prompted vast ecological change, transforming the Central American region from subtropical forest to an agricultural export economy by clearing and planting, pushing the frontier, and exhausting the soil. Cattle were introduced, making further claims on land. Land held by the Catholic Church or publicly held Indian lands called *ejidos* came to be seen by liberal free market reformers as constraints on further development of the export economy. By 1880, every Central American country had titling laws granting coffee growers rights to land formerly held by Indian communities. Exports surged, but so did the devastation of indigenous groups. The confiscation of traditional lands led Indians to the ecologically more fragile mountains or lowlands, compounding environmental problems. When coffee estate owners faced labor shortages, the government forced communities to provide workers for the labor-intensive harvest through the *mandamiento* program, often under brutal working conditions. The expansion of banana production in the 1920s and 1930s increased pressure on the land and local food crops as firms dominated by multinationals competed with less powerful *campesinos* for the best high-nutrient soils.

Devastation was not limited to Central America. Brazilian B. F. Brandão provided one of the earliest accounts of environmental destruction in 1865 in this description of his youth on a Brazilian *fazenda*:

> At six o'clock in the morning the overseer forces the poor slave, still exhausted from the evening's labor, to rise from his rude bed and proceed to his work. The first assignment of the season is the chopping down of the forests for the next year's planting. . . . The next step is destruction of the large trees. . . . They set fire to the devastated jungle, and then they cut and stack the branches and smaller tree trunks which have escaped the fire . . . and could hinder development of the crop. . . . Centuries-old tree trunks which two months before had produced a cool, crisp atmosphere over a broad stretch of land, lie on the surface of a field ravaged by fire and covered with ashes, where the slaves are compelled to spend twelve hours under the hot sun of the equator, without a single tree to give them shelter.[42]

Initially trees were burned in a short-term effort to increase soil fertility; they were also felled because they were thought to compete with coffee for limited moisture.[43] Over time, the result was economic devastation.

In mining, industry, and some agricultural activities, local governments allowed control by foreign multinational firms. As characterized by Eduardo Galeano, Latin America's open veins of tin and copper poured into multinational coffers with little commitment to sustainable environmental policy. For example, a New York firm was granted a concession to mine in the Cerro de Pasco region of Peru's Central Andes. It constructed a network of roads, railroads, smelters, mining camps, hydroelectric plants, and haciendas to serve the mines; in 1922 it opened a smelter refinery using timber, promoting deforestation, and polluting air and rivers with sulfuric acid and iron-zinc residues. Products were sold globally, but the devastation was local.

But foreign capital was not entirely to blame. In the 1940s Brazil's president expressed the following philosophy: "To conquer the land, tame the waters and subjugate the jungle, these have been our tasks. And in this centuries-old battle, we have won victory upon victory."[44] Resource-based growth was premised on taking advantage of the riches the land had to offer—at a clear cost to the environment. Even where an early consciousness of environmental protection existed, institutional resources for implementation were weak. The Brazilian government implemented a forest code in the 1930s, prohibiting deforestation along watercourses, limiting cutting on property, and protecting rare species. With limited financing, however, it was unenforceable.[45] Moreover, the demand for economic growth far outpaced environmental concerns.

THE ISOLATION OF THE WAR YEARS:
A BLESSING IN DISGUISE?

World War I had a profoundly dislocating effect on Latin America. The fall of the gold standard fomented financial instability. Oil-producing countries such as Venezuela benefited, but the confusion surrounding world war masked fundamental structural changes taking place in the global economy. As advanced industrial products were developed, the value of agricultural trade declined. New products such as synthetics displaced traditional raw materials. The Great Depression exacerbated global commodity market instability, leaving the externally oriented development strategy without robust markets for products. Growing protectionism abroad further limited export potential. The terms of trade—what a country receives for its exports relative to what it pays for its imports—fell between 21 and 45 percent when international markets collapsed. International capital inflows to fuel industrial development virtually dried up by 1929.[46]

But there was a silver lining to this cloud. As a result of these external shocks to the trade-driven model, Latin America was forced to adjust. It turned inward, adopting a set of economic policies called import substitution industrialization, the subject of chapter 3, to address the cycle of instability and vulnerability it faced under the externally oriented commodity export model. Although import substitution industrialization was not the solution to the puzzle of Latin American development, new strategies to meet growing internal and external economic challenges were introduced. Unfortunately, as we will see in the following chapters, a changed focus toward internal growth did little to change the fundamental pattern of asset ownership, reinforcing the highly unequal pattern of growth in the region.[47]

HISTORICAL LESSONS

To conclude our rapid tour of Latin American history, we have summarized some of the factors influencing growth in the region in table 2.8. Natural resource dependence, geography, unequal distribution of land, and labor, capital, and technological constraints shaped early development outcomes. What kind of lessons can we draw about these historical factors affecting Latin American development? We need to be very careful about concluding too much about historical causality, especially given the diverse set of circumstances in the region, but we can point to several legacies.

First, the colonial pattern of asset distribution in the region was unequal and tied to privilege. The political and economic power of the elites was replicated in the postindependence period and set the stage for contemporary policy. Persistent and rising inequality is the defining characteristic of the region's growth. Because international capital was relatively abundant, it did not have to turn to enhancing labor productivity as a source of growth. The poor in Latin America were rarely invested in.

Second, as a region rich in resources and blessed with agricultural abundance, Latin America first pursued a strategy of export promotion. Geography

**Table 2.8.   Stylized Characteristics of Early Growth Patterns
          in Latin America**

Natural resources	Resource abundant although often dependent on a single commodity Ownership was concentrated Geographic terrain and distance to markets Conditioned settlement patterns and institutions
Land	Land was initially distributed by the crown Landholdings were concentrated in large *latifundia* or *fazendas* Peasants did not hold clear title to the land they worked Land quality varied; lack of title for peasants decreased incentive for investment
Labor resources	Labor in agriculture and mining was scarce; slavery and Indian labor in addition to immigration relieve the labor constraint Low skill level; little investment in education Investment flows to Latin America were large and volatile
Financial capital	Part of the surplus was returned to Europe; concentrated ownership protected high returns in agriculture and resources creating little incentive for domestic investment in industry During periods of commodity booms, high returns in agriculture make investment in industry risky A domestic savings gap creates international financial dependency
Technology	Weak science and technology infrastructure Domestic technological gaps begin to emerge between industrial North and Latin America Technological control by the North begins High asset inequality allowed elites to build institutions to protect privilege
Policy environment	The golden age of exports gives way to import substitution in the post–World War II period International protection through trading companies limited export options

Source: Patrice Franko.

mattered enormously. Financial resources were drawn to the dynamic export sectors, to the neglect of balanced development strategies. Colonial inequality was reinforced by the region's successful integration into the global economy and its access to relatively cheap external capital and technology. Government efforts were focused not on improving the local human capital of the peasants but on attracting external capital as the source of growth.[48] The *encomienda* system established the pattern of depleting and not replenishing the region's human capital.[49]

Third, given the openness to world trade, Latin America was unable to protect itself from external shocks in the global economy. When the booms turned to busts and prices fell, entire economies suffered. The Great Depression and the war years produced dramatic structural changes in Latin America that forced a reconsideration of the externally oriented primary product model.

Finally, the commodity export model exacted a high environmental and social price. The dislocation of indigenous communities and devastation of the land had enduring consequences. Pristine forest lands and diverse wildlife fell under the reign of sugar-, coffee-, and banana-exporting economies. Contemporary patterns of social conflict in the region—for example, the thirty-six-year civil war in Guatemala or the movements of the landless people in Brazil—certainly find their roots in the historical pattern of unequal land distribution.

The dissatisfaction arising from the externally oriented commodity export model gave rise to a new model of development in Latin America: import substitution industrialization. Import substitution industrialization located the answer to the question of why Latin America stagnated after the war period while Europe and the United States took off in the vulnerability of external orientation and dependency on international primary product markets. As we will see in the next chapter, the focus on substituting imports with a wider array of domestically produced goods was envisioned as a means of diversifying the source of growth and harnessing the emerging locomotive for growth: technological change.

Key Concepts

backward linkage	*encomienda*	*hacienda*
caciques	Engel's law	*latifundia*
commodity lottery	export pessimism	*mandamiento*
declining terms of trade	*fazenda*	*minifundia*
Dutch disease	forward linkage	*repartida*
ejidos	golden age of primary	
enclave	product exports	

Chapter Summary

Growth Patterns

- Growth patterns demonstrate that disparities between industrialized nations and Latin America did not develop until the twentieth century.
- Historical factors including geography, natural endowments, the allocation of factors of production, policy frameworks, and macroeconomic environments have determined patterns of growth in Latin America.
- Geography conditions settlement patterns and trade profiles; it also shapes institutions associated with extractive industry.

An Extractive Economy

- Throughout the colonial period, Spanish and Portuguese conquistadors extracted abundant natural resources from Latin America. Their exploitative techniques utilized indigenous populations and imported slaves under the *encomienda* decree as well as marginalized peasants and concentrated land-holdings under the *latifundia* system. These methods resulted in elite control of capital and political power, a weak internal market, and severe income disparities.
- Despite the opportunity to alter rules of property rights during the period of Latin American independence, the political elite maintained concentrated landholdings. During the late 1800s and early 1900s, Latin America benefited from agricultural exports. The boom, however, was short-lived. Development policy was driven by the export sector, ignoring domestic production, and demand for exports was determined abroad.
- Single-commodity exports faced various problems. First, Dutch disease promoted unbalanced development. The dependence on any one export proved problematic when prices declined and revenues diminished.
- Second, single-commodity exports of primary products faced inelastic demand—that is, despite significant increases in consumer income, the consumption of a particular product may only rise slightly. Growth potential is therefore limited.
- Third, Latin American countries largely failed to reinvest profits from single-commodity exports. Furthermore, the characteristics of export commodities did not stimulate production in other sectors of the economy through forward or backward linkages. The influx of foreign capital, moreover, failed to foster the development of domestic financial institutions.
- Finally, the environmental costs of single-commodity exports in extractive economies were high. Conquistadors interrupted traditional agricultural practices and substituted environmentally unsustainable methods. World War I and the Great Depression forced Latin America to address the cycle of instability and vulnerability it faced under the externally oriented export model and to decrease its dependence on single-commodity exports.

Notes

1. Suggested starting points are Bradford E. Burns, ed., *Latin America: Conflict and Creation: A Historical Reader* (Englewood Cliffs, NJ: Prentice Hall, 1992); and Benjamin Keen, *Latin American Civilization*, 3rd ed. (Boston, MA: Houghton Mifflin, 1974). Even a few hours dabbling in these readers will help capture the rich and complex regional history. New work in the economic history of Latin America has been spurred by the confluence of research by the New Institutional Economics (led by Douglas North) and the work on the New Economic History, which analyzes technological and institutional sources of growth. For an overview see Stephen Haber, *How Latin America Fell Behind* (Stanford, CA: Stanford University Press, 1997), chap. 1.

2. Leandro Prados de la Escosura, "Colonial Independence and Economic Backwardness in Latin America," *GEHN Working Paper Series, Working Paper No. 10/05,* www.lse.ac.uk, February 2005, favorably compares Latin American growth to other African and Asian cases, indicating that the decline in Latin America was relative to the United States—and not to more geographically comparable cases.

3. Inter-American Development Bank, "Why Geography Matters," box 1.2 in *Latin America at the Turn of the New Century, Economic and Social Progress in Latin America 2000 Report,* 21.

4. Luis Bertola and Jeffrey Williamson, "Globalization in Latin America before 1940," *NBER Working Paper* No. W9687, May 2003, 4.

5. Prados, "Colonial Independence and Economic Backwardness in Latin America," 18.

6. John Luke Gallup, Alejandro Gaviria, and Eduardo Lora, *Is Geography Destiny?* (Washington, DC: The Inter-American Development Bank, 2003).

7. Bertola and Williamson, "Globalization in Latin America before 1940," 15.

8. Daron Acemoglu, "Root Causes: A Historical Approach to Assessing the Role of Institutions in Economic Development," *Finance & Development,* June 2003, 27–30.

9. Gallup, Gaviria, and Lora, *Is Geography Destiny?*

10. See, for example, Bill Weinberg, *War on the Land: Ecology and Politics in Central America* (Atlantic Highlands, NJ: Zed, 1991).

11. Colin M. Lewis, "Industry in Latin America," in *Dependency and Development in Latin America,* eds. Fernando Henrique Cardoso and Enzo Faletto (Berkeley: University of California Press, 1979).

12. Bertola and Williamson, "Globalization in Latin America before 1940," 15.

13. Stanley Engerman and Kenneth Sokoloff, *Factor Endowments, Institutions, and Differential Paths of Growth among New World Economies: A View from Economic Historians of the United States,* National Bureau of Economic Research Historical Paper No. 66 (Cambridge, MA.: NBER, 1994).

14. Thomas E. Skidmore, "Brazil's Persistent Income Inequality," *Latin American Politics and Society* 46(2) (2004): 138.

15. Prados "Colonial Independence and Economic Backwardness in Latin America," 4.

16. Kenneth Sokoloff, "Inequality and the Evolution of Institutions of Taxation: Evidence from the Economic History of the Americas," in *Growth Institutions and Crises: Latin America from a Historical Perspective,* ed. Sebastian Edwards (Cambridge, MA: NBER, 2005).

17. Engerman and Sokoloff, *Factor Endowments,* 30.

18. Prados, "Colonial Independence and Economic Backwardness in Latin America," 7.

19. John Coatsworth, "Notes on the Comparative Economic History of Latin America and the United States," in *Development and Underdevelopment in America,* eds. Walther Bernecker and Hans Werner Tobler (New York: Walter de Gruyter, 1993).

20. Acemoglu, "Root Causes," 29.

21. Prados, "Colonial Independence and Economic Backwardness in Latin America," 9.

22. John H. Coatsworth and Jeffrey G. Williamson, "Always Protectionist? Latin American Tariffs: Independence to the Great Depression," *Journal of Latin American Studies* 36(2) (May 2004): 205–232.

23. There is some inconsistency in the historical data. Although estimates of Latin American income at the time were almost certainly biased upward, Bulmer-Thomas, *The Economic History of Latin America since Independence,* 27, notes that "Latin America's relatively privileged status within what is now the third world at the end of the 18th century is difficult to dispute." (New York: Cambridge University Press, 1995).

24. Bulmer-Thomas, *The Economic History of Latin America since Independence,* uses the term "commodity lottery" to describe the effects of export orientation in the 1800s. Much of the discussion of economic history in this chapter relies on Bulmer-Thomas's illuminating text.

25. Michael Bordo and Christopher Meisner, "Financial Crisis 1880–1913: The Role of Foreign Currency Debt," in Edwards, *Growth Institutions and Crises.*

26. Rosemary Thorp, *Progress, Poverty, and Exclusion: An Economic History of Latin America in the 20th Century* (Baltimore, MD: Johns Hopkins University Press/Inter-American Development Bank, 1998), 49.

27. Daniel Farber, *Environment under Fire* (New York: Monthly Review Press, 1993), 34.

28. Simon Hanson, *Economic Development in Latin America* (Washington, DC: Inter-American Affairs Press, 1951), 107.

29. Ibid., 106.

30. Bertola and Williamson, "Globalization in Latin America before 1940," fig. 2.

31. Prados, "Colonial Independence and Economic Backwardness in Latin America," 9, citing Bulmer-Thomas.

32. Bertola and Williamson, "Globalization in Latin America before 1940," 18–23.

33. This section draws heavily from Alan Taylor, "Foreign Capital in Latin America in the Nineteenth and Twentieth Centuries," March 2003 *NBER Working Paper* No. W9580, which later appears as a chapter in the *Cambridge Economic History of Latin America*, edited by Victor Bulmer-Thomas, John Coatsworth, and Roberto Cortés (Cambridge, UK: Cambridge University Press, 2006). This short section hardly does justice to the rich detail in the article.

34. Thorp, *Progress, Poverty, and Exclusion*, 69.

35. Lewis, "Industry in Latin America," 295.

36. Thorp, *Progress, Poverty, and Exclusion*, 56.

37. Nathaniel H. Leff, "Economic Development in Brazil, 1822–1913," in *How Latin America Fell Behind: Essays on the Economic History of Brazil and Mexico, 1800–1914*, ed. Stephen Haber (Stanford, CA: Stanford University Press, 1997).

38. Gerardo Della Paolera and Alan M. Taylor, "Finance and Development in an Emerging Market: Argentina in the Interwar Period," in *Latin America and the World Economy in the Nineteenth and Twentieth Centuries: Explorations in Quantitative Economic History*, eds. John Coatsworth and Alan Taylor (Boston, MA: Harvard University Press, 1998), 12.

39. Ibid., 18.

40. Thorp, *Progress, Poverty, and Exclusion*, 64.

41. Farber, *Environment under Fire*, 15.

42. Burns, *Latin America*, 40.

43. Thorp, *Progress, Poverty, and Exclusion*, 57.

44. John Ryan, "The Shrinking Forest," *NACLA Report on the Americas* 25(2) (September 1991): 19.

45. Thorp, *Progress, Poverty, and Exclusion*, 21.

46. Vittorio Corbo, "Economic Policies and Performance in Latin America," in *Economic Development: Handbook of Comparative Economic Policies*, eds. Enzo Grilli and Dominick Salvatore (Westport, CN: Greenwood, 1994), 299.

47. Thorp, *Progress, Poverty, and Exclusion*, 6.

48. Coatsworth, "Notes on the Comparative Economic History of Latin America and the United States," 24.

49. Timothy Yeager, "Encomienda or Slavery? The Spanish Crown's Choice of Labor Organization in Sixteenth-Century Spanish America," *Journal of Economic History* 55(4) (December 1995).

CHAPTER THREE

IMPORT SUBSTITUTION INDUSTRIALIZATION

Looking Inward for the Source of Economic Growth

Many countries—including coffee producers—linked their growth to the commodity lottery. *(iStock/Arnoldophoto)*

At the beginning of the twentieth century Argentina was one of the world's wealthiest nations. Why did the elegant and luxurious buildings in Buenos Aires begin to seem locked in time as other nations modernized? Why did much of Latin America, despite its rich natural resources, experience slow growth? The export-led model discussed in chapter 2 did not deliver the anticipated growth. Distribution also had not improved. Why were the peasant *campesinos* stuck in a cycle of poverty? Emerging from the Great Depression and the world wars, Latin America lagged behind its neighbors in the Northern Hemisphere. Once behind international competitors, how could Latin American nations ever hope to catch up?

Hoping to answer these questions, Latin American policymakers compared the performance of the region with that of North America and Europe; they also looked with interest at the takeoff of the Soviet Union. Two answers to the puzzle of slow growth emerged: first, an explanation for Latin America's falling behind and, second, a prescription for what to do about it. Political economists such as Paul Baran and Andre Gundar Frank suggested that Latin America was not falling behind but was being *pushed* back by the exploitative development process in the powerful industrial countries. Raúl Prebisch and those at the Economic Commission for Latin America and the Caribbean (ECLAC) defined the development problem as the need to promote growth in the face of an international system controlled by the center countries. This chapter explores these tools of inward-looking development in the policy of **import substitution industrialization (ISI)**. It treats the role of the state as a developmental actor and introduces the exchange rate and trade tools used to promote industrialization. It concludes by evaluating the performance of ISI as an answer to the puzzle of how to promote development in Latin America. The following questions form the core of our investigation:

- How did theorists make sense of Latin America's declining position in the world economy?
- How did the theory of ISI propose to overcome the constraints on Latin American economic development?
- What were the key elements in the ISI toolbox?
- Was the approach successful in practice?

Understanding ISI is an important step in unraveling the puzzle of Latin American development. This gives us a sense of the historical backdrop to contemporary policy; it also locates one end of the policy spectrum with respect to the role of the state in development against which we can evaluate current practices. Box 3.1 provides a glimpse of the evolution of thought on development in the region by looking at the life of one significant contributor, Raúl Prebisch.

BOX 3.1.   RAÚL PREBISCH (1901–1986)

The Argentine economist Raúl Prebisch was born in 1901 in the town of Tucumán.[a] He was strongly influential in the development of Latin American economic policy, and his contributions to development economics broke with the neoclassical. Although later

continued

criticized, his views and ideas questioned the extent to which the free market and free trade could solve the problem of underdevelopment.

Prebisch was educated at the University of Buenos Aires,[b] and during the 1920s he worked as a statistician for the Sociedad Rural, a stockbreeder's association.[c] Toward the beginning of his career, Prebisch believed in neoclassical economics, but the Great Depression and the writings of economist John Maynard Keynes shattered his faith in the free trade model.[d] Prebisch began to formulate different theoretical views in the early 1940s. This shift was first manifested in *The Economic Development of Latin America and Its Principal Problem,* written in 1949.[e] By this time Prebisch had served as director general of the Argentine Central Bank (1935–1943) and had witnessed the devastating effects of the Depression on Argentina, which suffered from falling prices and debt payment difficulties. His 1949 manifesto reflected the effect of these external influences on economic development.

Prebisch divided the world in two, labeling one part the center and the other the periphery. The center referred to advanced economies, producing primarily industrial goods; the periphery included developing countries, producers of primary products. Prebisch defined a skewed relationship between the two, with the center gaining at the expense of the periphery. For Prebisch, productivity gains in the North (the center) were translated into rising wages, not falling prices, due to the market power of business and unions. In the South (the periphery), surplus labor kept wages low, and slow productivity growth in agriculture and mining acted as a drag on the economy.[f] The unequal distribution of economic gains was due primarily to **declining terms of trade**, as developing countries would have to export more and more to be able to import the same quantities as before. It is clear that by this point Prebisch rejected the idea that comparative advantage was the answer to growth for developing countries and opted for other policy prescriptions.

In 1948, the UN Economic Commission for Latin America was created; Prebisch became its influential chairman in 1949.[g] Prebisch's diagnosis for the causes of underdevelopment led him to advocate ISI. From 1964 to 1969, Prebisch was the secretary-general of the UN Conference on Trade and Development (UNCTAD).[h] During this time period, Prebisch put aside his theoretical thinking and formulated policies that were later ignored by both the developed and the developing worlds. When Prebisch returned to his theoretical endeavors after the UNCTAD years, he suggested that a post-ISI policy was required, including removing protection from certain industries and encouraging nontraditional exports. He pointed to the need to develop internal savings to decrease reliance on external debt, suggested institutional changes in the labor market and financial sector, and advised budgetary reforms to consolidate change in Latin America.[i]

---

a. Gerald M. Meier and Dudley Seers, *Pioneers in Development* (Oxford: Oxford University Press, 1984), 173.

b. Meier and Seers, *Pioneers in Development,* 173.

c. Ronald V. A. Sprout, "The Ideas of Prebisch," *CEPAL Review* 46 (April 1992): 178.

d. James L. Dietz and James H. Street, eds., *Latin America's Economic Development: Institutionalist and Structuralist Perspectives* (Boulder, CO: Rienner, 1987), 81.

e. Meier and Seers, *Pioneers in Development,* 176.

f. Henry Bruton, "A Reconsideration of Import Substitution," *Journal of Economic Literature* 36 (June 1998): 905.

g. Meier and Seers, *Pioneers in Development,* 176.

h. Sprout, "Ideas of Prebisch," 179.

i. Ibid., 182; and Nancy Birdsall and Carlos Lozada, "Recurring Themes in Latin American Economic Thought: From Prebisch to the Market and Back," in *Securing Stability and Growth in Latin America,* eds. Ricardo Hausmann and Helmut Reisen (Paris: OECD Publications, 1996).

Dependency Theory: An Explanation
for Backwardness

For some analysts, answering the question of why some nations were growing and others were stagnating required looking not at countries in isolation, as individual plants in a garden, but rather at how countries interacted with each other in the international system. Proponents of **dependency theory** postulated that a country did not thrive or falter simply because of its own national endowments. Rather, progress could be attributed to the power it had to set the rules of the international economic game. **Center** countries, or the industrialized countries, defined the rules; the **periphery**, or developing countries, were pawns in the international pursuit of profit. As dependency theorist Andre Gunder Frank postulated, underdeveloped countries were not developed countries in the making; rather, industrial countries had caused underdevelopment in other nations in the process of economic expansion. For Frank, underdevelopment was generated by the same historical process that produced economic development: the march of capitalism.[1] Industrialized countries had access to cheap inputs for growth through the extraction of resources, the export of minerals, and the exploitation of cheap labor in the underdeveloped world. Rich countries became rich by making other countries poor.

The owners of the resources—the wealthy in the underdeveloped region—benefited from the international market. According to dependency theorist Paul Baran, local elites formed alliances with international capitalists, hindering long-term, dynamic growth in favor of short-term profits. Baran pointed to the feudal coherence of the *latifundia* system and the monopolistic market structure as impediments to vigorous long-run growth.[2] A social glue bonding local and international elites cemented economic privilege for the upper class. Those with power had no interest in sharing it. Relatively concentrated markets weakened competitive pressures. For Baran and for Frank, while the periphery was tied to the center, there was no possibility of sustainable growth. As long as traditional elites remained in power, periphery countries would be shackled to center country interests. Revolution, therefore, was in order.

Other theorists, such as Fernando Henrique Cardoso and Enzo Faletto, disagreed with the revolutionary prescription. Although concurring with the assessment that the center countries controlled the dynamic of growth, Cardoso and Faletto argued that autonomous development was indeed possible within the periphery. It would, however, involve an active state policy to counterbalance the greedy hand of the international market. A powerful state acting in the national interest could counteract the strength of local and international economic elites to promote genuine development in the periphery.

From Dependency Theory to Development Policy:
ECLA and the Structuralist School

The dependency theorists' critique of the international economic system informed but did not completely define the position of the **structuralists** at the United Nations Economic Commission for Latin America (ECLA).[3] Under the leadership of Raúl Prebisch (see box 3.1), ECLA analysts looked at the disappointing economic performance of Latin America in the first half of the century, focusing on the volatility of primary product exports and the progressive difficulty of paying for more technologically sophisticated (and expensive) products with limited agricultural returns.[4] Technological progress was controlled by the powerful center-industrialized countries and spread slowly into the periphery. ECLA researchers in the 1950s were also fascinated by a seeming correlation between the interruption of normal trade patterns with the industrialized countries during the war periods and accompanying robust internal growth in Latin America. Isolation from the international system apparently helped growth at home.

In part, the disadvantaged position of periphery countries in the international system derived from the kind of goods they offered. Developing countries principally traded primary products, such as raw materials and agricultural goods, for more technologically advanced products in the international arena. Within this unequal framework, they faced what was seen as declining terms of trade for their products. There are only so many bananas that people want to eat or so much coffee that they can drink. Given the low income elasticity for agricultural products, as the global economy grows, the relative demand for primary products declines. Instead, rewards tend to accrue to those engaged in technological entrepreneurship. Technological sophistication adds value to a good, increasing its market price well beyond the cost of basic inputs. Declining terms of trade for primary products reflected the argument that as the prices of sophisticated goods rose, developing countries would need to export more and more oranges or wheat to pay for the more expensive technological machinery. Without mastering technology, countries had little hope of advancement.

In addition to the position that all goods do not generate equal rewards, structuralists also offered a view contrary to that of traditional economists on how economies functioned. Challenging the tenets of neoclassical economic theory, which assumes that rational, self-interested profit maximizers operating in open and competitive international markets will produce the greatest good for all, structuralists argued that the economy was shaped by power and politics. For the structuralists, economic activity is conditioned by interest-group politics. Markets in Latin America are controlled by concentrated oligopolies in which firms are price makers and elites establish patterns of consumption. Powerful advertising conglomerates shape global tastes; elites tend to demand sophisticated goods produced by industrial economies. Importing these items would do little to spur local growth. The promises of trickle-down economics hold no magic for the masses of the poor in the developing world. In the structuralist's eyes, the development process is not a movement toward equilibrium but rather is driven by imbalances and tension. Although the neoclassical model predicts benefits for poor countries from international trade, structuralists contend that international trade exacerbates inequality between and within nations because those countries and companies with control set the rules of the game in their favor. For the structuralist, the neoclassical model does not conform to the hard, cold facts of the international economy. Of course, neoclassical economists hold a different view, one suggesting that the dependency approach repackaged reality to fit its worldview. Some economic historians suggest that the unexpected growth under postwar isolation that prompted the strategy was neither as dynamic nor as isolated as the stylized facts of the dependency theorists suggest.[5]

From Structuralism to ISI

The arguments of the dependency theorists and the structuralists shaped the ISI policy package widely adopted in Latin America. Perceiving the international game as stacked against them and with multiple external shocks repeatedly destabilizing the economy, Latin American policymakers turned inward to promote internal sources of economic growth. Instead of relying on the international economy as the engine of growth, ISI policies sought to develop industries in a protected environment. The goal was to create industries capable of producing substitutes for expensive imports while simultaneously promoting industrial growth and the expansion of internal economies. The notion was that ISI would induce a process of learning driven by exposure to new ideas and processes that would dynamically spill over into the whole economy.[6] Raúl Prebisch and ECLA structuralists placed the role of technological change at the center of the development process and identified a strong role for the state in promoting national technological capabilities.[7] Without mastering technological processes, developing countries had no chance to catch up. The only economic actor strong enough to counterbalance the weight of multinational corporations was the state.

The strategy of ISI was informed by Albert Hirschman's concepts of bottlenecks and linkages. For Hirschman, imbalances in the system, such as supply shocks and bottlenecks, were central to development as signals for investment.[8] Hirschman characterized the development process as a bottle with a thin neck. Inputs—land, labor, capital—were constrained from freely flowing from the bottle by the constricting neck of scarce complementary factors such as technology, infrastructure, or entrepreneurial capital. If the state could break the bottlenecks in crucial industries, resources would flow back up the production chain, stimulating the demand for intermediate inputs, or they would flow forward in the consumption pattern to create the demand for new products. Therefore, by promoting a steel sector, for example, **backward linkages** such as those to the iron ore and smelters would stimulate the growth of these supplier industries, while **forward linkages** would stimulate the auto or machine industries. If the state could target those industries with the largest backward and forward linkages, it could act as an engine of development.

A strong state was critical to the structuralist program. ISI theorists pointed to a simple fact: if the market could work on its own, why had it not been successful in promoting growth in Latin America? **Market failure** to produce sustainable growth provided the rationale for state intervention. Given the weak private sector and the large economies of scale attached to industrial endeavors, an active state was viewed as a necessary complement to the market economy.[9] The ability of the state to deliver on public project investments contributed to the perceived need of governments to also meet the demand for social projects. This emanated from the highly unequal income distribution in Latin America.

The political demands of populism, of attending to the broad needs of the domestic population in the name of social peace, were consistent with the ISI economic theory. Populism drew on the charismatic power of leaders such as Juan Perón of Argentina or Getulio Vargas of Brazil to mobilize support within labor and industrial elites in the service of a nationalist development strategy. Traditional populist strategies encouraged support for a developmentalist model to meet the changing needs of society without explosive class conflict. By co-opting key labor and industrial groups into the quest for change, support for interventionist policies could be maintained. **Economic populism**, a term applied to the developmental strategies of the 1950s, 1960s, and 1970s, emphasized growth and redistribution of income to the neglect of internal and external constraints. That is, as long as financing was available, the state kept attempting to buy off each group in the conflictual process of development. Labor, politically powerful, was given strong protection under the law. Industrialists were favored with development schemes. State-led strategies to reduce poverty and promote infrastructure were pursued to keep local political leaders happy. But constraints on development—inflation, fiscal deficits, external imbalances—were often ignored until it was too late and crisis erupted.[10] Political demands to moderate the distributional tensions of development were consistent with the state-led ISI model.

THE ISI TOOLBOX

ISI relied on a variety of economic tools to achieve its aim. The toolbox can be broken down into three categories: active industrial policy, protective international instruments, and accommodationist fiscal and monetary policy complemented by a careful program of transnational participation. It is important to note that although these tools were at the disposal of all policymakers in the region, they were applied in varying degrees in each country. We will discuss these three broad tools in turn.

Active Industrial Policy: The Role of SOEs

Industrial policy was anchored in the formation of state-owned enterprises (SOEs) throughout the region. Under the assumption that the state was the only able domestic actor with the resources to produce in relatively underdeveloped markets, state firms were formed in a wide range of heavy industries, including oil, petrochemicals, telecommunications, steel, and aircraft. In some cases these enterprises were wholly owned by the state, and in others they operated as mixed enterprises, incorporating state and private capital. State firms had access to public funds for investment, research, and development. Backed by sovereign guarantees, they also had easier access to international financial markets to borrow for large development projects. State ministries could assist in the negotiation of international technology transfer packages to jump-start production. Such firms had the resources to hire some of the brightest national scientists, engineers, and managers to run operations. Additionally, the pressures of producing initial annual profits were relieved as state firms were able to extend their time horizon for investment returns.

Although the public enterprise status held many advantages, there were also restrictions. Hiring and pay scales were subject to national standards, sometimes placing a ceiling on the pay for skilled labor. State firms were subject to the whims of politicians and often became agencies for employing large numbers of constituents. Furthermore, the services of industries in basic infrastructure, such as the electrical or telecommunications sectors, were often underpriced to provide cheap inputs to stimulate the growth of the private sector. Cheap inputs allowed for a local manufacturing boom; however, underpricing electricity or phone service led to losses that were absorbed by the SOEs. As resources became increasingly constrained, underpricing also resulted in underinvestment over time. Because firms were carrying losses, they couldn't afford to expand to meet demand.

Despite the difficulties that SOEs confronted, they proliferated rapidly from the 1950s to the 1970s in Latin America. In table 3.1 we see what types of industries were most subject to state ownership and ISI policies in the case of Brazil. High rates of state ownership existed particularly in industries that required significant investment, such as public goods enjoyed by all citizens and critical industries, including national security enterprises.

In an analysis of the causes for state intervention, Tom Trebat identifies six reasons for state enterprises: a weak private sector, economies of scale, public externalities, dynamic public managers, natural resource rents, and public historical factors. In steel, electrical energy, and telecommunications, state-owned firms were formed after private-sector failures. Particularly in Brazil, developmental nationalists believed that state intervention was the pragmatic response to the failure of the free market. Economies of scale and the need for large investments to lower costs provided further grounds for state activity. In industries with clear public value, such as railroads, energy, and ports, it was argued that there were benefits to state provision of these services, especially when private providers had not emerged in the market. Because of public visibility and prestige, some state enterprises were able to attract the most dynamic managers. Finally, where industrialization was resource based, such as in oil and mining, it was argued that these resources belonged to the nation and should therefore be managed on the public's behalf.[11] Thus, there was an economic rationale (although perhaps not always a compelling one) for state activity in the industrial sector.

The High Tariff Walls of ISI: Protectionism as a Tool of ISI

International economic tools facilitated the industrialization process. If your grasp of international economics is rusty, box 3.2 provides a quick review of terms. The growth of state and private enterprises was encouraged under the protection of high tariff and trade restrictions. These protective walls were designed to give less-competitive national industries, conceived of as infant industries, the chance to develop without the competition of large multinational firms. There was a perceived need for protection while an economy developed the necessary condi-

Table 3.1.   State Enterprise Share in the Brazilian Economy, 1973

	Proportion of Assets in State-Owned Firms
High Degree of State Participation (≥50%)	
Railways	100
Port services	100
Water, gas, and sewers	99
Telegraph and telephone	97
Electricity	79
Mining	63
Developmental services	51
Chemicals	50
Medium Degree of State Participation (20–49%)	
Water transport	45
Banking and finance	38
Metal fabrication	37
Services	36
Air transport	22
Low Degree of State Participation (<20%)	
Construction and engineering	8
Rubber	6
Road transport and passengers	6
Agriculture and forestry	4
Nonmetallic mineral	2
Transport equipment	2
Food and beverages	1
Machinery	0
Wood products and furniture	0
Textiles and leather products	0
Tobacco	0
Printing and publishing	0
Radio and television	0
Commerce	0

Source: Adapted from Peter Evans, *Dependent Development* (Princeton, NJ: Princeton University Press, 1979), 221, table 5.1.

tions to promote learning and innovation within the firm.[12] The policy objective contraction to ignore exports; rather, the hope was that temporary protection would lead to the development of new products.[13] We can measure the degree of protectionism by looking at tariff rates. Average nominal protection over consumer and manufactured goods was 131 percent in Argentina, 168 percent in Brazil, 138 percent in Chile, 112 percent in Colombia, 61 percent in Mexico, and 21 percent in Uruguay in 1960.[14] In the case of Mexico in 1970, the effective rate of protection—the nominal tariff rate adjusted for the protection also present in the purchase of intermediate goods used to produce the final good—was as high as 671 percent for fertilizer and insecticides, 226 percent for synthetic fertilizers,

---

BOX 3.2.   A REVIEW OF THE TOOLS OF PROTECTIONISM

export subsidy   A fiscal incentive, sometimes in the form of a tax break, for reaching export targets. Export subsidies promote the development of export industries at home, arguably to unfair advantage compared to the international firms.

foreign exchange controls   To restrict the quantity of imports or to direct imports to certain sectors, the government may ration foreign exchange. This generally involves compelling exporters to sell foreign exchange to the government at a fixed price. Selective importers of key goods are offered preferential prices for foreign exchange, whereas importers of luxury items or those wanting to travel pay more local currency for their dollars, yen, or pounds. Foreign exchange controls are therefore linked to a system of multiple exchange rates. Not surprisingly, as there are therefore different prices for the same commodity—money—a "black" or a "parallel" market often develops. The black market price can sometimes be used as an indicator of how far the exchange rate has been taken off course by policy distortions.

import licensing   The legal requirement to obtain a license to import a certain kind of good. Import licensing boards evaluate national availability of goods to assess whether the import is critical or whether the need can be met by national production.

industrial incentives Direct payments or tax breaks to a firm engaging in a particular line of production. These credits act as a protectionist device if an international competitor cannot meet the lower, subsidized price in the local market.

quota   A quota is a quantitative limit on imports. A quota presents a fixed limit on the quantity of goods that may be imported. Quotas may be assigned to suppliers or they may be auctioned, creating revenue for the central government.

tariff   A tariff, the most common type of protectionism, is a tax on imports. A tariff works best when the demand for the good in question is elastic or price sensitive. If buyers do not respond to the higher price, a tariff will not limit imports. With a tariff, the central government collects revenues. Nominal tariff protection is measured by looking at the tariff rate on the final manufactured good. Effective rates of protection adjust this rate for tariffs on intermediate inputs.

---

206 percent for pharmaceuticals, 102 percent for automobiles, and 67 percent for electrical equipment. Across the board, for durable consumption and capital goods in Mexico in 1970, effective protection rates averaged 35 percent.[15] Import licenses were used in intermediate and consumer durable goods to encourage growth.[16] High import tariffs often induced multinational firms to set up factories within the country. In 1970 in Mexico, 62 percent of the machinery sector, 49.1 percent of transport vehicles, and 79.3 percent of electric equipment were dominated by foreign enterprises.[17] Although ownership was not national, labor learned new production techniques, and the technological level of production was raised.

Somewhat ironically, in the first stages of ISI, national imports usually rose. Steel, for example, could be produced only with huge furnaces, and they had to be bought somewhere. To promote the import of these critical inputs, states tended to maintain **overvalued exchange rates**, making imports relatively cheaper to purchase. Imports and access to this underpriced foreign exchange were often licensed to limit imported goods to those critical to the industrialization process. As reviewed in box 3.2, import licensing boards evaluated the quality and availability of national substitutes, their prices, and their importance in the production process before allocating cheap foreign exchange.[18] International trade and foreign exchange tools insulated the economy from rival foreign firms dominating the market. Box 3.3 contrasts the effects of various exchange rate regimes in development strategies.

BOX 3.3. EXCHANGE RATE POLICY AND DEVELOPMENT

An exchange rate is simply the price of one currency in terms of another. Ideally, exchange rates should equate the value of one nation's goods with those of another.[a]

There are three broad types of exchange rate regimes: fixed, flexible, and crawling pegs. Under the gold standard (1870–1914) and the Bretton Woods systems (1945–1973), countries fixed their currencies to an anchor—gold or the US dollar. A fixed exchange rate has the advantage of promoting stability. A critical economic price—the price of domestic goods in terms of international goods—is fixed. The rules of a fixed regime require that a country running a balance of payments deficit must clear its accounts by exporting gold or defend its rate by selling dollars or reserves. Because money supplies are anchored to dollars or gold, the decrease in money contracts the economy and fewer goods are imported. The economy should therefore expand only at the rate of its accumulation of real reserves—that is, gold or dollars in circulation. The best way to understand this concept is to visualize the old trade rules: if France imported more from Great Britain, it had to send or "export" gold to pay for it, thus lowering the national money supply. In the next period France could buy less—and Britain more—balancing imports and exports.

Today many countries pursue a floating exchange regime. Under a floating system, if a country is running a balance of payments deficit, the price of foreign exchange adjusts or depreciates. Rather than a country exporting gold, the market changes the value of national money. The price of the currency is determined by the demand for a country's goods. As imports surge, residents sell their own currency to buy the foreign currency needed to purchase the imported goods. As a result, imports become more expensive and exports appear cheaper in international markets. If consumers are responsive to price changes, flows should begin to balance. A large stock of reserves is not needed to defend the rate. Nevertheless, whereas the fixed exchange rate promotes price stability, a floating exchange rate may exacerbate inflation. Depreciation makes crucial imports more expensive, exerting an upward pressure on domestic prices.

Finally, some countries attempt to have both the stability of a fixed anchor and the flexibility of floating rates with the use of a crawling peg. Under this exchange rate system the currency is set to a central value but is allowed to fluctuate around that target in the short run.

What is the "right" exchange rate in the long run? Essentially, the same good should sell for the same price in two different markets. If it does not, and transportation costs are minimal and trade is free, some enterprising person will buy goods in the cheaper market and sell them where they are dear. Not surprisingly, using the exchange rate as a tool of industrial promotion interferes with arriving at the "right rate." Imbalances emerge that become difficult to sustain over time.

---

a. This is based on the theory of purchasing power parity and the law of one price. Two sweaters should sell for the same price in two markets (adjusted for transportation costs). If they didn't, some enterprising person would buy sweaters where they are cheap and sell them where they are dear.

Additional Tools of Industrial Policy: Targeted Lending, Multinational Activity, and Passive Monetary Policy

Ownership was not the only tool of industrial policy in Latin America. Industrial policy was accommodated by monetary and fiscal measures. The state provided subsidies to domestic firms, and it granted tax credits and soft credit to jump-start the national industrial motor. National development banks were formed, such as Chile's Corporación de Fomento de la Producción (CORFO) and Brazil's State National Development Bank (BNDES), to target investments in the economy. A national development bank has an advantage over commercial lenders in planning strategic investment projects. As a state bank, it has a longer return horizon and is able to be active in more risky sectors because bottom-line profits are not the objective. Key industries such as machinery, automobiles, shipbuilding, and telephones were targeted as central to industrial growth. In Mexico, the Law of New and Necessary Industries provided select tax exemptions to promote growth in a limited number of unrepresented but critical sectors in the economy. Economic policy flexibility adjusted to changes in product and monetary markets. Governments saw budget deficits as reasonable investments in the future, financing them either through borrowing or running the printing presses. Quite simply, economic policy supported a countercyclical dimension—an approach untenable in later years of macroeconomic crises.[19]

ISI contributed to the development of manufacturing such as this Brazilian auto parts manufacturer. *(Photo by Patrice Franko)*

In "strategic" sectors such as autos or steel, **transnational corporations** were welcomed as providers of needed technology and capital within the ISI model. In table 3.2 we can see the significant role played by multinational corporations in manufacturing. In or about 1970, 24 percent of manufacturing in Argentina, 50 percent in Brazil, 30 percent in Chile, 43 percent in Colombia, 35 percent in Mexico, 44 percent in Peru, and 14 percent in Venezuela was under foreign control. Some of this participation predates the ISI period, but the strong involvement of transnationals, particularly in industrial production, was seen throughout the postwar ISI period.[20]

The entry of transnational corporations was somewhat paradoxical. ISI, after all, was attempting to reduce dependency on the international structure of production. However, there was also a degree of pragmatism at work. Transnationals provided critical financial capital and technology. The goal became to utilize these assets selectively, employing state bargaining power to transform the rules of the game. ISI policies set new rules: to produce and sell in the domestic market, transnational companies had to commit to technology transfer and the training of labor. Under the threat of market closure to the sale of their products, transnational firms agreed to joint ownership arrangements and the use of local inputs. In the automobile industry in Brazil, for example, GM do Brasil was a joint venture between Brazilian capital and General Motors (GM). Along with Ford, Volkswagen, and Fiat, it sparked the development of an industrial park. With high tariff rates, local production was the only viable way to sell cars nationally. Multinational firms defended market shares against the possibility of being shut out through local manufacturing. If a multinational corporation did not participate according to local rules, its international competitors would. Development of local parts suppliers was promoted by requiring 99 percent local content by weight for passenger cars produced locally.[21] Mexico was able to prod concessions in creating national joint ventures in the electrical industry by playing one multinational against another.[22] In addition to local content laws, contracts often stipulated the training of local managers to improve national managerial capacity, an assurance of transfer of technological processes (not simply sending the more sophisticated parts preassembled in the United States or Europe), and limits on the repatriation of profits to promote local reinvestment of revenues.

Table 3.2.   Foreign Share of Selected Industries, circa 1970 (percentages)

	Argentina	Brazil	Chile	Colombia	Mexico	Peru	Venezuela
Food	15.3	42.1	23.2	22.0	21.5	33.1	10.0
Textiles	14.2	34.2	22.9	61.9	15.3	39.7	12.9
Chemicals	34.9	49.0	61.9	66.9	50.7	66.7	16.5
Transport equipment	44.4	88.2	64.5	79.7	64.0	72.9	31.1
Electrical machinery	27.6	83.7	48.6	67.2	50.1	60.7	23.2
Paper	25.7	22.3	7.9	79.3	32.9	64.8	20.1
All manufacturing	23.8	50.1	29.9	43.4	34.9	44.0	13.8

Source: Excerpted from Rhys Jenkins, *Transnational Corporations and Industrial Transformation in Latin America* (New York: St. Martin's, 1984), table 2.4.

A large domestic market enhanced national bargaining power in establishing contract terms with the multinationals. Clearly, Brazil and Mexico had greater bargaining power than Ecuador or Paraguay, as there were many more likely Brazilian or Mexican buyers of locally produced cars. Yet even in the Mexican and Brazilian cases, exports of locally manufactured multinational products were necessary to take advantage of economies of scale. Despite technology and export earnings, multinationals were not welcomed in all sectors. Even where bargaining power was strong, nationalist sentiments reserved strategic industries, such as oil in Mexico, to wholly local ownership.

For the most part, a loose monetary policy greased the fiscal wheels of development. From the mid-1960s to the 1980s, the dominant political system in Latin America was an authoritarian government. Developmental nationalists saw it as their mission to promote development as a critical element of security. Rules were changed to decrease the autonomy of central banks, forcing them to accommodate fiscal spending programs. Nonetheless, in areas of monetary, fiscal, or international affairs, reliable data about developing nations were sorely lacking, and many macroeconomic decisions were made by guesswork and intuition.[23]

THE PERFORMANCE OF ISI

How well did ISI work? Box 3.4 summarizes the tools at work. By the barometer of average annual growth rates of 5.5 percent over the period 1950 through 1980, one could call import substitution a successful strategy. Throughout the 1950s, Latin

---

BOX 3.4.   ISI TOOLBOX: A SUMMARY

INDUSTRIAL POLICY

Form state-owned firms
Form mixed economic enterprises—part state, part private
Require government purchases from national firms
Require foreign firms to establish joint ventures
Pressure foreign firms to increase local content

INTERNATIONAL INSTRUMENTS

Tariffs on final goods
Quotas on imports
Exchange rate overvaluation
Exchange rationing
Import licenses

FISCAL AND MONETARY POLICY

Subsidies for cheap inputs such as electricity
Subsidies for public transportation
Tax breaks in production
Preferential interest rates
Accommodating monetary policy

American economies were growing comparatively faster than the Western economies, and between 1950 and 1970 Latin American gross domestic product (GDP)
tripled.

As illustrated in table 3.3, performance varied by country, with Brazil,
Ecuador, and Mexico exhibiting the strongest growth rates over the ISI years of
roughly 1950 to 1980. The production of basic consumption goods was widespread throughout the region, and some countries successfully initiated heavy-
machine goods industries as well.[24] Production outstripped population growth,
making progress on this problem (identified in Chapter 2). While the population
of the region roughly doubled over the period 1945–1980, GDP in real terms
quintupled.[25]

Import performance was uneven. Most countries did not see a decline in
imports as a ratio of GDP. Brazil was more successful, as indicated in a comparison
of 1964 with 1949. Imports in the Brazilian economy decreased substantially as
a percentage of total national supply, ranging from 19.0 percent in 1949 to 4.2
percent in 1964. Predictably, during the first stages of ISI in Brazil, the import
of capital producer goods doubled from 1949 (15.8 BCR) to 1959 (29.2 BCR)
as machines were needed to produce other goods. However, by 1964, imports of
capital producer goods had fallen to nearly half the rate of the 1949 levels. Over the
same period, domestic production of consumer and producer goods rose substantially, with national production of all manufactured products increasing 266 percent
from 1949 through 1964.[26]

Table 3.3. Percentage Growth in GDP per Capita

Country	1941–1949	1950–1959	1960–1969	1970–1979	1980–1989
Brazil	1.6	3.6	2.8	6.1	0.8
Ecuador	4.1	2.4	1.8	7.0	−0.1
Mexico	3.7	3.1	3.5	3.2	−0.3
Dominican Republic	3.0	3.4	1.4	4.6	0.7
Panama	−2.2	1.8	4.8	1.9	−0.6
Costa Rica	4.7	2.8	2.2	3.3	−0.8
Colombia	1.6	1.8	2.1	3.2	1.6
Peru	2.5	3.0	2.5	1.2	−2.1
El Salvador	9.3	1.8	2.2	1.8	−2.6
Guatemala	0.3	0.5	1.9	3.1	−2.1
Paraguay	0.6	−0.7	1.1	5.0	0.9
Argentina	2.3	0.8	2.8	1.3	−2.3
Honduras	1.5	−0.1	1.8	2.4	−1.0
Chile	1.5	1.3	1.9	0.6	1.9
Uruguay	2.5	1.0	0.3	2.5	0.1
Nicaragua	4.2	2.4	3.6	−2.5	−3.8
Bolivia	0.6	−1.7	3.2	1.9	−3.0
Venezuela	6.7	2.9	0.0	−0.1	−3.4

Source: ECLA data as found in Vittorio Corbo, "Economic Policies and Performance in Latin America,"
in *Economic Development: Handbook of Comparative Economic Policies*, eds. Enzo Grilli and Dominick Salvatore (Westport, CN: Greenwood, 1994), 308.

Less-tangible gains also accrued.[27] Import substitution created forces for the development of an urban middle class, which demanded infrastructure entitlements in public utilities such as water and sewage systems. A national business class and a parallel labor union movement emerged, changing the agrarian balance of power. This coalition supporting the model, however, often intervened in policy making to thwart changes such as exchange rate valuations that might have prevented the accumulation of large fiscal imbalances.

The Crisis of ISI

Despite the apparent gains, ISI was both unsustainable over time and produced high economic and social costs. In theory, ISI should have developed an internal momentum, expanding industrialization through interindustry linkages. Employing his concept of linkages, Hirschman predicted that industrial growth should have occurred based on targeted investments. However, some contend that given the limited size of the internal market in Latin America, ISI became "exhausted." It was postulated that as one moves to ever more sophisticated production, especially heavy machinery, the minimum plant size increases. Successful substitution would therefore be limited to sectors in which the internal demand for the good exceeded plant size—or where exports could make up the difference. The export vent, however, was largely closed due to the unfavorable exchange rates and less competitive industries. One study suggested that with such a high degree of income inequality, a massive devaluation to make Latin American exports globally competitive would have been politically and socially explosive.[28] Some programs were successful, such as the Brazilian BEFIEX (Special Fiscal Benefits for Exports) scheme, which provided incentives for exports. In many cases nationally manufactured goods did not meet international quality standards after growing up under protective tariffs, and firms were not forced by competition to become efficient. ECLA economists advocated economic integration within the region to expand the economies of scale, but the integration process was stalled. Economic performance was too varied across the region, the base of consumers with an ability to pay was too small, and political differences made subregional integration difficult at times.

Others explained the crisis of ISI in political and sociological terms. Because the industrial process was largely in the hands of elites, it failed to create a new entrepreneurial class that would have given the process greater dynamism. Given elite power, ISI may have provided more support to industrialists than to industry.[29] Many of the tools used to manage ISI—import licenses, investment permits, and government contracts—created the possibility of profitable personal rents for those able to control them.[30] Corruption became economically expedient under the ISI model. This led to the views of the new political economists (which will be discussed in chapter 5), suggesting a minimalist role for government.

ISI exacerbated inequality in the region. With more than a third of the region's population living in poverty, internal demand was severely limited. Consumption patterns imitated those of the center elite instead of attending to the needs of the masses. ISI may also have been a more reactive and a less-coherently implemented strategy than is often supposed. That is, the policy-making process frequently may have been responding to balance of payments crises in erecting tariffs rather than proactive protection.[31] Finally, instead of promoting risk-taking behavior, the comfort of state ownership and international protection coddled the business culture. ISI fostered the creation of inefficient economic institutions that have persisted into the contemporary period.[32]

With resources focused on industrialization, agriculture was neglected. Necessary investments in agricultural infrastructure were not made as capital was directed to the industrial sector. Labor also gravitated toward urban industrial regions, pressuring cities. In some cases the decline in agricultural production meant an increase in the quantity of food imports, further pressuring the balance of payments. The neglect of agriculture weakened not only a source of profits but also the food security of nations. The urban, industrial bias was unsustainable. ISI was an imbalanced strategy.

Inefficiencies and inconsistencies abounded under ISI. Even Raúl Prebisch, founder of the ECLAC school, was not blind to the emerging challenges in the region in the late 1960s and early 1970s.[33] Prebisch noted that overvalued exchange rates biased growth against the export sector. Where exports are a source of international or hard currency, this introduces a foreign exchange gap to finance development. Differences in domestic expenditures and revenue in state-owned firms lead either to persistent deficits or to monetary expansion that results in inflation. We will consider these inflationary biases in Chapter 5. Internal and external resource gaps were met through external borrowing, adding annually to debt obligations (see Chapter 4). As long as international financial markets were willing to extend financing, the model could be sustained; however, once the spigots of international finance were turned off, internally driven industrialization ground to a halt.

Lessons for Development:
Was ISI Inherently Flawed?

Does the failure of ISI in the 1980s mean that it was a misguided policy from the start? Some contend that the triumphant adoption in the 1990s of the neoliberal model throughout the region testifies to the inherent flaws of ISI. Others such as economist Werner Baer suggest that ISI was the appropriate policy for the period but that times changed.[34] Indeed, it could be argued that the development of the industrial sector under ISI made the dynamic private-sector model possible in the 1990s. The international environment also changed substantially, with expanding globalization. After we look more closely at the neoliberal model in Chapters 6 through 9, consider the counterfactual question: Would industrial development have been so successful without ISI? Although we will come to no definitive conclusion, entertaining this question may foreshadow some of the future needs in Latin America with respect to the role of the state.

Remember Gabriel García Márquez's warning (see Chapter 2) about the repetitious cycles in Latin American history. Before we discard the goals and tools of ISI forever, we might do well to consider that in the future the past may reappear, with a stronger need for the state to address some of the problems of market failure.

But this is getting well ahead of our story. In the next chapter we will look more carefully at some of the problems associated with the later ISI period: macroeconomic instability and the debt crisis. This will then position us for a careful look at the neoliberal model, with a strong role for the private as opposed to the public sector.

Key Concepts

backward linkages	economic populism	overvalued exchange rates
center	forward linkages	periphery
declining terms	import substitution	structuralists
of trade	industrialization (ISI)	transnational corporations
dependency theory	market failure	

Chapter Summary

The Dependency and Structuralist School

- The dependency theory states that the center (industrialized nations) expanded at the expense of the periphery (developing nations). Capitalism therefore created underdevelopment. Local elites forged alliances with international capital, blocking development.
- The structuralist school, as defined by the UN Commission for Latin America described two main characteristics of growth in the region. First, declining terms of trade hindered economic development for Latin America. Second, concentrated oligopolies and elites determined prices and consumption patterns that proved incompatible with growth for the region.

Import Substitution Industrialization (ISI)

- In response to dependency theory and the structuralist school, Latin America pursued ISI. This inward-oriented approach sought to promote and protect domestic industries through an interventionist state that would attack bottlenecks and market failures.
- ISI relied on various tools to promote industrialization:
  - active industrial policy through the use of SOEs;

- protective international instruments such as tariffs, quotas, import licenses, foreign exchange controls, industrial incentives, and export subsidies to protect infant industries;
- targeted lending to industries such as machinery and automobiles;
- subsidies and tax exemptions for particular industries, including transnational corporations that provided critical financial capital and technology;
- strict investment rules such as local content laws and minority foreign ownership;
- and passive monetary policy to finance projects under ISI.
- Although data show that ISI had a positive effect on growth until the 1980s, there were also negative consequences. Nationally manufactured goods often failed to meet international quality standards, making them uncompetitive in the global market. ISI exacerbated inequality by preserving the power of the elite and failing to create an entrepreneurial class. In addition, the agricultural sector was neglected, which weakened a source of profit and food security. There was also a bias against export growth through overvalued exchange rates, leading to differences in domestic expenditures and revenue that contributed to persistent deficits and inflation.

Notes

1. Andre Gunder Frank, *Capitalism and Underdevelopment in Latin America* (New York: Monthly Review Press, 1967).

2. Paul A. Baran, "On the Political Economy of Backwardness," *Manchester School* 20(1) (1952); reprinted in *The Economics of Underdevelopment*, eds. A. N. Agarwala and S. P. Singh (New York: Oxford University Press, 1963), and in *Political Economy of Development*, ed. Charles K. Wilber (New York: Random House, 1973). See also the classic piece written by Gabriel Palma, "Dependency: A Formal Theory of Underdevelopment or a Methodology for the Analysis of Concrete Situations of Underdevelopment?" *World Development* 6(7–8) (July–August 1979): 881–924.

3. The Spanish acronym for ECLA is CEPAL, the Comisión Económica Para América Latina. ECLA later became ECLAC, with the "C" reflecting the incorporation of the Caribbean.

4. Enrique V. Iglesias, ed., *The Legacy of Raúl Prebisch* (Washington, DC: Inter-American Development Bank, 1994).

5. Stephen Haber, *How Latin America Fell Behind* (Stanford, CA: Stanford University Press, 1997), chapter 1.

6. Henry Bruton, "Import Substitution," in *Handbook of Development Economics*, vol. 2, 3rd ed., eds. Hollis Chenery and T. N. Srivivasan (New York: Elsevier, 1996), 1609.

7. Vittorio Corbo, "Economic Policies and Performance in Latin America," in *Economic Development: Handbook of Comparative Economic Policies*, eds. Enzo Grilli and Dominick Salvatore (Westport, CN: Greenwood, 1994).

8. Charles K. Wilber and Steven Francis, "The Methodological Basis of Hirschman's Development Economics: Pattern Modeling vs. General Laws," *World Development*, Special issue 14(2) (February 1986): 181–191.

9. For a discussion of the role of the state in economic development, see Thomas Trebat, *Brazil's State-Owned Enterprises: A Case Study of the State as Entrepreneur* (New York: Cambridge University Press, 1983).

10. Rudiger Dornbusch and Sebastian Edwards, "The Political Economy of Latin America," in *The Macroeconomics of Populism in Latin America*, National Bureau of Economic Research

Conference Report, eds. Rudiger Dornbusch and Sebastian Edwards (Chicago, IL: University of Chicago Press, 1991), 9. See also Alan Knight, "Populism and Neo-Populism in Latin America, Especially Mexico," *Journal of Latin American Studies* 30 (1998): 223–248.

11. Trebat, *Brazil's State-Owned Enterprises.*

12. Bruton, "Import Substitution," 1607.

13. Rosemary Thorp, "Import Substitution: A Good Idea in Principle," in *Latin America and the World Economy: Dependency and Beyond*, ed. Richard J. Salvucci (Lexington, MA: Heath, 1996), 140–146. The Salvucci book is a good reader to accompany Chapters 2–3 of this text.

14. Victor Bulmer-Thomas, *The Economic History of Latin America since Independence* (New York: Cambridge University Press, 1994), 280. "Nominal" refers to the tariff rate on the final good without adjusting for tariffs on intermediate inputs.

15. Adriaan ten Kate and Robert Bruce Wallace, "Nominal and Effective Protection by Sector," in *Protection and Economic Development in Mexico*, eds. Adriaan ten Kate and Robert Bruce Wallace (Hampshire: Gower, 1980), 122, 151.

16. Gerardo Esquivel and Graciela Marquez, "Some Economic Effects of Closing the Economy: The Mexican Experience in the Mid-Twentieth Century," in *Capital Controls and Capital Flows in Emerging Economies: Policies, Practices and Consequences*, ed. Sebastian Edwards, *NBER*, June 2005.

17. Tom Warts, "Protection and Private Foreign Investment," in *Protection and Economic Development in Mexico*, 198.

18. Robert Bruce Wallace, "Policies of Protection in Mexico," in *Protection and Economic Development in Mexico.*

19. Petro Lains illustrates this idea in "Before the Golden Age: Economic Growth in Mexico and Portugal, 1910–1950," p. 7 in Edwards, "Growth Institutions and Crises: Latin America from a Historical Perspective." Table 4 shows total public debt rising from 2.48 percent a year to 12.97 percent from 29–39 to 39–50 and M1 growth from 4.14 percent to 19.18 percent over the same period (p. 23).

20. Rhys Jenkins, *Transnational Corporations and Industrial Transformation in Latin America* (New York: St. Martin's, 1984), 40.

21. Gary Gereffi and Peter Evans, "Transnational Corporations, Dependent Development, and State Policy in the Semiperiphery," *Latin American Research Review* 16(3) (1981): 31–64.

22. Richard S. Newfarmer, "International Oligopoly in the Electrical Industry," in *Profits, Progress, and Poverty* (Notre Dame, IN: University of Notre Dame Press, 1984), 147.

23. Henry Bruton, "A Reconsideration of Import Substitution," *Journal of Economic Literature* 36 (June 1998): 910.

24. Robert J. Alexander, "Import Substitution in Latin America in Retrospect," in *Progress toward Development in Latin America: From Prebisch to Technological Autonomy*, eds. James L. Dietz and Dilmus James (Boulder, CO: Lynne Rienner, 1990).

25. Albert O. Hirschman, *A Propensity to Self Subversion* (Cambridge, MA: Harvard University Press, 1995), 156.

26. Bela Belassa, "Brazil," in *The Structure of Protection in Developing Countries* (Baltimore, MD: Johns Hopkins University Press, 1971), table 6.2, p. 107.

27. This paragraph draws from Rosemary Thorp, *Progress, Poverty and Exclusion: An Economic History of Latin America in the 20th Century* (Baltimore, MD: Johns Hopkins University Press for the IADB, 1998), 197.

28. James E. Mahon Jr., "Was Latin America Too Rich to Prosper? Structural and Political Obstacles to Export-Led Industrial Growth," *Journal of Development Studies* 28(2) (1992): 242.

29. Alan M. Taylor, "On the Costs of Inward-Looking Development: Price Distortions, Growth, and Divergence in Latin America," *Journal of Economic History* 58(1) (March 1998): 20.

30. Bruton, "A Reconsideration," 923.

31. Bruton, "Import Substitution," 1616.

32. Taylor, "On the Costs of Inward-Looking Development," 21.

33. Enrique V. Iglesias, "The Search for a New Economic Consensus in Latin America," in *The Legacy of Raúl Prebisch*, ed. Enrique V. Iglesias (Washington, DC: IADB, 1994).

34. Werner Baer, "Changing Paradigms: Changing Interpretations of the Public Sector in Latin America's Economies," *Public Choice* 88 (1996): 365–379.

CHAPTER FOUR

LATIN AMERICA'S DEBT CRISIS

The Limits of External Financing

Populism disposed Latin America to debt-driven growth.
(iStock/Golden Brown)

The debt crisis in Latin America was a development crisis. It called into question the viability of the import substitution industrialization model of development and shaped the economic future of the region.

How did the crisis come about? Borrowing to finance development is not in itself a bad thing. Developing countries are by definition capital poor. Funding is needed for investment and growth. If a country, like a person, wants to grow or expand, borrowing provides necessary capital for change. As a student, you might be borrowing money to finance educational expenses in anticipation of a better future. This is rational behavior. Borrowing becomes a crisis when an individual or a country fails to make payments on the outstanding value of the loan. If the investment you make in your education doesn't generate a decent salary by the time your first loan payment is due, you will have a personal financial crisis. For a nation, if the returns on the investments don't match the debt obligations when they come due, a crisis also ensues. Unfortunately, the development model in Latin America was dependent on a continuous infusion of capital, with new lending required to finance the development of long-term projects. When conditions in the international market changed dramatically in the early 1980s, Latin American economies, one after another, collapsed under the mountain of external debt. The debt crisis transformed economic policy in the region—at a very high price.

In this chapter we begin by analyzing how borrowing to support import substitution industrialization became an unstable foundation for growth. We then consider the problem of debt-led growth and why a change in external conditions brought inward-looking development to a halt. Finally, we turn to the changes in development policy that enabled economies to survive the crisis, and we analyze the economic and social costs to the region. Questions that will shape our analysis include the following:

- What fueled the accumulation of external debt?
- What role did internal and external factors play in precipitating a crisis?
- How did countries and the international financial community respond to the crisis?
- What are the legacies of the debt crisis?
- Is the Latin American debt crisis over?

THE MOUNTAIN OF DEBT: AN UNSTABLE FOUNDATION FOR DEVELOPMENT

Economic growth under the import substitution model of development was fueled by external savings. With thin domestic financial markets, by 1982, Latin America had borrowed more than US$300 billion from the rest of the world. Figure 4.1 shows this accumulation of Latin American total disbursed external debt during 1980–2004. Under the import substitution model, the first stage of industrialization was driven by the import of capital goods—particularly machinery—to be used to produce goods domestically. In many cases, the capital was also used to finance large infrastructure projects such as roads, electricity, telecommunications, or water supply, all of which

Figure 4.1. Total External Debt of Latin America

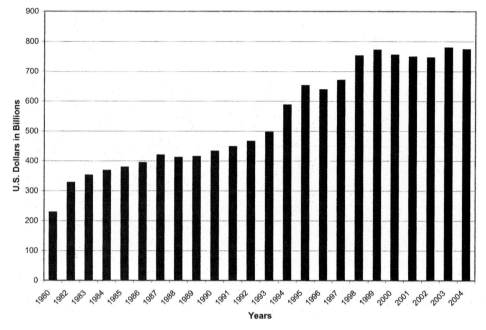

Source: World Bank, *World Debt Tables* (various years) and *Global Development Finance 2005*.

are vital to a nation's advancing growth. Borrowing in itself is not a bad strategy. Problems arise, however, when the borrowing requirements for long-term projects outpace the ability to repay past loans. Crises may erupt due to the mechanics of borrowing or the **debt trap** (unproductive investments or investments with very long time horizons that do not generate returns in time to help service loans), internally inconsistent economic policies that impede the success of projects, or external shocks that derail the domestic economy. Let's consider these causes in turn.

It is easy to fall into a debt trap when lending is for long-term projects but obligations to repay begin in the short term. This problem is made clear with a simple mathematical example. Assume the following (rather lenient) borrowing conditions. You contract to borrow $1,000 dollars a year for a project that is going to take ten years. You agree to pay $50 a year back in principal for each $1,000 borrowed over twenty years at an interest rate of 10 percent per year on the outstanding balance of the debt. As can be seen in table 4.1, in the first year you receive $1,000 and repay $50, leaving a balance of $950. At 10 percent interest your net outflow, the interest plus the principal, is $95 plus $50 or $145. In the second year you again receive $1,000 of new money to continue your project, pay $100 in principal (the first and second $50 principal payments), leaving $185 of interest to be paid on the balance of $1,850. Your principal plus interest therefore totaled $285. Your annual net transfer, the $1,000 coming in minus the $285 going out, is $715.

This formula of new money minus principal and interest payments goes on for several years. Notice that each year, because of the obligation to pay the principal

Table 4.1.   The Debt Trap: Long-Term Project Lending

Year	New Lending	Total Debt Incurred	Principal ($50/year for twenty years)	Out-standing Debt	Interest Payment (10%)	Total Net Outflow = Interest + Principle	Transfer = Disbursement Outflow
1	1,000	1,000	50	950	95	145	855
2	1,000	2,000	100	1,850	185	285	715
3	1,000	3,000	150	2,700	270	420	580
4	1,000	4,000	200	3,500	350	550	450
5	1,000	5,000	250	4,250	425	675	325
6	1,000	6,000	300	4,950	495	795	205
7	1,000	7,000	350	5,600	560	910	90
8	1,000	8,000	400	6,200	620	1,020	−20
9	1,000	9,000	450	6,750	675	1,125	−125
10	1,000	10,000	500	7,250	725	1,225	−225
11	1,000	11,000	550	7,700	770	1,320	−320

Source: John Charles Pool, Stephen C. Stamos, and Patrice Franko, *The ABCs of International Finance*, 2nd ed. (Lexington, MA: Lexington Books, 1991).

on past loans and the increasing interest burden, the net transfer—the amount of money coming in after payments have been made—substantially dwindles. Indeed, by the eighth year the $1,000 of new money doesn't even cover your payments on past obligations, much less fund new investment. If your multiyear project is incomplete or if it is not yet generating significant returns, you would need to borrow even more just to make payments. You have landed flat in the debt trap.

Mismatched Projects and Returns

Import substitution was fueled by regular infusions of capital not unlike our example above. In part, the import substitution industrialization model was driven by the failure of the private sector to provide critical goods and services in the economy. We remember that this took place most frequently in industries with large economies of scale and in sectors in which the complementary infrastructure was not available. This led to state investment in sectors with high capital requirements for entry as well as in large-scale projects to develop needed infrastructure in energy, telecommunications, and transportation. Unfortunately, the payback period for these multiyear investments was not always consistent with the terms of commercial lending. Furthermore, the returns to social investments by the state are not easily captured in state tax coffers for repayment of debt obligations.

Even when lending for large-scale infrastructure projects was efficient and well managed, multiyear development projects were not easily financed. If a road, for example, is constructed over a ten-year period and then it takes another ten years for businesses to move into the area and pay taxes, the project itself may not generate returns—and repayment of debt—until well into the future. Debt-generated investment should create the ability to service that debt in the future. Investments must have a sufficient rate of return within a compatible term structure. When this is not possible in huge undertakings, the government often steps in with public lending. Although it is a function of government to sequence projects and manage these flows, the magnitude of large-scale investments under import substitution industrialization left Latin American governments vulnerable to the willingness of capital markets to finance the gap between the period of investment and the long-term returns on the project. Given sovereign guarantees and the low likelihood of countries defaulting (as opposed to companies), markets were willing to lend. Debt was accumulated to service past debt.

Unsustainable Domestic Policies

In addition to the simple mathematical lesson of the debt trap, the intersection of politics and economics promoted debt-led development. Latin America has a long history of populism, or the use of political rhetoric to mobilize the masses. Old-style populists, such as Juan and Eva Perón of Argentina, charismatically co-opted labor and middle-class groups as well as domestic industrial elites to maintain power. But buying off the masses costs money. As we saw in Chapter 3, **economic populism** in the 1970s emphasized growth and income redistribution and de-emphasized the risks of inflation and deficit finance, external constraints, and the reaction of economic agents to aggressive nonmarket policies.[1] The populist political culture encouraged spending, which was made possible by favorable conditions in the international financial markets.

Unfortunately, the large state-run development model also lent itself well to inefficiency and corruption in lending. In some instances, lending was for pharaonic megaprojects with limited utility for social development. The history of Latin America contains numerous stories of a state firm's payrolls padded with dead people, construction taking place only on paper, and misguided attempts at development such as the Transamazonian Highway. Debt was incurred for projects that would never generate the ability to repay.

External Shocks

Of course, at some level, politicians understood that one day they would have to pay the piper. However, extraordinarily attractive international prices for capital played into the short-term political incentive to borrow. Real international interest rates—that is, interest rates adjusted for global inflation—were negative from 1974 until 1977. As shown in table 4.2, the US prime rate adjusted for inflation (the real prime rate) ranged between –2.2 and –1.4 percent. If someone asked you whether you would like to borrow money today, have the use of that money for some period

Table 4.2.   Real International Interest Rates, 1974–1984

Year	US Nominal Prime Rate (%)	US Inflation Rate (%)	US Real Prime Rate (%)
1974	10.81	13.1	−2.2
1975	7.86	11.1	−2.9
1976	6.84	8.3	−1.3
1977	6.83	8.5	−1.4
1978	9.06	7.2	1.7
1979	12.67	9.2	3.2
1980	15.27	11.9	3.0
1981	18.85	10.1	8.1
1982	14.77	7.5	6.8
1983	10.81	5.1	5.5
1984	12.04	4.8	6.9

Source: ECLAC, *Economic Survey of Latin America and the Caribbean* (Santiago, Chile: ECLAC, various years); IMF, International Financial Statistics, 1987 (Washington, DC: IMF, 1987), 113.

of time, and repay less than what was borrowed, how would you respond? Although much of the lending was on a floating rate basis—that is, each year your interest rate would change to reflect market conditions—after several years of negative real rates and the possibility that you wouldn't even be in office when repayment time came around, the decision to borrow could be seen as a rational response to price. It would be as if the interest rates in the debt trap example presented earlier were −2 percent rather than +10 percent. At that rate it would take twenty-one years, perhaps five different government administrations, for net flows to become negative. Within that time, the project might be bearing returns. Given those conditions, it would be hard for a politician to do anything but incur the loan!

Although the demand for finance was driven by developmental needs as defined by the import substitution model and the populist politics of its implementation, lending would never have taken place on such a broad scale without an ample supply of global cash. During the 1970s banks needed to recycle the proceeds from the quadrupling of oil prices, called petrodollars. Unless banks lent these petrodollar deposits, they would be unable to pay interest to the OPEC creditor nations. Many lenders simply saw it as easier and more lucrative to advance megaloans to state-owned enterprises (SOEs), backed by sovereign governments, than to package small business or agricultural loans in the United States. The competition to lend was ferocious.

Distinct Patterns, Same Result: Crisis

It is important to note that Latin American countries pursued a variety of economic strategies during this time period—yet all were strongly hit by crisis. Table 4.3 compares three cases: Mexico, Brazil, and Argentina. The Mexican debt crisis was driven by an attempt to expand the oil sector while maintaining social peace at home through domestic spending programs. International bankers were only too

Table 4.3.   Debt and Distinct Patterns of Development

Policy Instruments	Mexico	Brazil	Argentina
Long- and short-term external debt (billions of 1985 US$)	96.8	106.1	50.9
Fiscal policy	Overexpansion of fiscal policy driven by investments in the oil sector; new oil discoveries led to expanded investments by Pemex; fiscal deficit exploded to 17% of GDP	Responded to global recession with growth of domestic demand; maintained high protective tariffs; wages increased	Inconsistent fiscal policy; 1976 military regime adopted orthodox model
Monetary policy	Loose monetary policy with low interest rates led to massive capital flight; outflows reached US$8.4 billion in 1981 and US$6.6 billion in 1982; inflation soared	Economy indexed to respond to inflation; money supply passively accommodated expansionary fiscal policy	High peso interest rates initially generated strong capital inflow; when confidence was lost, capital flight ensued
Exchange rate policy	Maintained fixed exchange rate policy despite inflation; overvaluation resulted	Limited devaluation of cruzeiro to 50 percent despite inflation rates twice as high; overvaluation resulted	Overvalued exchange rate depressed exports and accelerated imports; acute reserve loss led to borrowing just to maintain the exchange rate
Exogenous shocks	Tightening US monetary policy raised real interest rates; oil prices plunged	Oil crisis pressured balance of payments; high interest rates; commodity price shock; contagion effects from Mexico	Tight US policy raised cost of capital
Comments	As an oil exporter, Mexico had access to capital; its problem derived from its attempts to limit social conflict through state spending while simultaneously expanding the oil sector	Brazil attempted to maintain state-led development model despite changes in the international economy; its large size allowed it to pursue this strategy too long	Argentina pursued an aggressive liberalization policy with exchange rate priced to restrain inflation— not promote exports; the model was therefore internally inconsistent

Source: Derived from information presented in SBC Warburg Dillon Read, *The Latin American Advisor* (February 1998).

happy to lend to Mexico because the loans were collateralized by the black gold of new oil discoveries. Domestic expansion exploded into inflation, which the government attempted to restrain through a fixed exchange rate. This exchange rate became overvalued, compromising the ability of the non-oil export sector to perform. As described below, Mexico sounded the first alert to the international community of the debt crisis in August 1982 when it announced its inability to meet its financial obligations.

Brazil also enjoyed easy access to international finance. Because it was one of the ten largest economies in the world, lenders believed that investments in this emerging powerhouse were well placed. Loans to state enterprises were seen as backed by the **sovereign guarantee** of the government of Brazil—investors thought that the government would not default on obligations. As international financial conditions changed in the 1980s, Brazil's size also slowed the incentive for its adjustment. It was able to maintain its inward-looking model of development and turn to domestic money creation to service external debt. Inflation soared, but a sophisticated system of indexing interest rates, wages, and prices minimized the pain for economic agents. We will consider these macroeconomic responses in Chapter 5. A rate of devaluation of the exchange rate slower than the rate of inflation was designed as a brake on rising prices but had the unfortunate effect of reducing export performance.

Whereas debt accumulation in Brazil and Mexico was driven by investments through state firms, Argentina's inward-looking development model ran out of steam under the populist Peronist regime. The military took over in 1976 and radically opened the economy. Unfortunately for Argentina, borrowing was used for financial purposes and did not result in an increase in the productive capabilities of the nation. Instead, a misguided attempt to maintain an overvalued exchange rate led to borrowing to defend the fixed currency price. Money flowed into the country in the form of short-term loans used to support the exchange rate, but those same dollars quickly exited in private portfolios betting against the ability of the Argentine government to restrain inflation and jump-start growth. At the crux of the Argentine problem was the fact that the overvalued exchange rate, used as an anchor for inflation, could not simultaneously promote exports. Box 4.1 provides a review of overvalued exchange rates.

Despite these differences in internal development models, Mexico (an oil exporter), Brazil (a nation inwardly focused on its large domestic market), and Argentina (an economy open to the international economy) were all rocked by changes in the international economy that transformed a heavy debt profile into an insupportable burden. Unsustainable domestic policies left each nation vulnerable; external pressure exposed the fragility of the debt-led development model.

The Crisis Builds: External Shocks and Capital Flight

The accumulation of external liabilities to finance development is not a crisis. However, external conditions changed radically, and evidence began to mount that called into question the ability of governments to service their debt. In 1979 US

Box 4.1. Overvaluation of Exchange Rates and the Debt Crisis

An overvalued exchange rate can be seen as both a cause of the accumulation of debt and an effect of the macroeconomic instability perpetuated by the debt crisis.

Before explaining the economic cause and effect of an overvalued rate, we should clarify what is meant by an overvalued exchange rate. An overvalued exchange rate exists when the currency is artificially too strong, allowing the purchase of more foreign currency than trade patterns might indicate. With a strong currency, people buy more from abroad. An undervalued rate is "too weak," favoring exports. Imports become prohibitively expensive, and exports are cheap. Most overvaluation exists when the price of a currency is established under a fixed exchange rate system.

The Goldilocks question of figuring out which rate is "just right" goes back to a theory of exchange rate determination called purchasing power parity, or PPP. In its simplest form, PPP argues that a good should sell for the same price in two countries when prices are adjusted for the exchange rate. Holding transportation costs constant, if Costa Rican coffee does not sell for the same price in San Jose, Costa Rica, and San Jose, California, people will buy it where it is cheap (Costa Rica) and sell it where it was dear (California), driving the price up in Costa Rica and down in California. Because one would need *colones* to purchase the coffee in Costa Rica, this would drive up the value of the *colon* until the value of the two goods was identical in the two markets. If the exchange rate were set by the government (rather than being a floating market rate), the "right" price for the currency should generate one price for coffee. However, if tastes changed and people drank less coffee and demanded fewer *colones* to buy it, an unadjusted exchange rate would become overvalued.

Alternatively, if the Costa Rican government increased the money supply, the *colon* should be worth less than the US dollar. For example, if prices in Costa Rica were rising at 20 percent per year but in the United States they were rising by only 5 percent a year, this means that Costa Ricans could purchase 15 percent (20 – 5) less a year with the same income as those in the United States. Under a floating system, this should be reflected in a 15 percent fall in the value of the currency, or the exchange rate. Once again, if the exchange market isn't functioning smoothly or if the government intervenes to fix a currency price and does not allow the devaluation to take place, we would say that this currency is overvalued.

A look at table 4.4 shows that from 1979 through 1981, currencies became significantly overvalued in Latin America. The numbers presented are indexes that set 1980–1982 as a base year. By 1981, for example, Argentina's currency was 7 percent too

Table 4.4.   Real Exchange Rate Indexes (1980–1982 = 100)

	Argentina	Brazil	Chile	Mexico	Venezuela
1976–1978	73	116	75	98	95
1979	101	96	79	98	94
1980	116	85	95	104	93
1981	107	103	108	114	100
1982	76	112	97	82	110
1983–1985	74	85	86	86	98

Source: Selected from Rudiger Dornbusch, *Stabilization, Debt, and Reform: Policy Analysis for Developing Countries* (Englewood Cliffs, NJ: Prentice-Hall, 1993); original source Morgan Guarantee, World Financial Markets.

continued

continued

strong, Brazil's 3 percent, Chile's 8 percent, and Mexico's 14 percent; only Venezuela's was "just right." (We see, however, not for long.)

Why would a country allow overvaluation to take place? First, if the country is pursuing import substitution, the strong currency value allows companies to purchase intermediate inputs at a lower cost. Because the policy was often to discourage the importation of final consumer goods, import licenses at these preferential rates were sometimes required. Second, countries may choose to link their currency to a vehicle currency such as the US dollar as an inflation-fighting anchor. Just as global currencies were set to the US dollar under the Bretton Woods system following World War II or under the gold standard, developing countries have at times viewed the link as a stabilizing force. Currency boards have also been used to establish a one-to-one link, constraining the growth of the domestic money supply to the number of US dollars held in reserve. Whether the link is firm or whether the government uses the US dollar value as a guide to monetary policy, under a fixed exchange rate regime this should be anti-inflationary. Nonetheless, if all inflation is not immediately squeezed out of the economy and a rate is fixed, when the local currency should be losing value to reflect inflation but it isn't, overvaluation is taking place.

Finally, even when a country knows that a devaluation is indicated, at times it is reluctant to do so. In addition to incurring a political cost (citizens concluding that the government was unable to control inflation), the devaluation can serve as an additional inflationary shock because imports now become more costly. The vicious circle between inflation causing the need for devaluation and then a devaluation increasing prices in the economy pressuring for a further devaluation is the economic minister's nightmare.

Capital flight makes the pressure toward devaluation worse. If indications point to the possibility of a devaluation, investors will move their assets out of the country. The rationale is clear. Say you have 1,000 pesos in the bank and that initially they can buy you US$1,000 worth of goods at a 1:1 exchange rate. Now assume that you have a 20 percent devaluation of the peso. This means that to buy the same US$1,000 worth of goods, you will have to come up with 1,200 pesos. Therefore, if you think there will be a devaluation, you will sell pesos and hold US dollars (perhaps in a Miami bank account or perhaps under your bed). Selling pesos, not surprisingly, weakens the peso. Under a fixed exchange rate, the government must intervene in the market, selling US dollars and buying pesos to maintain the value. It is forced to sell the US dollars that it holds in reserves for such foreign exchange transactions. However, a fall in reserves in the balance of payments numbers erodes confidence. Everyone knows that reserves are dwindling and that a devaluation is inevitable because the central bank does not have infinite resources to defend the currency. Capital flight accelerates in the face of a possible devaluation, making that change in the currency value inevitable. Pressures on overvalued exchange rates resulted in many countries moving from a fixed to a floating rate.

president Jimmy Carter appointed Paul Volcker as chairman of the Federal Reserve Board. Volcker's inflation-taming efforts drove the US prime rate to 18.8 percent in 1981. Floating rate obligations skyrocketed to a real, or inflation-adjusted, positive 12 percent. In addition to facing escalating interest payments, countries found it difficult to generate the hard currency—usually US dollars—to pay the debt. Debt in Latin America was generally dollar-denominated, because no international bank would issue a loan in pesos when the peso was likely to be devalued. To repay the loan, the country therefore had to earn or buy US dollars. The most direct means of augmenting dollar holdings was to sell Latin American goods in the United

Table 4.5.   Capital Flight from Selected Latin American Countries (billions of US$)

	1979	1980	1981	1982	1983	1984
Argentina	2.2	3.5	4.5	7.6	1.3	−3.4
Brazil	1.3	2.0	−1.4	1.8	0.5	4.0
Mexico	−1.1	2.2	2.6	4.7	9.3	2.6
Venezuela	3.0	4.8	5.4	3.2	3.1	4.0

Source: Robert Cumby and Richard Levich, "On the Definition and Magnitude of Recent Capital Flight," Working Paper 2275 (Cambridge, MA: National Bureau of Economic Research, 1987); cited in Sebastian Edwards, *Crisis and Reform in Latin America: From Despair to Hope* (New York: Oxford University Press and World Bank, 1995), 23.

States. Unfortunately, Volcker's inflation-fighting tools also generated recession, shrinking the United States as a market for Latin American goods. The slowdown became global, and the region found itself with increasingly burdensome obligations and a limited ability to earn the money owed.

Evidence of the unsustainability of the debt began to mount. Table 4.5 shows the capital flight from unsustainable policies in Argentina, Mexico, and Venezuela from 1979 through 1984. Capital flight as a percentage of total external debt reached 76.9 percent in Argentina, 73.3 percent in Mexico, and 131.5 percent in Venezuela. Capital flight takes place when a national makes a deposit or investment outside its home country. On one hand, capital flight is simply good international investing. A Brazilian economist once commented, "Why is it that when an American puts money abroad it is called 'foreign investment' and when an Argentinean does the same it is called 'capital flight'? Why is it that when an American company puts 30 percent of its equity abroad it is called 'strategic diversification' and when a Bolivian businessman puts only 4 percent abroad it is called 'lack of confidence'?"[2] On the other hand, if one's portfolio preference is decidedly against domestic investment or if investors or savers actively circumvent laws to prevent scarce capital from leaving the country, capital flight has taken place. Capital votes with its feet. Many Latin American families, for example, have savings accounts in Miami to guard against the possibility that the value of all of their savings would be decimated by poor economic management, followed by a devaluation. As shown in box 4.1, overvaluation of a currency contributes to capital flight because agents do not want to be caught holding assets denominated in a currency that is likely to be devalued. In some cases corruption exacerbated capital flight. Dollars coming in as loans to SOEs found their way out of the countries in the coffers of corrupt public agents.

Capital flight further destabilizes macroeconomic management. In an attempt to bribe capital to stay at home, interest rates may be set too high and retard investment. When capital leaves the tax base, the government's ability to raise revenues is weakened. There is stronger incentive for **seignorage**, the process of printing money to cover the deficit. Because people want to sell the local currency and trade it in for US dollars, the excess supply of the local currency is inflationary. We will come back to this problem in Chapter 5.

Table 4.6.   Debt Indicators for Latin America and the Caribbean, 1980–1990

Year	Total Debt/Exports of Goods and Services	Total Debt/GNP	Total Debt Service/Exports of Goods and Services	Interest/Export of Goods and Services	Interest/GNP
1980	206.0	36.2	36.9	19.6	3.4
1981	210.9	37.8	21.6	11.1	2.0
1982	269.1	46.9	47.6	30.3	5.3
1983	309.1	58.6	43.0	29.8	5.6
1984	291.4	59.3	39.9	27.2	5.5
1985	312.9	61.3	38.2	27.9	5.5
1986	376.6	63.2	43.6	27.5	4.6
1987	377.6	66.1	37.4	23.0	4.0
1988	332.6	56.7	39.6	24.1	4.1
1989	293.3	50.1	32.1	16.6	2.8
1990	277.4	45.0	26.3	13.0	2.1

Source: World Bank, *World Debt Tables* (Washington, DC: World Bank, various years).

Other measures of indebtedness fueled uncertainty, aggravating capital flight and the loss of confidence in economic management in the region. Because export earnings finance debt payments, it is important to look at the weight of debt to exports as well as debt service—the interest and principal that must be paid for by exports. A measure greater than 200 percent in the level of total external debt to exports or a debt service to export ratio over 40 percent is unhealthy, pointing to great pressure on exports for debt payments and leaving little capital for other investment. We can see in table 4.6 that by 1982 total debt over exports had reached 269 percent and that total debt service over the exports of goods and services was edging toward 50 percent. Interest payments alone ballooned to 30 percent of exports, without reducing future liabilities. Latin America was in trouble.

CAN'T PAY, WON'T PAY

In August 1982, Mexico announced to the international financial community that it could no longer service its debt. When the financial community saw that the sovereign government of Mexico would not or could not make good on its obligations, confidence in all developing countries eroded. It was a crisis for Mexico that quickly spread through the region and all developing countries and threatened the international finance system. At the time that Mexico signaled the international financial community of the severity of the crisis, exposure to debt was a problem not only for the countries but also for the banks. As can be seen in table 4.7, the exposure of the nine major banks to six highly indebted countries exceeded an average of 174 percent of shareholders' equity in the banks. Exposure to either Mexico or Brazil alone would have been approximately half of shareholders' capital.

Table 4.7. Exposure of Nine Major US Banks to Six Highly Indebted Countries, 1984

	% of Shareholders' Equity (common and preferred)
Manufacturers Hanover	268.5
Chase Manhattan	212.7
Citicorp	206.7
Chemical	196.7
Bankers Trust	177.6
Bank of America	150.9
Morgan Guarantee	143.5
Continental Illinois	129.9
Wells Fargo	129.8
First Chicago	126.9
Average	174.3

Source: John Charles Pool, Stephen C. Stamos, and Patrice Franko, *The ABCs of International Finance*, 2nd ed. (Lexington, MA: Lexington Books, 1991), 113.

The International Monetary Fund (IMF) Approach

When Mexico rang the alarm bell on the mountain of external debt accumulated by developing countries, the depth of the problem was poorly understood. The international financial community diagnosed the difficulty primarily as a liquidity crisis. The *World Development Report* of 1983 noted, "Debt problems of most major developing countries are caused by illiquidity, not by insolvency."[3] Returning to the analogy of personal finances, **illiquidity** might mean that because you were laid off from your job or because you went wild with your credit cards, you cannot make your payments when due. However, with time and budgeting, you could honor your commitments and not be forced into bankruptcy or insolvency. In the banking world, the assumption was that debtors would regain creditworthiness through a combination of internal adjustments and more favorable global economic conditions. Box 4.2 reviews other debt-related terms.

BOX 4.2. KEY DEBT TERMS

arrears   The amount of past-due payments (interest and principal) on outstanding debt owed by any given debtor.

bilateral loans   Loans from governments and their agencies, from autonomous bodies, and from official export credit agencies. These differ from private creditors (commercial banks and bonds) who did the bulk of the lending leading to the debt crisis.

concerted lending   Involuntary lending by a bank. When the Mexican crisis began in 1982, large banks formed bank advisory committees to represent all banks and to keep them informed of debt negotiations. These committees, along with industrialized countries and the IMF, pressured smaller banks to continue lending to prevent defaults.

continued

continued

debt service   The sum of principal repayments and interest payments actually made.
disbursements   Earnings on loan commitments during the year specified.
LIBOR (London Interbank Offer Rate)   Traditional benchmark interest rate for international lending by private European banks.
loan default   A bank declaration that a borrower is not expected ever to repay its debt, usually following an extended cessation of principal and payments by the debtor.
long-term external debt   Debts with a maturity of more than one year owed to nonresidents, payable in foreign currency, goods, or services.
moratorium   A declaration by a debtor country of its intent to stop principal and interest payments to its creditors.
net flows   Disbursements minus principal repayments.
net transfers   Net flows minus interest payments during the year.
sovereign default   A government's decision to default on its external debt obligations.

REFERENCES

Biersteker, Thomas J. *Dealing with Debt.* Boulder, CO: Westview, 1993.
Krugman, Paul R., and Maurice Obstfeld. *International Economics: Theory and Policy.* 3rd ed. New York: HarperCollins, 1994.
World Bank. *World Debt Tables, 1995–1996.* Washington, DC: World Bank, 1996.

The internal adjustments were, for most countries, tough medicine to swallow. The presumption was that countries were living beyond their means and therefore had to reduce domestic **absorption** of resources. If fewer goods were consumed at home, more could be exported to service the debt. If we allow Y to represent national income and A to stand for the domestic consumption of goods and services (including imports), we can see in the simple formula $Y - A = B$ that B (the balance) is the residual. A trade surplus, then, would help restore financial health by decreasing the need to finance imports, leaving the balance to pay off the debt. Absorbing less at home left more for hard currency-earning exports.

The Absorption Approach: $Y - A = B$

How should domestic absorption be decreased? The IMF prescription for achieving balance revolved around decreasing government and personal absorption of resources and increasing the attention to the international sector. In contrast to the state-centered import substitution strategy, the IMF recommended that states decrease spending on public works, privatize SOEs, and eliminate subsidies on goods and services. To combat inflation, monetary policy should be contractionary. If wages were indexed to a public minimum wage, it was generally suggested that wage increases be minimal. Devaluation was indicated to adjust overvalued exchange rates, and liberalization of markets through the reduction of tariffs and quotas was favored. The devaluation was designed to change the relative price of goods, making imports more expensive and exports cheaper. This creates incentives for expenditure switching by raising the opportunity cost of tradable goods. Fewer tradables will be consumed at home, and more will be released for sale abroad. Rather than borrowing, foreign investment was seen as the vehicle for the capital necessary for growth. The overriding principle was to get prices right. Resources should be directed to their most productive use through accurate price signals.

The IMF package was inherently contractionary, premised on decreasing fiscal spending and monetary emission. The hope was that the infusion of capital from abroad and initiative from the local private sector would fuel growth. The program generated a good deal of economic dislocation. Workers in bloated SOEs were laid off. Recipients of state-subsidized milk or tortillas faced dramatic price increases. The price of public transportation rose, and spending on infrastructure fell. Companies that had grown up behind the protection of high tariff walls found it difficult to compete with international firms. Tight money meant high interest rates, which retarded investment. Devalued exchange rates sent price shocks through imported consumer goods. Agricultural exports were rapidly promoted, often at high environmental cost.

But the bitter IMF pill was seen as necessary if countries were to maintain access to finance. When a country found itself unable to make payments on its external obligations, banks would lend no more until the country had signed a letter of intent with the IMF to implement the tough economic policies. Targets for macroeconomic performance would be set, and if countries adopted the conditions specified to achieve these goals, IMF funding would be released. **Conditionality**—the adoption of strict fiscal, monetary, and trade policies in exchange for the release of funds—was designed to alert the private sector that substantial change in the spending habits of the country was under way. This signaled a green light for further lending.

The lending, however, was not fresh money for new projects. Instead, given the severity of the financial crisis, the loans were intended to provide the capital to make payments on past liabilities coming due. For a price—and at a higher interest rate—old loans were rolled over into new loans with maturity dates further in the future. The presumption was that when these repackaged loans came due again, the benefits of the tough economic medicine would be available to service the obligations. Called **involuntary lending**, this rolling over of obligations was designed to provide financial breathing room until payments could be made from more productive economies.

Unfortunately, international macroeconomic conditions did not cooperate. Real interest rates did not decline rapidly, and the prices that countries received for their exports—primarily agricultural commodities—were depressed. By 1985 Latin American countries had not returned to good standing in the international market. The problem was clearly more than a short-term liquidity issue. But was the IMF approach wrong?

Criticism of IMF conditionality packages centered on the IMF's diagnosis of the problem as well as the policy measures to bring about change. In Latin America, the theoretical debate was led by the structuralist school. It faulted the IMF approach as too standardized. The same IMF recipe, based upon the assessment of the need to reduce excess demand, was applied in all cases. The structuralists focused instead on the particular economic characteristics of each country. They puzzled at how a country with an unemployment rate of 15 percent and a capacity utilization rate of 75 percent could have excess demand. Furthermore, they challenged the IMF proponents to explain how a crisis triggered by the external shock of high global interest rates and expensive oil imports could be solved by domestically reducing aggregate demand. The structuralists argued that IMF programs were unnecessarily recessionary and increased inequality. They contended that the restrictive short-run targets set by the IMF exacerbated the negative impacts. Finally, the structuralists argued that the international financial community played a significant role in the accumulation of debt and should therefore bear some of the adjustment burden.[4]

Despite the standardized prescriptions, this first stage of the debt crisis was defined by a case-by-case approach to the resolution of the problem. That is, a regionwide approach was rejected by creditors. The politics of the case-by-case strategy on the part of the IMF, the World Bank, and the creditor countries may explain in part why Latin America did not default on the debt. Despite the fact that at the outset the debtor countries had some bargaining power given the exposure of money center banks, collective action was not effective. In the Declaration of Quito (1984), Latin American countries called for an immediate response from the creditor countries to ameliorate the dramatic fall in living standards. In June 1984 the Cartagena Consensus Group of debtors argued that the burden of Latin American foreign debt threatened both the very stability of the international monetary system and the emergence of democracy in the region. But the Declaration of Quito was all talk and no action. Although some countries such as Peru declared a partial moratorium, stating that it would devote no more than 10 percent of exports to debt, and Brazil announced in 1987 a unilateral moratorium on the payment of interest of US$68 billion of medium- and long-term money, the carrots for good behavior—the flow of new money into countries—were sufficiently enticing to keep countries largely in line.[5]

The Market Reacts to the Continuing Crisis

While countries were engaged in difficult adjustment measures, the financial sector quietly found ways to reduce its exposure to debt. Through the process of **provisioning**, or setting aside profits before dividend payments against risky loans, banks set aside the capital to guarantee their positions in the event of a default. Banks also found means to reduce their exposure to unwanted debt through innovative new market instruments. A **secondary market** for debt developed. Because loans were assets, they could be resold to other, more risk-inclined, buyers for a discount. The new holder of a US million-dollar loan to Mexico might have paid only US$510,000 for this asset if it were purchased in August of 1987. The value of the discount would be steeper the lower the likelihood the country would ever repay the full amount. As we can see in table 4.8, by 1987 expectations were so low that Peru would ever make good on its external obligations that its debt could be purchased for between two and seven cents on the dollar.

Beyond allowing those who were more risk-averse—particularly the medium-sized regional banks—to exit, the secondary market produced another innovation,

Table 4.8.   Secondary Market Prices of Latin American Debt (% of face value)

Country	July 1985	January 1986	January 1987	August 1987	October 1987
Argentina	60–65	62–66	62–65	45–47	34–38
Brazil	75–81	75–81	74–77	52–54	35–40
Chile	56–69	65–69	65–68	64–66	52–56
Colombia	81–83	82–84	86–89	80–82	75–80
Ecuador	65–70	68–71	63–66	41–43	31–34
Mexico	80–82	69–73	64–57	51–53	46–49
Peru	45–50	25–30	16–19	7–10	2–7
Venezuela	81–83	80–82	72–74	72–74	50–54

Source: George Anayiotos and Jaime de Piniés, "The Secondary Market and the International Debt Problem," *World Development* 18(2) (1990): 1655–1660.

debt-for-equity swaps. For example, a firm wishing to build a factory in a Latin American country could use the secondary market to purchase the debt note. In August 1987 a firm wanting to invest in Chile could purchase US$100,000 worth of debt for about US$64,000. The country then owed the firm instead of the bank. However, the firm could turn to the government and say, "I don't need to be paid in dollars (hard earned through exports). In fact, in setting up this factory, I need pesos to buy supplies and pay my workers locally." In this way the debt purchased at a discount could be presented at the central bank for payment in local currencies. If the country had a strong bargaining position, such as good firm location, it too could negotiate a deal and agree to pay only US$90,000 worth of pesos to the firm. Firms were satisfied because the secondary market gave them access to discounted funds, and governments could pay in local currency, not scarce foreign exchange.

On the surface, debt-for-equity swaps are a win-win proposal. The banks sell their poorly performing loans; the company makes a profit on the difference between the discount and the local payment; and the country, in addition to reducing its debt in hard currency, gains in jobs through the foreign direct investment. Indeed, Chile reduced 10 percent of its external obligations this way. However, it was not the perfect scheme. It is important to identify how the local currency was raised. If the central printing presses were simply run a little longer, there could be inflationary impacts. If the government borrowed internally to finance the pesos, indebtedness hadn't really changed—the holders just switched from international to domestic lenders. It was also questionable whether the investments by firms would have taken place anyhow—perhaps bringing hard currency into the country. Some critics raised concerns over sovereignty, charging that foreign firms were using cheap money to compete against local entrepreneurs. (Domestic firms were prevented by international banking conventions from buying back their own debt.) Finally, use of debt-for-equity swaps was a strategy suited for only the best performers. Logically, it would work only if multinational corporations wanted to operate in the host country. If economic adjustment had not been substantial, it was unlikely that foreign capital was going to be banging down the doors.

Despite these drawbacks, the appeal was strong. The secondary market was also used to facilitate **debt-for-nature swaps**. In this instance, rather than purchase materials, international organizations purchased the discounted notes and offered cancellation or partial payment in exchange for the country's promise to establish a nature preserve. As discussed in box 4.3, Costa Rica, in particular, pursued this alternative.

Box 4.3.   Debt-for-Nature Swaps

Although the debt crisis was catastrophic for Latin America, it had a silver lining for international environmental nongovernmental organizations (NGOs) trying to persuade Latin American governments to adopt sustainable development policies. Third world debt, in the form of debt-for-nature swaps, gave NGOs a bargaining tool to influence the creation of environmental measures. Some countries were persuaded to implement environmentally sound projects and policies in exchange for a reduction in their outstanding debt.

Debt-for-nature swaps were first proposed in 1984 by the then vice president of the World Wildlife Fund, Thomas Lovejoy. Yet it was not until 1987 that Bolivia, Costa Rica, and Ecuador engaged in this form of debt reduction. Pointing to the negative environmental effects of debt service through natural resource exploitation to earn dollars, Lovejoy and others argued for a pro-environmental policy. Debt-for-nature swaps could reduce hard currency indebtedness while making investments critical to the environment.

To carry out a debt-for-nature swap, three requirements must be met. There must be a donor, usually an NGO, who funds the initiative by purchasing a portion of a developing country's debt from the secondary market. In addition, the country's central bank must be willing to accept the debt note and able to finance the negotiated environmental programs. Finally, a private or governmental agency must carry out the environmental programs. Two types of debt-for-nature swaps have taken place: bond-based programs, where the interest on government bonds is used to pay for environmental and conservation activities, and policy programs, where the government commits to implementing a series of environmental policies. The process for both types is similar. The donor negotiates with the debtor government on the terms and then purchases debt from the secondary market at a price lower than the face value of the outstanding debt. The debtor country now owes the donor instead of the creditor. If a bond-based program was negotiated, the purchased debt is converted to government bonds issued in the name of a local NGO that receives the interest over the life span of the bond. On the other hand, if a policy program is negotiated, in exchange for the debt note, the government agrees to implement environmental policies such as creating environmental reserves or ensuring that forests are managed sustainably. Finally, the funds are transferred to a local private or government agency for the implementation of negotiated projects.

Although debt-for-nature swaps sound like fabulous deals that benefit every party involved, they have limitations. They reduce little debt. In fact, the maximum debt reduction took place in Costa Rica, where less than 5 percent of external debt was reduced. There is a fear that the central bank will engage in money creation, triggering inflation. Further, conservation projects may take precedence where other, more critical sustainable development projects are needed. This also raises the question of sovereignty among nationalists who see foreign NGOs dictating the national environmental agenda.

Despite these restrictions, Costa Rica made good use of debt-for-nature swaps. The major reason for Costa Rica's success is the high level of government participation. To safeguard against inflationary tendencies, officials set a ceiling on the number of

continued

swaps allowed yearly. Costa Rica demonstrated that used properly, debt-for-nature swaps can help reduce some of its external debt. More important, debt became an instrument to achieve another policy goal: promoting environmental sustainability.

REFERENCES

Caldwell, Laura. "Swapping Debt to Preserve Nature." *Christian Science Monitor*, 11 September 1990.
Patterson, Allen. "Debt for Nature Swaps and the Need for Alternatives." *Environment* 21 (December 1990): 5–32.
World Bank. "Other Financial Mechanisms: Debt-for-Nature Swaps and Social Funds," www.esd.worldbank.

Beyond Muddling Through: The Baker Plan

"Muddling through" (as some called the first period of adjustment to the debt crisis) did not work to restore creditworthiness and growth to the region. Adjustment under IMF programs was largely unsuccessful. The burden of debt service had become painfully obvious. As seen in figure 4.2, high debt service costs resulted in a persistent outflow of resources from Latin America from 1982 through 1990. This loss of capital resulted in the flat growth in gross national product (GNP) seen over the same period in figure 4.3. As growth slowed, unemployment rose in the 1980s, and real wages did not increase to improve the standard of living for the masses.

The costs of adjustment were enormously painful. As will be discussed in later chapters, poverty increased and environmental damage was exacerbated. Political and social dislocation led to labor strikes, supermarket looting, and bus burnings in response to depressed wages and higher prices. Fragile democratic regimes were

Figure 4.2.   Net Flows and Resource Transfers

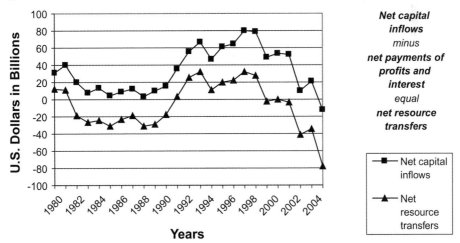

Source: ECLAC on the basis of figures from the IMF and national sources.

Figure 4.3.   Gross National Product of Latin America and the Caribbean, 1980–2000

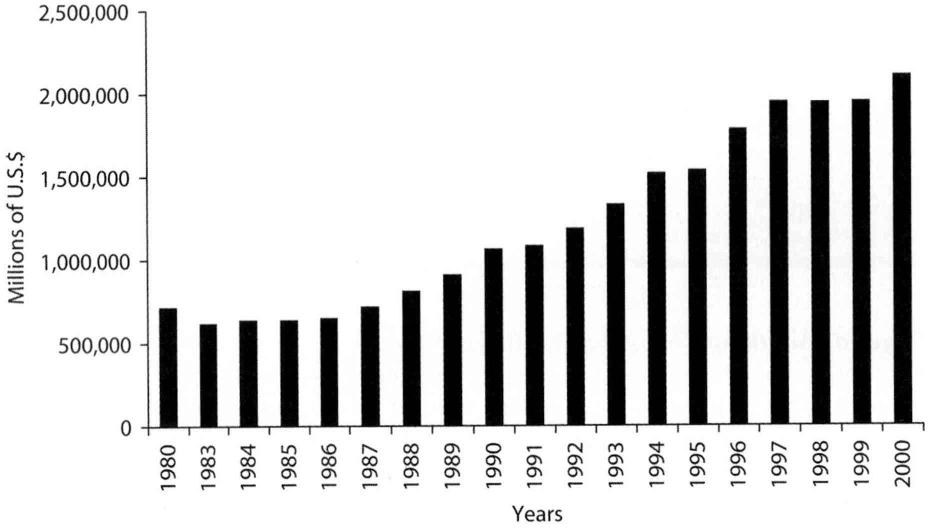

Source: World Bank, *Global Development Finance* (Washington, D.C.: World Bank, various years).

threatened as people began to idealize the stability and prosperity of military rule. To promote prosperity and stability, in 1985 US Treasury secretary James Baker announced a plan designed to jump-start growth. The premise of the Baker plan was that countries could not continue to service their debt through contractionary policies. Growth and adjustment became linked. The Baker plan targeted fifteen less-developed countries for US$29 billion of new money, US$20 billion from commercial banks and US$9 billion from the IMF and the World Bank.

The Baker plan was important in shifting policy from austerity to growth. It also identified a new role for the World Bank in promoting institutional change. The failure of traditional IMF measures to resolve the debt crisis changed the understanding of the debt crisis from a short-term liquidity problem (with primary responsibility lodged in the IMF) to a long-term problem of **structural adjustment**. Debt came to be understood as a development problem, and the World Bank was charged with assisting in the management of the adjustment process. As a result, the World Bank began to engage in macroeconomic policy, formerly the purview of the IMF, and the IMF was forced to design lending facilities to support long-term structural change. There was general agreement that adjustment with growth would be led by the export engine, but there was a greater appreciation for the fact that severely contractionary monetary policy would not favor investment, the deepening of markets, or democracy.

This conceptual shift was important, but the Baker plan itself was too little, too late. Twenty-nine billion dollars may have made a difference if it were targeted toward one or two countries, but given the almost trillion dollars in external obligations on the part of developing countries at the time, it was inconsequential.

Furthermore, commercial banks were unconvinced that new lending to debtor countries made any sense. In their view, why throw good money after bad?

Registering its "no confidence" vote for the success of the Baker plan, in 1987 Citicorp announced that it would allocate $3 billion from the loan loss reserves it had been setting aside against its developing country debt portfolio. Some had feared that such a move would lower Citicorp's stock value (since its assets are its loans, which were now worth less); instead, the stock market greeted the news with applause. The consensus was that the banks were prepared to take a realistic position on developing country debt: it would never be repaid in full. Accompanied by a $200 million write-off in the same year by the Bank of Boston, this was seen as the death of the Baker plan. Jump-starting growth would not work until the debt burden was reduced two years later under the Brady plan.

The Social and Environmental Costs of Debt Adjustment

The burden of adjustment to the debt crisis may have fallen disproportionately on women. Several studies showed that in poor households, women were responsible for changes in work, child care, and consumption patterns. Household incomes were maintained by increasing the number of workers per home. Unlike the effects of the Great Depression in the United States, where women tended to withdraw from the workforce in favor of men, in Latin America women entered the workforce during austerity to help meet family needs; their entrance appears permanent.[6] Skilled men were eligible for unemployment compensation; their wives sometimes went into the informal sector to compensate for income loss. The entrance of men into the informal sector of unregulated, poorly compensated jobs tended to be inversely related to skill level.[7] Girls often assumed more domestic tasks, including child care of younger siblings, sometimes leaving school to do so. People cut back on food expenditure, eating fewer meals and consuming less protein and fresh vegetables. Health care was also postponed, often until a medical condition became severe. Households were forced to dig into savings, pawn their possessions, and borrow from relatives or loan sharks. Pressures to make ends meet took an emotional toll on families as they struggled to survive the adjustment to the debt crisis.[8]

From Adjustment through Growth to Debt Reduction:
The 1989 Brady Plan

The 1989 Brady plan addressed the need for debt reduction as a necessary step toward stable growth in developing countries. The Brady plan offered three options: decrease the face value of debt, extend the time period of obligations, or infuse new money. Countries were officially able to decrease the face value through buybacks in the secondary market. Whereas earlier buybacks were considered cheating and not sanctioned as indicating good performance in servicing loans, countries such as Costa Rica were able to reduce official debt by US$1.1 billion.[9] Alternatively, countries were able to swap old loans for thirty-year bonds with a 30–35 percent discount on the face value

at a variable interest rate or swap loans without the discount but at a fixed interest rate
of 6.25 percent. The longer time period of the Brady bonds made them consistent
with the long-term strategies needed for growth. A novel feature of Brady deals were
the guarantees to the lender. The United States, Japan (a primary financier), and the
developing country put up guarantees (usually in the form of US Treasury bonds) to
safeguard payment in the event of default, encouraging investor confidence. Finally,
new money could be extended to cover interest in the early years and smooth the transition to the market economy. To be eligible for any of the three options, countries had
to show political will and a strong track record in economic reform.

The Mexican Brady deal in 1989 restructured US$48 billion of its liabilities by
floating US$20.8 billion in bonds that had been discounted from the face value at
35 percent and US$22.4 billion in par value bonds at 6.25 fixed interest. In addition,
Mexico received $4.4 billion in new money at the rate of LIBOR plus 13–16 per-
cent.[10] The World Bank estimated that this debt relief reduced net transfers by US$4
billion per year, nearly 2 percent of the gross domestic product (GDP), from 1989
through 1994.[11] Box 4.4 recalls the tough economic road Mexico faced up to the debt
relief of the Brady plan, underscoring how crisis drove policy throughout the decade.

The commercial sector responded more enthusiastically to the Brady options
than it did to the Baker plan. The former's realistic appraisal of the need to reduce

BOX 4.4.   MILEPOSTS IN MEXICAN DEBT

Date	Event
1978–1981	Three-month London Interbank Offer Rate (LIBOR) jumps from 8.8 percent to 16.8 percent
February 1982	President Lopez Portillo vows to "defend the currency like a dog" but is forced to devalue
August 12, 1982	Moratorium placed on US dollar–denominated deposits held in Mexican banks
August 15, 1982	Mexico announces it can no longer meet interest payments on foreign debt
Fall 1982	Mexico signs standby agreement with the IMF
1986	Peso devalued
October 1987	Mexican stock market collapses, losing 74 percent of its value in less than forty days; inflation at annual rate of 159 percent
December 1987	Unsuccessful Baker plan provides only US$1.1 billion in debt relief for Mexico
April 1989	Mexico signs three-year, US$3.64 billion loan agreement with the IMF
July 1989	US Treasury secretary Brady introduces collateralized Brady bonds, reducing Mexican debt to foreign banks by US$48.5 billion and cutting annual debt payments by US$3 billion for next four years

Source: Helen Shapiro, *Mexico: Escaping the Debt Crisis*, Harvard Business School Case (Boston:
Harvard Business School, 1991).

the debt overhang, as well as its insurance guarantees, made it appealing. Investors found the plan pragmatic and less risky than the traditional short-term financial commitments. It is also important to note that by 1989, Latin America had already undertaken substantial reforms and was emerging as an intriguing investment arena. Brady bonds arrived as a vehicle for investment in a region that, after much painful adjustment, was beginning to be viewed as ripe for growth.

Is the Debt Crisis Over in Latin America?

Tough adjustments in Latin America appear to have paid off in the region. Data for the 1990s in figure 4.2 mark the return of positive net transfers in the region. Table 4.9 shows the decline in the ratio of external debt to exports of goods and services, as well as interest as a percentage of exports of goods and services. By 2000 total external debt had reached the manageable level of 38.5 percent of GNP, and exports, or the ability to earn hard currency, had expanded while interest rates had fallen, bringing down the drain of interest payments on the export bill to 11.8 percent. This is not to say that Latin America is no longer vulnerable to its external obligations. When international financial crises in Asia, Russia, and Brazil hit the region in the late 1990s, the burden of debt servicing increased as well. Nonetheless, crisis was averted. As we will see in Chapter 7, international capital has returned to the region, but it has been unpredictable in both magnitude and type of capital flow.

Latin America's recovery from the debt crisis has been a long and painful process. The turnaround in the region is quite dramatic. Many nations are emerging as major players in the world's debt and equity markets. Some countries have initiated their own stabilization and emergency funds to circumvent the need for a future

Table 4.9.   Debt Indicators for Latin America and the Caribbean, 1980–2003

Year	Total Debt Stocks/ Export of Goods and Services	Total Debt Stocks/GNP	Total Debt Service/Export of Goods and Services	Interest/Export of Goods and Services	Reserves/ Months
1980	201.0	34.4	36.2	19.2	4.3
1990	254.5	44.6	24.4	12.2	3.6
1995	212.9	40.0	26.4	12.2	4.8
1996	201.0	38.0	31.3	11.7	5.2
1997	190.8	36.6	35.6	11.2	4.7
1998	212.7	41.1	34.0	11.9	4.2
1999	208.4	41.8	41.6	13.0	4.0
2000	172.6	38.5	39.0	11.8	3.5
2001–2003 averages	205.8	?	23.6	7.7	5.3

Source: World Bank, World Debt Tables & Global Development Finance (Washington, DC: World Bank, various years).

return to the IMF. As we will see in Chapter 7, financial flows have moved away from loans to bonds, portfolio stock flows, and foreign direct investment.

A second important sign of the maturity of Latin American markets is the shift in focus of Latin American firms to domestic markets to raise capital. Many Latin American firms are turning to the region's private pension and mutual funds for financing. Care must be taken, however, not to simply replace international liabilities with domestic debt. Internal debt can also be a cause for serious concern. In the Brazilian case, for example, the total net public debt exploded from 30 percent of GDP in 1984 to more than 60 percent in 2002. Only about 30 percent of this debt is in US dollars, but the internal obligation ties the hands of the government. The Brazilian government must maintain a fiscal surplus to keep interest rates down or risk a debt-led collapse of the Brazilian economy. The key to predicting the stability of Brazilian debt is estimating the tolerance of domestic institutional investors. The debt to GDP ratio in Italy and Belgium has exceeded 100 percent. Do Brazilians have this kind of confidence that their government will honor its obligations?[12]

These changes in the Latin American markets point to an overall increase in confidence for developing nations. Although there is still much progress to be made, recent trends suggest that Latin America may be ready to take on a more influential position in the world market. However, underneath the shiny new exterior, the mountain of external debt still remains to be paid in full.

Debt Relief for the Region's Poorest Countries

The postcrisis return to the financial market did not reach the poorest countries in Latin America. Table 4.10 shows debt burdens by income classifications. As a result of pressure from the international community, the World Bank and the IMF launched the **highly indebted poor country (HIPC) initiative** in 1998. Unlike earlier refinancing that actually increased the debt stock of poor countries, HIPC reduces the stock of debt to sustainable levels. A 1999 reform accelerated the relief given to countries with track records of credible reform. Countries receiving HIPC assistance must directly link debt relief to assistance to the poor with poverty-reduction strategy papers (PRSPs) developed in consultation with civil society. Comprehensive, well-targeted, and credible PRSPs include measures to achieve job-creating growth, especially in agriculture; realignment of public expenditure toward poverty reduction; improvements in access to basic health and education; action to improve governance; transparency and accountability; and processes to maintain the engagement of civil society.[13] The strategies are intended to be country-owned, developed as a result of national consultation, and implemented collaboratively with other development agencies, especially the UN system.

HIPC lending proceeds in two phases. At the end of the first period of adoption of structural reforms, a decision point is reached based on an analysis of **debt sustainability**; if a country's debt obligations as a percentage of exports exceed 150 percent, it qualifies for assistance. Once eligible, the country must establish a further track record of adjustment and adopt a national PRSP; compliance is rewarded with full debt relief. Financing of the debt obligations largely falls

**Table 4.10.   Latin American Economies by Income Group and
Indebtedness, 2003**

Income and Debt Classification	Severely Indebted PV of Debt/XGS >220% or PV Debt/GNP >80%	Moderately Indebted PV of debt/XGS> 132% and <220% or PV Debt/GNP >132% and < 80%	Less Indebted PV of Debt/XGS <132% or PV Debt/GNP <48%
Low income: pc GNP <US$765			Haiti, Nicaragua
Lower middle income: pc GNP US$766–US$3,035	Brazil, Ecuador, Peru	Bolivia, Colombia, El Salvador, Honduras, Paraguay	Dominican Republic, Guatemala
Upper middle income: pc GNP US$3,036–US$9,385	Argentina, Belize, Panama, Uruguay	Chile, Venezuela	Costa Rica, Mexico

Source: Extracted from The World Bank, *Global Development Finance 2005*, statistical appendix, Table A50.
Note: PV is the present value of debt which is the sum of all future debt service obligations (interest and principal) on existing debt discovered by the market interest rate.

to the IMF and other multilateral institutions with money from the proceeds of gold sales. The national process of consultation embodied in the PRSP is designed to promote accountability and to decrease the chances that debt relief will only benefit corrupt politicians or become fungible money for military spending. Funding is then allocated through the Poverty Reduction and Growth Facility (PRGF), the IMF's low-interest lending facility for low-income countries.

Evidence suggests that the poorest HIPC-eligible countries are spending more on social services than on debt service. Others suggested that the definition of sustainable debt levels is sensitive to the volatile external market shocks that poor countries face. For example, sustainable debt to export ratios can quickly become burdensome if foreign markets dry up. The calculation is also cumbersome; the World Bank's online handbook to advise countries on document presentation runs more than one thousand pages. The fear that relief was too slow and not substantial enough to alleviate the current misery of the poor motivates opposition to HIPC.[14] Frustration exists as well as commercial creditors have not delivered sufficient debt relief. Critics also point to inadequacies in the consultative process with civil society. Authentic participation takes time to develop—time that may not be consistent with the timetables of the IMF.[15] Some believe that HIPC is a good step, but only a baby step given the desperate lives of those living on less than US$1 a day.

In Latin America four countries qualified for HIPC: Bolivia, Guyana, Nicaragua, and Honduras. Bolivia, in 1998 the first country in the world to reach the so-called completion point—the successful completion of negotiations over progress indicators—received nearly US$2 billion in debt relief, reducing its external debt by half. Debt service as a percent of exports fell from 23 to 16 percent, releasing funds for poverty programs.[16] Guyana, Nicaragua, and Honduras qualified in 1998,

Table 4.11.   Nicaragua's Measures to Reach the Completion Point under the HIPC

Poverty reduction	Prepare a fully participatory poverty reduction strategy paper and implement it for one year
	Use interim savings from HIPC to implement the PRSP
Macroeconomic stability	Maintain stable macro frameworks and performance under PRGF
Human capital & social protection participation	Approve school autonomy law encouraging parental participation
	Approve health regulatory changes to grant autonomy to hospitals and local health systems
	Adopt action plan to introduce social protection
Strengthen governance	Implement a civil service law to reduce political interference in hiring/firing
	Introduce sound management of public-sector procurement
	Strengthen the comptroller's office
	Introduce legal reform and training programs for penal procedures
Pension reform	Create supervisory authority for pension funds with adequate staff; restructure social security administration
Privatization	Divest ENITEL
	Privatize electricity-generating units of ENEL

Source: IMF.org.

2004, and 2005, respectively. Table 4.11 provides a summary of the measures Nicaragua implemented to achieve the completion point debt relief. In 1999, Nicaragua's debt to exports ratio was 540 percent; debt relief of US$3.267 billion was achieved by 2004, despite adverse economic circumstances in the country. Additional support in the amount of US$129 million from 2002–2005 under the PRGF was allocated by the IMF to promote poverty-reducing growth. Budgetary savings from debt relief led to a US$165 million increase (approximately 4 percent of GDP) in spending on poverty programs in 2002–2003, with a focus on education, health, water, housing, and protection for vulnerable groups. Debt to exports fell to 161 percent—a significant decline, but still above the 150 percent benchmark commonly accepted as manageable.[17] It is not clear, however, that the job of debt relief is complete. Countries that did not qualify for HIPC, such as Peru or Brazil, but which still fight persistent extreme poverty under the burden of debt payments remain pressured by their financial liabilities.

LESSONS OF THE DEBT CRISIS

What are the lessons of the debt crisis? The most salient and the most painful lesson is that strong fundamentals matter. Unlike the populist policies of the past, countries must attend to price stability and budget constraints. Responsible fiscal policy—keeping the domestic house in order—has clear effects on a country's external balance. This is perhaps more important today in highly integrated capital markets. Information travels quickly, and negative performance on critical indicators carries a high price. Maintaining the confidence of the market is a vital ingredient for success. Without credible and predictable policies, capital will quickly respond to uncertainty by fleeing to less risky instruments. Politics and market psychology are intertwined with sound economic policy.

But generating the necessary macroeconomic stability in the region was no easy task. In the 1980s and early 1990s, several countries in the region had annual inflation rates exceeding 1,000 percent. In the next chapter we will consider how governments in Latin America took on the inflation problem. Tied to the ability to restrain inflation has been a reengineering of the role of government. In contrast to the central role of the state under ISI, Latin American governments had to redefine the boundaries between the public and the private sectors. The transformation of the inward-oriented model to an export-driven growth strategy has engendered strategic changes in the behavior of firms and states in the region. We tackle development challenges in the context of a globalized economy in Chapters 6, 7, and 8. These radical changes in the rules and goals of the economy in Latin America have not been without cost. Poverty rose throughout the region, and the environment suffered from the natural resource export drives—the subject of Chapters 10 through 14. As we explore these issues, we will see that the resolution of the debt crisis fundamentally transformed the development model in the region.

Key Concepts

absorption
capital flight
conditionality
debt-for-equity swaps
debt-for-nature swaps
debt sustainability

debt trap
economic populism
highly indebted poor
  country (HIPC) initiative
illiquidity
involuntary lending

provisioning
secondary market
seignorage
sovereign guarantee
structural adjustment
  programs

Chapter Summary

The Accumulation of Debt

- The debt crisis was a natural consequence of spending practices in the 1950s, 1960s, and 1970s. Careless borrowing for large-scale projects with high capital requirements was partly responsible for the accumulation of debt in Latin America. Many of these multiyear investments, with unpredictable returns, led to a debt trap. Economic populism, inefficiency, and corruption contributed to further unnecessary and extravagant fiscal spending financed through more loans.

- Negative real interest rates and the influx of petrodollars into the banking system made borrowing attractive and easy during the 1970s. In real terms, countries had to pay back less than what they borrowed and had seemingly unlimited funds.
- As evidenced by the cases of Mexico, Brazil, and Argentina, not every Latin American country pursued the same policies. The end result of accumulated debts, however, was the same.

On the Road to Crisis

- In 1979 the Federal Reserve Bank of the United States raised interest rates. The effects were detrimental for Latin America. While countries' interest payments for past loans increased, the US market for Latin American exports fell, effectively limiting the foreign exchange needed to repay loans.
- The excess supply of local currency fueled inflation. Locals deposited their money abroad in hopes of higher returns, and capital flight ensued. Governments' ability to raise revenues was therefore greatly weakened.
- Mexico's inability and unwillingness to pay its debt signaled to the international community that the economies of Latin America were on the verge of crisis.

Responses to the Debt Crisis

- Under the assumption that Latin American countries needed to reduce domestic absorption, the IMF prescribed a decrease in fiscal spending, tight monetary policy, and strict trade policies. What has become known as IMF conditionality spurred criticism from various circles, including the structuralist school, for unnecessarily contracting the macroeconomy without addressing its structural problems.
- In response to the crisis, a secondary market for debt developed. The secondary market was used to facilitate debt-for-equity and debt-for-nature swaps.
- The Baker plan was "too little, too late," representing a shift away from IMF conditionality. A new role was given to the World Bank, focusing on structural adjustment.
- The Brady plan decreased the face value of debt, extended the time period of obligations, or infused new money.

After the Crisis

- The return of international capital to Latin America, the shift toward domestic markets for financing, and an increase in the degree of trust in domestic currencies are signs of an increase in the maturity of Latin American markets.

- The HIPC initiative links debt reduction for the poorest countries with poverty alleviation measures.
- Debt sustainability: Under the enhanced HIPC initiative debt burden thresholds were adjusted downward, enabling a broader group of countries to qualify for debt relief.

Notes

1. Federico A. Sturzenegger, "Description of a Populist Experience: Argentina, 1973–1976," in *The Macroeconomics of Populism in Latin America*, eds. Rudiger Dornbusch and Sebastian Edwards (Chicago, IL: University of Chicago Press, 1991), 79.

2. John T. Cuddington, *Capital Flight: Estimates, Issues, and Explanations*, Princeton Studies in International Finance, No. 58 (Princeton, NJ: Princeton University Press, 1986), 10.

3. Sebastian Edwards, *Crisis and Reform in Latin America: From Despair to Hope* (New York: Oxford University Press, 1995), 17.

4. Patricio Meller, "IMF and World Bank Roles in the Latin American Foreign Debt Problem," in *The Latin American Development Debate: Neostructuralism, Neomonetarism, and Adjustment Processes*, ed. Patricio Meller (Boulder, CO: Westview, 1991).

5. "'Til Debt Do Us Part," *The Economist*, 28 February 1987, 85.

6. Irma Arriagada, "Unequal Participation by Women in the Working World," *CEPAL Review* 40 (April 1990): 83–98.

7. Helena Hirata and John Humphrey, "Workers' Response to Job Loss: Female and Male Industrial Workers in Brazil," *World Development* 19(6) (1991): 671–682.

8. Frances Stewart, *Adjustment and Poverty: Options and Choices* (London: Routledge, 1995), 189. Stewart summarizes results of studies published in the late 1980s.

9. US Department of State, *1996 Country Reports on Economic Policy and Trade Practices*, a report submitted to the Senate Committee on Foreign Relations, the Senate Committee on Finance, the House Committee on Foreign Affairs, and the House Committee on Ways and Means, January 1997 (available at www.state.gov/www/issues/tradereports/latinamerica99/costarica96.html).

10. Edwards, *Crisis and Reform*, table 4.3.

11. Ibid., 81.

12. "Brazil: Domestic Debt Dynamics and Implications," *ING Barings Emerging Markets Weekly Report*, March 5, 1999, 1–3.

13. Statement of US Treasury secretary Lawrence H. Summers at the Joint Session of the International Monetary and Finance Committee and the Development Committee, Prague, Czech Republic, September 24, 2000, www.imf.org.

14. Drop the Debt, "HIPC Initiative Offers No Guarantee against Future Debt Problems," www.dropthedebt.org.

15. Dijkstra presents a comprehensive and thoughtful analysis of the weakness in the process. Geske Dijkstra, "The PRSP Approach and the Illusion of Improved Aid Effectiveness: Lessons from Bolivia, Honduras and Nicaragua," *Development Policy Review* 23(4) (2005): 443–464.

16. World Bank News Release 2001/369/S, "Bolivia: World Bank and IMF Support US$1.2 Billion in Additional Debt Service Relief for Bolivia under Enhanced HIPC Initiative," www.worldbank.org. See also "Debt—Undermining Development," www.globalissues.org and www.oxfam.org.

17. "Completion Point under the Heavily Indebted Poor Countries Initiative," *Inter-American Development Bank* 8 (March 2004).

CHAPTER FIVE

MACROECONOMIC STABILIZATION

A Critical Ingredient for Sustained Growth

The region grappled with debilitating inflation in the 1980s and 1990s.
(iStock/swisshippo)

Inflation plagued Latin American economies from the 1980s through the first part of the 1990s. Imagine the difficulty—as was experienced in Argentina, Brazil, Nicaragua, and Peru—of living with inflation rates exceeding 2,000 percent per year! These were not isolated exceptions; as we can see in table 5.1, only Costa Rica, Panama, and Bolivia had rates under 20 percent in 1990, and as we will see, Bolivia paid a huge social price to achieve this ratio and tame inflation in the mid-1980s.

Inflation exacts a high cost. Real wages—earnings after the inflationary bite—fall, reducing purchasing power. Inflation hits the poor particularly hard; the wealthy can insulate themselves through financial mechanisms indexed to the inflation rate. Macroeconomic instability creates uncertainty and undermines the investment climate. Inflation compromises the business environment, complicating long-run decision making. It erodes tax earnings and reduces the ability of the government to provide public services. It promotes consumption today, reduces savings, and creates environmental pressure. Inflation hurts nearly all economic actors.

Despite these costs, excessive inflation persisted in Latin America for nearly fifteen years. Our discussion in this chapter revolves around several questions:

- Why was Latin America so inflation prone?
- What caused inflationary pressures in the region?
- Why was inflation so intractable?
- What mechanisms were used to bring inflation under control in the region?
- What worked?
- Is inflation in Latin America now gone for good?

Table 5.1. Inflation of Latin American Countries, 1990

Country	Hyper (>2000%)	High (>30%)	Medium (>20%)	Low (<20%)
Nicaragua	7,485.0			
Peru	7,481.5			
Brazil	2,937.0			
Argentina	2,313.7			
Uruguay		112.5		
Guyana		63.6		
Ecuador		48.5		
Guatemala		41.2		
Venezuela		40.6		
Paraguay		38.2		
Colombia			29.1	
Mexico			26.6	
Chile			26.0	
El Salvador			24.0	
Honduras			23.3	
Suriname			21.7	
Costa Rica				19.0
Bolivia				17.1
Panama				0.8

Source: IADB, Economic and Social Progress in Latin America (Washington, DC: Johns Hopkins University Press, various years); and IMF, *World Economic Outlook 1997* (Washington, DC: IMF, 1997), 148.

Latin America has been a virtual laboratory for macroeconomic experiments. This chapter will address these issues of macroeconomic stabilization, underscoring the causes and costs of inflation and highlighting the measures used to address it. It will look at the range of policies introduced to provide some insight on the difficult problem of maintaining stable prices while an economy is going through the complex and sometimes tumultuous process of economic growth.

THEORIES OF INFLATION: MONETARISTS VERSUS STRUCTURALISTS

Policies to attack inflation rest on an understanding of inflation's causes. Two broad schools of thought address the problem: the monetarists and the structuralists. For monetarists, or orthodox theorists, the cause of inflation is rather simple: too much money chasing too few goods. Monetarists such as Milton Friedman and the Chicago School look to the equation of exchange as a key to the cause of inflation. With M representing the quantity of money, V equal to the velocity or the number of times per year a unit of currency is used to purchase final goods and services, P as the price level, and Q standing for national output or gross domestic product (GDP) in real terms, monetarists argue that

$$M \times V = P \times Q$$

If the rate of growth of output and velocity are assumed to be constant in the short run, prices are determined by the quantity of money in circulation. A rising level of money in circulation causes price acceleration. Although in the short run resource price shocks or shortages may accelerate prices temporarily, monetarists perceive that inflation over time is caused by excess liquidity in the system. Understanding persistent inflation for the monetarist involves highlighting why monetary authorities would continue to make policy errors by increasing the money supply in the face of rising prices. Monetarist explanations for such excess in Latin America include irresponsible deficit financing, erosion of the tax base, and mismanagement of the debt crisis. Let's consider these in turn.

Deficit Financing

If a government is spending more than it is taking in, the deficit must be financed. This can be done in three ways: print money, issue domestic debt, or borrow from foreign sources. As John Maynard Keynes pointed out in 1923, a government can live for a long time by printing money.[1] A government's ability to buy goods and services by printing money is called **seignorage**. Indeed, if the economy is growing at a strong pace, the quantity of goods and services available increases and the price effect may be moderate. However, once growth slows, there is too much money chasing too few goods. Deficits in Latin America imply different dynamics than in the United States. The US dollar is the world's most important reserve currency. If the Federal Reserve issues more dollars—and if the world continues its appetite for dollars as a safe investment—investors throughout the world absorb the dollars and reinvest in America's sophisticated capital markets. If the Bank of Mexico issues pesos, a strong international demand is far less likely. The value of the peso erodes, confidence vanishes, and a crisis erupts. There may come a time when the demand for dollars weakens sufficiently to present binding constraints. For now it is enough to appreciate that tough budget problems in Latin America resolved by printing money are more likely to result in inflation and balance of payments crises.

The alternative to printing money is issuing debt to finance government spending. Governments are often precluded from issuing domestic debt—the equivalent of a US Treasury bond—by underdeveloped local capital markets. If the public cannot be induced to hold bonds, a government must borrow externally or print money. When the debt crisis hit Latin America in the early 1980s, the external borrowing option dried up, and the simplest response to deficits was to monetize them.

We can observe the pattern of macroeconomic instability in Latin America up to the 1990s in tables 5.2, 5.3, and 5.4. In table 5.2, we note the trend of strong and persistent fiscal deficits throughout the region from 1982 to 1990. Only two countries—Chile and Paraguay—had surpluses nearly as often as deficits. Brazil's consistent deficit averaged 10 percent of GDP over the period. Although we should be careful

Table 5.2. Overall Fiscal Surplus or Deficit in Latin American Countries, 1982–1990 (percentage of GDP)

Country	1982	1983	1984	1985	1986	1987	1988	1989	1990
Argentina	−3.7	−10.1	−5.7	−2.9	−3.2	−4.4	−3.8	−2.6	−1.7
Bolivia	−13.7	−17.0	−18.3	−9.3	−1.7	−3.7	−5.0	−2.0	−1.3
Brazil	−3.1	−4.3	−5.0	−11.1	−14.0	−12.6	−16.3	−17.5	−6.2
Chile	−2.6	−3.7	−3.0	−1.9	−0.5	2.3	3.6	5.0	1.4
Colombia	−2.0	−1.0	−4.3	−2.7	−1.3	−0.5	−1.4	−1.7	−0.1
Costa Rica	−3.2	−3.4	−3.1	−2	−3.3	−2.0	−2.5	−4.1	−4.4
Ecuador	−4.4	−3.0	−0.6	1.9	−2.2	−6.2	−2.0	0.4	3.5
El Salvador	−5.9	−4.1	−3.2	−2	−3.6	−0.9	−3.0	−3.7	−1.5
Guatemala	−4.7	−3.6	−3.7	−1.8	−1.5	−1.3	−1.7	−2.9	−1.8
Guyana	−34.3	−40.1	−44.5	−56.1	−58.8	−42.4	−31.6	−6.6	−22.9
Honduras	−9.7	−9.0	−9.8	−7.2	−6.0	−5.8	−4.1	−6.0	−4.1
Mexico	−11.9	−8.2	−7.2	−7.6	−13.1	−14.2	−9.7	−5.0	−2.8
Nicaragua	−13.3	−30.0	−22.5	−21.3	−14.5	−16.0	−25.1	−3.5	−18.7
Panama	−11.4	−6.2	−7.4	−3.4	−4.5	−4.2	−5.2	−6.9	6.8
Paraguay	−1.5	−4.7	−3.5	−2.3	0.0	0.4	0.6	2.4	3.2
Peru	−3.1	−7.3	−4.4	−3.0	−4.3	−6.9	−3.9	−6.3	−3.5
Suriname	−1.7	−17.6	−18.4	−21.4	−26.0	−24.8	−21.3	−14.0	−6.3
Uruguay	—	−4.2	−5.8	−3.1	−1.3	−1.3	−2.0	−3.4	−0.1
Venezuela	−2.1	−0.6	2.8	2.0	−0.4	−1.6	−7.4	−1.0	−2.1

Source: IADB, *Economic and Social Progress in Latin America* (Washington, DC: Johns Hopkins University Press, various years).

Table 5.3.   Average Annual Rates of Growth of Money Supply in Latin America, 1982–1990

Country	1982	1983	1984	1985	1986	1987	1988	1989	1990
Argentina	154.2	362.0	582.3	584.3	89.7	113.5	351.4	4,168.2	1,023.2
Bolivia	228.8	207.0	1,798.3	5,784.6	86.1	36.6	35.3	2.4	39.5
Brazil	68.5	102.7	204.1	334.3	330.1	215.4	426.9	1,337.0	2,333.6
Chile	2.8	15.6	22.8	24.2	43.3	21.0	46.5	17.2	23.3
Colombia	25.4	23.4	24.1	10.7	—	—	25.7	—	—
Costa Rica	70.3	38.9	17.6	7.7	31.0	0.3	53.2	−2	3.9
Ecuador	14.0	31.9	39.6	25.6	20.1	34.7	52.7	43.8	59.0
El Salvador	3.7	−1.3	13.8	27.0	19.1	−0.4	8.1	13.5	22.3
Guatemala	1.4	6.0	4.3	54.9	19.5	9.8	14.4	20.7	33.0
Guyana	25.3	17.4	20.2	20.3	19.4	51.4	54.8	34.0	54.5
Honduras	13.5	13.6	2.5	−3.2	8.2	26.6	11.9	20.0	23.6
Mexico	62.6	40.3	60.0	49.5	67.2	118.1	67.8	37.3	63.1
Nicaragua	25.7	67.1	83.5	162.8	252.2	637.0	11,673.4	2,368.3	6,286.7
Panama	5.4	−1.8	2.2	7.5	9.8	−1.6	−31.3	1.0	41.0
Paraguay	−3.6	25.6	29.4	28.0	26.7	53.6	34.8	31.7	28.3
Peru	40.4	96.5	104.4	281.2	88.0	122.0	515.0	1,654.9	6,710.0
Suriname	17.7	8.0	26.9	52.5	39.6	27.1	24.5	11.3	4.0
Uruguay	19.8	9.0	48.4	107.6	86.1	58.1	63.7	72.9	101.0
Venezuela	4.5	25.0	27.0	8.9	5.3	40.8	22.7	22.2	54.6

Source: IMF, *International Financial Statistics 1996* (Washington, DC: IMF, 1996), 81.

Table 5.4.   National Interest Rates in Latin America (central bank discount rates, end of period in percent per annum)

Country	1982	1983	1984	1985	1986	1987	1988	1989	1990
Brazil	174.0	194.0	272.0	380.0	89.0	401.0	2,282.0	38,341.0	1,083.0
Colombia	27.0	27.0	27.0	27.0	33.8	34.8	34.3	36.9	46.5
Costa Rica	30.0	30.0	28.0	28.0	27.5	31.4	31.5	31.6	37.8
Ecuador	15.0	19.0	23.0	23.0	23.0	23.0	23.0	32.0	35.0
Guatemala	9.0	9.0	9.0	9.0	9.0	9.0	9.0	13.0	18.5
Guyana	14.0	14.0	14.0	14.0	14.0	14.0	14.0	35.0	30.0
Honduras	24.0	24.0	24.0	24.0	24.0	24.0	24.0	24.0	28.2
Nicaragua	—	—	—	—	—	—	12,874.6	311.0	10.0
Paraguay	—	—	—	—	—	—	10.0	21.0	30.0
Peru	44.5	60.0	60.0	42.6	36.1	29.8	748.0	865.6	289.6
Uruguay	83.7	112.7	133.2	145.1	138.4	143.4	154.5	219.6	251.6
Venezuela	13.0	11.0	11.0	8.0	8.0	8.0	8.0	45.0	43.0

Source: IMF, *International Financial Statistics 1996* (Washington, DC: IMF, 1996), 96.

not to overinfer about the cause of the growth of the money supply, we can see that in the countries with strong and persistent deficits, the average annual rates of growth of the money supply are startling. In Brazil, Argentina, Nicaragua, and Peru, the rate of growth of the money supply exceeded 1,000 percent in 1990. In an attempt to raise money internally to finance deficits as well as to stem capital flight, national interest rates in 1990 exceeded 1,000 percent in Brazil and were above 30 percent in eight countries. But this was something of a losing battle. Although these interest rates were necessary to attract money for debt servicing, they also made borrowing for business investment problematic. The result was simultaneous inflation and recession.

Inflammatory financing of the fiscal deficit creates a vicious circle. Persistent inflation lowers the cash balances that people want to hold, because the value of the currency is declining quickly. People prefer to purchase goods to retain the value of their earnings, driving up prices in the market. Inflation therefore begets inflation. A second perverse effect has also been identified. Whereas deficit spending in most industrial countries is countercyclical, in Latin America it has largely been procyclical. That is, instead of spending to stimulate the economy during a recession, Latin American governments tend to contract during recession. This is tied to access to funds. As recession erodes the government's ability to raise money in international markets, it must reign in spending. Unfortunately, such procyclical policies, by their very nature, exacerbate macroeconomic volatility.[2]

The Tax Connection

If a government has lost credibility or if its population is very poor, tax collection as a percentage of government expenses is very low. Furthermore, as inflation rises, the real value of tax collection falls. Taxes for 1986 are due in 1987; because they are paid in 1987 dollars, they are worth less after inflation. The phenomenon by which inflation eats away at the value of tax receipts is called the **Olivera-Tanzi effect**. An extreme case was Bolivia, where by 1984 only 2 percent of government expenditure was covered by taxes.[3] More printed money was therefore needed to cover the deficits. Inflation, as a result, exceeded 8,000 percent. We will return to the problem of taxation in the region in Chapter 6.

Effects of the Debt Crisis

As access to foreign loans dried up, there was more pressure to raise money domestically to service existing debt. This left printing money as the most popular action to purchase the foreign exchange to make the interest payments on debt. This was the case in Argentina after 1982.[4] Furthermore, the devaluation often required in International Monetary Fund (IMF) stabilization packages increased the value of the external debt in domestic terms. That is, as the currency became worth less, it took more of it to buy the US dollars to service the external debt. This increased the temptation to print money to service the debt. Running up a down escalator may be a good metaphor for this type of policy.

Is Inflation Too Much Money?

At the center of the monetarist explanations for inflationary financing were profligate governments running budget deficits. The monetarist solution to restrain inflation in the region was therefore quite straightforward: decrease government spending. If the monetarists are right and inflation is tied to excessive government spending, the solution is clear: eliminate deficit-driven policies. Yet this was easier said than done. Deficit reduction proved politically tough.

Why do governments run large fiscal deficits despite the inflationary risks associated with them? The research in this area indicates that countries with less stable political systems are more likely to engage in deficit financing. As political instability increases, politicians see it in their own interest to buy political favor and to avoid making hard choices.[5] Politically threatened governments find it difficult to carry through on promises of fiscal responsibility. Political change can therefore make economic stabilization more problematic. Clearly this plays out in cases such as Peru or Nicaragua. Political change from an authoritarian government to a democracy was taking place over this period for countries such as Brazil and Argentina. Instability likely played a role in the capacity of states to follow sound economic programs.

In contrast to these monetarist explanations, for the **structuralists** the explanation of deficit-led instability was too simple. Structuralists do not deny that excess liquidity or budget deficits can cause inflation, but they do not believe that these are the sole or even central causes of inflation in Latin America. Attention to monetary variables is complemented by the study of a host of other factors. Because structuralists add other factors to the orthodox focus on the money supply, their policy is sometimes called **heterodox**. Structuralist or heterodox explanations focus on the structure of the underdeveloped economy as the propagating mechanism for inflation. Instead of making the equilibrium assumptions of the classical model upon which the monetarist theory is based, structuralists contend that economies in Latin America can best be understood as incomplete markets that do not automatically tend toward full employment equilibrium. For the structuralists, bottlenecks in both the agricultural and the industrial sectors create price pressures. If input markets cannot quickly adjust to price signals to meet supply requirements, inflation will result. External price shocks from the international economy can also introduce or exacerbate instability in the domestic market.

Cost-Push Elements

Cost-push elements were therefore central to the structuralist explanation. Internal shortages and external price shocks such as the oil crisis interact with the structure of industry and labor organization to fuel an inflationary struggle. In contrast to the perfect competition assumption in neoclassical models, both output and labor markets in Latin America are highly concentrated. Under oligopolistic conditions, prices are sticky downward. Shortages ratchet up prices, but during periods of slack demand or recession, prices rarely fall. Furthermore, firms may engage in markup pricing to maintain profit margins. Large firms often have internal sources of capital as well, circumventing the need to pay high interest rates for money. When prices increase, powerful labor unions demand wage increases—which firms are able to cover because they pass the cost on to the consumer. Inflation then reflects the distributive conflict between capital and labor. If all agents assume inflation, each side wants to build predicted price increases into its share of the pie.

Monetary authorities may passively accommodate the demand for money. Central banks in the region were often not independent of the executive branch and were therefore subject to political pressure. In Brazil the central bank was ordered by the military government to finance the public deficit automatically from 1971 to 1974; from 1974 until 1994, the politically dependent minister of finance had overwhelming control of the central bank. In 1994 Brazil finally formed a National Monetary Council as a supervisory and coordination organ for money policy, accountable not only to the presidency but also to Congress.[6] For the structuralists, underdeveloped political systems, the lack of accountability of military governments, and later nascent democracies unable to handle competing demands contributed to inflationary tendencies.

In the structuralist model, inflation becomes embedded in the economy. People begin to anticipate inflation. Such **inertial inflation** results when economic agents come to expect inflation and automatically adjust for it in their wage demands and pricing patterns. Not surprisingly, expected inflation is a self-fulfilling prophecy as people adjust behaviors accordingly. However, for the structuralist, inflation was an unwelcome but not unexpected result of the conflicts inherent in the process of economic development. Because markets in developing countries had unique characteristics that did not favor equilibrium, the recessionary costs of forcing austerity under these circumstances were just too high. Structuralists were willing to live with inflation as a price associated with growth in the developing world. The policy challenge became reducing the costs of living in an inflationary society.

PERPETUATING INFLATION: INDEXATION, INFLATIONARY EXPECTATIONS, AND VELOCITY

In the 1980s structuralist thought dominated much policy making in the Latin American region. Given that inflation was seen as a function of the structure of the economy, measures were introduced to minimize the costs of inflation. Most wages were indexed to a public minimum salary that was adjusted monthly to accommodate inflation. A teacher's contract might, for example, be written for seven times the national minimum wage. As the minimum wage rose each month, salaries tracked inflation. Some prices were also indexed to inflation. If you got into a taxi in Rio de Janeiro, you would not pay the price on the meter. Rather, the meter reflected a price on a *tabela*, or list of prices, that could be adjusted by decree. In stores, clothing was tagged with letters of the alphabet. Although K might mean a Cr$50 dress one day, a week later a buyer might have to come up with Cr$65. Interest on bank accounts was also indexed. Checking accounts were interest bearing (similar to US NOW accounts), and borrowers had to pay the real rate of interest plus inflation. Rents were likewise increased alongside interest and bond rates through this inflation adjustment, sometimes euphemistically called the "monetary correction."

In some periods the official rate of **indexation** was set at less than the rate of inflation to act as a brake against future inflation. But people quickly figured this out, and they took it into account in setting wage demands and prices. Ironically, although indexation was introduced as a defense against inflation, it made the transfer of inflation from the present to the future automatic, even when the government tried to manipulate expectations by lowering the percentage adjustment for inflation. Because it was built into the system, people came to expect it. Indexing made inflation easier to live with while inadvertently reinforcing its place in the economy.

Vicious Circles

Although indexation was designed to mitigate the costs of inflation, it created unintended inflationary side effects. **Inflationary expectations** became ingrained in the culture. People expected inflation, the government accommodated inflation, and the public got inflation. Inflation today was equal to inflation in the past period plus additional demand pressures and the effects of any supply shocks. As inflation accelerated, it made tax collection less efficient, pressuring fiscal balances and often leading to a further increase in the money supply. Inflation complicated exchange rate management. If the exchange rate was fixed, the erosion of the value of domestic money made it worth less relative to international or hard currencies. If the fixed rate was not adjusted, the currency was posted at an overvalued rate, creating a bias against exports. If the rate was devalued or if the currency was allowed to float freely, the higher prices of imported goods introduced additional inflationary pressures in the economy. To account for inflation and risk, nominal interest rates were high, often retarding investment.

The **velocity of money** changed in response to economic agents learning to live with inflation. A review of velocity will help illuminate this problem. Velocity is the number of times money turns over in a system each year. If the payment for a dinner to a restaurant owner is quickly used to purchase linens for a beach house, and those receipts are rapidly used (in concert with other receipts) by the curtain maker to buy a new sewing machine, and that revenue in turn is immediately used to pay workers, a given physical quantity of money is supporting the purchase of many goods. Velocity is a measure of how much output is supported by the stock of money, or GDP divided by the money supply (M). If velocity is increasing—that is, if a decreasing stock of money supports a given amount of output—increasing that stock of money without changing the productive capability of the economy will result in inflationary pressures.

In an inflationary economy, people have the incentive to transform their rapidly worthless currency into goods. If a worker in Brazil waited until the end of the month to buy groceries or other goods from a monthly paycheck, in 1990 prices would have risen by approximately 70 percent by the month's end, leaving 70 percent less in the grocery basket. It made good sense to buy quickly. Of course, shortages that the "buy now" behavior created spurred further increased prices.

The banking system may respond to the pressure to turn money over quickly, further increasing velocity. If you deposit a check and it takes three days to clear, you may not use that money for three days without bouncing another check. However, if your checks clear instantaneously, it is time to go shopping again! A higher velocity will support the purchase of more goods and services per dollar. Once a system has adapted to a higher velocity rate, modest increases in the money supply will have a stronger expansionary effect. If supply constraints prevent the rapid provision of goods and services in response to the increase in the money base, inflation will be ignited.

The velocity numbers are dramatic in the Brazilian case. During an inflationary period the velocity of money in Brazil was an astounding 125, compared to 16 in the United States. The highly efficient system of interest-bearing transactions balances allowed money holders to escape from the direct use of currency through something similar to checkable money market funds. The Brazilian money supply therefore supported a higher volume of goods and services per dollar than that in the United States. Changes in the money supply would be magnified in inflation rates.

How Much Inflation Is Too Much? Timing and Adjustment Problems

The monetarist versus structuralist policy debate in part boils down to a decision as to how much macroeconomic imbalance is tolerable in the medium term. Monetarists argue that imbalances should be swiftly redressed. Excesses in external accounts or in fiscal deficits should not be tolerated because they will quickly aggravate inflation. Structuralists contend that it is not that simple. Given the underdeveloped nature of markets in the developing world, they expect imbalances in domestic accounts or in external spending. Harsh and rapid adjustment, for the structuralist, is too high a price. Rapid reductions in the money supply to reduce domestic absorption might also have the effect of strangling long-term growth.

Monetarists and structuralists also had different views of the degrees of freedom of countries in their abilities to isolate themselves from the effects of the "inconsistent trinity" or "trilemma." Recall that most Latin American countries in this period adhered to a fixed exchange rate system. Policymakers face inevitable tensions in balancing goals of domestic monetary policy, fixed exchange rates, and capital mobility.[7] A country cannot have all three. Under a fixed exchange rate regime, if international capital is mobile and governments accept the rules of the game—that is, that a current account deficit will result in a decrease in money supply—autonomy in domestic monetary policy is forfeited. If a fixed exchange rate is maintained to preserve an international price anchor, capital controls and sterilization may give temporary relief, but exchange rate crises will certainly erupt if adjustment is incomplete. Governments might be tempted to pump up the money supply, but this will result in ballooning trade deficits. If nations want to pursue monetary autonomy they can certainly abandon the fixed rate and let the exchange rate float, but without high credibility in international markets this is likely to introduce an inflationary bias into the economy. Unless markets believe that the government is pursuing a stable monetary policy, the expected depreciation of the currency will raise import prices and foment inflation. Facing this trilemma, monetarists largely counseled abandoning domestic monetary policy and linking to a hard international currency; structuralists suggested exchange controls to preserve domestic autonomy. Rather than forfeit autonomous monetary policy or the exchange anchor, structuralists preferred to restrain capital mobility. Box 5.1 summarizes this trilemma of open economies. It is worth recalling that such capital controls were before the days when globalization and liberalized markets were the trademarks of sound policy.

How did stabilization policies play out in practice in Latin America? Drawing on elements of both schools, Latin American nations adopted a variety of approaches to macroeconomic stabilization. The fixed versus floating rate constraint was softened somewhat in practice by using intermediate exchange rate solutions such as crawling pegs or exchange rate target zones and other forms of managed exchange rate regimes. In these cases a target is set—either pegged to a hard currency such as the US dollar or set within a range, with a ceiling and a floor between which it can fluctuate. Depending on pressures on the currency, the monetary authority intervened by buying or selling to stabilize the currency but was not bound to defend a fixed price. This kind of flexibility accounted for the fact that inflation in developing countries is generally higher than in the industrial world.

BOX 5.1. MACROECONOMIC POLICY TRILEMMA

Tool	Objective	Conflict
Domestic monetary autonomy	Activist monetary policy to shorten recessions and restrain inflation	Under fixed exchange rate, "rules of the game" (deficit requires decrease in the money supply) weaken independent monetary policy; if domestic capital is not also mobile, central bank can perform offsetting domestic interventions (sterilization)
Fixed exchange rate	Price anchor—tie exchange rate to a firm anchor and force real adjustment	Lose monetary independence; could float exchange rate but lose price anchor; if capital is immobile, can create different domestic prices for money
Capital mobility	Encourage international investment; buoy confidence	Interest rates must be equal to international rates plus inflation; lose interest rate wedge in monetary policy; could float, but lose inflation anchor

Flexibility in exchange rate policy promotes competitiveness in international markets. However, if the central bank lacks credibility, inflation will resurge. The trade-off between credibility and competitiveness has shaped exchange rate policy in Latin America as countries struggle to produce stable growth fueled by export engines.[8] Table 5.5 illustrates the pros and cons of a fixed versus a flexible rate. In the late 1980s and early 1990s, raging, uncontrollable inflation led many countries to pursue **exchange rate–based stabilization programs**. By tying a country's currency to another, stable international currency, countries tied their own hands and their own ability to pursue independent monetary policies. Some suggest that these programs were a necessary medicine to create the conditions for price stability.[9] However, once stabilization of the exchange rate and prices was achieved, new problems emerged. Linking one currency to another—either through a hard link such as dollarization or a softer approach in a firm fix—means that real prices must adjust. That is, if a country is less productive than its anchor partner, real prices must actually fall to make that country's goods competitive on international markets. If prices don't adjust, the fixed exchange rate becomes overvalued and a target for financial runs. Exchange rate crises in the late 1990s led to an increasing preference for floating systems in the first decade of the twenty-first century.

Table 5.6 shows the choices of monetary frameworks and exchange rate regimes in 2005. Some countries retain an exchange rate anchor to monetary policy. Whether they have dollarized, such as El Salvador and Ecuador, or require central bank intervention to maintain a fixed or crawling peg as in Venezuela or Costa Rica, the anchor provides a foundation for price stability. Domestic monetary autonomy is sacrificed, and competitiveness must be achieved through real changes in the economy. You will notice, however, that the countries pursuing an exchange rate anchor tend to be smaller countries with strong bilateral trade with the United States. Venezuela is an exception in this respect, but recall that internationally, petroleum sales are largely priced in US dollars, hence the need for a strong dollar link. Under the pressure of currency crises in the late 1990s, several countries have abandoned exchange rate stabilization for firm and transparent monetary policy rules to promote credibility in central bank operations. Called inflation targeting, this has been defined as a framework for policy decisions in which the central bank makes an explicit commitment to conduct policy to meet a publicly announced numerical inflation target within a particular time frame.[10] Allowing the exchange rate to float to reflect market value, the central banks of Brazil or Peru, for example, set a preannounced target for inflation and adjust money supplies to meet that target. Transparency in inflation targeting regimes circumvents any market suspicion that politics, not sound economics, is driving national money machines. Other countries such as Paraguay do not follow strict targets; Argentina is a case where relatively flexible targets remain. A full-fledged targeting system with tight, preannounced bands requires a leveling out of macroeconomic variables, greater credibility by markets, and enhanced autonomy of the central bank.

A crawling peg or target zone can allow for small, regular devaluations to take inflation differentials into account and prevent an overvaluation of a currency.

Table 5.5.   Advantages and Disadvantages of Fixed versus Floating Rates

	Fixed Rate	*Floating Rate*
Advantages	Limits exchange rate risk for international transactions	Neutralizes the impact of external shocks
	Lowers risk premium and therefore cost of access to international financial markets	Neutralizes the impact of real shocks
	Decreases domestic interest rates as domestic rates need not include exchange rate premiums	Neutralizes the effect of inflation on export competitiveness
	Facilitates disinflation with an exchange rate anchor	Cheaper export prices promote competitiveness
	Impedes monetary financing of the fiscal deficit because monetary policy is impotent	Price mechanism (e.g., an exchange rate depreciation) reallocates resources from the nontradable to the tradables sector
Disadvantages	Credibility is fragile; subject to speculative attacks in currency markets	Source of imported inflation through increasing import prices
	In case of crisis, adjustment may be costly	Negative effect of strong volatility on trade and financial transactions; agents like predictable prices
	Dependence on the monetary policy of the peg country; may not meet national needs	Countries can engage in competitive devaluations, creating regional instability
	Strong sensitivity to external and real domestic shocks; a fall in global demand, for example, must be matched by a fall in the money supply to maintain the promised peg rate	Can lead to postponement of required structural adjustments; the change in prices may mask underlying rigidities
	Risk of real exchange rate appreciation; if national inflation exceeds the peg's inflation rate, the local currency becomes overvalued	In case of crisis, can make the servicing of external and internal debt unpredictable; more local currency units are needed to repay obligations
	An overvalued currency creates a current account imbalance; countries would have to lower costs to maintain competitiveness	Hyperinflationary past may impede necessary central bank credibility
	Current account imbalances will require financing; if confidence dries up, a crisis ensues	Stability is only as strong as underlying central bank institutions

Source: Adapted from Helene Poirson, "How Do Countries Choose Their Exchange Rate Regime?" IMF Working Paper WP/01/46, April 2001, www.imf.org, 26, table A3.

Table 5.6.   Monetary Policy Framework and Exchange Rate Regime

	Exchange Rate Anchor	Monetary Aggregate Target	Inflation Targeting Framework	IMF-supported or Other Monetary Program	Other (monitor various indicators)
Dollarized	Ecuador Panama El Salvador				
Conventional Fixed Peg Crawling Peg	Belize Venezuela Bolivia Costa Rica Honduras Nicaragua				
Managed Float with no predetermined path		Guyana Jamaica	Colombia Guatemala Peru	Argentina Haiti	Paraguay
Independently Floating		Uruguay	Brazil Canada Chile Mexico		United States Dominican Republic

Source: IMF Annual Report 2005, Appendix, Table II.13.

There is some suggestion that the exchange rate regime conditions inflation. In a fixed regime, inertial factors weigh more heavily. Countries under a fixed regime should pay close attention to labor market rigidities and corporate structure. Under a floating regime, deficit financing predominates. This may lead to a resurgence of inflation in the region as more countries have abandoned fixed anchors.[11] A radical alternative to either fixed or floating is no exchange rate at all—that is, simply dollarize and give up your currency. This option is discussed in box 5.2. There are rich lessons in the experience of macroeconomic stability in Latin America. Here we consider three cases: structuralist policies in Brazil, a monetarist approach in Bolivia, and a change from a structuralist to a monetarist stance in Argentina.

HETERODOX APPROACHES TO INFLATION STABILIZATION IN THE 1980S: BRAZIL

Brazilian policymakers diagnosed inflation in the 1980s as structural. The external oil price shocks of 1973 and 1978–1979, in conjunction with the interest rate shocks of the early 1980s, intersected with a highly concentrated industrial sector able to pass on cost increases to the public. Maxidevaluations of the currency in 1979 and 1983 took place because of current account pressures, fueling price increases.

Box 5.2.   Dollarization

In the midst of the debate on fixed versus flexible exchange rates, one option that has garnered attention is abandoning national currencies—and the question of the appropriate exchange rate—and adopting the US dollar.[a] Exchange rate pegs can be seen as invitations to speculative attacks, pushing countries to abandon the exchange rate anchor or float. The US dollar, an international currency, is not subject to the same kind of speculative attacks and currency runs. By taking away exchange rate uncertainty—and not leaving domestic monetary policy subject to political manipulation—nations could decrease the cost of borrowing in capital markets. Proponents point to the falling cost of capital for European nations such as Italy with the adoption of the euro and suggest that, as it did in Europe, a single currency would hasten regional integration. Dollarization enhances credibility, making tough changes irreversible.

Dollarization is not without its drawbacks. It implies a loss of seignorage, the money that a government makes by issuing money. Printing money that can be used for schools, roads, and hospitals is equivalent to a no-interest loan to the government. The central bank can also use currency, which does not bear interest, to purchase interest-bearing assets, such as foreign reserves. These show up as central bank profits and are transferred to the government. Clearly, dollarization implies a loss of monetary autonomy, including the ability of the central bank to provide liquidity to the banking system. Dollarization can also threaten competitiveness. The dollarized real exchange rate can become overvalued for the country in question. Real devaluation must be achieved through a fall in wages and prices. If labor markets are not flexible, such price reduction is problematic. Finally, dollarization may be a high-risk strategy for rebellion. Trashing the local currency challenges nationalist pride.

Approaches to the process of dollarization differ. Some recommend slow, evolutionary dollarization. With a starting point of complementary banking, fiscal, and trade reforms, dollarization would be the coronation after a long period of preparation. But those driven to dollarization by crisis may benefit from shock treatment. Rapid dollarization will force labor market adjustments—there is no choice but for unions to recognize that there are few alternatives. It hardens the government's fiscal constraint. The hope is that the term structure of debt will lengthen with less risk and the country will have enhanced access to commercial credit lines. Dollarization should create synchronization of business cycles through the interest rate.

Rapid dollarization is called the Nike approach—just do it. Countries most likely to benefit from dollarization are those most highly integrated with the United States, including a wide degree of informal dollarization through US dollar–based savings and transactions. The optimal currency literature suggests that the best candidates include those with small size, a high degree of openness, a high degree of cross-border trade, similar shocks, and US dollar–based debt structures. Williamson suggests that by these criteria the small Central American countries are strong candidates for dollarization; the Andean countries are an intermediate case. Mexico, an oil-based economy, is subject to different shocks, and **Mercosur** countries in search of a monetary anchor might better think of creating their own monetary union than tie their fates to the distant US dollar of the north.[b]

Panama adopted the US dollar as legal tender in 1904, leaving the balboa as a symbolic relic. It has a low rate of inflation and low cost of capital and has eliminated exchange rate risk. But dollarization isn't a magic wand. Due to its inability to control public finances and a high rate of external borrowing, Panama unpleasantly claims the second-largest number of IMF programs in the world. No exchange rate regime—not even a nonregime—can avoid the tough problems of reconciling the demand for government services with weak revenues.

continued

continued

After proclaiming a few days before that dollarizing was "a jump into the abyss," Ecuador's President Jamil Mahuad switched to the greenback in January 2000. It cost him his job two weeks later, but the results have been more successful than most analysts expected. Ecuador had run out of options. It faced erratic oil prices, debilitating capital flight, bank failures, international loan defaults, and devastating floods. Nearly half its twelve million people were considered impoverished by World Bank standards. The sucre had plunged from 7,000 to 25,000 per US$1, igniting price explosions. Without consulting the IMF, Ecuador moved to a US dollar standard. Ecuador dollarized at a discount, opening the door to international competitiveness. An IMF program in 2000 consolidated the gains of dollarization and further pushed structural reform, including the fiscal accounts and banking reform. By 2001, growth hit 5 percent, inflation was under 25 percent, and the people felt the benefit in the positive growth in the real minimum salary. Nonetheless, a delicate banking and financial system, vulnerability to oil prices, the weight of external debt, and falling global demand leave Ecuador's recovery fragile to external shocks. The boost from the initial devaluation has weakened; competitiveness will be contingent on improvements in productivity, labor reforms, and privatization in telecommunications and electricity—very tough microeconomic changes to engineer.[c]

a. Andrew Berg and Eduardo Borensztein, "The Dollarization Debate," *Finance & Development*, March 2000.

b. John Williamson, "Dollarization Does Not Make Sense Everywhere," Institute for International Economics, Speeches 2000, available at www.iie.com.

c. ECLAC, "Balance preliminar de las economías de América Latina y el Caribe, 2001," available at www.eclac.cl/publicaciones/DesarrolloEconomico/3/LCG2153PE/lcg2153sur.pdf and www.imf.org/external/np/sec/nb/2001/nb01129.htm.

Orthodox policies to reduce inflation had been tried under the military governments with painful social results. Sectoral conflicts between industry and agriculture, as well as social conflicts between powerful labor and industrial organizations, were thereafter resolved through spending. The state itself played an active role in the economy through state-owned enterprises (SOEs), especially in the provision of infrastructure such as electricity and key inputs such as steel. In these sectors, prices were held down to spur development of industry, but the difference was made up in deficit spending. As inflation accelerated, bonds, credit, and wages were indexed with increasingly frequent intervals. The lack of independence of the Bank of Brazil from the Treasury left it in a passive role to accommodate expansion.

When monthly inflation hit 459.1 percent in January 1986,[12] a radically different stabilization plan was called for. The **Cruzado Plan** included a general price freeze and a partial freeze on wages following an 8 percent readjustment. If the consumer price index increased more than 20 percent, wage increases would be permitted. Indexation of contracts with less than one year's duration was prohibited. A new currency was created called the cruzado, set equal to 1,000 cruzeiros. After a devaluation, the cruzado was fixed at 13.84 cruzados to the US dollar. Popular favor was cultivated as Brazilian president José Sarney deputized all Brazilians as *fiscais*, or price inspectors, to police the price freeze in supermarkets and shopping malls. Citizens could arrest store managers for raising prices. People felt empowered by the fight against inflation. The goal was to eliminate the inertial aspect of inflation, creating expectations for price stability rather than inflation.

The price of a currency is a key macroeconomic variable.
(Photo by Patrice Franko)

The preliminary results were dramatic. By April prices fell 4.5 percent, and in May they rose only 1 percent. Because inflation was not eating away at paychecks, Brazilians enjoyed a real wage increase for the first time in years, and economic growth was led by the strong demand for consumer durables. However, Brazilian industry was not able to meet the surge in consumer demand, and the economy began to overheat. Shortages emerged. The sustainability of the plan was called into question. As businesses lost faith in the plan, they withheld goods from the market, anticipating that the price freeze could not last indefinitely. Fiscal reform was limited, and monetary policy accommodated the deficit pressures. With state and gubernatorial elections in the fall of 1986, politics would not permit austerity. By December 1986 monthly inflation was back in triple digits. Following the elections, adjustments were made to the price framework, and a crawling peg for the exchange rate temporarily relieved the pressure for devaluation. Contracts were once again indexed to ease the costs of inflation. But credibility was destroyed, and a year and a half after the introduction of the plan, inflation topped 1,000 percent. Although the plan worked initially to reduce inflation dramatically, when the economy was unable to respond to the increased demand, credibility eroded in the government's ability to manage the economy.

Brazil continued its heterodox experiment with the **Bresser Plan** in mid-1987. The Bresser Plan also froze wages, although the caps were designed to be readjusted every ninety days to minimize misallocation and shortages. The exchange rate was managed through a series of mini devaluations. Interest rates were targeted above inflation to keep the lid on the consumer boom that overheated the economy under the Cruzado Plan. Finance Minister Luiz Carlos Bresser Periera placed heavy emphasis on controlling the public deficit in theory but was unable to realign the political priorities of the Sarney administration. A follow-up "summer plan" included another revaluation of the currency, lopping off three zeros once again and calling it the novo cruzado. However, it did little to change the underlying politics of the Brazilian situation. Fiscal pressures continued, inflation accelerated, and confidence was low.

In 1990 a new president—the first directly elected by the people in nearly thirty years—came into office with a strong mandate to "kill inflation with a single bullet." President Fernando Collor de Mello engineered the most dramatic of stabilization plans, with both heterodox and orthodox elements. With annual inflation nearing 3,000 percent, and consistent with prior stabilization plans, Collor froze wages and prices, and once again readjusted the monetary unit, renaming it the cruzeiro. Agreeing with the monetarists that inflation indeed had a strong monetary component, Collor implemented a radical liquidity freeze, immediately reducing the money stock by 80 percent. All bank accounts in excess of US$1,000 were frozen. Brazilians were shocked. People who had, for example, sold one house but were in the process of buying another could not go ahead with their purchases. By law, they were not allowed access to their own money. The economy—including prices—was essentially at a standstill. These drastic measures were accompanied by planned reductions in the shape of government, including privatizations and layoffs of government employees.

The plan backfired. Rather than change expectations toward a low-inflation economy, it eroded confidence in the government as a guarantor of the rules governing the economic game. If the government could step in and freeze a family's life savings, what would it not do? The powerful business lobby, represented by the Federation of Industries of São Paulo (FIESP), was not consulted in the plan, leaving an angry and alienated industrial sector. The plan collapsed with a loss of legitimacy; Collor himself later fell to charges of corruption and was impeached. Changing the shape of government had not addressed some of the personalistic privileges that government officials had usurped. Nonetheless, this early test of Brazilian democracy led, after the interim presidency of Itamar Franco, to the election of Fernando Henrique Cardoso on the platform of price stabilization.

As Franco's economics minister, Cardoso introduced the **Real Plan**. The Real Plan was a pragmatic mix of orthodox and heterodox elements. Its premise was heterodox in spirit: eliminate the inertial elements of inflation to break out of a cycle of indexed price increases that adjusted for past inflation. The preliminary stage of the plan lasted three months. It began in December 1993 by identifying disequilibria, eliminating price distortions, and introducing emergency fiscal adjustments. In March monetary reform was introduced. All wages, prices, and taxes, and the exchange rate, were redenominated in a new accounting unit, the real unit of value (URV), roughly set at par to the US dollar. The URV was a kind of superindex as an intermediate step on the path back to using money as the measure of value.

Indexation to other rates was prohibited, and the money supply was tightened, indicating a monetarist bent. By July a new currency, the real, was introduced; it was tied initially one to one to the URV accounting unit. Once again this new currency was designed to erase the inflationary memory associated with the old unit. What was different in the case of the real was that the policy changes implemented in association with the Real Plan were credible to the public. The gradual, preannounced nature of each step served to calm expectations. Furthermore, after more than two decades of unsuccessfully battling inflation, the public was simply ready to bite the bullet. Expectations of inflation were changed. As President Cardoso said on the second anniversary of the Real Plan, "Brazil used to be like a casino. Everyone, not only banks, speculated here. This is coming to an end."[13] By 1996 the inflation rate was the lowest in Brazil in thirty-nine years. As we can see from the data in table 5.7, growth resumed, buoyed by consumer confidence, and unemployment did not rise.

Table 5.7.   Macroeconomic Indicators for Brazil, 1982–2006

Year	Consumer Prices	Growth	Urban Unemployment
1982	100.3	0.6	6.3
1983	178.0	−3.4	6.7
1984	209.1	5.1	7.1
1985	239.0	8.0	5.3
1986	58.6	7.5	3.6
1987	394.6	3.4	3.7
1988	993.3	0.3	3.8
1989	1,863.6	3.2	3.4
1990	1,584.6	−4.2	4.3
1991	475.8	0.3	4.8
1992	1,149.1	−0.3	5.8
1993	2,489.1	4.5	5.4
1994	929.3	6.2	5.1
1995	22.0	4.2	4.6
1996	9.1	2.5	5.7
1997	4.3	3.1	5.7
1998	2.5	0.1	7.6
1999	8.4	0.7	7.6
2000	6.0	3.9	7.1
2001	7.7	1.3	6.2
2002	12.5	1.5	11.7
2003	9.3	0.6	12.3
2004	7.6	4.9	11.5
2005	5.7	2.3	9.8
2006*	4.0	2.8	10.0

Source: ECLAC, *Economic Survey of Latin America and the Caribbean* (Santiago: ECLAC, various years). Data for 2005 from David Fleischer, Brazil Focus e-newsletter, email fleischer@uol.com.br.
*Forecasts.

The real was a stable anchor against inflation through mid-1998, but imbalances began to emerge in the Brazilian economy. Government deficits, fueled by a lack of fundamental restructuring in fiscal outlays, became alarming. Strong spending—led by workers finally able to save enough to buy consumer durables—created trade balance problems. The real was becoming overvalued relative to economic fundamentals. As we will discuss in Chapter 7, when currency crises shook Asia and Russia, the unstable Brazilian economy was unable to withstand the capital outflows. The government abandoned the fixed exchange rate, allowing the currency to float on international markets. The associated 30–40 percent depreciation raised fears of igniting another inflationary round in Brazil.[14]

Restraining the resurgence of inflation was a top priority. Under pressure of financial turmoil and the loss of an IMF rescue package, President Cardoso was able to extract important fiscal reforms from Congress and restrain inflation to about 10 percent, a significant achievement given the country's hyperinflationary past. This was no small task in Brazil, where the 1988 constitution hampers the president's ability to change a complex system of taxes and entitlements controlled by a powerful Congress. A tightening of monetary policy by the central bank sent interest rates soaring to 43 percent by March 1999—a strong signal that the government was serious about fighting inflation without an exchange rate anchor.[15]

Without the fixed exchange rate anchor (or its second cousin the crawling peg), Brazilian monetary authorities had to generate market confidence in their ability to manage the independent monetary policy associated with a float. The third central bank president in as many weeks, Arminio Fraga, brought his Wall Street experience to Brasilia. The central bank announced a transparent commitment to inflation targets. Concerned about the inflation pass-through from the devaluation (estimated to be approximately 30–40 percent), interest rates were raised to 45 percent to restrain the impact of import price escalation. Fraga hit the international financial markets with forceful international economic diplomacy, successfully garnering external financial support. Inflationary expectations fell, and interest rate pressures were relieved. Panic behind it, the Brazilian central bank was able to lengthen the term structure of the government's domestic debt and regularize publication of inflation targets and performance on its website (www.bcb.gov.br).[16] By mid-1999, Brazil adopted an inflation-targeting scheme with strict targets that enhanced the credibility of the new regime. Despite pressure from the East Asian crises (discussed in Chapter 7), the devaluation of the Brazilian real and the dismantling of the exchange rate–based stabilization scheme did not lead to a full-blown currency crisis in 1999, in large part because the monetary move was accompanied by substantial reform.[17]

To reign in public finances, Brazil passed a fiscal responsibility law in 2000 that sets limits on borrowing by states and municipalities, forbidding the expenditure of more than 60 percent of revenues on wages. Aimed at budgetary balance, unintended effects included hiring fewer doctors, teachers, and security guards. Offending mayors can be banned from office. The federal government is also forbidden to bail out states and cities in trouble. By limiting fiscal excess and promoting more efficient tax collection, Brazil promoted international credibility and improved its bond ratings in international markets, lowering the cost of capital critical for growth.

The 2002 elections of Luiz Inácio "Lula" da Silva, the left-leaning Workers Party candidate, rocked Brazilian markets, resulting in a 40 percent depreciation of the real and a US$30 billion IMF lifeline in the face of an uncertain economic direction for Brazil. To the surprise of many, however, Lula turned to pursue conservative fiscal and monetary policies, bowing to the pressure of international markets to maintain budget and trade surpluses. From a nominal fiscal deficit in 1999 of 14 percent of GDP, Brazil reduced this measure of the burden of government in the economy to 10 percent in 2000 and 2–2.5 percent in 2005.[18] If interest payments owed by the government are held aside, Brazil posted a 2005 primary surplus of 5.1 percent. Brazil's ability to promote growth remains constrained by its need to maintain financial market credibility. With government debt at a weighty 51.7 percent of GDP, Brazilian growth is highly sensitive to bringing down interest rates. A 2005 move by the Brazilian central bank to lower the interest rate to 19 percent was greeted with praise for those looking to pump up the economy—but caution emerged as well to not move in the opposite direction of US interest rates. If the extravagant spread between riskier Brazilian investments and safer US options shrinks too much, foreign investment in Brazil may suffer. If falling investment increases the risk factor of investing in Brazil, this premium will be reflected in rising rates—just what the government is trying to avoid.[19]

What lessons for inflation stabilization can we take from the Brazilian case? Clearly, heterodox policy alone is not enough. Simply focusing on expectations and taming the inertial component does not eliminate the imbalances creating the expectations. Fiscal and monetary fundamentals also need to be adjusted. Without reshaping the fundamentals, it is not possible to generate confidence that the imbalance in the domestic economy has been corrected. A pure orthodox approach was simply not dramatic enough to generate confidence and support. In the Brazilian case, merely restraining the money supply had perverse effects. When the money supply was cut and interest rates rose as a result, economic agents perceived this as a rise in the nominal interest rate—or a signal that inflation was heating up again. They therefore increased their demands for higher wages or prices to adjust for expected future inflation. Without a change in expectations of inflation, without a clear sense of a change in the rules of the game, inertial aspects of inflation will plague the orthodox strategy.

The fight for shares, the struggle to adjust to inflation by stepping on the back of other economic agents, was indeed prevalent in the Brazilian case. In an economy characterized by a high degree of inequality and structural constraints on the road to equilibrium, this battle between capital and labor cannot be ignored. With Brazil's relatively closed economy, agents did not have to look to the external sector for competitive price setting. By the same token, resolving the problem of conflict over social shares cannot be passed around like a hot potato by ineffective government. Confidence in the ability of government to mediate this conflict, to stabilize the playing field, is crucial to a compact on the part of all agents in restraining inflation. Not surprisingly, this confidence begins at home, with a transparent and credible plan for managing fiscal accounts.

Solving chronic budgetary problems is the key to sustainable prices over time. By accompanying monetary with fiscal change, Brazil was able to move from an exchange rate–based stabilization program to an inflation target. Although the exchange rate–based stabilization program was likely necessary to overcome inflationary expectations and launch a credible currency, the real, an increasingly overvalued exchange rate constrained Brazil's international competitiveness. With a worsening current account, the Brazilian government had to raise interest rates to attract capital to finance the international imbalance—choking off domestic growth in the process.[20] Although Brazil must continue to pay attention to an international balancing act between the need to attract capital and a pro-growth interest rate, an inflation target combined with a floating exchange rate has given the country a bit of breathing space to promote growth through exports. Brazil's success in the short term of restraining speculative attacks on the real under the float will be cemented only by a long-term commitment to resolving the tough distributional issues that drive Brazil's deficits.[21]

EARLY MONETARIST APPLICATIONS: BOLIVIA

The Bolivian stabilization experience provides an interesting orthodox contrast to the Brazilian case. Bolivia had also embarked on a period of hyperinflation by 1985. External factors such as the crash of international tin prices from US$6 to US$3.5 between 1982 and 1985 severely contracted tax revenues. Tin export earnings fell from US$234.8 million to US$75.1 million. At the same time, foreign debt service requirements increased from 0.4 percent of GDP in 1979 to 10.8 percent in 1983. As in other developing countries, due to the debt crisis, there was virtually no access to new funding in international markets. In addition to the fall in revenues, inflation was eating away at the value of tax receipts. Because the government was pursuing an expansionary policy, financing the internal and external deficits required monetary emissions, or increases in the money supply. By 1984 the government deficit had risen to nearly one-fifth of gross national product (GNP). The jump in the money supply, or seignorage to finance government spending, mirrored the decline in resource flows from abroad. In contrast to the Brazilian case, wage and price indexation was not widespread. In a futile attempt to provide a monetary anchor, the exchange rate was fixed. Rather than price stability, the result was an overvalued exchange rate. When an exchange rate is fixed and exchange controls are imposed to restrict the amount of hard currency in the system, international currencies are strongly demanded in black—or, as they sometimes were called to reflect the openness of the transactions, parallel—markets. In Bolivia by 1985 the controlled rate was at 67,000 bolivianos per US dollar while the free black market rate was running at 1,143,548. This 1,600 percent overvaluation made legal exports unprofitable. Underground transactions therefore emerged as evidenced by oddities in international data. Peru, for example, despite its lack of tin mines, became a tin exporter (of illegal Bolivian exports) during this period. Of course, illegal exports were not taxed, further eroding the ability of the Bolivian state to finance its affairs. Speculation in foreign exchange became quite profitable. If a person could buy the overvalued official boliviano (sometimes illegally), money could be made in selling cheaply acquired US dollars on the black market. Politically, Bolivia had a weak government trying to adjudicate increasing claims on the state to address problems of poverty and inequality. A powerful military and labor movement pressured the spending arm of the state. Falling external prices made these constraints that much more acute.

In 1985, Victor Paz Estenssoro came to power and announced the New Economic Policy to address the extreme macroeconomic deterioration (shown in table 5.8). A devaluation of the exchange rate followed by managed floating addressed the priority of getting international prices right.[22] The state-led development strategy was abandoned. Enterprises were privatized or scaled down, resulting in a reduction of the public-sector wage bill. In particular, COMIBOL, the powerful state tin producer, reduced its employment from thirty thousand in 1985 to seven thousand in 1987. Public-sector revenues were increased through tax reform.

Table 5.8. Macroeconomic Indicators for Bolivia, 1982–2005

Year	Consumer Prices (annual % change)	Growth Rate of GDP (annual % change constant 2000 US$)	GDP/Capita (US$)	Public Deficit as % of GDP
1982	296.5	NA	1,069.0	–13.7
1983	328.5	–5.3	986.0	–15.7
1984	2,176.8	1.2	972.0	–17.6
1985	8,170.5	–0.1	945.0	–9.0
1986	65.9	–1.9	902.0	–1.6
1987	10.6	2.6	901.0	–3.6
1988	21.5	–1.3	809.0	–4.5
1989	16.6	3.8	822.0	–1.8
1990	18.0	4.6	840.0	–1.0
1991	14.5	5.3	864.0	–1.4
1992	10.5	1.7	857.0	0.8
1993	9.3	4.3	872.0	–1.0
1994	8.5	4.8	891.0	–4.2
1995	10.6	4.7	911.0	–3.8
1996	9.9	4.5	926.0	–1.9
1997	6.7	4.9	942.0	–3.3
1998	4.4	5	966.0	–4.0
1999	3.1	0.3	947.0	–3.8
2000	3.4	2.3	1,019.0	–3.7
2001	0.9	1.6	952.0	–6.9
2002	2.5	2.7	905.0	–9.0
2003	3.9	2.4	872.0	–7.0
2004	4.3	3.9	1.6	–5.4
2005	4.9	4.1	1.8	–3.5

Source: ECLAC, *Economic Survey of Latin America and the Caribbean* (Santiago: ECLAC, various years); and IADB, *Economic and Social Progress in Latin America* (Washington, DC: Johns Hopkins University Press, various years).

Greater confidence in the government also resulted in higher compliance with tax obligations. Debt was rescheduled, and funding from multilateral institutions and foreign governments was secured in exchange for the adoption of these orthodox economic policies. Widespread liberalization of trade and capital accounts was implemented to attract private capital inflows. An amnesty was declared for the return of US dollars that had fled abroad. US dollar deposits were also legalized without proof of origin, permitting the entry of coca dollars into the economy.[23]

The immediate result of this austere package was a call for a general strike. However, after three years of hyperinflation, the public chose to support the government rather than the workers, and the tough package was upheld. To minimize the social costs of adjustment, an emergency social fund (ESF), financed by the Inter-American Development Bank (IADB) and the World Bank, was implemented. It provided funds for small-scale, labor-intensive projects proposed and implemented by local nongovernmental organizations. The projects financed were mostly in infrastructure; they are estimated to have created nearly forty-one thousand jobs and added 2 percent to the GNP over the period.[24] We will return to the use of social funds in Chapter 11, which discusses poverty.

Despite the innovations of the ESF, the costs of inflation stabilization in Bolivia were enormous. Although inflation was dramatically controlled, the price was a long period of recession. Over the period 1985–1996, the rate of growth of GDP per capita ranged from –10.21 percent in 1988 to +2.86 percent in 1991. If the goal of development is to improve the well-being of its population, falling or stagnant rates of GDP growth do not present opportunities for economic advancement. By 1994 GDP finally climbed back to the 1982 level—a lost decade of development for Bolivians. GDP per capita in 1996 did not reach 1982 levels. The Bolivian orthodox strategy eradicated inflation, but at a high price for growth.

The Case of Argentina: From the Austral Plan to the Convertibility Plan

Stabilization in Argentina was conceptually path-breaking with its heterodox attempt in the 1980s and its orthodox plan in the 1990s. The Argentine **Austral Plan** of 1985 provided many of the elements followed by Brazil. Inflation was diagnosed as having a strong inertial component. A decade of failed stabilization attempts taught economic agents to expect inflation and adjust for it in wage and price setting. The Austral Plan therefore froze wages and prices (including the exchange rate) and introduced a new currency with a promise not to print money. Fiscal adjustment was the third element of the plan. There was a close relationship between fiscal deficits and money creation in Argentina. Eliminating deficits would stem the need for seignorage, or money printing, as the last resort for financing. Initially the plan succeeded as inflation decreased from 350 percent in the first half of 1985 to 20 percent in the second.

Nonetheless, the Austral Plan collapsed as signs of disequilibrium emerged. The exchange rate became overvalued, and external accounts deteriorated. The government made adjustments for price flexibility, but the credibility of the plan was undermined. Argentines needed to have their expectations grounded in a firm and credible long-run strategy. They found this in the 1991 **Convertibility Plan** introduced by Minister Domingo Cavallo in the Menem administration. President Carlos Menem succeeded President Raúl Alfonsín as the second democratically elected president after years of military rule. International markets held their breath because Menem was a renowned populist of the Peronist Party. However, the old style of populist spending to appease conflicts between industry, labor, and the military was surprisingly transformed into a personal populism that allowed Menem to introduce one of the toughest austerity programs in the region. The Convertibility Plan locked the Argentine peso to the US dollar. Through a currency board independent of the Treasury, by law the money supply could be increased only if the US dollars held in reserve were to rise. This took the central bank out of the position of being the lender of last resort and removed the temptation to finance domestic deficits with new money creation. Monetary policy was nondiscretionary, fixed to the long-run performance of the external sector. Liberalization of the economy promoted exports and the inflow of foreign investment to increase the stock of US dollars in Argentina. The peso, which formerly lost value daily, became indistinguishable from the US dollar. Indeed, in bank machines in Buenos Aires one could select whether to receive cash in US dollars or pesos. Fiscal adjustment was dramatic but incomplete. The government embarked on a large-scale privatization program, putting fifty-one firms on the auction block between 1989 and 1992 and generating approximately US$18 billion.[25] Tax reform increased revenues to balance government books. Smaller government demanded less inflationary financing.

As we can see in table 5.9, inflation tumbled in Argentina from the peak of more than 3,000 percent to an astoundingly low rate of 0.1 percent in 1996. Domestic and international capital believed in the long-run commitment of the plan. International capital flowed to Argentina, convinced of the sustainability of the program and lured by the values of the privatized firms on the stock exchange. The plan was remarkable. Despite high social costs of 17 percent unemployment, Cavallo was tough and held firm on the Convertibility Plan. When the Mexican peso crisis of 1994–1995 rocked the international financial community's faith in Latin America, Argentina stuck to the plan even as capital temporarily fled the region. Cavallo left the administration in July 1996 with the economy contracting at a rate of 4.6 percent in 1995; nonetheless, the new economics minister, Roque Fernandez, continued to ground the Argentine peso firmly in the value of the US dollar. Despite the recession, Fernandez attacked the budget deficit, increasing taxes and cutting spending. These tough policies were the cost of not erasing the inflationary memory.

When its trading partner, Brazil, let the real float in 1999, fragilities in the Argentine model were exacerbated. The accompanying devaluation of the Brazilian real improved competitiveness and the Brazilian trade balance; at the same time, the strengthening US dollar compounded the overvaluation of the peso. External accounts deteriorated, unemployment remained stuck at socially unacceptable levels in the range of 18 percent, and fiscal deficits were not brought under control. As we will see in Chapter 7, challenges from Brazil, the inability to restrain fiscal spending by the provinces, and rising external debt burst the viability of the peso-dollar lock, and Argentina tumbled into economic chaos.

Table 5.9.   Macroeconomic Indicators for Argentina, 1970–2006

Year	Inflation (average annual growth of consumer prices)	Annual Growth Rate of GDP	Urban Unemployment
1970	13.6	—	—
1971	34.7	—	—
1972	58.4	3.1	6.6
1973	61.2	6.1	5.4
1974	23.5	6.5	3.4
1975	182.9	−1.3	3.7
1976	444.0	−3.0	4.5
1977	176.1	6.4	2.8
1978	175.5	−3.4	2.8
1979	159.5	7.1	2.0
1980	100.8	1.4	2.3
1981	104.5	−6.2	4.5
1982	164.8	−5.2	4.8
1983	345.0	2.6	4.2
1984	627.5	2.4	3.9
1985	672.5	−4.4	5.3
1986	85.7	6.0	4.6
1987	123.1	2.1	5.3
1988	348.3	−1.0	6.0
1989	3,080.5	−1.9	7.6
1990	2,314.7	−6.1	7.4
1991	171.7	0.0	6.5
1992	24.9	8.8	7.0
1993	10.6	5.9	9.6
1994	4.2	5.8	11.5
1995	3.4	−2.9	17.5
1996	0.1	5.5	17.2
1997	0.3	8.0	14.9
1998	0.7	3.8	12.9
1999	−1.8	−3.4	14.3
2000	−0.7	−0.6	15.1
2001	−1.5	4.4	17.4
2002	41.0	−10.8	19.7
2003	3.7	8.7	17.3
2004	6.1	9.0	13.6
2005	12.3	9.2	11.6
2006*	11.0	8.5	—

Source: ECLAC, *Preliminary Overview of the Economy of Latin America and the Caribbean*, various years (Santiago: ECLAC, various years); Economic Commission for Latin America and the Caribbean, *Statistical Yearbook of Latin America and the Caribbean*, various years (Santiago: ECLAC, various years); and IADB, *Economic and Social Progress in Latin America* (Washington, DC: Johns Hopkins University Press, various years).
*Forecast.

A perfect storm hit Argentina in 2001. Still weak from financial contagion of the Asian currency crisis and the Brazilian real crisis, Argentina began running into balance of payments difficulty. Tied to the US dollar, the exchange rate anchor became a dead weight on the Argentina economy without significant internal improvements in productivity and competitiveness. As credibility eroded, capital rapidly flowed out of Argentina. Debt obligations became unsustainable as interest rates soared and growth slowed. Despite radical changes in the shape of the state under President Menem, tough adjustments in fiscal accounts lagged behind. Given that its monetary hand was tied by the convertibility law, the government should have adopted greater fiscal conservatism during periods of growth to cushion the fall during a downturn—but it wasn't so prudent. The IMF, perhaps a bit too tied to Argentina as its Washington Consensus poster child, extended additional loans without requiring stronger fiscal adjustment. An emergency loan called the "blindaje" or armor was arranged to protect the Argentine economy against external shocks.[26] Money market managers were drawn to the high returns that risky Argentine assets offered. So long as they could convince markets of the viability of future gains in Argentina, money poured in to make more money. Of course the US$14 billion loan was not a grant—increasing Argentina's indebtedness in a desperate attempt to save the Convertibility Plan and promote growth.

Yet investors began to suspect that the one-to-one link of US dollars to pesos couldn't hold. There was significantly stronger demand for US dollars—a demand that the central bank could not meet with its meager reserves. Argentines began to withdraw pesos from the system, running on banks to the tune of US$15 billion in the second half of 2001. As GDP growth ground to a halt, the debt to GDP ratio, an indicator of the ability to pay, rose, indicating an impending crisis. The only way to generate more growth was to issue more debt—creating a debt time bomb with exploding debt dynamics.[27] The unsustainability of the program became apparent— but as confidence waned, an exit strategy from the Convertibility Plan became more problematic. Convertibility was legally binding—if this promise was broken, what could markets trust?[28]

To stem the tide, the Argentine government imposed a little fence or "corralito" on funds, placing a US$1,000 a month ceiling on bank withdrawals. The public became furious and took to the streets to protest. Political uncertainty spiked investor anxiety, and funds continued to flee Argentina. Governments tumbled, as four presidents took office in Argentina and resigned in as many weeks. By February of 2002 Argentina was forced to default on US$155 billion of public debt, the largest default of any country in history. Desperate attempts to impose credibility on the system backfired. The announced zero deficit policy to restrain fiscal spending came at just the wrong time to wring a 13 percent cut in expenditure, as the economy was already in a painful contraction. Average income fell to almost a quarter of its level reached in the late 1990s, and more than half of the Argentine population sank under the poverty line.

By 2003, the IMF attempted to stave off default of an additional US$6.6 billion coming due to the fund from Argentina. Rewarding it for tough measures to reduce the deficit following default, the IMF was helping the government of President Eduardo Duhalde to stay in good stead at the IMF until a new government was elected that spring. Incoming President Néstor Kirchner and his economy minister

Roberto Lavagna then played hardball with markets. Using funds that would have gone to meet interest and principal payments to invest in the Argentine economy, growth recovered to 8 percent in 2004. Arguing that creditors who piled money into Argentina should bear some of the risk, in June 2005 the government forced hundreds of thousands of bondholders of the defaulted debt to take a huge "haircut"—a shaving of 66 percent on the US$103 billion outstanding liabilities, exchanging the defaulted paper for new discounted offerings. Given the megadevaluation versus the US dollar, this is the amount that Argentina felt it could reasonably repay. Argentines, tired of tough adjustment policies, rallied to the defiance of markets, reducing social tensions at home.

Despite the dire warnings that a default would preclude new capital flows to Argentine, by July 2005 a new bond issue of US$500 million was oversubscribed. Argentina's unprecedented primary budget surplus of 4 percent of GDP, its current account surplus, and low global interest rates left markets enamored, once again, with the Argentine financial tango.[29] Nonetheless, with a less than independent central bank, monetary emissions and a weak exchange rate were fueling the inflation engines to approximately 12 percent for the year.[30]

Argentina provides us with a case study of an effective instrument of stabilization—the one-to-one convertibility of the US dollar to the peso—that later became a debilitating liability. Once inflation was tamed, the value of the peso reflected underlying conditions in the US dollar–based economy—not those in Argentina. Because real productivity was dramatically different, Argentina became overwhelmingly constrained in its efforts to grow.

LESSONS FOR STABILIZATION

Box 5.3 summarizes the variation of the stabilization experiences we have just studied. What lessons can we draw from these cases of stabilization in Latin America? As Jeffrey Sachs notes, there are three components to inflation reduction: (1) finding a solution to chronic budgetary problems at the core of high inflation; (2) identifying a means of eliminating inertial inflation, principally wage and price indexation; and (3) introducing one or more nominal anchors to the price level at the start of stabilization to ground expectations and the behavior of central bank authorities.[31] In all the cases, without clear and credible attention to the fiscal crisis, inflation will resurge in the economy. Fiscal imbalances will prevent stabilization, and the government will likely respond by monetizing the difference.

Restructuring the role of government in the economy has an additional benefit: creating the perception that business as usual has changed. Generating the confidence that the government is serious about reform and will—and can—remain committed to a stable policy is critical to success. This involves erasing the inflationary memory, the backward-looking behavior of agents that reflexively drives price increases. Tying the currency to an anchor—either firmly as in the case of Argentina or loosely in terms of a crawling peg to the US dollar—provides monetary restraint. But with this stability comes a loss of flexible exchange rate changes to reflect different macroeconomic conditions. Beyond these tools, the population

Box 5.3.   Variations on the Stabilization Experience

	Brazil's Cruzado Plan 1986	Brazil's Real Plan 1994	Argentina's Convertibility Plan 1991	Bolivia's New Economic Policy 1985
Diagnosis of inflation	Structural; inflation is a fight over social shares; address inertial inflation	Provide nominal anchor tied to exchange rate, de-index economy, and correct fiscal imbalances	Erase inflationary memory and control expectations; provide firm price anchor	Monetary emissions to accommodate government spending; fall in tax revenue forces seignorage; exchange rate overvalued
Fiscal policy	Reform unsuccessful	Short-run emergency adjustment; long-run change stalled in Congress	Restrictive; cut expenditures; strong privatization; tax increase	Tax reform; increase public-sector prices; cut SOEs
Monetary policy	Increases due to fear of raising nominal interest rate giving inflation signal	Contractionary	Nondiscretionary; tied to US dollar reserves	Tight
Exchange rate policy	Fixed at 13.84Cr = US$1	Crawling peg set to US dollar	Fixed on par with US dollar; money supply tied to reserves	Establish stable, unified rate; devalue then dirty float
Wage and prices	Freeze	Flexible	Flexible	No controls
Currency	1Cz = 1,000Cr	New currency real tied to URV loosely set to US dollar	Peso interchangeable with US dollar	
Political	Price inspectors			Restrain influence of labor unions
Trade	Continued internal orientation	Temporary erection of tariffs	Aggressive liberalization	Liberalization

continued

continued

	Brazil's Cruzado Plan 1986	Brazil's Real Plan 1994	Argentina's Convertibility Plan 1991	Bolivia's New Economic Policy 1985
Indexation	Prohibit contracts of less than one year with indexation clauses	All indexation except to new URV prohibited	None	
Initial results	Inflation falls from 22 percent monthly in February to 0.3 in May; growth surges led by strong consumer durables	Inflation lowest in nearly forty years; consumption exploded with increase in real income; some tightening	Dramatically low inflation	Drove hyperinflation out
Persistent imbalances	Shortages, withholding of goods; plan collapses as expectations escalate	Fiscal imbalance; real structural change awaits congressional approval	Unemployment at 17 percent	High social costs; anemic growth rates
Balance of payments	Trade surplus shrinks; reserves fall; exchange rate held fixed too long to maintain internal-external balance	Loss of export dynamic due to overvalued currency		

needs to believe in the benefits of inflation fighting. In Argentina the public was so tired of struggling to live with inflation that it was willing to quit cold turkey. Much like an alcoholic, the public understood that one little ounce of price inflation would tip the economy into an inflationary binge. Over time, however, the objective of a credible anchor gave way to the need for job creation and competitiveness. Bolivians, also subject to ravaging hyperinflation, were willing to swallow the tough contractionary pill. In Mexico the support was negotiated through El Pacto, providing a framework for sharing the burden of stabilization. Brazilians have been able to stave off some of the more dramatic social conflicts, perhaps in part due to the size of their economy and the ability to insulate it to some degree from the shock of international competitiveness. Whether this will prove to be a good thing in the long run remains to be seen.

Resolving deficit financing involves putting an end to persistent deficits. Expenditures have outpaced volatile revenues in Latin America. An Organization for Economic Cooperation and Development (OECD) study shows that industrialized countries collect an equivalent of 23 percent of GDP, while Latin American governments take in less than 15 percent—of generally smaller GDPs.[32] The ability to raise tax collection is crucial to enhancing education, health, and technology systems. Fiscal policy in Latin America also tends to be procyclical, fueling booms and protracting recession. In addition to tough questions of taxing politically powerful elites versus the penniless poor, questions of corruption and legitimacy plague reform efforts. Tax reform is a difficult balancing act, invariably asking some group to give more for the sake of the public good.

Sustained stabilization may also involve the development of new financial markets. One of the defining features of underdeveloped economies is the lack of a long-term capital market. In part this is a self-fulfilling prophecy—instability decreases the incentive for long-term investments. But this makes macroeconomic stabilization in the short term problematic. Without long-term confidence, bond markets cannot be used as an effective instrument of open market operations to smooth cyclical variations in the economy. This lack of monetary instruments places increasing pressure on governments to use the blunt tools of decreasing fiscal expenditures to stabilize growth.[33] Banking systems are also in need of reform. Banks in Latin America are more vulnerable during crises because most deposits are short-term (due to lack of confidence in the government's policies), banking institutions tend to put a great share of assets in land, and the value of their holdings of government securities is more volatile. During crises, banks find it hard to raise external financing; this is exacerbated by the fact that domestic capital markets are thin.[34] As banks struggle with bad loans and missed payments during a downturn, confidence in the banking system's financial health is called into question. Macrocrises are exacerbated by these fragilities of banking systems. Many countries have therefore adopted reforms in the banking sector. They have tightened prudential guidelines for lending, established minimum capital requirements that banks must hold relative to their loan base, and adopted monitoring systems to assess loan quality and risk. Banks are subject to wider supervisory review and are required to provide more comprehensive financial information consistent with international standards. There is, however, a wide degree of variance in regional banking reform. Brazil's banking sector was able to withstand the pressure of the depreciation of the real in part due to reforms of the mid-1990s; Argentina and Chile are also leaders in reform efforts. Other nations need to improve supervisory capabilities, including the ability to monitor cross-border operations for those with significant offshore financial sectors.

From Stabilization to Growth

The dramatic achievements in price stabilization are evidenced in table 5.10 with a fall in the increase in consumer prices from an annual rate of 440.8 percent in 1990 to approximately 8.1 percent in 2000. Imagine the benefits of this price stability to

Table 5.10. Selected Latin American Macroeconomic Indicators

Year	Increase in Consumer Prices (%)	New Data	Increase in Real GDP per Capita (%)	New Data	Increase in Real GDP (%)	New Data
1990	440.8	87–96 avg. 181.9	−1.6	87–96 avg. 0.9	0.6	87–96 avg. 2.7
1995	36.0	97–06 avg. 8.0	−0.6	97–06 avg. 1.3	1.7	97–06 avg. 2.8
1996	21.2		2.0		3.6	
1997	12.9	11.9	3.5	3.6	5.3	5.2
1998	9.9	9.0	0.6	0.7	2.3	2.3
1999	8.8	8.2	−1.1	−1.1	0.2	0.4
2000	8.1	7.6	2.5	2.4	4.2	3.9
2001	6.2	6.1	−1.1	−1.0	1.7	0.5
2002	4.9	8.9	1.5	−1.5		x
2003		10.6		0.7		2.2
2004		6.5		4.2		5.6
2005*		6.3		2.7		4.1
2006*		5.4		2.4	3.6	3.8

Source: ECLAC, *Preliminary Overview of the Economies of Latin America and the Caribbean* (Santiago: ECLAC, various years).
* Forecast.

agents trying to plan for the future. Real GDP growth accelerated to a high of 5.3 percent before falling to 0.2 as a result of the global slowdown in 1999; regional output grew at a slow 1.7 percent in 2001, again reflecting a sharp slowdown in global conditions. Growth in per capita GDP is lower, however, reflecting the mismatch between the rate of growth of the economy and the needs of growing populations in the region.

The process of economic stabilization has not been smooth. The IADB's 1996 report characterizes the pattern of reform in five phases: stabilization and implementation of reforms; economic recovery or boom; stress; correction or crisis; and post-reform growth.[35] As in Brazil's or Argentina's first packages, successful stabilization measures discussed above created consumer and investor confidence that leads to economic recovery or boom. Growth increases at a rate 4 percent higher than normal, and the resulting increase in income tax revenues improves fiscal balances. The boom, usually lasting about three years, creates imbalances. Credit tightens and interest rates rise. Higher domestic spending leads to an appreciation of the currency, squeezing exports. The economy slows, and fiscal deficits emerge. Investors, including foreign capital, become wary. Confidence erodes, and the economy enters into a period of stress. Pressures are often exacerbated by political factors. The reform process can be temporarily derailed by the crisis. However, if corrections are swift and credible, although slower growth can be expected, the downturn need not be traumatic. Chile provides an example of a country that, after more than twenty years of reform, has entered into the final stage of post-reform. This is not to say that the economy is perfectly functioning. Challenges, particularly the social challenges of poverty and inequality, require response. But policy making has achieved a level of continuity and normalcy that encourages measured, long-run responses.

THE PRICE OF PRICE STABILITY: THE CHALLENGE OF RESOLVING THE SOCIAL DEFICIT

Despite stabilization, the magic of the market has not completely fulfilled the promise of development in Latin America. It is important to recall the huge human cost of austerity measures designed to stabilize inflationary economies. Like adjustment to the debt crisis, policies to reduce inflation come at the expense of current consumption—and for the poor, reducing a thin margin means human suffering. The fragility of this model was clearly demonstrated as strikes and demonstrations have evidenced frustrated expectations of growth. Domestic difficulties call into question the ability of governments to continue to apply tough austerity measures at home in hope of maintaining investor confidence abroad.[36] Large portions of the populations are left out of the process of growth. The social deficit—the enormous unmet need in the region for education, housing, medical services, transportation, and other public services—may not be resolved by the market. Contemporary social and political tension in Bolivia today can be traced to two decades of struggle. Women have borne the brunt of macroeconomic stabilization. As the guardians of the family, they are left with the task of designing strategies of survival. They must do more with less. Because they are forced outside the home for long hours to make up lost income, their daughters must fill motherly roles with younger siblings. Macrocrises can be considered a social "tax" on women's time.[37]

The road to economic reform in Latin America has been rocky. In all cases the social costs of stabilization have been the daily reality of Latin Americans. Poverty and inequality in the region rose, and human capital investments have suffered from the cuts in government programs in education, health, and social services. Macroeconomic equilibrium is seen as a necessary but not sufficient condition for development. Development, as we remember from Chapter 1, revolves around the question of structural change. Several problems must be addressed to move from stability to growth. Sufficient savings must be generated and channeled into productive investment, resources must be allocated efficiently, and a setting must be developed that is conducive to generating the incentives to find new, potentially better ways of doing things.[38] The broad framework should move beyond macroeconomic policy reform to address trade liberalization, private-sector development, innovative policies for technological change, and reform of the state, focused on greater equity, efficiency, participation, and environmental sustainability.[39] We will take up these issues in the following chapters.

Key Concepts

Austral Plan	heterodox	Real Plan
Bresser Plan	indexation	seignorage
Convertibility Plan	inertial inflation	structuralists
cost-push elements	inflationary expectations	velocity of money
Cruzado Plan	Mercosur	
exchange rate–based stabilization programs	Olivera-Tanzi effect	

Chapter Summary

Monetarist Theory of Inflation

- Monetarists believe that persistent inflation in Latin America was caused by irresponsible deficit financing, the erosion of the tax base, and the debt crisis. With weak capital markets, and with foreign sources of capital drying up after the debt crisis, Latin American governments financed their deficit through seignorage, or the printing of money, inducing inflation. Unable to generate revenue with a deteriorating tax base, governments again looked at seignorage as a form of financing deficits. The debt crisis exacerbated conditions, making it difficult to finance the deficit through other means. The monetarist solution was to decrease government spending—although this was politically difficult.

The Structuralist Theory of Inflation

- The structuralists focused on cost-push elements as the main factors inducing inflation. Bottlenecks causing shortages, oligopolies, external shocks, and labor interacted to push prices up and prevented them from falling under normal market conditions. The political power of business and labor made it difficult to resist accommodating money demands. Inflation then became imbedded in the system and, for the structuralists, a necessary price for growth in the developing world.
- With ingrained expectations of inflation, some countries adopted indexation to adjust to the increase in prices. At the same time, indexation propelled inflation as price increases were automatically passed around the economy. Inflationary expectations also increased the velocity of money. With higher velocity, an increase in the money supply has a stronger expansionary and inflationary effect.
- Latin America is a laboratory of inflation-fighting policies. Brazil, characterized by a culture of inflation, began its fight against inflation with the Cruzado Plan, which initially was successful. It failed due to a loss of credibility and political pressures. The next attempt was the Bresser Plan in 1987, which fell to shortages and balance of payments pressure. President Collor tried to bring the economy to a standstill by eliminating inflationary expectations but succeeded only in eroding credibility. Using a mix of heterodox and orthodox measures, Finance Minister (later President) Cardoso introduced the Real Plan, which managed to bring down inflation. The fixed exchange rate aspect of the plan was abandoned, however, as international capital was wary of the lack of fundamental reform in the wake of the Asian crisis. Inflation appears to have stabilized.
- The decrease in foreign capital in the mid-1980s induced Bolivia to finance government spending through seignorage. To reduce the inflationary effects of its policies, Bolivia adopted a monetarist approach by devaluing the currency, privatizing, instituting tax reform, liberalizing trade and capital accounts, and rescheduling the debt. The austerity package brought about a general strike, but the government was able to uphold its package. Tough contractionary measures resulted in low growth throughout the 1980s and into the 1990s.
- The 1985 Austral Plan to bring down inflation in Argentina initially succeeded but, like the Cruzado Plan in Brazil, ultimately collapsed as inflationary expectations resurged. Populist president Carlos Menem surprised the country by introducing an austerity program to fight inflation in 1991. Menem tied the Argentine peso to the US dollar to limit any increases in money supply and liberalized the economy. Although inflation fell from 3,000 percent to 0.1 percent, Argentina continues to suffer social costs of high unemployment. The Convertibility Plan collapsed in 2001 under the weight of fiscal deficits, weak competitiveness, and extreme debt.
- Lessons for stabilization include the need for fiscal sustainability, confidence in the ability to tackle tough choices, and the development of new sources of finance. The human and environmental costs of stabilization have been high, resulting in a huge social deficit and environmental degradation.

Notes

1. Rudiger Dornbusch, *Stabilization, Debt, and Reform: Policy Analysis for Developing Countries* (Englewood Cliffs, NJ: Prentice Hall, 1993), 19.

2. Michael Gavin, Ricardo Hausmann, Roberto Perotti, and Ernesto Talvi, *Managing Fiscal Policy in Latin America and the Caribbean: Volatility, Procyclicality, and Limited Creditworthiness*, IADB, Office of the Chief Economist Working Paper No. 326 (Washington, DC: IADB, 1996), 4.

3. Victor Bulmer-Thomas, *The Economic History of Latin America since Independence* (New York: Cambridge University Press, 1994), 393.

4. Dornbusch, *Stabilization, Debt, and Reform*, 20.

5. Sebastian Edwards, "The Political Economy of Inflation and Stabilization in Developing Countries," *Economic Development and Cultural Change* 42(2) (January 1994): 235–266.

6. G. Tullio and M. Ronci, "Brazilian Inflation from 1980 to 1993: Causes, Consequences and Dynamics," *Journal of Latin American Studies* 28 (October 1996): 635–666.

7. Obstfeld and Taylor refer to these as the macroeconomic policy trilemma for open economies. As cited in Alan M. Taylor, "On the Costs of Inward-Looking Development: Price Distortions, Growth, and Divergence in Latin America," *Journal of Economic History* 58(1) (March 1998): 22.

8. Jeffrey Frieden and Ernesto Stein, *The Currency Game: Exchange Rate Politics in Latin America* (Washington, DC: Johns Hopkins University Press for the IADB, 2001), 9.

9. Anoop Singh, Agnés Belaisch, Charles Collyns, Paula De Masi, Reva Krieger, Guy Meredith, and Robert Rennhack, "Stabilization and Reform in Latin America: A Macroeconomic Perspective on the Experience since the Early 1990s," Occasional Paper 238, International Monetary Fund, February 2005.

10. Federal Reserve Bank of San Francisco, "U.S. Inflation Targeting: Pro and Con," FRBSF Economic Letter 98–18, May 29, 1998.

11. Prakash Loungani and Phillip Swagel, "Source of Inflation in Developing Countries," IMF Working Paper 01/198 (Washington, DC: The International Monetary Fund, December 2001).

12. Inflation series from Donald V. Coes, *Macroeconomic Crises, Policies, and Growth in Brazil, 1964–90* (Washington, DC: World Bank, 1995), table A.10.

13. Interview with President Fernando Henrique Cardoso on the occasion of the second anniversary of the Real Plan, as reported by the Foreign Broadcast Information Services, Latin America (FBIS-LAT-96 -129, July 3, 1996), first appearing on Rede Globo (the Brazilian television station) at 10:30 Greenwich Mean Time, July 1, 1996.

14. The range for the depreciation depends on the day it is measured. On January 30, 1998, for example, it had depreciated 37 percent from its initial value.

15. Edmund Amann and Werner Baer, "Anchors Away: The Costs and Benefits of Brazil's Devaluation," *World Development* 31(6) (2003): 1040.

16. Arminio Fraga, "Monetary Policy during the Transition to a Floating Exchange Rate: Brazil's Recent Experience," *Finance & Development* 37(1) (March 2000), www.imf.org, and Victor Bulmer-Thomas, "The Brazilian Devaluation: National Responses and International Consequences," *International Affairs* 7(4) (1999): 729–741.

17. Amann and Baer, "Anchors Away," 1042.

18. Viviane Monteiro, "Fiscal Resolve Is Crucial to the Economy, Says Finance Minister Palocci," *Noticias Financieras*, Groupo de Diarios America Invest News (Brazil), September 13, 2005.

19. "Coming Up Roses," Latin American Economy & Business, Intelligence Research Ltd, October 25, 2005.

20. Amann and Baer, "Anchors Away," 1044.

21. Eliana Cardoso, "Brazil's Currency Crisis," in *Exchange Rate Politics in Latin America*, eds. Carol Wise and Riordan Roett (Washington, DC: Brookings Institution Press, 2000), 70–92.

22. "Managed floating" refers to an exchange rate policy in which the price is largely market determined; the government may intervene in the market by buying and selling currency to stabilize the value.

23. Adapted from Juan Antonio Morales and Jeffrey Sachs, "Bolivia's Economic Crisis," in *Developing Country Debt and the World Economy*, ed. Jeffrey Sachs (Chicago, IL: University of Chicago Press, 1989).

24. Diana Tussie, *The Inter-American Development Bank*, vol. 4 of The Multilateral Development Banks (Ottawa: North-South Institute, 1995), 112.

25. Sebastian Edwards, *Crisis and Reform in Latin America: From Despair to Hope* (New York: Oxford University Press, 1995), 196.

26. For a gripping insider account of the bankrupting of Argentina, see Paul Blustein, *And the Money Kept Rolling In (and Out)* (New York: Public Affairs, a member of the Perseus Group, 2005). The blindaje is discussed on p. 106.

27. Blustein, *And the Money Kept Rolling In (and Out)*, 80, quoting IMF official El-Erian.

28. Blustein, *And the Money Kept Rolling In (and Out)*, 96.

29. Peter Hudson, "Issue by Argentina Is Greeted Warmly," *Financial Times* news alerts, July 20, 2005.

30. Mary Anastasia O'Grady, "Argentina Land of the Incredible Shrinking Peso," *Wall Street Journal*, October 21, 2005.

31. Jeffrey Sachs and Alvaro Zini, "Brazilian Inflation and the Plano Real," *World Economy* 19(1) (January 1996).

32. Federal Reserve Bank of Atlanta, "Imbalances in Latin American Fiscal Accounts: Why the United States Should Care," *Econ South* 2(1), www.frbatlanta.org.

33. José María Fanelli and Roberto Frenkel, "Macropolicies for the Transition from Stabilization to Growth," in *New Directions in Development Economics: Growth, Environmental Concerns and Government in the 1990s*, eds. Mats Lundahl and Benno J. Ndulu (London: Routledge, 1996), 46.

34. Robert Rennhack, "Banking Supervision," *Finance & Development* (March 2000): 27.

35. As characterized by Michael Gavin, "Surviving Economic Surgery," *The IDB* (December 1996): 4–5.

36. "A New Risk of Default," *Euromoney*, September 1996, 283.

37. Lance Taylor and Ute Piper, *Reconciling Economic Reform and Sustainable Human Development: Social Consequences of Neo-Liberalism*, United Nations Development Programme Discussion Paper Series (New York: UNDP, 1996).

38. Fanelli and Frenkel, "Macropolicies," 41.

39. Colin Bradford Jr., "Future Policy Directions and Relevance," in *The Legacy of Raúl Prebisch*, ed. Enrique V. Iglesias (Washington, DC: IADB, 1994), 164.

PUBLIC AND PRIVATE CAPITAL FLOWS TO LATIN AMERICA

C H A P T E R   S I X

The challenge with open capital markets is locking in a stable value for currencies in the Latin America. *(iStock/Vergani_Fotografia)*

After the long period of painful structural adjustment to the debt crisis, Latin America became a magnet for international finance in the mid-1990s. Macroeconomic stability, the opening of closed economies to international markets, lucrative privatizations, and subregional integration enticed private foreign capital to Latin America. By 1997, net resource transfers, a measure of net capital flows minus payments of capital and interest, topped US$32.6 billion. After a decade of isolation, Latin America was again a darling of international investors. Yet five short years later, capital was again flowing out of the region, as Latin America became a net capital exporter. Fast forward to 2009, and Latin America's recovery from the Global Financial Crisis surprised analysts as capital returned to the region following the worst of the crisis. What have been the causes and the consequences of cyclical capital flows to the region? How has Latin America performed in a world of tightly integrated capital markets always looking for the next best thing?

Understanding stability and capital flows in the region involves distinguishing the types of capital in question. This chapter will begin with a discussion of the different kinds of private capital flows—debt flows through bank loans or bond, direct or equity investment. How do the different kinds of capital—**short- and long-term portfolio investments** as well as long-term **foreign direct investment (FDI)** through multinational corporations (MNCs)—affect development prospects in the region? Although new capital is of course a welcome way to spur growth, rapid inflows raise questions about sustainability and volatility. Are funds being channeled to improve the productive capacity of the region, or are they fueling asset bubbles or consumption booms? Are there ways of minimizing vulnerability while maintaining the confidence of international capital? How did Latin America fare during the Global Financial Crisis and the Great Recession?

In addition to private capital flows, **official flows** in the service of development are also important to consider, particularly for the poorest countries in the region. Who are the top international donors and recipients in the region? What kind of development programs are financed with international assistance? How can international dollars be leveraged for a stronger developmental impact?

Finally, you may be surprised to note that the largest source of capital flows into Latin America comes from Latin Americans themselves. In 2017 worker **remittances**—money sent home to families and communities in Latin America—accounted for more than 10 percent of national gross domestic product (GDP) in four countries: Nicaragua, El Salvador, Guatemala, and Honduras. The US$75 billion sent back to the region has grown nearly as much as exports.[1] The importance of remittances has more than doubled over the past ten years. What explains these flows—and are they an important source of development financing in Latin America?

Understanding the changing nature of capital flows to the region will enhance our understanding of the promise and the limitations of liberalization as a strategy for Latin American economic development. Like trade, which we will study in the next chapter, the free flow of capital brings opportunities for growth but may be accompanied by an increase in uncertainty and volatility. Unlike the inward-looking model of import substitution industrialization, financial and trade liberalization make a nation more sensitive to changes in the global economy—the good and the bad. We will consider the following questions:

- Across all types of global capital flows, what are key elements of sound macroeconomic management for Latin America?
- How does domestic saving complement global inflows to promote sustainable investment? Are savings sufficient to support productive investment?
- How can countries adopt macroeconomic strategies to reduce vulnerability to external shocks?
- How does the need to access global capital constrain domestic monetary policymaking?

AN INTRODUCTION TO THE BEHAVIOR OF CAPITAL FLOWS

The neoliberal market model places private capital flows at the center of development finance. Capital, it is argued, will flow to its most productive uses, where rates of return are highest. Tough austerity measures that transform the productivity of an economy should therefore be rewarded by improved access to international capital markets. This has, to some extent, taken place in the Latin American region. Capital flows in the 1990s were roughly 200 percent larger than those in the 1980s. Against the backdrop of the lost decade of debt in the 1980s, this was an extraordinary vote of confidence on the part of international markets in Latin American economic reform.

By 2001, however, Latin America had again become a net capital exporter to the rest of the world. Inflows stalled as Argentina entered crisis. Additionally, like other developing countries, Latin American nations began using current account surpluses to build up reserves against possible future currency crises and to pay down on past debt accrued.[2] New investments into the region were not sufficient to compensate for past debts accrued. Money was being drawn elsewhere.

To understand the nature of rapid capital reversals it is useful to analyze what drives the demand for foreign assets. As we have noted, the restructuring of Latin American economies created new growth potential. Remember that investors buy assets today in anticipation of returns in the future. Unlike buying a car or a computer, where you can pretty well predict what the good will be worth next year, financial investments carry an uncertain future value. Purchases are made based on *expected* value. Do you think the value of the asset will rise or fall over the term of the investment? This applies to investments in stocks, bonds, or commodities such as copper or tin. If there is a high degree of uncertainty as to the future performance of an asset, investors must be compensated for additional risk. If the asset is denominated in a foreign currency, the possibility that the currency may lose value over the term of the investment must be taken into account. Stability, confidence, and predictability are key to promoting sound financial investments.

Because international investment decisions are made one versus another—that is, investors evaluate *relative* returns—the policy or performance in Latin America may not be the sole factor. Relative returns on other assets—perhaps the US dollar or maybe investments in Europe or Asia—could become more lucrative. Investors consider Latin America versus other investment options. The rise of China as an arena for FDI and the allure of former East European countries in the bond market have drawn capital flows to other regions. In part (depending on the type of capital), these trade-offs are accentuated by investor decisions to retain a certain portion of portfolios in riskier emerging market assets. Balancing risk against more stable industrial market returns may mean moving out of one emerging market as a portfolio becomes weighted in another. With expectations at play, emerging markets are especially vulnerable to shifts in investor sentiment. Alternatively, Latin America may be interesting because returns in other regions (or in industrial economies) are low—not because Latin economies are performing particularly well. But a country can't control what is happening in the rest of the world. Periods of plenty and times of scarcity are subject not only to country performance but also to relative preferences of investors.

Even for the winners in attracting investment, capital inflows may have unintended costs. Too much of a good thing (capital inflows) can be a bit like an abundance of dessert at a holiday that lead to aches and sluggishness. If capital—say, US dollars—flows in, the supply of this foreign currency increases—and its price falls relative to the national currency. If the national currency then becomes stronger, this may compromise the ability of the country to pursue an aggressive export drive. Capital's "helping hand" may instead choke off the growth of exports. Although initially cheap foreign capital may have greased the wheels of growth, strengthening of the domestic exchange rate can distort export engines. We will explore whether policy instruments are needed to balance capital flows in emerging markets, but first we need a better understanding of the types of capital and how they might influence development.

The Short and Long of Capital Flows: Debt, Equity, and Private Transfers

The flow of capital into the region takes six forms: loans, bond purchases, FDI, portfolio equity flows, remittances, and lending directly to support trade.[3] Bank lending went from the predominant source of capital in the 1960s and 1970s to being a drain on regional resources as interest and principal payments on accumulated debt. Beyond debt drag, other forms of capital flows also have downsides. As Latin American countries learned in the late 1990s, **portfolio bonds** and **equity investments** can be transitory. Foreign investors might purchase portfolio bonds, which may be government issues similar to US Treasury bonds to finance public investments, or they may be corporate offerings. Remember that bonds are essentially a promise to pay in the future—an obligation incurred irrespective of whether the investment has generated returns. Moreover, developing country bonds have a second built-in risk, so-called original sin or the inability of emerging markets to borrow abroad in their own currencies.[4] Investors leery of purchasing bonds issued in local currencies look instead to hold bonds tied to, say, the Mexican economy—but payable in safer US dollars. The risk in bonds is piled on the issuer. If the local currency weakens (ostensibly by bad policy decisions as in the past), the bondholder doesn't normally pay for this. Instead, the developing country must come up with more units of national currency to meet the obligations on the bond.

Bonds are also more attractive than bank loans in that they are more liquid and hence tradable. Some developing countries, nonetheless, moved beyond original sin to issue bonds in local currency units. In 2004 Colombia was the first issuer of a global bond denominated in Colombian pesos; in 2005 Brazil launched a US$1.5 billion offering priced in the real, transferring currency risk to investors.[5] The benefit of greater macrostability is incurring less risk in raising capital via instruments denominated in national and not foreign currency units.

Equity investments—the sum of country funds, depository receipts,[6] and direct purchases of shares by foreign investors—decrease risk for the issuing country. Equity investments, or the purchase of stocks, are liquid, short-term capital, particularly if the holder maintains less than a 10 percent share. Equity or stock investments allow a company to share risk with investors. Short-term capital such as portfolio investments can leave as quickly as it arrives. In contrast, if an economy or a firm experiences a downturn and the stock value plummets, stockholders lose. When hard times hit a company that has financed expansion through bonds (or through commercial bank loans), the firm or nation must still make good on the face value of that obligation or face the ramifications of default. Stocks, therefore, spread risk from firms to investors.

In addition to spreading the risk from borrowers to creditors, stock markets help to diversify risks among investments. Most people wealthy enough to hold a financial portfolio keep an array of assets—a bank account, bonds, stocks, and real estate. From the borrower's perspective, corporate bonds or stock provide an important, cost-effective alternative to bank borrowing or internal profits to raise capital for investment. But stock and bond markets are weak in Latin America (and the rest of the developing world). Size is a key constraint. Market capitalization, the total value (shares times current price), as a proportion of GDP in middle-income countries is about one-third of that in industrial countries. Stock exchanges in developing countries tend to lag technologically, making trading, clearance, and settlement problematic. Stock institutions are built on clear, credible rules; developing country institutions are more prone than industrial country institutions to corruption and weak regulation.[7]

Despite the potential for risk sharing, capital markets in Latin America remain underdeveloped.[8] Latin American capital markets, characterized by dollarization, short-termism, and illiquidity, have lagged behind those in East Asia and Eastern Europe. The bond markets that have developed in Latin America tend to be dominated by public-sector debt, much of it with short maturities. Firms have de-listed and large companies have migrated to international exchanges. Although economic reforms have precipitated capital market deepening in other regions, in Latin America domestic trading has languished. Instead, the process of internationalization—where Latin American companies are listed on foreign exchanges—seems to have replaced heartier domestic development of exchanges. The offshoring of stock markets in the region may be traced to relatively illiquid domestic exchanges (where it is hard to exit to rebalance a portfolio), the region's history of macro turbulence, and a lack of confidence in corporate governance and stock market management.[9] In one sense listing abroad is logical—capital costs are cheaper in international markets where capital is more plentiful. However, thin domestic markets make it difficult for small and medium-sized firms less able to list on international exchanges to raise capital.

We can measure market capitalization or market value by taking the share price times the number of shares outstanding on an exchange. Market size is an important predictor of a country's ability to mobilize capital and diversify risk. The level of stock market development closely tracks a country's overall development level. The growth of stock markets may increase liquidity and diversify risk.[10] Market capitalization in Latin America is roughly a third of the level in the United States and Canada. Only a few Latin American firms are capable of issuing securities in amounts that will support ample liquidity; on the buy side there are only a few institutional buyers, driven in large part by domestic pension funds, further limiting liquidity in the market. Investors tend to buy and hold. The highly concentrated nature makes for an illiquid market. It is also a market easily affected by political news, leading to strong volatility. To overcome the limits of size, countries are experimenting with financial integration; the Pacific alliance nations of Chile, Colombia, Mexico, and Peru have launched the Integrated Latin America Market (MILA) and the Brazilian stock exchange has bought 8 percent of the Santiago exchange.[11] For the time being, underperforming capital markets constrain the ability of firms to increase investment.

Drivers behind Short Capital Flows to Latin America

Short-term (less than one year) capital with the exception of loans to finance trade is broadly characterized as speculative or "hot" money. It is this stateless, agile capital that concerns policymakers. As we learned in Chapter four on the debt crisis in the 1980s, financing long-term development on short-term capital is a risky venture. Portfolio flows create problems for long-term sustainability. But access to this hot capital can also generate important growth in the region. Think for a moment about the landscape of US growth minus our stock and bond markets—quite a bleak picture. Bonds and equity investments provide funding for projects. When interest rates are low in the United States, fund managers are desperate to obtain additional returns where they can chase capital investments around the globe. Not surprisingly, questions of volatility and sustainability arise.

A variety of factors explain hot money flows to Latin America relative to other regions. Beginning with the supply side, international flows responded to changes in international markets, following global integration. Technological changes facilitating the transfer of money and ideas made the world a smaller place, reducing transaction costs for international investment. With better information and changes in the US legal code, new groups of institutional investors such as pension and insurance funds have internationalized investment opportunities.[12] The aging baby boomers created a pool of capital in search of high returns. Low interest rates in the United States make domestic investments less attractive; fund managers are desperate to scavenge additional returns where they can. Excess global savings have continued to keep interest rates low despite the strong demand for money in the United States since 2001. These external supply factors, including developments in international financial markets, have been shown to be the primary determinant of capital flows to the region.[13] More investors are looking for productive opportunities around the globe. However, as discussed above, they prefer to make these purchases of foreign companies on the New York Stock Exchange rather than directly in regional markets.

Why invest in Latin America instead of other regions? In addition to the factors that have increased the global supply of capital, structural changes in Latin America pulled financing into the region. Tough austerity measures improved financial solvency in the 1990s. In most countries in the region, changes in investment codes and macroeconomic policy are perceived to be permanent. National exchange rate regimes are less susceptible to megadevaluations. Investors have greater confidence in their ability to predict the long-term macroeconomic environment for business. Legislation has favored international investment, and privatization created new investment opportunities. Simultaneous political reform and the deepening of democracy reduced the political risk associated with investment. We can summarize these factors by saying that the relative yield of countries' assets as well as financial solvency improved, while political instability and potential losses due to devaluation or nationalization declined. In short, Latin America became a good investment risk in the 1990s.[14] Nonetheless, it is important to remember that no matter how well structured Latin America's reforms are, international capital chooses a home based on relative appeal: opportunities for profit not only have to be good, but they must be better than expected returns and adjusted for uncertainty and risk everywhere else. Latin America may be better placed to absorb capital than it was in the 1980s—but investors may find returns even more attractive anywhere on the globe. We saw this with the heating of Latin American financial markets following the Global Financial Crisis. When the Chinese-driven commodity boom made Latin markets hot, capital flowed South in search of higher returns. But investors need strong stomachs as markets were quickly again deflated by corruption scandals that undermined their institutional credibility.[15]

REWARDS AND RISKS OF NEW CAPITAL FLOWS TO LATIN AMERICA

Hot money flows, or short-term capital investments, although used to finance investments and spur growth, introduce questions of volatility. What are the implications of short-term capital flows to Latin America? New capital flows to the region are the financial rewards for the painful process of structural adjustment. Greater global integration can be seen as a movement toward the more efficient worldwide utilization of capital. For advocates of new capital flows, maintaining access to international financial markets is simply the result of sound domestic economic management. They see international inflows as complementary to national capital. The infusion of funds will spur growth, which will then encourage savings.

Is money moving to the region because it is most efficiently employed in Latin America as compared to other investment alternatives? To evaluate the arguments of proponents of capital inflows, it is important to situate the theoretical argument in the context of the reality of Latin American markets. Latin American markets are not exactly like the Wall Street variety. As markets are relatively thin and uncompetitive, efficiency gains are limited. Furthermore, the price signals driving capital to certain markets may be flawed. Given that finance deals with future information, expectations and opinions dominate over facts in decision making—and information about developing country markets may be less available than developments in more mature economies. Herding behavior and contagion may result as buyers jump on bandwagons with weak fundamentals. Informational bottlenecks and the institutional peculiarities of investors may interfere with market efficiency. Many new investment instruments are complex and not completely understood by participants, increasing the underlying risk. Transactions in many markets are unregulated, accounting standards are lax, balance sheets are inscrutable, and financial disclosure is not as strictly enforced as in the United States. With incomplete information, the globalization of capital may not generate as much efficiency as claimed.[16] Capital may be more fickle and less efficient than is sometimes assumed.

Some policymakers in Latin America are wary of long-run dependency on capital inflows, particularly **short-term money**, because of its volatility and how it affects other variables. Because the decision to invest is made on relative rates of return, a country continuing to pursue a sound policy course might find itself out of favor in the international market as another nation or region becomes the Wall Street flavor of the month. A long history of negative effects of external price changes—such as the oil price and interest rate shocks precipitating the debt crisis of the 1980s—makes policymakers nervous concerning external vulnerability. Uncertainty is built into the structure of financing. For example, bonds with an average maturity of four years are a major source of capital supporting infrastructure expansion. What if they are not renewed at expiration?[17] Can development planning be creatively financed with short-term inflows?

Given bandwagon effects and herding, capital flows tend to be procyclical. Money pours in during boom periods—and quickly exits with the bust. The lack of access to capital during periods of crisis further limits the government's ability to use countercyclical policies to manage a crisis. Evidence suggests that procyclical financial markets compounded by procyclical macroeconomic policies have exacerbated the costs of volatility on growth. Major reversals of capital flows may have resulted in a decrease of 25 percent in the income of developing countries for a total of between US$100 billion and US$150 billion in lost GDP.[18]

In addition to volatility and a procyclical bias, capital inflows may adversely affect other economic variables. In particular, some economists are concerned about the degree to which capital inflows are consistent with sustainable levels of the exchange rate and the interest rate. Because capital inflows change the supply of money available for investment, they also change the price of money—both nationally, as measured by the domestic interest rate, and relatively, as measured by the exchange rate. If inflows are strong, finance becomes cheaper, and the interest rate falls. International money is more abundant, and therefore the local currency, relatively scarcer than it was before, appreciates. Low interest rates could have a negative effect on national savings rates, discouraging local sources of financing. An appreciated exchange rate may stand in the way of pursuing an export orientation.

In particular, if financial markets are shallow and uncompetitive, they may not be able to intermediate the capital surges effectively, exacerbating instability. If capital surges accelerate demand beyond the capacity of the economy, they may also create inflationary pressures. For some countries, the boom in capital flows is a high-risk venture that threatens national control over key monetary variables.

Financial innovation and international capital flows have decreased the degrees of freedom available to Latin American policymakers.[19] The speed of international capital markets requires greater flexibility in economic instruments; paradoxically, it also demands stability. Instantaneous movement of capital implies that markets are overly responsive to small policy mistakes, increasing the tendency toward instability.[20] The policymakers' tightrope is more threatening in international markets. Capital inflows, while acting as a spur to development, can also have a high cost.

International Capital Flows and Domestic Banking

A strong banking system can serve to dampen domestic macroeconomic instability and the challenges of short-term capital flows. Bank lending is the more traditional alternative to bond and stock markets in the region. Under a sound banking system, if domestic investors decide to sell long-term financial assets, they can move into domestic bank deposits. That is, if in the United States you are uncertain about the performance of the stock market or long-term mutual funds, you might opt for the safety of a certificate of deposit (CD). As people move into CDs, the greater availability of funds makes it easier to lend to companies, and expansion is encouraged, counteracting the downward trend in the market. However, if there is a lack of confidence in the banking sector, the substitute is international instruments, or capital flight.[21] When banks fail to provide domestic intermediation, the effects of crises are magnified. Furthermore, as has been demonstrated in the Asian financial crisis of 1997–1998, if domestic loans to large conglomerates—or, in the Latin case, *grupos*—sidestepped sound accounting procedures, a downturn may result in a resounding crash. The Chilean crisis in 1982–1983 and the Mexican crisis were exacerbated by loans made to huge conglomerates riding high on overinflated asset prices without corresponding real collateral to secure the megaloans. When the crisis hit in each country—and later in Asia—the high percentage of nonperforming loans magnified the contractionary effects on the economic system. Weak banks exacerbated rather than minimized the crisis.

THE COMPLEXITY OF TRANSNATIONAL INVESTMENT

One way to address balance of payments pressures without contracting spending or printing to purchase hard currency is to attract international capital. We recall that global capital flows come in two basic forms: portfolio and foreign direct investment. Portfolio capital flows—using stock or bond investments—can be welcome infusions of global cash. When well directed to productive investment by firms, they can propel capital projects. But short-term capital flows can also be dangerous; the inflow of so-called hot money can pressure exchange rates toward appreciations that work against export sales.

A defining feature of the global economy is **financialization**—or the enormous power of cross-border capital flows. Flows gush during good times and retreat rapidly in bad. In part this is driven by the short-term timeframe of money managers who herd in for part of the action on a good investment. Keep in mind that capital flows respond to *relative* returns. During the Global Financial Crisis, central banks in the United States and Europe were trying to stimulate economies through approaches called quantitative easing. Cash, however, spills across borders, looking for the highest interest rate. With near zero interest rates in New York and London, investors were more interested in São Paulo and Bogota—with the unintended effect of creating demand for Brazilian reais and Colombian pesos. The appreciation of the local currency then worked against export diversification and facilitated Latin American imports of American goods. Overhead space on flights out of Miami was at a premium as Latins traveled north to fill suitcases with cheaper American goods largely made in China. Guido Mantega, as finance minister of Brazil, coined the term "currency war" to characterize how monetary decisions in Tokyo or Washington were constraining options in Brasilia as it "imported" these excess US dollars. In 2010 the Brazilian real appreciated 25 percent, causing chaos in import pricing. By 2016 the excess of riches had disappeared with the "caipirinha crisis;" the Brazilian real hit a twenty-year low against the US dollar in the face of weak oil prices and a corruption scandal engulfing Petrobras, its flagship petroleum company. The challenge is for both private agents as well as the state to manage wide fluctuations in prices with exchange rate changes—and to make the macro economy more resilient to external shocks.

Foreign direct investment (FDI) is less volatile but has a fraught history in Latin America, conjuring experiences of companies like United Fruit and its engagement in national politics. As a large economy, Brazil accounts for 40 percent of regional FDI, but the impact of foreign investment is stronger in smaller countries. Regionally it accounts for 3 percent of GDP.[22] Around 40 percent of the earnings of foreign firms are reinvested, with the bulk repatriated.[23] Led by Canada—with strong interest from China—much of FDI is drawn into natural resources. China has defined a strong complementarity between its resource-intensive growth and the abundance of mineral and agricultural products in Latin America. To facilitate this, Chinese FDI in the region has been focused on acquiring large firms in natural resource–based industries.[24] In addition to the extractive sector, Chinese banks finance US$40.3 billion in infrastructure projects.[25]

Determinants of FDI

The decision by a transnational firm on where to build factories or buy businesses—FDI—is affected by many different factors as compared to short-term portfolio debt or equity flows. Foreign investment itself serves different purposes.

Does the country want access to a market, raw materials, improved efficiency, or technological assets? Is the company in the goods or services sector? Table 6.1 details these strategies of transnational corporations (TNCs) by sector. Some transnationals search raw materials, often available only in a given location. Petroleum and gas producers in Andean countries are a good example. Quite often the capital costs of exploration and development of the resource are beyond local private capital. TNCs might also profit from natural resources through tourism.

Beyond resources, the TNC might be looking to enhance efficiency in manufacturing by drawing upon lower-priced labor as in the clothing, electronics, or automotive sectors. Generally, this investment becomes part of a globally integrated production chain for export and depends upon the quality and cost of human resources, physical infrastructure, and international trade agreements. It is important to note that low wages are not in themselves a draw; the key is total compensation (which includes indirect costs from labor legislation) per unit of output. Low wages for low productivity are not a bargain. It has become clear that Latin America cannot compete on the basis of wages—it will be continuously trumped

Table 6.1.   Latin American and Caribbean Strategies of Transnational Corporations

Sector	*Efficiency Gains (labor costs) with Export Objectives*	*Natural Resource Seeking*	*Local Market Access*
Goods	Automotive: Mexico Electronics: Caribbean Basin, Mexico Clothing: Caribbean Basin, Mexico	Oil/gas: Argentina, Bolivia, Brazil, Colombia, Venezuela Minerals: Argentina, Chile, Andean	Automotive: Mercosur Agribusiness: Argentina, Brazil, Mexico Chemicals: Brazil Cement: Colombia, Dominican Republic, Venezuela
Services	Back office services, Costa Rica	Tourism: Mexico	Finance: Argentina, Brazil, Chile, Colombia, Mexico, Peru, Venezuela Telecommunications: Argentina, Brazil, Chile, Peru Electric power: Argentina, Brazil, Central America, Chile, Colombia Natural gas distribution: Argentina, Brazil, Chile, Colombia Retail trade: Argentina, Brazil, Chile, Mexico

Source: ECLAC, *Foreign Investment 2004*, Table I.6.

by China or other low wage economies. Instead, the focus in the region must be on efficiently raising the output of workers per wage through investments in human capital.

Alternatively, a TNC might want access to a market closed either by a tariff or reduce geographical constraints such as distance. Country size as expressed by GDP adjusted for the "effective market"—those consumers who can be reached with strong infrastructure such as good roads or ports—and distance from investors are two key factors that influence FDI decisions.[26] Automobiles were produced in Brazil for both reasons—to escape tariffs and to cut down on transportation costs of shipping heavy vehicles overseas. Infrastructure—particularly electric power, telecommunications, and electricity and gas distribution—are important service areas for transnational firms. Infrastructure investment depends on the regulatory environment in providing for after-contract services in areas such as telecommunications or water management.[27] Global retailers such as Walmart have made strong inroads in the service sector in the region. Finally, TNCs might seek out technological advantages by locating in a country or region with a strong science and technology base. Latin America experiences little FDI of this type.

Across the four different types of FDI—natural resources, efficiency, market access, and technology seeking—several additional factors are at play. Distance works as a pro and con, depending on whether the company wants to sell either goods or infrastructure services in the foreign market (local production cuts down on transport costs) or desires to re-export to the home or other markets (where proximity to the target market is key). Legal codes that guarantee intellectual property right protection and investment dispute settlement mechanisms are important in decreasing a country's risk profile. The degree of transparency in a country's institutions is an important factor. One study suggested that on average a country could expect a 40 percent increase in FDI with a one-point increase in its transparency rankings.[28] Rather than grease the wheels, corruption adds to the burden of taxes and **capital controls**.

Who invests in Latin America? Figure 6.1 shows that the United States is the principal investor in the region, concentrating on manufacturers in Mexico and services such as electricity and gas distribution and telecoms in Mercosur. European firms are a growing presence in Mercosur and Chile in telecoms, energy financial services, automotive, agroindustry, and retail trade. The new kid on the block, Spain, is a significant investor in telecoms, financial services, electricity generation and distribution, and petroleum. Those seeking market access in manufacturing are interested in Argentina, Brazil, and Mexico, and firms taking advantage of liberalization and privatization of services have moved in throughout the region.[29] The Netherlands features as an outsized player in the data as many global companies of different national original headquarter there for tax purposes. Japan has limited investment in the region.[30] Firms seeking efficiency gains and lower wages tend toward the automotive and electronics sectors in Mexico and the Caribbean Basin. With policies to attract foreign capital, Chile is a top destination for renewable investments, especially solar. With a high percentage of the world's metallic mineral reserves concentrated in Latin America and the Caribbean (66 percent of its lithium, 47 percent of its copper, 45 percent of its silver, 25 percent of its

Figure 6.1.   Inward Flow of Foreign Direct Investment, 2014 (millions of dollars)

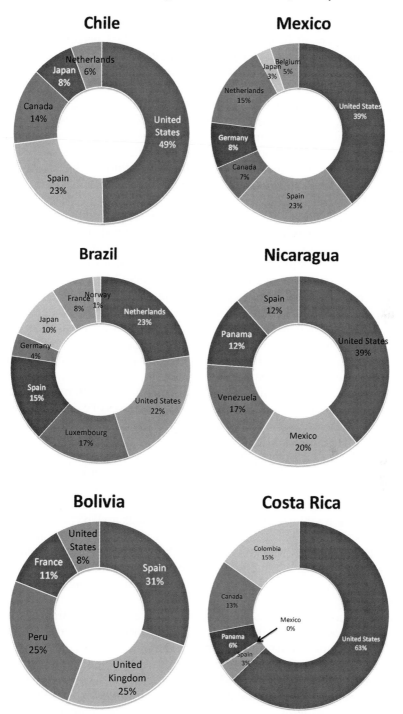

Source: ECLAC, Foreign Direct Investment in Latin America and the Caribbean, 2014.

tin, 23 percent of its bauxite, 23 percent of its nickel, and 14 percent of its iron), natural resource–seeking investors are attracted to Venezuela, Colombia, Bolivia, Argentina, Chile, and Peru. The weight of natural resources in total FDI increased from around 17 percent in the 1990s and 2000s to 22.3 percent in 2010–2014. Increasingly these investors are Chinese. Although still modest as compared to global mining giants from Australia, the United Kingdom, Switzerland, Canada, and the United States, Chinese mining firms have entered Peru and Brazil. The Peruvian Ministry of Energy and Mines estimates that roughly a third of mining is in Chinese hands, 17 percent with US companies, and 15 percent with Canadians.[31] Chinese companies increased mineral extraction and demanded more minerals on the international market, including Latin America; it is also aggressively investing in smelting and refining to moving up the mining/metallurgy value chain. The challenge for Latin American nations is to move up the value chain from exporters of ore to global players in refined metals.

An increasingly important phenomenon in the region are the multi-Latinas or the trans-Latinas—emerging Latin American transnationals that have made direct investments outside their home countries.[32] From a meager annual average of approximately US$52 million between 1970 and 1974, forty years later outward investment from Latin America is approximately US$47.362 billion per year. This growth is substantial from decades past, but represents a 15 percent drop between 2014 and 2015.[33] Although outward investment by developing countries is dominated by Asian transnationals, Mexican and Brazil firms such as Cemex (cement), América Móvil (telecommunications), Petrobras (petroleum), CVRD (mining), Gerdau (metals), JBS (meat), Grupo Bimbo (food), and Gruma (food) make it to the top fifty of nonfinancial transnationals from developing countries. Other important trans-Latinas are from Argentina and Chile. In most cases, internationalization of firms has been market-seeking and has involved purchases of existing assets. Nonetheless, the existence of these firms demonstrates that multi-Latinas can indeed be competitive on a global scale.[34]

Worldwide, US transnationals sell about two-thirds of their output in the host country, suggesting that the motivation for exports driven by cheap labor only adheres in a smaller percent of cases. In the Andean region, host-market serving and infrastructure arguments are even more compelling. US manufacturing affiliates reach a striking 90 percent in Peru and Venezuela and average 75 percent for other nations, indicating that export orientation as a rationale for investment is limited.[35] This constrains foreign investment, because the number of consumers is relatively small. Despite a good deal of activity in natural resource-related activities, Andean countries will be limited by market size in attracting technology-based investment in manufacturing.

Although the importance of single firms such as Chiquita Brands or General Motors in the economies of the subregion is not inconsequential, FDI is not the solution for all countries that want to spur development. That is, transnationals do not necessarily want to produce where conditions are unstable or the infrastructure is incomplete. They are also attracted to large markets such as Brazil or Mexico to sell the cars or machines produced there and avoid transport costs. FDI can be seen as preferable to short-term capital flows in that it reflects a long-term commitment to the nation. It should in fact translate into an increase in a country's productive potential—but it may work best where the country's industrial base is already relatively developed. On the negative side, however, transnational investment raises other questions with respect to balanced development, dependency, and domestic entrepreneurship. Foreign firms repatriate more than half of their profits and often exhibit weak linkages with local industries.

TNCs are extraordinarily powerful, accounting for one-third of world production, with total sales exceeding the value of world trade. Table 6.2 shows the activity of the top TNCs in the region. Compared to 1997, when auto and oil concerns dominated, between 2003 and 2013 we see greater participation of telecoms such as Telefonica and America Movil and retailers including Walmart and Carrefour. Brazil accounts for 40 percent of FDI; but FDI tends to have a stronger impact in smaller countries. Overall, FDI accounts for about 4 percent of Brazilian GDP, 8 percent Chilean, and 6 percent in Nicaragua, Honduras, and Costa Rica.

This penetration of firms into developing country markets raises the question of power and balance. Worldwide, ranked by output, fifty-one of the top one hundred "countries" are MNCs. That is, Walmart is larger than the GNP of Peru, and Nestlé's sales exceed the GDP of Costa Rica. In addition, more than half of world trade consists of transnational firm trading activity, largely of an intrafirm nature.[36] This means that half of world trade is associated with firms such as Coca-Cola or Nike sending subassembly materials and final products among their own subsidiaries. Some worry about the cultural content contained in globalized products; others herald the arrival of cheaper, higher-quality products through retailers such as Walmart. Walmart is the largest retailer and one of the largest employers in Latin America. One study credits Walmart's everyday low prices with ending a long history of hefty margins by national retailers and helping to reduce Mexico's inflation rate.[37] Others are less sanguine; Multinational Monitor called Walmart one of the ten worst corporations in 2004 for its labor practices in the United States.[38] As its reputational value is damaged by bad publicity, Walmart has implemented programs throughout the region to partner with communities and governments to promote sustainable business practices.

Transnational production brings benefits—but with costs. Transnationals may provide technology, improve efficiency, and create jobs. They can encourage the adoption of best production practices across borders. Some transnationals invest abroad to take advantage of cheaper labor or less stringent environmental standards. Producers of textiles, for example, have long moved to where unskilled workers, often women, can be paid a tenth of the going wage in the United States. Profits—made in part through the exploitation of cheap labor—are remitted to the home country rather than supporting growth in the local economy. Environmentalists worry that companies set up shop in countries with lax pollution laws, a phenomenon called environmental dumping. Governments, afraid of losing jobs and investment, may retreat from stricter environmental codes, promoting a race to the bottom of the environmental ladder. Evidence on this theory is incomplete; there is some suggestion that pollution costs are not a critical factor in location decisions and that at the national level governments tighten regulations as income rises.[39]

Table 6.2. Latin America and the Caribbean: Economic Groups with the Highest Share of Announced Foreign Direct Investment and Associated Job Creation, 2003–2013

	Capital Investment Announced			Job Creation Announced		
Economic Group	Country of Origin	Industry	Economic Group	Country of Origin	Industry
1. Telefónica	Spain	Telecom	1. Walmart	United States	Retail
2. Repsol YPF	Spain	Oil	2. Telefónica	Spain	Telecom
3. ThyssenKrupp (TK)	Germany	Steel, manufacturing	3. General Motors	United States	Automobile
4. BHP Billiton	Australia	Mining	4. Arcelor-Mittal	Luxembourg	Steel
5. Arcelor-Mittal	Luxembourg	Steel Production	5. Carrefour	France	Retail
6. Fiat	Italy	Automobile	6. Fiat	Italy	Automobile
7. Chevron Corporation	United States	Oil	7. BHP Billiton	Australia	Mining
8. América Móvil	Mexico	Telecom	8. Volkswagen	Germany	Automobile
9. Walmart	United States	Retail	9. Techint	Italy; Argentina	Manufacturing
10. General Motors (GM)	United States	Automobile	10. LG	South Korea	Electronics
11. Anglo American	South Africa	Mining	11. Ford	United States	Automobile
12. Techint	Italy; Argentina	Manufacturing	12. Falabella	Chile	Retail

Source: ECLAC, *Foreign Direct Investment in Latin America and the Caribbean, 2013.*

The degree to which TNCs contribute to local environments may be a function of the ability of the government to promote key backward linkages in the economy.[40] Overall, TNCs will employ technologies that best suit their own business needs. However, if a TNC is given incentives to source inputs locally, transfer of process and product information may take place. Government may play a key role in reducing the information gap between players by providing information about local producers, supporting the establishment of standards, testing and patent registration, and upgrading local human resource and technological capabilities.

The good news in enhancing the positive effects over the costs of transnationals is that globalization of information systems has decreased the ability of transnationals to get away with social and environmental abuse. As the Internet and CNN bring corporate activities into stockholders' living rooms, firms have been forced to comply with new standards. For example, after celebrity Kathie Lee Gifford was charged with exploitation of female workers in Central America in the production of her clothing line for Kmart, the negative publicity generated a fall in the stock price. The firm was forced to adopt codes of corporate conduct that improve the lives of workers. As dismal conditions and low wages have become well documented, college students across America have pressured for changes in sweatshop practices and adoption of a fair labor code by boycotting bookstore apparel.[41] Globalization of production has increased the transnational's reach but has made its activities more transparent.

Does the surge in transnational investment improve the productive capabilities of Latin American economies? One study of foreign production in Mexico shows that a high transnational presence is correlated with an increase in productivity in locally owned firms and that the rate of catch-up with international productivity standards is positively associated with the degree of foreign concentration in the industry. This suggests spillovers from transnational production to less-efficient local firms. Transnational firms may act as a catalyst to productivity growth, speeding up the convergence in productivity levels between developing and industrialized countries.[42] The authors warn, nonetheless, of extrapolating too much from the Mexican case because there is extensive movement of labor and capital between Mexico and the United States, especially in border production. Other studies of the Mexican case point out that the technology transferred may be too capital intensive and that subsidies provided by the Mexican government to attract firms may divert scarce resources from social investments.[43] Foreign investment along the border has significantly contributed to the development of two Mexicos—its modern North and lagging South. It is perhaps no surprise the Mexico has a love-hate affair with foreign capital!

The gains and the costs of transnational production should be evaluated on a case-by-case basis; the costs and benefits vary by the reason for the transnational's presence and the strength of the state in providing a positive regulatory environment. One study showed that the positive effects of transnational transfer of technology were strong only when there was already a well-developed human capital base.[44] Some of the issues we consider in later chapters on social development and education may therefore play a key role in shaping costs and benefits. Government policy in establishing the rules of the game for transnationals is important in evaluating outcomes. The size and number of other firms in a market also condition transnational behavior. If a transnational company is the only employer in a small town, it is less likely to treat workers well. If, however, if it is in competition with a large number of firms, it is more likely to provide good working conditions.

An ethical dilemma arises in considering labor standards for transnational production. Should home country or host country labor codes be employed? Labor standards in poor countries may approximate conditions in industrial countries 50 years ago. Should US transnationals meet US safety and health standards in a Guatemalan plant? Some contend that best practices should apply worldwide; others suggest local standards as a baseline while developing countries catch up. Proponents of FDI contend that although standards and wages may not match industrial country standards, they most often exceed the conditions and the pay in local factories. Sorting out the effects of transnational production poses tough ethical and policy dilemmas. Are workers worse off than they were without the new paychecks? How far can governments go in insisting on higher standards without driving investment and jobs away?

Liberalization of global trade rules also encouraged FDI in telecommunications and financial services. The gains from the privatization of state monopolies were greatest when competition could be introduced or an effective regulatory structure implemented to limit private monopoly pricing. Yet the challenges for effective regulation and competition policy in markets dominated by large transnationals are especially difficult for developing-country officials. Regulators in developing countries must deal with multiple social objectives. They are still struggling with issues such as improving access to phones in rural and poor areas and guaranteeing basic levels of quality. The international dynamism in mobile cellular communications and Internet services introduces a whole set of complicated regulations. With generally weaker institutions, less experience, and fewer resources, regulatory agencies in developing markets must carry out traditional and new tasks. In doing so, regulators come up against some of the titans of the global marketplace—large and powerful megacorporations. In many cases—particularly those of the early privatizers—the rush to privatization granted long periods of exclusive operation to foreign investors in exchange for commitments to expand basic services. As these frameworks expire, the regulatory challenge will be to develop coherent sectoral strategies to achieve national policy goals as well as corporate objectives through an upgrading of the regulatory institutions themselves.[45]

Nonetheless, despite potential costs from flows and unintended consequences, increasing access to international capital is on most national policy agendas. Latin American politicians often see expanding FDI as a key policy tool for growth. How can countries, particularly those that have not been the largest beneficiaries in the past, attract FDI? How does the policy environment affect the location decision of transnational companies? Policy recommendations for attracting productive new international investments include lowering trade costs, improving export processing zones, investigating the further use of incentives, promoting dialogue with investors on business climate issues, and investing in education.[46] Foreign firms must have some advantage in producing abroad that justifies additional coordination costs and risks in a foreign business climate.

REMITTANCES: PEOPLE MOVING NORTH, MONEY MOVING SOUTH

In Latin America the largest source of international capital flowing into the region comes not from transnationals, investors, or development agencies but from Latinos themselves. How is Latino capital international? The largest source of foreign funds in Latin America is the money that emigrant workers send home.[47] In 2013, the volume of remittances overtook official development assistance by three times.[48] Why have remittances seen explosive growth? What is the impact of this capital flowing south? Can this money be better channeled for developmental purposes? This section takes up some of these questions.

Global money remittances from the forty-one million adults born in Latin America living outside their country of origin to Latin America and the Caribbean soared from US$11.7 billion in 1995 to US$79 billion in 2017.[49] Three quarters of that originated in the United States.[50] For those adult Latinos living in the United States, 54 percent send money home regularly, usually between US$100 and US$300 a month.[51] Although remittances declined 5 to 20 percent during the Global Financial Crisis (2007–2008), flows have since recovered. The Global Financial Crisis was a painful period for migrants living in the United States who lost work in the informal economy yet were too afraid to return to their home countries, fearing the tightening of the Patriot Act. Since 2008, remittance flows experienced growth and in 2015 alone, family remittances grew 6 percent across Latin America.[52] Data for 2017 may reflect a buildup of savings in home countries as undocumented workers in the United States fear needing resources if deported to their home countries.[53]

Remittances are becoming an important source of local income. Eighteen percent of all adults in Mexico, 23 percent in Central America, and 14 percent in Ecuador are remittance receivers. Most are women. These links between husbands, fathers, and sons in the United States and communities at home give rise to a new phenomenon, transnational families.[54] Immigrants send home about 10 percent of their wages—but for poor families in Latin America this can constitute 50–80 percent of household income. Unlike traditional migrations from Europe to the United States, people are not leaving Latin America primarily in search of a better life in a new country; instead, they are leaving to support their families back home. The out-migration from Latin America is a response to the lack of economic opportunity and the high levels of violence in home countries, but it is also very much a means to support families back home.[55] Countries now depend on these flows to sustain survival and even build prosperity. Family remittances account for 10 percent of each Latin American country's GDP on average.[56] Remittances account for more than 10 percent of GDP in El Salvador, Honduras, and Nicaragua; in Mexico only petroleum exports provide more foreign exchange. It has been suggested that migration is now not just an escape valve; it is also a fuel pump.[57] Nonetheless, it is a pump primed by the fact that there are not enough high-income jobs in the region. People are indeed moving north, draining towns of human capital but sending more money south.

Out-migration in search of better earnings is a key factor behind the surge in remittance dollars. The late 1990s saw record flows of immigrants from Latin America to the United States. The number of Latinos residing in the United States rose from 11.8 million in 1995 to approximately 26 million in 2013.[58] Strong relationships among transnational families are in part behind the more than doubling of remittance flows since 2000.[59] But the US migrant population has grown by only 16 percent during this period.[60] Other factors including technology, competition, and legal changes have propelled the rapid rise in fund transfers.

Traditionally, migrants sent money back either through informal networks of contacts returning home or through companies such as Western Union and Money Gram. As banking services—such as the ubiquitous ATM machine—have become more prevalent even in the poor and rural sectors of Latin America, technological solutions have driven the market shares of wire transfer companies down. Banks have gotten into the business of offering binational banking services, increasing competition in the money transfer market and lowering the costs of sending money to family at home. As a result, the cost of transferring money has fallen from approximately 15 percent of the value of the transfer to 7 percent. The World Bank estimates that a reduction in remittance prices from 10 to 5 percent results in an additional US$16 billion each year in the pockets of migrants and their families.[61]

Legal changes have also facilitated banking the unbanked immigrants in the United States—making it possible for them to send money through formal channels. The US Patriot Act allows financial institutions to accept both the Individual Taxpayer Identification Number (ITIN) and consular cards issued by the national consulate office in the United States as valid identification for opening a bank account.[62] This legal change created inroads to economic citizenship in the United States—the ability to bank earnings and send them to loved ones at home. More recently, Western Union launched a platform called "Quick Pay" in which remittance payments are made by phone or website as a convenient and fast way to send money, using partner banks and agents, which in turn banks the "unbanked."[63] There is still much unmet potential in the remittances market especially in regards to financial inclusion, expansion of human and economic capital, and hedging against risk.[64] Moving the money through formal sectors also helps officials maintain better records of remittance flows—inserting a note of caution in the seeming explosion in remittance data. The dramatic rates of growth may also reflect money missed in balance of payments data as it passed through informal hands.

Whether the rate of growth of remittances is as robust as the data indicate is probably less important, however, than understanding and exploiting the impact of remittance dollars. Overall, the IMF in its *World Economic Outlook* found that remittances can play an important role in boosting growth, contributing to macrostability, easing the impact of adverse shocks, and ameliorating poverty in developing countries. Remittances allow households to smooth consumption in hard times, augment it during better periods, and finance education or set up small businesses.[65] In association with microcredit organizations, there is some evidence that remittances are being channeled into business start-ups. But some research suggests the impact is overstated, demonstrating that remittance dollars do little to promote growth.[66] In fact, by mobilizing the existing and informal savings of remittance recipients, an additional US$2 billion in savings in Central America alone could be introduced.[67] Furthermore, it should be recalled that the call of US dollars leaves towns empty and depletes human capital pools. It is often the most motivated and energetic who emigrate, leaving those with fewer human capital assets at home. There is also an increasing concern that remittance dollars are creating inequality between families who receive support from absent relatives and those who do not.

Despite these problems, the benefits of remittance dollars are substantial as a source of foreign exchange and income support. Policymakers are investigating ways not only to improve the efficiency of the transfer but also to enhance the ways that remittance flows can truly make a contribution to development. The unofficial status of many immigrants leaves 40 percent of migrants in the United States not using bank services to send money home—and forcing them into more expensive wire transfers or less reliable informal means.[68] Recipients also lack strong banking infrastructure; two-thirds of remittance receivers are without bank accounts. Twenty percent of Salvadorans received remittances in 2014, but only 3 percent actually used bank accounts to receive them. Additionally, although 27 percent of Mexicans have bank accounts, only 7 percent saved formally in 2011, which demonstrates the great need for a stronger strategy to promote savings.[69] There is a need to strengthen the banking infrastructure in rural and peri-urban areas in Latin America and through education to build a financial culture among both senders and recipients. Democratization of the financial systems of countries of origin will not only strengthen the security of flows and lower costs, but may also create other positive externalities such as prompting an increase in the rate of savings.[70]

An example of technologies reaching the marginalized includes a binational credit card via Citicorp's acquisition of Banamex. Both the US cardholder and the designated Mexican beneficiary are issued a Banamex credit card that can be used throughout Mexico; the sender can adjust the credit limit, and the beneficiary can also use it at an ATM. With this product, the number of Banamex bank transfer accounts soared 1,500 percent in the first half of 2004.[71] A game changer in the remittance marketplace, AirPak operates throughout Central America to offer a wide range of financial payments. BanPro, a Western Union representative in Nicaragua, opened 1,500 payment points that include partnerships with many small businesses as a way to make "bankarization" friendlier.[72] The Inter-American Dialogue's financial education model offers financial counseling to migrants and remittance recipients online. Serving over 200,000 people, it helped open 50,000 bank accounts for those sending and receiving remittances.

Since 2010, the percentage of migrants using the Internet to send money tripled.[73] With that, ownership of smartphones also skyrocketed. Mobile money services are now entering the market. In response to market competition and a need to differentiate its product, Digicel Haiti launched a new product in 2015 called "Mon Cash" with a wider network of vendors and service points for cellular transaction facilities. Accounts are free to open with a minimum initial deposit. Two years after its creation, Digicel Haiti already served over 500,000 users. Safe, convenient, and fast, these mobile money services directly address the unbanked.[74]

Beyond ease and cost of transfer, remittances can be leveraged to stronger developmental gains. A gaping social deficit in Latin America is the insufficient and unsafe, substandard housing stock. In contrast to the building blocks of middle-class America, in Latin America owning a home tends to be the purview of the rich. With a history of inflation and weak banking services, manageable, long-term mortgages are difficult to obtain. Programs such as Mi Viviendo's (my home's) Quinto Suyo efforts are changing this by tapping the US$1.7 billion sent home by Peruvians to build homes.[75] After saving 5 percent of a home's value in an overseas account, a government-backed mortgage can be obtained by Peruvians. The default rate is a low 0.3 percent, encouraged by a 20 percent government discount on monthly payments if the first six installments are made on time. Carlos Bruce, Peru's minister of housing, estimates that the strong initial interest in this program could translate into ten thousand housing units annually. Mexico and Ecuador offer similar programs. Rather than being tempted to spend remittance dollars on consumption, families are encouraged to build capital for when the immigrant returns home.

In addition to mortgage schemes, some Mexican states offer two- or three-to-one matches for money sent back to the municipality by one of the 623 Mexican clubs or hometown associations registered in the United States.[76] These collective remittances are used for paving roads or providing clean drinking water—with hopes of decreasing the amount of out-migration in the region. Programs such as Microfinance International Corporation's Mi Pueblo offer integrated banking facilities including account, money transfer, credit, loan, and money management services to Latin immigrants. The Inter-American Development Bank (IADB) is partnering with similar microfinance organizations to begin to tap the 15–20 percent of remittance dollars channeled toward savings—with hopes of marshaling this money as a fund for entrepreneurs and new small business start-ups to leverage the developmental impact of remittances. Recently, the IADB backed the "Light up Haiti" initiative in which remittances are funneled into renewable energy products for the 72 percent of Haitians without access to electricity. Using the Western Union Quick Pay platform, sending solar light kits is fast, convenient, and economical.[77]

Remittances have seen expansive growth in recent years. Many Latin Americans continue to emigrate for economic opportunities, education, and safety, yet despite the associated drain on human capital, remittances are being funneled into sustaining and improving the quality of life in the region. Although many Latin Americans remain unbanked, progress is being made to make the remittance flows more secure and accessible through the formal economy. This provides hope for regional development.

OFFICIAL DEVELOPMENT ASSISTANCE

Given the cold fact that capital will simply not flow to economies where abject poverty and low levels of human capital will retard returns, financing for development must also include official concessional flows. Official development assistance (ODA) plays an important role in bridging the gap between local resources and developmental needs in Latin America. ODA includes grants or loans by the official sector with the goal of promoting economic development and welfare; this excludes military assistance. Approximately 68 percent of the ODA to Latin America is in the form of grants (as opposed to loans).[78] Whereas aid in the 1990s was directed at economic infrastructure, the focus has now shifted to support for social services, environmental investments, and social infrastructure.

Net aid per capita to the region is low, US$16 per person as opposed to nearly US$50 per capita in Africa or the global average of US$27. Overall Latin America attracted 6.8 percent of official global aid dollars in 2014.[79] Colombia has experienced an uptick in aid to promote adjustment under its recent peace accords—yet as a percent of gross national income (GNI) it reaches only 0.3. Nonetheless, for poorer countries in the region such as Nicaragua, Honduras, and Bolivia, aid dollars are important in financing development, reaching between 2 and 3 percent of GNI. Of aid coming into Latin America, just under a quarter is channeled through multilateral organizations such as the IADB or the World Bank; the balance of the aid is bilateral, delivered on a country-to-country basis.[80]

The downward trend in official development aid was reversed in 2003 following the signing of the Monterrey Consensus. This conference reaffirmed the need for assistance by wealthier countries to jump-start investments in support of reaching the millennium development goals (MDGs) of reducing extreme poverty by half in 2015. Although the MDGs were not completely met, the UN adopted seventeen sustainable development goals (SDGs) for 2030.[81] Whereas the MDGs lacked an inclusive consultation process during formation, the ODA policy going forward will focus more on the private sector and host country contributions as key elements of innovative sustainable development financing.[82] Nonetheless, even in the best cases such as Germany at 0.53 percent of GNI or Switzerland at 0.52 percent aid levels are a stretch from the 0.7 target that some suggest is necessary to achieve the SDGs.[83] As shown in table 6.3, top donors to Latin America include the United States, Germany, and France, which gave 18, 18, and 12 percent of regional totals respectively. Table 6.3 also shows the top ten recipients of aid, with Colombia, Haiti, and Brazil heading the list. It is perhaps interesting to note that aid is not perfectly correlated with need, as defined by GNI per capita. Other factors, including strategic concerns, enter into the aid allocation equation. Assistance to the region is primarily used for investment in social infrastructure and services. Education, health, population, water, civil society, employment, and housing programs receive 46 percent of the aid dollars, with another 11 percent going to infrastructure and 10 percent to agriculture, industry, and trade and tourism promotion. Other categories for assistance include multisector projects, program assistance, emergency assistance, and actions related to debt relief.

In the United States, bilateral official aid to Latin America is administered through the US Agency for International Development (USAID), which focuses on policy in six areas: biodiversity, democracy, economic growth, education, health, and eradication of illegal narcotics. Assistance ranges from emergency response to natural disasters, which affected more than 57 million people between 2005 and 2012,[84] to investments in a US$73 million trust fund to preserve the Amazon Basin,[85] to facilitating the spread of microfinance in the region. Descriptions of policy objectives and case stories can be found at usaid.gov. Since 2008, the World Bank has been transitioning to an advisory role to Mexico and Brazil instead of a focus on financial assistance.[86] USAID is promoting partnerships, such as that with Microsoft to bring computer training to disadvantaged Brazilian youth to expand the skill base in the region. USAID also partners with nongovernmental organizations (NGOs) such as Mercy Corps, Accion, and Project Concern in delivering

Table 6.3. Top Ten Aid Donors and Recipients in the Latin America and Caribbean (LAC) Region

Top 10 Donors to LAC, 2014				Top 10 Recipients in LAC, 2014			
Donor	To LAC (USD Millions)	% All Aid to LAC	% Each Donor's Aid World Total	Recipient	(USD Million)	% of Total LAC Aid	GNI Per Capita, 2014 USD
Germany	1,816	18	16	Colombia	1,221	12	7,970
United States	1,749	18	10	Haiti	1,083	11	820
Inter-American Development Bank (IDB) Special Fund	1,719	17	n/a	Brazil*	912	9	9,850
France	1,145	12	15	Mexico	807	8	9,860
EU institutions	710	7	7	Bolivia	672	7	2,910
Canada	408	4	20	Honduras	604	6	2,280
Norway	342	3	18	Nicaragua	430	4	1,870
International Development Association (IDA; part of the world Bank)	256	3	n/a	Peru	325	3	6,370
Switzerland	228	2	14	Guatemala	277	3	3,410
Russia	196	2	n/a	Cuba	262	3	n/a
Other donors	1,378	14	3	Other	3,356	34	
Total	9,949	100	10	Total LAC*	9,949	100	5,658

Source: OECD, *Development Aid at a Glance, America,* 2016.
* World Bank Database

emergency relief, sustainable development, and civil society programs in the region. Either in partnership with bilateral or multilateral organizations or through their own fund-raising, NGOs play a large role in building human and social capacity in the region. Unofficial or private funding nearly doubles the US foreign assistance budget. In 2015 giving to international affairs by individuals, foundations, charities, and corporations was about US$15 billion—in a year when there was not a major humanitarian disaster.[87]

The debate on development aid is fraught with controversy. Should aid be given to the neediest countries or to those that might assist in the donor's strategic interest? What conditions should be imposed on countries in return for the receipt of development assistance? Some overarching principles of economic justice might suggest allocating aid to the neediest—but if those in most need are governed by corrupt rulers, will the aid simply be flushed through private coffers? Finally, how can aid be administered to strengthen institutions and not promote dependency on continual flows from donors? These are but some of the many questions swirling in the aid debate that also apply to the Latin American context.

Macro Policy in a Globalized Economy: Limiting Volatility and Promoting Economic Inclusivity

The Global Financial Crisis of 2007–2008 and its aftermath laid bare Latin America's accomplishments as well as its vulnerabilities in macroeconomic management. With hyperinflation largely tamed, when international capital markets crashed and trade flows plummeted, Latin America once again imported a crisis not of its own making. But this time was different; instead of applying the proverbial saying "The United States catches a cold and Latin American contracts pneumonia," the region rebounded. As shown in figure 6.2, annual growth rates exhibited a V-shaped recovery from the crisis. We now turn to explaining why this happened—as well as why the growth rates throughout the following decade have been disappointingly anemic. To foreshadow this rocky macro terrain, we note that the hard work of stabilization of the 1980s and 1990s paid off during the financial crisis as the region employed countercyclical tools to address the global contraction. Recovery then garnered positive tailwinds from the voracious demand of the Chinese economy for Latin American commodities. But, as we will conclude, more difficult macro adjustments lie ahead to create virtuous circles of savings and investment to promote sustainable, inclusive growth.

The Global Financial Crisis and Its Aftermath

The immediate effects of the Global Financial Crisis were severe in Latin America. As credibility crumbled and credit dried up around the globe, those in the Latin American region felt shock waves through both financial and trade channels. A crunch in lending in money centers such as New York and London resulted in a doubling of the cost of borrowing for Latin American firms. Although the

Figure 6.2.   Global Financial Crisis's Effect on GDP

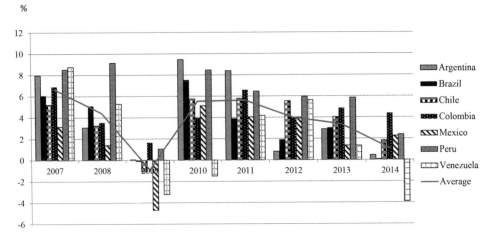

Source: OECD Latin American Economic Outlook (LEO).

epicenter of the financial crisis was the way that subprime mortgages from the United States were repackaged and sold globally, panicked investors fled back to the safety of guaranteed US Treasury bonds, rejecting higher yields in emerging markets when faced with intense global uncertainty. Corporate issues of Latin American debt and equities halved and inward foreign direct investment severely stalled. Smaller countries such as El Salvador and Honduras that are heavily dependent on remittances reeled as relatives working in the United States were laid off in the Great Recession. The engine of trade sputtered as consumers around the world hunkered down to prepare for the unknown. Positive trade performance in the region in the first half of the 2000s quickly went sour.

What was different this time is that despite the deep global contraction, Latin America quickly bounced back. Once global capital was assured that recession wasn't morphing into depression, money began to return to emerging markets, including Latin America, for higher returns. Latin American economies offered real value. In response to the macro shocks of the 1980s and 1990s, countries had pursued macro-prudential measures in both overall management and in market supervision. By 2002, 88 percent of countries had a supervisory agency and 94 had insider trading laws.[88] Fiscal responsibility laws reined in excessive government deficits and contained debt dynamics. Monetary policy was largely transparent and credible, based in many cases on rules insulated from political influence. Bank balance sheets were healthy from tighter loan-loss provisioning and limits on open positions of financial institutions. Reserve requirements reined in financial expansion in the system.[89] External public debt had declined from around 60 percent of GDP in 1990 to under 20 percent by 2008. Current account balances had extraordinary swings from deficits on the order of 50 percent in the 1990s to surpluses hovering around 40 percent by 2006. Exchange rates, largely floating with light-handed management, favored exports in US dollar–based terms as the crisis broke. In short, financial reform paid off. Figure 6.3 showcases the positive performance from 2001 through 2010.

Figure 6.3.   Primary Fiscal and Current Account Balances in Latin America

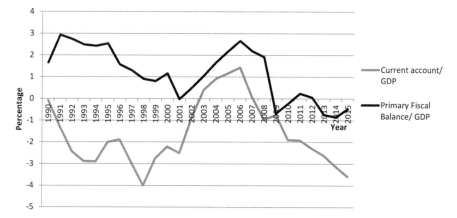

Source: Primary Fiscal Balance Source: Latin Macro Watch, 2016, IADB (Inter-American Development Bank). Current Account Source: World Economic Outlook Database, 2016, IMF (International Monetary Fund).

Most important, as the great recession choked growth, Latin American economies had the fiscal space to pursue countercyclical policies. As shown in table 6.4, we don't observe radical cuts in social spending following the crisis. Unlike earlier crises where the IMF conditioned lending on imposing contractionary policies further depressing growth, with strong fiscal positions and healthy reserves, governments in the region had policy options to counter the downturn with an infusion of spending in infrastructure, housing, and incentives for small businesses and farmers. Justin Lin, the World Bank chief economist at the time, highlighted the key role of developing countries as drivers of global recovery. The BEMs—Big Emerging Markets including Brazil, China, India, and Mexico—were a fresh source of global demand. Alicia Barcena, head of ECLAC, characterized the importance of emerging markets as a new political geometry with shared commitments in the global economy.

Beyond the entry of emerging global players, the rules had also changed. Barcena also heralded the "collapse of the neoliberal system" as indicating a "need to establish a greater balance between the State, the market and citizens so public management may be better organized."[90] As Western economies were using instruments of state investment to shore up anemic growth, this provided a validation for expanding public industrial policies worldwide. The halo around neoliberal, market-driven models was tarnished as economies saw the need to supplement the market crash with active intervention. As what had been heretical, interventionist policies became dominant approaches, Latin American governments, like those around the world, primed economies with state investments.

Initially this hybrid model of market and state met with strong success as regional growth rates topped 5 percent from 2003 to 2011. For many countries the domestic injection of funds received a boost from the external sector—the vigorous commodity demand by China. The speed with which China ramped up its integration into the global economy was perhaps unprecedented, rocketing from imports of 70 million metric tons of iron ore in 2000 to 932 million in 2014.

Table 6.4. Variation in per Capita Social Spending and GDP Growth

	1993		1998		2003		2008		2013	
	Rate of Growth of GDP (%)	Change in per Capita Social Spending (%)	Rate of Growth of GDP (%)	Change in per Capita Social Spending (%)	Rate of Growth of GDP (%)	Change in per Capita Social Spending (%)	Rate of Growth of GDP (%)	Change in per Capita Social Spending (%)	Rate of Growth of GDP (%)	Change in per Capita Social Spending (%)
Argentina	5.7	0.3	3.9	−6.5	8.8	−18.2	4.1	5.4	2.3	12.6
Brazil	4.9	13.8	0.3	10.2	1.1	2.1	5.1	5.6	3.0	6.8
Chile	7.0	8.8	3.2	8.8	3.9	−2.0	3.7	17.7	4.0	3.3
Colombia	5.7	11.6	0.6	1.4	3.9	−4.1	3.5	3.3	4.9	7.5
Mexico	2.0	9.5	5.0	8.8	1.4	2.5	1.4	−0.3	1.4	n/a
Venezuela	0.3	−17.5	0.3	−10.7	−7.8	−6.8	5.3	−7.6	1.3	−16.1

Source: ECLAC, *Economic Commission for Latin America and the Caribbean 2016.*

Similar patterns were felt in copper markets, as Chinese purchases rose from 12.6 to 40.1 percent of world imports. As the Chinese engine sucked in minerals, oil, and agricultural products, the commodity super cycle pushed regional growth rates upward. Crude oil, copper, and soybeans—key exports from South American economies—soared. We recall the high percentage of metallic reserves in the Latin American region: 66 percent of global lithium, 47 percent of copper, 45 percent of silver, 25 percent of tin, 23 percent of bauxite, 23 percent of nickel, 14 percent of iron. Chile produces 31 percent of mined copper; Peru 7.5 percent. Countries significantly dependent on exports to China include Argentina, Brazil, Chile, Colombia, Costa Rica, Peru, and Venezuela. Global growth, led by the Chinese engine, demanded these primary inputs to production as well as agricultural exports such as soya. Figure 6.4 shows the volatility in commodity prices as a result of these changing demand pressures. This was a dramatic positive external shock for commodity exporters in the region.

It is important to recall the effects of commodity booms on primary product exporters. Export concentration can be dangerous. The China shock radically changed the export basket with Peru and Chile moving from 40–45 percent of exports to 60 percent and above concentrated in minerals in under ten years. As more of a commodity is sold, national budget revenues swell either through taxes or sales by state-owned commodity exporters. But what goes up can decline quickly. In Ecuador, for example, 16 percent of fiscal revenues came from nonrenewable resources in 2011; by 2015 this was roughly halved.[91] During a boom, democratic governments pressured by social-sector needs find it difficult to resist spending to meet political demands. Consumers, with more money in their pockets, are able to buy goods they hadn't been able to afford for years. Consumer-led spending results in price spikes as well as pressure on the balance

Figure 6.4.   Real Commodity Prices, 1999–2015

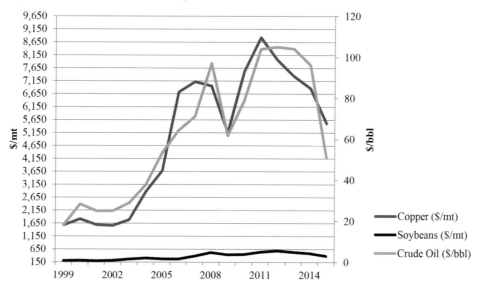

Source: World Bank Commodities Price Data Pink Sheets 1999–2016.

Figure 6.5.   Latin American and Caribbean Growth

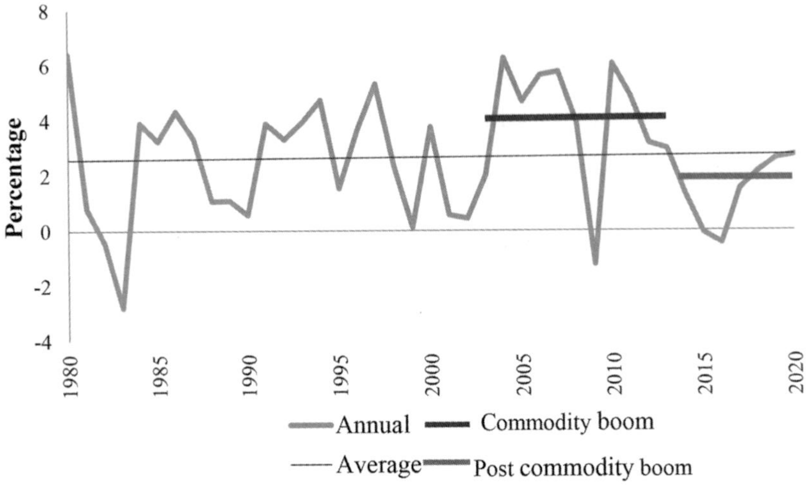

Source: World Economic Outlook Database, 2016, (IMF) International Monetary Fund.

of payments for the TVs, cars, and cellphones imported from abroad. Import binges are facilitated by exchange-rate appreciations caused in part by the demand for the nation's commodities.

At first, growth rates responded to the combined external demand for commodities and expansionary internal government and consumer spending. Many believed that the Latin American decade of stable, inclusive growth had arrived. Despite the effects of the global recession, growth rates during the commodity boom were in the 5 percent range. But as seen in figure 6.5 the macro sweet spot soon soured. The commodity tailwinds ebbed as China began its shift to a slower, more sustainable growth pattern. When commodities such as crude oil tumbled to a quarter of its high or copper valuations were halved, resource based exporters lagged. This was reinforced by slow or stagnant growth in the United States and Europe—important markets for non-commodity exporters, especially Mexico and Central America. By 2015, South American growth had sagged to a dismal negative 2.5 percent. Imagine the psychological effect of this rapid rise and brutal fall. The exuberant expectations of a growing nation dissolved into the morning after hangover of slow growth life as usual. The hopes of a growing middle class were dashed.

With the boom largely ended by 2015, countries now need to adjust to a low growth environment. The region is struggling to adapt to a growth model driven less by external factors by pivoting away from consumption-led growth (dependent on external infusions) to investments in competitiveness and productivity. Not all countries have the same performance pattern. ECLAC forecasted growth for 2018 at 2.2 percent—a rate insufficient to improve the standard of living of most Latin Americans.[92] Commodity exporters such as Chile and Peru moderated commodity downturns with a widening export palate, engaging with other Pacific Rim nations. But even these "good" performers were producing below potential.

THE MACRO NEW NORMAL: BETWEEN A ROCK AND A HARD PLACE

As the external sector rather abruptly shifted from providing tailwinds through exports to presenting headwinds from bulging current account deficits, the policy mix switched to an internal focus. Policymakers in the region were obviously happier with an expansionary macro policy to jumpstart growth; politically it is pleasurable to create programs whereas it is painful to cut them back. But external constraints can force policymakers to a contractionary stance, compelling a tightening of domestic spigots despite political resistance to fiscal adjustment, putting them between a rock and a hard place.

An expansionary monetary policy is often recommended to fuel growth during a downturn. Latin American economies followed North American and European counterparts by pursuing an expansionary stance to counter the Great Recession. Outcomes, however, are a bit more unpredictable in the global South. When money is injected into a system with weak domestic supply elasticities—that is with a weak ability to increase nationally produced goods to meet the new demand—two problems emerge. First, current accounts will be further pressured by imports to fulfill domestic wants. As people have more money they might spend it on importing electronics, toys, or clothing. Secondly, domestic prices will rise as too much money is chasing too few goods. Throughout the region we could see inflation pushing upward by 2015, particularly in Venezuela, Brazil, and Colombia. But as shown in figure 6.6, there is a high degree of regional divergence, largely driven by different inflation management regimes. We recall that in response to the hyperinflation of the 1980s and 1990s, some countries such as Ecuador imposed a fixed rate—indeed dollarized—regime. Six others—Brazil, Chile, Colombia, Mexico, Peru, and Uruguay—adopted transparent rules reinforced by greater central bank

Figure 6.6.   Selected Inflation Data

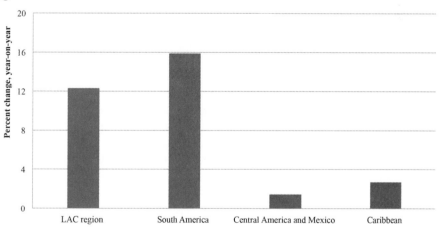

Source: ECLAC, Economic Commission for Latin America and the Caribbean, 2016.

independence for inflation targeting within clear, pre-announced bands. Finally, some countries fall in the middle, implementing intermediate regimes that allow for more permissive monetary expansion during slow growth periods. Inflation management in Latin America is a tricky business, made more complicated by the long historical memory of citizens who suffered through the pain of hyperinflation. When prices begin to edge up, some overreact, creating the need for the central bank to further tighten the money supply. This can have additional unintended effects. Increasing interest rates, used to dampen domestic demand, also raise the local cost of servicing domestic debt. This effect, called fiscal dominance, constrains the hands of central bankers because rate increases can also weaken government balance sheets. Policy falls into a vicious circle as the expansionary efforts promote inflation, brakes on inflation call for an increase in interest rates, and rising rates make public debt more vulnerable.

Inflation can also gain momentum as an unintended effect of an exchange rate depreciation. Under a flexible exchange rate system, a country running a balance of payments deficit should see its currency weaken. This cheaper currency should spur exports as well as signal home residents to decrease purchases of now more expensive imports—automatically correcting the trade imbalance. Flexible exchange rates should therefore be a shock absorber, using price signals to change the composition of exports and imports. But in an import-dependent economy, things can go awry. First, exports might not be sensitive to the depreciation. That is, if coffee is cheaper, it might not be the case that people around the world will drink more coffee. But if imports are more expensive, domestically people might not cut back on imported products either as final goods or intermediate inputs in value chains. The result of this can be that overall prices will rise as the effects of the exchange rate depreciation pass through the system.

The Fiscal Balancing Act and Capital Inflows

Countercyclical policy is complicated; spending to ignite growth must be financed. If countries saved during the boom period by building up reserves, these can be drawn down during a bust. Chile's copper stabilization fund is a good example of this type of economic smoothing. But when democracies face very present needs to address poverty and alleviate human suffering, it is harder to postpone the investments in health, education, and infrastructure so badly needed today for some future date. Politicians want the votes—and with money in the bank, literally, why not make everyone happy? Boom-time spending was also susceptible to irregular practices; as large-scale investments were made, who would miss a few million or so? Unlike the response to the Global Financial Crisis, which was a quick, sudden shock, the countercyclical policies implemented to address structural changes in the global economy with the slowing of China and secular stagnation in industrialized economies were largely on shaky fiscal grounds.

As shown in figure 6.7, by 2015 the regional fiscal balance had largely shifted to a deficit as the region adjusted to a low-growth global economy. Fiscal deficits require financing, especially if the inflationary option is cut off. Although

Figure 6.7. Change in Primary and Overall Balance, 2014–2015

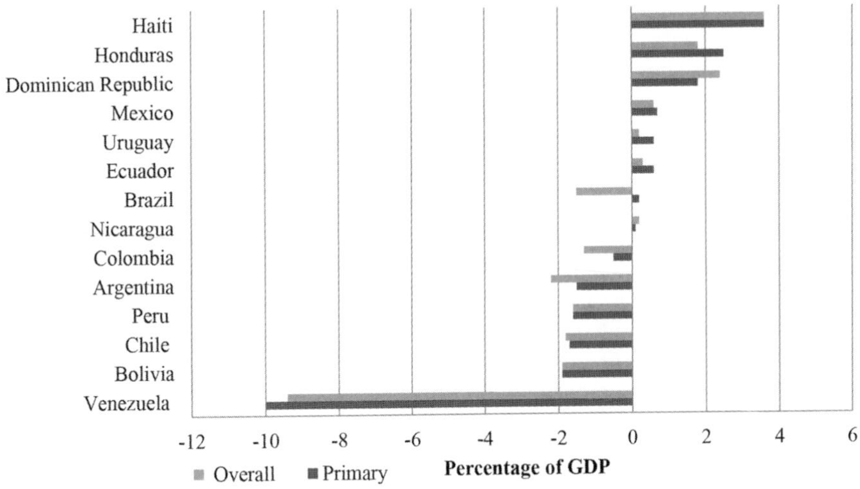

Source: International Monetary Fund *Fiscal Monitor* 2015.

capital markets in Latin America have deepened significantly since the debt crises of the 1980s to allow greater domestic intermediation of deficits, rising public debt—both domestic and international—will at some point need servicing. Investors are only willing to lend when they see responsible fiscal and monetary policies. Poor macro management will affect the private sector as well as investors shy from putting money into environments with poor macro fundamentals. In countries with a weak macro reputation, interest rates become exorbitantly high to account for the risk of default by a country repeatedly spending more domestically than it is making. Remember that the position of Latin American nations differs from that of the United States. While US creditors—especially the Chinese—may come knocking at some point in the future, loans written in US dollars will be repaid in US dollars. The United States can "repay" creditors, if needed, with dollars printed to service the debt. Latin American nations, in contrast, must earn the dollars through export sales to service dollar-denominated debt. They therefore must don what Tom Friedman called the "golden straitjacket"—a suit of responsible monetary and fiscal policies to continue to entice capital markets to lend.[93]

Macro Policy toward 2020

Latin America broadly faces four macro dilemmas and a trilemma as it looks toward 2020.[94] Dilemmas are choices between two outcomes; in a globalized economy they are further bound by a three-way choice or a trilemma. First, on the domestic monetary front, nations must choose between the credible, inflation-fighting monetary policy implemented after the crises of the late 1990s versus more expansive approaches to stimulate growth and unemployment adopted following the Global Financial Crisis. Second, in their fiscal stance, governments can choose to avoid political conflict by boosting short-term activity or they can preference long-term sustainability by raising taxes or cutting government expenditures. Third, on external balance, nations focusing on expansive policies can let current accounts widen when spending at home exceeds production or the choice can be made to depress domestic absorption to release a surplus. The final dilemma that governments must struggle with is attending to deep social deficits, especially the health and education needs of citizens, in the face of an erosion of the social gains achieved during the past decade of easier macroeconomic times.

These tough choices are made even more difficult by what Dani Rodrik calls the inescapable trilemma of the world economy.[95] With a trilemma, one must choose two of three conditions; Rodrik points our attention to choices among democracy, national sovereignty in macro policies and global economic integration. Given the deep transition to democracy in Latin America, it can either maintain autonomous national policies or it must commit to global markets for trade, finance, and production. Latin American history is shaded by trying to turn inward to promote domestic political stability. As global capital markets have become more fully integrated, it is difficult to ignore the opportunities access to capital brings. What nations must therefore in part give up is autonomy in national macro policies. They must don the "golden straitjacket" of fiscal and monetary responsibility to court global capital— sometimes very tough medicine. The long run objective is maintaining policies that may loosen the straight-jacket a bit, making economies more resilient and less bound by macro dilemmas in the context of a globalized economy. At the heart of creating more resilient macro foundations in Latin America is tackling the domestic savings deficit. It is to this problem that we now turn.

RAISING DOMESTIC SAVINGS: A KEY TO RESILIENT MACRO ECONOMIES

Before asking Latin Americans to save more, we should ask why nations in the region tend to save less than other parts of the world. In figure 6.8, we can see that as a region Latin America saves significantly less that those living in advanced economies as well as in emerging Asia. Empirical studies suggest that savings rates are conditioned by country-level variables such as macroeconomic volatility, weak institutions, or meager household income. The legacy of inflation in Latin America has worked against savings habits: Why save when the real value of your money may be quickly eroded by inflation? Investments in real assets—real estate, a new machine for your microenterprise—were more valuable stores of your wealth. People came to distrust financial institutions, most especially central bankers. If the value of your savings could be eroded overnight through a megadevaluation, it was far smarter for those with access to keep an offshore account in Miami. Finally, it is difficult for the poor to save. With many family needs ranging from daily food expense, annual fees for children's educational supplies, to unexpected health crises, it is difficult to defer consumption today in the hopes of a better tomorrow. The poor, however, do manage to put bits away for emergencies, family celebrations, health, and retirement.

Figure 6.8.   Gross National Savings as a Percentage of GDP

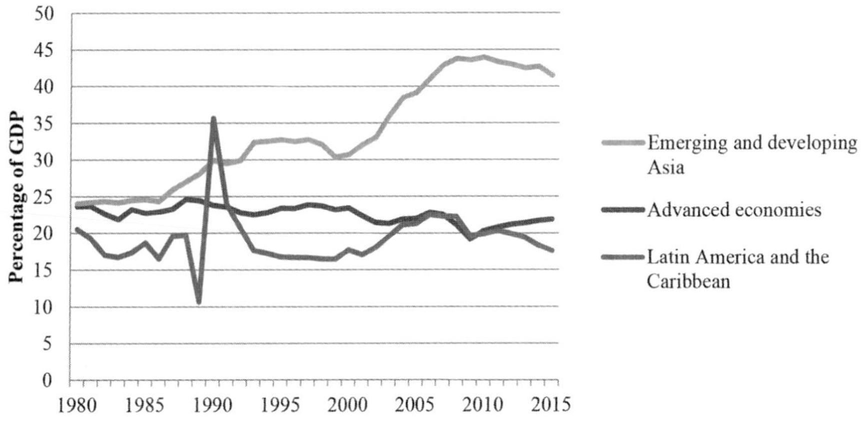

Source: IMF, World Economic Outlook

But poor people do manage to save more in other cultures. Even after controlling for demographics, income per capita, and growth performance, advanced economies and countries in Emerging Asia save, on average, 3 and 9 percentage points of GDP more than countries in Latin America and the Caribbean.[96]

What is different? At one level, Latin Americans might be more like North Americans in enjoying a consumer culture. Tomorrow will be tough enough—let's enjoy what we have today—often appears to be the refrain. Another aspect is the degree of forced savings in many economies. Although at certain stages in your life cycle you might prefer to buy a cellphone or a car, you are forced to save when in the United States your social security contribution is taken out of your paycheck. In many Latin American countries, the dominance of the informal sector (we'll talk about this more in our chapter on competitiveness) means that around half of the population is not contributing to a pension plan—otherwise known as being forced to save through legally mandated automatic deductions. As you might guess, informal workers also evade other taxes that could be allocated to provide key public services.

At the same time, there is a relatively generous approach to paying out pensions in the region. For those who have contributed—for example government workers, the military, and teachers—many countries have extraordinarily low retirement rates and generous benefits paid to widows and daughters. In Brazil, for example, there are the so-called Viagra brides—young girls married to fifty- and sixty-something men who will continue to draw a pension long after the husband is deceased. Many are paid not a portion of what they have paid in, but rather a percentage of their former salary—sometimes even 100 percent. Such noncontributory pensions are now one-third of all pensions in the region. For the present this system is sustainable because of a sweet demographic window—there are more young workers in the formal sector than there are pensioners drawing down on their contributions. As shown in figure 6.9, this window is set to narrow by 2050, creating a looming crisis over the horizon. Tackling the pension problem while the demographic bonus is in play—both in terms of formalizing contributions today and revising the payouts—is essential to addressing saving in the region.[97]

Figure 6.9.   Age Profile in Latin America

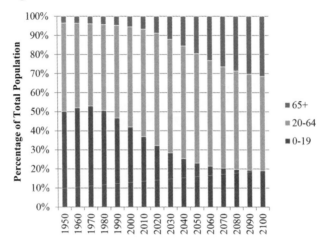

Source: Eduardo Cavallo, Tomás Serebrisky "Saving for Development: How Latin America and the Caribbean Can Save More," Inter-American Development Bank, 2016.

Government is also another source of savings. As shown in table 6.5, in emerging Asia, where total savings is 29.9 percent of GDP, public savings constitute 7.9 percent of the effort. Of Latin America's regional saving rate of 21 percent, only 2.8 percent is public.[98] Governments can save out of revenue. Much of the flexibility for countercyclical interventions following the global financial crisis came from stabilization funds such as Chile's sovereign wealth fund that invests in other assets during a boom to have a spending account when copper prices are soft. Savings can also be achieved by reducing leakages in current public spending on social assistance. Streamlining delivery, better targeting of needy populations, and transparency measures against corruption can create a cushion to be reinvested in the social sector during an economic downturn. Government savings might also be directed toward investments in infrastructure with high payoff for future productivity.

Beyond asking people and governments to save more, perhaps policy incentives can make it easier for them to do so. Savings cultures can be promoted in

Table 6.5.   Savings Rates, 1980–2015 (% of GDP)

Components of Saving	LAC	Emerging Asia	Sub-Saharan Africa	Advanced Economies
Gross national saving	17.5	33.7	13.8	22.8
Gross public saving	2.8	7.9	2.8	1.5
Gross private saving	14.7	25.8	10.9	21.2
Foreign saving	3.5	–3.8	5.4	0.8
Total saving	21.0	29.9	10.2	23.6

Source: Francesco Grigoli, Alexander Herman, and Klaus Schmidt-Hebbel (IMF), *Saving in Latin America and the Caribbean: Performance and May 2015.*

schools to encourage children and teens (many of whom work) to set aside a portion of earnings in savings accounts. Teaching kids—and their parents—about savings can help build the culture. Changes in regulations to encourage the development of new financial instruments can help move savings from informal to formal mechanisms. The poor do save some—they must to survive economic shocks. In Mexico, Peru, and Colombia, for example, of the 16–30 percent of those who report saving, only about 25 percent save through formal instruments. There appears room to provide more structured savings opportunities in the region. For other poor investors, the return on a refrigerator, truck, or other durable good is higher than interest on savings—so it is rational for these self-employed people not to save. For some, access to a bank is the problem. When was the last time you saw a (picture of a) bank in a slum? Only about a quarter of households in the lowest income decile have a neighborhood financial institution.[99] Poor people may need more ready access to their savings—and yet how many financial institutions want to place ATMs in neighborhoods where it is hard to service the machine?

Efforts to promote financial inclusion might have a macro effect on savings. Only in Brazil, Chile, and Costa Rica do more than half of the adult population own a bank account; in Honduras, Peru, and Nicaragua only one-third of adults are served.[100] A new data source on financial inclusion, Findex, shows that of Latin American adults with an account, only one-third saved in the last year. There is certainly much room to help poor individuals engage in intertemporal allocation of resources and manage risks. Weak rule of law may account for some of the poor performance as people don't trust financial protection. Although technology could help here, the Latin American region lags in using mobile phones as instruments to save. Tigo's mobile money in Paraguay is an exception, providing vehicles to control finances through mobile money, making it possible for the busy poor clients to avoid coming into a bank.[101] More nonbank, nontraditional suppliers may help address the supply shortage in offering financial services to the poor. Some may benefit from informal arrangements, such as saving groups or rotating saving and credit associations (ROSCAs). Savings circles promote commitment devices to change people's decision to save; scheduled saving plans and commitment accounts that provide incentives and penalties could be effective instruments to bank the unbanked and help them increase their saving balances.

The Investment Mirror of Savings

Increasing savings would facilitate raising investment rates in the region without relying on large foreign infusions of capital. As a mirror to low saving, Latin America underinvests. Based upon an analysis of thirteen economies that grew on average 7 percent a year for at least 25 years between 1950 and 2005, the Commission on Growth and Development estimates that 25 percent is the minimum investment level compatible with long-term growth.[102] As seen in figure 6.10, Latin America is sadly far from the 25 percent benchmark. To reach it at current rates of domestic savings,

Figure 6.10.   Average Gross Savings and Investment

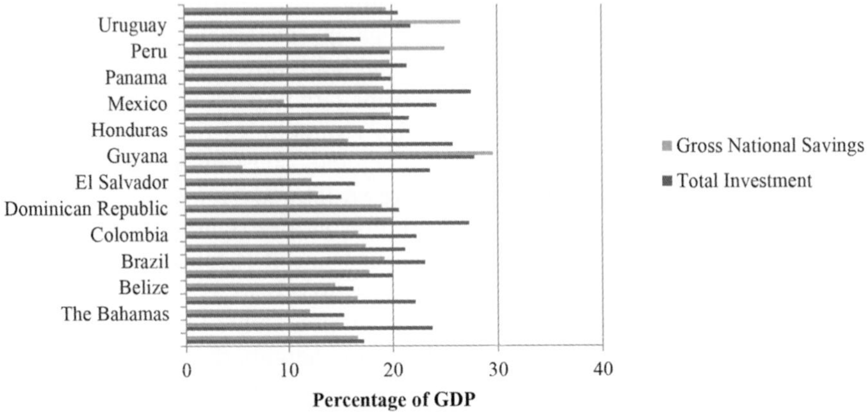

Source: IMF, World Economic Outlook 2015

the region would need to double foreign borrowing, increasing vulnerability to external shocks. Augmenting domestic sources of saving would allow Latin America to invest the recommended benchmark of 5 percent of GDP in infrastructure. India meets this target and China exceeds it at 8.5 percent; in comparison the average of sixteen countries in the region providing data is a paltry 3.7 percent.[103]

VIRTUOUS CIRCLES: CAN LATIN AMERICA PROMOTE MORE RESILIENT GROWTH?

To conclude our tour of macro policy in Latin America in a globalized economy, it may be helpful to think about the elements of strong growth giving rise to a virtuous circle as depicted in figure 6.11. A key lesson of the 1980s and 1990s was that macro fundamentals matter—low inflation combined with a fiscal balance will promote a current account balance and avoid the buildups and blowups of the earlier periods. With a firm macro foundation, global capital is attracted to the region, reducing the cost of capital for investment by firms. As firms expand, jobs create the income to increase domestic demand. But there are multiple pressures on the virtuous circle. External shocks—such as the Global Financial Crisis or commodity busts—interrupt national growth. As internal and external balance is unhinged, exchange rates come under pressure. To smooth over instability, there is the temptation to postpone adjustment by taking on domestic or foreign debt. Shocks might also come from inside the virtuous economy. With underdeveloped productive capabilities, burgeoning demand and an appreciated exchange rate can also lead to a deluge of imports. Maintaining a virtuous cycle of growth is a tricky art with less resilient productive systems. Weak micro foundations lead to ruptures—with significant adjustment costs. In later chapters we will turn to consider how these micro foundations might be strengthened to support sustained productivity and structural change.

Figure 6.11.   Virtuous Cycles of Growth

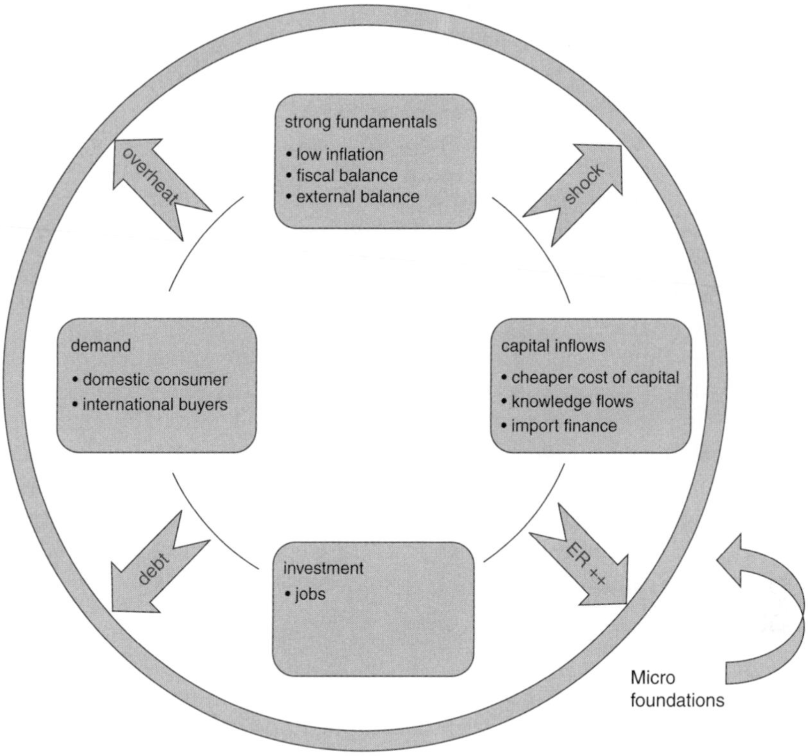

Source: author

K e y   C o n c e p t s

capital controls
equity investments
financialization
foreign direct
   investment (FDI)
official flows

portfolio bonds
remittances
short- and long-term portfolio
   investments
short-term money
Trilema of the world economy

C h a p t e r   S u m m a r y

Capital Flows

Defining Capital Flows

- Financial liberalization makes a nation more sensitive to changes in the global economy—the good and the bad.

- The neoliberal model places private capital flows at the center of development finance. Capital will flow to its most productive uses; therefore, tough austerity measures that transform the productivity of an economy should be rewarded by improved access to international financial markets. However, capital reversal has been rapid in Latin America because *relative returns* drive demand for foreign assets.
- Capital flows come in seven forms: loans, bond purchases, FDI, portfolio, equity flows, remittances, and lending directly to support trade. Bonds and equity investments decrease risk for the issuing country by transferring risk to investors. However, stock and bond markets are underdeveloped in Latin America since size is the key constraint and market capitalization remains relatively low. Despite the potential for risk sharing, the outlook for capital markets in Latin America remains weak, since capital markets are characterized by dollarization, short termism, and illiquidity.
- On the supply side, drivers of capital flows include: global integration, technological changes, better information, changes in the US legal code, excess global savings, and low interest rates in the United States and Europe. On the demand side, structural changes in the 1990s improved relative yields of assets and financial solvency, and decreased political instability and potential losses drive capital.

Risks Associated with Capital Flows

- Access to short-term capital can help generate important growth in the region, but financing long-term development on short-term capital is a risky venture. Advocates of new capital flows believe the infusion of funds will spur growth, which will then encourage savings. However, in Latin America efficiency gains may be limited due to incomplete information. Relying on capital inflows may also be risky due to their volatility, procyclical bias, and ability to adversely affect other key monetary variables.
- A strong banking system can serve to dampen domestic macroeconomic instability and the challenges of short-term capital flows. However, when banks fail to provide domestic intermediation, the effects of a crisis are magnified. If domestic loans to large conglomerates sidestepped sound accounting procedures, a downturn may result in a resounding crash.
- One way to address balance of payments pressures without contracting spending or printing to purchase hard currency is to attract international capital. Financialization—the enormous power of cross border capital flows—leads to risk since flows gush during good times and retreat rapidly during bad times.
- FDI is less volatile than other forms of capital but has a fraught history in Latin America. There are four different types of FDI: natural resources, efficiency, market access, and technology seeking. The United States is the principal source of FDI in the region, followed by the European Union. Chinese investment has increased dramatically, driven by demand for natural resources. Additionally, an increasingly important phenomenon are multi-Latinas.

- Penetration of transnational companies in developing country markets raises the question of power and balance. Globalization of production has increased the transnational reach, but has made its activities more transparent.

Other Sources of Capital

- In Latin America, the largest source of international capital flowing into the region comes from Latinos themselves. Many Latin Americans continue to emigrate for economic opportunities, education, and safety, yet despite the associated drain on human capital, remittances are being funneled into sustaining and improving the quality of life in the region. Although many Latin Americans remain unbanked, progress is being made to make the remittance flows more secure and accessible through the formal economy. This provides hope for regional development.
- Although net aid per capita in the region is low, Official Development Assistance plays an important role in bridging the gap between local resources and developmental needs in Latin America. In recent years, the focus of aid has shifted from economic infrastructure to support for social services, environmental investments, and social infrastructure.

Macroeconomic Landscape

- The Global Financial Crisis of 2007–2008 and its aftermath laid bare Latin America's accomplishments as well as its vulnerabilities in macroeconomic management. In contrast to previous financial crises, in the face of an external shock, the region rebounded. Following the hard work of stabilization, the region had the fiscal space to employ countercyclical tools to address the global contraction.
- Regional growth rates were strong in the first decade of this century, in part due to the positive external shock of increased Chinese commodity demands. However, the commodity booms largely ended by 2015, and countries are now faced with adjusting to a low growth environment.
- Macro policy exists in a new normal between a rock and a hard place as external constraints can force policymakers to take a contractionary stance, tightening fiscal spending despite political resistance to fiscal adjustment. Although expansionary monetary policy is often recommended to fuel growth during a downturn, the results of such policies are unpredictable in Latin America, in part because of inflation management regimes that came out of reforms in the 1990s and import dependent economies. Fiscal policy requires a balancing act in the face of capital inflows. Countercyclical policy is complicated because spending to ignite growth must be financed. Political pressures often force policymakers to spend during boom times, increasing fiscal deficits which require financing. Furthermore, rising public debt will need servicing at some point.
- Policymakers face four macro dilemmas:
  - Credible, inflation-fighting monetary policy versus more expansive approaches to stimulate growth and unemployment

- Avoiding political conflict by boosting short-term activity versus prioritizing long-term sustainability by either raising taxes or cutting government expenditures
- Pursuing expansive policies at the expense of increasing current account deficits versus depressing domestic absorption to release a surplus
- Attending to deep social deficits in the face of an erosion of the social gains achieved during the past decade
- Additionally, policymakers must work within the trilemma of the world economy which states that governments must choose two of three conditions among democracy, national sovereignty, and global economic integration.
- At the heart of creating more resilient macro foundations in Latin America is increasing domestic savings.

Notes

1. Manuel Orozco, "Remittances to Latin America and the Caribbean in 2017 The Inter-American Dialogue," www.thedialogue.org/wp-content/uploads/2018/01/Remittances-2017-1-2.pdf.

2. World Bank, *Global Development Finance 2004: Harnessing Cyclical Gains for Development* (Washington, DC: World Bank, 2004), 7.

3. Lending directly to support trade includes bank letters of credit that provide financing for exports in transit until the importer pays for the goods as well as commercial bank lending.

4. Barry Eichengreen and Ricardo Hausmann, "Original Sin: The Road to Redemption," www.nber.org, revised January 2005.

5. Paul J. Davies, Joanna Chung, and Kevin Allison, "Brazil Raises $1.5bn," *Financial Times*, September 20, 2005, www.ft.com.

6. Depository receipts represent purchases made through another exchange. A depository receipt is a security issued by a US bank in place of the foreign shares held in trust by that bank. Essentially, it is a mechanism for listing on the US exchange. For example, American depository receipts (ADR) could represent shares of Brazilian Telebras bought on the US stock exchange. Each Telebras ADR that is traded on the New York Stock Exchange represents one thousand preferred shares held by the Bank of New York. An advantage of the ADR is that the liquidity and visibility of the stock increase. Some American retail investors, by their own rules, are not permitted to buy emerging market shares but can purchase an ADR. In some countries, to control capital inflows and outflows, only qualified institutional buyers approved by the central bank can invest in local shares. To qualify for an ADR, the foreign firm must file with the Security and Exchange Commission (SEC) and abide by SEC rules. The costs associated with filing (e.g., registration, lawyers, and investment bankers) are high, and the requirements for listing in terms of transparency and reporting are stringent. However, the gains in increasing market size are often worth the cost.

7. World Bank, *Global Development Finance 2004*, 95.

8. Augusto de la Torre and Sergio Schmukler, *Whither Latin American Capital Markets?* Sponsored by the Office of the Chief Economist, World Bank (Washington, DC: World Bank, October 2004), and Augusto de la Torre and Sergio Schmukler, *Financial Development in Latin America and the Caribbean: The Road Ahead,* (Washington, DC: World Bank, 2012).

9. Ibid.

10. World Bank, *World Development Indicators, 1997* (Washington, DC: World Bank, 1997), table 5.3, "About the Data."

11. IMF Staff Report, Financial Integration in Latin America March 2016.

12. As of October 1992, US authorities approved increasing the number of institutional investors, including pension plans and insurance funds, allowed to invest in privately placed securities. Standardization of legal and accounting practices between the United States and Mexico has also helped.

13. Sebastian Edwards, *Capital Flows into Latin America: A Stop-Go Story?* National Bureau of Economic Research Working Paper No. 6441 (Cambridge, MA: National Bureau of Economic Research, 1998), available at www.nber.org/papers/w6441. Edwards cites a 1993 IMF staff paper by Guillermo Calvo and a 1997 World Bank study on capital flows.

14. Adapted from José Angel Gurría, "Capital Flows: The Mexico Case," *Coping with Capital Surges: The Return of Finance to Latin America*, eds Ricardo Ffrench-Davis and Stephany Griffith-Jones (Boulder, CO: Rienner, 1995), 189.

15. Ney Hayashi Cruz and Eduardo Thomson, "Latin America's Boom-Year Promises Unravel in Stock-Market Bust," Bloomberg.org, August 18, 2015.

16. Masood Ahmed, Timothy Lane, and Marianne Schulze-Ghattas, "Refocusing IMF Conditionality," *Finance and Development* 38(4) (December 2001), as accessed at www.imf.org.

17. This is not weighted by the share of a country's GDP in regional GDP; it is a straight average of FDI taken as a percentage of 1995 GDP. World Bank, *World Development Indicators, 1997*.

18. Several studies, including those by Barry Eichengreen, Joseph Stiglitz, Stephanie Griffith Jones, and William Easterly, are summarized in *The United Nations, World Economic and Social Survey 2005, Financing for Development*, Chapter 3, "International Private Capital Flows."

19. Ian Katz, "Snapping up South America," *Business Week*, January 18, 1999, 60.

20. Nader Nazmi, "The Internationalization of Capital in a Small and Vulnerable Economy: The Case of Ecuador," *Foreign Direct Investment in Latin America*, eds. Werner Baer and William R. Miles (New York: Hayworth, 2001), 119–139.

21. Shatz, "Expanding Foreign Direct Investment," 7.

22. ECLAC 2016.

23. ECLAC 2016.

24. Augusto de la Torre, Cristian Aedo, and I. Walker, *Latin America and the Caribbean's Long-Term Growth: Made in China* (Washington DC: World Bank, 2011), http://documents.worldbank.org/curated/en/208581468266159691/Latin-America-and-the-Caribbeans-long-term-growth-made-in-China.

25. Kevin P. Gallagher and Margaret Myers, *China-Latin America Finance Database*, (Washington, DC: Inter-American Dialogue, 2016).

26. Warburg Dillon Read, "The Impact of the Asian Crisis," July 14, 1998, 2, fax newsletter .

27. Diana Jean Schemo, "Brazilians Fret as Economic Threat Moves Closer," *New York Times*, September 20, 1998, online edition.

28. Paul Lewis, "Latin Americans Say Russian Default Is Hurting Their Economies," *New York Times*, October 6, 1998, online edition.

29. Lewis, "Latin Americans," A13.

30. Mac Margolis, "Hat in Hand," *Newsweek*, October 12, 1998, 32B.

31. ECLAC Foreign Investment in Latin America and the Caribbean 2016.

32. Michael Mortimore, Álvaro Calderón, Pablo Carvallo, and Márcia Tavares, "Foreign Investment in Latin America and the Caribbean," ECLAC Unit on Investment and Corporate Strategies, Briefing Paper 2005.

33. ECLAC Foreign Investment in Latin America and the Caribbean 2016.

34. Laura Alfaro and Eliza Hammel, "Latin American Multinationals," World Economic Forum: Latin America Competitiveness Report, Geneva, Switzerland, April 2006.

35. "Brazil's Affluent Are Hurt by Crisis," *Washington Post*, January 25, 1999, A18.

36. Remember that a Latin American government—just like the US Fed or the Bank of England—issues domestic debt to finance fiscal expenditures. If the Fed raises the interest rate, the cost of financing the US debt goes up; correspondingly, when a Latin American government raises interest rates, it increases the cost of financing domestically held debt.

37. Diana Farrell, Jaana K. Remes, and Heiner Schulz, "The Truth about Foreign Direct Investment in Emerging Markets," *The McKinsey Quarterly* 1 (2004).

38. Russell Mokhiber and Robert Weissman, "The Ten Worst Corporations of 2004," *Multinational Monitor* 25(12) (December 2004), multinationalmonitor.org.

39. Ricardo Ffrench-Davis, "Policy Implications of the Tequila Effect," *Challenge*, March–April 1998, 36.

40. Ian A. Goldin and Kenneth Reinert, "Global Capital Flows and Development: A Survey," *Journal of International Trade and Economic Development* 14(4) (2005): 9–11.

41. Economic Survey of Latin America and the Caribbean, 2000–2001, www.eclac.org.

42. This problem is discussed in José María Fanelli and José Luis Machinea, "Capital Movements in Argentina," *Coping with Capital Surges: The Return of Finance to Latin America*, eds. Ricardo Ffrench-Davis and Stephany Griffith-Jones (Boulder, CO: Rienner, 1995), 183.

43. In Richard N. Haass and Robert E. Litan, "Globalization and Its Discontents," *Foreign Affairs* 77(3) (1998): 4.

44. José Antonio Ocampo, "Towards a Global Solution," *ECLAC Notes 1* (November 1998): 2.

45. Communiqué of ECLAC on the international financial crisis, September 15, 1998, Available at www.cepal.org.english/coverpage/financialcrisis.htm.

46. Howard Shatz, "Expanding Foreign Direct Investment in the Andean Countries," CID Working Paper No. 64 (Cambridge, MA: Center for International Development at Harvard University, March 2001), 3.

47. Dan Glaister, "Emigrants Provide Lifeline," *The Guardian*, March 31, 2004, Internet edition.

48. "Remittances to Latin America Grow, but Mexico Bucks the Trend Faced with the US Slowdown," *The World Bank,* October 8, 2013, www.worldbank.org/en/news/feature/2013/10/04/remesas-latinoamerica-crecimiento-mexico-caida.

49. Manuel Orozco, Laura Porras, and Julia Yansura, "The Continued Growth of Family Remittances to Latin America and the Caribbean," *The Inter-American Dialogue,* February 16, 2016, www.thedialogue.org/wp-content/uploads/2016/02/2015-Remittances-to-LAC-2122016.pdf.

50. "Remittances to Latin America Grow, but Mexico Bucks the Trend."

51. D'Vera Cohn, Ana Gonzalez-Barrera, and Danielle Cuddington, "Remittances to Latin America Recover—But Not to Mexico," *Pew Research Center,* November 15, 2013, www.pewhispanic.org/2013/11/15/remittances-to-latin-america-recover-but-not-to-mexico/.

52. Orozco, Porras, and Yansura, "The Continued Growth of Family Remittances."

53. World Bank, Migration and Development Brief, October 28, 2017, www.knomad.org/sites/default/files/2017-12/Migration%20and%20Development%20Report%2012-14-17%20web.pdf.

54. Roberto Suro, "Remittance Senders and Receivers: Tracking the Transnational Channels," Joint Report of the Multilateral Investment Fund (MIF) and the Pew Hispanic Center (PHC) (Washington DC, November 24, 2003).

55. Enrique Benavides and Gloriana Sojo, "Migration & Development in Central America: Perspectives for the Alliance for Prosperity," *The Dialogue,* January 14, 2016, www.thedialogue.org/resources/migration-development-in-central-america-perspectives-for-the-alliance-for-prosperity/.

56. "Remittances to Latin America Grow, but Mexico Bucks the Trend."

57. Ibid.

58. Ibid.

59. Cohn, Gonzalez-Barrera, and Cuddington, "Remittances to Latin America Recover—But Not to Mexico,"

60. John Authers, "Mortgage Scheme Offers a Tiny Piece of Mexico," *Financial Times*, September 1, 2005, 8.

61. Manuel Orozco and Julia Yansura, "Confronting the Challenges of Migration & Development," *The Dialogue*, January 13, 2016, www.thedialogue.org/resources/confronting-the-challenges-of-migration-development/.

62. M. Frias, "Linking International Remittance Flows to Financial Services: Tapping the Latino Immigrant Market." Supervisory Insights Winter 2004, Federal Deposit Insurance Corporation.

63. "Western Union Launches a New Product Called Quick Pay," *Metropole Haiti*, July 9, 2015, www.metropolehaiti.com/metropole/full_poli_fr.php?id=26731.

64. Orozco and Yansura, "Confronting the Challenges of Migration & Development."

65. IMF Survey, July 18, 2005, 212.

66. Ralph Chami, Connel Fullenkamp, and Samir Jahjah, "Are Immigrant Remittance Flows a Source of Capital for Development?" *IMF Staff Papers* 52(1) (2005).

67. Orozco and Yansura, "Confronting the Challenges of Migration & Development."

68. Ibid.

69. Ibid.

70. SELA, "Current Trends in Migrants' Remittances in Latin America and the Caribbean," Regional Seminar "Migrants' remittances: An alternative for Latin America and the Caribbean?" Caracas, Venezuela 26 and 27 July 2004 SP/SRRM-UAALC/Di N° 3/Rev. 1 SELA/CAF: 18.

71. Frias, "Linking International Remittance Flows to Financial Services."

72. "RIO July, 2015 Newsletter," *The Dialogue*, July 2015, www.thedialogue.org/wp-content/uploads/2015/10/RIO-July-2015-Newsletter.pdf.

73. Miriam Jordan, "Remittances to Latin America Rose in 2014," *The Wall Street Journal*, February 25, 2015, www.wsj.com/articles/remittances-to-latin-america-rose-in-2014-1424901951.

74. "Digicel Haiti Revamps Mobile Money as 'Mon Cash,'" August 18, 2015, www.telegeography.com/products/commsupdate/articles/2015/08/18/digicel-haiti-revamps-mobile-money-as-mon-cash/.

75. Lucian Chauvin, "With Money Sent from U.S., Peruvians Buy Homes," *Christian Science Monitor*, July 13, 2005, 4.

76. Ibid.

77. "Western Union and Sogexpress Innovate: Remittances to Fund Renewable Energy in Haiti," *Investor Relations*, July 23, 2015, http://ir.westernunion.com/News/Press-Releases/Press-Release-Details/2015/Western-Union-and-Sogexpress-Innovate-Remittances-to-Fund-Renewable-Energy-in-Haiti/default.aspx.

78. Steven Kennedy, *A Global Partner for a Region on the Rise: The World Bank in Latin America and the Caribbean*, (Washington, DC: The World Bank, 2010).

79. OECD, www.oecd.org/dac/stats/documentupload/3%20America%20-%20Development%20Aid%20at%20a%20Glance%202016.pdf.

80. Ibid.

81. "2030 Agenda for Sustainable Development," *The United Nations Development Programme*, 2015, www.latinamerica.undp.org/content/rblac/en/home/post-2015/sdg-overview.html.

82. "Building the Post-2015 Development Agenda," *The United Nations Development Programme*, April 21, 2015, www.latinamerica.undp.org/content/undp/en/home/librarypage/mdg/building-the-post-2015-development-agenda/.

83. Jeffrey D. Sachs, *The End of Poverty* (New York: Penguin, 2005), 299.

84. "2030 Agenda for Sustainable Development," *The United Nations Development Programme*, 2015, www.latinamerica.undp.org/content/rblac/en/home/post-2015/sdg-overview.html.

85. Kennedy, *A Global Partner for a Region on the Rise*.

86. Ibid.

87. "Giving USA 2016" as discussed at www.cafamerica.org/remarkable-rise-international-giving/.

88. De la Torre and Schmukler, *Whither Latin American Capital Markets?*

89. Augusto de la Torre, Alain Ize, and Sergio L. Schmukler. *LAC Success Put to Test*. (Washington, DC: World Bank, 2011, http://documents.worldbank.org/curated/en/401231468270863901/LAC-success-put-to-test.

90. ECLAC, Social Panorama 2007.

91. See the structural fiscal balance databases from the IDB, https://publications.iadb.org/handle/11319/6979.

92. ECLAC, *Latin American and Caribbean Economies Will Show a Moderate Recovery in 2018 and Grow 2.2% Preliminary Overview of the Economies of Latin America and the Caribbean 2017*, 14 December 2017.

93. T. Friedman, "The Golden Straitjacket," *The Lexus and the Olive Tree* (New York: Anchor Books, 2000), 101–111.

94. Augusto de la Torre, Federico Filippini and Alain Ize, "The Commodity Cycle in Latin America: Mirages and Dilemmas," LAC Semiannual Report (Washington, DC: World Bank, 2016), https://openknowledge.worldbank.org/handle/10986/24014 License: CC BY 3.0 IGO.

95. Dani Rodrik, *The Inescapable Trilemma of the World Economy*, http://rodrik.typepad.com/dani_rodriks_weblog/2007/06/the-inescapable.html

96. Eduardo Cavallo and Tomás Serebrisky, *Saving for Development: How Latin America and the Caribbean Can Save More*, Inter-American Development Bank, 2016.

97. Saving for Development IADB report.

98. Francesco Grigoli, Alexander Herman, and Klaus Schmidt-Hebbel, *Saving in Latin America and the Caribbean: Performance and May 2015*, www.imf.org/external/pubs/ft/wp/2015/wp15108.pdf.

99. Cavallo and Serebrisky, *Saving for Development*.

100. Liliana Rojas-Suarez, "Financial Inclusion in Latin America: Facts and Obstacles," Volume 439 Working Paper (Center for Global Development) Washington, DC: Center for Global Development, 2016

101. "Financial Inclusion in Paraguay: New Mobile Money Regulation July 2014," www.gsma.com/latinamerica/financial-inclusion-in-paraguay-new-mobile-money-regulation.

102. Cavallo and Serebrisky, "Saving for Development."

103. Time to Act.

CONTEMPORARY TRADE POLICY

Engine or Brakes for Growth?

CHAPTER SEVEN

Trade in agricultural products is central—but perhaps not enough—to sustain exports. *(Courtesy of the Inter-American Development Bank)*

After the debt crisis of the 1980s and the global shift towards open markets, trade liberalization became the center of economic reform in Latin America. Without cheap external financing, the internal orientation of import substitution industrialization (ISI) was not viable over time. Liberalization of trade was seen as the new engine for growth. Yet even without the financing constraint, many analysts argued that an open trading regime is preferable to a closed model. As globalization of trade, finance, and production came to define the international agenda, an external orientation was widely adopted as the only strategy compatible with global trends. This chapter provides the theoretical framework to evaluate the free trade argument.

But some of the concerns of the ISI period about the vulnerability of less-powerful nations competing in a trading arena dominated by industrial giants remain. We will consider these objections and analyze policies consistent with an open trading regime that may mitigate some of the costs. To enhance the gains from trade, some policymakers advocate economic integration with other regional partners. We will therefore analyze the benefits of subregional integration as well as the progress toward a hemispheric free trade agreement. Different strategies have different risks and opportunities. Free trade with a large number of partners should be weighed against the possible trade-diverting effects of integration. The effects of trade policy choices on the environment and equitable growth will also be discussed.

The following questions will orient this chapter:

- What are the theoretical benefits of free trade?
- What concerns do some analysts have with the free trade model?
- What has been the record of liberalization in the region?
- Who trades what and why?
- Why and how have countries entered into subregional trading arrangements?
- Who wins and loses with trade?

THEORETICAL BENEFITS OF FREE TRADE

Economists have long been enamored with the gains from free trade. In 1776 Adam Smith posited trade as the answer to a central development question: How do nations become wealthy? In contrast to the mercantilist, state-centered policies of the seventeenth and eighteenth centuries in Europe, Smith countered that nations become wealthy through open trade with each other. For Smith, open markets encouraged individuals to pursue greedy self-interest—the surplus of which could be traded for overall gain, generating good for all.

David Ricardo, in the nineteenth century, provided the conceptual underpinnings for the theoretical argument for free trade: the **theory of comparative advantage**. In a classical model, where all factors of production can be reduced to the labor required to produce them, Ricardo showed that if each country produces the good it is relatively best at producing, world output would increase. Even if a country is absolutely better in both growing wheat and producing engines, if in comparison to another country it is relatively better at engine production, it should build engines and leave wheat to be grown elsewhere. The gains derive from the benefits of specialization.

To understand the gains, first imagine that there is no trade. Each country must produce both wheat and engines. Given scarce resources (a fixed supply of labor), a certain quantity of each good can be produced. Because there are only two goods in this hypothetical model, we can create an internal trading price of how much wheat it would take to buy an engine. For example, we might find that each engine costs one hundred bales of wheat, or each wheat bale trades for one one-hundredth of an engine. Now drop our imaginary trade barriers. In another country, each engine might cost two hundred bales of wheat or each wheat bale one two-hundredth of an engine. An engine costs more here, but wheat costs less—one two-hundredth rather than one one-hundredth of an engine. By specializing in the product you are relatively better in, you can produce that product more cheaply than in the other country. Furthermore, your country may produce both goods more efficiently than the other. In this case it should produce the good it is relatively best at; because you are not using scarce labor to produce the good that you are only second best at, your labor can focus on engines, your star performer.

This is analogous to the often-told story of the lawyer who can type faster than her secretary. Should the lawyer type her own briefs? The answer is no, because the secretary can't appear in court to try the cases. With each person doing what she is relatively best at, the law firm will make more money. The same logic is extended to countries. Even if the United States can produce textiles and cars more cheaply than Guatemala, if textiles can be produced relatively less expensively in Guatemala, there are gains from trade.

The **Heckscher-Ohlin theorem** extends the concept of comparative advantage to a two-factor model, incorporating capital with labor. In the Heckscher-Ohlin model, factor proportions determine the direction of trade. A country relatively well endowed with labor should produce and export labor-intensive goods; the country with a larger proportion of capital than labor should focus on capital-intensive products. Relative costs once again drive the two-factor model. In a country where labor is abundant relative to capital, the excess supply of labor will make for lower wages, and the scarcity of capital will exact higher interest rates. Producing labor-intensive products will allow the labor-abundant country to bring the cost advantage of the cheaper labor to the international market.

Two corollaries to the Heckscher-Ohlin theorem extend its range to include distributional implications. The **Stolper-Samuelson effect** indicates that if a labor-abundant country produces cheap labor-intensive goods, over time the increased international demand for these goods will raise their price and by association the price of their key input, labor. The Stolper-Samuelson effect therefore predicts that trade will initially benefit the least well-off—the poor workers. As more people in the world demand Guatemalan textiles, workers should share in the rewards. A second corollary, the **factor price equalization theorem**, suggests that as wages increase in the labor-abundant country (and fall in the capital-rich country), international prices of labor and capital will each converge. Therefore, at least in theory, there should be greater equality of prices for each factor in the international economy: both wage rates and interest rates should be nearly equal in all markets. Of course, this implies that there may be a social price, including unemployment, in the country where wages are rising. Of course developing countries—for example Mexico—might not be satisfied with the outcomes of a model that reinforces the status quo—low capital versus labor. The Heckscher-Ohlin theorem is static—it begins with existing stocks of capital and labor and not the future flows of increased capital to which capital developing countries aspire. More on that shortly.

Does Liberalization Deliver Promised Gains?

Free trade advocates therefore contend that by producing in accord with comparative advantage, global output and income distribution will improve. In May 1978, Carlos Díaz Alejandro, a Cuban economist teaching at Columbia, wrote an article in the *American Economic Review* questioning the theory of free trade in practice.[1] Using the construct of a Martian landing on Earth, he challenged readers to explain why, if the theory of free trade is so compelling, hadn't the gains from trade been more apparent in developing countries? Why were countries still so poor? Why were the poor workers in these countries still suffering? Why hadn't the prices of capital and labor equalized?

The results of the free trade model as applied to the real economy motivated ISI. Many economists in the developing world believed that free market trade theory wasn't benefiting the least well-off. Indeed, the theory itself doesn't predict necessarily which country will gain from the increased production in trade but simply that there will be gains to global welfare. In practice, developing countries perceived that the gains were accruing to the powerful industrial countries, leaving the periphery further and further behind. In particular, we remember the problem of declining terms of trade from Chapter 2's discussion of dependency theory; control of technology in the center made it more and more difficult for the periphery countries to export a sufficient quantity of goods to purchase the high-tech products. For the South, trade was therefore impoverishing. Dependence on commodity exports left countries open to export price instability. Furthermore, rather than trade improving the lives of poor workers, the belief was that multinational corporations were exploiting the cheap labor in the periphery and keeping the additional profits for themselves.

In addition to the dependency critique, three other negative assessments of the results of trade emerged: the environmental, gender, and welfare dimensions. Environmentalists fear that specialization in accord with comparative advantage further encourages countries to base their economies on agricultural export crops such as timber, bananas, soya, or coffee, that can be environmentally damaging. Pressures to export create unsustainable burdens on the environment. Environmentalists are also concerned that in an open global trading system, companies seeking to reduce production costs will flee to those countries in the developing world with the lowest environmental standards or lax enforcement. Some point out that global standards may actually improve when trade agreements explicitly engage these targets. Those concerned about the gender implications of free trade point to the cases of multinational production exploiting a cheap female labor force in the developing world. With double obligations in the home and in the factory, women find it difficult to organize; low wages and poor working conditions result. The gender critique is part of a larger literature questioning the welfare effects on trade.

Despite the theoretical predictions of benefiting the least well-off, some contend that trade accentuates poverty and inequality with an overall decline in national welfare. As countries open to trade in the global value chain, production may move to the lowest price producer. The poor lack the assets of education and training that contribute to higher value-added exports—and they fall further behind. Commodity exports also tend to reward a small group of skilled workers in mining, leaving others outside the boom. Empirical evidence, however, is inconclusive—perhaps due to the interactions of opening to trade and finance as well as the important role of domestic policies in managing the welfare effects of trade.[2] As some in an economy benefit from globalization, others are left behind. Indigenous populations and national cultures lose local vibrancy in a world flattened by McMinimization and Walmart sourcing. Those marginalized are all too frequently women. Box 7.1 illustrates some of the trade-offs between trade in accord with comparative advantage and negative externalities of trade in the case of cut flowers in Ecuador.

BOX 7.1.   FLOWER POWER OR TAINTED COLORS? MANAGING THE EFFECTS OF SOCIAL EFFECTS OF TRADE IN ECUADOR

The flower industry in Ecuador has blossomed. A wide variety of microclimates, the equatorial sun, and the country's cool Andean Valley make for prime growing conditions. The industry got its boost in 1991 when the Andean Trade Preferences Act opened tax-free exports to the United States. Fresh cut flowers went from almost 0 to 9 percent of Ecuador's export earnings—third place behind traditional exports of oil and bananas.[a] Ecuador provides 20 percent of US flower imports, a market segment growing as supermarkets and discount stores have brought competitively priced flowers to fill American vases. Niche products of tropical varieties are also giving a boost to biotrade from the Andean region. The development agency of the Andean Community of Nations, CAF, has been working with small- and medium-size growers, rural communities, and indigenous groups to promote sustainable agroexports.[b]

Valentine's Day is the peak of the selling season. Approximately three hundred Ecuadorian growers, many owned by Dutch or Colombian partners, gear up for the homage to love. Crop management is labor intensive, particularly with roses, Ecuador's top floral product. Workers carefully monitor the plant's progress, providing irrigation and protection from disease. The plants are carefully harvested, hydrated, and wrapped and within twenty-four hours are placed on a plane for Miami. There they clear customs, particularly the strict US Department of Agriculture (USDA) animal and plant inspection for pests or disease. Firms such as UPS's Big Brown maintain the "cool cycle" until they arrive to the delighted recipient—"'Nothing would ruin a Valentine moment faster than dried up flowers,' said a company spokesman."[c]

But the reality of the flower industry is far less romantic. Peak harvesting is exhausting, as lax labor legislation and weak unions keep workers in the field for 60 grueling hours a week. Flower workers normally have short-term fixed contracts without job security, pensions, maternity leave, or health insurance.[d] The minimum wage of US$145 a month barely covers subsistence—and overtime is not paid. Pushed to work quickly to make production quotas, rose thorns prick workers' hands. Because only edible crops are inspected by the USDA for pesticide residue, intensive chemicals are applied daily. Workers are generally not well protected; the International Labor Organization (ILO) found that only 22 percent of workers were familiar with chemical safety techniques. The Pan American Health Organization (PAHO) has documented a nearly sevenfold increase in pesticide intoxication cases since 1990.[e] Pesticide poisoning raises the rate of spontaneous abortion and premature birth.[f] Pesticides also contaminate rivers and water systems.

continued

continued

The ILO estimates that 20 percent of the seasonal flower workers are children. Approximately 70 percent of the workers are women. Although the flora culture export sector has opened new off-farm work opportunities for women, harassment and illegal pregnancy testing have been documented in the firms. Flower companies strongly retaliate against attempts at unionization to improve workers' conditions.[g] "The companies are organized among themselves and they have a list on the Internet of the people who have tried to unionize or have unionized," said Olga Tutillo, a labor union leader at one of the four farms that are unionized. "If someone tries to create a union, the company threatens to fire them and says they won't be able to find another job. These are the famous blacklists."[h]

Is the flower trade therefore bad for Ecuadorian workers? Were the workers better off unemployed or in lower-paid jobs? Two important lessons can be taken from this case. First, opening up to the international sector without adequate institutions to manage the opportunities and minimize the damage of trade is likely to impose new social costs. For example, the Ecuadorian government is now launching a campaign to reduce child labor and strengthen inspection and monitoring of conditions. Stronger labor legislation and enforcement can help improve the lives of the flower workers.

Second, markets themselves can also help. Germany, for example, launched the Flower Label Program in 1999 to require growers to sign an International Code of Conduct for the socially and environmentally sustainable production of cut flowers. Life for workers in the 10 percent of Ecuador's companies covered by the certification standards has improved.[i] None of these firms use prohibited pesticides, and workers are protected by permanent contracts. One example is the Bouqs company; it requires its growers produce third-party certification from fair trade groups such as the Rainforest Alliance that they are not using any "red label" or highly toxic chemicals. Bouqs buys directly from the farmers, eliminating middle markets and returning more to small communities.[j] But the demand for certification of fair labor standards—or for flowers produced under organic conditions—has been weak in the United States. Until American consumers decide they are willing to pay for "sustainable" romance, Ecuadorian workers are likely to be the ones to suffer.

---

a. Larry Sawers, "Nontraditional or New Traditional Exports," *Latin American Research Review* 40(3) (October 2005): 1.

b. "Ecuadorian 2004 Flower Exports at \$314 M," *Latin America News Digest*, January 13, 2005.

c. "On Valentine's Day, Cupid Is Dressed in Brown," *Canada NewsWire*, February 10, 2005.

d. ILRF, "Codes of Conduct in the Cut-Flower Industry," Working Paper, September 2003, www.laborrights.org/projects/women.

e. "Share the Love with Flower Workers," Pesticide Action Network Updates Service (PANUPS), February 7, 2006.

f. PAHO Basic Indicators Data Base Educator, accessed March 2006.

g. "Do We Not Bleed?," *Multinational Monitor* 26(1/2) (January–February 2005): 37–40.

h. "Respect the Rights of Cut-Flowers Workers," www.unionvoice.org/campaign/RosasDelEcuador.

i. Stephanie Cuttler, "Valentine's Day Consumer Alert #2: Cut Flowers," *Calvert News*, January 31, 2006, www.calvert.com/news.

j. Michelle Z. Donahue, "These Flowers Come Straight from the Farm to Your Door," Read more: www.smithsonianmag.com/innovation/these-flowers-come-straight-farm-your-door-180962151/#z1fcFlwKf7tY8KSb.99.

It is important to focus policy attention on the intersection between trade and economic inequality. As Diana Tussie notes, trade policy is an inherently distributive instrument. That is, employment in import-competing sectors is exchanged for employment in export-oriented sectors—creating both losers and winners. These trade-offs need to be made more explicit within the context of domestic policy making. Markets are social constructions, embedded in sociopolitical systems, advises Tussie. With globalization, developing-country governments face less and less flexibility in establishing the domestic parameters within which their markets function. Attention to the effects of trade on poverty and social exclusion is critical in considering policy interventions to improve the position of the losers in the global trading arena.[3]

HAS TRADE PROMOTED GROWTH?

The record of liberalization throughout the world has raised the question of when greater openness has promoted growth. This has been an important policy question without convincing answers. A slew of empirical studies measured the effects of openness on growth, but a definitive relationship has not been established. Part of the problem is that the empirical relationship is full of nuances, the database is imperfect, it is difficult to define just what is meant by openness, and countries whose incomes are high for reasons not related to trade may have high trade ratios.[4] There is a great deal of heterogeneity in the extent to which growth rose after trade,[5] and trade opening is not implemented in isolation but as a part of a package of policy initiatives. Three seminal studies have framed the policy debate on trade and growth. David Dollar found that higher levels of trade distortion were associated with lower levels of growth. His research underscores the theoretical lesson of the free trade argument. Among globalizing developing countries in the period 1970–1990, those with open trade regimes grew at 5.0 percent per capita; nonglobalizing developing countries struggled along at 1.4 percent. The conclusion of this body of work indicates that trade does seem to create higher growth.[6] This protrade stance was confirmed by Jeffrey Sachs and Andrew Warner who, after controlling for other policy variables such as investment and government spending, find their openness index to be related to the growth rate of per capita gross domestic product (GDP).[7] Incorporating new data, Wacziarg and Welch suggest that over the 1950–1998 period, countries that liberalized their trade regimes experienced average annual growth rates that were about 1.5 percentage points higher than before liberalization. Post liberalization investment rates rose 1.5–2.0 percentage points, confirming past findings that liberalization fosters growth in part through its effect on physical capital accumulation.[8]

Francisco Rodriguez and Dani Rodrik criticize the findings that trade brings growth, showing instead that there is no guarantee of faster growth with trade.[9] They suggest that these findings are less robust than claimed due to complexity in measuring openness, statistically sensitive specifications, the colinearity of protectionist policies with other bad policies, and other econometric problems. The results of the Rodriguez and Rodrik studies have focused attention on the complexity of the trade and growth relationship. Simply lowering trade barriers will not increase growth. Rather, as Robert Baldwin concludes, to promote growth changes in trade policy must be complemented by prudent macroeconomic management and corruption-free, transparent policies.[10] Of particular importance is the management of the exchange rate such that appreciation does not choke off export price competitiveness and encourage a flood of imports. This was the case Christoph Ernst reports in Brazil and Argentina, where an emerging specialization in dynamic manufacturing was slowed by exchange rate appreciations driven by primary and semi-processed exports booms.[11] Latin American commodity exporters with currencies buoyed by Chinese demand for minerals and food found strong exchange rates a barrier to competitiveness in the manufacturing sector. But it is hard to come up with the counterfactual in the modern global economy of closed and insulated economies growing faster than open markets. The giant leaps of the Chinese economy stand as an example of the effects of opening. However, as with the experience of China, it is not trade alone but the set of complementary policies that will shape the long-term growth rate and the welfare implications for the nation.

In addition to the predicted gains in resource allocation from trade in accord with comparative advantage, new protrade arguments began to dominate the liberalization debate. Openness to the international market brings with it better access to technologies and inputs to production and a wider array of intermediate and final goods. An economy producing for the international market is also better positioned to take advantage of economies of scale in production. Also important is the fact that opening borders to the influx of new products as well as investment by multinational firms encourages competition in the domestic market. Oligopolistic power to set prices enjoyed by large firms in protected domestic markets is pressured by the competition of international markets. Production under conditions of competition not only encourages lower prices but also provides incentives to produce goods more efficiently. The shake-up of domestic industries from the challenge of international competition may create a Schumpeterian effect as firms adapt to the new business environment.[12] Participation in the international market opens firms to new ideas and the transfer of knowledge that define success in the global economy. Indeed, improvements in productivity rates have been correlated with periods of liberalization in Latin America.[13]

How Should Trade Liberalization Be Implemented?

No country has grown over time by turning its back on trade and capital flows. However, simply opening up to trade without building institutions to manage its social and environmental costs is a risky approach.[14] Despite the gains from liberalization over time, there are also short-run costs. Tearing down trade barriers can decimate inefficient firms, putting large numbers of employees out of work. The costs to the losers in trade have increasingly become political dynamite. Global trade has come under attack from protectionist and nationalist fronts pushing back against globalization. The time path of liberalization is therefore important. How quickly should it proceed? Should industries gradually adapt to international price signals, giving them time to modernize or become more efficient? In contrast, does a gradualist approach prolong the agony of adjustment, suggesting that a quick, tough shock, although painful, might be preferable? Some research indicates that a staged process of tariff reduction works best. In the first stage, tariffs might be brought down to a uniform rate of, say, 50 percent. After industries adapt to this structure, tariffs could be lowered to an across-the-board 10 percent rate. However, others suggest that a quick and thorough opening of the external sector is an important element in establishing credibility in the seriousness of the reform process.

In addition to the question of the time path, liberalization should be seen in the context of a package of policies to maximize its benefits. Trade liberalization without an appropriate exchange rate is dangerous. If a currency is or becomes overvalued and trade barriers are low, the country will face an explosion of imports, and exporters will find it difficult to sell goods internationally. Trade liberalization may also need to be accompanied by short-term incentives from the state (perhaps financed through multilateral agencies) for export promotion. The Asian export model does not indicate a pure free market but rather one in which the state selectively promoted the growth of the export sector. In particular, firms that have been producing for domestic consumption need to learn international marketing. They may also need state assistance in the form of trade missions and financing to establish themselves abroad. This selective model allows trade to benefit from social networks. Trade opportunities don't just magically appear; networks such as ethnic Chinese business networks and/or regional production networks with Japan take cultivation. Whether its nationwide or selective, trade liberalization works best when it is preceded by fiscal reform. If internal consumption—either public or private—is too high, the surplus for export disappears. Relieving pressures on the internal balance facilitates the generation of an external equilibrium. Without fiscal reform, internal interest rates may become too high, attracting short-term financial capital, leading to an appreciation of the exchange rate, and thwarting export efforts. It is clear that trade liberalization must be seen in the context of overall structural reform.

The Record of Liberalization in Latin America

Despite growth and equity concerns, in the 1990s liberalization was on the agenda of nearly every nation in the region. Why? Economic imbalances had built up under ISI. The overvalued exchange rates typical of the period resulted in a bias against exports. By 1981, regional current account deficits had reached US$42 billion annually. In 1982, no country had a positive current account balance. If you import more than you export, someone has to pay for it. As capital dried up due to the debt crisis, current account deficits became unsustainable without external financing.

In contrast to deteriorating performance in Latin America stood the successful export-oriented growth model in Asia, which was capturing the attention of multilateral agencies as well as governments. Although the Asian model also relied in good part on an active role for the state, the International Monetary Fund (IMF), the World Bank, and the Inter-American Development Bank (IADB) came to promote trade liberalization as an engine of growth. It is also important to note the change in the global context. The process of globalization—the integration of production and trade structures, the expansion of international financial markets, and the information revolution that knows no borders—had transformed the way states and firms participated in the international economy. The game went global. The world had changed, and Latin America needed to change with it.

Average tariff rates in Latin America declined significantly following adjustment to macroeconomic crises in the early 1980s and 1990s. The average tariff for the region was nearly 50 percent in 1985, with rates as high as 80 percent in Brazil and Colombia. By 2002, average tariffs in the region had come down to just above 10.4 percent, a radical transformation in the structure of the economies. There is far less dispersion in rates, signaling the consensus view that open economies are more conducive to growth. In table 7.1 we can see the high rates and variability in the tariff structure in the pre-reform period. Although Argentina, Brazil, Mexico, and Peru retain higher than average tariff rates, they are relatively close to the low tariff countries of Bolivia, Chile, and Paraguay. Most of the reductions were introduced gradually over the period to soften the adjustment effects on industries, but in cases such as Peru, the tariff surgery was radical and swift, with rates falling from 68.05 percent in 1990 to 17.63 percent in 1992. Since the early 2000s, tariff rates have remained more or less constant. There has been less variability in tariff rates; in 2014 the highest rate was Argentina at 15.9 and the lowest was Peru at 3.2 (which has continued to decline since the 1980s). The majority of rates in Latin American countries were between 6 and 10 percent, still much higher than the global average of 2.88 in 2014.[15]

Table 7.1.   Average Tariff in Latin America: Selected Years, 1985–2014 (percentage)

Country	Mid-80s	Late 80s	Mid-90s	2000–2002	2010	2014
Argentina	28.0	43.7	14.0	12.2	16.0	15.9
Bolivia	20.0	18.6	9.7	9.3	9.9	10.7
Brazil	80.0	50.6	12.6	12.3	11.4	11.6
Chile	36.0	15.1	11.0	7.0	6.0	6.0
Colombia	83.0	47.6	11.4	11.7	12.0	6.5
Costa Rica	53.0	n/a	11.7	6.0	7.2	6.4
Ecuador	50.0	39.9	11.2	11.3	10.1	10.1
El Salvador	23.0	n/a	9.2	7.3	6.2	6.2
Guatemala	50.0	n/a	10.8	6.9	5.9	6.0
Honduras	n/a	41.9	17.9	6.1	6.4	6.1
Mexico	34.0	10.6	13.7	16.4	6.9	6.1
Nicaragua	54.0	n/a	17.4	5.1	6.2	6.1
Panama	n/a	33.0	n/a	8.9	8.3	7.9
Paraguay	71.7	19.3	9.4	10.7	8.8	8.8
Peru	64.0	67.8	16.3	13.5	5.0	3.2
Uruguay	32.0	27.0	9.6	11.4	9.3	9.5
Venezuela	30.0	33.8	11.8	12.2	n/a	12.0
Latin America	49.98	33.99	12.35	10.43	n/a	8.31

Source: Data from IADB. Available online at www.iadb.org.
Note: The tariff history of each country corresponds to different years, depending on the availability of information.

   Lower tariffs and free access of goods to the region without high taxes were accompanied by a surge in growth of exports of goods and services from the region. With liberalization in the mid-1990s, as import barriers came down the goods came pouring in, leading to current account deficits throughout the region. The strong demand that China has exerted in international markets propelled export growth above imports. Table 7.2 shows the dramatic changes in most countries of the importance of exports in the overall economy that occurred between the 1980s and today, particularly in Central America. But as remarkable as the growth was in the 1990s, Latin America remained less export driven than Asia. China's entrance into the global trading arena in 2001 substantially changed trade geography. Despite declining growth, China is still exerting influence in the region, particularly as the West becomes increasingly isolationist. We'll come back to China's role in a bit.

   Although Latin America accounts for 8.2 percent of global economic activity, it only registers 5.1 percent of global exports of goods and services. The region is less open than other developing areas, with imports and exports together only representing 44 percent of GDP.[16] Considerable variable exists, with openness ranging from 25 to 125 percent of GDP. In Brazil and Argentina—despite being global agricultural players—exports and imports only account for 27.5 percent and 24 percent of GDP, while small Central American countries are more reliant

Table 7.2.   Exports of Goods and Services (% of GDP)

	1985	1990	1995	2000	2005	2010	2014
Argentina	11.7	10.4	9.7	11	20.9	17.4	14.8
Bolivia	19.0	22.8	22.6	18.3	35.5	41.2	43.3
Brazil	12.2	8.2	7.4	10.2	15.2	10.7	11.5
Chile	28.1	34.0	29.3	29.3	38.4	38.1	33.8
Colombia	13.8	20.6	14.5	15.9	16.8	15.9	16.0
Costa Rica	27.1	30.2	37.6	48.6	48.5	38.2	35.1
Ecuador	19.7	22.8	21.3	32.1	27.6	27.9	28.6
El Salvador	22.3	18.6	21.6	27.4	25.6	25.9	25.8
Guatemala	11.9	21	19.3	20.2	25.1	25.8	23.1
Honduras	25.1	37.2	43.7	54.0	59.0	45.8	46.9
Mexico	15.4	18.6	25.2	26.3	26.6	29.9	32.4
Nicaragua	14.8	24.9	16.1	20.1	16.6	38.4	42.3
Panama	68.6	86.8	100.7	72.6	75.5	70.6	n/a
Paraguay	n/a	n/a	61.7	46.8	58.2	55.1	46.8
Peru	27.5	16.1	12.9	16.8	26.6	26.6	22.4
Uruguay	26.8	23.5	19	16.7	30.4	26.3	23.4
Venezuela, RB	24.1	39.5	27.1	29.7	39.7	28.5	n/a
Latin America & Caribbean	n/a	n/a	n/a	n/a	n/a	n/a	22.9

Source: World Development Indicators database.
Definition: Exports of goods and services represent the value of all goods and other market services provided to the rest of the world. They include the value of merchandise, freight, insurance, transport, travel, royalties, license fees, and other services, such as communication, construction, financial, information, business, personal, and government services. They exclude labor and property income (formerly called factor services) as well as transfer payments.

on imported goods and services. Nicaragua and Honduras have openness indicators in excess of 100 percent. Mexico, although large, has parlayed integration with the United States into an open trading profile with 66.53 percent in 2012. This variation is important in understanding differing responses in the region to trade shocks.

Trade Imbalances

Liberalization of trade does not, of course, imply that a country's trade accounts will be balanced. Improvement in exports will still result in a deteriorating trade balance if outpaced by an increase in imports. Unless this trade deficit is matched by strong inflow of capital to finance the gap, the country may quickly find itself with balance of payments problems. Throughout the mid-1990s, the strong increase in exports of goods was accompanied by continued demand for the import of services, leaving the region with a negative balance on goods and services. Financial inflows compensated for this balance in 1995 and 2000. By 2002, rising commodity prices pushed exports over imports. However, by 2015 China's slowdown prompted a drop in commodity prices that hurt Latin American economies.[17] Promoting a sustainable global balance that does not draw down reserves or necessitate IMF interventions is a delicate process. External variables, including the performance of the global economy, play havoc with national accounts. One mechanism to attempt to decrease some of the extra regional effects of trade disturbance has been to pursue regional trade integration. However, as we will see below with the effects of the Brazilian currency crisis on **Mercosur**, there may be some unintended effects in the transmission of disturbances within the region.

Chile provides an interesting example of trade liberalization. From an average tariff level of 105 percent at the time of the military coup in 1973—with some tariffs reaching more than 700 percent—Chile unilaterally implemented a 10 percent tariff rate within four years of the start of the Pinochet government. How did such a radical and rapid restructuring of the economy take place?[18] Five stages distinguished the Chilean process. After a dramatic reduction of trade barriers as part of a comprehensive stabilization package that included a real exchange rate devaluation in the first stage (1974–1979), the second stage (1979–1982) was characterized by exchange rate overvaluation when the peso became the anti-inflationary anchor. During the third stage (1983–1985) Chile suffered through a temporary reversal during a deep economic crisis and suffered deindustrialization, while in the fourth (1985–1990) liberalization accompanied recovery. With the transition to democracy in the final stage (1991–), Chile began its turn to preferential trading agreements to complement its unilateral liberalization; to date it has entered into twenty-seven agreements. The Chilean government subsidized agriculture to ease the transition and promote the sale of Chilean products such as wine and salmon abroad. Chilean performance confirms Rodrik's proposition regarding the need for an enhanced role for the state in an open economy. The government's involvement also facilitated the infrastructure necessary for trade growth—as will be discussed in our competitiveness chapter.

Composition of Goods

As shown in figure 7.1, the type of goods that Latin America is exporting to the rest of the world has changed over recent decades. With the aid of the **North American Free Trade Agreement (NAFTA)** and strong liberalization policies, Mexico has diversified significantly. Mexico is also concentrated in oil, but its integration into the North American automotive manufacturing market further defines its export list. Mercosur shows significant diversification, with a mix of primary products such as soy and poultry with manufactured exports in passenger motor cars and aircraft. The commodity boom of 2002–2012, however, redirected production toward the agricultural sector. Natural resources—crude petroleum, gold, and coal—form the base for the Andean nations, with agricultural exports comprising the bulk of their other exports. Likewise, Chile has a very strong concentration in copper and its derivatives; more than half its exports are tied to the commodity. Nonetheless, it has also managed to develop other high-value export markets in fish and wine. Panama remains grounded in fish and agricultural products, while the Central American common market countries furthered diversification into light machinery, textiles, and medical supplies. Diversification matters; a 25 percent reduction in product concentration can increase the region's per capita growth by 1 percentage point. As we enter into lower GDP growth rates, this is significant.[19]

Figure 7.1.   Composition of Exports by Sector

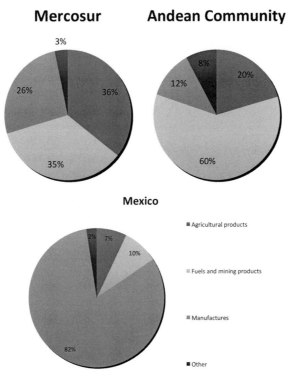

The historical problems of geographic market concentration and export price instability discussed in Chapter 2 continue to plague the region. As shown in Table 7.3, Latin America sends the bulk of its exports—nearly half—to the large North American market. About one-fifth of its trade is with Europe. An increasing amount is being sent to Asia, particularly the voracious Chinese market, which grew from 1.8 percent of merchandise exports in 2000 to 8.8 percent in 2015. This increase came from both the North American and the intraregional shares. Figure 7.2 shows the dramatic changes in commodity prices over time. In inflation-adjusted dollars,

Table 7.3.   Latin America's Top Five Trading Partners

Export Market	(US$ Mil)	Import Source	(US$ Mil)
United States	376,265.5449	United States	267,621.7100
China	73,503.41814	China	150,600.3150
Brazil	21,719.14478	Germany	33,391.5967
Netherlands	18,962.22606	Brazil	33,362.6312
Canada	18,623.9116	Japan	28,739.6632

Source: World Bank, UNCTAD, UNSD and the WTO: World Integrated Trade Solution (WITS) https://wits.worldbank.org/about_wits.html.

Figure 7.2.   Export Prices of Primary Commodities, 2005–2016

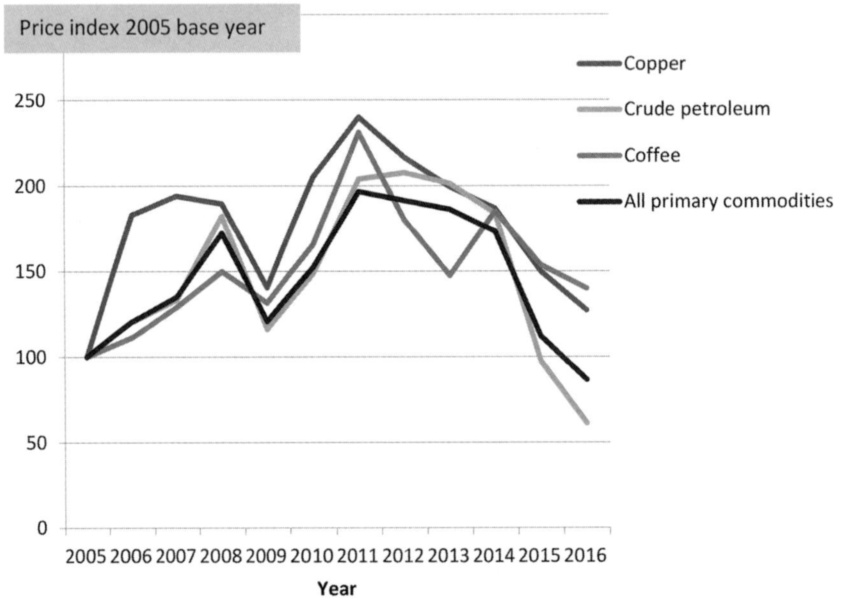

Source: World Trade Organization, wto.org, Table A67.

coffee peaked in 2011 then dropped to about two-thirds of its price in 2013; copper fell from its 2011 peak by half in 2015. For small farmers in particular, losing 50–65 percent of income is devastating.[20] Copper has taken the most dramatic ride in prices. Chinese integration into the global economy bid up the prices of raw materials and agricultural commodities. Sugar prices continue to trend upward propelled by multiple uses for the commodity not only as a sweetener but also as an energy crop. The question, of course, is how sugar producers will manage the wide swings in price variation.[21] Even these price booms of copper, soy, and crude oil have the downside of Dutch Disease, sucking resources into these sectors while depleting others.

THE NEW GEOGRAPHY OF INTERNATIONAL TRADE: WHERE TO FOCUS TRADE OPENING

Latin American nations have incorporated trade as a central element of their development strategies. In a globalized world, the question is no longer one of inward versus external orientation but rather how Latin America will trade with the world. Trade generates winners and losers. How a country pursues the process of liberalization shapes the distribution and the timing of gains and losses. In Latin America, the first stage of opening to the international arena was driven in large part by IMF mandate or the desire to signal a change in the model of development. Chile and Mexico were among the early liberalizers, unilaterally reducing trade barriers to benefit from the inflow of cheaper imports and investment flows. Other countries such as Colombia and Peru were pushed toward liberalization by structural reform packages.

The period of the liberalization driven by policy decree has ended. The new approach engages trade liberalization by negotiation. With average tariff rates hovering at 3 percent, the gains from further liberalization must be achieved not by the benefits of lower-priced imports but rather by improving access to other countries' markets. Access is best achieved by negotiation on multilateral, regional, or bilateral levels. Trade policy, then, is no longer a simple economic calculation of tariff rates but rather a political balancing act of exchanging domestic opening (which may hurt certain sectors) for access to broader markets (which may help export sectors). Trade negotiations are a complicated calculus of bargaining power and market potential constrained by the bureaucratic capacity for intricate consultation and effective implementation. The key question facing Latin American nations is whether liberalization is most effectively pursued through multilateral negotiations through the World Trade Organization (WTO) or bilateral and subregional arrangements. Multiple tracks may be pursued, but Brazil, Argentina, and Venezuela in particular have chosen to strengthen subregional integration to enhance bargaining power at the hemispheric and global levels. Let us consider progress and pitfalls in each arena to assess the potential gains from liberalization for the region.

Nontraditional export crops have opened new opportunities for women but also added to their burden. *(Courtesy of the Inter-American Development Bank)*

Global Trade: Doha and Beyond

In 2001 trade ministers from WTO member countries meeting in Doha, Qatar, began a long and arduous process of trade negotiations with an important central focus: addressing the problems that developing countries face in international trade. The so-called Doha Development Agenda principally aimed to lower the barriers that developing countries face in highly protected agricultural markets in the industrial world—areas where many developing countries should have a comparative advantage—in exchange for opening of markets for investment and services in the South. Some analysts argued that the world would gain between $250 billion and $650 billion (half of which would accrue to developing countries) if high tariffs and subsidies, particularly those on protected agricultural commodities, were reduced. Other analysts have suggested that the gains are more modest, on the order of a one-off increase in world income of between US$40 billion and US$60 billion.[22]

The road to Doha was full of disruptions and detours. The power of the 100 developing countries of the 148 participating in this trade round distinguished it from earlier efforts at trade liberalization. Key Doha issues for Latin America included increasing the effectiveness of market opening, especially for agriculture; maintaining policy space for development through the WTO convention of the special and differential (S&D) treatment of developing countries; liberalizing of services, particularly the service of labor and movement of persons; and developing a transparent institutional framework to support trade.[23] Overall, the profound differences in priorities and approaches of WTO countries brought the Doha round to a shallow end. The failure of the Doha round undermined the legitimacy of multilateral agreements; as WTO director Roberto Azevedo argues, there will be costs with overly complicated and overlapping regional trade agreements. Only a global trade deal will effectively tackle issues like agricultural subsidies that affect every country.[24]

Although the Doha efforts to improve the rules for developing countries largely failed, some success was achieved in cases brought by developing countries pressuring the United States and Europe to uphold existing trade rules in sugar, cotton, and bananas. The 2010s show gains for developing countries. In February 2017, a historic deal called the Trade Facilitation Agreement struck in Bali entered into force for two-thirds of WTO member nations. This agreement reduces border bottlenecks and modernizes customs procedures, potentially delivering global economic gains of up to US$1 trillion annually, most of which benefit developing countries. Furthermore, this agreement contains provisions for technical assistance and capacity building in customs processing. While these cases are encouraging, there's still a long way to go in reducing what Roberto Azevedo refers to as long-standing distortions in the global trading system.[25]

The Chinese Challenge—Or the Asian Opportunity?

The rapid rise of China dramatically changed Latin America's insertion in international markets. Bilateral trade between China and Latin America grew exponentially since the early 2000s—from US$12 billion in 2000 to US$289 billion in 2013.[26] By 2015 China replaced the European Union as Latin America's second largest trading partner. As shown in table 7.4, exports to China are highly concentrated, primarily commodities from Argentina, Brazil, Chile, Peru, and Venezuela. Latin American imports of Chinese goods are largely manufactured goods, mimicking old North-South trade dependencies—but with a South-South twist.[27] Initially, China's rise generated an increase in commodity prices as its investment-intensive growth model drew heavily on raw materials. China accounted for one-third of the upsurge in global demand for petroleum and worldwide oil consumption. It represents more than half the demand for base metals. For the Latin American exporters of commodities—Brazilian soybeans, Chilean copper, and Venezuelan oil—China has been a great boon to export growth as it represented more than half of global demand for major base metals in recent years. Its large market size made China an international price maker, placing between first and third in the world as a market for copper, fertilizers, iron and steel, oilseeds; oils, plastics, electronics, optical, photographic, and medical devices.

But there are also pitfalls for the countries enjoying the commodity price boom. Students of Latin American history will recall the problems of Dutch Disease, with commodity price peaks sucking resources away from other sectors only to suffer a crash during a trough. The appreciation of Latin American currencies driven by the demand for their soya, beef, metals, and minerals made manufactured exports less competitive. As often happens with Dutch Disease, China invested heavily in the primary good sectors in these Latin American countries, exacerbating the problem.[28] Policymakers fear a recommodification of the region's exports, with a return to the region's historical dependence on natural resources and a resurgence of the commodity lottery. The structural change in the region's economy that reduced the percent of natural resources in the export from 52 percent in the early 1980s to 27 percent in the late 1990s is potentially being reversed with resource-based exports surging above the 50 percent mark again. As with earlier afflictions of Dutch Disease, the pull toward exports biases against imports; in this case, the particular Chinese variant is that Latin America's import of manufactured goods competes directly with manufacturing in the region.[29] That is, there is greater

Table 7.4.   Latin America and Caribbean Trade with China: Top Five Exports and Imports

LAC Exports to China		LAC Imports from China	
Soybeans and other oilseeds	19.2%	Telecommunications equipment	9.7%
Iron ore and concentrates	16.8%	Data processing machines	3.8%
Crude petroleum	11.8%	Optical instruments, apparatus	3.3%
Copper	11.4%	Ships, boats, floating structures	3.3%
Copper ores, concentrates	10.0%	Other electrical equipment	2.3%
Total, top 5	69.2%	Total, top 5	22.5%

Source: UN Comtrade as reproduced by Rebecca Ray and Kevin P. Gallagher, *China-Latin America Economic Bulletin* 2017-1, BU Global Economic Governance Initiative.

similarity in the export profiles of Latin American and China as compared to the region and the US; this can create displacement.

Although Mexico does not struggle with commodity prices as much as South American countries, China challenged its manufactured exports. Both Mexico and China export heavily to the US market and their export baskets look remarkably similar. While they are both working to diversify, China has diversified more thoroughly and invested heavily in its technology. As of 2013, China accounted for 32 percent of worldwide patent applications. China has yet to truly steal the American market from Mexico, but it remains a fierce competitor.

China's heavy share in primary products has had an adverse environmental effect in Latin America. South America exports mostly oil, minerals, metals, and agricultural products, all sectors that require large amounts of water, emit greenhouses gases, and deplete the natural resources. Overall, exports to China consume twice as much water for every dollar exported than the region's exports to the other parts of the world. Chinese companies have come to the region with investments in extractive industries to facilitate its resource pipeline. Chinese firms have been especially engaged in developing Peru's copper mining sector, investing more than US and Canadian firms combined.[30] Latin America's weak regulatory frameworks and generally inadequate governance, coupled with China's relative unfamiliarity with the region, has led to multiple socio-environmental conflicts between Chinese companies and surrounding communities. These conflicts reveal a need for a larger commitment to social and environmental issues. The region may find solutions in better coordination within Latin American governments, a larger commitment to corporate social responsibility in Chinese companies, or through increased supranational regulations.

In 2015 8 percent of Chile's GDP, 5 percent of Peru's, and 2.5 percent of Brazil's was tied to exports to China. China's transition to a more sustainable consumption-driven growth path will therefore impact mineral export countries. There's still positive news; if the current trend of integrating rural people into Chinese cities continues, agricultural exports from Latin America to feed urban dwellers in Beijing or Shanghai will still be needed.[31] China has 19 percent of the world population but only 7 percent of the world's farmland. As China continues to urbanize, this disparity likely will only increase. While agricultural exports to China have boomed, they are problematically concentrated in certain products from certain countries—largely soy, with its attendant environmental consequences. Latin America represents a strategic potential partner for China to meet agricultural demand—and therefore has expressed interest in expanding trade and investment in Latin America. President Xi vowed to double trade with Latin America and has taken steps towards this goal.

Expansion in the Chinese private banking sector has also increased Chinese investment in Latin America; as Gallagher notes, it surpassed the World Bank's and the Inter-American Development Bank's individual lending in 2016.[32] Although some fear increasing trade leads to an increase in inequality, the relationship between Chinese trade and inequality in Latin America has been complex. Surprisingly, Chinese trade has seemed to reduce inequality in some countries by boosting wages in primary product sectors while simultaneously dampening wages in manufacturing sectors. Though the latter likely hurts Latin America's long-run development, the former is certainly positive news for Latin America.[33]

As China and Latin America integrate further, it will be important for policymakers to take steps to mitigate the effects of Dutch Disease as well as improve environmental and social issues in the region. As Carol Wise points out, the twenty first century structural characteristics of Latin American economies differ from the period of classic North-South dependency. Deeper linkages to industrial production coexist in commodity export economies.[34] There are policies that governments might consider to mitigate the downsides of the China boom. Trade delegations and information-clearing mechanisms for Chinese markets, with special attention to the needs of small and medium enterprises, can be encouraged. The costs of exploring the Chinese market are high; grants to those who propose collaborative projects might generate new opportunities. The Chilean government taxes copper exports and invests this fund to promote innovation and competitiveness in research and development in nontraditional, agriculture-based exports and industries in which Chile has a comparative advantage.[35] Finally, it is important to recognize Paul Krugman's dictum that countries don't compete with each other—companies do. The growth of China need not be at the expense of Latin America, particularly if Latin governments use this period to build stronger institutions to support market-based growth of their firms.[36] As the Trump administration backs away from Latin America, China has only grown stronger in its commitment to the region. China has already surpassed the United States as South America's largest trading partner, will it eventually lead in all of Latin America?[37]

Subregional Building Blocks or Stumbling Blocks to Liberalization?

One response to Chinese challenges or American neglect is regionalism. **Regional integration** may assume different forms depending on the penchant for forfeiting national sovereignty in search of synergies and economies of scale in unification. There are four broad categories of trade integration: a **free trade area (FTA)**, a **customs union**, a **common market**, and an **economic union**. In a FTA, trade restrictions are abolished between participating countries, but each country maintains an independent trade policy and separate tariff rates with the rest of the world. In a bit of an ironic play on words, a FTA is actually a step away from pure free trade. Economists define free trade as an open, multilateral system in which countries do not define preferences for partners but simply buy the cheapest goods available in the global market. A FTA negotiates preferential status for member countries, diverging from pure unfettered trade. A customs union takes preferential arrangements a step further, establishing a common external tariff (CET) for the group, and a common market advances cooperation in other policy-making measures, such as agriculture and the social sector. Full economic integration, including a common monetary policy and a common currency, is an economic union. Because trade integration tends to occur on a regional basis to take advantage of geographic proximity, the different forms are sometimes lumped together as regional integration arrangements; **preferential trade agreements (PTAs)** take account of the fact that countries not sharing a geographic space are increasingly interested in opening new avenues for trade. To these categories of formal integration agreements we can also add less formal arrangements to promote cooperation.

Why pursue regional economic integration? Regional integration may create special opportunities to take advantage of economies of scale, allowing export diversification by producing for a larger market without producing for a global market. Absent trade restrictions and in the presence of a stable currency, trade might proceed as if it were between Massachusetts and Connecticut. Where labor training, technology, and long-term capital are scarce in developing markets, economies of scale may offer new opportunities to strengthen markets and create new sources of international competitiveness.[38] Regional trading arrangements may also be a means of moving beyond opening markets for goods to promote "deep integration" in trade in services, harmonization of regulatory regions, and the coordination of macroeconomic policies.[39] Regional trade arrangements may also be seen as a protective step toward freer trade. That is, countries gain some of the benefit from a larger market, but if they associate with partners with similar development levels, their industries will not be overwhelmed by more advanced and competitive international providers. Others worry about the losers in trade agreements; Box 7.2 shares the story of corn farmers in Mexico.

WTO Director Roberto Azevedo contends that PTAs are a step on the path toward free trade.[40] A free trade agreement can work to open protected markets, creating new sales opportunities. In particular, PTAs are pursued where market potential in services such as telecommunications and investment may open opportunities not covered by simply lowering tariffs. Countries with similar tastes and cultural

---

BOX 7.2.   SMALL CORN FARMERS IN MEXICO

TARA BRIAN

Ninety-year-old José says he is an antique: not because of his age but because of his profession. The weathered man is one of several million Mexican corn farmers who struggle to survive in the difficult reality of Mexico's rural sector. In 2006, José and his son received only 25 cents per kilogram of corn (2.2 pounds), a price that has been more than halved since NAFTA came into effect in 1994. "Who wants to work all day in the sun and earn so little?" asks José, "All the younger people now look for jobs in factories or construction. Either that, or they go to the United States." Many accuse NAFTA of exacerbating the plight of Mexico's small producers as they have been forced into competition with the subsidized goods of their more economically dominant northern neighbors. To many, corn is emblematic of NAFTA's agricultural problems. The average Mexican consumes about 280 pounds of corn a year, the second-highest per capita consumption in the world. The food is Mexico's primary crop, and sustains some 15 million people, two-thirds of whom are small-scale producers. Although NAFTA provided a 14-year schedule to reduce tariffs, Mexico liberalized corn markets well ahead of schedule and cheap US imports have poured into the market. Adding to the challenges faced by Mexican farmers, while the US highly subsidizes corn growers—something left unchecked by NAFTA—Mexico has remained committed to reducing its own extensive systems of support. While a US corn farmer may receive up to US$20,000 a year in subsidies, his

continued

continued

Mexican counterpart only pockets the equivalent of about US$100. Further disadvantaging small producers, subsidies and supports in both the United States and Mexico disproportionately favor large commercial producers. The price of corn has fallen by roughly 50 percent in Mexico since 1994, contributing to trends of rural out-migration and prompting over 25 percent of the rural sector to supplement their agricultural income with temporary work in cities and at tourist sites. Although there are many contributing factors, difficulties in the rural sector have also led to increased rates of migration to the United States, which have more than doubled since NAFTA began. Although slightly less than a quarter of Mexicans live in rural areas, almost half (44 percent) of all Mexican migrants to the United States come from rural communities.

The plight of corn farmers is not confined to economics; in Mexico, the cultivation of corn is a way of life and the crop holds tremendous cultural and spiritual significance. Farmers have carefully selected seed for generations and still cultivate more than fifty-five different native varieties. Today, as it becomes cheaper to buy corn than to grow it and as genetically modified seed threatens to contaminate local varieties, Mexico, the origin of the crop, risks losing this incredible biodiversity. Mexico's food dependency has grown dramatically under NAFTA, as American corn exports to Mexico have nearly quadrupled and now represent about 40 percent of Mexican production, compared with 15 percent between 1984 and 1993.

The Mexican government is suggesting small-scale corn producers begin growing more marketable crops that will make the county more economically competitive. Yet, José's son Casto raises some crucial concerns with the idea: "They say we should grow broccoli and asparagus, but where's the training program? Do they expect us to take on new methods, invest in new tools, and then suddenly find a new market for our goods?" As Harley Shaiken of UC Berkeley's Center for Latin American Studies notes, "There's no way peasant farmers in Oaxaca are going to be competitive with highly subsidized, very productive farms in Iowa." Some Mexican farmers have been successful, however, and the country has seen exports to the United States of seasonal fruits and vegetables triple. However, it is not the little guys that have benefited from the liberalized borders but the big commercial producers. Furthermore, because of the capital-intensive nature of large-scale farming, job creation in Mexico's rural sector has been scant.

Despite differing views on the effects of NAFTA, policymakers can agree that the issue of rural poverty must be addressed for a sustainable and mutually beneficial partnership in North America to evolve. Roughly 60 percent of Mexicans who live in extreme poverty also live in rural areas, and rural poverty is one of the principal reasons for the development gap between Mexico and the United States. Furthermore, poverty in the countryside is a major push factor in Mexican migration to the United States and it strains the social fabric in Mexico, leading to political strife and unrest.

So what can be done?

While widespread rural poverty must first and foremost be addressed by Mexican policymakers, there is also need for considerable reform to NAFTA to address the continuing asymmetries between Mexico's agricultural systems and those of its NAFTA counterparts and to restore public policy flexibility, primarily in Mexico. All told, policies must seek to improve food security, reduce rural poverty and migration, and address environmental and biodiversity concerns. Some, such as the World Bank and the Inter-American Development Bank, are considering ways to create incentives that will direct remittances to productive activities in rural communities. Other scholars agree that governments must seek out creative opportunities to invest in rural communities through credit, technical assistance, and infrastructure development. Amazingly enough, despite the extreme poverty in rural areas of Mexico and the declining price of corn, small-scale production of corn has increased as indigenous peasants refuse to give up their livelihoods. It seems José is not so much an antique as he is one of millions in need of substantial reforms that will finally recognize the value of Mexico's peasant lifestyle.

predispositions as well as common language ties may find invigorating marketing opportunities. Opening to trade through regional integration may meet less political resistance than unilateral tariff reductions. The perception of neighborliness and reciprocity may serve to soften the price of sectoral reform. As new competitors emerge in the regional context and as the dislocation that always accompanies the change in the trading rules of the game dissipates, new players may be better positioned in the global economy. The learning curve in terms of international marketing and shipping infrastructure can be extended to the world marketplace.

Free trade agreements have proliferated around the world, accounting for 84 percent of trade agreements. Of the 274 trade agreements globally, eighty-seven involved countries in the Western Hemisphere as of 2013. Mexico and Chile are both leading the PTA pack with fourteen and twenty-seven trade agreements, respectively.[41] Western Hemisphere PTAs are more diverse than those involving European nations in that they have more different-sized players who do not always share similar national objectives.[42] Integration in Latin American countries beginning to liberalize may also have an effect on the expectations of investors, promoting credibility in the permanence of reforms. This is due to the difficulty of rolling back trade liberalization after it has been locked in by a treaty with another country. For example, when Mexico suffered from the 1994–1995 peso crisis, it raised tariffs on 550 products—except for those exported to **NAFTA** partners. The political costs of abrogating a treaty may exceed the short-term pain of economic adjustment.

The gains or losses from economic integration may be assessed in light of the existing distance from a free trade ideal. If a free trade agreement opens a country further, it is said to have a trade-creating effect. If a country trades more—and in the process makes more efficient use of its own resources—welfare will increase. If, however, the treaty serves to create an economic enclave, it is trade diverting, as purchases are now made from a partner, not the most efficient global producer. Some have suggested that trade integration in the region has diverted trade from its most efficient sources. Traditional suppliers of textiles from the Caribbean countries, for example, may have suffered from Mexico's improved access to the US market under NAFTA.[43] Economists such as Jagdish Bhagwati and Anne Kruger believe that FTAs are by definition discriminatory; the degree of **trade diversion** is a function of the **rules of origin** restricting trade. As most FTAs embed domestic content rules to prevent the FTA partner from becoming a back door to duty-free access from other countries, they contend that the higher the domestic content requirement, the greater the efficiency loss. For example, with the **Central American Free Trade Agreement** (**CAFTA**), proponents of the accord argued that because Central American countries would be restricted in sourcing the fabric for their clothing from US mills, jobs would be gained. Of course, from an efficiency standpoint if the Central American clothing manufacturer could procure cheaper textiles from China, it should. The rules-of-origin requirement creates a tangled spaghetti-like arrangement that could limit the trade-creating potential of the hard-earned PTAs.[44]

Other economists such as Robert Lawrence, Jeffrey Schott, and Fred Bergsten look at FTAs as steps toward liberalization.[45] FTAs can lead to reductions in barriers

Trade is dependent on export infrastructure such as the Panama Canal. *(Photo by Patrice Franko)*

on services and other activities not covered in multilateral WTO negotiations, creating dynamic welfare effects. Able to address tough trade problems, they can be considered a pragmatic second best when multilateral routes are not working. Robert Zoellick, the former USTR (US Trade Representative) and former President of the World Bank, likened preferential trade agreements to riding a bike. A country engaging in PTAs is much like the person biking—so long as one keeps moving forward, momentum creates progress. Once you stop, you fall. For many, whether the FTA has a positive or negative effect depends on the design and implementation of the accord. When embedded in a consistent and credible reform strategy, FTAs can lead to positive outcomes. However, their very success may precipitate failure. The proliferation of agreements is leading to a weakened ability by governments for implementation and enforcement. If different agreements have different liberalization schedules and different rules of origin, enforcement becomes a customs nightmare.[46] It is also problematic for business, as each new rule in each PTA represents a new policy for firms to consider in their export, outsourcing, and investment decisions.[47] Genuine free trade avoids these bureaucratic costs; however, genuine free trade is hard to come by.

Despite the complications of FTAs, the free trade ideal may not be the most practical benchmark to assess efforts. One of the difficult parts of weighing the impact of regional trading arrangements is figuring out what would have happened in its absence. Would there have been more movement toward the pure trade model or greater protectionism? Analysis of regional economic integration parallels the joke about the economist who is asked "How is your love life?" and replies "Relative to what?"[48] Evaluating integration involves a benchmark: should the benchmark be the free trade ideal or increasing global isolation? The IMF points out, however, that if Latin America could increase its intra-regional trade from its current level of 15 percent of exports to the 55 percent evident in the highly integrated Asia-Pacific region, it could increase real per capita growth by 1.3 percentage points.[49] Another study by the Inter-American Development Bank concluded that the hemispheric PTAs that cross North-South lines (NAFTA and CAFTA) created more trade than those limited to Latin American members (CAN, CACM, MERCOSUR).[50] Let us consider the wide range of integration efforts in the region to evaluate this proposition.

The Andean Region

The **Community of Andean Nations (CAN)** has a long but uneven history. A modern realization of independence hero Simón Bolívar's vision of unification, the treaty was signed in 1969. It provided for free commerce and a common external tariff among Bolivia, Colombia, Ecuador, Venezuela, and Peru.[51] The hope was that subregional production would overcome the limitation of economies of scale faced under ISI. Problems in the early stages of the Andean Pact derived in large part from political disputes as well as very different domestic economic policies and goals. An ambitious emphasis on industrial planning and joint industrialization was more than the meager sums dedicated to the projects could support, particularly as disputes arose between the more powerful countries and the smaller nations. Policies governing foreign capital were also controversial. International investment disputes led nations to ban foreigners from investing in activities that would compete with existing firms; strict controls were also placed on foreign ownership and profit remittances.[52]

With greater contemporary homogeneity in economic policies, there are improved prospects for the development of subregional trade. Trade in goods between Bolivia, Colombia, Ecuador, and Venezuela is fully deregulated, allowing any goods originating in a partner country to enter duty free; Peru is becoming part of this through a liberalization program. So far, lowering these barriers seems to have led to **trade creation**, as opposed to trade diversion, a positive outcome for the agreement. The regional market appeared to play a key role in promoting export expansion. Scale economies in intra-industry trade between Andean partners are preparing firms for competition in the global marketplace.[53] The CAN embraces the concept of supranationality, which means that its regulations apply in all member countries and supersede national laws if in conflict. Its institutional structure parallels that of the European Union, including a formal Andean Presidential Council, a Court of Justice with supranational powers, and an Andean integration system that incorporates all the Andean integration agencies. Plans include promoting a customs union, reinforcing dispute resolution mechanisms, establishing joint investment particularly in energy and agroindustry, and providing special support for Bolivia as a poorer partner. However, these ambitious plans may encounter problems in part caused by the political divide between market-oriented and state-leaning countries. We have already seen economic and political setbacks among member nations that have occasionally led to the use of unilateral, trade-distorting measures that pressure the system.

The biggest challenges for deepening integration within the CAN at this time appear to be its extra-pact trade negotiations. The Andean-Mercosur and Peru-Mercosur free trade agreements are precursors to the South American community of nations envisaged in the 2004 Cuzco declaration of the South American summit to unite the two trade blocks. Nonetheless, this is complicated by the fact that Colombia and Peru have signed free trade agreements with the United States with deeper and broader commitments than those with Andean or Mercosur partners. Colombia and Peru have opened their agricultural markets to imports from the United States in exchange for continued preferential access to the lucrative US market. This introduced tension with Venezuela, not exactly a huge fan of the United States, as well as Brazil, which is using South-South integration as a bargaining chip in multilateral trade and foreign policy arenas.[54] President Chavez pulled out of the AC in 2006, proposing instead a union of Bolivarian nations, **ALBA** (the Bolivarian Alternative of the Americas). This regional trade association not allied with the United States has grown to include among Caribbean states Bolivia, Ecuador, and Nicaragua; Iran and Syria are observer countries.[55] ALBA's developmentalist's precepts of solidarity and state-driven trade stand in contrast to the open regional approaches of Peru and Colombia in the Pacific Alliance.[56] Venezuela's withdrawal, along with the creation of the Pacific Alliance, which Peru is a member of, has left the CAN in an uncomfortable place. Costoya characterizes the AC versus ALBA as an ideological battleground for the two visions of trade that have come to the fore in Latin America: the open neoliberal model and deep integration of a Bolivarian state, exemplified by ALBA.[57]

Created in 2011, the **Pacific Alliance** (**PA**), is an agreement between Chile, Colombia, Mexico, and Peru to promote and deepen integration and free trade. The Latin American four constitute 39 percent of the region's GDP, 54 percent of Latin America's overall global trade in goods, and are home to 217 million customers.[58] The Pacific Alliance was in some ways born from the Pacific Rim Agreement, which helped eleven Latin American countries harmonize their trade and strengthen regional integration before addressing potential trade with Asia Pacific. Unable to reach consensus on tariff reductions, the Pacific Rim Agreement failed slowly, and effectively ended when PA negotiations began in 2012. These negations lasted until 2014 at which point all four countries had successfully created a timetable for the reduction of tariff and nontariff barriers. They also reached agreements on e-commerce, telecommunications, dispute settlement, and financial services. PA nations have also been successful in reducing barriers to immigration and harmonizing their financial institutions. Their intra-regional export profiles are more heavily concentrated in manufacturing than their extraregional commodity and agricultural baskets.[59]

Despite their geographic diversity, the member countries all have strong economies and strong free trade policies. Additionally, they have lower unemployment and lower inflation rates than the rest of the region. Furthermore, the countries all lead in regional competitiveness and The World Bank's Doing Business Index. So far, 90 percent of trade between PA countries has been liberalized. Despite these impressive numbers, the intraregional trade has fallen from 3.5 percent in 2013 to 3.2 percent in 2016. Some believe that this lack of intraregional trade is due to the incompatibility of their exports, whereas others believe it may be caused by Mexico's reliance on the United States. Though intraregional trade is somewhat low, the foreign direct investment (FDI) linkages between the countries are high. Mexico and Chile have net FDI outflows to Colombia and Peru. The proliferation of trans-Latins has helped create this FDI increase. Of the fifty largest trans-Latins in 2012, sixteen were Mexican, eleven were Chilean, and six were Colombian. The Pacific Alliance engages a broader range of policy issues for economic integration, including cross-border investment, financial integration, and environmental, social, and technological exchanges.[60] Overall, the Pacific Alliance has generated positive responses in its first four years.

Not only does the Pacific Alliance represent a pivot towards Asia with its name, but its uniquely large number of observer nations, more than ten times the number of full members, also features many major Asian economies. For the Asian and European nations, full acceptance into the FTA is highly unlikely, but their interest in the Alliance is promising. Additionally, the Pacific Alliance may have an interesting role to play in the future of broader agreements such as the Trans Pacific Partnership or TPP. However, trade patterns between PA countries and major Asian economies still vary widely, calling into question the ease of transition. Furthermore, coordinating pre-determined PA policies with broader TPP policies could prove challenging. The success, or failure, of the merging of these agreements will help us determine whether regional agreements can serve as building blocks.[61]

Andean Agreements with the United States: US-Chile, US-Colombia, and US-Peru FTAs

When the US-Chile Free Trade Agreement went into effect on January 2004, Chile joined a select group of only five other countries with an FTA with the United States: Canada, Mexico, Jordan, Singapore, and Israel. The United States is Chile's second largest single trading partner, accounting for 14.1 percent of Chilean exports and 17.42 percent of its imports. For the United States, Chile's role is smaller, ranking thirty-fourth as a destination for US exports and thirty-sixth in imports. The United States largely sells Chile capital goods and imports copper, fruit, nuts, fish, wood, and wine. The negotiation process that began in 2000 opened market access, with 85 percent of bilateral trade in consumer and industrial products eligible for duty-free treatment immediately and other tariff rates reduced over time. Other key issues included environment and labor provisions, more open government procurement rules, intellectual property, and the creation of a new e-commerce chapter. For the United States, Chile was seen as a strategic foothold in Latin America supporting US interests. Its economic and political stability, transparency, and steadfast commitment to market economics made it attractive to US business. The Chilean FTA was considered as a template for other negotiations.[62]

The US negotiated the US-Colombia Trade Agreement beginning in 2004 and ending in 2012. The agreement eliminated over 80 percent of tariffs on US exports of consumer and industrial products to Colombia upon entry into force. The agreement also included important labor protection and environmental protection. Finally, the agreement includes provisions to ease investor dispute settlements, thus encouraging increased FDI. Trade has expanded between Peru and the US under a US trade agreement decreasing tariffs and nontariff barriers, committing to environmental protection, and increasing investor dispute settlement protections.[63] Total trade has roughly doubled between the United States and Peru, from close to $9 billion in 2009 to more than $22 billion in 2016.[64]

Central American Region

The **Central American Common Market**, formed in 1960, was an early attempt at integration. Unsurprisingly, it has had a rocky history. The treaty signed in 1961 by Guatemala, El Salvador, Honduras, and Nicaragua established a secretariat for Central American economic integration that Costa Rica joined in 1963. Progress toward integration in the 1970s was set back by geopolitical struggles and civil war in the region. Although by 1970 intraregional trade had reached 26 percent, small market size and social revolutions turned the clock back. The 1990s saw new resolve to exploit the economies of scale offered by integration. Both business and civil society have taken leadership roles in propelling integration efforts forward. Given that most countries in the Central America region had already pursued unilateral trade liberalization, convergence at a low common external tariff (CET) between 0 and 20 percent was achieved. Countries opened their capital accounts, and investment returned to the region. Nonetheless, progress was stalled by macroeconomic instability, weak infrastructure, and unskilled human capital. Priorities of the new regional economic integration program included strengthening the legal and institutional framework, instituting joint actions to reduce debt, and promoting cooperation on sectoral issues such as upgrading infrastructure in transport, energy, and telecommunications. Mexico and the Central American countries have announced an infrastructure strategy, the Plan Puebla Panama, that would also incorporate social and environmental dimensions.[65] Although imperfect, integration has advanced substantially.

US Agreements in Central America: In 2003 El Salvador, Guatemala, Honduras, and Nicaragua began talks with the United States to pursue stronger integration with the United States via CAFTA; Costa Rica joined the negotiations in January and the Dominican Republic in March 2004. With the addition of the Dominican Republic, the FTA became known as DR-CAFTA. The agreement promised to boost regional GDP by between 0.8 and 2.3 percent, sending a strong signal to investors of the potential of Central America's forty-five million consumers close to the US border. On both sides of the border the political push to complete DR-CAFTA was framed in terms of competition with China. Within this framework, proponents argued geography matters in the global supply chain. That is, textile producers in Guatemala or Costa Rica are more likely to use yarns and fabrics produced in the United States, whereas the Chinese would source from South East Asia. Central Americans feared job loss to cheaper Chinese labor, while the United States wanted to remain a Central American supplier of choice. Support on the US side also came from quarters within US agribusiness—particularly pork, poultry, dairy, and corn—hoping to open key segments of the Central American market and double exports to the region.[66]

Opponents in the United States cited the weak enforcement provisions for legal compliance with ILO standards for freedom of association, collective bargaining, elimination of child labor, and nondiscrimination of employment.[67] The United States engaged in trade capacity building with the partner countries to enhance the implementation of local law, but funding in the US Bureau of International Labor Affairs was lacking.[68] In the United States, the vote on the treaty was a close 217 to 215, with the Bush administration pushing hard as a symbol of its commitment to international trade liberalization. Opposition also emanated from Central America, where the potential market gains by the United States are translated into local job losses. According to Guatemala's lead negotiator, Guido Rodas, "rice, pork, corn, beer, telecommunications, and generic medicates are among the losers who will pick up the tab of the CAFTA negotiations largely through job loss."[69] CAFTA was designed to come into effect on January 1, 2006; implementation, however, was delayed until legislatures overcame their issues with trade union rights and enforcing intellectual property rights. This opposition was ignited by local businesses and peasant farmers fearing impoverishment. Eventually, El Salvador joined on March 1, 2006; Honduras and Nicaragua joined on April 1, 2006; Guatemala joined on July 1, 2006; the Dominican Republic joined on March 1, 2007; and, finally, Costa Rica joined on January 1, 2009. CAFTA is a telling example of the potential gains and losses in negotiating free trade agreements.

With the effects of the global financial crisis looming large over trade, it is perhaps still early to evaluate outcomes. One World Bank study done by request of the Costa Rican government pointed to increasing exports as well as foreign direct investment. Intellectual property agreements and market opening in telecommunications as well as high-tech sectors such as medical devices led to multinational interests.[70] The rise of China has seemed to affect trade between the United States and South America much more than trade between the United States and Central America. According to ECLAC, North-South trade agreements like NAFTA and DR-CAFTA have succeeded in increasing trade more than their South-South counterparts.[71] For instance, two-way trade between the United States and the six DR-CAFTA countries has increased by over 50 percent between 2005 and 2015; the US holds a slight (5 billion US$) surplus.[72]

Shortly after the Chilean FTA went into effect, Panama and the United States began working toward a bilateral free trade agreement that entered into force in 2012. Panama's historic relationship with the United States, including the return of the canal to Panamanian control in 1999, sets it apart from other Central American countries. Although a small US trading partner, Panama has benefited from significant preferences through the Caribbean Basin Initiative, which it made permanent through the FTA. The United States sought to go beyond WTO standards in advancing its interests in standardized rules for services trade, investment, intellectual property rights, and government procurement. As with DR-CAFTA, US labor groups challenged Panama's working conditions and enforcement capability.[73] The Chilean and Panamanian FTAs are small treaties for the United States from an economic perspective but have been negotiated to build commitment to the free trade movement between the United States and its southern neighbors.

NAFTA: North American Integration

In 1991 the United States, Canada, and Mexico began negotiating NAFTA, the North American Free Trade Agreement, making it the first formal regional trading agreement that involved both developed and developing countries. A potential Canada-US trade agreement, CUSFTA, helped spark interest in NAFTA from a newly liberalizing Mexico, who feared losing a key trading partner. Additionally, Mexico saw NAFTA as a means of solidifying new liberal economic policies and securing more international capital. As for the United States, NAFTA had the potential to decrease political tensions with Mexico as well as strengthen economic relations and reduce illegal immigration. After long negotiations, NAFTA was signed in 1994.

Unlike the EU, or even Mercosur, NAFTA is almost an entirely economic agreement with very limited supranational institutions. The centerpiece of NAFTA was the gradual elimination of tariffs over a ten-year period, including the elimination of restrictions in textiles and apparel in the United States and Canada.[74] Intellectual property rights were also strengthened. To prevent the abuse of the free trade status by nontreaty countries, the legislation includes tough rules of origin specifying what proportion of the value of a product must be added locally and imposing strict domestic content rules for the purchase of inputs. Computers, for example, could not be assembled in Mexico with imported components from around the globe and qualify for NAFTA trade preferences. For autos, the 62.5 percent content requirement means that some parts and components that would otherwise be purchased from Asia or Europe are instead purchased in the NAFTA region.[75] Other key elements of the NAFTA accord include changes in agriculture, manufacturing, and services. The accord provided for liberalization of the export of fresh fruits and vegetables from Mexico into the United States and corn and other grains from the United States to Mexico. It promoted lowering of tariffs and quotas on textiles and apparel. It removed tariffs on cars imported into Mexico over a five- to ten-year period, and it opened the Mexican telecommunications and government procurement markets. Finally, it sped implementation of WTO intellectual property rights and provided national treatment to investors of other NAFTA countries.[76] NAFTA makes no provision for the free movement of labor within the bloc. It is notable that the only sectors where the new regime explicitly benefits Mexico are concessions in the US markets for fruit, textiles, and clothing. The more industrialized partners realized significant gains in lucrative telecommunications and government markets. In an effort to gain credibility with international investors, Mexico may have given up more than it got in the NAFTA negotiations. Liberalization with industrialized partners came at a relatively high price for Mexicans.

The signing of NAFTA generated a great deal of controversy. In the United States and Canada, opponents were concerned about the potential loss of jobs as manufacturers moved south of the border to take advantage of cheaper labor. In assessing the effects of cheap labor, it must be remembered that low wages do not magically guarantee a profit. Low wages may be the result of low levels of productivity such that the cost per unit of product is not reduced. In fact, although wages in the United States are at points roughly eight times the wages paid in Mexico, US workers produced only 8.2 times as much as Mexicans in *maquila* plants. This is not to say that if cheaper Mexican workers can be made more productive with better education and equipment Mexico wouldn't be more of a threat but rather that the claims for the widespread job loss in the United States, given Mexican productivity levels, were somewhat exaggerated. Profit increases only when productive labor is paid less than it is worth. Opponents of NAFTA often forgot that Mexico had already engaged in substantial liberalization prior to the agreement. NAFTA was more of a way to lock in liberalization reforms. Mexico had joined the WTO and already decreased its tariff rates to around 14 percent, such that the decrease in tariff rates was not particularly dramatic, with the exception of changes in agriculture and government services. Additionally, those opposing NAFTA failed to point out that international capital, mainly US capital, had already entered Mexico through the *maquiladora* program. This twin-plant program, which began in 1965, has allowed foreign firms to import components without duty so long as the final product was re-exported. Capital that wanted to be in Mexico because of the cheap labor platform largely was already there.

In the United States, the American Federation of Labor-Congress of Industrial Organizations, an organization of affiliated labor unions, charged that NAFTA helped keep inflation-adjusted average hourly wages of US workers flat, at approximately twelve dollars per hour. What NAFTA may have done is make the threat of plant relocation to Mexico more real to American workers and therefore depress wage demands in collective bargaining. One study found that 60 percent of union-organizing efforts after NAFTA were met by the threat of plant closings, compared to 29 percent before.[77] Nonetheless, NAFTA does not change the fact that multinationals could always threaten to move abroad; if it wasn't Mexico, it would be Malaysia or China. It's important to note that job creation or job loss is difficult to measure, in part because you can't tell which workers are dedicated to "NAFTA production" and which are making goods sold elsewhere. We know that when workers are laid off from jobs due to firms moving to Mexico, they may register for benefits under the NAFTA Transitional Adjustment Assistance (NAFTA-TAA). Roughly 366 thousand workers—about one quarter of 1 percent of the US workforce—qualified for adjustment assistance.[78] There is probably some understatement in this figure in that not all workers displaced applied for TAA, but this may be balanced by the fact that not all the firms that moved to Mexico or Canada did so explicitly because of liberalization—there may have been other business reasons. To put these numbers in context, every quarter an average of 10.5 million jobs are displaced in the United States. According to the Public Citizen's NAFTA-TAA database, after NAFTA was enacted, between 1994 and 2013, roughly 44,500 jobs were lost to Canada or Mexico. At most only about 5 percent of US job displacement can be attributed to NAFTA. In the midst of this churning process, the effect of job loss has been small compared to the overall turnover in the US market.[79] Jobs also have been created through integration. Transportation sector jobs such as trucking have also benefited, as goods are moved over land between the NAFTA countries. In cases such as the US Fisher-Price Corporation, a job-creating effect of NAFTA was relocating production from Hong Kong to Monterey, because firms such as Celadon Trucking, which move goods from Mexico into the US market, must hire drivers.[80] Mexico's exports to the United States contain 40 percent US content—raw materials, technology, or assembly.[81] There is the possibility that NAFTA created as many jobs as it may have lost, albeit in different sectors or geographic areas. In short, it's not possible to see whether NAFTA has increased US unemployment. For the most part, it is macroeconomic conditions and not trade agreements that determine the level of employment in an economy.[82] National levels of income determine aggregate demand; changes in the sectoral distribution of which country is producing each item will not determine an overall job loss. Unfortunately, where jobs are lost the damage is geographically concentrated in communities devastated by plant closings. The pain is magnified on a local level and this local pain feeds into anti-trade sentiments. A study conducted by the Pew Research Center in 2010 found 55 percent of respondents believed FTAs lead to US job losses.[83] This widespread belief has been magnified by President Trump and placed NAFTA in a precarious position.

Another reason the aggregate job loss hasn't been as high as predicted is the domestic content regulations. Prior to NAFTA, firms (particularly those that had set up in the maquiladora zones) had imported components from Asia; now they must purchase from American suppliers. Exports to Mexico may have been higher had the peso crisis not sent the Mexican economy into a tailspin.[84] By 1999, Mexico had indeed become the second-largest US export market after Canada, surpassing Japan. By 2005, two-way trade had nearly reached a record $300 billion. As shown in table 7.5, US exports to Mexico reached $240.2 billion in 2014. Imports were $294.1 billion, leaving the United States with a trade deficit with its southern partner. It is interesting to note that the top goods traded have a great deal of overlap between imports and exports. The top four imports were the same as the top four exports (but ranked differently), and included vehicle parts, electric machinery, nuclear machinery, and mineral fuel/wax. Mexico's duty on American goods has fallen from its pre-NAFTA rate of approximately 10 percent to less than 2 percent, allowing more than 80 percent of US goods to enter duty free. Half of Mexico's job creation is in the export sector; jobs here pay 40 percent more than the national average. US employment supported by exports to NAFTA countries reached over 2.8 million jobs, with these paying 13–18 percent more than the average US wage.[85] Total exports to our NAFTA partners Canada and Mexico supported over 2.8 million jobs (1.7 million by exports to Canada and 1.1 million by exports to Mexico), which represents 24 percent of all jobs supported by exports in 2014.

As for Mexico's expectation of growth, it is difficult to separate out the direct effects of the trade agreement, the unrelated negative macroeconomic effects of the peso crisis and its aftermath, growth cycles in the United States and Mexico,

Table 7.5. Trade between NAFTA Partners

2-Digit End-Use Code (in Thousands of Dollars) Merchandise includes all tangible goods—e.g., manufactures, raw materials, and unprocessed agricultural commodities.

	US Exports to Mexico		US Imports from Mexico		US Exports to Canada		US Imports from Canada	
	End-Use Code	Value 2014	End-Use Code	Value 2014	End-Use Code	Value 2014	End-Use Code	Value 2014
Total	**Total**	**240,248,662,812**	**Total**	**294,074,053,415**	**Total**	**312,420,805,048**	**Total**	**347,797,986,092**
	84—nuclear reactors, boilers, machinery etc.; parts	43,131,731,580	87—vehicles, except railway or tramway, and parts etc.	67,872,460,794	87—vehicles, except railway or tramway, and parts etc.	51,422,480,154	27—mineral fuel, oil etc.; bitumin subst; mineral wax	117,044,308,447
	85—electric machinery etc.; sound equip; tv equip; parts	38,317,241,559	85—electric machinery etc.; sound equip; tv equip; parts	58,143,025,648	84—nuclear reactors, boilers, machinery etc.; parts	46,781,154,454	87—vehicles, except railway or tramway, and parts etc.	55,947,648,751
	27—mineral fuel, oil etc.; bitumin subst; mineral wax	23,666,597,848	84—nuclear reactors, boilers, machinery etc.; parts	45,008,380,687	27—mineral fuel, oil etc.; bitumin subst; mineral wax	32,804,219,993	84—nuclear reactors, boilers, machinery etc.; parts	21,085,549,311
	87—vehicles, except railway or tramway, and parts etc.	21,261,777,990	27—mineral fuel, oil etc.; bitumin subst; mineral wax	30,253,394,987	85—electric machinery etc.; sound equip; tv equip; parts	27,676,180,756	98—special classification provisions, not elsewhere specified or indicated	12,078,074,043

continued

Table 7.5. (Continued)

End-Use Code	Value 2014	End-Use Code	Value 2014	End-Use Code	Value 2014	End-Use Code	Value 2014
39—plastics and articles thereof	16,439,246,278	90—optic, photo etc., medical or surgical instruments etc.	11,561,324,993	39—plastics and articles thereof	13,796,024,686	39—plastics and articles thereof	11,282,120,194
98—special classification provisions, not elsewhere specified or indicated	7,394,960,430	94—furniture; bedding etc.; lamps not elsewhere specified or indicated etc.; prefabricated	9,696,351,870	90—optic, photo etc., medical or surgical instruments etc.	9,217,795,721	44—wood and articles thereof; wood charcoal	8,499,565,306
29—organic chemicals	6,437,473,945	98—special classification provisions,	6,665,292,572	73—articles of iron or steel	7,642,476,183	88—aircraft, spacecraft, and parts thereof	7,954,905,918
90—optic, photo etc., medical or surgical instruments etc.	6,369,105,258	71—gems (pearls, precious stones) etc.; coin	5,724,783,918	88—aircraft, spacecraft, and parts thereof	7,570,684,867	85—electric machinery etc.; sound equip; tv equip; parts	7,897,906,011
73—articles of iron or steel	5,499,846,799	07—edible vegetables & certain roots & tubers	5,124,949,830	98—special classification provisions, not elsewhere specified or indicated	7,414,094,956	76—aluminum and articles thereof	7,330,679,526

Category	Value	Category	Value	Category	Value	Category	Value
72—iron and steel	4,395,049,776	39—plastics and articles thereof	4,612,276,433	72—iron and steel	6,274,235,384	48—paper & paperboard & articles (incl paper pulp)	6,832,719,096
48—paper & paperboard & articles	3,858,931,000	08—edible vegetables & certain roots & tubers	4,479,789,897	94—furniture; bedding etc.; lamps not elsewhere specified or indicated etc.; prefabicated	5,488,965,616	71—natural pearls, precious stones, etc.; coin	6,490,411,731
76—aluminum and articles thereof	3,802,027,822	73—articles of iron or steel	4,293,890,767	48—paper & paperboard & articles	5,094,097,109	72—iron and steel	5,670,738,099
02—meat and edible meat offal	3,706,732,402	22—beverages, spirits and vinegar	3,860,195,747	38— miscellaneous chemical products	4,569,647,607	29—organic chemicals	4,603,334,972
10—cereals	3,580,470,417	62—apparel articles and accessories	2,508,641,695	40—rubber and articles thereof	4,503,255,651	30— pharmaceutical products	4,395,581,362
40—rubber and articles thereof	3,556,211,366	72—iron and steel	2,264,298,481	29—organic chemicals	4,455,592,118	73—articles of iron or steel	4,082,363,326

Source: US International Trade Administration Trade Stats Express, tse.export.gov.

and the historically positive binational atmosphere that NAFTA has generated. Isolating the effects of the trade agreement from a 45 percent devaluation of the peso, a 7 percent drop in Mexican output, and a 22 percent fall in Mexican real wages staggers even the economists' imagination.[86] Given the small size of trade with Mexico relative to the US economy (two-way trade at 3 percent of US GDP), changes in trade patterns did not generate large impacts on the US economy. More surprising, studies of the Mexican economy have found the impact to be complex. A World Bank study found unequal effects across regions and income levels but also showed that Mexican per capita GDP would have been 4–5 percent lower, exports 25 percent lower, and foreign direct investment down 40 percent.[87] NAFTA spurred diversification away from oil, moving from oil dominating 75 percent of exports pre-NAFTA to today manufacturing exports representing 80 percent of total exports (oil less than 10 percent).[88] Nearly half of all jobs created in Mexico in the last 20 years were due to foreign trade—and Mexican workers in export activities obtain wages that are 40 percent above the rest of the economy, and most of these workers are unionized. NAFTA may have also accelerated the growth of the middle class in Mexico by providing consumers with lower cost, high-quality goods.

Negative effects have also been reported. The opening of the agricultural market in Mexico to the inflow of cheaper US foodstuffs has been good for urban populations, but the rural sector has borne the brunt of the adjustment. Overall NAFTA's effect has increased the North-South divide already present in Mexico. The North tends to be more industrialized and integrated into the global economy while the South remains largely rural and often neglected—creating a two-speed economy that is difficult to govern. This regional inequality within Mexico could potentially be linked to increased trade and its inherent distributive effects. Real wages are lower today in Mexico than they were when NAFTA took effect. The causality of this, however, is in dispute, as the 1995 peso crisis and competition from China have undoubtedly depressed wages.[89] Given the economic crisis in Mexico and the threat of job loss from China, the Mexican government has been unable to develop sufficient safeguards and social insurance schemes to compensate those hurt by trade opening and to invest in employment and education to improve competitiveness. Although the poverty rate declined from 42.5 percent in 1995 to 16.7 percent in 2014, NAFTA cannot be fully credited with this progress.[90] Even the World Bank concludes that NAFTA alone is not enough to ensure economic convergence among North American countries and regions.

The overall effects of NAFTA are still unfolding. It is, in a certain sense, a work in progress. Total US trade with NAFTA partners increased significantly over the past eleven years, rising from $293 billion in 1993 to $1,154 billion in 2013. It is important to note, however, that an increase in trade with NAFTA partners is not in itself evidence of an increase in trade with NAFTA. That is, trade everywhere has grown, even without preferential agreements; however, trade with NAFTA countries has grown slightly more than trade with the rest of the world. Estimates of causality vary greatly—from 5 to 50 percent of two-way trade. Liberalization began before the pact, but the agreement is likely to have extended and deepened the process. Trade in NAFTA is asymmetrical. The United States is Mexico's most significant trading partner; approximately 90 percent of Mexico's exports go the United States, and about 60 percent of its imports come from the United States; Canada is Mexico's far second cousin, with 2 percent of each. To diversify, Mexico has entered into a total of twelve trade agreements with more than forty countries but is still largely dependent on the United States.[91]

The environment was another key tension in the signing of NAFTA. Environmental advocates on both sides of the border were fearful of the motives of big business in relocating to avoid tougher environmental regulations in the North. In Mexico there was the apprehension that the *yanquis* would invade again, exploiting Mexican labor and putting Mexican corporations out of business. The border between the United States and Mexico has long suffered environmental deterioration from sewage problems in Tijuana, inadequate waste disposal from *maquilas*, and copper smelting in Sonora and Arizona. NAFTA heightened fears of greater damage. US firms in conformance with environmental regulations did not want to be put at a disadvantage with respect to firms located in Mexico, and Mexicans themselves did not want to breathe dirtier air or drink more polluted water courtesy of multinational capital. As a result of tough lobbying, NAFTA also included important side agreements concerning labor and the environment. The nations agreed to an upward harmonization of environmental standards but gave no authority to any country to enforce domestic environmental standards beyond its borders.[92] Under the United States–Mexico Border Program, five-year goals were set for achieving a cleaner environment. Nine binational groups were created to work on reducing vehicle emissions at border crossings, tracking transport of hazardous wastes, minimizing the risk of chemical spills, reducing solid waste, monitoring children's health risks from pesticide exposures, and reducing the impacts of growth on fish and wildlife resources. Two institutions were set up under NAFTA to promote sustainable environmental practices: the **Border Environment Cooperation Commission** (**BECC**) and the trinational Commission for Environmental Cooperation (CEC). An interesting innovation in the international legislation makes it possible for citizens and nongovernmental organizations (NGOs) to make direct complaints to the CEC.

Unfortunately, dissatisfaction remains as to the efficacy of the environmental agreements in practice. Some have argued that the institutions are underfunded and that the political attention in Mexico given to macroeconomic stabilization took away from progress on the environmental front. Those defending the record argue that the BECC received funds from the US Environmental Protection Agency and the Mexican Ministry of Social Development and has provided more than $30.2 million in aid to the development of 230 water, sewage, and municipal waste projects in 131 communities on both sides of the border. Recent activities can be viewed at the BECC web site, www.cocef.org.[93] The NADBank, or North American Development Bank, that was set up to finance capital requirements of environmental projects, has been slow to review project proposals and has approved funding for only a handful of projects. Environmental conditions along the border are making people sick. Rates of hepatitis, diarrheal diseases, and gastroenteritis are two to six times the Texas state average—and things are worse on the Mexican side. With a doubling of the border population in the past decades, sanitary ser-vices are pressed beyond capacity.[94] New mechanisms may be needed to facilitate lending, as the bank's charter limits it to projects viable on commercial terms. It may need a special concessional window to attend to the needs of the poorest and most vulnerable communities, expanding projects to include some of the structural causes of environmental degradation such as housing and poor sanitation.[95] Finally, some analysts are concerned that under NAFTA institutions basic principles such as "polluter pays" are absent. Although a fine may be levied, it is not calculated on the basis of environmental damage, and it is paid by the government as opposed to the industry.[96] Nonetheless, the environmental side agreement within NAFTA can be seen as an accomplishment in that it exists at all; it is the first to go beyond WTO provisions to address ecological interests. Although this first "greening" of a trade agreement is far from coherent and effective, institution building in environmental cooperation is important.[97] Trade related damages from invasive species along with transportation-driven emission of pollutants have been identified. [98]Audley, Polaski, Papademetriou, and Vaughan conclude that the fears of the race to the bottom have been unfounded but that the overall $36 billion in annual environmental damages accelerated pressures already inherent in the Mexican growth process.[99]

Now that NAFTA is almost 25 years old, many provisions could stand to be updated, and, due to President Trump's dissatisfaction with the agreement, on May 18, 2017, the United States announced its intention to commence negotiations to update NAFTA. Ideally these negotiations could bring NAFTA into the twenty-first century by updating the agreement to include more e-commerce regulations that help protect property and consumer privacy as well as updating the dispute settlement clauses. Additionally, these negotiations could simplify the rules of origin regulations that some argue are overly complicated and deter businesses. Long-standing issues like labor rights and environmental policy could be updated to improve standards across the board. However, these changes may be difficult to achieve seeing as the Trump administration's main goal is to reduce the US trade deficit and stands on the opposing side of many of these issues, particularly the rules of origin.[100]

Mercosur: The Southern Cone Market

The second-largest trading agreement in the region after NAFTA is Mercosur. The groundwork for Mercosur began with a bilateral program signed in July 1986 between Argentina and Brazil for industrial integration. Extending from Bra-zil's tropical jungles to the sub-Antarctic zone of Argentina in Tierra del Fuego, Mercosur countries account for approximately half of the Latin American land-mass and GDP, 43 percent of the population, and 33 percent of regional trade.[101] Because Mercosur countries include some of the world's richest agricultural and mineral resources, there are ample opportunities for growth and production. The 1991 Treaty of Asunción, which included Uruguay and Paraguay, expanded this bilateral agreement to include progressive, automatic tariff reduction and a CET in eleven tiers ranging from 0 to 20 percent with an average level of 13.5 percent and harmonization of macroeconomic policies. Exceptions were made for four years to the free trade in textiles, steel, automobiles, and petrochemicals. Mercosur eventually developed the lofty goal of creating a common market that it continues to work toward.

Administratively, Mercosur is governed by six institutions. Its Council, a political leadership group, is composed of the foreign relations and economics ministers of the four member states and oversees all other Mercosur institutions, with decision-making authority over member state institutions. The Common Market Group, or the executive organization of the community, has both policy-making and administrative responsibilities. The Mercosur Commerce Commission is divided into eleven working groups charged with monitoring the common commercial policy, including the CET and competition policy. The joint Parliamentary Commission is an advisory commission representing national legislatures; the Forum, a consultative body, reflects the views of various sectors such as producers, consumers, workers, and merchants; and a small secretariat with a permanent staff of about thirty professionals headquartered in Montevideo, Uruguay, completes the list. In comparison to the autonomy built into European Union (EU) institutions, political control in Mercosur resides in the hands of the member states. In the European Union, European delegates are elected by popular vote; in Mercosur, institutions are staffed by national representatives. Despite the existence of these institutions, negotiations between the members are fraught by conflict and often compromised by tensions between Brazil and Argentina.

Although Mercosur has only four full members, other countries have been involved with the trade bloc to varying degrees. Chile initially did not join the agreement because it wanted to maintain a lower external tariff than the Mercosur countries, although in 1996 it signed a bilateral agreement with the union as an associate member. Bolivia, Colombia, Ecuador, and Peru are also associates, with preferential duty treatment for their products. They do not necessarily abide by the CET. Venezuela officially joined the bloc in 2012, but lost its membership in 2016.[102] Bolivia was invited to join the bloc in 2012, but negotiations are ongoing. The bloc is also heavily influenced by China, a major trading partner of Brazil. The Chinese market has played a major role in increasing commodity dependence and decreasing manufacturing in Mercosur countries, posing more long-term problems.[103]

While Brazil and Argentina hoped to use the trading bloc to enhance their global bargaining power, the internal disharmony in Mercosur has hindered their ability to negotiate. Since 2000 Mercosur and the European Union have held a series of talks that could lead to a free market agreement. The European Union's two-way trade with Mercosur totaled topped US$105 billion in 2016; in light of the turn inward by the United States, Europe seeks an opening with Latin America.[104] In particular, Europe is active in the infrastructure arena, buying telephone companies and utilities in Brazil, Chile, Peru, and Argentina. Seven of the ten largest private companies in Brazil are European-owned; only two are dominated by Americans.[105] Nonetheless, the European Union and Mercosur have struggled to reach a trade agreement, in part due to incoherent internal agenda but also due to sensitive negotiations over agriculture.[106] Still there is new hope that these blocs will reach an agreement after negotiations were re-launched in 2016; parties are targeting 2018 for signature.

Mercosur is still not a true common market. Although members have achieved a customs union, full market status awaits progress in the coordination of economic, legislative, environmental, infrastructure, and technology policies. Member countries face the hard task of harmonizing standards and establishing a supranational bureaucracy beyond the national control of member states. Evaluated by the criteria of common market, Mercosur is still a bit thin. Additionally, Mercosur had high nontariff barriers. Nonetheless, the achievements of Mercosur are important, particularly in locking in progress toward free trade in the region.[107] It is also important to remember that the European Union has been decades in the making; slow progress in negotiating tough international issues is rather predictable. Some suggest that the weak role of strong countries in Mercosur—as compared to China in East Asia—accounts for weaker regional trading hubs in Latin America.[108]

Trade within Mercosur quadrupled since 1990, growing from approximately US$4.1 billion in 1990 to more than US$37 billion in 2016, constituting 13.12 of total exports. Argentina sells more than one-third of its exports—especially agricultural and natural resource products—to Brazil, making Brazil Argentina's largest trading partner after the United States. Brazilian multinationals have set up shop in Argentina. International automakers have taken advantage of the new scale economies to expand auto production in the region. Despite this boom, intraregional trade as a percentage of total exports has fallen in the past few years; this is in part driven by soya exports to Asia by all member countries. However, given relatively steady export levels within the Mercosur group, this decline has more to do with the rise in total exports in 2003 and 2004 driven by the boom in China. Tension between Brazil and Argentina as well as Brazil's protectionist nature have hurt the bloc's internal trade. Additionally, Latin America as a whole, and Mercosur in particular, has been slow to integrate into global value chains. Despite a 12.5 percent increase in Argentina's global value chain (GVC) participation and a 14 percent increase by Brazil's between 1995 and 2011, the countries still hover around 30 percent GVC participation while Mexico and Asia's participation register around 50 percent. This low GVC participation may be problematic as many believe GVCs are key to increasing access to new technologies.[109]

Harmonization of monetary and tax policies has had less success, partly due to economic volatility. Common industrial policies to direct resources toward new areas have also lagged. The asymmetrical nature of the economies makes noncompliance difficult to address. Brazil's economy overwhelms that of Argentina—not to mention tiny Uruguay and Paraguay. For example, the increase in output in one year of Brazil's beer giant Brahma was equal to Argentina's entire consumption of brew. Given its size, Brazil can act without much regard for the effects that a policy may have on Mercosur partners. Relatively weak enforcement institutions make unilateral actions on Brazil's part unpunishable.

Macroeconomic instability has rocked Mercosur. Brazil's move to a floating exchange rate in 1999 pressured the already fragile Argentine economy. The collapse of the Argentine Convertibility Plan in 2001–2002, along with its ensuing economic chaos, has led to a sharp decline in intraregional trade. Mercosur holds promise but also pitfalls for participant countries. In the wake of the Brazilian crisis of 1998–1999 and the Argentine collapse of 2001–2002 Mercosur may be behaving slightly more like a FTA than a common market, turning outward to Chinese, European, and US markets as a source of dynamism. Mercosur countries, pressured by crisis, pushed for reductions on tariffs in industrial countries on agricultural policies, with the hopes of easing recession through traditional export markets.[110]

This macroeconomic volatility precipitated renewed protection. Throughout the union there are too many tariff exceptions, the most recent being refrigerators in Argentina. Argentina is also complaining about Brazilian textiles, footwear, and televisions hindering its national reindustrialization. For its part, Brazil alleges that Argentine chickens, dairy, wheat, rice, and sugar are derailing domestic production. To address these tensions, Brazil and Argentina set up a bilateral dispute mechanism—contravening the spirit of the multicounty accord. The mechanism for competitive adaptation, integration, and balanced trade expansion will allow the application of protectionist measures in case a productive sector of Argentina or Brazil proves to the state they sustain lasting damages.[111] Argentine president Néstor Kirchner was able to leverage this concession from Brazilian president Luiz Inácio "Lula" da Silva as a means to protect Argentina's most vulnerable industries, notably car manufacturing, textiles, and shoemaking.[112] President Macro lifted in 2017 many of the tariffs imposed to protect jobs. High prices for TVs, computers and cell phones were driving Argentines to purchase them abroad illegally—weakening the intent of job protection. Macri called Mercosur the most protectionist block in the world—and urged it to open to improve competitiveness.

The accession of Venezuela has been another sticking point for Mercosur and has driven members farther apart. Venezuela joined the group in 2012 as part of a largely political deal supported by the leftist Brazilian and Argentinian governments. When those governments changed in 2015–2016, the bloc was much less in favor of Venezuelan membership, and finally, in 2016, Venezuela's membership was suspended after it failed to commit to protecting human rights consistent with the bloc's 1998 Ushuaia Protocol, which was implemented to ensure all members remained democratic nations.

Mercosur suffers from a fundamental implementation deficit. The goals are ambitious, but the mechanisms for attaining them are weak. Institutions lack transparent rules for rule making and managing differences.[113] In 2006 Uruguay and Argentina were locked in a dispute over two paper mills being built on the Uruguayan side of the river. Argentine protestors claim that these giant Spanish and Finnish factories will pollute the river, cause acid rain, and hurt local tourism, farming, and fishing. The International Court of Justice at The Hague ruled against Argentina, and a Mercosur arbitration tribunal found that the roadblocks contravened the government to the free movement of goods—but no penalty was assessed.[114]

Despite internal disruptions, Mercosur has paradoxically also become stronger, or at least more necessary, to its dominant member, Brazil. When countries look outward, they can gain leverage in multilateral negotiations by carrying the clout of a trade union. This potential to enhance political prestige encourages Brazil to maintain Mercosur, if only for political purposes. Gary Hufbauer, a senior fellow at the Institute for International Economics, notes that "Mercosur was already stumbling as an economic agreement. Now Brazil has evidently decided to make the Mercosur first and foremost a diplomatic pact."[115] If Brazil is able to use this weight to leverage concessions from the developed countries in terms of their agriculture policies, space may be created by growth to strengthen the institutional capacity of Mercosur. Indeed, 2017 brought new hope for this union, at least in terms of its political prowess. Early in the year, Michel Temer, the Brazilian president, and Mauricio Macri, the Argentinian president, expressed interest in pursuing closer ties with Mexico and moving forward with the Mercosur-EU trade deal.[116] In the wake of multiple corruption scandals, Brazil faces new political instability that draws into question their ability to recommit to Mercosur. This torturous road to trade liberalization has already taken unintended (and protectionist) detours, and it is likely to take more. While the story of Mercosur is filled with failures that draw into question the ability of South-South trade blocs to aid development, there is potential for this Mercosur to turn itself around.

CONCLUSION: NEW GEOMETRIES OF TRADE—OR ERECTING IMPEDIMENTS

As evidenced by the details in this chapter and in figure 7.3, Latin America has no shortage of integration efforts. In the late 1800s, Simon Bolivar envisioned an integrated Latin America; the current intraregional trade levels of between 15 and 20 percent pale in comparison to this vision (or to the rates of integration in Europe

Figure 7.3.   Regional Trade Agreements in the Western Hemisphere

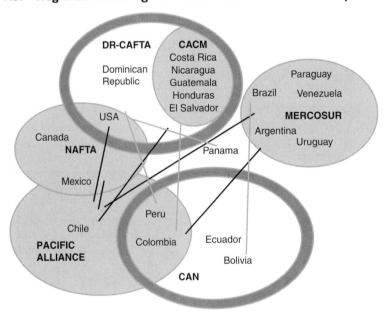

of 65 percent or Asia at about 50 percent). The most recent of integrational aspirations is CELAC (Community of Latin American and Caribbean States), a regional alternative to the political Organization of American States (OAS)—minus the United States and Canada.[117] Without deeply structured institutions, CELAC serves as a platform for regional dialogue and agenda-setting. There is, indeed, much to discuss with the turn away from open trade and the Trump administration's talk of walls to separate the United States from partners in the region. The next five years will likely redefine trade geometries. The appreciation of the gains from market opening to exploit economies of scale is clear in the proliferation of regional agreements. The distinction between ambitious arrangements such as Mercosur that have had fewer trade achievements as compared to more flexible arrangements such as the Pacific Alliance will become clearer. Could the region integrate more simply into a single Latin American and Caribbean Free Trade Agreement (LACFTA)? The Inter-American Development Bank suggests that the benefits of harmonization and coordination of regional trade outweigh the costs.[118] We will also be cautiously watching extraregional trade partnerships. Will trade toward 2025 edge Latin America toward its Pacific partners or will there be a consolidation of existing Western Hemispheric regional agreements?

Key Concepts

Bolivarian alternative of the Americas (ALBA)
Border Environment Cooperation Commission (BECC)
Central American Common Market
Central American Free Trade Agreement (CAFTA)
common market

Community of Andean Nations (CAN)
customs union
economic union
factor price equalization theorem
free trade area (FTA)
Heckscher-Ohlin theorem
Mercosur
North American Free Trade Agreement (NAFTA)

Pacific Alliance (PA)
preferential trade agreements (PTAs)
regional integration
rules of origin
Stolper-Samuelson effect
theory of comparative advantage
trade creation
trade diversion

Chapter Summary

The Theory of Free Trade

- The theoretical underpinning of free trade is the theory of comparative advantage, which states that countries should trade those goods that they can most efficiently produce to maximize global output. Neoclassical trade theory posits that trade will benefit the least advantaged through raising the price of labor in developing countries and will bring factor prices into global equilibrium.

- Critics of free trade contend that, in practice, there are few gains from trade for developing countries. From a dependency, gender, and environmental standpoint, critics believe that free trade can actually damage a country's overall welfare by perpetrating trade in commodities with low value added that pressure fragile environments.
- Although Asia prospered from export-oriented growth during the 1980s, Latin America experienced deteriorating current account deficits. Based on Asia's success, trade liberalization was promoted by the international community as a way of improving growth conditions in Latin America.
- Policymakers pursuing trade liberalization should consider an adequate time frame, appropriate exchange rates, trade adjustment assistance, and fiscal reform.
- Reduced tariffs in Latin America have effectively increased the flow of exports and imports in the region. The composition of goods has changed somewhat, although primary products continue to play a dominant role in the export sector.
- China presents both a challenge (to product competing countries) and an opportunity (for those exporters to the huge Chinese market).

Integration: Trade Creation or Trade Diversion?

- There are four ways a country can integrate its markets: by establishing an FTA, a customs union, a common market, or an economic union. Integration encourages economies of scale, opens markets, and promotes credibility within the region. If trade diversion occurs, however, the costs of integration may be high.
- CAN fully deregulates trade between Bolivia, Colombia, Ecuador, and Peru.
- The oldest integration unit in Latin America, the Central American Common Market, has achieved significant liberalization and has been engaged in infrastructure integration through the Plan Puebla Panama. Member countries have negotiated a parallel agreement, CAFTA, with the United States to take advantage of free access to the large North American market.
- NAFTA, a regional trade agreement among the United States, Canada, and Mexico, sought to decrease tariffs over a ten-year period and thereby increase trade in the region. The controversy surrounding the agreement was based upon fears that NAFTA would lead to job loss in the North, contribute to environmental degradation, and put domestic corporations out of business in the South.
- Mercosur is a customs union comprised of Brazil, Argentina, Uruguay, and Paraguay with Chile and Bolivia as associate members (Venezuela has been suspended for human rights violations). Since the inception of Mercosur, trade has increased not only among the member states but with the European

Union as well. Harmonization of policies has, however, proved difficult, and dispute settlement mechanisms are weak.

- Chile and Panama have negotiated FTAs with the United States. The Chilean agreement has been described as a template for negotiations between richer and less industrialized partners in the region. The Panama FTA is of interest to the United States because of the service trade through the Panama Canal.

Notes

1. Carlos Díaz Alejandro, "International Markets for LDCs: The Old and the New," *American Economic Review*, May 1978, 254–269.

2. International Monetary Fund, Trade Integration in Latin America and the Caribbean, IMF Country Report No. 17/66, March 2017.

3. Diana Tussie and Cintia Quiliconi, "The Current Trade Context," HDR Publications, Background Papers, 2005, http://hdr.undp.org/publications/.

4. Robert E. Baldwin, "Openness and Growth: What's the Empirical Relationship?," National Bureau of Economic Research Working Paper No. 9578, March 2003.

5. Romain Wacziarg and Karen Horn Welch, "Trade Liberalization and Growth: New Evidence," National Bureau of Economic Research Working Paper No. 10152, December 2003.

6. David Dollar and Aart Kraay, "Trade, Growth and Poverty," Development Research Group, the World Bank, June 2001, Research paper posted at www.worldbank.org.

7. Baldwin, "Openness and Growth" and Romain Wacziarg and Karen Horn Welch, "Trade Liberalization and Growth: New Evidence," *The World Bank Economic Review*, 22(2): 187–231.

8. Baldwin, "Openness and Growth."

9. Wacziarg and Welch, "Trade Liberalization and Growth."

10. Baldwin, "Openness and Growth."

11. Christoph Ernst, "Trade Liberalization, Export Orientation and Employment in Argentina, Brazil and Mexico," Employment Strategy Papers 2005–15, International Labour Office, 2005.

12. Schumpeter argued that shocks to an industry, like crises in the life of an individual, might force the sector to grow and adapt. Industries, like people, he suggested, sometimes need to be pushed to try something different.

13. Sebastian Edwards, "The Opening of Latin America," *Crisis and Reform in Latin America: From Despair to Hope* (New York: Oxford University Press, 1995).

14. Dani Rodrik, "The Global Governance of Trade as if Development Really Mattered," United Nations Development Programme, October 2001, accessed at www.undp.org.

15. World Bank, Tariff rate, applied, weighted mean, all products, http://data.worldbank.org/indicator/TM.TAX.MRCH.WM.AR.ZS.

16. International Monetary Fund, Cluster Report – Trade Integration in Latin America and the Caribbean, IMF Country Report No. 17/66, March 2017, https://www.imf.org.

17. Esteban R.Brenesa Arnoldo R.Camachoa LucianoCiravegnab Caleb A.Pichardoa, "Strategy and innovation in emerging economies after the end of the commodity boom—Insights from Latin America", *Journal of Business Research*, http://www.sciencedirect.com/science/article/pii/S014829631630265X#bb0170.

18. This section summarizes the findings of Sebastian Edwards and Daniel Lederman, *The Political Economy of Unilateral Trade Liberalization: The Case of Chile*, National Bureau of Economic Research Working Paper No. 6510 (Cambridge, MA: National Bureau of Economic Research, 1998), available at www.nber.org/papers/w6510.

19. IMF Cluster Report 2017.

20. Warburg Dillon Read, *The Latin American Adviser*, July 9, 1998, 16 (fax newsletter).

21. "Prices Soar as Brazil's Flexfuel Cars Set the Pace," *Financial Times*, FT News Alerts, March 26, 2006.

22. Sandra Polaski, *Winners and Losers: Impact of the Doha Round on Developing Countries* (Washington, D.C.: Carnegie Endowment, 2006).

23. ECLAC, "Latin America and the Caribbean in the World Economy, 2005 Trends," Santiago Chile, United Nations, 2005.

24. Roberto Azevêdo, "Why We Need A Global Trade Deal," *Americas Quarterly* Summer 2015. www.americasquarterly.org/content/why-we-need-global-trade-deal.

25. Azevêdo, "Why We Need A Global Trade Deal" and Trade Facilitation, www.wto.org/english/tratop_e/tradfa_e/tradfa_e.htm.

26. Anthony Elson, "Dragon among the Iguanas," Finance & Development, *IMF Magazine* 51(4) (December 2014).

27. Ibid.

28. ECLAC, "Latin America and the Caribbean in the World Economy: The Regional Trade Crisis: Assessment and Outlook," 2015, 61–77.

29. Elson, "Dragon among the Iguanas."

30. Elson, "Dragon among the Iguanas."

31. Eduardo Lora, "Should Latin America Fear China?" Inter-American Development Research Department Working Paper No. 531 Bank, May 2005, www.iadb.org.

32. Kevin P. Gallagher and Magaret Myers, China-Latin America Finance Database, www.bu.edu/pardeeschool/research/gegi/program-area/chinas-global-reach/china-in-latin-america/china-finance-and-investment/china-latin-america-database/.

33. Inter-American Development Bank, Andrew Powell editor, "Latin American and Caribbean Macroeconomic Report: Routes to Growth in a New Trade World," 51–52, https://publications.iadb.org/bitstream/handle/11319/8203/2017-Latin-American-and-Caribbean-Macroeconomic-Report-Routes-to-Growth-in-a-New-Trade-World.pdf?sequence=9.

34. Carol Wise, "China and Latin America's Emerging Economies: New Realities amid Old Challenges," *Latin American Policy*, 7 (2016): 26–51. doi:10.1111/lamp.12087.

35. "China Ascendant: A Snapshot of Economic Performance," *Ideas* 6 (January–April 2005), www.iadb.org.

36. Lora, "Should Latin America Fear China?"

37. Kevin Gallagher, http://latinamericagoesglobal.org/2016/11/trump-builds-wall-xi-builds-bridges-latam/.

38. Ricardo Ffrench-Davis, comment on L. Allan Winters, "Assessing Regional Integration," in *Trade: Towards Open Regionalism*, proceedings of the 1997 World Bank Conference on Development in Latin America and the Caribbean (Washington, DC: World Bank, 1998), 73–74.

39. Sarath Rajapatirana, *Trade Policies in Latin America and the Caribbean: Priorities, Progress, and Prospects* (San Francisco, CA: International Center for Economic Growth, 1997), 15.

40. Roberto Azevêdo, "Why We Need A Global Trade Deal," *Americas Quarterly* Summer 2015, www.americasquarterly.org/content/why-we-need-global-trade-deal.

41. M. Angeles Villarreal, "Mexico's Free Trade Agreements," CRS Brief April 25, 2017, https://fas.org/sgp/crs/row/R40784.pdf for Mexico, all other info from WTO.org. Western Hemisphere info from SICE, the Foreign Trade Information System at the OAS, http://www.sice.oas.org/agreements_e.asp.

42. M. Angeles Villarreal, "Trade Integration in the Americas," Congressional Research Service Report RL33162 Washington, DC, Library of Congress, November 22, 2005.

43. Jagdish Bhagwati, "The FTAA Is Not Free Trade," in *Trade: Towards Open Regionalism*, proceedings of the 1997 World Bank Conference on Development in Latin America and the Caribbean (Washington, DC: World Bank, 1998).

44. Antoni Estevadeordal and Kati Suominen, "Is All Well with the Spaghetti Bowl in the Americas?" *Economía* 5(2) (2005): 63–103.

45. William H. Cooper, "Free Trade Agreements: Impact on US Trade and Implications for US Trade Policy," Congressional Research Service Report RL31356, Washington, DC, Library of Congress, December 6, 2005.

46. World Bank, *Global Economic Prospects 2005: Trade, Regionalism and Development Annual Report*, Chapter 3, "Regional Trade Agreements: Effects on Trade," www.worldbank.org.

47. Estevadeordal and Suominen, "Is All Well with the Spaghetti Bowl in the Americas?"

48. L. Allan Winters, "Assessing Regional Integration."

49. IMF Cluster Report 2017.

50. Inter-American Development Bank, "Routes to Growth in a New Trade World."

51. Venezuela joined in 1973; Chile was a member between 1969 and 1976. Peru has had difficulty with adoption of the common external tariff.

52. Devlin and Estevadeordal, "What's New in the New Regionalism in the Americas?" Intal Working Paper (6) 2001: 24.

53. Juan José Echavarría, "Trade Flow in the Andean Countries: Unilateral Liberalization or Regional Preferences," in *Trade: Towards Open Regionalism*, proceedings of the 1997 World Bank Conference on Development in Latin America and the Caribbean (Washington, DC: World Bank, 1998), 95.

54. Bruce Odessey, "U.S. Announces Completion of Free-Trade Agreement with Colombia," Washington File, http://usinfo.state.gov/wh/Archive/2006/Feb/27 - 250339.html.

55. Venezuela quits Andean trade bloc, *BBC News*, http://news.bbc.co.uk/2/hi/business/4925056. stm; also see Barbara Kotschwar and Nicolas Albertoni, "How We Trade in the Hemisphere," *Americas Quarterly*, americasquarterly.org/charticles/how-we-trade-in-the-hemisphere/.

56. albainfo.org/what-is-the-alba/.

57. Manuel Mejido Costoya, "Politics of Trade in Post-neoliberal Latin America: The Case of Bolivia," *Bulletin of Latin American Research*, 30(1) (2011): 80–95.

58. AS/COA weekly chart: The Numbers of Pacific Alliance Trade, www.as-coa.org, September 14, 2017.

59. Ibid.

60. IMF Cluster Report.

61. ECLAC, "The Pacific Alliance and Its Economic Impact on Regional Trade," International Trade Series No. 128.

62. J. F. Hornbeck, *The U.S.-Chile Free Trade Agreement: Economic and Trade Policy Issues*, Congressional Research Service Report RL31144, September 10, 2003, www.opencrs.cdt.org.

63. https://ustr.gov/trade-agreements/free-trade-agreements/peru-tpa.

64. Ibid.

65. Eduardo Lizano and José M. Salazar-Xirinach, "Central American Common Market and Hemispheric Free Trade," *Integrating the Hemisphere, 1997: The Inter-American Dialogue*, eds. Ana Julia Jatar and Sidney Weintraub (Santa Fé de Bogotá, Colombia: Tercer Mundo, 1997).

66. "CAFTA Accord," *Oxford Analytic*, Latin American Daily Briefs, February 2, 2004.

67. Kimberly Ann Elliott, "Trading Up: Labor Standards, Development and CAFTA," CGD Brief 3(2) (May 2004).

68. Elliott, "Trading Up."

69. "CAFTA's Missed Opportunities," Bulletin of the Washington Office on Latin America, March 2004.

70. Koehler-Geib, Friederike; Sanchez, Susana M.. 2015. *Costa Rica Five Years after CAFTA-DR: Assessing Early Results*. Directions in Development—Trade; Washington, DC: World Bank. © World Bank. https://openknowledge.worldbank.org/handle/10986/22013 License: CC BY 3.0 IGO.

71. Gary Clyde Hufbauer (PIIE), Cathleen Cimino-Isaacs (PIIE), and Tyler Moran (PIIE), *NAFTA at 20: Misleading Charges and Positive Achievements Policy Brief* 14–13 May 2014.

72. America's USTR Office of the Western Hemisphere, M. Angeles Villarreal Ian F. Fergusson, *NAFTA at 20: Overview and Trade Effects*, April 28, 2014, www.crs.org.

73. Mark P. Sullivan, *Panama: Political and Economic Conditions and U.S. Relation*, Congressional Research Service Report RL30981, February 15, 2006, www.opencrs.cdt.org.

74. Domestic lobbies in both countries kept the tariffs on textiles high.

75. Caroline Freund, *Streamlining Rules of Origin in NAFTA*, Peterson Institute for International Economics, June 2017, https://piie.com/system/files/documents/pb17-25.pdf.

76. Arvind Panagariya, "The Free Trade Area of the Americas: Good for Latin America?" *World Economy* 19(5) (1996): 496.

77. "NAFTA: Where's That Giant Sucking Sound?" *BusinessWeek*, July 7, 1997, 45. Cites study by Kate Bronfenbrenner of Cornell University.

78. Gary Clyde Hufbauer and Jeffrey J. Schott, *NAFTA Revisited: Achievements and Challenges* (Washington, DC: Institute for International Economics, 2005), 41

79. Ibid.

80. "NAFTA: Where's That Giant Sucking Sound?"

81. Robert Koopman, William Powers, and Zhi Wang, et al., *Give Credit Where Credit is Due: Tracing Value Added in Global Production Chains*, National Bureau of Economic Research, Working Paper 16426, Cambridge, MA, September 2010.

82. Employment Policy Foundation, "Open Trade: The 'Fast Track' to Higher Living Standards," *Contemporary Issues in Employment and Workplace Policy* 111(10) (October 1997), Internet publication available at epfnet.org.

83. Gary Clyde Hufbauer, Cathleen Cimino, and Tyler Moran, "NAFTA at 20: Misleading Charges and Positive Achievements," Peterson Institute for International Economics.

84. Sidney Weintraub, "In the Debate about NAFTA, Just the Facts, Please," *Wall Street Journal*, June 20, 1997, A19.

85. Elizabeth Schaefer and Chris Rasmussen, "Jobs Supported by Export Destination 2014," International Trade Administration, Department of Commerce June 18, 2015, www.trade.gov/mas/ian/build/groups/public/@tg_ian/documents/webcontent/tg_ian_005478.pdf.

86. Data from Lustig's comment on Jeffrey J. Schott, "NAFTA: An Interim Report," Annual World Bank Conference on Development in Latin America and the Caribbean, 1997: Trade, Towards Open Regionalism: Proceedings of a Conference Held in Montevideo, Uruguay: 125.

87. "Lessons from NAFTA for Latin America and Caribbean," World Bank, 2003.

88. John Paul Rathbone, "Mexico and Nafta at 20. Why it Went Wrong for One of 'Tres Amigos'," FT editorial, www.ft.com, February 18, 2014.

89. Sandra Polaski, "Jobs, Wages, and Household Income," Chapter 1 in John Audley, Sandra Polaski, Demetrios G. Papademetriou, and Scott Vaughan, *NAFTA's Promise and Reality: Lessons from Mexico*, Carnegie Endowment Report, November 2003.

90. OECD Data, Poverty Rate, https://data.oecd.org/inequality/poverty-rate.htm.

91. M. Angeles Villarreal, "Trade Integration in the Americas," Congressional Research Service Report RL33162, November 22, 2005, www.opencrs.cdt.org.

92. Claudia Schatan, "Lessons from the Mexican Environmental Experience: First Results from NAFTA," *The Environment and International Trade Negotiations: Developing Country Stakes*, ed. Diana Tussie (New York: St. Martin's in association with International Development Research Center, 2000).

93. See www.cocef.org/ingles.php.

94. Sam Howe Verhovek, "Pollution Problems Fester South of the Border," *New York Times*, July 4, 1998, online edition.

95. Data from Lustig's comment on Jeffrey J. Schott, "NAFTA: An Interim Report," 127.

96. Schatan, "Lessons from the Mexican Environmental Experience," 178.

97. Ibid., 184.

98. Environmental Assessment of NAFTA by the commission for Environmental Cooperation, 2011, www.cec.org.

99. Polaski, "Jobs, Wages, and Household Income."

100. "A Guide to Renegotiating NAFTA," https://piie.com/blogs/trade-investment-policy-watch/guide-renegotiating-nafta?utm_source=update-%20newsletter&utm_medium=email&&utm_campaign=2017-06-19_nafta.

101. Data do not include new member Venezuela.

102. "Venezuela: Accession Will Not Affect Mercosur's Economy," *LatinNews Daily*, January 26, 2006.

103. Latin America Special Report, Mercosur's move towards flexibility, Latin American Newsletters SR-2016-06, November 2016.

104. Bloomberg, "Europe Closes In on a Latin American Trade Deal Amid Trump Protectionism," www.bloomberg.com/news/articles/2018-01-28/europe-closes-in-on-fresh-trade-deal-as-trump-puts-up-barriers.

105. John Templeman, "Is Europe Elbowing the U.S. Out of South America?" *BusinessWeek*, August 4, 1997, 56.

106. Mario E. Carranza, "Can *Mercosur* Survive? Domestic and International Constraints on *Mercosur*," *Latin America Politics and Society*, 2003.

107. *Argentina Business: The Portable Encyclopedia for Doing Business with Argentina* (San Rafael, CA: World Trade Press, 1995).

108. IMF Cluster report.

109. ECLAC, Latin American and the Caribbean in the World Economy 2016: 21.

110. Diana Jean Schemo, "A Latin Bloc Asks U.S. and Europe to Ease Trade Barriers," *New York Times*, February 23, 1999, online edition.

111. "Argentina, Brazil Agree on Regulating Bilateral Trade," *La Nacion—Argentina*, distributed by Latin America News Digest, February 2, 2006.

112. "Kirchner Gets What He Came for in Brazil," *LatinNews Daily*, January 19, 2006.

113. Pedro da Motta Veiga, "Mercosur: In Search of a New Agenda," *The Challenges of a Project in Crisis, INTAL-ITD*, July 2004, www.iadb.org.

114. "Mercusor Tribunal Rules on Paper Mills," *LatinNews Daily*, September 7, 2006.

115. Alan Clendenning, "From Wine to Washing Machines, South American Trade Zone Faces New Challenges," *Associated Press*, February 15, 2006.

116. Daniela Estrella Morgan, "Trade Developments in Latin America and the Caribbean," IMF, 2017.and Trade in Value Added and Global Value Chains. Data From: WTO Statistics Soto, Alonso "UPDATE 1-Brazil, Argentina push for closer trade with Mexico in Trump era," *CNBC,* February 7, 2017, www.cnbc.com/2017/02/07/reuters-america-update-1-brazil-argentina-push-for-closer-trade-with-mexico-in-trump-era.html.

117. Brendan O'Boyle, "What Is CELAC?" www.as-coa.org/articles/explainer-what-celac, January 27, 2015.

118. Inter-American Development Bank, " Routes to Growth in a New Trade World."

CHAPTER EIGHT

MICROECONOMIC FOUNDATIONS FOR GROWTH AND COMPETITIVENESS IN THE GLOBAL ECONOMY

Corrupt institutions are a tax on productive growth; citizens, such as these Argentines, are beginning to demand accountable services. *(iStock/ AndresRuffo)*

Micro foundations in Globalized Economy

Latin American per capita GDP has stagnated at roughly 30 percent that of the United States while the Asian region has exhibited greater convergence to American standards of living. In an age of globalization when technology and capital can quickly cross borders, why has Latin American growth not gained momentum? Every good micro principles student knows that the key to enhancing the welfare of a population is improving the economy's productivity. More money in an economy will likely result in higher prices. If wages rise but output is constant, the price of goods will only go up, and no one is better off. The only genuine way to improve people's standard of living is to increase the quantity of goods and services produced per unit of input such as labor, or to decrease the costs associated with production. Absent government transfers, people have to be able to make more in order to have more. Improving productivity is fundamental to the elusive quest for growth.

Our basic microeconomics can again be helpful in thinking through the factors associated with rising productivity. We recall that total product, or our production function, is determined by the combination of land, labor, and capital. In this chapter we analyze the contributions of labor and capital to increasing industrial production in Latin America; in Chapter 9 we will consider some of the issues associated with agricultural change. From the economics literature we know that in addition to our primary inputs of labor and capital, we also need to account for the ways they are combined—total factor productivity or the degree of efficiency, and the way technology enhances output growth. Technological change is devilishly hard to measure. Often considered the residual after measuring how increases in labor and capital affect output, it is the secret source of growth.

Infrastructure such as roads and telecommunications as well as the logistical systems for delivery are complementary accelerators of growth. Our production function must also take into account differences in the national policy environment. Do government policies send the correct incentives to firms to produce more efficiently, or do they act as a drag on innovations increasing output? As Daron Acemoglu argues, countries with strong economic institutions sending appropriate signals will invest more in human and physical capital and will use these factors more efficiently.[1] This chapter will consider how this mix of input conditions—labor, capital, technology, infrastructure, and government policies—creates the wealth of Latin American nations.

Benchmarking Competitiveness

How far behind is Latin America by global standards of productivity and competitiveness? The answer is a rather depressing: most countries lag significantly. The World Economic Forum's annual Global Competitiveness Report makes a big splash each year as papers around the world cover star performers or bemoan the results for laggards; the news is rarely positive in the region.[2] Its **Global Competitiveness Index (GCI)** attempts to capture the collection of factors, policies, and institutions that can determine the level of prosperity of an economy. It is important to note that its use of the term "competitiveness" does not imply a race where a winner captures the gains and excludes the losers. Competitiveness is not defined as a zero-sum game or a dominant share of markets. Rather, by highlighting the quality of key inputs contributing to growth, the index is designed to propel all countries to excel, a win-win proposition for global prosperity.

Based in part on the work of Harvard Business School competitiveness guru Michael Porter, the GCI provides a composite of the effects of factor input conditions, the context for firm strategy and rivalry, the quality of local demand conditions, and the presence of local and supporting industries. Each point of Porter's diamond (described in figure 8.1) creates synergies with the others. With this conceptual backdrop, the GCI incorporates a broad range of factors, including health, education, labor market rigidities, and the sophistication of financial institutions. We have highlighted three areas that constrain competitiveness in Latin America: the legacy of macro instability that we have just covered, the social deficit that we will investigate in our closing chapters, and the market rigidities that we will explore in this section.

The GCI recognizes that countries at different stages of growth can enhance productivity (and therefore output) for different reasons. It posits that growth in less sophisticated economies is driven by the condition of basic factors of production, especially labor. Once countries improve the primary levels of health, education, and infrastructure, in the second stage growth is derived from improving efficiency. Finally, when the gains from efficiency enhancers reach diminishing returns, to

Figure 8.1. Porter's Productivity and the Business Environment

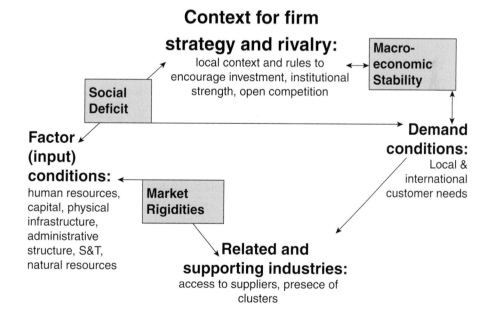

continue to improve productivity countries in the third stage must focus on elements that enhance business sophistication and innovation. Although all factors matter to all countries, enhancing productivity in Bolivia or Nicaragua is likely to be more successful by targeting factor policies such as education. Colombia or Peru are in the transition between factor-driven and efficiency-driven competitiveness, while sustained strong growth in Brazil or Chile is most likely to result from efficiency enhancers. Recognizing country differences, the index weights the factors by a country's place in the stages of development. That is, a little like a handicap in golf, improvements in basic factors will help a poorer country compete in the rankings with a wealthier country focused on components of technology and innovation.

The rather dismal results (with the exception of Chile) for Latin American economies are presented in table 8.1. Chile is the top performer in the region—but doesn't make the top 25 global list. Panama, a global shipping hub, has improved its business sophistication and innovation. Mexico and Costa Rica hover at the 50 mark. Large gaps in infrastructure, institutions tarnished by **corruption** and labor market (in)efficiency leave most of the region underperforming relative to GDP. Venezuela, pursuing a program of resource nationalism, scores poorly on sub-indicators of market freedom; it lands at the bottom of the regional pack. Overall, with low competitiveness rankings, many countries in Latin America operate at the low end of the global value chain, focusing on commodities, resource-based manufacturing and low technology products that constitute more than half of total exports.

Despite the appeal of the indices in the global competitiveness report—after all, who doesn't like a good race—caution should be taken in interpreting the

Table 8.1.   Global Competitiveness Index

Country Name	Country Rank
Chile	33
Panama	42
Mexico	51
Costa Rica	54
Colombia	61
Peru	67
Uruguay	73
Guatemala	78
Brazil	81
Honduras	88
Ecuador	91
Nicaragua	103
Argentina	104
El Salvador	105
Paraguay	117
Bolivia	121
Venezuela	130

Source: The Global Competitiveness Report 2016–2017.

results with respect to answering the important question of why some countries grow faster than others. The index reflects a rich mosaic of data. However, economists grounded in strong economic techniques take issue with the causal relationships between the data presented and changes in productivity or the rate of growth of output.[3] In an economic model, regression techniques allow us to highlight the contribution of a factor to changes in output—that is, to establish causality between independent and dependent variables. The GCI does not weight its factors—or indeed collect its data—in a controlled environment. The specificity of an index and annual leader-of-the-pack rankings stretch is attractive; more complicated but less glitzy causal models don't sell newspapers. Despite these methodological weaknesses, the index is a useful reminder of the key factors that we need to consider in understanding the foundations for productive growth.

The World Bank's publication *The Ease of Doing Business* also collects data on how impediments in the business environment may weaken productivity. In the map in figure 8.2, we see the predominance of dark shading in the graphic—indicating low performance. Table 8.2 identifies some of the background metrics that restrict business in the region. Imagine you want to open a small pizza parlor like Sei Shiroma, an immigrant to Brazil from New York, aspired to do. To be part of the legal economy, you must get permits; it takes over a hundred days to open a business in Brazil. You must go from one bureaucrat to the next, getting each legal piece of paper notarized. Finally, Mr. Shiroman had to hire a fixer—a common middleperson—to negotiate the paperwork nightmare.[4] Luckily pizza parlors don't export; he therefore didn't have to confront the delays in customs where firms spend five times the number of hours filling out paperwork to sell goods abroad.

Although Latin America performs poorly in the business environment, some countries in the region have made strides in easing impediments to business activity. Although improving the business environment may seem straightforward, there

Figure 8.2.   Ease of Doing Business

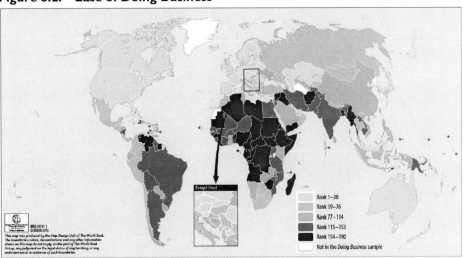

Source: Doing Business database.

Table 8.2.   Comparison of 2017 World Bank Ease of Doing Business Indicators

Indicator	Latin America and Caribbean	East Asia and Pacific	OECD High Income
Time Spent Paying Taxes (hours per year)	342.6	198.0	163.4
Time to Start a Business (days)	31.6	23.9	8.3
Cost of Starting a Business (% of income per capita)	31.5	19.0	3.1
Cost of Getting Electricity (% of income per capita)	999.0	714.6	62.5
Time to Register Property (days)	68.6	74.4	22.4
Time Spent Dealing with Construction Permits (days)	181.3	134.1	152.1
Time to Export: Border Compliance (hours)	63.5	57.0	12.4

can be unintended effects. With a complex set of causes that include high costs to legally register your firm, as well as tax evasion, bringing firms into legal compliance requires a multidimensional strategy. Quickly cracking down on unregistered firms could have inadvertent consequences. Primarily run by poor and poorly educated people, they may not transfer easily over to the formal economy. Carrots—such as lowering the barriers to small business registration as well as universal health care—are more successful first steps. Information and training can help those with a primary education to file for legal certification. Regulatory reform doesn't imply no regulation; instead it is the creation of rules to facilitate rather than hinder business. The World Bank packages this as SMART business regulations—Streamlined, Meaningful, Adaptable, Relevant, Transparent—not necessarily fewer regulations.

A more effective business environment should target micro- and medium-sized enterprises. Even small costs can loom large for the poor—and included in this is the cost of time for the hard-working entrepreneurial poor. Reducing the costs to become legal is therefore important. Chile's Business In One Day and Guatemala's Easy Service Window cut down on the transactions costs of compliance. In Brazil, an individual micro entrepreneur program allows workers in small firms to pay a reduced rate (5 percent of the minimum wage) for the right to a tax registration number. One cost that governments have been reticent to address is reducing the difficulty of laying workers off. As a legacy of populist policies to co-opt workers, labor legislation in some countries such as Mexico and Brazil is more stringent than in most of Europe. But protection can perversely work against some workers. Firms are reluctant to hire when they are bound by the court complexities when firing; they therefore prefer own-account workers who unfortunately fall outside the formal labor market.

Governments can also increase the perceived benefits of formalization by ramping up legal services for small firms, creating a benefit to offset the costs of compliance. Brazil, Ecuador, Mexico, and Peru have required that firms supplying the government must be formally registered—including, in some cases, pushing down the supply chain to be sure that the large computer services or paper government contractor is using formal-sector sub-suppliers. These small changes in the business environment can work toward enhancing competitiveness and promoting productivity. Let's now take a deeper dive into these productivity challenges dogging growth in the region.

A Profile of Micro Foundations for Productive Growth in Latin America

The notion that people can only be made better off by creating more output with fewer inputs is elegantly simple. Creating an environment to enhance how nations produce and combine these inputs to promote a prosperous economy is devilishly complex. Development economists have long held that sustained growth is tied to improvements in productivity. You might remember the classic production function from a principles class:

$$TP = f(K, L, L)$$

Total product (TP) grows as we add K (capital such as machines) or L (labor that can be adjusted for skills and education) and combine it with L (land and natural resources). By adding capital and labor we can expect more output or production. But factor-intensive growth is expensive—you need to pay for additional capital, hire workers, or invest in resources. The key to improving well-being is improving output without adding additional inputs—or the magic sauce at play: **TFP**, or **total factor productivity**. As depicted in figure 8.3, this is the effect on growth (econometrically speaking the "residual") when we combine our capital and labor, magically creating knowledge and innovation.

Think about a simple example of a soccer ball factory. If you add more machines or more workers, you will likely increase your output. Of course you need to pay for both, so you may not be better off. But if you can put your labor and capital together more efficiently with innovative know-how, you can produce a larger number of soccer balls with the same set of workers and machines. Knowledge is key to increasing output without adding more labor or capital—and adding to your costs. If output goes up but costs are held down, this simple society will have more soccer balls. The million-dollar question is how to encourage investment in innovation, people, and the physical plant to promote productive, sustainable growth while also containing costs. Some countries are clearly better than others at promoting an incubating business culture. Frustratingly, we will see that the enabling environment for innovative, sustainable growth in Latin America has been alarmingly weak.

As TFP is very difficult to measure, estimates are not widely available. We can see in figure 8.4 data limited to the United States and Brazil. While Brazil in this period exhibited stronger growth in labor productivity, the magic dose of TFP is actually negative. In another study for the Inter-American Development Bank, it was estimated that if Mexico's TFP had been able to keep pace with that of the United States

Figure 8.3. Total Factor Productivity: The Key to Growth

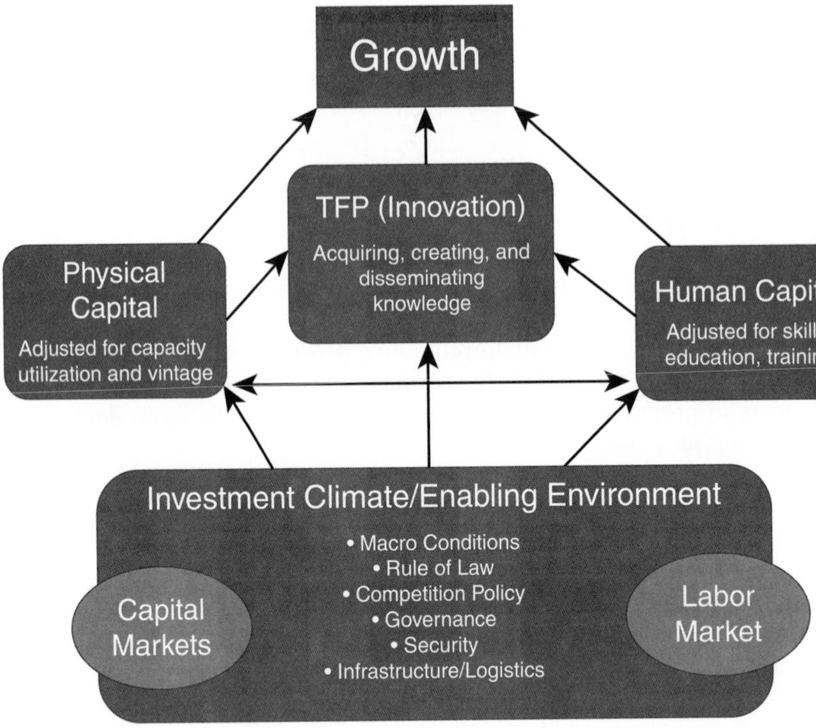

Source: Diagram adapted by the author from The World Bank: Knowledge and innovation for competitiveness in Brazil (2008)

over roughly the past 50 years, the relative per capita income of Mexicans would be 24 percent higher today.[5] To promote sustainable increases in Latin American living standards we need to think about elements that will raise the efficiency of workers while shifting inventives toward knowledge and innovation economies.

Labor productivity data is a bit easier to gather. Here, too, Latin American lags in productivity rates to generate sustainable growth. By 2013, workers in Colombia and Brazil were only about 16 percent as productive as those in the United States; as shown in figure 8.5, Mexico and Chile performed better, edging over 30 percent. The average growth of labor productivity economy wide in Latin America has only been a weak 1.2 percent as compared to 4.2 percent globally.[6] Labor productivity is the baseline for how much people can be paid; a firm will go out of business if it pays its workers more than the value labor creates for the firm. The pathway to rising incomes is therefore through rising productivity.

Latin America's labor productivity is about half its potential.[7] But a country can still be competitive with low labor productivity—so long as its wages are commensurately priced. Of course cutting wages is never a popular political policy—so the key is in increasing productivity. As one can surmise from the wage data in figure 8.5, with the possible exception of Mexico, Latin America does not offer a competitive value in labor when adjusted for the output per worker. If Argentina's

Figure 8.4.   Labor Productivity Growth and Total Factor Productivity in Brazil and the United States, 2007–2012

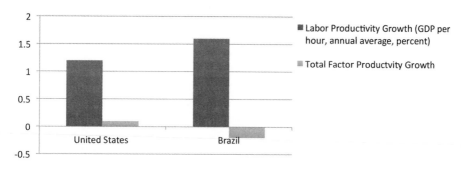

Source: The Conference Board Total Economy Database, Summary Statistics, 1997–2014.
Note: Series is through 2011 for TFP and 2012 for Labor Productivity.

Figure 8.5.   Hourly Compensation Costs in Manufacturing: Argentina, Brazil, and Mexico

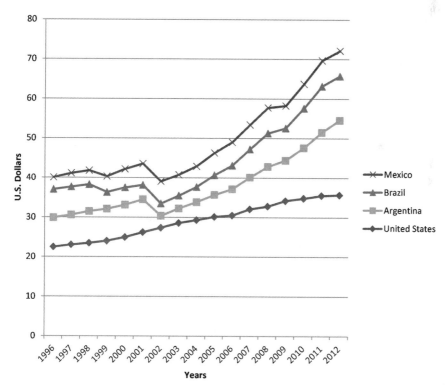

Source: US Bureau of Labor Statistics, International Labor Comparisons, August 2013.

productivity is less than a third than that of the United States but its workers are paid about half the rate of the American worker, firms are at a competitive disadvantage. As the wages of workers rise (largely a good thing as they can afford to buy more goods and enhance their material well-being) but productivity lags, countries get caught in the **middle income trap** (**MIT**). Unlike nations with abundant and cheap labor, they can't compete globally by producing cheap goods—but they also have not moved up the ladder of technology and efficiency to offer knowledge-intensive goods on the global market. Countries caught in the MIT face a prolonged slowdown as they are unable to engineer a structural change from cheap labor to innovation driven economies.[8] This chapter explores the impediments to this structural shift—including the dominance of a low-productivity informal sector, weaknesses in rule of law, and rent-seeking behavior. To date, only Chile and Uruguay are escaping the MIT.[9]

Macro Roots of Micro Fragility

Why does Latin America lag in productivity? Macro instability and the contractionary effects of the debt crisis had a profound impact on industrial performance in Latin America. High rates of inflation and associated uncertainty thwarted long-term strategic decision making and investments in the capital stock. Capital formation was stalled by the lack of available finance. Survival depended on financial ingenuity, not investments in plant and equipment. During this period, dramatic global changes in information technologies transformed the frontiers of business practice, largely leaving Latin American firms behind. The technological lag in automated production and in new inventory systems set firms at a competitive disadvantage. Sluggish domestic demand and neoliberal policy prescriptions forced a new orientation toward the export sector as opposed to production for the domestic market; the focus was largely on agriculture and natural resource-based products, not higher value-added technological items. Trade liberalization and associated import competition had negative effects on textiles, footwear, and the metal and machinery branches.[10] Small and medium-sized enterprises were hard hit; some weathered the crisis by becoming subcontractors to large transnational firms. As demonstrated at the beginning of this chapter, lagging institutional environments for business—large bureaucracies creating delays in registering businesses—created inefficiencies. Insertion into the international economy as a competitive exporters depends upon institutional change in domestic markets for labor, technology, and infrastructure.

Most Latin American nations do not demonstrate comparative advantage in the international market through cheap labor. Keep in mind that with globalization, Latin American workers compete against those in Asia and Africa to produce in the global factory. Central Americans and Mexicans were particularly hard hit as China became the world's assembler post-2000; in 2001 Mexico and China's shares of the US import market were about equal at 12 percent; by 2008 China had risen to over 25 percent of the US import bill. But as wages in the Asian value chain have risen, some wage competiveness has been restored.[11]

Adjusting for prices and foreign exchange, when China first contested the US market, annual real wages in Mexico were about six times those of a Chinese worker; by 2011 they were only 40 percent higher. Nonetheless, the key to sustaining an increase in well-being isn't in depressing wages but in elevating

Table 8.3.   Hourly Compensation Costs in Manufacturing, US Dollars, and as a Percentage of Costs in the United States

| | Hourly Compensation Costs | | | |
| | in US dollars | | US=100 | |
	1997	2012	1997	2012
United States	23.04	35.67	100	100
Spain	13.95	26.83	61	75
Argentina	7.55	18.87	33	53
Brazil	7.07	11.20	31	31
Mexico	3.47	6.36	15	18

Source: US Bureau of Labor Statistics, International Labor Comparisons, August 2013.
Note: 1997 is the first year data for all countries are available to BLS. See technical notes at www.bls.gov/ilc/ichcctn.pdf/.

Figure 8.6a.   Comparative Productivity in Latin America (growth rates)

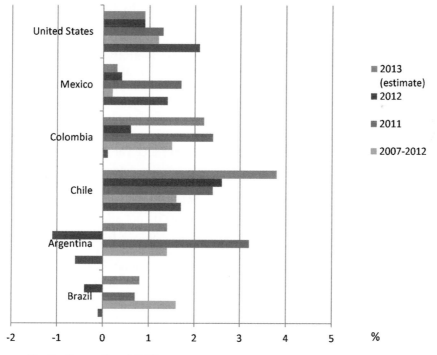

Source: The Conference Board, 2013.

Figure 8.6b.   Comparative Productivity in Latin America (% of US)

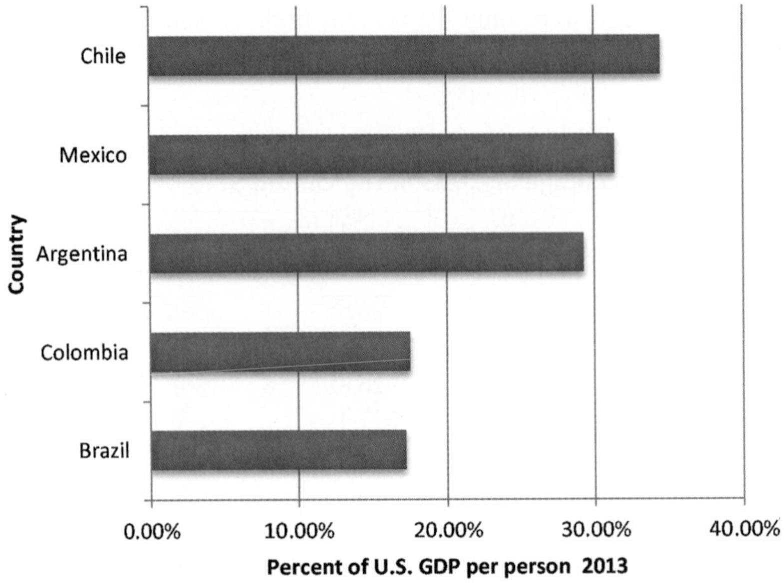

Source: The Conference Board Total Economy Data Base 1997–2014

the efficiency of workers in the region. As suggested by table 8.3, compensation at less than 31 percent of US workers for Brazil when labor productivity (as in figure 8.6) is less than 20 percent of the American rate does not add up to competitiveness. Mexico, in contrast, exhibits productivity at roughly 30 percent of the US rate while workers are compensated at about 20 percent of the wages north of the border—making it an attractive manufacturing destination, especially given geographic proximity.

LABOR MARKETS: GOOD JOBS WANTED IN HIGH PRODUCTIVITY SECTORS

How labor and capital are combined—TFP—is low in the region; this inefficiency is exacerbated because labor markets in Latin America do not allocate resources well. Reform requires a two-pronged approach: moving workers from low-productivity jobs to more productive sectors as well as upgrading the productivity of each worker's job. Under forces of globalization and neoliberal deregulation, workers increasingly find themselves in precarious, unproductive sectors. Survival strategies have sent workers scrambling for subsistence in an informal sector not covered by insurance, benefits, or regulations. Women in particular are concentrated in the low end of the labor market. Moving workers to stable, high productivity jobs is an economy-wide shift in where people work; the second challenge involves firm level adjustments to make working people more productive.

Reducing **informal sector** is the new challenge of structural change. In addition to underinvestment in infrastructure, **logistics**, and research and development, the large size of the informal sector acts as a drag on productivity in Latin America. Informality can be measured from the perspective of either the firm or the worker. A firm that is completely informal might not register its activity, pay taxes or comply with regulatory structures. Some firms might be officially registered but evade taxes or hide workers. Finally, a firm may be in compliance with tax and labor laws, but may rely on self-employed contract workers to avoid paying for social security. From the worker's perspective, informal employment measures unprotected labor—those employed by firms in both the formal and informal sectors plus those in domestic service who aren't covered by social insurance. Although some workers may be trying to evade paying taxes, the International Labor Organization (ILO) points to the lack of formal-sector opportunities as the primary driver for performing insecure labor. That is, if you were offered the chance to pay some taxes but receive social security or evade taxes but have a very uncertain old age, which would you choose?

Although figure 8.7 shows that the informal sector has shrunk from 50.1 percent in 2009 to 47.7 percent in 2012, 130 million Latin Americans are found in the low-productivity informal sector where they perform activities not covered by national labor regulations. In Costa Rica, Uruguay, and Brazil, fewer than 40 percent of workers are in the informal sector; El Salvador, Honduras, and Guatemala have more than two-thirds of their labor force in the low-productivity informal sector. Although informal workers tend to concentrate in small firms, informality in the region is complex as even large modern firms hire non-salaried contract workers paid by the piece, accounting for 11.9 percent of the workforce.

Domestic work accounts for an additional 4.9 percent of jobs with the balance of 30.5 percent as unprotected workers in off-the-books firms.[12] Half of working women have no formal labor protection. For those with only a primary education, 63 percent find themselves in the informal sector; a secondary education reduces the pool to 47 percent and only about a quarter of university graduates work in unregistered capacities. As education maps into income, 75 percent of the poorest toil in the non-agricultural informal sector compared to 31 percent of those in the top 20 percent.[13] Sectorally, the largest concentrations are in construction (69 percent), transportation (57 percent), trade (56 percent), and social and personal services (42 percent). Perhaps not surprisingly, informality is tied to firm size. Nearly 60 percent of small firms (with between one and ten workers) employ workers informally, whereas in firms with over ten workers only 14.6 percent of workers are informal.

Regional reductions in informality were greatest in those countries that experienced commodity booms through 2013. Nearly 90 percent of the reduction in informality—30 million jobs—was a windfall of the positive terms of trade for commodity producers. Unfortunately, the end of the commodity super-cycle is likely to reverse this. The evolution of a vibrant middle class in the region is also contingent on increasing formality. Roughly half of the emerging middle class making between US$10 and US$50 a day—and the vulnerable class (between US$4 and US$10 a day)—still work in the informal sector and are not covered by social security/pension provisions. Middle-class aspirations will be rapidly dashed as these workers retire without social protection and re-enter into poverty. Sustained reduction of informality will only continue through structural change and firm level adjustments.[14]

Causes of Informality

What pushes firms to the informal sector? Some small entrepreneurs find the burden of registering a business or filing taxes to be beyond their time or technical capacity. Some firms believe they cannot cover the labor costs of formality, including payments into social security as well as health benefits. Others are put off by the 71 days it takes to start a business in the region, the 434 days in Venezuela to get a construction permit, or the 400 hours it takes to file income taxes.[15] Rather than focus on issues of productivity or technology generation, managers' attention is often dragged toward resolving bureaucratic red tape. In addition to regulations and rigidity, managers also must confront social and political problems of corruption, crime, and policy uncertainty that weigh down competitiveness in the region. Given these obstacles, it is perhaps surprising that businesses perform as well as they do. Firms such as Embraer in Brazil or Cemex in Mexico demonstrate the ability to contest the international market. Embraer has become a global leader in the export of medium-range aircraft; Cemex is truly multinational in the production and distribution of cement. Both show that strong technological systems adapted to

Figure 8.7.   Non-agricultural Informal Employment in Latin America

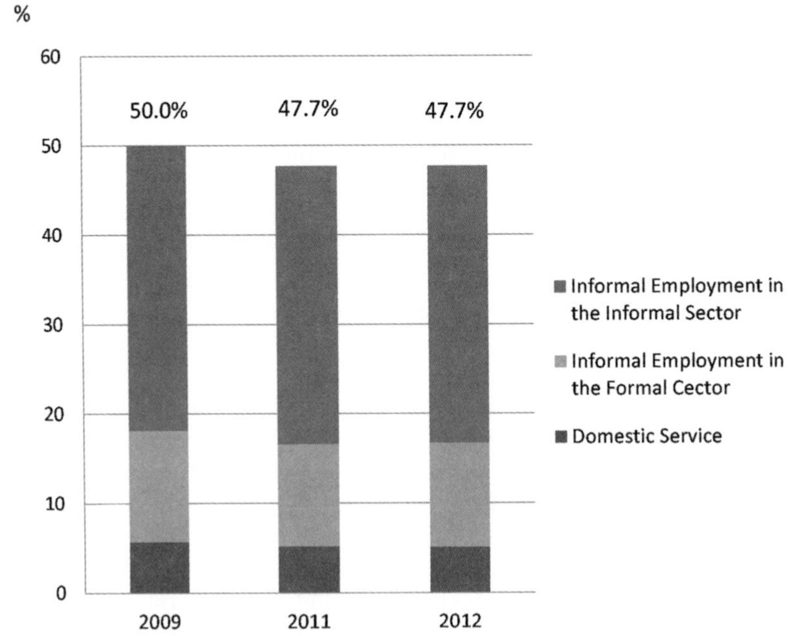

Source: ILO, based on household surveys

local markets can create success. Imagine the productivity and creativity within the Latin American business sector if these constraints were reduced!

Informal firms tend to be small and unproductive in comparison to larger formal-sector firms. The lack of registration normally means they are unable to apply for loans. In addition to a financing gap, informal firms have limited access to government training or protection of property rights through court settlements. To secure protection they tend to rely on payments to gangs as opposed to police support. Large in numbers, it is nearly impossible for authorities to crack down on all extra-legal operations. Without public services, informality rates correlate to a fall in productivity. The World Bank finds that in Latin America each 10 percent increase in tax and social security evasion rates is related to a 7–10 percent decline in total factor productivity. On a macro level, if 50 percent of your economic activity is outside the tax collection system, this huge gap in fiscal revenues is a significant loss to potential investments in health, education, or sustainability. Informality creates a vicious cycle; underfunded education systems poorly prepare workers for knowledge-intensive higher paying jobs. In part, this is caused by the firms in the informal sector escaping tax obligations; workers in these same firms are not usually covered by social security systems, shifting the burden of caring for aging populations without pensions to the government.[16]

Informality is the New Development Challenge

Reducing informality is a process of structural change. Shifting low-productivity activity to the formal sector can be seen as a parallel to earlier transitions in development from backward agriculture to modern industrial sectors—with some adjustments. Early models of economic development such as the Lewis-Ranis and Fei approaches focused on shifting workers from low-productivity agricultural activity to higher productivity modern manufacturing. In twenty-first century economies, export agriculture is highly productive whereas service sectors lag in efficiency. In manufacturing, large frontier firms operate much like their multinational cousins around the globe, while small and medium-size enterprises have not adopted the efficiency enhancing systems found in advanced economies. The service sector in middle-income countries tends to lag and remains disconnected from global standards of information technologies.

A study by the consultancy McKinsey highlights this dualism in Mexico. The productivity of Mexico's modern powerhouse firms is strong, growing at 5.8 percent a year since 1999—but productivity in small traditional (and largely informal) enterprises has been falling 6.5 percent a year and midsize firms have struggled with under 1 percent a year growth. Overall, McKinsey finds that the gains of the modern companies have been offset by the traditional sector, with economy-wide productivity at 0.8 percent since 1990. Compounding this problem is the fact that the efficient producers in high-growth sectors such as electronics and autos are investing more in automation and robots than in training new workers.[17] Poorly educated unskilled workers will lose either way.

A visible example of this is in restaurants. Unlike northern counterparts, orders are largely taken on paper and passed onto the kitchen. It is charming, but less efficient than a computerized system that feeds backward and forward into ordering supplies and delivering dinners. Where service deliverers in food, finance, and transportation logistics don't adopt the powers of cloud computing, they act as a drag on efficiency. This switch is a key element in enhancing national competitiveness.

THE PERSISTENCE OF INFORMALITY: LABOR MARKET RIGIDITY

Why does the informal sector persist despite efforts to reduce its size? Ironically, informal and vulnerable employment is a result of state efforts to protect workers. Countries in the region have high safeguards in place to protect dismissed workers; 17 of 18 national constitutions guarantee a minimum wage and half mandate compensation for dismissed workers.

Beyond legal labor market rigidities, other characteristics introduce frictions into matching workers with more highly productive firms. Search measures are largely based in informal networks of relatives and friends.[18] Workers in the informal sector have few opportunities to raise their productivity; in the region only 14.2 percent of all workers receive training, far less than an overall of 56.3 percent across all OECD countries.[19] Firms don't demand workers who are less productive—and workers find few opportunities to raise productivity to contend for formal sector jobs.

Firms find it difficult to ascertain a job candidate's productivity, often using poor proxies such as race or ethnicity that lead to bias in hiring. The region experiences one of the widest gaps between the skill set of the workforce and the attributes demanded by firms: over 50 percent of firms report difficulties in hiring for appropriate skills.[20] A low-skills trap sends all the wrong incentives. Low productivity and a weak skill set deter higher value-added investments—and the resulting lack of good jobs creates the disincentive to invest in human capital. Labor markets are failing to send the right signals. To overcome the low skills trap in a globalized economy, selective state intervention may be required to promote a different work ethic. Three types of skills have been identified by the Andean Development Bank. Socioemotional skills, such as perseverance and determination, are the most positively correlated with labor-market participation, physical health, and happiness. Cognitive skills—what the brain uses every day to learn, remember, calculate, and reason—are more closely associated with labor income and the quality of work. Physical skills interact positively with every result concerning the overall quality of human capital.[21] The deficit of these skills creates barriers to growth and reinforces barriers between the informal and formal sectors.

Young workers are especially challenged in landing their first jobs as their productivity can't be ascertained via prior employment. New workers sometimes take internships to establish credentials—but only those with financial resources can afford to work without income. Despite constituting about a quarter of the region's population, 64 percent of youth over the ages 15–29 live in poor or vulnerable households exposed to a range of threats and vulnerabilities. Roughly one in five young people work in informal-sector jobs. But this number masks differences by class. Of all the working youth in the informal sector, 40 percent are the extreme poor, 30 percent are moderately poor, 20 percent are from the vulnerable class, and less than 10 percent are middle class. This labor market segmentation is that much more worrisome as after one year, 60 percent of workers in an informal job will remain in these relatively dead-end positions with low pay. Youth become discouraged. At age 29, three out of ten are NEETS (neither working nor in education nor training, NINI in Spanish), four out of ten are in the informal sector, two in the formal sector, and the rest are students or working students. Of the NEETS, less than one in three have received some education at a college, university, or higher level technical school; another third has not completed secondary education. Technical training is weak in the region, rarely preparing workers for high-level formal-sector jobs. These breakdowns in labor markets for young entrants have persistent effects of excluding the cohort from systems of inclusion—schooling and decent jobs—that build strong societies. Instead, these labor market failures contribute to the intergenerational transmission of poverty by relegating workers to low-productivity informal sectors. Policies are called for that promote smart, inclusive growth that encourages the development of lifelong learning skills responsive to the marketplace to create an endogenous engine of growth.

The relatively young age structure of the population in the region requires substantial new job creation. Youth unemployment has rocketed. The youth bulge of half the population under the age of twenty-five requires that people entering the workforce, roughly from ages fifteen to twenty-four, make the transition from school to jobs.[22] Varying by country, currently 15–40 percent of those young workers seeking employment are unemployed. One program, called Entra 21, is designed to benefit disadvantaged unemployed youth across the region by training young job entrants in the information technology field. Set up by the International Youth Foundation, it runs thirty projects in twenty-one countries in a multisector partnership among business, schools, and the civil sector. Benefitting more than 135,000 youth from 2001 through 2011, Entra 21 focuses on technical and life skills demanded by the labor market. In addition to financial support, corporate donor partners (such as Lucent Technologies, Nokia, Merrill Lynch, Gap, Nike, Telefonica, Accor Hotels, Walmart, Monsanto, Shell, and Microsoft) partner with NGOs and multilaterals such as the Multilateral Investment Fund (an autonomous fund administered by the Inter-American Development Bank) and USAID to provide training services, job opportunities, and technical assistance. Broad partnerships are critical to addressing labor market failures to deliver productive employment more inclusively in the region.

POLICY INTERVENTIONS FOR LABOR MARKETS IN A GLOBALIZED ECONOMY

High unemployment and underemployment may be attributed to structural rigidity in wage adjustments and job security. Latin American countries have long used labor legislation as a tool of social policy.[23] Minimum wages and measures to protect jobs, such as heavy required severance packages or laws against hiring replacement workers, were seen as political vehicles for income transfers and the protection of the poor. The unintended result, however, was labor market rigidity. **Labor market distortions** in Latin America include government intervention in setting wages, high costs of dismissal, high payroll taxes, and the nature of labor-management relations. There is a long tradition of protecting job security. Workers may contest dismissals in court and may be awarded large severance packages. All these factors reduce the flexibility of management and make restructuring difficult. Studies show that an increase in job security results in a decrease in economy-wide employment.[24] Furthermore, the impact more squarely falls on the employment prospects of young, female, and unskilled workers, contributing to rising inequality. The policy dilemma becomes how to protect income security for the employed—who tend to have political power—and simultaneously open labor markets to new entrants and improve global competitiveness.

Union activity is concentrated in the urban formal sector. The union movement in Latin America has often been the path to political power. Labor unions along with the military have historically been among the few interest-group power centers with the organizational structure, leadership capacity, and defined objectives to affect policy outcomes.[25] However, labor union influence has varied historically. Beginning in the 1920s, many Latin American governments began enforcing workers' rights. Legislation and public controls to address employment issues and resolve labor conflicts fit with the populist political paradigm. Governments were directly involved in collective bargaining, promoting a close alignment between political parties and labor. Through legislative changes, formal-sector employees obtained a number of guarantees, most important among them job security. Ground was lost in the 1970s when military governments restricted labor organizing. The return to democracy in the 1980s was also accompanied by financial austerity, limiting gains on the labor front. Trade liberalization brought global competitors in the 1990s, further constraining labor's bargaining power. With weak representation on the factory floor, unions failed to deliver economic outcomes.[26] Union membership declined in industrial countries from 39.7 percent of the workforce in the 1980s to 31.2 percent in the 1990s; in Latin America the fall was from 24.6 to 15.5 percent.

Despite the weakened bargaining power of unions, labor markets remain rigid. In most countries in the region, dismissing a worker after one year carries a severance penalty of more than one month's wages; with ten years' seniority, the cost rises to between six months and one year's salary. Temporary hiring practices have traditionally been constrained in the region in the interest of job security; this interferes with firms' ability to meet cyclical global demand. Finally, in the absence of strong social legislation, health, social security, and unemployment compensation schemes have been directly tied to the wage bill. In Argentina, Brazil, Colombia, and Uruguay this tax tops 30 percent of the cost of labor; throughout the rest of the region it ranges between 15 and 30 percent.[27] High social taxes on labor distort whatever advantage abundant labor might confer in the international economy. On average, the costs of mandatory job security provisions in Latin America were nearly three months of wages; this is nearly double the average Organization for Economic Cooperation and Development level.[28] In a globalized economy there are trade-offs between job-based social protection and factor-based competitiveness.

Formal-sector workers are required to contribute to social security funds, which provide workers with pensions, health care, and accident insurance. The difficulties with these funds include their encouragement of early retirement, payments unrelated to individual contributions, and expensive health care packages that exclude the nonworking poor. Pension systems in the region tend to be organized on a pay-as-you-go basis, placing the burden for payments to pensioners today on current workers in the system. In Chile a program of mandatory payments into individual accounts with minimum benefits guaranteed by the government have replaced the pay-as-you-go scheme. Workers may choose among different investment accounts, generating competition in the market. Similar schemes have been adopted in Argentina, Colombia, Mexico, and Peru.[29] Using the market to create the individual incentive for retirement may not only take the burden off firms but also raise national savings rates and decrease reliance on capital inflows, a point we made in Chapter 7. However, some worry about the future ability of the funds to support the needs of an aging population.

Labor market reforms have not followed a uniform direction in the region. Some countries, such as Colombia, Nicaragua, and Argentina, have worked to increase flexibility. Others such as Chile have traded measures for decreasing the costs of labor to the firm (such as the use of private retirement accounts) for greater protection for workers, including part-time and seasonal workers. Chile pushed through the labor reform bill of 2001, which reduced the workweek and extended labor protection, arguing that Chile must have labor legislation in step with the modern world in order to enter into trade agreements.[30] This tension between labor market flexibility and international standards is a difficult national problem.

To address both informality and uncompetitiveness, nations are working to promote job creation rather than job protection. These programs tend toward labor-intensive public works projects or subsidies to private firms to hire more workers. They are financed by central governments and are often executed by local agents, either public or private through NGOs. But public employment programs such as workfare can distort private labor markets, and supplements to private firms may simply subsidize hires that would have taken place anyway. Training programs are also popular. Chile Joven, a pioneering youth training program, combines scholarships for classroom training with private-sector apprenticeships. In 2006 the Chilean government of Michelle Bachelet proposed a 50 percent subsidy of the salaries of four thousand young workers under age twenty-five as an incentive to incorporate them into the job market. But training programs tend to be expensive on a per-beneficiary basis, and they may in fact attract youth away from continuing formal education. For those who otherwise would be working, scholarships must be set low enough so that they don't discourage job search. Finally, both employment generation and training schemes often don't reach the poorest of the poor—those without the basic requisites for labor market entry.

We know that labor markets are not functioning well in Latin America. Rather than promote efficiency, they tend to segregate workers into low-end informal or well-remunerated modern-sector jobs. What can be done to improve their efficiency—and ideally also promote greater equity? We can think about how people enter the labor market as well as what takes place once they are working. First job initiatives can facilitate the movement of NEETs into formal market positions. Internships and on-the-job training can be made more appealing to firms and more effective if linked to vocational training institutes responsive to labor market demands. Governments can provide subsidies for hiring new entrants; this can even be revenue neutral if a cash transfer is redirected from an entitlement to an enticement to work. Better information about labor markets can open opportunities to a wider set of applicants than found in informal personal networks. Active labor market policies are designed to promote adjustment within labor markets and the movement of unemployed workers to better positions. For people holding jobs, incentives to promote training can enhance productivity. In Latin America, a review of dismal protocols can enhance flexibility in markets and encourage firms to take a chance on new workers without fear that they can't let them go.

Lagging Investment

Addressing low productivity also requires capital investments; the investment rate is too low to promote healthy growth rates. A measure of investment is something called gross fixed capital formation—basically buying the machines we described before accounting for depreciation or the aging of machines. In the 1980s and 1990s, gross fixed capital formation averaged about 18 percent of GDP a year. By the mid-2000s, this regional investment rate had grown to 20.7 percent, which was about the rate from 1950 through 1970 and just below the high of 24.3 percent reached in the 1970s.[31] It is, however, a far cry from the Asian investment rate that reached 44.4 percent in 2013.[32] Investment in infrastructure, and the telecommunications, energy, and land transport networks linking production to market averaged around 2 percent of GDP, not nearly enough for global competitiveness.

SCIENCE AND TECHNOLOGY POLICY: ACCELERATORS OF PRODUCTIVITY

If growth in a globalized world can't be generated on the backs of low-wage Latin American workers, another key to raising incomes is targeted improvements in national systems for technology and innovation. Technology improves the productivity of labor and capital. Technology also allows companies and ultimately countries to move into a higher value-added world. Sustained economic growth involves a structural shift from low-value labor-intensive production to a high-value generation. When confronting the global marketplace, the problem isn't simply producing more but producing something better. Even low-wage Guatemala can't compete with China on wages; it can, however, attempt to identify a market niche where it can innovate, creating a product that is just a little bit different for which people are willing to pay more. For a typical less-developed country, this involves imitating activities that already exist—figuring out how to make t-shirts, coffee, electronics, call centers, or cut flowers better than someone else. Identifying the market niche is a process of self-discovery—but a process that, without the protection of patents, is likely to be imitated by another country or region. The key to sustained growth is creating an environment that continuously favors innovation and adaptation—a tall order for a poor country with competing priorities.

The 2016 Global Innovation Index paints a fairly dismal picture of the Latin American region. Not one country is an innovation achiever as defined by innovation performance greater than that predicted by its GDP. Chile, Costa Rica, Colombia, and Mexico are regional standouts; with weak distinction Panama, Brazil, Peru, Argentina, Paraguay, and Guatemala make it into the top 100 countries but Ecuador, Honduras, El Salvador, Bolivia, Nicaragua, and Venezuela fall at the bottom of global rankings. Research and development (R&D) spending doesn't pass 1 percent of GDP—unlike Israel at 4.3 percent, Finland at 3.9 percent, or the Republic of Korea at 3.7 percent. A positive spin on this dismal performance is that the region has untapped innovation potential.[33] There is also a science and technology gap among countries in the region. Argentina, Brazil, Chile, Mexico, and Venezuela are relatively advanced. Colombia, Costa Rica, and Uruguay have recently generated significant national capacity, but in the rest of the region there is an absence of policies and institutions for science and technology development. In technology generation, the number of patents granted ranged from 11 in Guatemala to 2,535 in Brazil.

The UN Millennium Task Force on Science, Technology and Innovation has placed technology innovation at the center of its view of growth. Characterizing development as learning,[34] it suggests that economic improvement is largely a result of the application of knowledge in productive activities and adjustments in social institutions. It notes that growth results from interactive learning involving government, industry, academia, and civil society. Learning or continuous improvement in the knowledge base is crucial to growth; technological innovation is not simply a matter of installing devices but also of transforming society and its value systems.[35] Half the growth in rich countries is attributed to technology. How can Latin America appropriate some of this dynamism?

Latin America's weakness in innovation reflects low university-industry collaboration, low quality of scientific research institutions, low company spending on R&D, weak intellectual property protection, and low capacity for innovation. Learning requires a culture of openness, criticism, and exploration—institutional qualities often lacking in Latin America's more traditional and hierarchical organizations. Argentina, Brazil, and Chile, the region's leading private technological investors, only spent US$50 per capita on R&D versus between US$200–US$700 in developed countries.[36] Raising standards of living involves the application of knowledge to transform countries from reliance on the exploitation of natural resources and labor to technological innovation as the basis for development. Finland and Ireland are two examples of small countries that have made this successful transition; can Latin America do the same?

Innovation engages a wide range of actors in a society who form a system of mutually reinforcing learning activities. Nonetheless, innovative activity in Latin

America is segmented. Latin America has traditionally been plagued by a splintering of capacity in science and technology systems. Businesses, universities, research institutes, and state providers of financing do not interact in a smooth technological system. Jorge Sabato conceived of a smoothly functioning technological system as a triangle in which industry, basic educational institutions, and science and technology centers constantly interact. Latin America has been plagued by gaps among these institutions, such that there is little communication between the private sector and the university or even between state-run research institutes and academic researchers. Across much of Latin America, the best scientific minds choose to work in academia over industry—or decide to live in North America or Europe. The connection between the academy and the industrial sector is extremely weak. Most of the limited R&D undertaken in the region is paid for by governments or foreign NGOs and performed by universities—yet much of the university work is unconnected to returns in the private sector.[37] Innovation capital is low in Latin America—only 13 percent of GDP versus 30 percent in OECD countries—and it is mostly in the stock of tertiary education as opposed to largely R&D expenditure in more advanced nations.[38] In developed countries, in contrast, 70 percent of R&D activity is supported by the private sector. In Europe 45 percent of researchers and technologists are employed in the private sector; in the United States, private-sector employment in technology-related jobs reaches 80 percent. In Latin America this percentage inverts; 80 percent work in the public sector, leaving only 20 percent in private innovation.[39]

In addition to segmentation, Latin America pursues a linear supply model for science and technology. Because technology and science are seen as public goods, state organizations are given money to develop knowledge. In the linear model, the state develops technology and sends it to the firms. In the United States, while investments are also made in knowledge as a public good, technology is primarily seen as a commodity. That is, information is something that firms buy and sell in the market in response to demand.[40] Market incentives drive investment. This is not to say that there isn't a role for the state in promoting science and technology. The role, however, may be more indirect as a provider or facilitator of risk capital as opposed to a producer in state-sponsored public universities. Demand-driven interactions are nonlinear, engaging a range of actors. States can participate in this dynamic network but are not the primary drivers of technology.

The need for public financing to promote vibrant technological systems may be explained by market failure. Basic scientific knowledge can be considered a public good that the state must provide to promote new activity. With such a low level of basic science and technology infrastructure, it is expensive for firms to span the gap between basic science and industrial applications. With few firms engaging in R&D, there are limited externalities or synergies created by a core of high-tech firms. It would be as if the high-tech corridor in Silicon Valley were distributed one firm at a time across the poorest counties in the mountains of Appalachia. Not only would low levels of educational attainment hinder innovation, but the clustering of suppliers and skilled labor would disappear. The challenge clearly has become how to overcome constraints of training, size, and geographical dispersion to improve productivity in Latin America.

Beyond linear, state-dominated structures, R&D in Latin America is more heavily weighted toward basic science as opposed to industrial applications where it can help productivity. In most countries in the region, activity has been fragmented and uncoordinated, with players and programs operating in isolation from one another. Lagging technological change means that it will take Panama 55 years, Honduras 79 years, and even our regional leader Chile 25 years to catch up to the US level of productivity growth. Although we don't want to make too much of the catch-up metaphor—countries may choose pathways different from that of the United States—it is a rough estimator of the low rate of productivity in the region, a rate that will continue to depress the well-being of its population.

Meeting the productivity challenge involves a clearer understanding of the nature of technology. Neoclassical theory tends to see technology as exogenous to the production system, a tradable recipe or input that incurs a short-run cost in production. Technological progress is viewed as continuous and cumulative, in a single-track race for dominance. Neostructuralists view technology differently. Relying in part on the views of Joseph Schumpeter, an economist who dedicated much of his work to thinking about technological change, neostructuralists see technology as tacit knowledge not easily transferred, a result of interactive learning and a synergistic process between producers and users. Progress is seen as both continuous and discontinuous, with windows of opportunity for acquisition opening—but abruptly shutting at critical junctions in the process of technological change.[41] The policy ramifications of the different views on technology are complex. Can technology be purchased like any input of production to increase output, or are institutional changes required to promote technological absorption into Latin America economic systems?

No matter what your theoretical perspective, the problem of catching up with the technological frontier involves the question of technological acquisition. Technology is an asset; it must be procured somewhere. Technology may be acquired through foreign direct investment, through licensing or turnkey plants, or through the promotion of national technological parks. Technological acquisition is often asymmetrical. The seller of a technology naturally has more information about the new product or process than the buyer. In the case of hard technologies (incorporated into machinery and equipment) as well as soft technologies (new management techniques, quality control, industrial relations, and just-in-time production), the seller of the technology may be the only agent who knows fully the nature of the commodity.

In a developing country, the next task is the assimilation of technology. Here our question of institutional change comes into play. Simply installing a modern factory does not result in technological acquisition. Technology can remain a black box poorly understood and unsuitable for adaptation and innovation. Improving productivity in an economy involves appropriating information about technological systems, assimilating this knowledge, and disseminating applications beyond the first user. Absorption of technology requires not only obtaining a machine but also training a labor force to run it. Sometimes companies are reticent to make such expensive investments in human capital, as well-trained people often leave the firm. Workers themselves, when poor, may not be able to afford the educational investments to become productive in the international economy. Financing of technological acquisition is also risky—investments often do not pan out. Thin venture capital markets in the developing world make it far more difficult to finance a good idea. Institutions—the set of rules and enforcement mechanisms that shape the behavior of organizations and individuals in society—do not effectively promote technology in Latin America. Poor regulatory quality, weak rule of law, corruption, and ineffective governance contribute to the widening productivity gap between Latin America and the rest of the world.[42] The capabilities of governments to promote technological change are limited not only by financing but also by effective governance. Unfortunately, the challenge of technological development was beyond the capabilities of most states, and most nations in Latin America fell further and further behind in the global arena. The private sector has not risen to fill the technology gap. Incentives must be changed to promote technological change in the region.

Given fiscal constraints, states must focus more on structuring incentives for private-sector investment in technology rather than directly investing in technology. Tax incentives favorable to R&D and strong laws protecting intellectual property rights are crucial in promoting a business environment conducive to the development of a science and technology infrastructure. Regulatory frameworks to encourage firms to finance and undertake more R&D must be designed. The state can also act as an arbiter of information, disseminating information about best practices. Collaboration can maximize the use of scarce resources. The state can work directly to redirect public resources in education to improve the quality of human capital. It can also take a leadership role in monitoring and assessing the national stock of technological assets.

Attention should be paid to the gender implications of investments in science and technology education. Good science and engineering indicators are crucial to informed adjustments in science and technology policy.[43] State promotion of investments in science and technology may help transform the problems of economies of scale and limited time horizons that firms face in allocating resources to technological activity. By adjusting incentives, risk may be minimized for these investments, which tend to have uncertain long-term payoffs.

Clearly, with limited resources in the area, incentives toward public-private partnerships might allow for exploitation of economies of scale in technological innovation and adaptation. Costa Rica stands out as an example of a country that has made the transition from a resource-based economy to one pursuing development through technology, viewing "software as the coffee of the new millennium."[44] There are approximately 150 firms in an information technology cluster supporting banking and finance, human resources, health, education, artificial intelligence, data migration, communications, tourism, and management. Half these firms export regularly; nearly 85 percent have used the external sector as a means to expand their markets and achieve scale economies. In addition, multinationals such as Motorola, Conair, and Sylvania had established plants in the Costa Rican free assembly zone. The sector, dominated by local capital, traces its success back to government initiatives in the 1960s and 1970s that transformed the environment for information technologies. Eliminating debilitating 133 percent taxes on personal computers created the demand for Spanish-language software applications for new imported hardware. The Costa Rican government also invested in two public universities to promote the development of human capital. The centers at the

University of Costa Rica as well as the Instituto Tecnológico de Costa Rica created clear rivalry to build computer departments. It also developed a new institution named CENFOTEC, a technical school that didn't duplicate the four-year degree but rather worked with industry to train workers to address the local skills deficit. The people engaged in software development were all at university together; they continue this network at the Costa Rican Chamber of Information and Communication Technologies, a private, not-for-profit business association.

NGOs and multilateral agencies partnered to promote computer literacy from the elementary level through technical institutions. Such investment in technology was not cheap; Costa Rica leveraged its funds with external financing from the IADB as well as the Canadian Initiative for Industrial Competitiveness in Costa Rica, USAID, and the United Nations.[45] Partnerships between public institutions and business encouraged firms to develop innovative applications that were not only appropriate for the client but could also be sold externally. Firms were also supported by the Costa Rican trade promotion agency Procomer's "Creating Exporters" program that helped firms with the processes and the search costs of identifying international clients.

Costa Rica's success in building upon this cluster of dynamic firms attracted Intel's 1996 investment in a microprocessor plant; this decision was a function of an ample supply of well-educated workers across the technical, maintenance, engineering, and management levels. As a small country, Costa Rica focused early on a limited number of technologies: information systems, environmental sciences, and the agricultural and forestry sectors, transforming these narrowly defined investments into international comparative advantage in these fields. By 1999 Intel came to account for 30 percent of exports. But in the fast-moving global economy, by 2014 the relative wage differential favored Asia. The company abandoned assembly in Costa Rica, releasing 1,600 workers but retaining a R&D center and a client computing group. Although some feared a major impact on growth, the strong science and technology foundations attracted new firms including an aerospace cluster and manufacturing for high-end apparel such as Lululemon.

Banquete, a food producer, built upon the country's global reputation as a tropical paradise to launch a line of specialized hot sauces in varieties of tropical fruit. Its experience in developing this product line underscored that success wasn't contingent on the acquisition of the physical capital—machines could be purchased at trade shows—but rather on the tacit knowledge involved in innovative product design and international marketing. Costa Rica is seen as an example of the gains of smart, modest investments in the technological arena generating long-term rewards.[46] Innovative institutional arrangements supported by strategic financing can promote dynamic technological development in the region.

INFRASTRUCTURE: A CRITICAL COMPLEMENTARY INPUT

Infrastructure is critical to smoothly functioning markets. If you are the most productive coffee farmer or producer of electronic keyboards, it hardly matters if you can't get your goods to market. Given its proximity to the huge US market, Central

America, for example, should have a greater geographic advantage in trade than it does; it is blocked from its potential by weak infrastructure linking productive facilities to the world.[47] In addition, intraregional connections are terrible, precluding a vibrant expansion of trade in the Central American Common Market. The weak infrastructure that exists is highly vulnerable to natural disasters of heavy rains, hurricanes, swampy soils, earthquakes, volcanic eruptions, and deforestation. The region historically has responded to destruction after the event—rather than preventative shoring up of areas of extreme vulnerability.

Infrastructure development in Latin America confronts an unfriendly geography. Although long coastlines are a plus, high mountains, dense jungles, dry deserts, and isolated urban centers pose enormous challenges. International rankings of transportation infrastructure place Latin America in the bottom seventy-fifth percentile. A movement from the bottom to the top quarter corresponds to a reduction of 9,000 miles measured in transportation costs. Traversing the Andes between Santiago and Buenos Aires is equivalent to nearly quadrupling the distance from 1,129 to 4,700 kilometers; transport costs rise as a function of closed passages in winter and the costs of driving at high altitudes. Trucks must detour about 1,500 miles around the Argentine pampas in the worst of winter. The Amazon basin consumes infrastructure. Intense rains wash out roads; only 30 percent of the jungle roads in which Peru invested in 1980 remain paved today.

Overall, the ratio of paved roads in the region is the lowest in the world. The Latin American average of just under 20 kilometers per 100 km^2 is nine times less than the density of roads in Germany and five times less than in Republic of Korea. As measured by kilometers per one thousand inhabitants, the United States has approximately fourteen times more roads. Costa Rica is the only country with more roads per km^2 than the OECD (2012) average. The accompanying photo in this chapter shows just how tough road conditions are in Latin America. Road systems fail to comply with basic standards for safe and effective traffic patterns. Only 26 percent of the main road network complies with legally required road width; 84 percent of broad secondary networks don't meet standard requirements. Maintenance is unsatisfactory, in part because funding for maintenance has not been prioritized in road-building projects. There is a strong need for self-funding maintenance programs.[48] Weak road infrastructure means weak connections between markets or between farms and tables or suppliers and firms.

Railway density is even worse. Germany's railway density is over one hundred times that of Latin America; even the dismal rail connections in the United States are twenty-seven times those of Latin America. In addition to inadequate roads throughout the region, railroad infrastructure was designed for requirements at the beginning of the twentieth century—not the global market of the new millennium. Regional integration requires a change in the institutional framework to encourage a long-term vision and promote technical cooperation among countries. Inefficient and lengthy customs and border requirements impede the smooth flow of goods, adding to high operating costs for users. Passenger and cargo regulations overregulate transport of passengers but undersupervise cargo transport. Poor technical expertise, credit limitations, lack of contractual liability, and poor social security benefits compound problems in the rail sector. Marine

Poor roads and mountains such as these in San Jose, Bolivia, create obstacles to transportation. *(Courtesy of David Edelstein)*

transport and ports are rendered less efficient by technical problems with fairway depth and the poor availability of equipment to load and unload. Again, the problems are not all with the physical machinery. Given poor roads, travel by sea is the preferred transport mode. Yet the potential of rivers for intra-Latin trade suffers from poorly connected river basins. Latin America has some of the most inefficient ports in the world, better only than South Asia and West Africa. One index of port efficiency places Europe at 5.41 and Latin America at a weak 3.37. Yet Latin ports charge almost twice as much for this poor handling service. Central America's proximity to the huge North American market confers advantage; nevertheless, delays equal to 40 percent of travel time add to costs. In Ecuador it takes 16.4 days to clear customs. Poor customs procedures, lack of electronic data processing, lack of coordination at crossings, confusing documentation, and poorly trained personnel impede trade. Good port performance in Latin America is possible—Chile and Costa Rica, for example, already achieve fast clearing rates to facilitate their export focus.

Logistics costs suffer when the different modes of transportation aren't well joined. If a logistician's dream is an efficient deep water port connected to a freight railway that unloads onto containerized trucking for the final miles, Latin America is the freight engineer's nightmare. A co-modal system reduces transportation costs by 57 percent and lowers social externalities such as pollution by 27 percent for a total savings of 42 percent that supports economic competitiveness as well as environmental sustainability.[49]

Electrical generation per one thousand inhabitants is less than one-fourth the level of OECD countries. Broadband subscriptions are one-third the level of Europe—and largely of poorer quality. Investment in infrastructure was more than halved in the debt and macro crisis years; although it recovered some by 2008, it is still 25 percent less than it was during the period of strong state investment under ISI. The only metric where Latin America is in the ballpark is with mobile phone subscriptions per one thousand inhabitants. Overall, Latin America suffers from a severe infrastructure deficit.[50] ECLAC estimates the need to invest 6.2 percent of annual GDP—more than twice the current level of 2.7 percent—to meet infrastructure demands to the year 2020.[51] To close the gap with East Asia, Latin America needs to invest 3.3 percent in land transportation alone.[52]

Linking Latin America to the Global Economy: Logistics and Competitiveness

Competitiveness isn't solely about making things. Instead, key elements of costs in a global economy is how you move things. One can be the most efficient producer in the world—but if the costs to bring your goods too market are too high, they won't sell. In a globally integrated economy, logistics, defined as the process for transporting inputs, goods, and services from the point of production to the final consumer, is crucial to growth and competitiveness. The World Bank has constructed a logistics performance index (LPI) to benchmark this performance and—perhaps no surprise at this point in our chapter—as shown in table 8.4 Latin America fares poorly.

Although Panama and Chile squeak into the top 50 ranking, once again there is a large set of outliers placing over 100 in the index. Logistics comprises multiple elements of "hardware" such as infrastructure as well as soft systems such as customs, tracking, and tracing. The improvement of the Logistics Performance Index of one point—for example, if Bolivia could achieve Chile's score in the LPI—is commensurate to a 35 percent gain in labor productivity.[53] Achieving gains in the LPI will differ by country. For some the key is transport infrastructure but for others customs regulations will top the list. For example, in Uruguay, an extra day's customs delay reduces the export growth rate by 2.8 percent.[54] Brazil could cut its excessive logistics costs by 16 percent if processing time at the port of Santos were reduced by four days.[55] The busy port of Santos processes about fifty containers per hour; the rate in Shanghai, China, nearly triples that.[56] Reduction in processing times could be achieved through the application of software systems to manage customs processes electronically. Logistical costs comprise between 18 and 35 percent of a product's value in Latin America; in OECD countries the average is 8 percent.[57] Logistics in Latin America are a weak link in competitiveness.

Not only is Latin America weak in logistics, but the products it sells to the rest of the world, such as agricultural commodities and minerals, are especially sensitive to poor logistics. The Food and Agricultural Organization reports that more than 50 percent of fruit produced in the region is lost or wasted before it reaches its

Table 8.4. The Logistics Performance Index (LPI)

Country	Overall Logistics Performance Index		% of Highest Performer	Customs Rank	Infra-structure Rank	Ease to Arrange International Shipments Rank	Logistics Quality & Competence Rank	Tracking & Tracing Rank	Timelines Rank
	Score	Rank							
Germany	4.23	1	100.00	2	1	8	1	3	2
Spain	3.73	23	84.55	24	25	22	23	23	26
China	3.66	27	82.49	31	23	12	27	28	31
Panama	3.34	40	72.47	42	38	16	45	63	41
Chile	3.25	46	69.70	35	63	43	56	34	44
Mexico	3.11	54	65.53	54	57	61	48	42	68
Brazil	3.09	55	64.72	62	47	72	50	45	66
Uruguay	2.97	65	61.21	58	61	69	53	74	59
Argentina	2.96	66	60.84	76	59	81	66	47	61
Peru	2.89	69	58.69	63	75	68	64	65	80
Ecuador	2.78	74	55.15	74	88	65	84	86	77
El Salvador	2.71	83	52.87	107	114	76	83	76	74
Costa Rica	2.65	89	51.12	113	107	73	94	77	101
Dom Rep	2.63	91	50.44	101	111	87	79	88	93
Colombia	2.61	94	49.98	129	95	103	81	96	78
Paraguay	2.56	101	48.40	103	92	96	78	126	107
Nicaragua	2.53	102	47.46	90	83	107	96	107	134
Guatemala	2.48	111	45.76	91	127	120	130	110	100
Honduras	2.46	112	45.34	126	143	97	110	99	108
Venezuela	2.39	122	43.11	145	102	113	122	106	127
Cuba	2.35	131	41.74	105	108	136	135	124	145
Bolivia	2.25	138	38.79	146	134	122	154	125	118

Source: The World Bank Logistics Performance Index. http://lpi.worldbank.org/about

final destination—largely during storage, packaging, and distribution with poorly coordinated logistical services. Although some such as the dairy company Dos Pinos of Costa Rica employ sophisticated and sanitary methods of collecting milk, processing by-products such as cheese while maintaining a cold chain throughout production and distribution, most lack the technical capability to preserve fragile foodstuff. Beyond spoilage, existing systems don't fully exploit information and communication technologies (ICTs) to lower costs. Handling and transportation for a pineapple sent to Saint Lucia via Miami is 43 percent of the product's final price—far more than the 10 percent for production costs. Sending wheat from Manta to Quevedo, Ecuador, is twice as expensive as the original shipment of wheat from Vancouver to Manta. Poor logistics increases food prices in the region by 30–100 percent through inefficient production and delivery. Bringing Latin America and the Caribbean's soft logistics infrastructure to OECD levels has the potential to increase agricultural exports 158 percent, equal to a tariff reduction of 79.3 percent in destination importing countries.[58] The World Trade Report 2013 noted that a 10 percent decline in average transport costs would result in an expansion of more than 10 percent of the number of products exported. As twenty-first century production takes place in a global factory linked by a logistics-intensive supply chain, transport costs are a main driver of competitiveness.

Improving logistics is one of the most cost-effective ways to generate benefits from trade, providing connections to global markets to both source inputs and sell output. With strong logistical systems countries without autonomous input sectors or small national markets can tap linkages for suppliers as well as buyers. Logistics cost more for small and medium-sized firms unable to ship large containers, buy in bulk, or self-supply through subsidiaries; this adds up to over 40 percent of total sales as opposed to 15–18 percent in large firms.[59] For example, small beef producers in Nicaragua face double the logistics costs of large suppliers from ranch to slaughterhouse—decreasing the competitiveness of smaller scale agriculture.[60] Globally, if every country improved just two supply chain barriers—border administration as well as transport and communications infrastructure—to only halfway toward the world's best practices, GDP could increase 5 percent. Under conservative estimates (just eliminating resource waste), even bringing operations halfway to world standards would increase GDP by 4.7 percent and trade by 14.7 percent.[61] For countries struggling with anemic growth rates, this is lush, low-hanging fruit to jumpstart growth.[62]

Soft Components of Logistics

Transforming Latin America's infrastructure gap is a daunting long-term problem. Despite the high risk and significant financial investment, actions can be taken in the short run to improve logistical outcomes including administrative and customs procedures, transportation organization and management, packaging, storage and stocking, tracking and tracing services, and the use of ICTs throughout the process.[63] Poor logistics often make interregional freight costs as expensive—as sometimes more so—than extraregional imports. Enhancing integration involves addressing the logical gaps in the region.

Not all improvements cost much money. In Latin America, a primary cause of delays in delivery is solicitation of informal payments and criminal activities involving stolen cargo. Nearly 20 percent of logistics operators surveyed in Latin America identified criminal activity and 33 percent pointed to bribes as delaying the delivery of goods. (This compares to 5 and 9 percent in OECD countries.)[64] Ironically, firms became accustomed to paying officials to speed customs procedures; this facilitation has now become a drag on the rapid processing of goods. In addition to reducing red tape in customs houses, introducing e-processing can reduce the opportunity for payments to grease the wheels of transport. In Mexico and Central America security costs also loom large, consuming between 15 and 20 percent of logistics spending.[65] Delivery trucks are often accompanied by security details to deter looting by illegal gangs.

COMPETITIVENESS BOOSTERS: INFORMATION AND COMMUNICATIONS TECHNOLOGIES

A key constraint in improving logistics is the regional lag in information and communications technologies. The digital economy is a complex cluster that includes the telecommunications infrastructure, the ICT industries (software, hardware, and ICT services) and the many economic and social activities that are facilitated by the Internet, cloud computing, and mobile, social, and remote sensor networks. It has three main components: the broadband network infrastructure, the ICT applications industry and the final users. ECLAC estimates that the digital economy accounts for 3 percent of Latin America's gross domestic product (GDP), as opposed to 5 percent in the European Union, 6 percent in the United States, and 7 percent in Japan.

More than 62 percent of Latin Americans use the Internet as opposed to 50.1 percent globally. Facebook is a big draw with more than 321 million regional users.[66] In 2008–2012, the region recorded the second fastest growth rate of the population that uses the Internet (15 percent annual average), after the Middle East-Africa. In terms of who uses the Internet, Latin Americans exceed global averages for social networks (96 to 81 percent), e-commerce (76 to 73 percent), and education (46 to 36 percent). But it lags comparatively in business and finance (48 to 57 percent) and e-governance (21 to 30 percent).[67] The Latin American digital footprint is a two-speed process. Although countries are at 75 percent of the OECD income average, they fall at 38 percent of the ICT development index. On a Global ICT Development index that runs to 10, only Uruguay, Argentina, Chile and Costa Rica are above 6.[68] (The United States, Germany, and the United Kingdom are all above 8; Spain is at 7.62.)

Gaps with the global digital economy constrain growth as the availability of networking tools is limited. Uruguay, Chile, Mexico, and Argentina have between ten and seventeen fixed broadband subscriptions per one hundred inhabitants as compared to thirty-two in the United States. At the far end of the spectrum, Honduras, Cuba, and Haiti all have less than one fixed broadband subscription per one hundred inhabitants. A skype call between Brazil and the United States is unlikely to support video for more than a few blurry minutes, and even a voice connection is likely to fall. Broadband can be excruciatingly slow. According to the International Telecommunications Union, although roughly 10 percent of Brazil's inhabitants can access broadband, only about 2 percent access the high speed that 20 percent of Americans—or over 40 percent of Koreans—enjoy. Chile is slightly better—but other Latin American countries don't even make the chart. Improving penetration, speed, and reliability is high on the policy agenda. With limited resources, however, it is likely to be successful only in partnering with the private sector to expand investment.[69]

Latin America's information and communications technology infrastructure is underdeveloped. This is probably not surprising. Industrial countries roughly spend twenty-five hundred dollars per capita on ICT; in Latin America, where average per capita income is far lower, this would mean spending a huge chunk on information technologies—as opposed to food, housing, or health.[70] Although information and knowledge are considered public goods, the ability to access these is increasingly tied to hardware, network infrastructure, and software—which have a private cost. Economies of scale define networks, there is a high degree of uncertainty tied to investments, and there is a need for strong legal and regulatory frameworks to ensure ongoing outlays. Small and medium-sized enterprises have a harder time restructuring processes to adopt new technologies. Inequalities of access are high by both income and geography, with the upper-income strata benefitting from near advanced country status but the lower income strata struggling to find public portals. A large divide also remains between the rural and urban sectors. Finally, a critical aspect of ICT policy in Latin America is not only the digital divide between rich and poor countries but also the important challenge of promoting social inclusion within countries. Clearly, the wealthy elite in Latin America have the latest in computing and information technologies; it is the large majority of low- and middle-class families who would most benefit from this productivity boost.

The Internet can be a powerful accelerator of growth and productivity. As a medium for information and exchange, it enlarges markets and minds Although efforts have been made to connect schools to the Internet, providing expanded access to content and online courses, progress is uneven. A key problem is annual maintenance costs of information technology systems, sometimes exceeding the initial capital investment. In the poorest countries the number of personal computers is low, and access to fast broadband services (most effective for business) is weak. There is much room for private social investment, such as initiatives by Microsoft, supporting new startups, and providing software and cash to nonprofits. This can be a win-win—creating new markets while promoting social good.[71] Nonetheless, to address the huge digital divide both between and within countries, it is likely that the market alone will reinforce existing social gaps and amplify social exclusion.[72]

Beyond the Internet, cellphones are a multiplier for economic activity. The expansion of mobile telephony is impressive. Mobile phone systems are easier to install in cities than running fixed lines through overcrowded slums; they cost 50 percent less than the equivalent fixed line segment. In addition, mobile phones better suit the payment abilities of the poor, allowing the possibility of pay-as-you-use card systems that can be purchased at kiosks as opposed to the more complicated monthly billing for service rendered in areas where informal housing may mean no fixed address. Access to phones is critically important in securing and maintaining a job. Think about your own process of landing a summer job or internship—or the difficulty of calling in when you are sick—without access to a phone. Mobile phones also have a public safety use; hurricane and disaster warning systems to alert populations will be enhanced with stronger connectivity. Of course, mobile phones are less functional in dispersed or rugged rural areas—as any drive through a mountainous zone in the United States will confirm.

Policy Interventions in Infrastructure and ICT

Investments in infrastructure and ICT can support economic growth, reduce poverty, and make development environmentally sustainable.[73] In considering reforms in infrastructure, three policy guidelines emerge: infrastructure should be managed like a business, not a bureaucracy; competition should be introduced; and stakeholders should have a strong voice and real responsibility.[74] In infrastructure reform there is a clear need for a public-private partnership. Profit opportunities create incentives for private participation to increase productivity and reduce costs. But incentives from the public sector are critical in reducing risks that make private-sector activity alone prohibitive.

Throughout the world, public-sector services no longer need to be conceived of as natural monopolies. Revolutions in telecommunications and in provision of electrical and energy services have made a smaller scale possible. Natural monopolies can be opened to the forces of competition, unbundling portions of the service or breaking up service areas geographically. Clearly, this must be done with an eye to equity. Profit-oriented telecoms, not surprisingly, are more interested in servicing high-priced business areas than low-income neighborhoods or rural sectors. Private activity in one area may need to subsidize access for all.[75]

Current shortcomings in transportation that result in high operating costs include limited capacity, poor conditions, and lack of maintenance for roads, airports, railways, and ports.[76] But the problem isn't purely one of physical infrastructure. A key constraint is access to funding. Given the long-term nature and the difficulty, in certain situations, of having users pay for the goods, infrastructure finance usually involves a strong state role. Restrictions in the access to public funding provided by international financial institutions make infrastructure investment in the region problematic. To create the appropriate incentives for infrastructure investment, changes are required in the legal and regulatory framework. Finally, new organizations bridging the public and private sector may be required to build infrastructure deficits. For example, Brazil has changed legislation under its Public-Private Partnership initiative to allow private providers of port services (under lease agreement with the state) to collect fees—a prohibited activity under prior legislation.

In the power and gas sector, population concentrations in urban areas make private investment lucrative. Indeed, Latin America has become a leader in electricity infrastructure privatization. Brazil, Argentina, and Colombia lead the list of developing countries in terms of private investments in the electricity sector. Cost savings are significant. In Bogota, Colombia, the private CODENSA electricity distribution company halved its losses from 24 to 12.5 percent, increased customers per employee from eight hundred to nineteen hundred, and reduced the frequency of service disruption 30 percent within two and half years.[77] Mexico embarked on a new energy strategy in 2014 to encourage private investments, particularly in the electricity sector. In transport, possibilities for private road concessions and maintenance are being pursued. In water and waste, public municipalities are accepting bids for lease contracts to private services. Most public-private partnerships (PPPs) remain at the national level—although municipalities and Brazil and Chile are developing the institutional capacities to manage their own projects.

PPPs introduce private-sector technology and innovation in the provision of public services and incentivize on-time delivery. Joint ventures judiciously negotiated by international firms can bring new expertise to lagging sectors. Risk, inherent in large-scale infrastructure, can be apportioned between the state and the private sector. By separating the functions of buyer/budgeter from deliverer of services, states can impose more fiscal constraints on private firms. However, state activity is critical in providing technical and financial assistance to the solid waste and wastewater disposal firms. Allowing private concessions a license to operate can provide a jolt of competition to state-owned enterprises, inducing these national champions to behave more efficiently. Creating less expensive bedrock services in energy and transport will facilitate the competitiveness of firms throughout the economy.

But PPPs are no panacea. They may incur a high political price as workers are dismissed in streamlined private companies or prices rise to market level. In some sectors, citizens have come to see goods such as clean water as public goods to which they are entitled—not commodities to be priced.[78] We will likely observe increasing regional disparities, as wealthier areas are most likely to attract private capital with higher returns. The rural sector, in contrast, will need more flexible accommodations. Public management of private projects is also fraught with problems. Mispricing a mega-project can be disastrous; the example of Mexican Toll Roads that went belly-up when the public did not want to pay for faster access is a cautionary tale. In Mexico, thirty-six hundred miles of highways were built from 1988 to 1994 at a cost of US$15 billion. These high costs resulted in government bailouts of forty-eight out of the fifty-two concessions granted.[79] Outrageous tolls scared away traffic, making cost recovery problematic. The tolls from Mexico City to Acapulco were a whopping US$63! The government stepped in, cutting average tariffs by 60 percent. In part the lesson of Mexican road concessions concerned the short time frame. Given contract periods of between 10 and 15 years, firms were attempting to recover costs too quickly with exorbitant prices. A longer concession period reduces these pressures, making the concessions more profitable.

Infrastructure is also subject to different time structures for the private versus public sector. Legally a private firm may be liable for compliance to a government that has changed in an electoral period. PPPs in developing regions often also involve multilateral actors such as the International Finance Corporation (IFC) of the World Bank to access credit. Since mega-projects need the bulk of their financing upfront, there is a need for a co-signer to obtain capital. Such participation by the World Bank often involves stipulations for social and environmental licenses—a long-run gain with some short-run obstacles to obtain.

We can think of PPPs on a continuum. If at one end we find fully public companies owned by the state or in joint ventures with private capital, we can move across the spectrum to management contracts, concessions, and fully private operations in a sector. Operations requiring partnerships—normally for technical or financial reasons—engender the need for regulatory changes. If a private firm were to engage in a ten-year investment into electrical distribution, it needs assurances that the terms of the contract (either for a concession or outright ownership) would not be abrogated during the project period. It requires assurances that regulatory agencies won't shift the rules of the game midstream and that access to capital will remain open. The Economist Intelligence Unit's Infrascope ranks countries by their readiness to engage in PPPs with Chile, Brazil, Colombia, Mexico, and Peru leading the regional pack with mature environments for investment. In contrast, the high degree of political uncertainty in Venezuela, Ecuador, and Nicaragua leave them as unattractive for long term infrastructure investment.

CORRUPTION: A GANGRENE ON SOCIETY

A key to raising competitiveness in Latin America is addressing rampant corruption. On my way into a Latin American city after a red-eye from the States, the taxi driver is my first source to catch up on what is on people's minds. In the 1980s and 1990s, the answer was always price inflation and austerity. Now, the first word is invariably corruption. Upon the simplest prompt, the driver will hold forth on how corruption is the cause of unsafe potholes, unfinished construction, unreliable policing, and unresponsive governments. Pope Francis, in a 2015 visit to Paraguay, called corruption the "gangrene of a people."[80] Corruption is also a key source of slow growth.

Transparency International defines corruption as "the abuse of entrusted power for private gain." This transgression occurs in the private sector, government, and in civil society. Individuals may behave in corrupt ways; systemic corruption appears to pervade all levels of society, weakening property rights and the rule of law, acting as a tax on growth, draining institutional capacity, and retarding economic and political development. Acts might be small—perhaps taking a box of bandages from a hospital—or involve massive payoffs such as those embedded in contractors to the Brazilian oil giant Petrobras. It may simply involve not showing up and still being paid. In Peru, 20 percent of surveyed doctors and nurses said absenteeism among their colleagues was "common." In Venezuela, researchers estimated that specialists and senior doctors were absent for around 30 percent of their contracted service hours, while residents and nurses missed 13 and 7 percent of their contracted time, respectively. Parallel behavior appears in schools or other government services.[81] Table 8.5 provides insight into corruption perceptions in the region. You might note that some of the best overall economic performers in the region also have the best scores on corruption.

Table 8.5.   The Americas' Corruption Perception Index

Country Rank	Country/Territory	CPI 2014 Score	Surveys Used	Standard Error	90% Confidence Interval	
					Lower	Upper
10	Canada	81	7	2.45	77	85
17	United States	74	8	3.74	68	80
21	Chile	73	8	1.74	70	76
21	Uruguay	73	6	1.41	71	75
47	Costa Rica	54	5	4.07	47	61
63	Cuba	46	4	4.46	39	53
69	Brazil	43	7	4.01	36	50
80	El Salvador	39	6	1.98	36	42
85	Peru	38	7	2.63	34	42
94	Colombia	37	7	1.68	34	40
94	Panama	37	6	3.49	31	43
103	Bolivia	35	7	2.98	30	40
103	Mexico	35	8	1.66	32	38
107	Argentina	34	7	2.42	30	38
110	Ecuador	33	5	3.56	27	39
115	Dominican Republic	32	6	3.30	27	37
115	Guatemala	32	6	2.96	27	37
124	Guyana	30	4	3.03	25	35
126	Honduras	29	6	3.49	23	35
133	Nicaragua	28	7	2.03	25	31
150	Paraguay	24	5	2.95	19	29
161	Haiti	19	5	2.86	14	24
161	Venezuela	19	7	1.69	16	22

Source: Transparency International 2014.

Is corruption in Latin America as large as people imagine? Measuring corruption is, by its very nature, problematic. Taking place behind closed doors, it is not easily observable. Researchers employ various strategies to document the extent of corruption. Some directly ask people, perhaps framing a question around whether the respondent or a family member has asked for or paid a bribe in the last year. For example, in Ecuador one survey showed 20 percent of adult citizens pay bribes when carrying out a transaction with a local official. Twenty-five percent of respondents report making under-the-table payments in the courts, a third of those using health facilities had to grease the wheels to receive medical services, and 40 percent of users of education pay to receive appropriate schooling.[82] Although the wealthy may pay (and receive) more in absolute amounts, the poor bear a greater burden of the corruption tax to access the public services to which they are entitled.

Measuring corruption is, however, complicated. Even accounting for the fact that bribes are not the only form of corruption, one runs into problems of under- and overestimation. Some—particularly those at the top of the economic ladder—may be reluctant to report paying bribes. It is, of course, normally illegal. Other surveys rely on perceptions of corruptions. The World Economic Forum, for example, does an executive survey that asks people to rank perceived corruption by country. If the chatter is that a country is especially corrupt—perhaps with a bad media story—it will be seen as corrupt even if practices haven't much changed. For corruption in public expenditures such as infrastructure, health, and education leakage studies are used; this is a methodology to track budgetary allocations against actual purchases and stocks in supply rooms.

Corruption acts as a drag on growth. On average, firms grow 3 percent more slowly in poor governance environments; all else equal, national income growth is 2–4 percent higher in countries with moderate as opposed to poor corruption rankings. Corruption is the equivalent of a 20 percent tax on foreign investment. A World Bank report suggests that in the long run, a country with an income per capita of US$2,000 that addresses corruption over time could expect its citizens to see a quadrupling of income to US$8,000.[83] One estimate suggests that corruption in Brazil between 2002 and 2009 has a price tag of about US$25 billion dollars.[84] Beyond outlays of cash to grease the wheels, corruption costs as it erodes confidence in individuals, government, and society. Well-functioning markets require trust in institutions; the belief that there is unequal (and paid for) access to economic and political resources will undermine growth and the legitimacy of democracy.

We can think about corruption as imposing efficiency losses. It acts as a barrier to entry—do you have the political access and the cash to back it up? It diverts investment from productivity-enhancing to rent-seeking behavior. Instead of managers focusing on how to make something cheaply, they are forced to think about who to approach to get needed inputs through customs. For foreign firms falling under corrupt foreign practices acts, it should be calculated as a risk. Corruption eliminates competition in bidding for contracts, landing a more powerful but perhaps less efficient firm with the contract. Corruption allows firms to maintain monopoly power. Pervasive corruption can lead to low rates of investment and slow growth.

In light of the high economic and political costs of corruption, why does it persist? At one level, the answer is simple—elites benefit from access to privilege and money. But we need to ask why it is that corruption is apparently stronger in Latin America than in some other parts of the world. One explanation, offered by Paulo Mauro, focused on the strategic complementarity in the decision to steal.[85] If corruption is commonplace, it is harder to be singled out as corrupt. Again, where stealing from the public is the norm, even if one is caught, it is not big news nor is the reputational damage high. Perversely, if corruption is perceived to be ingrained in institutions, individuals might feel that they might as well steal—because people think they are on the take in any case. If you are already judged as guilty, why not enjoy the rewards? If the legal system can also be manipulated, you will like get away with impunity. For the less powerful in society, a different logic may be at work. Imagine wages are low—and again the probability of detection is low because "everyone is doing it." If a little corruption is tolerated with the slap of the wrist, the costs of getting caught—the probability of detection multiplied by the fine—is minimal and the gains exceed the penalty. If the ultimate cost is losing your job—but your job pays pittance—why not risk the extra money for your family? If you followed this line of reasoning you can better appreciate why many low-paid police officers are able to be bought off in the region.

Given the interdependence of decision making, piecemeal reforms to address corruption are unlikely to work. Major institutional reforms are required so that when you are caught you stand out and face a meaningful price. What policy measures might be considered to break the cycle of corruption? We can think about policy interventions at the national and multilateral levels; both should, however, crucially engage the private sector. Transparency is a key element to combat corruption—and the Internet creates new mechanisms to shed light on secret deals. Local, state, and national governments can be pushed to implement measures of e-government. Bids can be posted and opened online, with video technology. Open data helps by publishing reference prices for hospital and educational supplies; these can be compared to actual outlays to see if the commonplace practice of over-invoicing to land a payment in a bureaucrat's pocket is taking place. Budgets can be made more readily available to citizens—and citizens, usually supported by NGOs, can track whether projects were commensurate with outlays. Evidence suggests that anti-corruption measures alone are less successful than institutional change and a rethinking of governance.[86] Instead, promoting rule of law, freedom of the press, and political competition can generate change. One example is participatory budgeting in Brazil. Incorporating citizen input—especially in poor communities—from the first stage of defining local priorities through the selection of bidders to evaluating outcomes not only improves health and education but makes city governments more accountable, transparent, and less corrupt.[87] Change is not just about weeding out the bad apples but altering the way the crop is grown.

As powerful global corporations are central actors—and also at times victims—of the corruption cycle, international conventions against corruption can be a potent tool. Corruption is a cost of doing business in weak institutional environments. There is an incentive for companies to decrease costs—but only if other large players are willing to put down their payoff arsenals as well. The United Nations Convention Against Corruption, signed in December 2003 in Merida, Mexico, was an important step to better global behavior. Industry agreements can also be effective. The World Bank advocates integrity pacts. Competitors for major bids in telecoms, for example, might pledge not to bribe local officials. Under the pact, if caught, the briber must pay damages to competitors as well as being blacklisted from future projects.[88] Integrity pacts were successful in reducing corruption in the El Cajón and La Yesca hydroelectric projects in Mexico. The private corporate sector can also be leveraged to appreciate the benefits of governance reform. In addition to abandoning bribery as a means of accessing political influence, the adoption of ethical standards can result in better financial performance. Well-governed firms receive higher market valuations, increasing capital inflows.[89] Poor governance and weak transparency undercut the development of deep capital markets.

Corruption is especially problematic in resource-intensive sectors such as oil and mining; industry standards for ethical practices such as the Global Mining Initiative provide cover for change in the private sector. If all firms adopt voluntary standards, one firm is not singled out by stockholders for social investments. US firms often complain they are at a disadvantage as they are at risk of prosecution under the US Foreign Corrupt Practices Act prohibiting the payment of bribes to foreign officials to obtain or retain business worldwide. Parallel global legislation could help to diminish the source of funds influencing political corruption.

Global data tracking can also help improve transparency, governance and the deepening of accountability. The World Bank, the Corruption Perception Index of Transparency International, and the Global Competitiveness program of the World Economic Forum provide import services in shining light on corrupt practices. Consistent data allow citizens the chance to benchmark their national environment against similar countries. If, for example, Chile and Uruguay can perform so well on Transparency's scores (and they do, at numbers 21 and 22 in 2014 globally they are right after the United States and scoring better than France, Portugal, and Spain),[90] then why can't Argentina, Ecuador, or Mexico bust out of the dark basement from being ranked behind one hundred other countries in the world? Civil society and the media can use such benchmarking to nudge national pride toward cleaner governance.

Citizen initiatives are central to promoting institutional change. But those in marginalized communities may need guidance in learning effective pressure points for change. In the Guatemalan municipality of Chinique de Las Flores, for example, when the water began to look like chocolate and children were falling ill, citizens turned to ALAC, or the Advocacy and Legal Advice Center, to navigate political rights. Despite risking personal safety in the face of violent political pushback, the community was able to uncover corruption in the construction of water systems and achieve redress.[91] Social accountability practices have enabled communities to reclaim the corruption tax and improve public services.[92] Cellphones with camera capabilities can become eyes to the world. Indeed, paired with the rise of a Latin American middle class demanding access to services, social media can be a powerful force of change.

Enhancing Productivity in Latin America: The Policy Mix

This chapter has surveyed the wide range of inefficiencies in the business environment in Latin America that leads to lower productivity. Our discussion of the informal sector, labor markets, underinvestment, infrastructure and ICT gaps, and weak institutions perpetuating corruption provides ample space for policy interventions. There is broad agreement that productivity improves with strong competition and enforcement of property rights.[93] A legacy of the oligarchic system of access in Latin America is a crowding out of new, entrepreneurial, and disruptive ideas. An open flow of intellectual and financial capital can encourage better functioning of markets. Interventions in the region will vary by level of development. Those economies that are more factor-driven will benefit from investments in human capital through changes in health and education. We will look more at these opportunities in closing chapters. More advanced economies in the region might focus on higher quality education, training, technological readiness—and the accompanying developments in capital markets to support innovative economies.[94] Institutional factors including weak rule of law and unenforced property rights will benefit from anti-corruption measures and capacity strengthening to build accountability in institutions. In a more certain environment where they are likely to reap returns, firms are likely to be more willing to invest in productivity-enhancing measures.[95]

Judicious opening to international markets can help to promote productivity. When firms are exposed to competition from at home and abroad, they must upgrade products and processes to survive. This disciplinary effect of imports can prompt firms to move to the technological frontier. Moving up the global value chain in production involves wise uses of imports and integration of new processes to secure competitive advantage. Foreign direct investment can provide an infusion of financial and technological capital to jumpstart growth.[96] Highly protected sectors—such as telecommunications in Mexico before reform—tend to extract rents from captive customers. Prices of cellphone services fell 30 percent following Mexico's telecom reform, returning a surplus to consumers. But openness and liberalization is not a guarantee. Competent competition authorities must remain vigilant to secure the best interests of citizens. An open economy can be facilitated and made more competitive with industrial policies that confront market failures in labor, technology, and infrastructure investments. Addressing the structural challenge of moving from low-productivity informal activity to higher productivity formal-sector production is an "all hands on deck" enterprise of governments, civil society and markets.[97] After we take up the specific case of agriculture in the next chapter, we will look at ways market gaps in the social sector might be reformed to promote sustainable, equitable and productive growth.

Key Concepts

corruption	informal sector	middle income trap (MIT)
Global Competitiveness Index (GCI)	labor market distortions logistics	total factor productivity (TFP)

Chapter Summary

Microfoundations for Growth Are Weak in Latin America

- While improving total productivity is important to sustain growth, econometric work suggests that an even more important element is the total factor productivity (TFP)—how knowledge and innovation improve the efficiency of combining labor and capital to create product. The way in which this knowledge and innovation are promoted in a society is the society's investment climate.

The investment climate in Latin America is extremely weak, contributing to the region's lack of growth.

- With wages in Latin America disproportionately higher than productivity, most of the region has been caught in the middle income trap (MIT). Wages are not low enough for the countries to compete globally by producing cheap goods, but technology and innovation are also lacking, leaving the countries unable to compete in the global market for knowledge-intensive goods. Nonetheless, the key to breaking out of this MIT is not lowering wages, but rather improving efficiency.
- Latin America's informal sector makes up just under half of the employment in the region, weighing down on productivity. The informal sector includes unregistered firms, registered firms evading taxes, and unprotected employees who lack both formal job security and retirement security. These informal firms are almost always less productive than larger formal firms, as they lack financing and government protection. Additionally, since these firms do not pay taxes, they deprive the government of much needed revenue that could be put towards health, education, or sustainability. Transitioning those employed in the informal sector into the more productive formal sector is key in increasing a nation's competitiveness.
- The competitiveness indices rank the competitiveness of the countries in relation to growth, business, and other factors. The Global Competitiveness Index suggests three levels of growth: improvement on basic development indicators, increasing efficiency, and business sophistication. However, indexes should be carefully analyzed because of differences in data collection.
- The competitive indices suggest that Latin America has largely divided itself into groups of high-achieving countries like Chile, low-achieving ones such as Nicaragua, and those in the middle of the pack. As a result, blanket strategies aimed at "Latin America" are no longer effective, and must be replaced by country-specific ones.
- Productivity in Latin America is low because of the lack of good institutions; capital accumulation alone does not explain the slow speed of growth. Labor productivity lags due to the lack of natural and physical capital and weak investment in technology. Latin American productivity is roughly the same as in the early 1990s, accounting for much of the poverty in the region. Although Chile, Mexico, Uruguay, and Costa Rica have reasonable or strong growth in productivity, for the majority of the region anemic or even negative productivity growth dominates. Reversing this trend is critical, as per capita productivity growth is essential to making all Latin Americans better off.

Labor Market Rigidities and Unemployment Constrain Growth

- The unemployment problem in Latin America is probably underestimated in the official unemployment statistics, given the difficulty in measuring those workers who are actively searching for jobs. Furthermore, the weak unemployment safety nets cause workers to take jobs for which they are overqualified. Increasing numbers of women and youth entering the labor force increase the need for faster growth to incorporate these new workers.

- Historically, strict labor legislation created a rigid labor market, with high social taxes on labor. Higher mandatory job security provisions undermine cheap labor advantages. The informal sector serves as a safety net for unskilled workers and avoids costly compliance to regulations. The informal sector also acts as a main source of jobs. This sector is divided into three areas: microenterprise employment, own-account workers, and domestic service. However, it tends to be a low-productivity sector because of its capital-poor definition, dragging down the overall productivity growth.

- Labor market regulation and oversight are falling; remuneration and collective organization of workers are also declining. Tension between labor market flexibility and international labor standards have made it difficult to promote job creation and protection in the region.

- Youth unemployment continues to persist, as only those with significant financial means are able to take the unpaid internships necessary to show productivity and experience to potential employers. As a result, many young people, especially those from poor backgrounds, are forced to work in the informal sector. Lack of education and technical training exacerbate this issue, making it even more difficult for youth to become productive members of the workforce.

Weak Investments in Technology Constrain Enhancing Competitiveness

- Latin America is weak on technological innovation as compared to the developed world. Latin America traditionally has had a fractured capacity for R&D with weak interactions between universities, research institutions, and businesses. Due to this lack of foundations, many scientists choose to either go into academia or leave the region, rather than dedicating their work to improving industry. The public sector accounts for an extremely large portion of the funding for research that is normally focused in basic science as opposed to industrial applications, where innovation can enhance productivity. Rather than a direct investment role, state institutions might rethink incentives for technological development, promoting investment and training workers for new global realities.

Infrastructure Gaps Reduce the Capacity for Growth

- Infrastructure in Latin America was damaged by the debt and macro crises of the 1980s and 1990s. The harsh physical environment of Latin America creates challenges for the construction of infrastructure. Public-private partnerships can enhance productivity with private investment and knowledge. Also, privatization in many sectors has improved the service; nonetheless, private monopolies need stronger regulation to avoid overpricing. Services in uneconomical areas might still be provided or subsidized by the government to attend to the populations in distant rural areas. The privatization of companies can provide a low cost and high productivity by easier acquisition of technology, but the social risks of privatization require careful policy initiatives.

Uncertainty in the Business Environment Retards Investment and Growth

- The products that Latin America exports, such as agricultural commodities and minerals, are especially sensitive to poor infrastructure and logistics. A large portion of the agricultural commodities exported are wasted due to inefficient handling and transportation, causing the region to lose potential profits and increasing food prices in the area. Improving these gaps in logistics is one of the simplest ways to increase benefits from trade for the region.
- The crisis of the 1980s led to a reduction in long-term capital investment, leaving Latin American businesses lagging behind. Growth and investment in technology and infrastructure require robust institutions. Bureaucracy, corruption, crime, and policy uncertainty rather than technology or productivity are consistently in the managers' agendas. Institutional reform is required to improve the long-term growth potential of the region.
- Corruption is a tax on doing business; transparency measure to improve accountability will enhance growth.

Notes

1. Daron Acemoglu, Simon Johnson, and James Robinson, "Institutions as the Fundamental Cause of Long-Run Growth," *Handbook of Economic Growth*, eds. Philippe Aghion and Steven Durlauf (Amsterdam: Elsevier, 2005), Chapter 6, accessed at elsa.berkeley.edu/~chad/Handbook.html.

2. Michael E. Porter, Klaus Schwab, and Augusto Lopez-Claros, *The Global Competitiveness Report 2005–2006: Policies Underpinning Rising Prosperity* (New York: World Economic Forum held by WEF at Geneva, Switzerland, published by Palgrave Macmillan, 2005).

3. See, for example, the important article by Sanjaya Lall, "Competitiveness Indices and Developing Countries: An Economic Evaluation of the Global Competitiveness Report," *World Development*, 29(9) (September 2001): 1501–1525.

4. Christiana Sciaudone and David Biller, "A New York Pizza Man's Brazil Nightmare and the Mess It Exposed," Bloomberg.org, July 7, 2015.

5. Matías Busso, María Victoria Fazio, and Santiago Levy, "(In)Formal and (Un)Productive: The Productivity Costs of Excessive Informality in Mexico," IDB Working Paper Series No. IDB-WP-341, August 2012.

6. Jorge Thompson Araujo, Ekaterina Vostroknutova, Konstantin M. Wacker, and Mateo Clavijo, "Understanding Latin America and the Caribbean's Income Gap," World Bank Report No. 97885-LAC, July 2015.

7. E. Fernández-Arias, "The Productivity Gap in Latin America: Lessons from 50 Years of Experience," InterAmerican Development Bank, paper series IDB-WP-692. https://publications.iadb.org/bitstream/.../The-Productivity-Gap-in-Latin-America-Less . . ..

8. Latin American Economic Outlook (LEO) 2017: *Youth, Skills and Entrepreneurship*, © OECD/CAF/ECLAC 2016.

9. LEO 2017.

10. Jose Miguel Benvente, Gustavo Crespi, Jorge Katz, and Giovanni Stumpo, "Changes in the Industrial Development of Latin America," *CEPAL Review* 60 (December 1996): 62.

11. Herman Kamil and Jeremy Zook, IMF's Western Hemisphere Department. Chapter 2 of the IMF's *2012 Selected Issues Paper for Mexico,* www.imf.org/external/pubs/ft/fandd/2013/03/kamil.htm.

12. Elizabeth Gonzalez, "Weekly Chart: Latin America's Informal Economy," *AS/COA* April 2015.

13. ILO, "Recent experiences of formalization in Latin America and the Caribbean," FORLAC Notes on Formalization, 2014.

14. Veronica Alaimo, Mariano Bosch, David S. Kaplan, Carmen Pagés, and Laura Ripani, *Jobs for Growth*, IDB 2015.

15. The World Bank, *Doing Business 2017.*

16. Mariano Bosch, Ángel Melguizo, and Carmen Pagés, "Better Pensions, Better Jobs: Towards Universal Coverage in Latin America and the Caribbean," *IDB*, October 2013.

17. Eduardo Bolio, Jaana Remes, Tomás Lajous, James Manyika, Eugenia Ramirez, and Morten Rossé, "A Tale of Two Mexicos: Growth and Prosperity in a Two Speed Economy," *McKinsey Global Institute*, March 2014.

18. *Jobs for Growth,* IDB 2015.

19. Ibid.

20. OECD Latin American Economic Outlook 2017, www.oecd.org/dev/americas/E-Book_LEO2017.pdf.

21. Pablo Sanguinetti, "Skilling Up Latin America," *Project Syndicate*, December 2016.

22. For a full list of partners in supported projects, please visit: www.iyfnet.org/section.cfm/5/24/800.

23. Shahid Javed Burki and Sebastian ETdwards, *Latin America after Mexico: Quickening the Pace* (Washington, DC: World Bank, 1996), 19.

24. James J. Heckman and Carmen Pages, Working Paper 7773, NBER Working Paper Series, www.nber.org/papers/w7773, June 2000, table 2, Summary of Existing Evidence on the Impact of Job Security in Latin America, 15.

25. Sebastian Edwards and Nora Claudia Lustig, eds., *Labor Markets in Latin America: Combining Social Protection with Market Flexibility* (Washington, DC: Brookings Institution, 1997), 32.

26. B. R. Schneider and S. Karcher, "Complementarities and Continuities in the Political Economy of Labour Markets in Latin America," *Socio-Economic Review* 8(4) (2010): 623–651. Web.

27. Inter-American Development Bank, *Latin America after a Decade of Reforms: Economic and Social Progress 1997 Report* (Washington, DC: Johns Hopkins University Press/IADB, 1997).

28. Inter-American Development Bank, *Competitiveness: The Business of Growth 2001 Report, Economic and Social Progress in Latin America Series* (Washington, DC: IADB), 113.

29. World Bank, *Labor and Economic Reforms in Latin America and the Caribbean: Regional Perspectives on World Development* (Washington, DC: World Bank, 1995).

30. Mark Mulligan, "Chile Labour Reform Secures Backing," *Financial Times*, September 5, 2001, Internet edition.

31. ECLAC, *Structural Change for Equality: An Integrated Approach to Development*, 2012.

32. Gross capital formation (formerly gross domestic investment) consists of outlays on additions to the fixed assets of the economy plus net changes in the level of inventories. Fixed assets include land improvements (fences, ditches, drains, and so on); plant, machinery, and equipment purchases; and the construction of roads, railways, and the like, including schools, offices, hospitals, private residential dwellings, and commercial and industrial buildings. Inventories are stocks of goods held by firms to meet temporary or unexpected fluctuations in production or sales, and "work in progress." http://data.worldbank.org/indicator/NE.GDI.TOTL.ZS Data point from www.tradingeconomics.com/east-asia-and-pacific/gross-fixed-capital-formation-percent-of-gdp-wb-data.html.

33. Cornell University, INSEAD, and WIPO, *The Global Innovation Index 2016: Winning with Global Innovation, Ithaca, Fontainebleau, and Geneva*, 2016.

34. Calestous Juma and Lee Yee Cheon, *Innovation: Applying Knowledge in Development*, UN Millennium Task Force on Science, Technology and Innovation, Belfer Center for Science and International Affairs, John F. Kennedy School of Government, 2005.

35. Juma and Cheon, *Innovation*, citing Sagasti.

36. Augusto Lopez-Claros, Latin American Competitiveness Review 2006, World Economic Forum on Latin America, 2006.

37. Andres Rodriguez-Clare, "Innovation and Technology Adoption in Central America," Research Department Working Paper Series No. 525, Inter-American Development Bank, July 2005.

38. LEO 2015.

39. RICYT, "El Estado de la Ciencia: Principales Indicadores de Ciencia y Tecnología Iberoamericanos/InterAmericanos 2004," Network on Science and Technology Indicators—Ibero-American and Inter-American—(RICYT), www.ricyt.edu.ar.

40. Mario Cimoli, João Carlos Ferraz, and Annalisa Primi, "Science and Technology Policies in Open Economies: The Case of Latin America and the Caribbean," Productive Development Series, No. 165 (Directors Office) October 2005, www.eclac.cl/.

41. Caroline Moser, "Gender Planning in the Third World: Meeting Practical and Strategic Gender Needs," *World Development* 17(11) (1989): 1799–1825.

42. Lauritz Holm-Nielsen, Michael Crawford, and Alcyone Saliba, *Institutional and Entrepreneurial Leadership in the Brazilian Science and Technology Sector,* World Bank Discussion Paper No. 325 (Washington, DC: World Bank, 1996).

43. World Bank, *Meeting the Infrastructure Challenge in Latin America and the Caribbean* (Washington, DC: World Bank, 1995), 10–11, gives data on infrastructure deficits.

44. Andres Rodriguez-Clare, "Innovation and Technology Adoption."

45. CAMTIC webpage, www.camtic.org/EN/camtic/proyectos_cooperacion/ICCI_en.phtml.

46. Statistics in this section from Jeffery Sachs and Joaquin Vial, "Can Latin America Compete?" *Latin American Competitiveness Report* (New York: Oxford University Press, 2002).

47. (ECLAC), Serie CEPAL, Recursos Naturales e Infraestructura, No. 97, September 2005.

48. Sanchez and Wilmsmeier, *Bridging Infrastructural Gaps in Central America.*

49. Gomes et al., 2010 in LEO 2014.

50. ECLAC, "Economic Survey of Latin America 2015."

51. ECLAC, "Countries in the Region Should Invest 6.2% of Annual GDP to Satisfy Infrastructure Demands," October 2014.

52. ECLAC and UNASUR 2012.

53. Latin American Economic Outlook (LEO) 2014 © OECD/UN-ECLAC/CAF 2013, p. 137.

54. Volpe Martincus, Carballo, and Graziano, 2013 in LEO 2014.

55. World Bank, IDB, and ECLAC, 2010, in LEO 2014.

56. ECLAC, Latin American and Asia: Productivity of Selected Ports 2008–2010 in ECLAC 2010–2011.

57. Guasch, 2011 in LEO 2014.

58. Nabil Chaherli and John Nash, *Agricultural Exports from Latin America and the Caribbean: Harnessing Trade to Feed the World and Promote Development.* (World Bank, Washington DC, 2013), https://openknowledge.worldbank.org/handle/10986/16048.

59. Fernández et al. (2011), Guasch (2011), Fries and Fernández (2012), Rodrigue (2012) in LEO 2014.

60. Fries and Fernández, 2012 in LEO 2014.

61. Weforum, Forum's Global Agenda Councils on Logistics & Supply Chains and Global Trade & FDI, "Enabling Trade: Valuing Growth Opportunities 2013," www3.weforum.org/docs/WEF_SCT_EnablingTrade_Report_2013.pdf.

62. WEF, Bain, and World Bank, 2013, as found in LEO 2015.

63. LEO 2014.

64. LEO 2014.

65. Pérez-Salas, 2013 in LEO 2014.

66. "Latin American Internet Users and Population Statistics 2016," Internet World Stats, December 2016.

67. ECLAC, "Main Internet Use in Latin America and the World 2012."

68. ITC Development Index 2016, ITU.

69. LEO 2012.

70. ECLAC, Division of Production, Productivity and Management, "Public Policies for the Development of Information Societies in Latin America and the Caribbean," LC/W.19 Junio 2005, www.eclac.

71. Read more at https://news.microsoft.com/features/how-technology-is-transforming-and-empowering-latin-america-one-person-and-organization-at-a-time/#8LvI3sj2DUhE4cOI.99.

72. Ibid.

73. World Bank, *Economic Growth and Returns to Work* (Washington, DC: World Bank, 1995), 17.

74. IADB, *Competitiveness: The Business of Growth*, 166.

75. Ibid., 186.

76. Sanchez and Wilmsmeier, *Bridging Infrastructural Gaps in Central America.*

77. Richard Lapper, "Policy under Pressure," *Financial Times*, October 6, 2002.

78. John Authers, Auther's Note, *Financial Times*, November 9, 2015

79. McKinsey Global Institute, *Productivity: The Key to Accelerated Development Path for Brazil 1998, Telecom Case 9* (São Paulo: McKinsey, 1998).

80. Francis X. Rocca, "Pope Francis Calls for Judicial Transparency in Front of Audience that Includes Paraguay's President," July 11, 2015, www.wsj.com/articles/pope-compares-corruption-to-gangrene-in-paraguay-speech-1436672901.

81. R. Di Tella and W. D. Savedoff, eds., *Diagnosis Corruption* (Washington, DC: Inter-American Development Bank, 2001).

82. Mitchell *Seligson* "The Measurement and Impact of Corruption Victimization: Survey Evidence from Latin America." *World Development*, February 2006, 34(2): 381–404.

83. The World Bank, *The Costs of Corruption April 2004*, http://web.worldbank.org/WBSITE/EXTERNAL/NEWS/0,,contentMDK:20190187~pagePK:64257043~piPK:437376~theSitePK:4607,00.html.

84. Iona Teixeira Stevens, "Brazil: Taking a Stand against Corruption," *Financial Times,* September 8, 2011, www.ft.com/content/b3ad6755-8d88-36a3-9272-99756634aba5.

85. Paulo Mauro, "The Persistence of Corruption and Slower Economic Growth," IMF Working Paper 2002.

86. Daniel Kaufmann, "Corruption: The Facts," *Foreign Policy* 107 (Summer) 1997: 114–113.

87. Brian Wampler and Mike Touchton, "Brazil Let Its Citizens Make Decisions about City Budgets. Here's What Happened," *Washington Post*, January 2014.

88. David R. Francis, "Why Fighting Corruption Helps the Poor," *The Christian Science Monitor*, November 13, 2003, and "Integrity Pacts in Public Procurement: An Implementation Guide," Transparency International, April 14, 2014.

89. *Why Corporate Governance*, IFC, http://www.ifc.org/wps/wcm/connect/0bfbd70043820680a101b9869243d457/Why+Corporate+Governance.pdf?MOD=AJPERES.

90. "Corruption Perceptions Index 2014: Results," Transparency International, www.transparency.org/cpi2014/results.

91. Coco McCabe, "Turning on the Tap of 'People Power' in Guatemala," Oxfam, March 23, 2015.

92. Reviewed Work: *Enforcing the Rule of Law: Social Accountability in the New Latin American Democracies* by Enrique Peruzzotti and Catalina Smulovitz, Review by John M. Ackerman, *Latin American Politics and Society* 50(2) (Summer, 2008): 192–194.

93. Stephen Weymouth and Richard Feinberg, "National Competitiveness in Comparative Perspective: Evidence from Latin America," *Latin American Politics and Society* 53(3) (Fall 2011): 141–159.

94. Cristobal Aninat, Jose Miguel Benavente, Ignácio Briones, Nicolas Eyzaguirre, Patricio Navia, and Jocelyn Olivari, "The Political Economy of Productivity: The Case of Chile," IDB-WP-105 Working Papers.

95. Thompson Araujo et al., "Understanding Latin America and the Caribbean's Income Gap."

96. Sebastian Faundez, Nanno Mulder, and Nicole Carpentier, "Productivity Growth in Latin American Manufacturing: What Role for International Trade Intensities?," MPRA Paper, University Library of Munich, Germany, 2011.

97. Mario Cimoli, Giovanni Dosi, and Joseph E. Stiglitz, "Industrial Policy and Development: The Political Economy of Capabilities Accumulation," Oxford Scholarship Online, February 2010.

CHAPTER NINE

LATIN AMERICAN AGRICULTURE

Achieving Sustainable and Equitable Rural Development

Small-scale farmers face challenges in the face of agroexports in the region.
(Courtesy of the Inter-American Development Bank)

The agricultural sector in Latin America is complex. It is a locus of dynamism but also one of slow growth. Latin America and the Caribbean offers the largest reserve of arable land in proportion to population in the world, with a total of 576 million hectares (ha) or 30 percent of the world's total arable land. Table 9.1 provides data on the heterogeneous agricultural sector.[1] Regional producers account for 50 percent of global soybean production, 44 percent of beef, 42 percent of chicken and 17 percent of pork exports worldwide.[2] It also is home to five of the ten countries with the greatest biodiversity. Agriculture not only produces food, but is also a source of livelihoods and exports; the sector's output defines its inhabitants' incomes. It holds the possibilities of equitable, sustainable growth—and its history is framed by inequality and **environmental degradation**. Full of contradictions, understanding the rural sector is central to our exploration of development in Latin America.

This chapter begins to unpack the complicated nature of agricultural production and rural life in Latin America. We start by looking at salient characteristics of agricultural markets. Growing beans or soya is not the same as making jeans or washing machines. After exploring market failures in agriculture, we characterize the dominant feature of the sector in Latin America: a highly dualistic market. We analyze the tensions between providing rural livelihoods and promoting food security versus the role that agriculture plays as an export engine, increasingly as part of a global agricultural value chain. Agricultural value chain. In the context of market gaps and productive opportunities, we evaluate policy options to promote strong and sustainable growth and improved livelihoods for nearly a quarter of the region's population.

This chapter analyzes the characteristics of Latin American agriculture and rural development. It also seeks to explain the opportunities and challenges that the region faces as it works to achieve productive, sustainable, and inclusive rural development policy. Throughout, it seeks to answer the following questions:

- What are the characteristics of agricultural markets in Latin America? How does agricultural production differ from manufacturing? Does this call for a different role for the mix between markets and the state?
- What is the nature of agricultural production in Latin America? Who owns or has access to the assets in the agricultural sector? What opportunities are there for smallholders versus corporate producers? How are production techniques and strategies changing? What linkages make up the global value chain?
- What is the impact on rural dwellers of trade liberalization? How has opening up to world export markets affected small- and medium-sized farmers as opposed to the corporate agriculture?
- How does technology intersect with the array of small and large producers in Latin America?
- What factors act as constraints to sustainable, inclusive, and productive agricultural policy and rural development?
- What agricultural alternatives exist to meet these challenges? How can *campesinos*, corporate agriculture, and other stakeholders cooperate to ensure more equitable access and production practices?

Table 9.1. Agriculture at a Glance: Characteristics of Agriculture in Latin America

Countries	Percent Share of GDP, 2009–2011	Percent of Workers in Agriculture, 2005–2010	Number of Tractors & Machinery, 2000–2009	Percent Arable Land, 2009	Hectares of Cropland per Capita, 2009	Exports, 2011 (1,000 US$)	Imports, 2011 (1,000 US$)	Capital Stock, 2007 (millions US$)
United States	1.2	1.6	4,389,812	40.3	0.5	139,891,089	107,109,145	619,125
Chile	3.4	11.2	53,915	8.1	0.1	10,374,887	5,330,276	22,663
Mexico	3.7	13.1	238,830	24.4	0.2	20,997,304	26,035,799	121,134
Panama	4.0	17.9	8,066	24.6	0.2	307,138	1,249,214	3,592
Cuba	5.0	18.6	72,602	54.8	0.4	720,637	2,169,504	24,317
Brazil	5.5	17.0	788,053	23.1	0.4	79,630,341	10,908,333	212,210
Dominican Republic	6.1	14.5	1,868	32.4	0.1	1,455,767	2,010,967	10,301

Source: FAOSTAT accessed at fao.org October 2013

A MULTIPLICITY OF MARKET FAILURES CONSTRAIN LATIN AMERICAN AGRICULTURE

What obstacles exist to achieving sustainable and equitable rural development policy in Latin America? Agriculture appears to lag under both import substitution industrialization (ISI) and open markets—leading us to ask whether there is something peculiar about the sector. The very essence of agriculture—production subject to the open air, reliant on water and good soil—is characterized by an array of risks. Agricultural production is subject to hydro-meteorological, geological, and biological risks. Farmers must contend with too much or too little rain, high winds, and the destructive power of tornados and hurricanes. Their carefully planted fields are disrupted by earthquakes, volcanic eruptions, and tsunamis, and they must be ever vigilant against crop disease and insect infestations.

Latin American subregions are all too familiar with these risks brought on by extreme climatic events. Central American and Mexican farmers are periodically wiped out by tropical cyclones with associated heavy rain, flooding, and landslides. The northern part of South America and the Pacific Coast of Central America face many of the extremes of El Niño's drought conditions while La Niña batters Colombia with flooding. Natural disasters make agricultural production an extremely fragile venture, particularly for small farmers without access to mechanisms for insurance. Not surprisingly, the unpredictability of risky agriculture also makes peasant farmers even more risk averse; adopting a new technology or a new seed that hasn't stood the storms of time may not make sense to the subsistence farmer whose family livelihood is on the line.

Beyond the risks presented by Mother Nature, agricultural markets exhibit other challenges. Agriculture requires a series of tightly linked activities from the suppliers of seed and fertilizer, to the farmer, producer groups, processors, exporters, and wholesalers.[3] For example, bananas—seemingly simple tropical fruits—call for carefully controlled temperatures over land and sea so that they arrive in European and North American markets unblemished and unspoiled. Distances from farm to the point of sale may be large and roads are likely to be poor in underpopulated areas. Produce, dairy, or meat products can easily spoil on long tropical journeys without expensive cold chain transportation facilities. Phytosanitary standards adopted in Western economies make it difficult for small farmers to access markets protected by a web of complicated regulations and certification procedures. Irrigation is uneven, and in remote agricultural areas electricity is unreliable. Farmers or fishing families may not have good information about prices in markets distant from home.

Capital for investment is often scarce, particularly in the lean times of planting before harvest. Access to credit is especially difficult in agriculture because of the unstable nature of returns. Seasonal agricultural activity yields products only at specific times of the year, and diversification is problematic. Unlike making shoes, growing coffee brings money only in season, threatening loan repayments out of the agricultural cycle. Credit markets to supply farmers with seed, machinery, and fertilizer are underdeveloped, leaving poor farmers to rely on expensive intermediaries. Latin American countries typically have segmented credit markets, charging borrowers different prices. Lack of access to formal-sector loans forces smaller holders to rely on friends and family, patron-client relationships, landlords, or professional moneylenders, often at higher than market interest rates.

Several supply-side factors also complicate lending: high bank costs to serving geographically dispersed customers, problems in contract enforcement, and a lack of trained and motivated financial personnel in the rural sector.[4] Transactions costs are higher in the rural sector as agents must travel long distances to borrow, lend, or sell produce. Where an urban microlender might be able to visit ten customers a day, rural distances decrease bank productivity. Small producers with uncertain harvests and a lack of collateral are therefore less likely to find formal-sector lending than large farms. Without credit, investments wither in orchards that bear fruit years later—or even in vegetable farming with no returns until the end-of-season harvest. Governments have attempted to intermediate, providing cheaper rural credit through agricultural development banks as well as offering rediscount lines at negative interest rates and frequent debt forgiveness. But the strict adjustment policies of the 1990s cut many of these traditional rural finance mechanisms. Overall, smaller producers find it difficult to overcome credit and finance constraints and often cannot absorb the transactions costs—the information, negotiations, monitoring, and enforcement—of international trade contracts. New technologies are costly— both to develop through research and to adopt for risk-averse small farmers. Prospects for peasant farmers are limited unless new forms of partnerships promote investments in microtechnologies and rural finance to bring peasant farmers into small-scale commercial sectors.[5]

In addition to credit, **water rights** act as a market constraint. Vital to the protection of local ecosystems, they are key in providing safe drinking water, sanitation, and irrigation for crops. Latin America contains approximately 31 percent of the world's freshwater.[6] However, there are dry regions in northern and central Mexico, the coastal and inland valleys of Peru, Chile, and Western Argentina, Northeast Brazil, the Yucatan Peninsula, and the Gran Chaco area of Paraguay, Bolivia, and Argentina.[7] The uneven distribution of water creates policy problems.

Although the region met its millennium development goal (MDG) of providing safe drinking water to 96 percent of the population, access to water remains unequal across rural and urban regions. The allocation of water and sanitation services is often prioritized for cities, but neglected in the countryside. As a result, rural sanitation is stuck at around 60 percent.[8] The poor are the most impacted during water crises such as droughts or floods. This issue of inclusivity and equality is exacerbated by surface water rights systems based on seniority. Such systems fail to encourage those with priority rights to conserve water, limiting availability to others. For groundwater, incentives must be created to prompt efficient use and conservation. In the case of surface water in rivers or streams, a market for water rights could be developed. Under this system, if those with priority rights were given a greater number of shares in a water rights system to head off political opposition, these shares could be traded to prompt more efficient allocation of this scarce resource.[9] Additionally, community-based infrastructure such as storage systems could be built to allocate water resources more inclusively.

Due to climate change's glacial melting, water scarcity is predicted to increase throughout certain regions, including in the Andes.[10] The economic costs of climate change are estimated—albeit with a high degree of uncertainty—at between 1.5 and 5 percent of the region's GDP.[11] This is staggering. As we will explore in chapter 13, Latin America faces asymmetrical effects in climate change; although only responsible for 9 percent of greenhouse gas emissions, Latin America's agricultural systems face catastrophic damages.[12] Soy is likely to fall in Brazil on the order of 30 percent and yields of corn could face significant declines in Mexico and Central America, while rice, a wetland crop that thrives at higher temperatures, could increase.[13] Adaptation measures, if properly funded, could help minimize the losses due to climate change.

Agricultural markets are failing to promote environmental sustainability. Protection of natural resources against environmental degradation is essential to promoting a healthy, equitable, and sustainable rural sector. Beyond climate change, expansion of agribusiness and intensification of production has created severe costs of deforestation, depletion of soil nutrients, pollution, and damaging use of fertilizers and pesticides. It is estimated that one hundred million hectares of lands were threatened throughout Latin America due to overgrazing, overexploitation of the soil, deforestation, and the use of degrading farming methods.[14] A glaring example of deforestation is in the Gran Chaco region in Paraguay, which is being called "genocide against the forests." Within the Chaco, it is estimated that over two thousand hectares are deforested per day, the highest rate in the world. This deforestation continues, despite an environmental decree (# 453) that prohibits the deforestation of the region to conserve natural resources. Overall, Paraguay has lost 85 percent of its forests in the past half century—loss driven by both large and small farms.

Despite environmental legislation, large-scale companies are often able to skirt regulations. Adhering to environmentally sustainable policy also can be unattractive for small farmers without assets; their priority is family subsistence. Illiteracy and poor sanitary training among uneducated workers have resulted in the poisoning of workers who spread pesticides by hand or eat without washing. One investigation showed that 39 percent of pesticides were applied without protective clothing, and 18 percent of workers admitted to not washing after completing the chore. Good environmental laws are not enough in the face of weak enforcement and strong incentives to deforest or save money on worker agrochemical education. We will look closely at environmental issues in chapter 13; it is important at this juncture to link environmental concerns with sustainable agriculture.

In many rural areas, **property rights** are poorly documented, removing the farmer's best means of collateral: legal title to land. In addition to blocking access to finance, the lack of secure property minimizes incentives for farming families to invest in sustainable agriculture. Why invest for future generations if you are uncertain if the land will remain in your family? Cuts in government budgets in the decades of neoliberal adjustment decimated **agricultural extension programs** that promoted approaches to sustainable farming. Geographic isolation makes the formation of agricultural support groups difficult. With this mountain of market failures, simply getting prices right will not promote equitable and sustainable agriculture. Efficient markets solve coordination problems—seamlessly connecting input suppliers to farmers to transportation logistics to markets along the agricultural value chain to deliver food to consumers. Broken links drain value, resulting in stagnant agricultural sectors. As we will discuss when we turn to policy options, addressing agricultural deficits involves innovations in institutions with an eye to new ways of partnering between farmers, private companies, NGOs, and governments to facilitate dynamic growth in the sector.[15]

Market failures and challenges to sustainable agricultural production in Latin America have exacerbated the historical legacy of unequal colonial land patterns resulting in a highly dualistic sector. Rich in natural resources, Latin America has a relative comparative advantage in the production of agricultural products, providing opportunities for welfare improvement of the least well-off. But all stakeholders have not shared fully in this growth. Small holders are severely constrained by market failures; large corporate farms have been able to leverage opportunities to expand. Let's turn to this dualistic agricultural landscape in Latin America.

DUALISM IN LATIN AMERICAN AGRICULTURAL MARKETS PERPETUATES UNEQUAL GROWTH

Latin American agriculture is highly dualistic. The concentration of large, export-oriented firms is in part the legacy of colonial land distribution. Rural oligarchies protected their access to large tracts of land, resisting redistribution after independence. The reliance on large export crops such as coffee and sugar—and the revenues these brought to national coffers—left central governments disposed toward concentrated agricultural production. Import substitution, with its neglect of agriculture, did little to disturb the status quo.

Agriculture plays a vital economic role in Latin America, ranging from 4 percent of total GDP in Panama to 40.5 percent in Guatemala. Agriculture presents two faces in Latin America, characterized on one side by the prevalence of small-scale farming, based on *campesino* and indigenous traditions, while the other expression is large-scale global agribusiness headed by billionaires such as Blairo Maggi, former billionaire soy king later appointed as Brazilian Minister of Agriculture.[16] As table 9.2 shows, agribusiness dominates landholdings, controlling up to 97.17 percent of the total arable farmland, as is the case in Argentina. Although this is not as extreme in countries such as Colombia and Ecuador, agro-industries nevertheless lead the agricultural system and reduce the presence of smallholders.

This dual presence of family and corporate agriculture has been conditioned by the legacy of the *latifundia* system. During the colonial *latifundia* era, immense plots of lands were allotted to Spanish or Portuguese inheritors, and peasants worked these tracts by means of sharecropping and credit, building paternalistic relationships.[17] Whereas historically the *latifundia* system of landowners and sharecroppers was characterized by cooperation and interdependence, the current divide between small- and large-scale producers is enormous. *Campesinos* have become marginalized from land, labor, and credit markets. They confront enormous market competition from large

Table 9.2.   Small-Scale versus Corporate Agriculture

Country, Year, Type	Number by Type	Area (ha)	% of Farm Land	% of Farms
Argentina (2002)				
Subsistence	63,621	283,868	0.16	21.39
Family	108,501	4,664,718	2.67	36.48
Corporate	125,303	169,859,978	97.17	42.13
Uruguay (2000)				
Subsistence	13,346	65,000	0.40	18.93
Family	36,045	856,000	5.21	51.14
Corporate	21,086	15,501,000	94.39	29.92
Brazil (2006)				
Subsistence	2,477,071	7,799,000	2.36	50.34
Family	1,971,577	62,893,000	19.06	40.07
Corporate	471,817	259,249,000	78.57	9.59
Colombia (2010)				
Subsistence	1,359,654	3,978,318	7.85	67.25
Family	553,865	17,499,253	34.51	27.39
Corporate	108,372	29,227,876	57.64	5.36
Chile (2007)				
Subsistence	165813	552921	1.09	59.5
Family	94487	2769274	9.3	33.91
Corporate	18360	26459491	88.84	6.59
Ecuador (2000)				
Subsistence	636375	1463212	11.84	75.5
Family	186950	5632243	45.58	22.18
Corporate	19557	5260375	42.57	2.32

Subsistence: 0–10 ha, Family: 10–100 ha, Corporate: <100 ha. Data calculated according to statistics in Julio A. Berdegue and Ricardo Fuentealba, "Latin America: The State of Smallholders in Agriculture." In *Conference on New Directions for Smallholder Agriculture* (Rome, IFAD HQ: IFAD, January 2011).

companies that can afford access to resources and technology that *campesinos* cannot. Crops traditionally grown by small-scale farmers, such as wheat, coffee, and cotton, are being produced increasingly by agro-industries, as local farmers are pushed out of this market.[18] Driven by the expansion of nontraditional crop production such as such large-scale plantings of soybeans in Brazil, Paraguay, and Argentina, small-scale farmers struggle to enter the growing commercial export market that increasingly dominates Latin American agriculture.

Let's take a closer look at these contradictions between traditional and modern agriculture in the region. The Latin American smallholder sector of approximately fifteen million family farms can be broken down into three segments of small-scale production. The first category, which makes up approximately 65 percent of small-scale production, comprises farmers reliant on nonfarming sources of income to complement their agricultural activities; this group is limited by little access to land and resources. Although farming is not the only source of income for this group, agricultural production is nevertheless vital for their survival and protection against shocks.[19] With restricted access to land, they are at once dependent on agricultural production for survival but must also supplement it with nonfarm sources of income. The second segment, made up of about four million farms that control approximately two hundred million hectares, encompasses family producers that are primarily or completely dependent on the income from their farms for survival, hiring little to no outside labor.[20] This group faces barriers to market access because of limited assets, infrastructure constraints, and the exclusive nature of markets. Finally, the third smallholder group, taking up about 8 percent of the smallholder sector and producing on approximately one hundred million hectares, occupies a space between family and corporate agriculture. Family members remain active on the farm, but the family also hires outside labor.[21] Overall, the distribution of these groups, which make up the face of small-scale agriculture, varies by region, with a greater number of the third category in the Southern Cone and the Andes.[22] This diversity of needs in the smallholder sector complicates rural-sector policies.

The viability of these farms is conditioned by location as well as size. Luckier firms fall within high productivity areas where land and agricultural assets are better connected into export value chains. Others, however, face depleted resource stocks or are isolated from markets by poor infrastructure. Rural households in these areas also tend to suffer from inadequate provision of public services such as health and education.[23] The heterogeneity of climate in the region contributes to a wide array of farming systems. According to the World Bank, sixteen different systems exist in Latin America, ranging from forest-based agriculture in the Amazon basin, through temperate mixed promoting livestock, coastal plantation zones of Central America, Colombia, and Venezuela producing export crops and aquaculture, and high-altitude farming in the Andes.[24]

Profits gained from the operation of these diverse value chains are often depressed by external subsidies that flood markets with low-priced products. The United States and the European Union are the biggest subsidizers, providing US$50 and US$100 million, respectively.[25] Nevertheless, Argentine economist Walter Pengue argues that removing subsidies within a global production context could actually hurt small farmers. As Latin American corporate farming expands to satisfy global markets, without strengthening local capacity, the boom could put additional pressure on small landholders, increase environmental degradation, and concentrate land ownership, motivating the mass migration of small farmers to the cities.[26]

Agricultural revenues are also sensitive to the exchange rate. Recall that under ISI, the overvalued exchange rate biased development against the agricultural sector. Industrial protection distorted the internal terms of trade between the domestic sectors. Very often, agricultural protection of competitive commodities was directly taxed as a means of raising revenue to support industrial expansion.

To offset this drain, politically powerful agricultural elites were sometimes able to garner favors in terms of subsidies or infrastructure support—but rarely did these benefits trickle down to the small producers.[27] Yet more competitive exchange rates under the neoliberal package have helped spur growth in agriculture. In some cases—Brazil in 2005, for example—the foreign exchange earned in the export boom led to an appreciation of the exchange rate, choking off growth. This demonstrates that maintaining a competitive exchange rate is a delicate balancing act.[28]

Shocks also render agricultural prices vulnerable to change. Agricultural prices of Latin America's major commodities fell to their lowest level of the century during the 1990s, as debt-laden countries adopted the neoliberal focus on agricultural exports.[29] Markets grew saturated, and excess supply drove prices down. In contrast, food prices doubled between 2006 and 2008 during the international food crisis, further demonstrating the volatility of food prices. Although international food prices have since declined, they are still considerably higher than prior to 2006, and are likely remain inflated for the next decade.[30] Looking forward, agricultural reforms may be important to removing distortions and reducing price volatility.[31] In contrast to the opportunities for corporate farming under export agriculture, small and medium-sized farms are increasingly vulnerable to shocks and market fluctuations. Critics argue that free trade agreements and structural adjustment programs contribute to the uneven playing field in which small-scale producers must compete. Critics also question the agro-export model's outcomes for social welfare; evidence suggests that large-scale production profits rarely trickle down to meet the needs of the masses.[32]

Neoliberal prescriptions for export revenues to address the debt transfer problem also reinforced the power of outward-oriented agriculture. The winners of the increasing network of free trade agreements have mostly been those large corporations able to reach global markets. Improvements in packaging and refrigeration for long-distance transportation, and the outcropping of global grocery stores, have also facilitated export interactions. The failure of trickle-down is evidenced in food security data. For example, in Paraguay, although Paraguayan agribusinesses produce enough food to feed approximately 70 million people in a country with a population of 6.7 million, 34 percent of the population still suffers from malnutrition, the highest rate in South America.[33] Farm labor also loses; agricultural employment opportunities have decreased in almost half of Latin American countries due to the adoption of large-scale high-technology displacing workers.[34] Thus, although fast-paced and considerably productive, corporate export models reinforce marginalization of the poor in the rural sector.

THE GLOBAL VALUE CHAIN: INPUTS, PRODUCTION, AND SALES

Globalization has reinforced **dualism** in Latin American agriculture. The form of global production has shifted to rely on agricultural value chains or the sequence of agricultural stages—from the input of seeds and fertilizer by the farmer, to storage and transportation logistics, to retail distribution that places food on people's tables around the world.[35] Growing demand from a global middle class for animal proteins and increased daily calorie intakes combined with a shifts in tastes in North America and Europe for year-round fruits and vegetables have linked Latin American agricultural systems to the global kitchen. It should not be surprising, however, that large producers have a decided edge in delivering high-quality produce and proteins to satisfy new markets.

The structure of agricultural production is based on the vertical integration of a few powerful input suppliers, large-scale producers, and middlemen, creating additional complications for traditional producers. Concentration of large-scale business is so great within the input stage of production that six corporations control 75 percent of pesticide, 63 percent of seed, and 75 percent of private biotechnology research.[36] This keeps prices high, making inputs and other assets for production inaccessible to a large portion of small-scale producers.[37] Small farmers are unlikely to have information networks to identify the latest food fads. How might, for example, a highlands farmer in Peru know that traditional quinoa has become hot new super grain or that a drought in California has spiked the price of avocados? Even if they had this information (which is increasingly possible with new information technologies or information and communication technology (ICTs) in agriculture), how can a small farmer link into systems of safe and quick transport (especially for those quick-spoiling avocados or bananas) to arrive on the shelf of the Walmart in the Boston suburbs?

It is probably not a startling fact that export production falls largely into the hands of corporate agriculture, requiring 90 percent of smallholders to focus on production for the domestic market in order to sustain local populations.[38] It also will not be a surprise to learn that as the demand for soy in China or asparagus in Europe escalates, rising prices of land and other inputs cause smallholders to give up production, selling out to large corporate farmers.

The concentration story is not simply one of global markets but also domestic retail outlets. Supermarket chains control approximately 50 percent of Latin American food sales; the top three account for 80 percent of the big-store market.[39] Smallholders find it increasingly difficult to place products on national shelves. A key impediment is new private quality standards adopted by transnational supermarkets. A case of e-coli on the shelves of a Walmart in Mexico City will quickly spark fears of buying the same lettuce in Chicago—and negatively impact sales and stock prices for Walmart. Reputational damage control will require an ability to trace and correct the problem—something that is far harder to do if the produce is sourced among many small growers.[40] The question, as we turn to policy, is whether and how smallholders can be integrated into the agricultural value chain. They do offer possibilities—especially for production of niche fruits, vegetables, and coffees for high-end global consumers. One example of successful integration of smallholders to a value chain is of Terra Fertil, a buying cooperative in Central America. But integration into the value chain is a complex process engaging a variety of public and private actors.

It should also be noted that Latin American–grown *multilatinas* are key players in the concentration of agricultural production in the region. In addition to global agro-industries like Cargill, regional powerhouses dominate. This control is so great that it has facilitated immense land inequality in countries such as Paraguay, in which 2 percent of the population owned 77 percent of arable land.[41] Within Brazil alone, there are approximately twenty agro-companies whose annual sales total over US$1 billion per year.[42] One particular Brazilian company, SLC Agrícola, became the first grain and cotton producer, in 2007, to list shares on the stock exchange, raising over US$181 million.[43] The Brazilian-owned JBS is the largest foreign meat company on US soil—and it is the world's top producer of beef and chicken, and one of the largest of pork.[44] In 2017 it became embroiled in a corruption scandal that threatens its global dominance.[45] Whatever the outcome, the power and reach of *multilatinas* is extraordinary.

Recent Production Shifts: Monocultures, Transgenic Crops, and Nontraditional Exports

Not surprisingly, the increasing concentration of Latin American agriculture has been accompanied by changes in crop composition with a new focus on monocultures, or single crops, on large tracts of land. In fact, in 2009 the International Assessment of Agricultural Knowledge, Science and Technology for Development argued that the most dramatic change in land use in the region since the turn of the century has been caused by the expansion of monoculture production of soybeans, specifically in Brazil, Paraguay, and Argentina.[46] In Paraguay, soybean production now constitutes more than 40 percent of total agricultural value and takes up 80 percent of cultivated lands. Overall, expansion of monoculture production throughout the region, though enabling large-scale and fast-paced production of high-demand crops, spurs the clearing of forests and the exhaustion of soil nutrients. As a result, this has taken a toll on biodiversity and the future potential of land fertility.

New technologies have made it possible to manipulate the genetics and reproduction of crops, introducing a dependence on transgenic crops and genetically modified organisms (**GMOs**). The private sector controls 85 percent of this complex agrotechnological investment, exacerbating the already immense imbalances between the community controlled and corporate driven agriculture. Reliance on agrotechnology has driven changes in the agricultural workforce, reducing demand for manual laborers and depressing agriculture's share of employment to between 0.8 percent in Peru and 36.1 percent in Bolivia (return to table 9.1). This has driven many to find work in cities, reducing the workforce available to farms.[47] This incorporation of transgenic practices has—like most places—been controversial in Latin America with diverging perceptions of the positive and negative impacts in relation to health, sustainability, and equitable and inclusive development. Brazil and Argentina follow the United States as the top producers of biotech crops.[48] With transgenics, certain crops have enabled a reduction in pesticide use through modified pest resistance. Argentina has been a leader in the adoption of transgenic varieties, covering nearly all planted soybean, corn, and cotton. In conjunction with other new technologies such as no-till farming and silo bags to preserve produce after harvest adopted by farmers, output more than doubled.[49]

But the costs are largely social. Transgenic production is concentrated in large monoculture tracts, often spurring deforestation and the corresponding displacement of local populations. Reliance on GMOs for production also threatens biodiversity and local variations of crops. In response to these perceived harms, certain regions and entire countries in Latin America have sought to ban the use of GMOs or the production of transgenics. Venezuela passed the 2002 "Ley de Semillas" or Seed Law that banned transgenics in the country and fought against the privatization of seeds.[50] President Hugo Chavez declared, "the people of the United States, of Latin America, and the world, ought to follow the example of a Venezuela free of transgenics."[51] Venezuela has continued to block the entrance of companies such as Monsanto because of the threat that they might introduce genetically modified practices within the country. In other places, rather than banning transgenics entirely, governments work to increase transparency and caution with production. The district of Montevideo, Uruguay, now requires all GMO and transgenic products to be labeled in supermarkets for "reasons of health, economics, the environment, religion, and ethics."[52] This transgenics debate underscores the difficult choices in exporting to earn hard currency and preserving the cultural and nutritional elements of food sovereignty.

The change in focus from concentrating on staples for local consumption such as manioc and maize and traditional exports, such as sugar, cocoa, and bananas, toward export products goes beyond transgenics to **nontraditional agricultural exports (NTAEs)** outside the historical pattern of tropical products such as sugar and coffee. NTAEs such as fruits, vegetables, flowers, nuts, and oils already constituted 15 percent of agricultural exports from Latin America in 2005.[53] NTAEs are especially lucrative, because reverse North American seasons make Latin American production complementary to the US and Canadian markets, creating a large demand. This demand is augmented as more North Americans replace meat with fruits and vegetables in their diets. Largely temperate products, these diversified exports are the result of Latin American suppliers exploiting a window of opportunity to meet market global market demand at a lower price. For example, blueberries were introduced in Chile in 1979. Incubated by the National Public Agricultural Research Agency (INIA in Spanish), the technology was passed on to private local producers. Government agencies encouraged investment in quality improvements, certification, logistics, and market development. In 2014 Chile was the top blueberry producer in the world.[54]

Not surprisingly, transnational corporations such as Chiquita (United Brands), Del Monte, and Dole (Standard Fruit) exert significant control over nontraditional export production.[55] However, some small family farms have become involved in nontraditional "niche" markets, such as organic coffee and Fair Trade markets, in which Latin America accounts for more than 60 percent of the world's certified producers.[56] Niche markets have become increasingly popular and successful as consumers demand differentiated products that demonstrate a dedication to sound and transparent practices, creating opportunities for small-scale producers. More on how niche markets might help address the extreme dualism in Latin American agriculture shortly.

SOCIOECONOMIC DEFICITS IN THE RURAL SECTOR

Before we consider policy reforms in agriculture, we need to broaden our lens to consider the socioeconomic characteristics of the rural sector. The economic activity of agricultural production takes place largely outside the health, educational, and infrastructure services of urban centers. Whereas the owners of the huge US Cargill or

Brazilian JBS might live in Minneapolis or São Paulo, smallholders largely live where they produce. In addition to these farmer residents, we also need to consider other rural citizens who survive on nonfarm production. How do those with few assets devise livelihood strategies? How does rural poverty constrain sustainable agricultural capacity? Are agricultural exit options recommended, and if so, who should they target?

Despite a decline of 25 percent in overall poverty in Latin America since 1980, rural poverty remains relatively unchanged. Despite fewer rural inhabitants—119 million, down from 124 million in the 1980s—roughly the same number (62 million) are stuck in poverty, half of these are unable to meet their food needs.[57] Although agriculture has grown at a rate of 3 percent per year (surpassing overall GDP growth for the region), growth has not been pro-poor.[58] According to the Food and Agriculture Organization in 2010, 52 percent of rural Latin Americans were impoverished, and the majority lacked secure access to necessary resources.[59] As shown in table 9.3, poverty rates vary from 10.8 percent in Chile to 71.4 percent in Guatemala; in Bolivia, Ecuador, Guatemala, and Paraguay roughly one-third of the rural population is unable to secure adequate nutrition. This paradox of malnourishment in the midst of agricultural plenty is tied to the lack of assets to invest in agricultural output, including the key element of property rights.

Rural residents suffer from multiple deficits.[60] Insufficient services limit the growth of human capital. Although healthcare has generally improved throughout Latin America, access is still severely inadequate in rural communities. Unpaved roads, large distances between communities and facilities, and lack of funding and medicinal resources are only a few of the constraints to suitable health care faced by countryside inhabitants. Educational quality is poor with limited access in many communities. Small and remote communities find it hard to attract quality teachers; shortages are especially acute at the secondary level. Bright young students are locked out of opportunity with tragic consequences on literacy and future employment opportunities. In Mexico, the rural illiteracy rate is 15.6 percent as opposed to the 4.3 percent in urban regions, greatly limiting employment options.[61] Despite overall growth in the agricultural sector, families completely reliant on farming have become less well off.[62] This surprising negative outcome is explained by the fact that export agriculture is not inclusive of family farmers, instead marginalizing them from the gains from trade. Households with members engaged in nonfarm rural employment do comparatively better—providing a bit of guidance when we turn to policy.

Rural poverty programs must consider the heterogeneity of the rural sector and address the needs of three key groups: farmers, landless agricultural workers, and rural nonfarm workers. The least well off tend to reside in **rural exclusive areas** with little or no infrastructure, few permanent structures, and low population density; options are different when the rural area is connected to local and international markets. Inhabitants of rural exclusive areas suffer the most abject poverty, whereas rural areas with access to larger markets have greater potential to develop more rapidly. Options to improve livelihoods are limited by the dearth of human capital and the lack of opportunity for nonfarm employment. Exit strategies from rural poverty must therefore provide a safety net for those trapped in poverty, permit migration of the young from remote low-density rural areas, stimulate the growth of rural nonfarm activities where possible, foster dynamic commercial agriculture in areas connected to markets, and intensify the productivity and income of the small-farm sector.[63]

Table 9.3. Rural Social Deficit Indicators

Countries	Gini for Income 2005–2011	Gini for Land 1990	Headcount at Rural Poverty Line (%) 2008–2012	Prevalence of Food Inadequacy (%) 2010–2012	Value of Food Production per Capita (US$) 2007–2009	Lack of Access to Safe Water (%) 2010	Property Rights (0–100) 2010
Argentina	44.5	0.83		9.6	968		20
Bolivia	56.3		66.4	35.6	290	12	10
Brazil	58.6	0.85		12.3	616	2	50
Chile	52.1		10.8	10.0	445	4	85
Colombia	55.9	0.79	46.1	20.2	284	8	50
Costa Rica	50.7		25.8	13.1	540	3	55
Cuba				<5.0	235	6	10
Dominican Republic	47.2		48.4	25.5	243	14	30
Ecuador	49.3		50.9	30.7	398	6	20
El Salvador	48.3		50.2	19.8	155	12	40
Guatemala	55.9		71.4	37.8	261	8	35
Honduras	57.0	0.66	65.2	15.1	216	13	30
Mexico	48.3		60.8	10.0	290	4	50
Nicaragua	40.5		63.3	28.3	219	15	20
Panama	51.9	0.87	50.4	19.2	258		40
Paraguay	52.4	0.93	44.8	36.4	599	14	30
Peru	48.1	0.86	56.5	20.1	258	15	40
Uruguay	45.3		4.6	12.2	1005	0	70
United States		0.74		<5.0	669	1	85
Venezuela	44.8			6.4	214		5
World				19.1	295	12	

Source: FAO. *FAO Statistical Yearbook 2013: World Food and Agriculture.* Rome, 2013, tables 12, 14, and 16. Property rights assess degree of guarantee, prevalence of corruption, and likelihood of expropriation (Heritage Foundation). Inequality in Agriculture Indicators: www.fao.org/docrep/018/i3107e/i3107e. Governance Indicators Database: Indicator at a Glance. www.iadb.org/datagob/index.html, and World Bank WDI: Agriculture and Rural Development, http://data.worldbank.org/indicator/SI.POV.RUHC.

Participation and Marginalization: Women in Agriculture

A crucial dimension of rural poverty is the gendered dimension of Latin American agriculture. How do barriers to access for women, the invisible contributors to agricultural production, constrain the potential for sustainable and equitable agriculture? Women's role and participation in the rural economy have grown in Latin America. This is often in response to increasing male migration to cities, leaving women in charge of farms and families.[64] The rural woman's day is consumed by responsibilities such as food preparation; collection of water and firewood; care of children, vegetable gardens, and domestic animals; clearing and plowing land; weeding, cultivating, milking cows, and processing milk and other foods to sell at market; and acting as business manager for the family enterprise.[65] Beyond adopting greater responsibility in their homes, rural women are increasingly engaged in non-own farm employment. Women are employed as laborers for large-scale export-based agribusinesses, which tend to prefer female laborers, because they are generally more available to work on a seasonal basis for lower wages.[66] Rural women also work in nonfarming sectors such as low-wage *maquila* production (largely in Central America), the service sector, and commerce, performing low-productivity activities such as cloth weaving, street vending, or domestic services to help support the household.[67] According to an ECLAC study of eleven Latin American countries, with the exception of Bolivia, rural women's participation in nonfarming activities was higher than men's. However, rural women's employment is still lower than that of urban women and rural men.[68] Nevertheless, their rising participation challenges traditional roles within the rural family.

Despite their increasing role in agriculture and the rural economy, rural women still face intense barriers to land access. This is commonly due to obstacles in the land market and gender bias in family, community, and state land-distribution efforts. Traditionally, in rural communities, promoting female land rights was considered unnecessary, because women relocated to live with their husbands and benefitted from their assets, as opposed to those of their own family. Land and property was traditionally passed down to male inheritors to keep assets within the family. This legacy, despite evolving familial roles, has continued to inhibit female access. As a result, women rarely represent more than 25 percent of landowners throughout Latin America, and in some countries this inequality is much greater.[69] For example, although women in Paraguay produce 80 percent of the food for consumption in the country, they do so with access to only 8 percent of the land.[70] This inequality of distribution of land and assets is exacerbated by legal constraints and male privilege in inheritance and marriage.[71] One such legal constraint can be seen in Mexico, where traditional legal practice made it so that only one person per household could hold land titles, spurring families to favor sons. This causes much conflict, as sons sometimes become beneficiaries of a father's estate to the detriment of surviving widows.[72] In the same way, women have often been excluded from the land decision-making process, which is normally operated by assemblies of men, who implement policy based on patrimonial patterns. This limitation of self-expression in the decision-making process is also exacerbated by high rates of illiteracy among the rural female population.

Recognizing constraints to equal land and asset access within the rural agricultural sector, some governments have attempted to address these issues by establishing agrarian laws to defend women's formal property rights. For example, laws in some countries now enable joint titling, permit dual household heads, and give women a larger say in inheritance and distribution.[73] Nonetheless, women have yet to achieve parity in landholdings. Under contemporary land redistribution programs in Brazil, for example, eligibility to receive land is dependent on many other factors such as an identity card, a registration number, a voter's card, a **land reform** receipt book, a rental contract, and a work permit—documents that can cost a month's salary for the poorest to obtain. And, although some organizations are cooperating with rural women to help register them as potential beneficiaries, the process is slow.[74] Social norms have changed slowly, and women's access to assets that confer power is only gradually opening.[75]

Other nongovernmental advocates for greater representation for rural women include the efforts of rural trade unions and social movements—such as the Brazilian National Rural Women's Movement; ANAMURI, a Chilean women's group; and CONAMURI, the women's food sovereignty network of Paraguay—to promote expanded access to land for women.[76] As highlighted in box 9.1, CONAMURI and other groups work toward more equitable access to land, property, and resources. Ensuring these producers fair access to land can empower women, and improve rural education and health standards.[77]

Box 9.1.   CONAMURI: Female Food Sovereignty to Empower Paraguayan *Campesino* Women

BRIANNE ILLICH

The January Paraguayan heat beats down mercilessly as the eleven representatives of CONAMURI—The National Coordinator of Rural, Working and Indigenous Women's Organizations—sit on the patio of Asunción headquarters. Headquarters operates as the umbrella coordinator for all the smaller CONAMURI district organizations throughout the country.[a] Here, the elected representatives of each district plan urban programs and events, such as radio and television specials, marches, conferences, and fairs that sell produce grown by CONAMURI *campesinas* to city consumers.[b] However, in these meetings, they also discuss the separate efforts that representatives run in their own communities. These include holding courses for women on sexual education, domestic abuse, and agro-ecological training, keeping community gardens, and managing seed banks. Overall, these women are the glue that links the rural and urban communities within CONAMURI together. CONAMURI, the national Paraguayan female food sovereignty network, promotes *campesino*, indigenous, and women's rights, especially within the context of the rural agricultural sector. Specifically, their movement has two focuses. First, they defend *campesino* food sovereignty rights, demanding equitable access to land, a reduction in illicit pesticide use and deforestation, and an end to *campesino* displacements and abuse. In doing so, they hope to give voice to *campesinos*, defend their way of living, and endorse agro-ecological and small-scale production and consumption against the neoliberal model. Second, they promote *campesino* and indigenous women's rights within a patriarchal society that frequently treats women as "subjects rather than protagonists," restricts their access to opportunities, and turns a blind-eye to domestic abuse.

CONAMURI embraces a feminine consciousness and recognizes the significance of its role as the only *women's* food sovereignty group in Paraguay, striving to facilitate female empowerment. The subordination of women in Paraguayan society has been reinforced by the legacy of the patriarchal colonial era, in which male heads ruled families.[c] Under this

continued

continued

social system, women "were subject to direct patriarchal control and forfeited their juridical persona, including administration of property to their…husband."[d] Even into the twentieth century, women were perceived by men as "lacking in rationality … [and] too weak and impulsive to be treated as … equals. They were therefore regarded as 'outside citizenship' and … in need of protection."[e] These historical values promoted by male interests continue to assert an influence on Paraguayan social and gender practices today.

Polarization of gender roles has created many challenges for female empowerment. Women are generally less educated and work less outside the home due to structural limitations, familial responsibilities, and cultural norms. Women's role as mothers makes it especially difficult for them to participate. Historians Sylvia Chant and Nikki Craske argue that motherhood in Latin American feminist theory has been conveyed as a position of "self sacrifice … presenting major obstacles to women's progress."[f] Marianismo, a gender ideology that began within the Catholic Church's adoration of Mary, has idealized feminine values of motherhood, offering "a series of beliefs about women's spiritual and moral superiority to men … to legitimate their subordinate domestic and societal roles."[g] In the same way, historian Evelyn Stevens describes that Marianismo has restricted women's ability to wield power in the public sphere outside of their role as mothers:

> Among the characteristics of this ideal are semidivinity, moral superiority, and spiritual strength. This spiritual strength engenders abnegation that is an infinite capacity for humility and sacrifice. No self-denial is too great for the Latin American woman … She is also submissive to the demands of the men: husbands, sons, fathers, brothers.[h]

Sofia, a CONAMURI secretary, agrees that motherhood has presented a challenge, not just regarding how society treats her, but also concerning her capacity to work outside the home. This emphasizes the divide between women's access to the public and private domain, and the relationship between gender and place. As her boisterous curly-haired two-year-old clambers up her lap, she laughs, "Her at my side … complicates things a lot."[i] According to the United Nations Population Fund, only 7% of Paraguayan women return to work after having their first child, and only 25% of students return to school after a pregnancy.[j] Those who continue to work outside the domestic sphere after having children face much criticism. A CONAMURI "grandmother," María, explains that when a woman is seen working outside the home, men sometimes call out, "What are you doing? Your house is dirty. Take care of your child."[k] This demonstrates that society still places boundaries on women's activity in Paraguay, and "social practices continue to relate gender to place."[l] Anthropologist Jane Nash explains,

> The "transgressions" of women in places dominated by men—the streets, public places in general—fertilize the gender antagonism that erupts in unpredictable ways … The male categories that define women as decent or not decent when they enter these restricted areas still dominate the discourse on sexuality.[m]

However, CONAMURI is working to facilitate an alternative discourse, in which femininity and motherhood become a source of pride that empowers their participation outside the home, rather than limits them to a particular role and space.

Forming their own creed and goals, CONAMURI denounces the oppressive female reality and declares, "Now we are convinced that violence is not natural, rather that it is naturalized in [our] society that conserves the cultural patriarchy of inequality between men and women. We adopt the challenge to search for social transformation and become the owners of our own history."[n] In this way, they are working to "*desalambrar*," or tear down, old norms that reinforce the society of gendered subordination and domination in order to create a new discourse on gender.[o] They also emphasize the importance of defending the rights of indigenous women, whom they consider to be some of the most marginalized members of society, due to their "double barriers of gender and ethnic restriction."[p]

continued

Overall, the CONAMURI cause is more than just a social movement for these women; for many, it is their life's work and a full-time job. Nine months pregnant, thirty-year-old Inés continues to attend representative meetings. Fanning herself half-heartedly, she shifts again, cradling her belly protectively. She doesn't know it yet, but her son will be born in two days. She continues to work, because the center is like her home, and CONAMURI members, her adopted family. This familial reality is augmented as her three-year-old daughter Amber and two-year-old Nacho scamper past the table in pursuit of cicadas.

CONAMURI, with a history of focusing on promoting female solidarity from within, is now looking outward. Although headquarters is a women's space, young men are increasingly getting involved. One might think that male participation, at an all-female led organization that focuses heavily on rural women's empowerment issues, might be an unwelcome intrusion. On the contrary, the presence of male "feminists" is encouraging. CONAMURI women believe that men must become involved in the fight for rural women's rights and against machismo, to prevent the organization from becoming a self-contained island. In the same way, CONAMURI now focuses on projecting their cause outward by connecting with the international community by means of conferences, alliances, and social media. This objective has been very effective. The doorbell rings often at headquarters, announcing the arrival of visitors and volunteers, not only from throughout Paraguay and the rest Latin America but also the world. Headquarters also hosts many large-scale events for La Via Campesina, the international food sovereignty network, to promote their message internationally. CONAMURI, as a woman's organization, takes pride in being highly regarded as a successful and influential food sovereignty group, and its members are invited to speak at and attend food sovereignty conferences throughout the world. CONAMURI is making large strides for women's and *campesino* rights. The movement has enabled *campesino* women to assertively participate, taking their situation into their own hands to find solutions.

a. Names have been changed for the privacy of the individuals.

b. BriAnne Illich, Anonymous Interview, Asuncion, January 14, 2014.

c. Elizabeth Dore. "One Step Forward, Two Steps Back: Gender and the State in the Long Nineteenth Century," *Hidden Histories of Gender and the State in Latin America* (Durham, NC: Duke University Press, 2000), 11, 1–32.

d. Ibid., 12.

e. Maxine Molyneux, "Twentieth-Century State Formations in Latin America," *Hidden Histories of Gender and the State in Latin America* (Durham, NC: Duke University Press, 2000), 44.

f. Sylvia Chant and Nikki Craske, *Gender in Latin America* (Piscataway, NJ: Rutgers University Press, 2003), 9.

g. Ibid.

h. Ibid.

i. BriAnne Illich, Interview with Diana Viveros, Personal Interview, Asuncion, January 22, 2014. "ella al lado…se complica mucho."

j. Perla Álvarez, Alicia Amarilla, Magui Balbuena, and Julia Franco, ÑE'ê Roky, ed. CONAMURI, Boletin 8, 1–11, Asuncion, March 2011.

k. BriAnne Illich, Interview with Hilaria Cruzabie, Personal Interview, Asuncion, January 14, 2014. "Qué estás haciendo? Tu casa está sucia. Cuida de tu hijo."

l. June Nash, "Gender in Place and Culture," *Gender's Place: Feminist Anthropologies of Latin America*, eds. Lessie Jo Frazier, Rosario Montoya, Janise Hurtig (New York, NY: Palgrave Macmillan, 2002), 289, 289–296.

m. Ibid.

n. Perla Álvarez, Alicia Amarilla, Magui Balbuena, and Julia Franco, *ÑE'ê Roky*, ed. CONAMURI, Boletin 9, 1–11, Asuncion, July 2011. "Ahora estamos convencidas de que la violencia no es natural, sino que está naturalizada en la sociedad que conserva la cultura patriarcal de la desigualdad entre hombres y mujeres… nos llama al desafío de buscar las transformaciones sociales y de ser dueñas de nuestra propia historia."

o. Hurtig, Montoya and Frazier, "Unfencing Gender's Place," in *Gender's Place: Feminist Anthropologies of Latin America*, eds. Lessie Jo Frazier, Rosario Montoya, Janise Hurtig (New York, NY: Palgrave Macmillan, 2002).

p. Nash, "Gender in Place and Culture."

The Land Question: Property Rights, Reform, and Landless Struggles

Reliable access to land is not solely a question of gender; others have been histori-cally excluded from this important asset. What factors exacerbate land inequality in Latin America? How do discrepancies in landholdings create a dynamic of unequal power and access to resources, and present a barrier to agricultural development and economic growth in the long run?[78]

Land, although fundamental to supporting rural populations, is hoarded and distributed unequally throughout Latin America. In fact, more than 30 percent of the rural poor are landless.[79] These landless peoples are often driven to migrate to cities in search of work, forming an urban belt of poverty. Weak, corrupt, or poorly enforced land rights push people off lands that may have been held communally. Property rights in the rural sector are often poorly defined, with official records frequently incomplete, conflicting, or nonexistent. Back in table 9.3 you may have observed a correlation of weak rights with rural poverty. A lack of computeriza-tion, insufficient staffing, or inappropriate storage facilities may contribute to poor record keeping. Conflicts emerge between nationally registered systems and de facto rights of occupancy by local squatters or customary rights of traditional com-munities, resulting in overlapping claims. This problem is exacerbated by lack of proper recognition of indigenous land rights that are sometimes mapped but often brushed aside or disregarded, despite constitutional recognition.[80] These conflicting or absent claims in regions lacking strong legal and police enforcement or trans-parency mechanisms make land rights all the more precarious, limiting transfer-ability or sale of rights. Unfortunately, secure land titles are often a prerequisite to obtaining access to credit. Additionally, uncertainty regarding the legitimacy or stability of a claim, hinting at the possibility of eviction, discourages farmers from investing in land for the long term or adopting more costly sustainable practices. In other words, this tenacity of land rights makes cheaper and environmentally degrading practices more appealing to those fearing loss of their lands.

In response to immense land inequality, *campesino* abuses, and frequent inad-equacy or lack of government reaction that establishes effective and inclusive reform, many groups representing landless populations have mobilized throughout Latin America. These movements promote *campesino* and indigenous human rights, demand recognition of structural inequalities and injustices that exclude minority populations from participation, and call for equal access to knowledge, technology, land, and other resources. One very influential landless movement in Brazil, the MST Landless Workers Movement, or Movimento Sem Terra, has, with the support of churches and international groups, occupied (or invaded) unproductive ranches to pressure for land reform in a country where 3 percent of the richest farmers own 66 percent of the land. Killings by police defending the land have made land reform in Brazil an international human rights issue. By forging connections between the rural and urban sector, the MST has been able to transform itself into the largest social movement in the region.[81] With a particular focus on reframing gender relationships, it is chipping away at traditionally male patterns of distribution.[82]

Maintaining secure and equitable property rights requires investment in tech-nical infrastructure to demarcate boundaries, maintain maps and land records, and invest in the social infrastructure in courts and conflict resolution mechanisms.[83] Institutions that enforce these land rights must operate independently of politically charged institutions in order to avoid corruption and favoritism. In the same vein, transparency and inclusivity of reform and enforcement is necessary. Protection of rights and enforcement of fair access certainly have the potential to positively influence agricultural prospects. Confidence in protection of land rights could motivate individuals to invest more into their properties and to adopt sustainable and efficient practices. More equitable access to land would incorporate more people into the formal market, and increase linkages and general agricultural efficiency.

Creating viable land reform is about more than parceling out additional hectares. As activist Perla Alvarez suggestions, "When we talk about integral land reform, we not only enter into speaking of the land, but also talk about what is related to our ... health, mode of production ... and our environment."[84] Land reform has been used in Latin America to address asset inequality in the rural sector, but how reform takes place is quite controversial. Should the government confiscate land? Should compensation be paid for land granted centuries ago? When land is not being productively used, does the state have the right (and at what price) to redistribute property? Can the market be used in land reform efforts? What is the optimal size of farms? As farms are broken up, will small peasant farmers have access to credit, technology, and new equipment to increase productivity? If the nation does not have idle land, whose land should be taken, and what kind of compensation should be offered? When the easy stage of capturing idle or uncolonized land is over, how will the confiscation affect the credibility of property rights in the economy? Should the process take place quickly to send signals of resolve, or does a slower, more measured program allow for the development of complementary infrastructure? How nations have resolved these questions defined the nature of their land reforms.

Extensive land reforms have been undertaken in countries including Mexico, Bolivia, Chile, Ecuador, El Salvador, Nicaragua, Honduras, and Peru. Unfortunately, they have generally failed to reduce the poverty of the peasantry. However, this is not to say that reform has not had a positive impact, or that there is not hope for the future. In Peru, the formalization of land ownership and strengthening of regulatory mechanisms has been especially effective in motivating households to become more involved in the formal economy.[85] Similarly, Honduras' Access to Land Pilot Project, PACTA, has worked to open access to land and promote the development of sustainable rural enterprises, making grants available to families for products. In doing so it has motivated investment in property, and expanded access to land and resources.[86]

Several lessons can be distilled from the experience with land reform and landless struggles. First, the easy stages of redistributing unproductive land are over. Land is in short supply, so redistribution now has a clear economic opportunity cost. The goal of increased production may be harmed, because taking land away from large owners may result in less land available for export sectors. Second, land reform has not helped the poorest of the rural poor. Those who were relatively better off were able to take advantage of changes in policy;

those on the margins of existence were less adept at working with authorities to transform property rights. Third, land reform works best when accompanied by ample credit and technical assistance. Simply owning land without the complementary inputs does little to raise productivity or incomes. The presumption in some land reform efforts that larger size was more efficient may have really been a proxy for the fact that larger farms had access to credit, not that larger farms are necessarily more efficient. To succeed, land reform therefore requires a comprehensive strategy for rural development. Fourth, policies adopted may have differential effects on small and large landowners. A policy package that reduces biases toward large holders and secures property rights of small peasants may help reduce rural poverty. This package could be supplemented with public investments to develop infrastructure and promote better exchange of information among small farmers to encourage broader-based growth. Picking labor-intensive crops to promote may direct growth toward the small farmer.[87] Fifth, this strategy must incorporate environmental as well as economic dimensions of reform. Environmental deterioration is closely tied to **insecure property rights**, inadequate credit, and poorly designed public infrastructure for water use, waste disposal, or transportation of goods to market. Reform requires changes in law as well as public and private investments. Public resources for an integrated rural development strategy might come from increased taxation of agricultural land, particularly unproductive land. Higher taxation of larger parcels might encourage private market sales to small-scale producers. Revenues from taxation can be used for public infrastructure as well as financing loans to prospective buyers. Multilateral and bilateral international assistance in agricultural reform can help in project lending for infrastructure, and NGOs can facilitate grassroots access to poor farmers to promote extension services well suited to local conditions.[88]

POLICY INTERVENTIONS FOR A SUSTAINABLE AGRICULTURAL SECTOR

Promoting dynamic, sustainable, and inclusive growth in the agricultural sector in Latin America requires concerted policy interventions to address market failures and incorporate marginalized family farmers. It implies an understanding of the heterogeneity of the rural producer and the complicated challenge of not only increasing agricultural output but also promoting livelihoods in the rural sector. This is a tall order! Evan Fraser describes four narratives that condition different policy frameworks to promote sustainable agricultural development.[89] As shown in figure 9.1, he positions these narratives along two axes: top down versus bottom up and individual versus collective action. Fraser characterizes the first approach to agriculture (bottom left) as a technocratic problem whose goal is to produce enough food by means of high technology to meet demand and promote growth, anticipating that growth will enable trickle-down in the long run. This market-based approach advocates a removal of governmental restrictions in the agricultural market, elimination of subsidies, strengthening of property rights, and an opening of markets to free trade. Those less trustful of the market might supplement it with the second approach (top left) that includes top-down government intervention to encourage sustainable and inclusive practices. The government in this context might reward good farming practices and discourage unsustainable activity by penalizing farmers that cause nutrient runoff, excessive carbon emissions, and residue pesticides.

Figure 9.1.   Fraser's Axis of Policy Narratives[90]

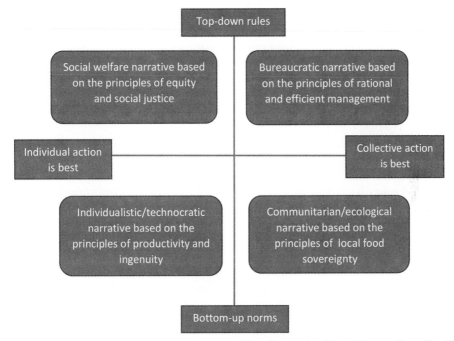

Source: Evan Fraser as found in Johan Bastianensen, "Non-Conventional Rural Finance," pp. 191–209 in Sustainable Agriculture in Central America, ed. Jan P. De Groot and Ruerd Ruben (London: Macmillan, 1997).

In contrast to these two approaches that place the individual at the center of the story, a third approach (top right) focuses on rural development and the food security agenda; this narrative seeks to increase access of the marginalized to necessary resources through collective action. It argues that the government should target spending on food and nutrition programs, improve distribution mechanisms, revamp agricultural credit systems, and fund food storage in preparation for crises. Finally, the fourth approach (bottom right) embraces a food sovereignty model. This narrative defends local and ecologically sustainable food systems, arguing that the power of food decision making and production should be put back in the hands of communities. It also embraces the view that policies must recognize class, ethnicity, and gender of market actors; without considering the local context of an agricultural system, policies will undoubtedly fail.

Too frequently in the literature, each of the four schools holds conversations in an isolated silo. Yet the complicated nature of dualistic agriculture in Latin America requires a dialogue among various stakeholders. No single narrative's suggestions are sufficient to enable the success of equitable and sustainable agricultural development in the long run. Fraser argues for a portfolio approach to policy acknowledging the role of all actors—each with limitations and trade-offs into play with one another.[91] When evaluating policy across the wide range of products and processes in the region, Fraser's matrix is useful in highlighting when a market, a state, or a community-based structure is most appropriate. It also reminds us that agriculture creates nonmarket outcomes with social and environmental value. These positive externalities must be valued in framing policy interventions. The key to strong agricultural policy is raising productivity while simultaneously focusing on sustainability and inclusion and cooperation of all stakeholders, especially the poor and marginalized, whose voice and needs must be recognized and respected.[92] With this holistic approach in mind, let's consider several policy options.

Localized Niche Production and Small-Scale Sustainability

We can begin a consideration of policy options with an appreciation of the entrepreneurial role of individuals. One promising approach to integrating small and medium-sized firms into the global value chain is the use of export platforms. Each platform consists of ten to fifteen firms; they are given international business training, information on market access, and access to trade missions. From Nicaragua, independent farmers were able to send chili peppers and mini corns to Mexican Americans, particularly after identifying the packaging in cans preferred by consumers. Gourmet coffee, guava, and plantain chips have also been successful exports.[93] Small farms do well in attending to a niche market; the key, however, is to develop the connective links between the farmer and the consumer.[94]

Policy interventions to promote small-scale rural activities need not be focused on external markets. Projects addressing food security in the rural sector while also fostering more livelihood opportunities are a win-win. Fisheries in Bolivia experienced income generation while also contributing to raising nutritional intake through a program of aquaculture encouraging technological innovation while reintroducing a native species into ponds.[95] The program focused on women entrepreneurs, addressed gender asymmetries in the Northern Amazon region, and empowered them in their homes and communities. In Peru, a participatory market chain approach to agriculture focuses on identifying market demand and joint production activities.[96] In Colombia, the introduction of new varieties of native potatoes for both the domestic and the export market resulted in dramatic increases in output. In Ecuador, Conpapa, a consortium of potato producers, joined with regional funder Fundagro and the national institute for agricultural research to identify the best native potatoes from among three hundred fifty varieties for nutritional content and resistance to disease. Information about planting techniques and seeds were distributed to members—with demand outstripping supply. The organization also worked to launch a new gourmet snack firm that developed a native potato flakes mix. Certification was obtained for Kosher, non-GMO, and non-gluten properties, opening markets for exports. Perhaps you have eaten Kiwa brand chips—a Quechua word for "green" that reflects both the firm's social and environmental sustainability. These interventions can be understood in Fraser's taxonomy as providing opportunities for collective action and state investment while also appreciative of the communitarian foundations and individual initiative.

Throughout the Andean region the revival of lucrative and sustainable family potato farming can be attributed to developing innovation and links among stakeholders in the agricultural value chain. NGOs, academic research institutes, private firms, governmental agencies, and multilateral donors have worked together to connect farmer and consumer, promoting competitiveness in this culturally and historically important crop: the potato.[97] Sales value soared between 174 and 433 percent with new potato-based products as well as increased yields. Another example of integrating small and medium-sized family farms is in the biofuels sector. In Brazil, a subsidiary of the state energy conglomerate Petrobras was tasked with enhancing engagement with smallholders. The firm has begun to deal directly with small-scale farmers, providing a wide range of support policies (technical assistance and free distribution of good quality seeds) and signing formal contracts.[98] It is also supporting the creation of local associations and the use of other biodiesel sources, including sunflower and cotton, to include more farmers and encourage mixed food and feedstock to diversify growers' risk. A representative from a social movement or organization signs the contract along with the smallholder to increase the farmer's bargaining power. As a result of the program, the purchase value by biodiesel industries from smallholders increased fivefold in two years, reaching US$635 million by 2010. Unfortunately, the fall in energy prices flattened the biofuels sector, underscoring the vulnerability of smallholders to external events.

Unable to compete with agricultural conglomerates in the production of traditional export crops and seeking to protect traditional low-capital and low-technology farming practices, some small-scale farmers support livelihoods by entering into the organic and fair trade markets. Organic production not only has a stronger upscale market but also can be better suited to the needs of the small farmer. It encourages small-scale and diverse production, and rejects the use of expensive fertilizers and other pesticides in favor of labor-intensive natural composting and weeding by hand.[99] Organic methods are environmentally sustainable, creating an economic incentive to produce without using inputs that interfere with the ecosystem.[100] While organic products are certified as not using agrochemicals for production, **fair trade labels** certify the production process. Fair trade labeling organizations establish standards of production and pricing that promote sustainable livelihoods for growers. One drawback, however, is the difficulty for the smallest or most remote farmers to form and maintain producer cooperatives. The small farmer doesn't just drop into the local Whole Foods supermarket to place products; it takes a value chain of certification, logistics, and retail connections to put products on supermarket shelves. Fair trade in this sense can leave out some of the neediest producers. Work may need to be done to promote the organizational skills of peasants in forming cooperatives to meet scale requirements.[101] Fair trade marketing may also have an unintended effect. If one assumes that most coffee drinkers are price sensitive, boosting the price for fair trade while stigmatizing drinkers of non-specialty coffee may in fact work to put more growers out of work. Nonetheless, with a supportive infrastructure, organics provide opportunities for smallholders in a globalized market.

The lesson spanning aquaculture, potatoes, and integration into the biodiesel chain is that civil society partnerships matter. Information, training, and coordination costs are most effectively shared between the private and public sector. Grassroots organizations more generally have the reach into and the trust of communities—and can also reach out to empower individuals to adopt technological change. Civil society organizations can provide key links between smallholders, large firms, and governmental agencies. Agricultural policy is an all-hands-on-deck endeavor.

Redressing Market Failure: Insurance, Risk Management, and Complementary Services

We began our chapter by analyzing how agricultural markets are different from a manufacturing effort such as making shoes. At the core of this characterization of agricultural production were market failures created by exposure to risk and missing markets in credit. Mitigating risk is a shared proposition among farmers, governments, and markets. The path to sustainable development faces roadblocks created by weak provisions for *insurance and risk management*. Insurance services are constrained by lack of information and resources, inability to pay high premiums, and inefficient government use of subsidies and relief funds. The government's role in providing the resources to measure, evaluate, and monitor risk is essential, especially as the region faces the consequences of climate change, natural disasters and global financial instability.[102] Government support can include improvements in forecasting and early warning systems for agricultural risk, regulatory and operational systems for the efficient use of credit information, and movable property as loan collateral to lower the risks related to rural lending.[103] In partnership with NGOs, governments also play a vital role in educating farmers to reduce and manage risk. They might do so by promoting sound practices including irrigation and storage, providing accessible resources, and encouraging knowledge-sharing through the use of ICTs.[104] Inclusionary finance mechanisms such as micro-insurance can help farmers self-insure. But the frequent larger, systemic losses require more government intermediation.

With weak statistics making actuarial predictions unreliable, agricultural insurance markets remain underdeveloped in the region.[105] Fortunately, governments in several countries have begun enhancing agricultural insurance programs, implementing subsidies or drafting new agricultural-sector policies that support preexisting systems or acknowledge risk conditions.[106] As in the case of Mexico's Agroasemex, the government might act as a reinsurer for private vendors to spread risk in the event of a catastrophic national event such as a major hurricane.[107] The Brazilian government implemented the Insurance Premium Subsidy Program, increasing the land insured in Brazil from seventy thousand hectares in 2005 to over five million hectares by 2011. Mexico has also issued a substantial number of policies, but only Argentina and Uruguay begin to approach the level of insured coverage protecting Europe.[108]

Policymakers must also consider other structural impediments to agricultural sustainability including the need for technical assistance, sanitary management, transportation logistics, and market information systems. To reduce high and often unaffordable transaction costs, governments might attempt to encourage stricter chain integration in order to ease smallholders' participation in the market. In the end, these policies should stimulate the transition to higher value-added and inclusive agricultural activities within Latin America. These technocratic fixes may lead to more efficient production among the actors needing it most—the rural poor.

Public-Private Partnerships for Sustainable Development

Transforming rural poverty requires innovative partnerships with both the public sector and agribusiness itself. The key to sustainable livelihoods isn't just sustaining small farmers but rather reducing poverty and creating rural opportunity. The sector needs to be seen as more than the sum of individual energies and measures to address market impediments. Long neglected under ISI and neoliberal strategies, transformation change requires a pro-poor approach to facilitate equitable and innovative rural development.[109] **Demand-driven rural investment funds (DRIFs)** are a tool governments can employ to achieve development aims. With DRIFs, central governments are able to transfer funds to local governments and communities. In order to receive funds, groups must meet specific eligibility requirements. After demonstrating need, communities can then use funds to address their particular development goals. Beneficiaries include neighborhood associations, women's groups, and producer associations or cooperatives.[110] Also, in areas affected by externalities and uses of common resources, government intervention is critical to provide incentives for cooperative voluntary action. In the agricultural sector, the new role for the state is to create enabling environments for private and voluntary action—not to deliver the goods or the technologies, as in the past.[111]

Agribusinesses can potentially contribute to the sustainability and inclusivity of rural development by acting accountably and adopting socially responsible practices. By operating in environmentally sustainable and conscientious ways, corporations might ensure the feasibility of small- and large-scale farming coexistence. For example, if governments require that agribusinesses use pesticides safely, treat the soil sustainably by rotating crops, and respect *campesino* rights to land, both small and large farms may be able to simultaneously function sustainably and successfully. Fortunately, there is hope that corporate social responsibility (CSR) self-monitoring in agriculture will increase. The market for ethical products is growing as consumers seek to purchase goods produced by companies known for their adherence to CSR. As a result, in order to get a competitive edge, certain transnational and large-scale food producers are promoting sustainable practices and enable their operations to be surveyed by civil society organizations such as Corporate Watch, increasing transparency.[112]

Agroecology and Rural Development

A common tactic of food sovereignty movements is to promote the adoption of agro-ecological and sustainable production practices, enabling communities to support themselves by means of small-scale production. Eric Holt-Giménez, the executive director of the Institute of Food and Development Policy, explains that agro-ecological techniques focus on "knowledge-intensive" rather than "capital-intensive" methods and create innovative farming strategies in a bottom-up rather than top-down fashion.[113] Agro-ecology, in an effort to be both productive and environmentally sustainable, tries to reduce community reliance on external inputs, and focuses on recycling nutrients, diversifying products, taking advantage of locally produced inputs, and diminishing the need for pesticides and fossil energy for production. Agro-ecological farming is labor intensive and usually limited to small and diverse farms. Thus, it is not a solution in all regions, and its adoption must incorporate techniques that are relevant to local context and needs. However, agro-ecological farming is beneficial for small-scale farmers who have little access to credit, resources, and technology, and are linked with other small farmers. Agro-ecological community successes throughout Latin America underscore the power of communities to adopt innovative techniques by means of community linkages, networks, cooperation, and outreach.

Final Considerations on Agricultural Development Policy: Market v. State

This chapter has underscored market and governance failures in the face of a complex, dualistic agricultural environment in Latin America. The agricultural sector may be an example where employing neat prescriptions may lead to policy failure, unless we are clear on the characteristics of the market. Policy remedies for **incomplete markets** include securing transferable property rights, creating enforceable contracts, removing subsidies, implementing market-based initiatives as opposed to command and control regulations, adopting green accounting methods and peer monitoring, and cosigning loans to decrease risk. In credit markets, mechanisms have been employed to reduce the risk to lenders of bad loans through relying on local leaders or group-lending schemes.[114] Positive incentives such as interest rebates for timely repayment and access to new benefits including longer time horizons may enhance enforcement of repayment. Negative sanctions such as legal proceedings may be useful, but the large number of small producers makes enforcement tough and costly. Local governance structures, such as cooperative lending to promote repayment, are more promising. Such unconventional rural finance can also facilitate the growth of horizontal civic rural institutions, enhancing the sustainability and equity of rural finance.[115]

The greatest challenge in any agricultural strategy is to create equitable pathways to rising farm productivity. Export-driven models do not guarantee benefits to the poor, and technological change costs money. Promoting sustainable agricultural development is about more than strengthening markets, getting prices right, and increasing productivity. A strategy to spur rural development must take a broad focus, moving beyond the narrow agricultural sector to include the entire rural productive system.[116] If the dynamism in the rural sector is going to extend beyond large corporate farms, a system of peasant credit is necessary to support advances in small-scale farming. Policies to improve productivity for peasant farmers must acknowledge the risk-averse nature of small-scale producers and provide flexible, extended terms to smooth the potential losses in any one year. Peasant farmers also need to be involved in determining the necessary changes in farming practices to solve local problems. New approaches to rural development underscore the importance of coordination and cooperation across sectors and among different stakeholders. In the end, rural development should embrace all dimensions of people's lives and subsistence strategies.

Key Concepts

agricultural extension programs

demand-driven rural investment funds (DRIFs)

dualism

environmental degradation

fair trade labels

GMOs

incomplete markets

insecure property rights

land reform

nontraditional agricultural exports (NTAEs)

property rights

rural exclusive areas

water rights

Chapter Summary

Latin American Agriculture: Diverse Structures and Performances

- Agricultural markets face risks of nature; they also suffer from the lack of complementary physical and financial capital, thin insurance coverage, poor logistics to connect remote farms to markets, and unequal distribution of assets. Climate change will exacerbate many of the physical risks and social consequences. Gender also conditions outcomes in agriculture.

- The agricultural sector in Latin America is characterized by its dualistic nature: corporate farming and small-scale, traditional peasant agriculture. Global value chains tie export monocrops to new demand but further squeeze small producers. The trend in many Latin American countries has been a shift away from production for local consumption to production for exports. Commercialization for exports has marginalized peasant farmers and increased migration from the rural sector into the cities.

- Although some Latin American countries have experienced slow growth in agriculture, many have seen moderate to rapid growth in production. Nevertheless, falling prices, international trade barriers and subsidies, overvalued exchange rates, and other forms of indirect taxation have placed constraints on the agricultural sector.

Problems for Small Producers

- Agriculture has not been able to generate sustainable incomes for the rural majority. Rural poverty contributes to a number of problems such as environmental degradation or harmful use of pesticides. Women's contributions to agricultural production are often unaccounted for, yet women play a major role in the agricultural sector. Weak capacity in agricultural ministries has led to poor input in integrating agricultural policy with an overall development policy. A fragile private sector cannot fill the gap as governments have moved out to make room for the market.
- The failure of the agricultural sector to generate adequate incomes for the rural poor is due to several factors. Previous policies and incomplete markets have been biased against the peasant farmer and in favor of the rural elite. Ambiguity with property rights, common in the region, has led to underinvestment, barriers in obtaining credit, and inefficiency in the use of land. Peasant farmers face more obstacles in obtaining much-needed credit due to their lack of collateral and the nature of agricultural activity. Policies to remedy the problem must use unconventional forms of allocating credit for the small farmer and address the issue of unequal landholding.

Niche Farming and Organic Production: Potential Solutions for Small Farmers

- In response to the price volatility, some small producers have looked for ways in which to differentiate their products, namely through organic production and fair trade certification. Policies encouraging small and medium-size farms to integrate on the global value chain can bring positive returns from globalization. A rising demand for organic products from consumers has led to higher prices on certified coffee beans, making organic farming more profitable for small farmers. In addition, it is ecologically sustainable and poses fewer health risks than large agro-industry. Fair trade is a process by which the middleman is eliminated so that farmers receive a larger percentage of profits from their produce. Although organic and fair trade certification has the potential to be very beneficial to small producers, there are some drawbacks. Certification processes can be difficult and expensive, especially given language and literacy barriers. However, rising demand for more environmentally and socially responsible products gives niche farming a positive future outlook.

Policy Options and Alternatives to Land Reform

- Historically, many Latin American countries have engaged in land reform to address the issue of inequality. The experience in the region has shown that land reform has done little to improve the quality of life of the rural peasant.

Its failure is due to a lack of complementary policies that will address problems such as the biases disadvantaging the poor relative to the elite, the problem of credit, and environmental sustainability.

- Agricultural policy must be multidimensional. Farm productivity must be raised, but policy needs to take into account the concerns and behavior of the poor small farmers, who tend to be risk averse. Policies that consider factors such as migration to urban sectors, infrastructure, credit, and landholding patterns will tend to be more successful in the long run.
- Agriculture in Latin America is a complex mosaic of farm structures and with varying products. Policy must attend to local characteristics; at times collective action is required to redress market failures. In other cases, interventions can best focus on providing technology and access to markets to release the entrepreneurship of small holders.

Notes

1. International Assessment of Agricultural Knowledge Science and Technology for Development, LAC Report.

2. P. Henriquez and H. Li Pun, eds., *Impactful Innovations: Lessons from Family Agriculture in Latin America and the Caribbean* (Costa Rica), Inter-American Development Bank (IDB); Inter-American Institute for Cooperation on Agriculture.

3. Marina Ruete, "Financing for Agriculture: How to Boost Opportunities in Developing Countries," Brief #3, IISD.org 4 2015.

4. Maurice Schiff and Alberto Valdes, "The Plundering of Agriculture in Developing Countries," 1994 draft paper, available at the World Bank home page at www.worldbank.org/html/extpb/PlunderingAgri.html. See also Anne Krueger, Maurice Schiff, and Alberto Valdes, *Political Economy of Agricultural Pricing Policy* (Baltimore, MD: Johns Hopkins University Press, 1991), cited in Hans P. Binswanger and Klaus Deininger, "Explaining Agricultural and Agrarian Policies in Developing Countries," *Journal of Economic Literature* 35 (December 1997): 1958–2005.

5. ECLAC and IICA, "Survey of Agriculture in Latin America and the Caribbean, 1990–2000," December 2001, 36, at www.eclac.cl.

6. "World Water Day: Latin America Leads in Water Management but Inequalities in Access Remain," *The World Bank Economic Review* (March 22, 2013), www.worldbank.org/en/news/feature/2013/03/22/world-water-day-latin-america-achievements-challenges (accessed March 5, 2014).

7. International Assessment of Agricultural Knowledge Science and Technology for Development, LAC Report.

8. Ibid.

9. Jacob Meerman, *Reforming Agriculture: The World Bank Goes to Market* (Washington, DC: World Bank, 1997), 38.

10. "World Water Day," *The World Bank Economic Review*.

11. ECLAC, "The Economics of Climate Change in Latin America and the Caribbean Paradoxes and Challenges," *Sustainable Development and Human Settlements Division Overview for 2014*, repositorio.cepal.org/bitstream/handle/11362/37056/S1420806_en.pdf.

12. ECLAC, "The Economics of Climate Change" 2014.

13. Erick C.M Fernandes, Ayat Soliman, Roberto Confalonieri, Marcello Donatelli, and Francesco Tubiello, *Climate Change and Agriculture in Latin America, 2020–2050: Projected Impacts and Response to Adaptation Strategies* (Washington, DC: World Bank, 2012), https://openknowledge.worldbank.org.

14. Orlando Milesi and Marianela Jarroud, "Soil Degradation Threatens Nutrition in Latin America," *Inter-Press Service*, June 2016, www.ipsnews.net/2016/06/soil-degradation-threatens-nutrition-in-latin-america/.

15. Steve Wiggins, Johann Kirsten, and Luis Llambí, "The Future of Small Farms," *World Development* 38(10) (October 2010): 1341–1348.

16. Kenneth Rapoza, "Brazil Senator Maggi Joins Forbes Billionaire List," *Forbes*, www.forbes.com/APR 10, 2014, and Alastair Stewart, "Brazil's Impeachment Brings Maggi to Ag Ministry," *DTN Progressive Farmer*, May 12, 2016, www.dtnpf.com/agriculture/web/.../brazils-impeachment-brings-maggi-ag.

17. *Mugged: Poverty in Your Cup*, Oxfam International 2002, www.maketradefair.com.

18. Lori Ann Thrupp, *Bittersweet Harvests for Global Supermarkets: Challenges in Latin America's Agricultural Export Boom* (Washington, DC: World Resources Institute, 1995).

19. Julio A. Berdegue and Ricardo Fuentealba, "Latin America: The State of Smallholders in Agriculture." In *Conference on New Directions for Smallholder Agriculture* (Rome, IFAD HQ: IFAD, January 2011).

20. Ibid.

21. Ibid.

22. Ibid.

23. Steve Wiggins, "Agriculture and Rural Development Reconsidered," *IFAD* 2016, 36.

24. Agricultural Insurance in Latin America—Developing the Market–International Finance Corporation Report no. 61963, www.ifc.org/.../Agricultural_insurance_in_LAC_20...

25. T. Christian Miller and Davan Maharau, "Coffee's Bitter Harvest," *Los Angeles Times,* as circulated by CENTAM-L@LISTSERV.BUFFALO.EDU, October 7, 2002.

26. Marcela Valente, "Latin America: End to Subsidies Also to End Rural Poverty?" *IPS Terraviva*, December 5, 2005.

27. Oxford Analytica, *Latin America Daily Brief*, Thursday, September 12, 2002, prodept@oxford-analytica.com.

28. Valente, "End to Subsidies."

29. "Worst Ever Coffee Crisis Hits Latin America," *Cepal News* 22(4) (April 2002).

30. International Fund for Agricultural Development, Rural Poverty Report Latin America, Rome, Italy, 2011.

31. The World Bank, *Agricultural Price Distortions, Inequality, and Poverty* (Washington, DC: The World Bank, 2010).

32. Maurice Lemoine, "El Reino Del Latifundio," *E'a* (January 21, 2014), http://ea.com.py/el-reino-del-latifundio/ (accessed January 24, 2014).

33. "Uno de cada quatro Paraguayos pasa hambre en Paraguay," *E'a* (October 18, 2013). http://ea.com.py/1-de-cada-4-paraguayos-pasa-hambre-en-paraguay/ (accessed February 28, 2014).

34. International Assessment of Agricultural Knowledge Science and Technology for Development, LAC Report.

35. Ibid.

36. ETC Group, "Breaking Bad: Big Ag Mega-Mergers in Play," www.etcgroup.org/files/files/etcgroup_agmergers_22oct2015.pptx_.pdf.

37. CONAMURI, "Soberania Alimentaria: Tierra," la Campana por la Soberania Alimentaria, October 14, 2013, video, www.youtube.com/watch?v=gWwA_SFuYek (accessed January 4, 2013).

38. Berdegue and Fuentealba, "The State of Smallholders in Agriculture."

39. Juan Delgado, "Market Structure, Growth and Competition in the Supermarket Sector in Latin America," prepared for Latin American Competition Forum, OECD 2015.

40. Ibid.

41. Lemoine, "El Reino Del Latifundio."

42. Kieran Gartlan, "The Global Power of Brazilian Agribusiness," *The Economist Intelligence Unit*, November 2010.

43. Ibid.

44. Bryan Gruley and Lucia Kassai, "Brazilian Meatpacker JBS Wrangles the U.S. Beef Industry," *Bloomberg Business Week,* September 19, 2013, www.bloomberg.com/news/articles/2013-09-19/brazilian-meatpacker-jbs-wrangles-the-u-dot-s-dot-beef-industry.

45. "World's Biggest Meat Producer Struggles with Bad Beef Allegations," *Bloomberg*, www. bloomberg.com/news/articles/2017-03-23/world-s-biggest-meat-producer-struggles-with-bad-beef-allegations.

46. International Assessment of Agricultural Knowledge Science and Technology for Development, LAC Report.

47. James Brooke, "Home, Home on the Range, in Brazil's Heartland," *The New York Times*, April 26, 1995.

48. Distribution of Biotech Crops by Country (International Service for the Acquisition of Agri-Biotech Applications, 2016), http://www.isaaa.org/resources/publications/pocketk/16/default.asp.

49. David Bell and Mary Shelman, Note on Agriculture in Argentina, HBS case 9-515-069 December 2014.

50. "Gran Revés Para Monsanto En Venezuela: Por Ley Los Transgénicos No Entrarán Al País," *Analisis 365 Revista Digital* (January 9, 2014).

51. Frederick B. Mills and William Camacaro, "Venezuela and the Battle against Transgenic Seeds," http://venezuelanalysis.com/analysis/10236 (accessed March 31, 2014).

52. Lopez Reilly and G. Cortizas, "IMM Obliga a Identificar Transgenicos," *Eco Portal* (January 9, 2014), http://www.ecoportal.net/Eco-Noticias/IMM_obliga_a_identificar_transgenicos (accessed January 12, 2014).

53. Johan Bastiaensen, "Non-Conventional Rural Finance and the Crisis of Economic Institutions in Nicaragua," in *Sustainable Agriculture in Central America*, eds. Jan P. de Groot and Ruerd Ruben (London: Macmillan, 1997).

54. Michiko Iizuka and Muli Gegreeyesus, "Discovery of Non-traditional Agricultural Exports in Latin America: Diverging Pathways through Learning and Innovation," *Innovation and Development* July 2017.

55. Canute James, "Caribbean Banana Producers See Future in Organic Farming," *Financial Times*, November 13, 2001, Internet edition.

56. Berdegue and Fuentealba, "The State of Smallholders in Agriculture."

57. Ibid., 7.

58. Panorama 2005, "El nuevo patron de desarrollo de la agricultura en america latina y el caribe," The New Pattern of Development of Agriculture in Latin America and the Caribbean, *ECLAC*, September 2005.

59. "Rural Poverty Remains Strong in Latin America in Spite of Agriculture Boom." *Merco Press* (November 8, 2010), http://en.mercopress.com/2010/11/08/rural-poverty-remains-strong-in-latin-america-in-spite-of-agriculture-boom (accessed March 5, 2014).

60. Cristobal Kay, "Rural Poverty Reduction Policies in Honduras, Nicaragua and Bolivia: Lessons from a Comparative Analysis," *European Journal of Development* 23(3) (April 2011): 249–265.

61. IFAD, *Born into Poverty—New Report Highlights the Harsh Inequalities Facing Latin America's Poor Rural People*, April 24, 2012, www.ifad.org/media/press/2012/30.htm.

62. The Outlook for Agriculture and Rural Development in the Americas: A Perspective on Latin America and the Caribbean 2014, www.fao.org/americas/recursos/perspectivas/en/.

63. World Bank, *Rural Poverty Alleviation in Brazil: Toward an Integrated Strategy* (Washington, DC: World Bank, 2003).

64. International Assessment of Agricultural Knowledge Science and Technology for Development, LAC Report.

65. IADB, "Invisible Farmers," in *IDB Extra: Investing in Women* (Washington, DC: Inter-American Development Bank, 1994).

66. Cristóbal Key, "Rural Development and Agrarian Issues in Contemporary Latin America," in *Structural Adjustment and the Agricultural Sector in Latin America and the Caribbean*, ed. John Weeks (New York: St. Martin's, 1995).

67. Carmen Diana Deere, "The Feminization of Agriculture? Economic Restructuring in Rural Latin America," *UNRISD* Occasional Paper #1, February 2005.

68. Gilles Cliché, *Rural Women's Empowerment in Nonfarm Employment Issues for ICT Initiatives and Territorial Policies in Latin America* (Accra: The United Nations, September 2011).

69. Carmen Diana Deere and Magdalena Leon, "The Gender Asset Gap: Land in Latin America," *World Development* 31(6) (2003): 925–947, and Carmen Diana Deere and Jennifer Twyman, "Poverty,

Headship, and Gender Inequality in Asset Ownership in Latin America," University of Florida Working Paper #296 March 2010.

70. Raul Zibechi, "Paraguay: Women at the Center of Resistance," January 10, 2014, www.cetri.be/Woman-at-the-center-of-resistance?lang=fr.

71. Deere and Leon, "The Gender Asset Gap."

72. Carmen Diana Deere, "The Feminization of Agriculture? Economic Restructuring in Rural Latin America," *UNRISD* Occasional Paper #1, February 2005.

73. Deere and Leon, "The Gender Asset Gap."

74. Julia Guivant, "Agrarian Change, Gender and Land Rights: A Brazilian Case Study," *United Nations Research Institute for Social Development*, PP SPD, June 14, 2003, www.unrisd.org), and Carmen Dianne Deere, "Women's Land Rights, Rural Social Movements, and the State in the 21st-century Latin American Agrarian Reforms," *Journal of Agrarian Change*, 17 (2017): 258–278, https://doi.org/10.1111/joac.12208.

75. Deere, "Women's Land Rights, Rural Social Movements, and the State."

76. "21 anos da morte de Margarida Alves," http://www.mmcbrasil.com.br/noticias/.

77. Klaus Deininger, *Land Policies for Growth and Poverty Reduction* (Washington, DC: World Bank and Oxford University Press, 2003).

78. Mexico, "Municipal Development in Rural Areas Project," July 2002, www.worldbank.org.

79. International Assessment of Agricultural Knowledge Science and Technology for Development, LAC Report.

80. John Weeks, "Macroeconomic Adjustment," as noted in "Latin America's Export of Manufactured Goods," a special section of *Economic and Social Progress in Latin America* 1992 Report (Washington, DC: IADB, 1992), 68.

81. Thrupp, *Bittersweet Harvests for Global Supermarkets*, 24.

82. Sônia Fátima Schwendler and Lucia Amaranta Thompson, "An Education in Gender and Agroecology in Brazil's Landless Rural Workers' Movement," *Gender and Education,* 29(1) (2017).

83. Deininger, "Land Policies for Growth."

84. Perla Álvarez, Alicia Amarilla, Magui Balbuena, and Julia Franco, *ÑE'ê Roky*, ed. CONAMURI, Boletin 2, 1–8, Asuncion, September 2009.

85. Deininger, "Land Policies for Growth."

86. Fernando Korczowski, Thomas Pichon, Francisco Reyes, and Hiska Galeana, "PACTA: Rural Development in Honduras through Access to Land and the Development of Productive Enterprises," *World Bank Note* 1(75) (July 2005).

87. Gabriel Keynan, Manuel Olin, and Ariel Dinar, "Cofinanced Public Extension in Nicaragua," *World Bank Research Observer* 12(2) (August 1997): 227.

88. World Bank, "Reaching the Rural Poor: A Rural Development Strategy for the Latin American and Caribbean Region," Box A4.1, Public/Private Partnerships in Research and Extension Projects, 2002, 83.

89. Evan Fraser, "High Tech Farming, Local Food Systems, Food Aid, or Strict Environmental Regulation?" October 2012 Centre for Climate Change Economics and Policy Working Paper No. 110 Sustainability Research Institute Paper No. 38, https://www.cccep.ac.uk/wp-content/uploads/2015/10/WP110-farming-food-american-dust-bowl-drought.pdf.

90. Adapted from diagram in Fraser 2012.

91. Fraser, High Tech Farming, 2012.

92. Charles Ameur, Agricultural Extension: A Step beyond the Next Step, *World Bank* Technical Paper No. 247 (Washington, DC: World Bank, 1994), 12–13.

93. Daniel Rodriguez Salvez, "Access for Latin American and Caribbean Agrifood Products to International Markets," *Communica* (January–July 2010).

94. Steve Wiggins, Johann Kirsten, and Luis Llambi, "The Future of Small Farms Special Section: Impact Assessment of Policy-Oriented International Agricultural Research," *World Development* 38(10) (October 2010), 1349–1361.

95. Martin Piñeiro, Eduardo Dante Bianchi, Laura Uzquiza, and Mario Trucco, *Food Security Policies in Latin America*, Series on Trade and Food Security, Policy Report 4 (2010). Available at SSRN: https://ssrn.com/abstract=1895648 or http://dx.doi.org/10.2139/ssrn.1895648.

96. T. Bernet, "Participatory Market Chain Approach (PMCA)," *International Potato Center*, http://cipotato.org/wp-content/.../003296.pdf.

97. Andre Devaux and Miguel Ordinola, "Innovation to Value Native Potatoes' Biodiversity in Dynamic Markets: The Case of the Andean Potato/INCOPA/CIP in Peru," congresosiica.org/.../consulta-cgiar-alc-2014-innovation-native%20potat...

98. Mairon G. Bastos Lima, 2013. "Adjusting Biofuel Policies to Meet Social and Rural Development Needs: Analysing the Experiences of Brazil, India and Indonesia," *Policy Research Brief 40*, International Policy Centre for Inclusive Growth.

99. Thrupp, *Bittersweet Harvests for Global Supermarkets*.

100. ECLAC and IICA, Survey of Agriculture in Latin America and the Caribbean, 1990–2000, December 2001 at www.eclac.cl, 152.

101. B. Lewin, D. Giovannucci, and P. Varangis, *Fair Trade and the Coffee Crisis Coffee Markets: New Paradigms in Global Supply and Demand* (Washington, DC: World Bank, 2004).

102. *Agricultural Insurance in Latin America*, Swiss Re, May 21, 2014.

103. World Bank, *Agriculture in Nicaragua: Promoting Competitiveness and Stimulating Broad-Based Growth* (Washington, DC: World Bank, 2003).

104. Ibid.

105. Ramiro Iturrioz, Aspen Re, *Agricultural Insurance in Latin America*. Casualty Actuarial Society – Seminar on Reinsurance New York, May 21, 2014, https://www.casact.org/education/reinsure/2014/handouts/Paper_3230_handout_2143_0.pdf.

106. Iturrioz, *Agricultural Insurance in Latin America*.

107. "Agricultural Insurance in Latin America: Developing the Market," International Finance Corporation Report no. 61963, www.ifc.org/.../Agricultural_insurance_in_LAC_20...

108. Iturrioz, *Agricultural Insurance in Latin America*.

109. Oliver De Schutter, "The Transformative Potential of Agroecology," *Food Movements Unite*, ed. Eric Holt-Gimenez (Oakland, CA: Food First Books, 2011), 223–237.

110. Alain de Janvry and Elisabeth Sadoulet, "NAFTA and Mexico's Maize Producers," *World Development* 23(8) (August 1995): 1349–1362.

111. Johan van Zyl et al. (1995), cited in Binswanger and Deininger, "Explaining Agricultural and Agrarian Policies in Developing Countries."

112. International Assessment of Agricultural Knowledge Science and Technology for Development, LAC Report.

113. Eric Holt-Giménez and Miguel A. Altieri, Agroecology, Food Sovereignty, and the New Green Revolution, *Agroecology and Sustainable Food Systems* 37 (2013): 1, 90–102.

114. Avishay Braverman and J. Luis Guasch, "Administrative Failures in Government Credit Programs," *The Economics of Rural Organization*, eds. Karla Hoff, Avishay Braverman, and Joseph Stiglitz (New York: Oxford University Press/World Bank, 1993), 53.

115. Fared Shah, David Zilberman, and Ujjayant Chakravorty, "Water Rights Doctrines and Technology Adoption," *The Economics of Rural Organization*, eds. Karla Hoff, Avishay Braverman, and Joseph Stiglitz (New York: Oxford University Press/World Bank, 1993), 478.

116. Karla Hoff, "Designing Land Policies: An Overview," *The Economics of Rural Organization*, eds. Karla Hoff, Avishay Braverman, and Joseph Stiglitz (New York: Oxford University Press/World Bank, 1993), 231.

POVERTY IN
LATIN AMERICA

CHAPTER TEN

Informal settlements, such as this one in Ciudad Bolivar, Venezuela,
present challenges of sanitation, transportation, and education.
(iStock/Sohadiszno)

Latin America entered the twenty-first century with twenty-five out of one hundred of its people living on less than US$2.50, an international **poverty line**; just over a decade later, only fourteen out of one hundred live with such limited access to income.[1] Using national poverty lines, around the arrival of the millennium more than 43 percent of Latin Americans were considered poor; a decade later, that figure had fallen to below 30 percent. At the turn of this century there were about 225 million poor people living in the region; about a decade later, despite population growth, the number had fallen to 168 million.[2] This is a dramatic improvement in the lives of Latin Americans. Inequality also showed significant improvement in the region. With the exception of Costa Rica (already one of the lowest in the region) and the Dominican Republic, Gini coefficients, a measure of inequality, fell—a first for a region defined by absurdly unequal incomes.

Yet progress is imperfect. There are still more poor people in Latin America than the combined populations of England, Italy, and Spain. Far too many people are doomed to lives of misery, unable to improve their own well-being. It is important to note that poverty isn't just about not having money. Most poignantly, it is about lacking the access to resources that empower people to make choices to achieve their potential. Although some poor people may find enough to eat or wear stylish sneakers, they are systematically excluded from the opportunity to invest in safe and sanitary housing, decent education, and adequate health care. They live precarious lives, just a bit of bad luck away from a truly awful existence. That is, poor people face barriers to the elements that the majority see as essentially human choices to improve their lot in life.

In this chapter we will explore dimensions of poverty and inequality in the Latin American region. After introducing monetary as well as multidimensional measures of poverty and analyzing the distribution of income, we will evaluate the policy options to reduce poverty and improve equality. As poverty and income distribution have complex roots, we will see that changing the pattern of development in the region to an inclusive, pro-poor approach will involve a range of stakeholders. Good policy begins with engaging the poor in identifying their priorities; it will embrace work for local and national governments, civil society, and the business sector.

Key questions include:

- What does it mean to be poor?
- How do we measure poverty?
- What is the record in lowering poverty in the region?
- What does the distribution of income look like in Latin America?
- What is the record on policy interventions to reduce poverty and inequality in the region?
- What challenges loom largest moving forward?

How Do We Understand Poverty?

Imagine the life of Bia. A child born of passion, her mom and half-brother live in a humble dwelling on the outskirts of Natal in the state of Rio Grande do Norte, Brazil. Her mom's big hug envelops her when her grandmother drops her home for the weekend. During the week she lives with her dad's family in the city, attending a private school and excelling in math and dance. Is Bia poor or wealthy? Certainly to meet her you'd be captivated by her rich spirit and contagious smile. But like the precarious positions she adopts in her beloved ballet, her life is a balancing act. Can she overcome a late start in school and permanently escape the vulnerability of her mom's life? Will she be truly welcome in privileged society?

Like Bia, many of the poor straddle lives of comfort and destitution. Cleaning ladies, door men, gardeners, and casual laborers migrate daily from outlying pockets of poverty to posh inner city neighborhoods throughout Latin America. Are these people the poor of the region? As measured against the typical North American family, the answer is yes. Compared to the images of starvation from the destitute countries of the world, Latin Americans are relatively well-off. Poverty is culturally and socially constructed. Beyond income measures, poverty may be experienced as relative deprivation. We also witness geographical areas of poverty, areas isolated from urban centers that suffer from a wide set of deprivations. Poverty in a major metropolis such as Buenos Aires will differ from that in a small remote village in the Andes. Many of those who have recently moved above the poverty line live perched above, vulnerable to fall back with the slightest life shock. How can we compare the diversity of experiences of poverty in a way that is helpful to good policy design?

Step One: Income Measures of Poverty

How is poverty defined? This is a controversial question. You may be familiar with measuring the world's very poor by those who live under US$1 a day. This powerful and shocking number was popularized by World Bank economists in the 1980s as they observed that a number of developing countries drew their poverty lines—the amount of money basically to stay alive—at US$370 a year. A little simple math by economist Martin Ravallion brought us the easily remembered number of a dollar a day.[3] Inflation has crept into this handy number, and we now count those who survive on US$1.90 a day as extremely poor and those who subsist on US$3.30 daily as poor. Even with this nod to inflation, it is powerful to imagine surviving on for a day what others spend on a black coffee at Starbucks. Actually, most of the poor don't make a consistent dollar a day; some days they make $10, and then go a week without earning anything. And of course the dollar will buy more in a small rural town in the Amazon than it does in New York City. Nor do they spend the full dollar on food; we know that people will often sacrifice food for family entertainment and celebrations.

Despite limitations, this measure of US$1.90 a day is useful in helping us envision the sad panorama of the global poor. Only 5.5 percent of Latin Americans live on this pittance; in contrast to 48.5 percent in Sub-Saharan Africa or 31 percent in South Asia, Latin Americans appear relatively well off.[4] The metric has also been instrumental in the millennium development goals, asking the global community to come together to cut in half the percent of the world's population who live on less than US$1.90 a day. It was clear and it was an achievable target.

On the World Bank's website povertydata.worldbank.org you can play with different poverty lines. Raising the bar to US$5.50 a day, the threshold for upper middle income countries, put about 27.1 percent or 166 million of the region's population in poverty in 2013.[5] International comparisons of poverty are complicated by cultural differences in defining human needs, the variety of local goods available at different prices, and a menu of government interventions. Counting the poor is extremely problematic, especially for those without permanent residences. Unlike the people enumerated in data generated by income tax payments in OECD countries, or census takers of those in formal public support programs, the very poor are often nameless. The data should be interpreted with caution. The good news is that in Latin America poverty has fallen in the past decade. Using a US$2.50 metric employed by SEDLAC, the Socio-Economic Database for Latin America and the Caribbean in figure 10.1 we can see that for seventeen of the eighteen countries in the region, poverty was lower in 2010 than it was at the turn of this century. In ten countries, poverty declined by more than 30 percent—a dramatic achievement in a decade. Nonetheless, there is significant variation. In the poorest countries in the region—Nicaragua, Honduras, and Guatemala—more than a third of the population continues to lack the income necessary to maintain physical well-being. In the map of regional poverty as measured by US$2.50 a day in figure 10.2, we can also see variation within country borders. Mexico and Brazil stand out for having extremes of wealth and poverty; such geographic dispersion of poverty complicates policy making.

Figure 10.1. Poverty in Latin America, 2000–2010

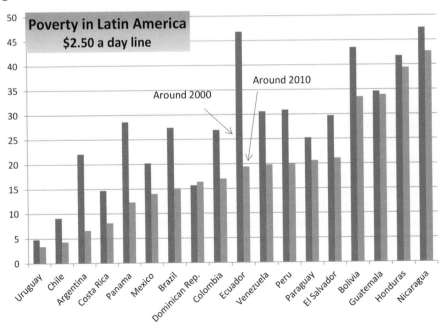

Source: Socio-Economic Database for Latin America and the Caribbean, CEDLAS and The World Bank, May2013.

Figure 10.2.   Poverty Map

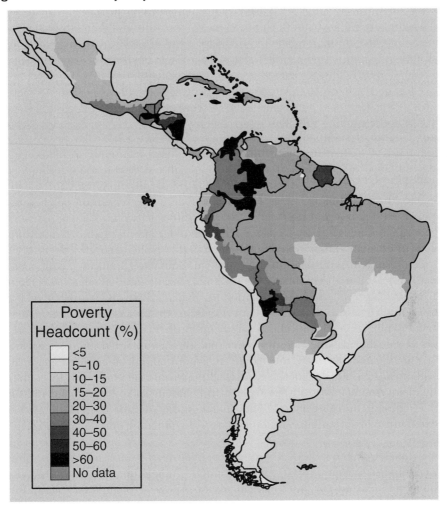

Source: Socio-Economic Database for Latin America and the Caribbean, CEDLAS and The World Bank, May2013 Based on the $2.5 dollars per day

We can think of these global cutoffs of US$1.90 or US$3.20 as absolute international poverty lines. They help us understand the sad reality that a larger portion
of Nicaraguans suffer deprivation as compared to Chileans. But many Chilean
families may experience poverty despite earning more than US$2.50 a day. Pov-
erty can be understood as a relative concept. The working poor in an urban slum
in New York make $7.25 an hour—and yet can fall below US federal guidelines
for poverty. Much like in the United States, Latin American governments establish national poverty lines that reflect a socially constructed view of the minimum
needed for human decency. Sometimes this is done by creating a composite of
housing and food costs; other times a simple percentage—often 60 percent—of

the median household income is used. We can then measure, using national census surveys, the portion of the population that falls below this nationally determined line. The data in ECLAC publications present these nationally determined figures. For example, in Colombia while those living on US$2.50 a day were about 17 percent of the population, the national poverty line characterized 37.3 percent as poor. Regionally, in 2012 28.8 percent of Latin Americans—or 167 million people— were classified as poor; of this group, according to national estimates, 11.4 percent or 66 million were indigent. This relative country by country measure is more useful in understanding the distribution of income within nations; a poor Mexican could of course be a middle income Honduran.[6]

Broadening Our Understanding of Poverty

Income measures of poverty of course only tell part of the story of poverty. One could be earning a decent wage but locked into a living situation that is characterized by deprivations in health, housing, or education. Beyond income measures we can therefore look to **multidimensional poverty measures**. Since 1990 the UNDP has measured poverty through the **Human Development Index (HDI)**. Using metrics for life expectancy (a proxy for health), mean years of schooling and expected years of schooling to complement per capita income, the HDI can paint a different picture. In Cuba, as we see in table 10.1, income is low but strong educational and health systems render a higher HDI as people live longer and are better educated. The Multidimensional Poverty Index (MPI) complements the HDI by characterizing overlapping deprivations suffered by individuals at the same time; by focusing on the intersection of gaps in health, education, and housing (access to clean water, floors, electricity), the deepest pockets of poverty can be targeted for interventions.[7]

What Does It Mean to Be Poor?

Beyond indices to compare multidimensional aspects of poverty, it is important for us to begin to understand what it means to be poor. Poverty is not simply the absence of sufficient income or the lack of access to private schools and glistening hospitals. Although poverty is certainly characterized by resource deprivation, perhaps its most debilitating aspects are the lack of empowerment and the vulnerability experienced by the poor. Impeded access to goods, services, and income are reinforced by a deficiency in voice, participation, and autonomy. The poor are often significantly marginalized from political and social life. They lead vulnerable lives, exposed to deprivation that can, from one week to the next, be exacerbated by a health or environmental shock. The poor live on the edge—of society, of safety, of personal well-being.[8]

Amartya Sen has deepened our understanding of poverty by characterizing it as the lack of *the beings* and *doings* as well as *functionings* to live a valued life. We might see "being" well-off as being well nourished, being comfortably housed, being educated, or being part of a community. Being well-off allows the space to "do" things that are important to us: travel, care for a child, take part in politics, or heat one's house.[9] *Capabilities*, or the opportunity set realistically available to people, shape personal prospects for being and doing. Having ample capabilities allows people the freedom to choose among this set of opportunities the life they value. Those who are poor are unable to freely choose their preferred life path. Instead, active membership in society is severely compromised.

Choice by the poor is restricted. Those who are poor face limited prospects for education; half of the indigent adults in Latin America have not completed a primary education. Most of the poor work; this is the only way to survive. In Latin America only about 8 percent of the indigent (very poor) and 6 percent of the non-indigent poor are unemployed.[10] Jobs, however, are squarely situated in the low-paying, low-productivity **informal sector**. Although access to electricity is widespread at rates of 86 percent of the indigent and 95 percent of the poor, the health of the indigent and the poor is compromised by uneven access to drinking water and sanitation. Among the indigent, 29 percent do not have access to drinking water and 53 percent lack adequate sanitation; 19 percent of the non-indigent poor cannot rely on clean water while 39 percent struggle with sanitation problems. Poor water connections and lousy sanitation contribute to the deprivation of the poor, particularly women. To combat health dangers, women must haul water or dispose of waste from community sources. Urban residents carting drinkable water into narrow shanty streets not only cuts into their time for things like childcare and homework but also into their budgets as the poor pay more for water than those who can load it into cars at the big box Walmart.

More than half the families in Guatemala, Nicaragua, Peru, Honduras, El Salvador, Ecuador, and Bolivia are homeless or live in poor-quality houses. Of the 130 million urban families in the region, 37 million live in dwellings lacking title, sewerage, adequate flooring, or insufficient space.[11] The problem extends beyond the walls of one's own home. Neighborhoods are defined by poor access to schools, recreation, or supermarkets. Poverty is also regional. Living in the South East of Brazil can resemble a European city; the North East, where the slave trade had its largest impact, is abjectly poor. In Peru the poor are still concentrated in the Andes, which is also home of the largest indigenous populations in the country. There is an interesting link between poverty and other sources of inequality and exclusion.

Inequality and Social Exclusion

Poor Latin Americans struggle not only with deprivation of incomes and social resources but also experience this in the context of one of the most unequal regions in the world. One measure of inequality is the Gini coefficient. To understand the quality of life, it is therefore important to measure the degree of income inequality. The **Gini coefficient** measures the difference between a hypothetical population with all income divided equally and the actual distribution in an economy. A forty-five-degree line represents the hypothetical situation of perfect equality. If the population is divided into quintiles from lowest to highest, in a perfectly equal society the first 20 percent of the population would hold 20 percent of the income, the next 20 percent would hold another 20 percent for a cumulative 40 percent, and so on.

Table 10.1. Human Development Index and Its Components

Country	Human Development Index (HDI) 2012 Value	Life Expectancy at Birth (years) 2012	Mean Years of Schooling (years) 2010	Expected Years of Schooling (years) 2011	Gross National Income per Capita (PPP$) 2012	GNI per Capita Rank Minus HDI Rank 2012	Non Income HDI (value) 2012
Very High Human Development							
1 Norway	0.955	81.3	12.6	17.5	48,688	4	0.977
3 United States	0.937	78.7	13.3	16.8	43,480	6	0.958
40 Chile	0.819	79.3	9.7	14.7	14,987	13	0.863
45 Argentina	0.811	76.1	9.3	16.1	15,347	7	0.848
High Human Development							
51 Uruguay	0.792	77.2	8.5	15.5	13,333	11	0.829
59 Cuba	0.780	79.3	10.2	16.2	5,539	44	0.894
59 Panama	0.780	76.3	9.4	13.2	13,519	1	0.810
61 Mexico	0.775	77.1	8.5	13.7	12,947	4	0.805
62 Costa Rica	0.773	79.4	8.4	13.7	10,863	12	0.816
71 Venezuela	0.748	74.6	7.6	14.4	11,475	-2	0.774
77 Peru	0.741	74.2	8.7	13.2	9,306	6	0.780
85 Brazil	0.730	73.8	7.2	14.2	10,152	-8	0.755
89 Ecuador	0.724	75.8	7.6	13.7	7,471	7	0.772
91 Colombia	0.719	73.9	7.3	13.6	8,711	-6	0.751

Medium Human Development

96	Belize	0.702	76.3	8.0	12.5	5,327	8	0.767
96	Dominican Republic	0.702	73.6	7.2	12.3	8,506	−11	0.726
107	El Salvador	0.680	72.4	7.5	12.0	5,915	−5	0.723
108	Bolivia	0.675	66.9	9.2	13.5	4,444	7	0.740
111	Paraguay	0.669	72.7	7.7	12.1	4,497	4	0.730
118	Guyana	0.636	70.2	8.5	10.3	3,387	11	0.703
120	Honduras	0.632	73.4	6.5	11.4	3,426	8	0.695
129	Nicaragua	0.599	74.3	5.8	10.8	2,551	10	0.671
133	Guatemala	0.581	71.4	4.1	10.7	4,235	−14	0.596

Regions

Arab States	0.652	71.0	6.0	10.6	8,317	—	0.658
East Asia and Pacific	0.683	72.7	7.2	11.8	6,874	—	0.712
Europe & Central Asia	0.771	71.5	10.4	13.7	12,243	—	0.801
LAC	0.741	74.7	7.8	13.7	10,300	—	0.770
South Asia	0.558	66.2	4.7	10.2	3,343	—	0.577
Sub-Saharan Africa	0.475	54.9	4.7	9.3	2,010	—	0.479
World	0.694	70.1	7.5	11.6	10,184	—	0.690

Source: Human Development Report 2013.

However, societies are not equal. The **Lorenz curve** measures the actual distribution. The Gini coefficient is equal to the area between the line of perfect equality and the Lorenz curve, labeled "a," and the whole triangle, or a + b. If a society were perfectly equal, the area "a" would be empty, because the distribution would be the same as the line of perfect equality, and a/(a + b) would therefore be zero. If a society were perfectly unequal, one person would hold all the wealth, so that the area "a" would take up the whole triangle, or a/(a + b) would equal one. Figure 10.3 shows a Lorenz curve that approximates the distribution in the region. Note that the area labelled "a" is about as large as area "b"—leading to a Gini of around 0.50.

The average Gini coefficient for the region is 0.50, the highest regional Gini in the world. (Note that sometimes the Gini is written as "0.50" and other times it is represented as "50.0." The two forms are parallel.) We can observe LAC Gini coefficients from 0.41 (El Salvador and Uruguay) to 0.53 (Colombia) in 2014—in contrast to 0.32 to 0.39 for non-LAC OECD countries. Figure 10.4 projects these data onto a map that his heavily shaded by intense inequality. Imagine the effect of these different worlds on the perception of fairness and opportunity in Latin American societies. The chasm that separates the haves and the have-nots not only creates social tension, but also acts as a drag on growth.

Figure 10.3.   Latin American Income Distribution

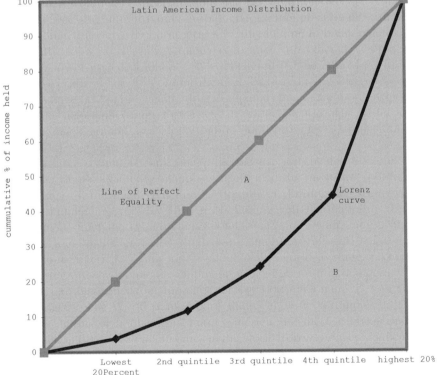

Figure 10.4.   Inequality in Latin America and the Caribbean

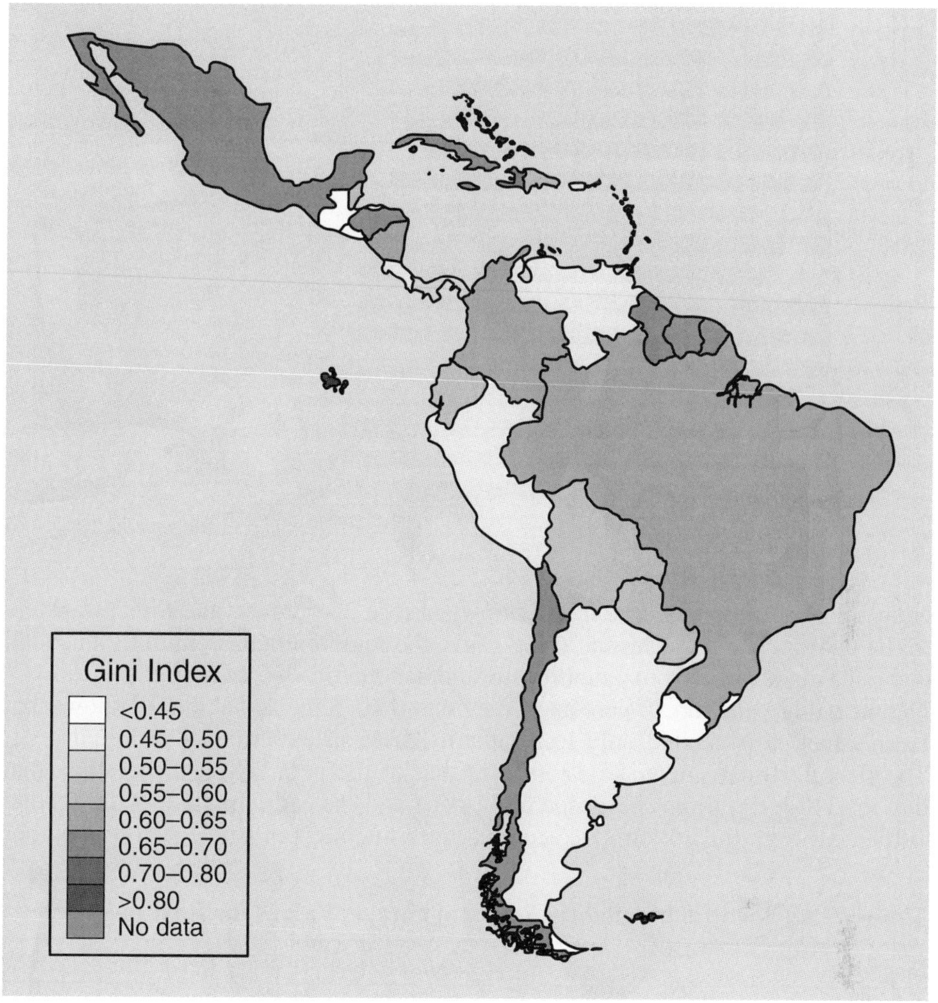

Source: Socio-Economic Database for Latin America and the Caribbean, CEDLAS and The World Bank, May2013.

There has been surprising good news regarding [change Ok and as meant?] decreasing inequality in the region. As figure 10.5 shows, most countries in the region experienced a decline in income inequality in the period 2006–2011. Unlike a macro indicator such as inflation, income inequality does not tend to change much in short periods of time. The data tell an encouraging tale for one of the most unequal areas of the world: regionally, from a peak of over 0.53 in 2002, the average Gini coefficient has fallen to 0.50.[12] Despite the challenges of the global financial crisis, strong regional growth and steady employment helped. Wages rose in the export sector, and the unequalizing effects of market reforms from the 1990s dissipated. As the state assumed a more active role, basic

Figure 10.5.   Improving Gini Coefficients in Latin America

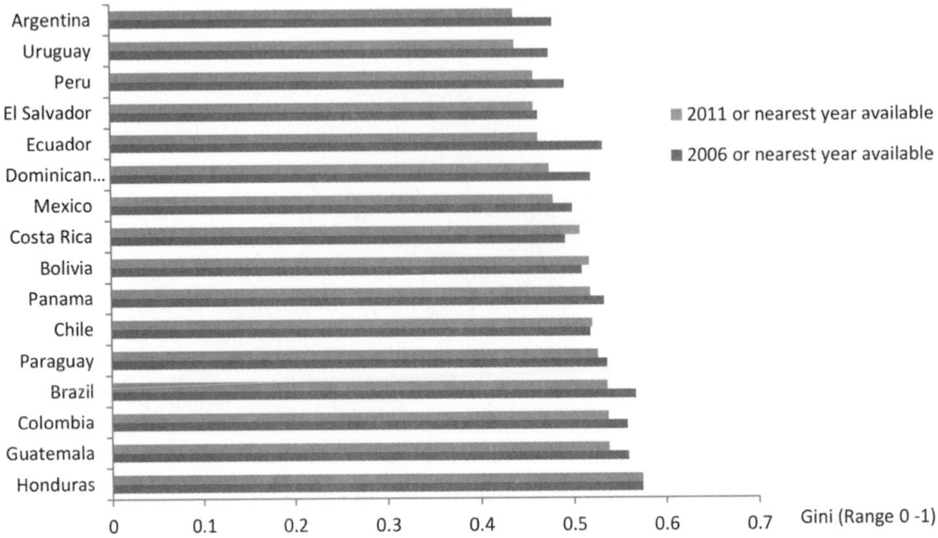

Legend:
- 2011 or nearest year available
- 2006 or nearest year available

Categories (top to bottom): Argentina, Uruguay, Peru, El Salvador, Ecuador, Dominican..., Mexico, Costa Rica, Bolivia, Panama, Chile, Paraguay, Brazil, Colombia, Guatemala, Honduras

X-axis: Gini (Range 0 -1), 0 to 0.7

education was expanded, the minimum wage rose 35 percent, and direct transfers to the poor increased.[13] Despite these gains, the region remains painfully unequal. Gabriel Palma directs our attention to another metric of inequality, the ratio of income held by the top 10 percent to the bottom 10 percent. Table 10.2 shows that Latin America is second only to Southern Africa in extremes of rich and poor. The richest 10 percent make 33.9 times that of the poor. Even if we allow that the bottom decile might be desperately poor and instead compare to the second 10 percent from the bottom, we see that the economic gap of the rich to the poor

Table 10.2.   Income Inequality: Regional Median Values for Rich to Poor

Region	Declie10/Declie1	Declie10/Decile2
Southern Africa	35.1	25.2
Latin America	33.9	19.4
Caribbean	16.6	10.5
Sub-Saharan Africa	15.5	10.3
East Asia	17.7	10.3
United States	19.8	9.3
Non-LA LDCs	13.1	8.9
North Africa	11.1	7.6
OECD-1 (not United States & Russia)	12.5	6.6
European Union	9.2	5.6

Source: José Gabriel Palma, "Homogeneous Middles vs. Heterogeneous Tails, and the End of the 'Inverted-U': It's All About the Share of the Rich," *Development and Change* 42(1) (January 2011): 87–153.

in the region is startling—or as Palma puts it, Latin America belongs on another planet when it comes to unequal incomes.[14]

New Class Dynamics in Latin America

As Latin America has grown in the past decade, its class structure has shifted. Rather than a large bottom of people classified as poor and a relatively small middle and exclusive upper class, countries in the region are developing broader middle classes. Now for the statistically minded, it is appropriate to note that there has always been a "middle" or a median in measuring income. One can line people up from poorest to richest, and draw a line at the middle. But this statistical approach is hard to compare across countries. What might be middle in El Salvador would be poor in Canada. Other definitions of middle class suggested it was a residual—if you weren't poor as defined by poverty lines or you weren't of the elite rich, you must be middle class. There was, however, something askew in this definition. Sociologists define middle class in terms of education, occupation, or asset ownership. In the United States one thinks about college aspirations, a good job, and a house. But this didn't quite fit the Latin American experience as housing markets are substantially different. Furthermore, people weren't comfortably settled into a new group; instead, after moving up, there was a distinct possibility of falling down hard. Is this truly achieving the middle-class dream?

Poverty researchers have therefore characterized an intermediate step in the income ladder: the vulnerable class. Using a poverty line of US$4, those over the line making up to US$10 per capita per day are now described as in the vulnerable or struggling class. The US$10 threshold was determined by the point at which the probability of falling back into poverty had been reduced to 10 percent; a family could feel fairly comfortable at this level that their assets and opportunities were not at risk. This US$10 a day also corresponds to the 68th percentile of income; that is, in Latin America 68 percent of the population is either poor or vulnerable. If your individual daily income hits between US$10 and US$50, you are considered middle class. For those who have lived in expensive Latin American cities, you know US$10 barely gets you past buying breakfast and a ride to work. However, in personal surveys, people self-describe as middle class in this bracket. Defining the end of the tail at US$50 was a bit murkier. Most people think of themselves as middle class at this level of around US$73,000 a year. The remaining part of the population then dubbed as rich amounts to between 1 and 5 percent—the elusive elite.

Based upon these metrics we observe the exciting good news story that the size of the middle class has expanded by 50 percent, growing from 103 million in 2003 to reach 152 million in 2009.[15] About 30 percent of the region enjoys middle-class status, but strong heterogeneities exist. You'll find a robust middle class in Brazil, Costa Rica, Chile, Argentina, and Uruguay; in Ecuador, El Salvador, and Honduras it remains weak, accounting for less than 20 percent of the population.[16] But being middle class in Latin America may not mean the same thing as it does in other parts of the world. Conventional wisdom suggests that a deeper middle class will have a stronger social glue binding society through community-based institutions, athletic teams, schools, and churches. Middle-class demands are thought to promote better services from politicians accountable to a large center. Early evidence in Latin America, however, suggests that the middle class, rather than unifying with its vulnerable roots, is behaving more like its aspirational elite class. It is sending its children to private schools and accessing private health services, requiring private security and even, as in the case of the Dominican Republic, relying on private electricity generation. It is also acquiring debt to do so. This is generating a vicious circle. As the middle class is opting out of the social contract, less pressure for quality public services decreases the demand for improvements in health and education. Preferring lower taxes to better public services, the middle class is voting with its feet toward the private sector. The resulting lower tax base not surprisingly generates poor services for the poor and vulnerable. To break this bad equilibrium, the middle class will need to be brought back into the social contract—but they are disturbed by the existing poor quality of education and health.[17] Indeed, they want more for their children.

Mobility in the Region Comes with Binding Strings

With strong economic growth rates and more effective poverty safety nets, about 43 percent of all Latin Americans changed social classes between the mid-1990s and the end of the 2000s; only 2 percent fell downward.[18] The moves are gradual—21 percent of the poor became vulnerable and 18.2 percent of the vulnerable are now considered middle class. Despite this positive transition to shared prosperity, a person's opportunities in life remain circumscribed by the family and the socioeconomic conditions one is born into. Predetermined traits such as race, gender, or birthplace squarely shape people's life achievements. For example, if a child is born to a poor family in Colombia, it is likely that he will have ten fewer years of education as compared to his upper-class counterpart. This educational deficit will severely compromise his ability to achieve his potential.[19] Although his family might struggle and become a bit better off, his predetermined circumstances of a poor as opposed to a wealthy birth act as an anchor on his opportunity set. Those in the bottom strata are systematically excluded from opportunities for access to quality education and health as well as financial mechanisms to invest in human and physical capital.

Theorists of economic justice worry about inequality that is caused by circumstances beyond an individual's control. In assessing whether outcomes in a society are fair, the unlucky draw of gender, race, of socioeconomic origin constrains whether hard work and good choices bring just rewards.[20] If two kids of equal abilities—one rich and one poor—try equally hard, should they not expect similar returns? Inequality of opportunity in Latin America accounts for between 20 and

Table 10.3. Human Opportunity Index (HOI)

Country	HOI for Education	HOI for Housing	HOI
Chile	90	93	91
Argentina	89	88	88
Costa Rica	79	94	86
Venezuela	84	89	86
Uruguay	85	85	85
Mexico	88	75	82
Colombia	78	69	74
Ecuador	80	69	74
Jamaica	90	55	73
Brazil	67	77	72
Dom Rep	77	65	71
Panama	81	57	69
Paraguay	74	59	67
Peru	83	49	66
Bolivia	83	41	62
El Salvador	65	46	55
Honduras	62	44	53
Guatemala	51	50	50
Nicaragua	59	34	46
Average	76	64	70

Source: Francisco H. G. Ferreira, Jose R. Molinas Vega, Ricardo Paes de Barros,, and Jaime Saavedra Chanduvi, *Measuring Inequality of Opportunities in Latin America and the Caribbean* (Washington, DC: The World Bank, November 2008).

50 percent of overall inequality in the region. As shown in table 10.3, the **Human Opportunity Index (HOI)** is an attempt to measure the degree to which exogenous circumstances such as family background predetermine outcomes. The HOI runs from zero to one hundred. A society enjoying nearly universal access to water, electricity, and sanitation as well as school enrollment and timely completion of the sixth grade would score closer to one hundred on the HOI. Assuming that children can hardly be responsible for their own circumstances, the HOI measures coverage of these proxies for opportunity and then adjusts it for how equitably access to these key inputs are allocated among socioeconomic groups.[21] What this tells us is that even if a nation has a relatively high rate of access to clean water or if most of its primary-age children are in school, if poor families face significantly different circumstances from those in wealthy neighborhoods, the HOI is discounted. A bright young child in Nicaragua or Guatemala is far more constrained in access to the basic opportunity set that will contribute to good health, education, and economic security as compared to a Chilean or Argentine. But we ought to be careful in interpreting this as a stamp of fairness. You might recall from the data above that Chile has one of the highest Gini coefficients in the region, indicating extreme inequality. Years of student protests certainly attest to the perception of inequality and associated lack of opportunity in

Chilean society. Part of this puzzle might be resolved by looking at the variables used to construct the HOI. By focusing on basic inputs—including school enrollment and completion of sixth grade—it misses the constrained opportunities in the richer countries. As countries progress, it is easier to meet this basic threshold and complete primary school or provide great coverage in water or electricity. Yet a Chilean from a poor neighborhood west of Central Santiago Centro, such as Quinta Normal and Independencia, might find that a sixth-grade education does little to improve her competitiveness with kids completing high school in the exclusive neighborhoods of Las Condes and Vitacura. Secondary education increases the chances that a person will remain out of poverty for the rest of their lives. Measures of inequality of opportunity in education—separable from overall opportunity— suggest that 35 percent of all disparities in educational achievement in Latin America are from circumstances beyond the individual's control. This rate, even in the best country cases, is much higher than European counterparts. The sad lesson is that in Latin America the wealthier your family, the better your test score results. A concept in economic justice called the compensation principle suggests that inequalities due to circumstances should be eliminated.[22] But this is even more complicated than in wealthier countries as the needs are greater and the budgets more constrained. Let's now turn to consider policies to redress inequality and alleviate poverty in the region.

ADDRESSING POVERTY AND INEQUALITY IN LATIN AMERICA

The progress in reducing poverty and redressing inequality in the region is encouraging—but much remains to be done. It is inspiring to appreciate that policy, well formulated, can improve the well-being of the poor and open opportunities for those less well-off in society. Despite the historic progress, we recall that 160 million people or approximately 27.5 percent of the regional population live in circumstances that limit their ability to choose pathways to greater well-being. For one in four Latin Americans, poverty is chronic, condemning people to lives with little opportunity. That is a huge loss of human potential.

Why has progress in poverty reduction been so slow in countries that possess significant wealth? Some such as Gabriel Palma suggest that elites in Latin America have been uniquely capable of protecting their economic and social privilege.[23] Political economists would point our attention to analyzing how politics shapes social policy. The so-called three I's of social protection—institutions, interests, and ideas—give us clues as to the slow progress in reducing poverty and promoting a fairer distribution.[24] Political systems, while largely democratic in the region, may not be responsive to constituent needs. Instead, a legacy of patron-client relations impedes systemic change. The interests of key actors—the political elites, bureaucrats, donors, or NGOs—may not align squarely with the needs of the poor. Ideas held by elites about the causes and consequences of poverty and the obligations of the state to provide a social safety net for the vulnerable may have prevented policy innovation. Most poverty policies in the past have not systemically incorporated gendered aspects of development, leading to distorted outcomes.

Another cause of unsatisfactory progress in reducing poverty and inequality is a knowledge gap. Despite over 50 years of development as a field of study and its application in practice, we know stunningly little in terms of what works. Countries have adopted various poverty-fighting tools consistent with national ideologies and institutions. For example, under import substitution industrialization, when industry was receiving subsidies, it appeared quite logical (and politically palatable) to subsidize the consumption baskets of the poor. Much of this was done by holding down the prices of basic foodstuffs such as tortillas or milk. But this turned out to be a very inefficient policy if the goal is to support the poor. When a government subsidizes an agricultural product, the difference is paid to the producer; it is perhaps no great surprise that politicians liked these payouts in anticipation of political payback from agro-producers. Consumers—both rich and poor—would find lower prices at the checkout line. One couldn't ask two different prices for the same item—grocery store chaos would ensue. In this way the wealthy were also benefitting from the low price of dairy or bread, a leakage from the stream of social spending that should have been directed to the poor. In adjusting to the debt and economic crises of the 1980s and 1990s, subsidies were slashed under the neoliberal model. But the global financial crisis delegitimized pure market approaches. A new approximation of state and market is taking place in the region, allowing for social innovation.

What Works in Reducing Poverty?

Even with this new political economy, we don't always know why certain interventions in the social sector work. We have, for example, an intuitive sense that education and health are good investments. But education takes place in various social and economic environments. A subset of development economics has advanced work in identifying what works in what environments by applying techniques most broadly used in the medical sciences. For example, one argument has been that putting computers in classrooms will improve educational outcomes. But do they? How? A randomized controlled trial (RCT) of the One Laptop per Child program in Peru found little improvement in conventional math and language skills (as assessed by standard testing) but measurable improvements in verbal fluency and general cognitive skills.[25] Another popular development measure has been to extend credit to the poor. An RCT study by Dean Karlan of Yale and Innovations for Poverty Action found that lowering the interest rate for clients in Mexico's Compartamos by 10 percent increased bank revenue because borrowers were very responsive and the demand for loans increased. Furthermore, Karlan pushed deeper to ask which groups of people were made better off—and which were made worse off—through increased borrowing.[26] Half receive a high rate, and half received a low rate, although everyone's rate was reduced a little bit. New clients were brought in, overcompensating for the loss of revenue from lowering rates. By creating a control group that did not receive the lowest rates, Karlan and his coauthors found that people who accessed micro credit were marginally better off—and certainly no worse off—than those who stayed out of the market. RCTs can help us understand why people behave in certain ways when basic conditions can be controlled. It is less useful, however, in cases of infrastructure investment or in assessing the distributional impacts of a policy.[27] The large scale and one-off nature make it difficult to set up control groups for study.

In addition to RCTs, other policy innovations are being experimented with to address poverty. One new idea gaining traction is yes, another acronym—or really two (or more)—RBF or COD. Results-based financing (RBF) and cash on delivery (COD) share a common aspect in that they look at the outcomes rather than focus on the programs. If the goal, for example, is to improve child and maternal health, RBF will pay for a decrease in maternal and child morbidity, or an increase in newborn weight. Care providers can be compensated at two stages—increasing the number of pregnant and lactating moms enrolled and then later for results. Such methods of pay for performance do of course have drawbacks. It is important to verify results such that care deliverers do not have incentives for misreporting. Counting quality outcomes can be problematic. Nonetheless, such schemes create incentives for caregivers to work with communities to improve outcomes.[28]

What Should Poverty Reduction Accomplish?

Several principles can guide our poverty reduction policy menu. It is important to design institutions that are fair and transparent to deliver quality goods and services. Shining the light of transparency is the best antidote to corruption that acts as a negative tax on public services. Institutional quality is critical. Providing bad services can sometimes be worse that providing no services as all as they can undermine trust in government. If people believe the government is inept they are reluctant to pay taxes that might be squandered—and public services further deteriorate without a sound fiscal base.

Policymakers need to be wary of unintended effects. For example, tightening regulations to draw more workers into the formal sector might actually drive firms into informal status—an undesired goal as informality is associated with low productivity. Providing too comfortable a safety net for the poor might depress savings and work effort.[29] The goal of social protection is to provide help to the most vulnerable while creating incentives to work and save. Programs ideally will be geared to smooth consumption during crises, prevent poverty, and promote investment in human capital.[30] Some programs should be designed to prevent social risks through investment in human capital and other interventions intended to cope with events that have already occurred. Attention should be paid to increasing risks from climate change, food price spikes, and gendered social vulnerabilities.[31]

Entitlements and Social Spending

It is important to remember that as in many countries, the bulk of social spending is not tied to the very poor but rather as protection against economic shocks and aging. Social spending in Latin America broadly breaks down into two categories.

Formal-sector workers—those working in registered firms—are largely covered by social security and unemployment insurance. As people age and are not working or workers are hit by a shock, these safety nets keep people out of poverty. Workers in the public and private formal sectors enjoy access to good health care, social insurance, and pensions to cover family needs as workers progress from the workplace to retirement. But these often super generous programs do not extend to half the workforce in Latin America; the poor and vulnerable are broadly excluded.[32] Countries in the region finance pensions through payroll taxes and contributions to social security; contributions from general revenues supplement the pot. Old-age income security programs draw about 3 percent of gross domestic product (GDP) in countries with smaller programs (such as Colombia, Peru, and the Central American countries) but up to 10 to 12 percent in countries with large systems (such as Brazil and Uruguay).[33] Retirement ages remain relatively early in the sixties, and some special pensions, such as those for the military, can also be drawn by adult daughters. As the demography shifts in the region, burdens of caring for the so-called "third generation" will further drag on future GDP growth.[34] Job protection policies in the region have often been categorized as overly rigid, making it difficult to hire and fire formal-sector workers without resort to large severance packages or legal claims. In exchange for loosening these restrictions (which adversely encourage firms to remain in the informal sector), countries are attempting to expand income protection programs such as unemployment insurance.[35] Nonetheless, these programs have limited coverage for formal-sector workers.

Beyond social spending to prevent the nonpoor from falling into poverty, governments directly invest resources in poverty reduction. The region has been a center for innovations in income support for poor families, dramatically lowering poverty rates. Programs called **conditional cash transfers** (**CCTs**) were pioneered by Brazil and Mexico in the late 1990s. They have now spread to eighteen countries in the region, benefitting 135 million people.[36] In Mexico, Colombia, and Brazil CCTs cover about 55 percent of those who would otherwise exist on less than US$2.50 a day. It is estimated that poverty would have been approximately 13 percent higher had these programs—that cost less than 1 percent of GDP—not existed. CCTs combine dual objectives of alleviating poverty in the short run through a cash transfer with encouraging long-run human capital development by imposing conditions of school attendance and health checkups.[37] The conditionalities vary across programs, but often require that students be present for 85 percent of school days and complete regular health checkups. In exchange, families receive a deposit of about US$15 per child in primary school—perhaps ranging to US$30 for secondary attendance—deposited to an electronic bank account, most often in the mother's name.[38]

Evidence on the success of these programs varies, but most studies suggest that CCTs are more effective in reducing poverty than in improving human capital. Success in poverty alleviation varies by whether the transfers are well targeted and transparently delivered. **Targeting** can be tricky; in informal settlements it may be difficult to accurately identify the poor as opposed to the vulnerable populations. Mexico's Prospera (formerly Progresa and then Oportunidades) CCT is one of the best targeted; it has added between eight and ten months of schooling and led to a decline of 11.8 percentage points in the incidence of anemia among children under age two.[39] Questions of progressive graduation from the program also arise. If someone has picked up an informal-sector job, how is that information transmitted to the social services agency to graduate the person off the transfer list? Corrupt practices risk that CCTs become political entitlements rather than safety nets. Transparency through electronic publication of those receiving transfers can help decrease abuses in the system. When CCTs are aptly targeted, governments get far bigger bang for the poverty reducing buck as compared to the broadly accessible food subsidies we discussed earlier. Some suggest the CCT payouts are too small—Latin American cities have become painfully expensive—but for those near the poverty line CCTs have succeeded in providing a supplement to exit the worst of deprivation.

A critical problem with CCTs has been unintended effects in the long-term development of human capital. CCTs may increase the incentive to remain in the informal sector to avoid the loss of the payment if one's reported income rises. The short-term collection of a CCT transfer means that the worker isn't investing in a formal-sector pension program. A second unintended effect has been that as CCTs have increased, so has the demand for education and health, and this has further overwhelmed weak quality in supply. As more students enroll in schools, outcomes in the already stressed education section are further enfeebled. CCTs are but one component in a suite of policies to promote human development. Supply-side coverage of health, nutrition, and education services needs to be enhanced.[40] Programs should be further tailored for the complexities of the urban setting and informal markets to promote genuine long-term change. When the Mexico Opportunidades was relaunched as Prospera in 2014, the program expanded beyond income to measures to promote social and productive inclusion of beneficiaries such as vocational training and micro finance.[41] One might conclude that the problem isn't with CCTs per se but rather the weak institutional mechanisms that complement their implementation; more needs to be done to give the poor a chance to achieve their potential.

Physical Government Investment in Poverty Alleviation

In addition to transfers to individuals, governments might choose to invest in infrastructure and services to promote human development. If in addition to enhancing infrastructure such as development of a clean water system or a new road, a community can build its capacity for governance and decision making, the project will have accomplished improving both the physical and the social infrastructure. Programs that promote community involvement, with local input from design to implementation, are important in encouraging ownership and voice for the poor.

Venezuela has pursued capacity building approaches over monetary transfers in its missions programs. Despite the wealth brought to Venezuela through oil, nearly half of the population lived in **extreme poverty** in 1999.[42] President Chavez mobilized financing through contributions from the nation's oil company, PDVSA, into a separate fund, controlled by the president, for social investment or missions.[43]

A portfolio of nearly forty programs attacked the ecology of poverty, including Mision Ribas for adult education, Mision Barrio Adentro to improve community health, and Mision Mercal to provide subsidized food markets.[44] In addition to the goal of delivering services, the missions were seen as a new form of community organization to build social capital as an alternative to market-driven neoliberal policies. By 2012, Venezuela had achieved the second strongest record of poverty alleviation in the region, to just over a quarter of the population, with extreme poverty reduced to 6.8 percent.[45] In the wake of the death of Hugo Chavez in early 2013, the sustainability of these achievements is in jeopardy. Weak oil prices and an antibusiness regulatory environment have stripped the country of its ability to deliver basic necessities. Many Venezuelans cannot get access to food and medicine tragically suffering from malnutrition and curable disease. Nonetheless, the direct government interventions stand as an example of the kind of work the state can do to complement market failures leading to poverty.

Labor Market Strategies

As one considers poverty in Latin America, it is distinguished from inadequate incomes in North America and Europe by the dominant presence of the informal market. As we discussed in Chapter 8, we do know that poverty is correlated with low productivity and low-productivity growth rates. Informality is not necessarily poverty; the sector is complex with continuous movement of people in and out.[46] If people are paid the value of what their work is creating (economists will recall that this is called the value of the marginal product or the marginal revenue product), remuneration will remain pitiful as long as productivity is low. If an employer pays above a worker's contribution to production, the firm would quickly go out of business. Improving productivity of workers is central to addressing long-run, structural causes of poverty.

Policies such as CCTs to address short-term income shortfalls are critical, but raising incomes above a poverty line may not fundamentally improve the quality of life if the multidimensional aspects of poverty and deprivation are not addressed. Having an extra US$50 a month helps; if, however, you are still in the same neighborhood with the same lousy-quality schools, undrinkable tap water, and insufficient sanitation services, you continue to be relatively deprived. You are poorly prepared to compete in the global economic market, and are probably prone to intestinal disease that compromises your performance. Productivity sags.

The central policy challenge of poverty reduction is improving the capacity of people to invest in their own skills and raise productivity. Youth born into neighborhoods defined by **chronic poverty** may benefit from **active labor market policies** (**ALMPs**) where governments intervene to help those unemployed find work. These might include training programs, apprenticeships, vocational schools and incentives to firms to hire riskier workers. By addressing market failures, ALMPS can improve job prospects for skilled workers and young people.[47] Think, for a moment, about a job search where your record of work, probably a long one since you were young, was not recorded. Imagine not having contacts through a social network to land a good interview and provide references. You may have significant skills developed on your informal job, but these skills are not certified or may not be the exact set needed in a formal workplace. Jobs are likely located a good distance from your home and the search cost on public transportation is high. ALMPs use public-private initiatives to compensate for the lack of social capital in low-income communities. Government job search assistance in collaboration with private-sector partners can help overcome these hurdles. The public sector might provide training to transform informal-sector skills into those demanded by larger businesses. It can certify applicable expertise already developed and offer financial incentives to firms to hire young workers. Work programs work best when driven by the skills demands by local employers. NGOs can help intermediate to develop the skills to make the jump from informal work to secured employment. An example of such a program is Jovenes in the Dominican Republic. It is training nearly thirty-eight thousand disadvantaged young people, placing them in subsidized internships. This cost-effective program—pretty cheap at between US$600 and US$2,000 per kid—shows that 80 percent of employers hire their young talent after the training period.

Private-Sector Initiatives

In addition to partnering with governments, the private sector has a role in poverty alleviation and social protection. Enhancing inclusive human development is an all hands on deck enterprise. In addition to public funding, complementary resources from the private sector are essential. What have been the drivers changing the relationship between business and society in the Latin America?

Beyond philanthropy, three broad reasons motivate businesses to engage in **corporate social responsibility (CSR)**: the business case, insurance and risk reduction, and the creation of genuine social value transforming the culture not only of society but of the firm.[48] Exploiting the business case for corporate social responsibility—investing in the three Ps of people, planet, and profits—has generated significant returns for some of the national and international firms operating in the region. The large size of the Latin American market creates opportunities to create new products and innovative business models with social returns. Reactive approaches employ CSR strategies to reduce business risks inherent in global production networks, in discords over fairness and in losing a social license to operate. The degree to which the product is branded, its vulnerability to supply chain operations, its exposure to stakeholders in international markets, and its need for reputational capital shape the risk functions differently for domestic and foreign firms. Commodity exporting firms focus less on reducing reputational risks and more on generating a broader social license to operate. In the process of investing in changing society's view of business, the goal of the firm is centrally, and perhaps surprisingly to a North American audience, to change society itself.

What is CSR? This is not a simple question—and how we define it has implications for measuring its success. For some, CSR is voluntary behavior beyond legal compliance in environmental, labor, and human rights standards, making investments serving a social purpose.[49] The corporate social responsibility initiative at Harvard's Kennedy School of Government (KSG) defines CSR strategically. Beyond lawful compliance and philanthropy, the KSG definition calls attention to how firms make profits and how they interact with various stakeholders in the workplace, the marketplace, the supply chain, the community, and the public realm. The World Bank and the OECD reject the voluntary or "beyond compliance" aspect of the CSR definition.[50] The World Bank defines corporate responsibility as the commitment of business to contribute to sustainable development; OECD guidelines encourage the positive contributions companies can make to economic, environmental, and social progress while minimizing the negative externalities created by their operations.

The OECD definition gives greatest space to the corporation's ability to maximize change and minimize harm in its operating environment. It creates the opportunity, according to Simon Zadek, to renegotiate and realign the role of business in society.[51] Under this formulation, responsible business is broadening its accountability beyond profits and shareholders to include social and environmental effects on stakeholders. A dynamic process, new business roles also change the expectations society has for corporate engagement, enhancing the value derived from new forms of collaboration with civil society. Practicing corporate responsibility, this may reinforce the foundation for social expectations, and ultimately the legal responsibility of firms.

The Drivers of CSR: The Business Case

Much has been made for the business case for corporate social responsibility. The San Francisco–based BSR (Business for Social Responsibility) and a myriad of other business-based CSR organizations have long pushed the business case of "Doing Well by Doing Good." The enlightened self-interest of firms can actually work to increase financial returns while promoting social good. Attention to the "triple bottom line"—profits, sustainability, and social return—can enhance performance across all three. Annual company CSR reports highlight achievements in delivering the "three Ps"—profits, planet and people—to their range of stakeholders.

One element of the triple bottom line is investing in your own "internal public," or your employees. Investing in workers may raise productivity and is simply good business, particularly if you are operating in a tight labor market. Engaging in corporate social responsibility, whether investing directly in your workers or in other aspects of the community, may be a special application of the efficiency wage hypothesis. One can think of CSR expenditures as a psychic increase in wages. By paying a "social" wage above the prevailing wage, a firm may be able to attract better workers, minimize turnover, and promote higher morale, resulting in higher productivity.

External certification may validate the claims of a positive environment for workers. Top Brazilian firms proudly note compliance with Brazilian market standards such as the ISE (Index of Sustainable Enterprise or Indice de Sustentabilidade Empresarial), or being listed in the Novo Mercado, a group of firms within the

BOVESPA, the Brazilian stock exchange, meeting international governance standards.[52] Achieving these verifiable standards allows firms the capability to signal a strong internal working environment, and encourage recruiting and retention of the most productive workers—a clear benefit to the triple bottom line. Companies such as the Brazilian aircraft manufacturer EMBRAER, the oil giant Petrobras, or banks such as Bradesco proudly display certifications on their websites, contributing to their reputations as one of the best Brazilian firms to work for.[53]

Large firms in the region are likely to have foundations engaging in community projects. With reputational value at stake, often through branded products, large firms are in part driven by the external public to invest in the social sector. Smaller firms, particularly suppliers to final manufacturers, find fewer incentives in the consumer market. They are more likely to become engaged as their customers in the supply chain demand stronger responsiveness to social concerns. Rather than work with community organizations, it is most likely that the focus of CSR efforts among small and medium-sized enterprises will be with the internal labor markets. Working with employees on better health, training, and safety may promote a goal of competitive inclusiveness, engaging the less advantaged workers in the process of sustainable development. This approach to engage lower income workers, however, will need to be driven by the top of the supply chain.[54]

In addition to pressuring small and medium-sized enterprises to adopt stronger internal labor practices, larger corporations may also see the upgrading of the supply chain as a sound business investment with positive social returns. Microenterprises, especially those within the informal sector, are often outside the regulated labor environment. Walmart do Brazil lists requirements for its suppliers, including legal compliance with work and salary laws, no slave or forced labor, child laws, respect for human rights, a healthy work environment, and observance of environmental legislation. Working with firms to upgrade labor and productive potential can add to the competitiveness of the final producer. Rather than focus on diffuse social projects outside the firm, a larger entity might choose to extend education, training, and finance to micro operators in their supply chain. For example, Orsa, a major Brazilian forestry company, has promoted the development of micro enterprises using recycled materials from its end stage production. This improves community relations—but also solves an end-waste problem while reducing costs. Implementing different social initiatives at different stages of the value chain may enhance competitiveness and the bottom line.

Working back through the supply chain has enormous potential in the agricultural sector. In Central America, one hundred farms in countries covering twenty-three thousand workers improved communications of basic standards regarding excess hours, fair pay, and child labor. Walmart in particular has worked with small suppliers to its grocery line to meet minimum health and safety standards. Beyond supplying locally, in cooperation with NGOs, its peasant farmers in Mexico are beginning to build export markets to the European Union. Large firms can also provide consulting services to smaller suppliers. Walmart, in its program of energy reduction, is using in-house technical support for energy assessments of its suppliers. By lowering the costs for its suppliers it improves its own competitiveness.

Attending to the three Ps of profits, planet, and people may also mean developing new markets for environmental or socially desirable goods. In Mexico Expedia is partnering with the UN Foundation, Alianza, and National Geographic to development sustainable tourism. It is working to improve the local capacity of employers, support local financial initiatives, and create opportunities for workers. Expedia's goal is to create an eco-tour brand that through its commitment to environment and community is distinguished from other environmental tourism producers.[55] The leader in Brazil's domestic cosmetics sector, Natura, has made its market by becoming the leading company in the sustainable use of Brazil's biodiversity.[56] Through its EKOS line made from raw materials gathered in a sustainable manner, Natura has marketed its product on the "well-being–being well" concept. The company was able to sell its beliefs of connecting to nature sustainably not only at home but also abroad. Starbucks is working with its suppliers around the world to promote responsible practices among the growers of its premium coffee. It has partnered with Conservation International to make coffee the world's first sustainable agriculture product. Investing in the social sector as well as expanding access to credit, technical assistance, and certification processes for growers can help both Starbucks and local communities enhance value in the coffee commodity chain.[57]

People may purchase a product because they believe in how the company does business. But it is difficult to verify sustainable practices. Unlike an automobile or fine wine (which economists sometimes call an experience good), a consumer can't directly observe a particular company's environmental performance. Consumers never learn fully about a key element of the product—how it is produced—even after buying and consuming the good.[58] Verifiable certification helps, but the average consumer is less attuned to the benchmarks for fair labor practices and environmental sustainability. Instead, the value of this so-called "credence good" is established in a different market—the market of public opinion shaped strongly by NGOs.

But socially sustainable practices may generate returns independent of a consumer's willingness to purchase a credence good. CSR can help form a company's social legitimacy; social legitimacy strengthens the brand's sustainable competitive advantage among key stakeholder groups, especially socially conscious consumers. Some firms play to the desire for social branding a company as "good" through positive labor and environmental practices; indeed, firms may use social causes as a mechanism to generate market share.

In contrast to a limited scope for cause-related marketing in Latin America, creating new markets attending to social needs has greater prospects. In its triple bottom line quest for investing in people, profits, and the planet, CSR can generate more than new markets—it can also generate new knowledge. Corporate social responsibility can be seen as a competitive necessity in utilizing the knowledge embedded in global networks. GlaxoSmithKline (GSK) and a small Brazilian biotech company signed a US$3.2 million contract to screen compounds of plant, fungal, and bacterial origin from several regions in Brazil; 25 percent of the royalties will go to community-based conservation, health, and education efforts and 25 percent to the university group. GSK will pay for all R&D costs and will have options on license. These kinds of partnerships would not likely have been developed under old business models of short-term profit maximization. Instead, corporate activities must adapt to take advantage of the learning and innovation in social networks.

The notion of developing markets among the world's poor as an expression of corporate social responsibility is perhaps more easily digested when those making the money from these endeavors include the poor. Connecting multinational business to social entrepreneurship among the poor can create new markets and new models of doing business. **Social entrepreneurship** refers to a growing number of organizations that are catering to basic human needs that existing markets and institutions have failed to satisfy. Combining the resourcefulness of traditional entrepreneurship with a mission of changing society, social entrepreneurship can create enormous social—and commercial—value. Traditional capitalists, NGOs, and multilateral organizations are teaming up and jumping on the social entrepreneurship bandwagon. The World Bank is creating mechanisms to put social entrepreneurs with poverty-fighting ideas into contact with private partners with the resources to help them implement their vision. The connection of capital and business management skills in traditional corporate enterprises with the energy and creativeness demanded by surviving poverty creates a value proposition for all.

CSR plays several roles in minimizing social risk. First, it provides intelligence. By partnering with civil society organizations, companies are engaging in cost-effective tool for generating strategic intelligence. Secondly, CSR provides a mechanism—one of the very few—to respond to attacks. The key, however, is not in responding in the midst of crisis, but to use the store of reputational capital with your stakeholders such that when a problem erupts, the company can respond with a credible campaign. Its track record of doing good becomes the asset for addressing the bad. Such long-term CSR involves effective management of stakeholder relationships. This does not imply manipulation of civil society, but rather provides stakeholders knowledge about corporate decision making, welcomes NGOs and governmental authorities to a process of dialogue, and builds trust between business and society.

License to Operate

In addition to risk management, some companies, largely as a function of industry, depend on CSR to acquire a social license to operate. The social license to operate is an intangible contract between a firm and a community to create a positive work environment for both. The social license may be required in a community hosting extractive operations such as timber or mining as the firm is dependent on the good will of the community for the ability to run operations. In an isolated area, operations can easily be shut down by acts of sabotage or vandalism. Becoming a corporate member of the community facilitates day-to-day operations as well as the ability to deal with crises. Participation may provide financial savings, competitive advantage, enable access to technical assistance, help firms pre-empt or weaken regulations, shape future regulations, and create a positive firm image.[59] Because of the distrust of extractive multinationals, this often requires the presence of a third-party actor. In Peru Newmont mining brought in the compliance

advisor/ombudsman of the IFC to mediate when a mercury spill contaminated villages. In this process the chief accountability officer brings together members of
the community, NGOs, and company officials to work through a plan of redress
that meets the needs of all stakeholders. As Newmont's senior vice president and
chief administrative officer notes, building relationships in advance of crisis and
maintaining a transparent, verifiable process in good and bad times is critical to
successful operations.[60]

Good practices, such as those advocated by BSR in its guidebook on the social
license to operate, must be distinguished from practices which are little more than
buying off sources of power in a community. Even if well intentioned, it is not
surprising that a project manager may respond to the powerful in the community
who pose the greatest threat to operations—not necessarily where the development
dollar is best spent.[61] Failing to involve community stakeholders in all stages may
also promote dependency, with the corporation becoming the parental sponsor.
Corporate responsibility may also threaten local government authority. A reason
companies are asked to build schools is because governments have failed. Providing these services reinforces the view of the weakness of government and the
efficacy of the private sector.

An intriguing urban example of needing a license to operate is LAMSA, the
private road contractor in Rio de Janeiro connecting the international airport and
affluent beach communities. The road cut right through communities—and ten-year-
olds could easily stop traffic by standing on an overpass and throwing rocks. The job
of INVEPAR, the institute associated with the private road concession, was to create
a sense of ownership of the road—and not opposition to its passing through.

A second intriguing and quite ambitious example of a license to operate is
Orsa's Jari project. Orsa Celulose, the second largest paper product firm in Brazil,
bought the infamous Jari project for US$1 plus its outstanding debts. At Jari, ship-
ping magnate Daniel Ludwig attempted to build a first-class paper facility based on
fast-growing eucalyptus trees. Covering an area half the size of Holland, it failed
despite huge infusions of cash and technology. Orsa's president, a social visionary,
is betting that he can generate profits by promoting investment not only in trees but
also in the social resources of the region. This bold bet to transform one of the biggest business failures in the history of Brazil into a profitable venture is a function
of not only creating optimal growing conditions but promoting the ingenuity and
entrepreneurship necessary to succeed in the competitive global paper business.
The community—both the thirty-five hundred workers plus the seventy thousand
people living in Monte Dourado—hold the key to Orsa's bet that it can transform
the project into a dynamic source of growth.[62]

Strategic CSR: Changing the Brazilian Business Environment—and the Firm

In contrast to risk management of reputation or obtaining a community license to
operate, offensive or strategic CSR changes the way that businesses engage in the
global economy. "Offensive" or more frequently called "strategic" CSR involves

changing the business environment to create shared value for all actors. Such an approach includes measures that transform both the firm and society. Strategic CSR leverages the core activities of the business to create, in Porter's terms, "unique value propositions"—things the firm can do that others cannot, unlocking shared gains by investing in aspects of the business environment that strengthen competitiveness.

A partnership is strategic when it involves the core business or program activities of both partners. Philanthropy, where businesses simply donate funds, is limited; strategic programs are created jointly and not simply "given" to the civil society partner.[63] More closely related to core competencies within the firm, its focused approach does not address a wide range of social problems. Rather, it looks to create shared value based on the specific advantages a firm can bring to the table.

The transformation of the business environment might indeed be led by a firm that is engaging in best- class responsibility practices that are limiting growth against lower cost, exploitative suppliers. Collaboratively working to raise social expectations of business in society will improve the firm's—and workers'—outcomes.[64] Fabio Barbosa, chairman of Banco Real, characterizes this focus for his organization as a new bank for a new society.[65] He sees social investment as part of a "wave of movement" from the individual to the firm to the market and to society. Strategic or "game changing" CSR involves picking the right issue, establishing concrete goals, reporting progress, deploying the company's key assets, and creating new cross-sector partnerships.[66] In the developing world, it may also mean the creation of new business models, investment strategies, and partnerships to strengthen institutions for good governance and private-sector development.[67] Businesses may develop forms of engagement in the social sector that are not purely profit seeking but are also not traditional philanthropy. These so-called "hybrid" projects may not generate commercial returns in the short term, but the investment in the social sector may generate business value in the long run.[68] For Banco Real, the programs range from recycling 98 percent of material, to investments in biodiesel and **microcredit** projects that engage a new model of saving for small forestry projects (Poupanca Florestal) among its 23,210 micro clients.

Companies in the region look to partnerships with the government to leverage social investments into genuine opportunities for change. That is, Cargill do Brasil does not want to donate money to schools—it wants to work with school officials to change education in the country. It is doing so through planting seeds of education—and developing materials for science learning. Indeed, the programs Cargill supports in its local areas—programs designed in part to acquire a social license to operate—would affect only a limited number of stakeholders without government participation. But by partnering with municipal education departments to deliver complementary inputs to education—not the foundational books everyone should by law have but the extra activity-based learning modules—Cargill can amplify its efforts and multiply its investment dollars.[69] In a parallel fashion, O Globo, a media giant in Brazil, works with governments and NGOs on national campaigns. Using its extended public presence, it promotes action on poverty through "Christmas without Hunger" or social service messages on drunk driving. It sees companies as responsible for addressing society's needs.

Across the board, companies need to see local governments as partners. This sometimes presents problems. Orsa, a Brazilian paper and products company, was shunned by a newly elected mayor who didn't want to be associated with the program of the defeated party. Nonetheless, the engagement of government widens a positive development footprint of companies. Stakeholders see the face of local officials working alongside company representatives. This modeling of public-private partnerships is a pragmatic means of effecting change in the fiscally constrained environments in the developing world.

Necessary but Not Sufficient

Private social investment has become a necessary ingredient in pursuing equitable, sustainable growth in the developing world. But CSR is not a panacea. It will never be a substitute for well-articulated public policy in the social sector. It is not comprehensive; that is, CSR is unlikely to help the poorest of the poor in that they are rarely stakeholders with voice.[70] The most marginalized in a society rarely find themselves within corporate reach. The poorest communities, often outside the geographical location of firms, are the hardest to reach. Third-sector organizations are limited in their contact with the poorest of the poor, leaving this cohort to public assistance when available.[71] Third-sector organizations are also relatively underdeveloped. The success of CSR will be tied to the professionalization of these delivery intermediaries.

Innovations such as **bottom of the pyramid (BOP) marketing** by large multinational corporations may also crowd out smaller providers of local services. BOP marketing provides products and services to low-income customers with packaging and payment plans tailored to those with limited budgets. For example, payment plans for health insurance may adapt to the unpredictable income of the poor—or laundry detergent may be developed for the limited access to water in many slums and sold in small packages. Because foreign direct investment is less appealing in the poorest countries of the world, CSR will also be absent there.[72] Both in terms of geographic coverage and areas of investment, firms will likely pick off the low-hanging fruit—the projects or issues that will deliver results most quickly. Firms are less likely to tackle ugly issues or the most intractable social problems.[73] Private investment in the social sector is not a comprehensive solution to gaping deficits in education, health, or the environment.

Despite these clear limitations, it is tough to see how sustainable development can be achieved without the engagement of the corporate sector. The need for fiscal balance is so strong in the developing world—and the social deficits so overwhelming—that both public and private actors must be engaged in the process. In addition to financing social development, the private sector is a key actor in developing new social norms. If businesses are not engaged in investing in the human capital of their workers, in reducing demands upon resources and energy, in replenishing the environment—or worse work against these ends—the possibilities for genuine, sustainable development are severely circumscribed. Firms operating in the Latin American environment—at least the largest—have identified innovative pathways to change. Although limited, they are indeed creating a new business environment in the region.

Key Concepts

active labor market
   policies
   (ALMPs)
bottom of the
   pyramid (BOP)
   marketing
chronic poverty
conditional cash
   transfers (CCTs)

corporate social
   responsibility (CSR)
extreme poverty
Gini coefficient
headcount ratio
Human Opportunity
   Index (HOI)
Human Development
   Index (HDI)

informal sector
Lorenz curve
microcredit
multidimensional
   poverty measures
poverty line
social
   entrepreneurship
targeting

Chapter Summary

Poverty

- During the first decade of the twenty-first century in Latin America poverty declined dramatically and inequality also showed significant improvement.
- It is important to note that poverty is not merely the absence of money; it is about lacking the access to resources that empower people to make choices to achieve their potential.
- Poverty is measured in a variety of ways. The World Bank defines the absolute international poverty lines as US$1.90 and US$3.20 a day. However, since poverty is a relative concept, countries also establish national poverty lines which are useful in understanding the distribution of income within nations.
- Additionally, since income is only one dimension of poverty, multidimensional poverty measures are a useful tool. The Human Development Index (HDI) uses metrics for life expectancy, mean years of schooling, and expected years of schooling in addition to per capita income. Poverty can also be characterized as the lack of the beings and doings as well as functionings to live a valued life.

Inequality and Social Exclusion

- The Gini coefficient measures the degree of inequality in a region and helps with understanding quality of life in the region. A Gini coefficient of 0 represents perfect equality and a coefficient of 1 represents perfect inequality. Despite a reduction in inequality, the average Gini for the region is 0.5, the highest regional average in the world. High degrees of inequality create social tension and act as a drag on growth.

New Class Dynamics

- Economic growth has created new class dynamics in Latin America. With strong economic growth and more effective poverty safety nets, 43 percent of Latin Americans changed social classes between the mid-1990s and end of the 2000s.
- Latin America's middle class has grown in the past decade. In Latin America, US$4 a day is defined as poor, up to US$10 a day is defined as the vulnerable class, and US$10–US$50 a day is defined as the middle class. About 30 percent of Latin America now falls in the middle-class category, but there is significant heterogeneity in the region.
- Unlike the middle class in other regions, the Latin American middle class is opting out of the social contract and putting less pressure on the government to provide quality public services.

Mobility in the Region

- Despite positive trends, people's opportunities remain shaped by predetermined traits such as race, gender, and birthplace. Citizens remain systematically excluded from opportunities for access to quality education and health care as well as financial mechanisms to invest in human and physical capital. The Human Opportunity Index attempts to measure the degree to which exogenous circumstances pre determine outcomes.

Addressing Poverty and Inequality in the Region

- Although progress toward reducing poverty and redressing inequality is encouraging, much remains to be done. Progress remains hindered by institutions, interests, and ideas. For example, political systems can be unresponsive to citizens' needs and patron-client relationships persist. Likewise, the interests of key actors can shape policy decisions. Additionally, a knowledge gap persists—little is known about what poverty alleviation programs actually work.
- One effort to reduce the knowledge gap is through randomized controlled trials, a technique most often used in medical sciences. Such trials help us understand why people behave in certain ways when basic conditions are controlled for. However, randomized control trials have their limitations and are less useful in cases of infrastructure investment or assessing the distributional impact of policies since they require control groups.
- Another policy innovation is results-based financing or cash on delivery programs which compensate participants based on program outcomes. These programs do face challenges including the ability to effectively monitor outcomes.

What Should Poverty Reduction Accomplish?

- Poverty reduction policies should help create fair and transparent institutions to deliver quality goods and services. Institutional quality is critical to engendering trust in the government, which also helps strengthen the fiscal base to support public services.
- Policymakers need to be careful of unintended effects. The goal of social protection is to provide help to the most vulnerable while creating incentives to work and save. Programs ideally will help smooth consumption during crisis, prevent poverty, and promote investment in human capital.

Entitlements and Social Spending

- Social spending is divided into two broad categories in the region—the formal and informal sectors. The formal sector benefits from generous social programs. However, these programs do not extend to half the workforce in Latin America; the poor and vulnerable remain broadly excluded.
- In addition to social spending, governments invest resources in poverty reduction. The region has been a center for innovations in income support programs for poor families dramatically lowering poverty rates.
- Conditional cash transfers, first pioneered in Brazil and Mexico in the late 1990s, alleviate poverty in the short run through cash transfers while encouraging long-run human capital development by imposing conditions such as school attendance of health checkups.
- CCTS are generally more effective in reducing poverty than improving human capital. Targeting remains a challenge. Additionally, unintended effects of the programs, such as overcrowded schools, have highlighted the need for complementary institutional strengthening.
- Government investment in poverty alleviation.
- Governments might choose to invest in infrastructure and services that promote human development in additional to other programs. Investment efforts can be paired with community level involvement, thereby building capacity and improving both physical and social infrastructure.

Labor Market Strategies

- A unique dimension of poverty in Latin America is the dominance of the informal sector. Although the informal sector and poverty are not directly correlated, improving the productivity of workers is central to addressing long-run, structural causes of poverty.
- Active labor market policies, an example of public-private initiatives, can help address market failures by matching job seekers to employers.

Private-Sector Initiatives

- The private sector has a role to play in poverty alleviation and social protection. Businesses can help supplement government resources and address significant social deficits. If businesses are not involved, the prospects for sustainable development are circumscribed.

Notes

1. Rebeca Grynspan and López-Calva, "Multidimensional Poverty in Latin America: Concept, Measurement, and Policy," in J. A. Ocampo and J. Ros (eds.), *The Oxford Handbook of Latin American Economics* (New York: Oxford University Press, July 2011).

2. ECLAC, "Social Panorama of Latin America 2012."

3. Ruth Alexander, "Dollar Benchmark: The Rise of the $1 a Day Statistic," *BBC News*, March 9, 2012.

4. World Bank WDI Poverty figures at data.worldbank.org, accessed May 2013. To change the poverty line go to http://povertydata.worldbank.org/poverty/region/LAC and under the graphic region poverty trends choose select a poverty line.

5. $4 a day is a commonly accepted baseline offered by ECLAC to meet the basics of nutrition given food prices in the LAC region. It is confusing, however, because $4 is also the threshold used by the World Bank for the vulnerable class. To compound confusion, there are also national poverty lines.

6. If you are confused about national versus international poverty lines you might consult the World Bank's page "Poverty & Equality Data FAQs," http://web.worldbank.org/WBSITE/EXTERNAL/TOPICS/EXTPOVERTY/0,,contentMDK:23012899~pagePK:210058~piPK:210062~theSitePK:336992,00.html.

7. The United Nations, "Multidimensional Poverty Index," http://hdr.undp.org/en/content/multidimensional-poverty-index-mpi.

8. These aspects of resources deprivation, lack of empowerment, and vulnerability draw upon the World Bank definition of poverty, http://www.worldbank.org/en/topic/poverty/overview.

9. For Sen's work I am indebted to Ingrid Robeyns, "The Capability Approach," in *The Stanford Encyclopedia of Philosophy, ed.* Edward N. Zalta (Summer 2011 Edition), plato.stanford.edu/archives/sum2011/entries/capability-approach/, for her lucid summary.

10. Data characterizing poverty from ECLAC, "Social Panorama of Latin America 2012, www.eclac.org/publicaciones/xml/4/.../SocialPanorama2012DocI.pdf.

11. IDB, "Room for Development in Housing Markets," in *Ideas for Development in the Americas (IDEA)* Volume 26 (September-December, 2011), https://publications.iadb.org/handle/11319/3989#sthash.G9RQUH6M.dpuf.

12. Leonardo Gasparini and Nora *Lustig,* "The *Rise and Fall* of Income Inequality in Latin America." *Oxford Handbooks Online* (September 18, 2012).

13. Gasparini and Lustig, "The Rise and Fall of Income Inequality."

14. José Gabriel Palma, "Homogeneous Middles vs. Heterogeneous Tails, and the End of the 'Inverted-U': It's All about the Share of the Rich," *Development and Change*, 42(1) (January 2011): 87–153.

15. Nancy Birdsall, "A Note on the Middle Class in Latin America," CGD Working Paper, 303.

16. Birdsall, "A Note on the Middle Class in Latin America."

17. Presentation on "The Rising Middle Class" by Julian Messina, Office of the Chief Economist, Latin America and the Caribbean Region, The World Bank, at LASA May 2013.

18. Francisco H. G. Ferreira, Julian Messina, Jamele Rigolini, Luis-Felipe Lopez-Calva, Maria Ana Lugo, Renos Vakis, Luis Felipe Lopez-Calva, and Renos Vakis, *Economic Mobility and the Rise of the Latin American Middle Class* (Washington, DC: World Bank, Top of Form 2012).

19. Data from J Messina, "Intragenerational Mobility in Latin America over the Past 15 Years," 2013, https://openknowledge.worldbank.org/bitstream/.../9780821396346.pdf 2013.

20. Francisco H. G. Ferreira and Je´re´mie Gignoux, "The Measurement of Educational Inequality: Achievement and Opportunity," *The World Bank Economic Review* (2013) doi: 10.1093/wber/lht004, First published online: February 20, 2013.

21. José R. Molinas Vega, Ricardo Paes de Barros, Jaime Saavedra Chanduvi, Marcelo Giugale, Louise J. Cord, Carola Pessino, Amer Hasan, 2012. "Do Our Children Have a Chance? A Human Opportunity Report for Latin America and the Caribbean," *World Bank*, 2012, https://openknowledge.worldbank.org/handle/10986/2374.

22. Paolo Brunori, Francisco H. G. Ferreira, and Vito Peragine, "Inequality of Opportunity, Income Inequality and Economic Mobility: Some International Comparisons," Policy Research Working Paper 6304, The World Bank, January 2013.

23. José Gabriel Palma, "Homogeneous Middles vs. Heterogeneous Tails, and the End of the 'Inverted-U': It's All About the Share of the Rich," *Development and Change* 42(1) (January 2011): 87–153.

24. Rebecca Holmes and Nicola Jones, "Rethinking Social Protection Using a Gender Lens," Working Paper 320, Overseas Development Institute, October 2010.

25. Jenna Burrell, "On the Overuse of Randomized Controlled Trials in the Aid Sector," October 30, 2012, www.globalpolicyjournal.com/blog/30/10/2012/overuse-randomized-controlled-trials-aid-sector, reporting on Julian Cristia, Pablo Ibarraran, Santiago Cueto, Ana Santiago, and Eugenio Severin, "Technology and Child Development: Evidence from the One Laptop per Child Program," Research Department Publications 4764, Inter-American Development Bank, Research Department, 2012.

26. Presentation by Dean Karlan on two studies on interest rate elasticity and the impact of microcredit. Both studies were conducted in Mexico in partnership with Compartamos Banco (presented on June 1, 2013), Evidence on Innovations in Financial Capability Conference—Lima, Peru.

27. Pranab Bardhan, "Little, Big: Two Ideas About Fighting Global Poverty," Bostonreview.net, May 20, 2013.

28. See Nancy Birdsall and William Savedoff, "Cash on Delivery: A New Approach to Foreign Aid 2010," www.cgdev.org.

29. *Shifting Gears to Accelerate Shared Prosperity in Latin America and the Caribbean,* World Bank, June 2013, www.worldbank.org/content/dam/Worldbank/document/LAC/PLB%20Shared%20 Prosperity%20FINAL.pdf, and Helena Ribe, David A. Robalino, and Ian Walker, *From Right to Reality: Incentives, Labor Markets, and the Challenge of Universal Social Protection in Latin America and the Caribbean* (Washington, DC: World Bank, 2012).

30. Ribe, Robalino, and Walker, *From Right to Reality.*

31. Jennifer Pribble, "Worlds Apart: Social Policy Regimes in Latin America," *Studies in Comparative International Development*, 46 (2011):191–216, and *Shifting Gears to Accelerate Shared Prosperity.*

32. Ania Calderon, "On Finding the Right Bundles: Social Policy, Growth, and Equal Development: An Interview with Santiago Levy," *Journal of International Affairs* 66(2) (Spring/Summer 2013).

33. Ribe, Robalino, and Walker, *From Right to Reality.*

34. Joe Leahy, "Brazil Pensions Blamed for Curbing GDP," *The Financial Times*, March 6, 2012.

35. Ribe, Robalino, and Walker, *From Right to Reality.*

36. Marco Stampini and Leopoldo Tornarolli, *"The Growth of Conditional Cash Transfers in Latin America and the Caribbean: Did They Go Too Far?"* IDB Policy Brief No. IDB-PB-185, November 2012.

37. S. Handa and B. Davis, "The Experience of Conditional Cash Transfers in Latin America and the Caribbean," *Development Policy Review*, 24(5) 2006: 513–536.

38. Michael Shifter and Cameron Combs, "The Politics of Poverty: South America's Conditional Cash Transfers," *World Politics Review,* May 14, 2013.

39. World Bank, "A Model from Mexico for the World," November 19, 2014.

40. Ribe, Robalino, and Walker, *From Right to Reality.*

41. Giles Constantine, "Mexico Rebrands Flagship Social Welfare Programme in BID to Help Working Poor," September 26, 2014, https://eyeonlatinamerica.wordpress.com/2014/09/26/mexico-prospera-welfare-programme-working-poor/.

42. ECLAC, "Social Panorama."

43. Andrew Downie, Whitney Eulich, and Andrew Rosati, "Chávez vs Lula: Two Distinct Approaches to Poverty Reduction in Latin America," *Christian Science Monitor*, 08827729, March 7, 2013.

44. Pia Riggirozzi, "Social Policy in Post-Neo-liberal Latin America: The Cases of Argentina, Venezuela and Bolivia," *Development* 53(1) (2010): 70–76. doi:10.1057/dev.2009.96.

45. Embassy of the Bolivarian Republic of Venezuela, ECLAC, "Venezuela Has Third-Lowest Poverty Rate in Latin America," January 13, 2012, http://venezuela-us.org/2012/01/13/eclac-venezuela-has-third-lowest-poverty-rate-in-latin-america/.

46. Ania Calderon, "On Finding the Right Bundles: Social Policy, Growth, and Equal Development: An Interview with Santiago *Levy*," *Journal of International Affairs* 66(2) (Spring/Summer 2013).

47. Ribe, Robalino, and Walker, *From Right to Reality.*

48. Jane Nelson, "Corporate Citizenship in a Global Context," Corporate Social Responsibility Initiative Working Paper No. 13 (Cambridge, MA: John F. Kennedy School of Government, Harvard University).

49. Krista Bondy, Dirk Mattern, and Jeremy Moon, "MNC Codes of Conduct: CSR or Corporate Governance?," International Centre for Corporate Social Responsibility, Nottingham, UK, No. 40–2006 ICCSR Research Paper series ISSN 1479–5124.

50. Cited in Tom Fox, "Corporate Social Responsibility and Development: In Quest of an Agenda," *Development* 47(3) (2004): 29–36.

51. Simon Zadek, "The Logic of Collaborative Governance: Corporate Responsibility, Accountability and the Social Contract," Corporate Social Responsibility Initiative Working Paper No. 17 (Cambridge, MA: John F. Kennedy School of Government, Harvard University, January 2006).

52. Novo Mercado at www.bovespa.com.br/home/redirect.asp?end=/Empresas/NovoMercadoNiveis/IndexNMP.asp.

53. Embraer, www.embraer.com/english/content/empresa/certifications.asp; Petrobrás, www2.petrobras.com.br/meio_ambiente/ingles/gestao/ges_iso.htm.

54. General conclusion from the IADB CSR conference, Guatemala City, Guatemala, December 2007.

55. IADB CSR conference, Guatemala City, Guatemala, December 2007.

56. Geoffrey Jones and Ricardo Reisen de Pinho, "Natura: Global Beauty Made in Brazil," HBS Case: December 12, 2006.

57. Starbucks, *Ethical Sourcing: Coffee*, www.starbucks.com/responsibility/sourcing/coffee and The Evidence Project "Starbucks and Conservation International: How a Sustained NGO-company Partnership Led to the Coffee Industry's First Sustainability Standard," 2017, http://evidenceproject.popcouncil.org/wp-content/uploads/2017/03/Case-Study-1-Starbucks.pdf.

58. Jason Scott Johnston, "Corporate Social Responsibility Initiative," Working Paper (Cambridge, MA: John F. Kennedy School of Government, Harvard University, November 2005).

59. Jennifer Howard-Grenville, Jennifer Nash, and Cary Coglianese, "Constructing the License to Operate," Corporate Social Responsibility Initiative Working Paper No. 27 (Cambridge, MA: John F. Kennedy School of Government, Harvard University, August 2006).

60. L. Kurlander, "Newmont Mining: The Social License to Operate," presentation to the Global Executive Forum, October 2001, Institute for International Business and Centre for International Business Education and Research, University of Colorado Denver, available from: www.cudenver.edu.

61. Jedrzej George Frynas, "The False Developmental Promise of Corporate Social Responsibility: Evidence from Multinational Oil Companies," *International Affairs* 81(3) (2005): 581–598.

62. Mark Milstein, Stuart Hart, and Bruno Sadinha, "Jari Celulose SA," Oikos sustainability case writing competition 2003, www.oikos foundation.unisg.ch; Sergio Amoroso and Robert Waack, "Developing Sustainability: The Orsa Group Approach in the Jari River Region," Grupo Orsa, Interview at Fundação Orsa.

63. Darcy Ashman, "Promoting Corporate Citizenship in the Global South," *Institute for Development Research*, 16(3) (2000), www.jsi.com.idr.

64. Zadek, "The Logic of Collaborative Governance."

65. Carlos Motto, presentation on Banco Real, Fiesp Mostra, Sao Paulo, August 2007.

66. Mark Kramer and John Kania, "Game Changing CSR," CSRI Working Paper No. 18, February 2006.

67. Jane Nelson, "Leveraging the Development Impact of Business in the Fight Against Global Poverty," CSRI Working Paper No. 22, April 2006.

68. Ibid.

69. Interview with Denise Cantarelli, Cargill do Brasil, Sao Paulo, 1 February 2007.

70. Rhys Jenkins, "Globalization, Corporate Social Responsibility and Poverty," *International Affairs*, 81(3) (2005): 525–540.

71. Interview with Silvia Morais, Hedging Grifo, Sao Paulo, 31 January 2007.

72. Michael Blowfield, "Corporate Social Responsibility: Reinventing the Meaning of Development?," *International Affairs*, 81(3) (2005): 515–524.

73. Blowfield, "Corporate Social Responsibility."

HEALTH POLICY
Investing in People's Future

Combatting diseases of poverty, such as mosquito-borne Zika, at the same time as modern challenges of cardiac disease or cancer, which affect all segments of a population regardless of ecominc status, strains health budgets. *(iStock/luizsouzarj)*

CHAPTER ELEVEN

Addressing poverty and enhancing human capital in Latin America rest on progress in health and educational systems in the region. As the World Health Organization (WHO) argues, the promotion of health is the process of enabling people to increase their control over improvements in their environment to reach a state of complete physical, mental, and social well-being. Beyond disease reduction, health promotion is critical not only to maintain a decent quality of life but also to achieve human and social potential. Education is central to transforming health trends and increasing human capital in the region. Education reform will determine Latin America's competitiveness in the global economy as well as the character of democratic political life and a more just economic distribution within each nation. Without a healthy, well-educated citizenry, Latin America will be left behind.

Our next two chapters consider the health and educational deficits in the region and identify strategies for reform. Chapter 11 begins by analyzing the good news and the bad news in the regional health profile. The good news is that substantial progress has been made, as measured by health indicators. The bad news is that improvement was stalled by the economic crisis of the 1980s and the new fiscal realities in the current period. Smaller public sectors leave less to invest in health and education. Given financial constraints, we then consider ways of organizing health care delivery systems that may be able to do more with less. Efficient and effective delivery of health services is the key to the future well-being of the over 645 million residents of the region.[1] Education has faced similar challenges. Chapter 12 will show that although literacy rates in the region measure signs of progress, high rates of repetition and unequal access to education limit the gains from education to society. Innovation in educational policy is critical for Latin American countries to compete in the global arena in the twenty-first century. Both health and education systems are challenged by how to accomplish more with limited resources.

Key questions to explore in this chapter include:

- What is the health profile for Latin America? What health conditions most threaten lives in the region?
- How do health needs of women and indigenous groups differ from those of the broader population?
- How have health challenges changed with globalization?
- What is the structure of health care delivery in Latin America, and how does this affect outcomes?
- How do health delivery systems differ in the rural and the urban sectors? Are centrally located urban hospitals a better health investment than rural community health providers?
- What is the experience of health care reform in the region?

THE PECULIAR NATURE OF HEALTH CARE AS A GOOD

Health is integrally linked into the human, social, political, and economic development of a country. The opportunities for human development condition the national health profile. As shown in Figure 11.1, health systems are built on complex

Figure 11.1.   WHO Health Systems Framework

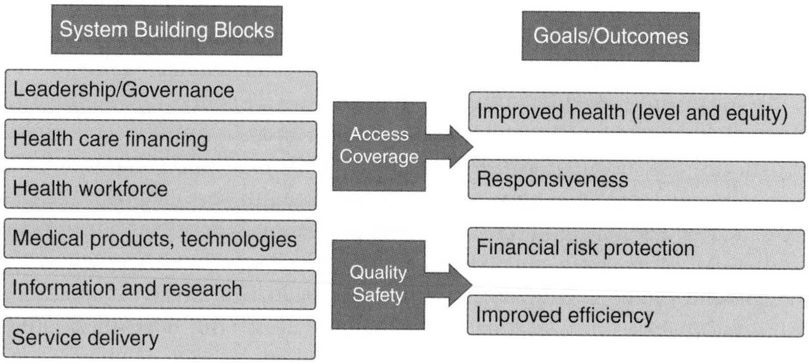

Source: World Health Organziation, who.int/healthinfo/systems/WHO_MBHSS_2010_full_web.pdf

interactions between governance, financing, medicine, and information delivery. Without the political will to provide health services as a basic human right, even the wealthiest of countries will have significant health deficits among the poor. Although the right to health care is defined in most Latin American countries in their constitutions or by law, quality delivery of health care impedes growth. The level of economic development in part determines the social resources available for health care as well as individuals' ability to invest in their own well-being. But in Latin America, weakness in the delivery of health care systems contributes to lower than expected performance given per capita gross domestic product (GDP).[2] A poor person has little control over the external environment of open sewage, polluted water and air, or safety from violence. A poor country has limited resources to provide health services and transform the social infrastructure into one that provides basic human needs for all. Avoidable mortality—deaths that could be prevented by improvements in basic health conditions—hover in the 45 percent range in the region. A startling 1.5 million persons under the age of sixty-five are dying each year from avoidable causes. Health care is in crisis in Latin America and, given new challenges on the horizon, will be woefully ill-equipped to provide opportunities for healthy lives to its citizens.

Similar to education, the production of health care has a few peculiarities that we should consider. Health care is considered a **merit good**. A merit good will be underconsumed in the market because individuals typically ignore the positive externalities created for others in society. Certain diseases, particularly the infectious variety, lead to the classification as a merit good. When people are healthy, the spread of disease is less likely. It is therefore in my interest for you to be vaccinated or taught good preventative health practices. But what if you value health differently? One may also derive some utility from knowing that the basic health needs of a population are met; healthy people are less prone to risky survival behavior such as prostitution or drug dealing that may also have an impact on others. Social returns can therefore exceed the sum of individual returns, meriting a role for government to invest in the provision of public health. But all health care does not have a social benefit. The appropriate mix of public support of health care is a question facing all societies—particularly as costs in health care have skyrocketed. In Latin America this question is even more pressing as the need for comprehensive access to basic health care overlays with modern disease challenges.

Although all aspects of health care do not meet the two criteria of public goods—nonrivalry and nonexcludability—certain aspects of health provision indeed can be considered a public good. With scarce dollars, consumption of hospital services by one person, for example, may preclude treatment of another person; people are also regularly excluded from health services for an inability to pay. However, the knowledge creation and dissemination critical to public health creates aspects of being a **public good**. A radio program to promote sanitary hygiene to stem the spread of dysentery does not exhibit rivalry or excludability; likewise, a safe sex campaign to prevent the spread of HIV benefits all. When the externalities of a public good transcend borders, as in the case of HIV, we consider this a case of a **global public good**. The presence of global public goods in health signals the need to strengthen governance for international health risks. Consider the Zika virus—spread by mosquitos that don't check in with border authorities. This international health problem can only be effectively addressed by cooperation between governments as well as through increased access to health care.[3]

In addition to having characteristics of a merit good and a global public good, the need for health care is distinguished by the **lack of predictability**. Unlike education, where it is fairly predictable when the services will be needed, it is more difficult to plan for illness.[4] Given the highly variable nature of demand, the question of insurance arises. Pooling the risk of illness and collecting modest sums to pay for the unlucky who fall ill is a rational response to the unpredictability of health problems. Our key policy question is how the payment for this risk should be organized—through public funds, private contributions, or a mix of both. The design of health care systems therefore breaks out into two central areas: How should health care be financed, and how should it be delivered? Some countries opt for public finance and private delivery, while others rely more heavily on private contributions to insurance accepted at both public and private hospitals. As we will see, in Latin America there has traditionally been a mix of both. The last decade has also seen a rise in universal programs of health care throughout the region. Let's turn to look at some of the characteristics of health (or lack thereof) in Latin America.

A Profile of Health in the Region

Dramatic Progress . . . and Large Gaps in Coverage

Health care can be seen as a proxy for the dramatic changes in the standard of living in Latin America over the past decades. Since 1960 life expectancy has risen from fifty-four to seventy-five years. In 1927 life expectancy in Costa Rica was about forty years; in the United States at that time people could expect to live to age sixty. Today Costa Ricans expect to live to age eighty, a year longer than Americans.[5] In 1960, 153 out of every 1,000 Latin American children did not make it to their fifth birthday; by 2011, that figure was 10. Unlike other regions, Latin America was able to continue to reduce infant mortality by 4 percent a year in the 1990s.[6] Dramatically, from 1970 to 2000, infant mortality fell by 72.42 percent in Brazil, and from 2000 to 2015, the rate fell an additional 13.5 percent. Table 11.1 presents mortality based on broad causality by country. Care should be taken in analyzing the numbers, as each country's reporting and statistical methods vary. Nonetheless, we can roughly correlate poverty with poor performance and see the huge regional diversity on morbidity indicators. Improved sanitation, measured as the greater availability of treated running water and sewerage and additional schooling, particularly by mothers, led to these falls in infant mortality. As shown in Table 11.2, countries with incomplete access to water and sanitation have higher morbidity rates.

We must look at national data with caution. The poorest regions of Brazil have decreased their rates of under-five child mortality from 75 for every 1,000 in 2000, to a rate of 42 for every 1,000 by 2009, but huge disparities remain as compared to the national rate of 13.7. Even for the more affluent southern region, rates are high compared to the accomplishments in Chile (of 8.2) in reducing child mortality to rates approximating industrial countries.[7] (The United States is at 6.9.) Problems of malnutrition and preventable diseases are tightly woven into problems of inequality

Table 11.1. Mortality and Life Expectancy Indicators

	Maternal Mortality Ratio (per 100,000 live births)	Infant Mortality Rate (per 1,000 live births)	Under 5 Mortality Rate (per 1,000 live births 2011)	Life Expectancy at Birth (2014)	
				Male	Female
Argentina	34.9	11.1	14	72.84	80.06
Belize	41.8	17.3	17	71.09	77.28
Bolivia	229.0	50	51	65.34	69.76
Brazil	61.6	14.6	16	70.64	77.84
Chile	17.2	7.4	9	77.41	82.91
Colombia	69.7	17.8	18	70.63	77.91
Costa Rica	17.0	8.7	10	78.01	82.36
Cuba	38.9	4.2	6	77.51	81.41
Ecuador	60.0	10.1	23	73.96	79.65
El Salvador	38.0	21.5	15	68.04	77.32
Guatemala	116.0	18.3	30	68.87	75.93
Honduras	74.0	24.0	21	71.86	76.45
Mexico	42.3	13.3	16	75.29	79.97
Nicaragua	50.8	20.0	26	72.15	78.21
Panama	64.9	14.3	20	75.04	80.68
Paraguay	84.9	14.7	22	70.13	74.7
Peru	93.0	16.0	18	72.48	77.87
Uruguay	16.0	8.8	10	73.88	80.68
Venezuela	73.3	15.0	15	71.91	77.84
United States	12.7	6.05	8	76.68	81.44

Source: Health Indicators Database, Pan American Health Organization (PAHO). Data taken from most recent report, all between 2007 and 2014.

Table 11.2. Population with Access to Improved Services

	Water Source %		Sanitation %	
	Urban	*Rural*	*Urban*	*Rural*
Argentina	98	80	91	77
Belize	99	100	93	86
Bolivia	96	67	34	9
Brazil	99	84	87	37
Chile	99	75	98	83
Colombia	99	73	81	55
Costa Rica	100	91	95	96
Cuba	96	89	94	81
Ecuador	97	88	96	84
El Salvador	94	76	89	83
Guatemala	98	90	89	73
Honduras	95	77	80	62
Mexico	96	87	90	68
Nicaragua	98	68	63	37
Panama	97	83	75	51
Paraguay	99	66	90	40
Peru	90	61	81	36
Uruguay	100	100	100	100
Venezuela	94	75	94	57

Source: PAHO, Health Situation in the Americas Basic Indicators 2009.

of access. Striking inequalities of access to quality health care between rich and poor, rural and urban residents, and indigenous and nonindigenous citizens pervade the region. In the Ecuadorian Amazon, life expectancy from 1995 to 2000 was 59.6 years, and an estimated 21 percent of the population would not survive more than forty years; in the wealthier Ecuadorian province of Pichincha, life expectancy was fifteen years longer—74.5 years—and only 6.8 percent were expected to die before age forty. In the urban area of Guayaquil, 7 percent of the mothers go without pre-natal care; in the remote Amazon, 34 percent have none. Five percent of deliveries in Guayaquil and Quito are at home; 50 percent of the mothers give birth outside medical care in the Amazonia.[8]

Countrywide data should, therefore, be interpreted with caution. Income inequality skews access to health care. If you are an affluent Mexican, for example, the chances of your baby dying in infancy are 13.4 per 1,000 live births; if you are poor, the odds escalate to a tragic 109.76. Rural Peruvian babies are about three times as likely to die as those in Lima. Malnutrition in Ecuador among children under age five ranges from 8 to 42.6 percent, depending on the socioeconomic district. In Peru, a mother with no education is three times more likely to have her child die than a mother with a secondary education or higher. A rural inhabitant in Brazil can expect to live twenty fewer years than a wealthy cousin in the city. Divergent rural and urban standards of living result in widely different health pro-files. Health ministries must therefore make tough choices about where to invest the nation's health resources. Should investments be made in cities to confront new challenges to health with technologically sophisticated systems? Or should resources be placed in the poorest rural sectors to address traditional disease threats?

Children who survive but are not properly fed often suffer from stunting, measured by two standard deviations below median height for age of the reference population. Rates of stunting in the countries worst afflicted have fallen from 32.5 to 25.2 percent of the age relevant cohort in Ecuador (1998–2012), from 19.7 to 12.7 percent in Colombia (1995–2010), and from 37.3 to 18.4 in Peru (1991–2012).[9] Stunting, largely attributed to protein-energy malnutrition and anemia as result of an iron deficiency, is more acute in the rural sector and among children whose mothers have no education. In Guatemala, for example, 69 percent of children of uneducated mothers and 66 percent of indigenous children are stunted.[10] In Ecuador, stunting continues to afflict 41 percent of the children in the rural highlands. Controlling for differences in education, housing, and economics status, discrimination and exclusion of these indigenous children through cultural and linguistic barriers, negative attitudes in health care delivery, and inappropriate educational curriculums are to blame for the retardation in growth.[11] In addition to the effects of stunting, childhood malnutrition severely jeopardizes, reduces, or impairs the prospects for productive social participation into adulthood.

Paradoxically, malnutrition exists side by side with obesity—with some of the same causes. The double burden of malnutrition reflects the coexistence of both undernutrition and overnutrition in the same population across the life course.[12] Babies from poor social backgrounds who have experienced intrauterine growth restrictions as a result of maternal malnutrition are prone to become obese as adults, since they develop thrifty metabolic mechanisms and are exposed to food of poor quality from an early age. The problem of nutrition in Latin America is characterized by the coexistence of excess and scarcity.[13] Between 17 and 36 percent of adolescents in the region in 2014 were considered overweight or obese.[14] With the exception of Haití (38.5 percent), Paraguay (48.5 percent) and Nicaragua (49.4 percent), half the population of the region is overweight.[15] Yet in Nicaragua and Guatemala, 29 and 25 percent of the population, respectively, is undernourished.

Malnourished children have an increased risk of hypertension, cardiovascular diseases, and diabetes and are less able to resist disease as adults and less likely to finish school and achieve economic stability.[16] Three of the four countries in the world with the highest percentage of overweight mothers and malnourished children are in Latin American: Guatemala (13 percent of households), Bolivia (11 percent), and Nicaragua (10 percent). Nutritional interventions in the early months of life can make a lifetime of difference—but to be effective these must be part of changes in the health/biological, the economic/food, and the social/cultural environment for health.[17]

The unfinished agenda in resolving the **epidemiological backlog** in Latin America exacts a high human toll. Despite strides made in reducing child and adult mortality, hunger afflicts approximately 8 percent of Latin Americans.[18] Increasing undernourishment, the condition of people whose dietary energy consumption is continuously below a minimum dietary energy requirement for maintaining a healthy life and carrying out a light physical activity, afflicts disproportionate numbers in a region where food is available. Table 11.3 shows how the degree of malnutrition is roughly correlated with achieving other millennium development goals (MDGs) in the region. The Food and Agriculture Organization (FAO) reports approximately 2.2 million Bolivians or 20 percent of the population as undernourished, the highest in the region; 14 percent of Guatemalans are also undernourished, which causes 31.77 percent of deaths in Guatemalan children under age five. Yet there is a degree of variation, even within Central America. Undernourishment is at 14 percent in El Salvador and 6 percent in Costa Rica, evidencing the scope for improvement in the worst-off cases. Region-wide, 7.7 percent of the population is undernourished.[19] Hunger and malnutrition lead to increased poverty; reduced school attendance; weakened immune systems; neonatal disorders of diarrhea, pneumonia, and malaria; and, of course, death.[20] Reducing the prevalence of underweight children by another 5 percentage points could reduce child mortality by 30 percent.

Box 11.1 highlights Mexico's struggle with obesity. Countries in the region are experiencing a food transition, where an increasing portion of diets is comprised of ultra-processed foods and animal proteins. Latin America is among the

Table 11.3. Undernourishment and MDG Indicators, 2013–2015

Country	Poverty Headcount Ratio Living on < $1PPP (MDG 1) (%) 2011–2013	Prevalence of Underweight Children <5 (MDG 1) (%) 2009–2013	<5 Mortality Rate/1,000 Live Births (MDG 4) 1990	2015	Maternal Mortality Ratio/100,000 Live Births (MDG 5) 1990	2013
15–18 percent undernourished						
Bolivia	7.7	5	124	38	510	200
Nicaragua	10.8	6	67	22	170	100
10–14 percent undernourished						
Ecuador	4.4	6	57	22	160	87
El Salvador	3.3	7	59	17	110	69
Guatemala	11.5	13	81	29	270	140
Honduras	18.9	13	58	20	290	120
Panama	2.9	7	31	17	98	85
Paraguay	2.2	4	47	21	130	110
5–9.5 percent undernourished						
Colombia	6.1	3	35	16	100	83
Costa Rica	1.7	1	17	10	38	38
Peru	3.7	4	80	17	250	89
<5 percent undernourished						
Argentina	1.8	2	28	13	71	69
Brazil	4.9	2	61	16	120	69
Chile	0.9	1	19	8	55	22
Mexico	2.7	3	47	13	88	49
Uruguay	0.3	4	23	10	42	14
Venezuela	9.2	3	30	15	93	110

Source: FAO, The State of Food Insecurity in the World 2015.

Box 11.1. The Economic Costs of Obesity in Mexico

KATELYN HAMILTON

A nutritional paradox plagues the poor and indigenous populations throughout Latin America.[a] In Mexico 35 percent of the country's children under the age of five are either overweight or obese.[b] One in three Mexican adults is obese with one in four suffering from hypertension and one in ten diagnosed with diabetes—two diseases not unrelated to weight. Mexico's obesity epidemic has made diabetes become the country's number one killer. The paradox is that many of these same dangerously overweight people are also poor and malnourished. Twenty million Mexican children live in poverty and over five million of those children live in extreme poverty.[c]

Two nutritional problems—malnutrition and obesity—exist within the same most vulnerable sectors—adults living in poverty and their offspring.[d] There are an estimated fifty-two million people affected by hunger in Mexico and the introduction of cheaper, processed foods is not effectively solving the hunger problem. Malnutrition is not necessarily the lack of access to food but rather the lack of access to the proper, nutritious foods needed to lead a healthy life. This is why both a starving person and an obese person can be considered malnourished. Malnutrition remains a real fear as the Mexican diet transitions into one that is high in salt, sugar, and saturated fats but low in fiber, protein, and other essential nutrients.[e]

With the expansion of global food chains and the signing of NAFTA in 1994, supermarkets have evolved from providing high price, luxury food items to selling mass-produced, canned, processed foods.[f] Over the past two decades, Latin America's dependence on cheap processed foods has greatly increased, which has contributed to the rise of the obesity levels throughout the region. Part of this is due to the improved trade; in addition to the US$50 billion a year in goods the United States exports to Mexico, America has shipped its supersized, cheap, processed goods south of the border.[g] Unhealthy beverage options have also become increasingly popular. Mexican children and adolescents drank 226 percent more carbonated sodas and sweetened beverages in 2006 than they did in 1999.[h] This increase in consumption of sweetened beverages has resulted in lower consumption of water, with the majority of Mexican children drinking water for only 26.5 percent of their liquids intake.[i] Children in urbanized Mexico are also alarmingly sedentary; 58.6 percent of children between the ages of ten and fourteen report doing no extracurricular activity—and 67 percent in the national survey confess to more than two hours a day in front of an electronic screen. Only one hour a week of physical education is mandatory in Mexican schools—and many neighborhoods lack open spaces and playgrounds for safe activity. Finally, there is a lingering belief in Mexican society that girls should not play sports but should be engaged in household chores. Other traditional impediments to healthier weights include the persistent perception that overweight or obese children have the appearance of health.[j]

Obesity pressures not only waistlines but also national budgets. The general obesity problem is also a large financial burden for Mexico, generating approximately 82 percent of projected health expenditure in 2012.[k] Health care spending in Mexico is already stretched thin but if current trends continue, more resources will have to be allocated towards diseases correlated with obesity. Today's estimates show that, without intervention, by 2050 only 12 percent of males and 9 percent of females will be of normal weight.[l] Additionally there will be more people who are obese than overweight by 2050. For the Mexican health care system, this means increased cases of diabetes and other noncommunicable diseases (NCDs). In 2010, the cost for thirteen of these obesity-associated NCD treatments was US$806 million.[m] This number is expected to increase to US$1.2 billion by 2030 and US$1.7 billion by 2050.[n] Reversing the trend and decreasing the

continued

continued

population's BMI by just 1 percent would save Mexico US$43 million in 2030 and US$85 million in 2050.[o] As Mexico's population becomes increasingly overweight it dramatically pressures the government's health care expenditure, thus creating a further strain on the country.

The obesity epidemic is not only affecting the health care system but it is beginning to impact labor productivity and school performance as individuals become more overweight. In a country where most citizens are at risk for becoming overweight and obese, a decrease in productivity levels could be catastrophic on Mexico's overall economic competitiveness. A report released by Mexico's health ministry in 2014 showed that Mexicans' productivity greatly decreases as their body-mass index (BMI) increases. An overweight person has the potential for a 28 percent loss in productivity as compared to a normal weight person. An obese person has a 34 percent potential loss in productivity and a morbidly obese person has a potential loss in productivity of 73 percent.[p] Considering the number of Mexicans at risk of developing obesity, this decrease in productivity could negatively impact Mexico's GDP per capita and other economic indicators, thus hindering its world standing.

Stunning statistics such as these on productivity loss and its economic impact have garnered the attention of politicians and civil society alike. One of President Pena Nieto's campaign promises was to combat the obesity epidemic in Mexico; he has successfully launched national efforts. Mexico was the first country to implement a national soda tax of approximately one peso per liter, which went into effect on January 1, 2014. Often considered the most radical way to combat widespread obesity, this program has already seen a 6 percent decrease in consumption of sweetened beverages such as coffee, juice, sodas, and energy drinks.[q] While the Mexican government has effectively implemented hard or concrete policies to combat obesity, they are also working on public health and educational strategies that will guide smaller stakeholders in their efforts to decrease obesity rates.

The National Strategy for Overweight, Obesity, and Diabetes Prevention and Control is another way the Mexican government has addressed rising obesity rates. This comprehensive report has a combined mission to unite the government, private sector, and society with one effective goal. In order to achieve this, the strategy has three pillars that focus on public health, access to policy, and regulatory policy combining coalitions of stakeholders, families, and policy makers. Only by working together can they accurately solve this problem. The National Crusade against Hunger (NCAH) and the National System against Hunger (NSAH) are two other organizations working to bring together stakeholders. The NCAH coordinates committees from different sectors to streamline efforts in four hundred of Mexico's poorest communities while the NSAH serves as the legal, administrative, and bureaucratic arm for the coordinating committees. Although previous administrations have attempted similar coordination efforts, the Pena Nieto Administration has been the most successful in helping such a wide range of communities.[r] The numbers do not lie. Mexico is facing increasing obesity rates and has not yet conquered the issue of hunger. If current trends continue, Mexico will continue to face incredibly undernourished populations with many chronic health problems. The costs of having an unhealthy population will wreak havoc on its financial systems of these countries. Working to solve the nutritional paradox of obesity and hunger now will not only help Mexico's economy but, more importantly, it will also help save people's lives.

a. Robert Stahl. "HEALTH: Starving, Stunted... Obese?," *Center for Latin American Studies (CLAS)*, The Regents of the University of California, 18 September 2015, Web. 22 February 2017.

b. S Barquera, I. Campos, and J. A. Rivera, "Mexico Attempts to Tackle Obesity: The Process, Results, Push Backs and Future Challenges," *Obesity Reviews* 14 (2013): 69–78, Web.

c. Ella Cady, "10 Facts about Poverty in Mexico," *The Borgen Project*, August 1, 2016, Web, February 22, 2017.

d. Ibid.

e. Abay Asfaw, "Does Consumption of Processed Foods Explain Disparities in the Body Weight of Individuals? The Case of Guatemala," *Health Economics* 20(2) (2009): n. pag. *Wiley Online Library*, Web, April, 10 2017.

f. Ibid.

g. Kate Kilpatrick, "Child Obesity in Mexico," *Al Jazeera America*, August, 15 2015, Web, February 15, 2017.

h. Magaly Aceves-Martins et al., "Obesity-Promoting Factors in Mexican Children and Adolescents: Challenges and Opportunities," *Global Health Action* 9 (2016): 10.3402/gha.v9.29625, PMC, Web, June 19, 2017.

i. Ibid.

j. Ibid.

k. Ibid.

l. Ketevan Rtveladze, Tim Marsh, Simon Barquera, Luz Maria Sanchez Romero, David Levy, Guillermo Melendez, Laura Webber, Fanny Kilpi, Klim Mcpherson, and Martin Brown, "Obesity Prevalence in Mexico: Impact on Health and Economic Burden," *Public Health Nutrition* 17(1) (2013): 233–239, Web.

m. Ibid.

n. Ibid.

o. Ibid.

p. *National Strategy for the Prevention and Control of Overweight, Obesity and Diabetes*, Publication. N.p.: Health Secretary, United Mexican States, 2014.

q. Magaly Aceves-Martins et al., "Obesity-Promoting Factors in Mexican Children and Adolescents."

r. Juan Henao, "Mexico's Crusade against Hunger," *Americas Quarterly*, January 29, 2013, Web, April 10, 2017.

most urbanized regions of the world—with little space for safe exercise in poor neighborhoods. Those without cars to drive to big box stores find it difficult to access fresh and healthy foods in the neighborhood bodega. Children increasingly consume electronic media—and are simultaneously targets of junk food and sugary drinks advertising.[21] Progress has been made, but there is still a considerable distance to go in improving the lives of children in the region.

A Demographic Window Is Opening

Gaps notwithstanding improvements in health and living standards have altered the general demographic profile in Latin America. Total fertility rates have fallen from 6 children per woman in the period 1960–1965 to 2.2 in 2013. Children are no longer as valuable as instruments of old age insurance, and as women have entered the workforce the opportunity costs of having children have also increased. As fertility rates have declined, the proportion of the working population aged fifteen to sixty-five has risen. In contrast to this productive group, the older population (6 percent in Latin America) as well as children under age fifteen (30 percent) are net consumers, especially when it comes to health care. In Latin America, this bulge in the working population will peak in the period 2010–2025. This will be a grace period, opening a demographic window for change, where the larger percentage of the working population will support fewer dependents.

Appropriate investments in health care and education complemented by growth-oriented policies can launch a new economic and social transformation.[22] After 2025, old age will begin to overwhelm the contributions of the working population, and Latin America will begin to look more like Europe, where a 16 percent dependency ratio by both the young and the old severely strains the system. Taking advantage of the demographic dividend will be crucial to the quality of human life in Latin America.

The Unfinished Agenda

Despite advances in the quality of life in Latin America, much work remains. There is a great deal of diversity in health performance in the region. As can be seen back in Table 11.1, life expectancy ranges from a low of 65.6 years for Bolivian males to a high of 83.1 for Chilean women. You may be surprised to see that women live longer in Chile and Costa Rica than in the United States. Bolivia and Guatemala are the worst performers on infant mortality, while Chile and Cuba have achieved low child-mortality rates. Hospital beds are scarce relative to high-income countries. In countries with either the political will or the money, significant strides have been made in creating health systems to treat these diseases. Countries such as Cuba and Costa Rica have gone through an **epidemiological transition** where communicable diseases are relatively under control; they have health profiles similar to developed countries. The least-developed countries, such as Bolivia, have truncated transitions and suffer primarily from infectious diseases, such as malaria, and diseases of deficiency, such as malnutrition. The middle- and high-income countries, such as Ecuador and Brazil, have begun their epidemiological transition but still suffer from an accumulation of both the infectious and deficiency diseases found in the less-developed countries while also confronting emerging, chronic, and degenerative diseases as a result of the demographic transition toward a more urbanized and aging society.[23] Known as an **epidemiological backlog**, this double health burden strains social welfare budgets. These systems must solve the problems of poorer countries while also being challenged by the health concerns of the wealthier world. Figure 11.2 shows countries by cause of death based on broad causality divided by those with higher rates of noncommunicable diseases which have undergone the epidemiological transition to those still managing communicable diseases. This epidemiological mosaic challenges countries to address health challenges on a variety of fronts at once.

Poor health is a disease of poverty. Malaria, a life-threatening parasitic disease transmitted by the bite of an infected mosquito, breeds in conditions of poverty—particularly stagnant, open sewerage and damp, tropical conditions. About 40 percent of the region's population is at risk of contracting this debilitating disease. This ancient scourge hits indigenous populations harder than other population groups, particularly those living in rural and heavily forested areas.[24] Where malaria is endemic, people are continually re-infected, developing immunity to treatment over time. Malaria increases the chance of maternal anemia, stillbirth, intrauterine

Figure 11.2.   Causes of Death

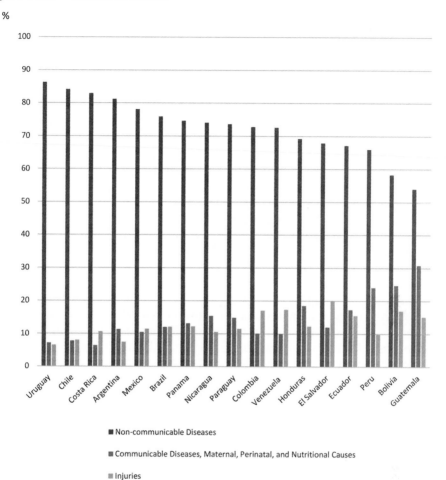

■ Non-communicable Diseases

■ Communicable Diseases, Maternal, Perinatal, and Nutritional Causes

■ Injuries

Source: Institute for Health Metrics and Evaluation, University of Washington, 2015.

growth retardation, and low birth weight. A severe episode of malaria can lead to stunting and brain damage, permanently constraining a child's growth and development. Malaria depletes not only the person but also the family, increasing health care expenditures and decreasing income. Outbreaks discourage foreign investment and tourism. Malaria can be prevented by spraying households with insecticide, using insecticide-treated mosquito nets, and eliminating mosquito breeding sites. These are relatively cost-effective measures to combat such a devastating disease but are measures that weigh heavily on the budgets of the poor. Contracted malaria can be treated, but drug therapies that overcome problems of resistance are expensive, excluding their use by most vulnerable populations.[25] The Bill and Melinda Gates foundation has donated US$168 million in the quest to find a vaccine for this deadly disease; until science advances, however, it is the poor who will suffer.

In 2015, the Zika virus, a largely neglected disease, came to international attention when its emergence was associated with birth defects. It is spread via mosquitos, but historically was found only in Africa and parts of Asia.[26] The first case of Zika in Brazil was confirmed in May 2015. Large swaths of South America and the Caribbean also confirmed outbreaks, which caused the WHO to announce a Public Health Emergency of International Concern in 2016. Zika is a significant threat to pregnant women and their unborn babies due to its direct linkage to a severe birth defect known as microcephaly. As with most infectious diseases, Zika is especially burdensome to poor women living in the affected regions, such as the favelas of Rio, who cannot afford protection against mosquitos. However, it also serves as a potential global health threat because it cannot be contained by geographic and socioeconomic boundaries alone.[27] Heartbreaking photos of babies with enlarged heads claimed international attention; the continued health costs of caring for these children will strain health budgets in the coming years. Brazil contained the virus by 2017 through aggressive house-to-house spraying and innovative technologies to mate Zika-carrying mosquitos with sterile partners. Vigilance, however, is called for against future mutations and outbreaks.[28]

Zika is not the only mosquito-borne disease to be active in Latin America. Another prominent disease of this nature is Dengue. Dengue is a virus transmitted by *Aedes aegypti* mosquitoes that causes flu-like symptoms and can be lethal.[29] It develops in tropical climates that are urban or semi-urban such as Brazil. The disease has now spread to over one hundred countries within the Americas, Middle East, Africa, and Asia-Pacific regions. About 2.35 million cases have been reported in the Americas alone and it is estimated that there will be approximately 50 million infections each year.[30] Another similar disease found in the region is Chikungunya. This is, once again, a mosquito-borne disease that leads to fever and joint pain.[31]

Chagas is another disease of poverty. Named after the Brazilian physician Carlos Chagas, who first described it in 1909, Chagas disease is unique to the American continent. The risk of infection is directly correlated with poverty: The blood-sucking triatomine bug that hosts the parasite lives comfortably in crevices in the walls and roofs of poor houses in rural areas and in the peripheral urban slums. The migration from rural to urban areas in the 1970s and 1980s changed the traditional epidemiological pattern of Chagas disease, transforming it into an urban infection that can be transmitted by blood transfusion. Chagas disease hits the poorest of the poor in Latin America. This tropical disease affects sixteen to eighteen million people, fifty thousand of whom die each year. It is estimated that as much as 25 percent of the Latin American population are at risk for Chagas disease; approximately a quarter of those infected will progress to irreversible cardiac, esophageal, and colonic pathology, imposing a heavy socioeconomic burden on countries with weakened or deteriorating economies.[32] Chagas disease can be addressed; the transmission in most of the Southern Cone has been eliminated, yet it has spread north to the United States. However, with little change yet in Central American and Andean countries, it is a disease of poor resources. Given that it primarily afflicts the poor, it is also a disease that international pharmaceutical firms have tended to ignore.[33]

Gender, Ethnicity, and Health

Health is not just about biological functions; it is also socially determined. The goal of health equity directs policymakers to provide opportunities for all to achieve their full health potential; removing systemic, avoidable, and unfair barriers becomes a matter of social justice.[34] In addition to biological differences, gender inequalities in health care are driven by differences in men and women's social roles and in their access to family and community resources. The denial of reproductive rights results in death.[35] Latin America contains some of the most restrictive laws regarding abortion, with several deeming it illegal even if the mother's life is at risk.[36] Uneducated women have unmet needs for contraception at twice the rate as those with at least a secondary education.

Maternal deaths throughout Latin America and the Caribbean are largely preventable with quality obstetric care during pregnancy, delivery, and postpartum. Systems make a huge difference as evidenced by the range of maternal mortality per 100,000 live births from 25 in Costa Rica to 150 in Nicaragua or 15 in Uruguay compared to Bolivia, where the maternal mortality rate is 206. Women die from hypertension, haemorrhage, abortion, and sepsis as well as indirect causes such as HIV, cardiovascular issues, anaemia, and other preexisting medical conditions such as malaria and tuberculosis—many of which are preventable. Lower socioeconomic position, mixed ethnicity, including Afro-descendence, and rural location of residence are linked to higher morbidity from pre-eclampsia, eclampsia, or hypertensive disorders.[37] Poor women also suffer disproportionately as they resort to unsafe methods when unable to pay for travel or an underground clinic.[38] Maternal health outcomes for those in marginalized service areas can be explained by a three delays framework: delay in seeking medical health care, delay in arriving at a health care facility, and delay in receiving the necessary care once they have reached the health facility.

Furthermore, poor women disproportionality suffer more in Latin America due to the illegality of abortion, as they are unable to pay for the procedure to be conducted in safe clinics (where wealthy women are able to access care), and instead must resort to unregulated and unsafe methods. Twenty-five percent give birth without the assistance of a skilled attendant and 27 percent have no access to prenatal care. Breast cancer incidence is the leading cause of cancer-attributed death for women in the region, with an estimated 43,200 deaths annually.[39]

Maternal malnutrition is a leading cause of both maternal and infant mortality. Without adequate prenatal care, an infant will not receive important nutrients for growth. Breastfeeding by well-nourished mothers transfers needed antibodies to their children to fight viral and bacterial infections, such as diarrhea and pneumonia, rashes, and allergies. In urban areas, many women, however, have been substituting more modern infant feeding practices for breastfeeding, leading to a decline in infant health.

An important element in health care is a woman's ability to control her own fertility. The region has one of the highest rates of adolescent pregnancies in the world, with Guyana, Dominican Republic, Nicaragua, and El Salvador having the highest concentration—again predominately among girls with the least education. Table 11.4 presents reproductive health statistics for the region. A Save the Children/Bolivian Mothercare project found that women identified their most urgent

Table 11.4. Gender and Health: Reproductive Statistics

	Estimated Total Fertility Rates						Contraceptive Use (women 15–49, all methods) (%)	Births Attended by Skilled Health Staff (% of total)
	1960–1965	1970–1975	1980–1985	1990–1995	2000–2005	2010–2014		
Argentina	3.1	3.1	3.2	2.8	2.4	2.2	78.0	98.0
Bolivia	6.6	6.5	5.3	4.8	4.0	3.3	61.0	84.0
Brazil	6.2	4.7	3.8	2.6	2.3	1.8	81.0	98.0
Chile	5.4	3.6	2.7	2.6	2.0	1.8	58.0	100.0
Colombia	6.8	5.0	3.7	3.0	2.6	2.3	79.0	99.0
Costa Rica	7.2	4.3	3.5	2.9	2.3	1.8	76.0	99.0
Ecuador	6.7	6.0	4.7	3.4	2.8	2.6	73.0	91.0
El Salvador	6.8	6.1	4.5	3.5	2.9	2.2	73.0	100.0
Guatemala	6.5	6.2	6.1	5.5	4.6	3.8	54.0	52.0
Honduras	7.4	7.1	6.0	4.9	3.7	3.1	73.0	83.0
Mexico	6.8	6.5	4.2	3.1	2.5	2.2	73.0	96.0
Nicaragua	7.3	6.8	6.0	4.6	3.3	2.5	80.0	88.0
Panama	5.9	4.9	3.5	2.9	2.7	2.5	52.0	94.0
Paraguay	6.6	5.7	5.3	4.6	3.8	2.9	79.0	96.0
Peru	6.9	6.0	4.7	3.7	2.9	2.4	74.0	87.0
Uruguay	2.9	3.0	2.6	2.5	2.3	2.1	78.0	100.0
Venezuela	6.7	5.1	3.9	3.0	2.6	2.4	58.0	96.0
Latin America	6.0	5.1	3.9	3.0	2.6			

Source: World Development Indicators database, www.worldbank.org.

health problem as having too many children.[40] All countries in the region are above the high-income fertility ratio of 1.7 children per couple. However, Brazil, Chile, and Costa Rica are nearly there and progress has been made across the region. The mean age of a Latin American mom for the first birth of a child is around 22 years as opposed to nearing thirty for Europe and North America.[41] As women have entered the marketplace in increasing numbers, the opportunity cost of children has risen. As some market women note, customers want to be waited on quickly and not be distracted by crying babies.[42] Use of contraceptives ranges from 80 percent in Nicaragua to less than 52 percent in Panama; demand (including unmet needs) is between 50 and 80 percent.[43] The most widely used method of contraception in the region has been female sterilization. According to the Brazilian health ministry, 21 percent of women between the ages of twenty-five and twenty-nine have been sterilized, reflecting a failure to provide other methods of contraception. In poorer regions of the northwest and center, these rates nearly double. Family planning, however, remains somewhat controversial, given both religious preferences and the position of some multilateral donor agencies. For some indigenous women, the thought of (mostly male) doctors poking inside them prevents them from seeking medical advice on family planning methods. Traditional men sometimes fear that contraception will encourage promiscuous behavior among their wives and daughters. Tragically, unwanted pregnancies are often terminated with self-induced abortions that threaten the lives of the mothers or leave deformities in the child should it be born. Some alliance between ethnomedicine (traditional healers) and biomedical practitioners might help alleviate the difficulties in providing health care to indigenous women. Biomedical practitioners need to better understand the role of patient attitudes and responses in improving the delivery of health services in traditional areas. Husbands need to be included in educational efforts at family planning to dispel widely held myths concerning the negative effects of family planning.

The health and nutritional levels of indigenous communities in Latin America are well below national averages. Viral diseases, including influenza, measles, dengue, and respiratory infections, frequently become epidemics under poor sanitary conditions in indigenous communities. Activities such as mining and oil exploration exact high costs in terms of the health of otherwise isolated indigenous groups. In addition to disrupting the environment, workers introduce diseases for which indigenous communities have not developed immunities. In the Amazon Basin countries, the most important challenges to the health of indigenous communities come from the overexploitation of resources. In Bolivia, indigenous people report more than twice the number of illnesses and injuries and miss twice as many workdays but receive less medical care than the general population. In Ecuador the rate of chronic child malnutrition was 58.2 percent compared to 24.2 in the nonindigenous cohort.[44] Life expectancy for the indigenous in Colombia is about ten years lower than national averages.[45] Cultural differences between health care dispensed in hospitals and traditional practices promoted by healers and midwives in indigenous communities also create a health services gap, particularly in practices such as childbirth that are highly sensitive to custom and tradition. In Guatemala, for example, the maternal mortality rate in the indigenous population is significantly higher than that for the nonindigenous population. Access to health care is often poor due to physical isolation as well as a weak relationship to government. Infants born to mothers without a secondary education are seven times as likely to die in El Salvador; three times as likely in Bolivia, Guatemala, Colombia, and the Dominican Republic; and twice as likely in Peru.[46] The Brazilian government spends just over US$7 a head on indigenous health care versus US$33 each for the country as a whole.[47] Despite a special segment of the national health care plan directed toward indigenous areas—and agreements with Cuba to bring medical practitioners to meet staffing gaps of rural health professionals—outcomes in indigenous areas still lag national statistics.[48] Stunting among the indigenous in Mexico, for example, is more than three times the rate in the nonindigenous population. This is likely tied to the weak coverage of health services for the indigenous as well as the lack of income for food.[49] Geographic isolation complicates health care in Guatemala, where about 60 percent of the population lives in rural areas; 80 percent of these in remote villages have almost no access to quality health care services. The rural population is comprised predominantly of the Maya, the indigenous people of Central America, most living in conditions of poverty. A dismal fact is that indigenous children exhibit extremely high malnutrition rates, even in countries that have otherwise virtually eliminated this problem. In Mexico, just 6 percent of children nationwide are underweight compared with almost 20 percent of indigenous children.[50]

But interventions have extended health care in the rural sector, shrinking the ratio between indigenous and nonindigenous deaths. For the indigenous peoples, humans are inseparable from nature; health care must therefore involve holistic approaches. To be effective, health delivery systems must be sensitive to cultural practices. The 1993 Pan American Health Organization (PAHO) workshop Indigenous Peoples and Health held in Winnipeg, Canada, set out guidelines for health promotion, advocating community participation, preservation of habitat and traditional lifestyles, evaluation and monitoring of the health status and living conditions of indigenous peoples, and formulation of national health policies to address the problems of indigenous communities. Nonetheless, as the communiqué initiating the meeting characterized, the health of indigenous peoples is "perhaps the most technically complex and difficult health issue of the day."[51] Indigenous health care remains lacking; improvements indicate the need for supplemental funding for nongovernmental organizations (NGOs) to reach indigenous populations, better data on indigenous health concerns, stronger preparation of health care workers in multicultural communities to attend to the needs and be respectful of the traditional practices of indigenous peoples, and improved dissemination of program efforts to illustrate best-case practices for other countries.[52] Policy measures will require patience and perseverance for success.

On the Unfinished Agenda: Health for All

The poor are particularly vulnerable to bad health shocks. Economic shocks such as the coffee crisis in Central America increased malnutrition rates in Guatemala to highs of 35 percent with severe malnutrition and 40–45 percent with significant but less severe food deprivation.[53] Natural disasters cause devastation, displacement, disease, accidents, and death, setting back national development for years.[54] In the competitive global economic scene the poor are most vulnerable; erosion of working conditions, expansion of the informal sector, and the explosion of urban slums make life exceptionally precarious. The deterioration of the physical environment, including the gaps in clean drinking water and basic sanitation, make homes breeding grounds for disease.[55] Poverty not only makes people more vulnerable to health shocks; health shocks also make people poorer. Without adequate insurance, the sick person, and most commonly the whole family, is dragged further into a vicious cycle of decline.

The unfinished agenda to fight preventable disease in Latin America is a battle of resources and political will. It is clearly lodged in providing universal access to basic health services. The objective of **universal health coverage** is to guarantee that all people have access to the services they need without risking financial ruin or impoverishment. **Primary health care (PHC)** was the foundation for the **Health for All (HFA)** strategy adopted at the 1978 Alma Ata joint WHO-UNICEF conference and endorsed by the WHO Assembly in 1981. This landmark document outlined programmatic health objectives as part of a new model for health care based on comprehensive PHC. These included water, sanitation, food supply, nutrition, mother and child care, family planning, immunization, control of local diseases, essential drugs, and education. Health for All encourages culturally sensitive plans that employ appropriate treatment and technology. Health should be integrated into national development plans to improve the social and economic development of the community. Education and active participation are seen as the keys to the promotive, preventive, curative, and rehabilitative services of PHC. The PHC approach is aimed at mobilizing individuals and communities to improve health systems to provide fair and equitable delivery of needed services. The issue of inequality is particularly important in Latin America; PAHO sees overcoming inequality as the major constraint in meeting the goal of universal access to basic health services for the inhabitants of the region.[56]

The strategies for achieving HFA and the subsequent emphasis on PHC are based on three pillars: participation, equity, and intersectoral cooperation. PHC emphasizes social justice, a broadly defined concept of health that includes lifestyle and environmental components, intersectoral integration, and community participation. PHC employs a holistic approach, embracing the individual's relationship with community and family. Participation is central to the implementation of effective health plans. It can be viewed as the first step toward the decentralization of local health systems.[57] Equity is threefold: between the first and third worlds, rural and urban areas, and genders. The call for equity is grounded in the fundamental right to health care. Intersectoral cooperation refers to the need to link health and development plans, as seen in PAHO's "health in development" and WHO's "health as a conditionality for economic development" strategies.[58]

Universal health care as articulated in the 2010 WHO World Health Report took the HFA commitment a step further, aiming to align financing mechanisms exist to bring about equality in health access. Universal access requires sustainable financing and an appreciation of the interactions with social, political, economic, and environmental status. Investing in health can at times involve tough choices. In Brazil, the Institute Materno-Infantil de Pernambuco (IMIP) faced such a tough trade-off. IMIP, a winner of a UNICEF award for a child-friendly hospital, had to decide whether to maintain its pediatric intensive care unit or engage in community outreach. With 95 percent of its financing coming from the Brazilian Ministry of Health (MOH), it had to match costs to average revenues set by the government. The intensive care unit cost more than the government was willing to pay. Furthermore, the children sent to the unit from all over northeastern Brazil were so sick and malnourished that the mortality rate remained high despite expensive interventions. A more cost-effective strategy to saving children's lives was pursued: close the intensive care unit and expand the network of small community health posts in slum neighborhoods of the major city of Recife. Indeed, infant mortality declined from 147 to 101 per 1,000 live births in those neighborhoods.[59] Local control and local initiative can work to reverse the devastating effects of neglect on children and families in poor rural regions.

Most countries have some elements of PHC in their MOH health care delivery systems and have decreased emphasis on the medicalization of health as well as the engineering model, which saw the body as a machine and good health as a question of getting it tuned correctly. However, due primarily to budgetary and political reasons, selective PHC programs, as opposed to comprehensive PHC programs, have been implemented. Weaker versions, limited to growth monitoring, oral rehydration, breastfeeding, immunization, family planning, food production, and female education, have been the norm. The poor have had an increasing burden of paying for health services out of pocket. With budget cuts, many health posts can no longer provide basic services. In Ecuador, for example, spending on health has come to absorb 12 to 17 percent of the family budget. Those unable to afford private-sector service are left without critically needed curative care and rarely invest in preventive care.[60] Public and private international donor agencies, led in part by WHO and PAHO, can facilitate a broader adoption of universal programs through partnerships with state and local governments to bridge the fiscal gap.

Emergent Diseases: The New Agenda

Overlaying problems of malnutrition and attendant diseases such as Chagas disease or malaria are a host of chronic diseases that are the effect of living in modern societies. Cardiovascular disease, cancer, AIDS, obesity, mental health, traffic deaths, and violence all place enormous burdens on health systems already buckling under the pressure of addressing traditional infectious diseases. The ability to attack both the old and new health agendas simultaneously calls for a transformation of health systems in the region. "This transformation will require addressing incentives, human resources, information technology, and public needs together in new ways," says Derek Yach, professor of global health at the Yale School of Public Health.[61] Developing country health systems are behind in the diagnosis and treatment of the rising tide of chronic disease; their health financing systems are ill-equipped to support the long-term care and services that those suffering from chronic disease demand. Because of underdeveloped health systems, chronic disease deaths occur at much earlier ages in low- and middle-income countries than in high-income countries.

For those between 25 and 64—a cohort that has escaped childhood disease and not yet confronted diseases of old age—the top three causes of mortality are heat disease, diabetes, and homicide.[62] South and Central America have some of the highest cervical cancer rates in the world, with incidence rates of between 20 and 80 per 100,000 throughout Latin American and the Caribbean four times the US and European rates.[63] This is avoidable; the rates in Costa Rica fell from 45 to 15 from 1992 to 2003 when the Costa Rican government implemented stronger screening initiatives. There are tragic trade-offs, however, in many of the poorer nations of the region. Should the government fund cervical screening or prenatal visits?

Globalization has brought its own disease vector. Approximately two million people—0.5 percent of the population—are living with HIV in Latin America. This reflects a 3 percent rise in rates from 2010 to 2015—following a more encouraging 20 percent fall in the previous decade. In 2015 there were approximately 100,000 new infections and 50,000 **AIDS**-related deaths.[64] Men who have sex with men, transgender women, and sex workers are particularly affected.[65] The highest prevalence in the population is in Belize, Guatemala, and Honduras, with approximately 1 percent of adults infected with HIV. Honduras is home to one-third of all HIV cases in the Central American subregion, with infection rates just under 2 percent; AIDS has become the number one cause of death among women of fertile age. The causes of the spread of HIV in Latin America are a combination of unsafe sex and intravenous drug use. In Mexico a man having sex with another man faces a one in three chance that his partner is HIV-positive. The epidemic is concentrated among the poor; 60 percent of those with HIV/AIDS have not completed primary school. IV drug users are another group at risk. In Mexico between 3 and 11 percent are infected; in Brazil and Argentina the rate reaches nearly 50 percent. The epidemic has spread to include women, who now account for one-fourth of all reported AIDS cases.[66]

Prevention is inextricably tied to education. Knowledge of AIDS prevention varies by socioeconomic class. In the poorest quintile in Latin America, only 46.8 percent of females have knowledge of AIDS as opposed to 81.8 percent in the wealthiest strata. A 2004 survey in Brazil showed that 36 percent of fifteen- to twenty-four-year-olds had sex before their fifteenth birthday, and only 62 percent knew how HIV was transmitted. Women whose husbands sleep with other men or women are at risk; the culture of machismo in Latin America makes it difficult even for wives to insist on condom use.

Brazil has led the region in providing antiretroviral drugs to all in need via the country's national health system. Beginning in 1996, Brazil implemented what is now considered one of the boldest and most successful AIDS treatment programs in the developing world.[67] Based on a constitutional guarantee, Brazil promises a virtually free HIV drug distribution program.[68] In response to the high price of antiretroviral medicines available largely in the United States, domestic companies in Brazil began the production of generic HIV drugs at low costs. Complementing the antiretroviral treatment is an aggressive education policy. Using a social marketing approach, the Brazilian government's strategy is to provide both education and condoms. During the famous Brazilian revelry of Carnival, for example, volunteers from more than eighteen hundred NGOs hand out millions of condoms paid for by the MOH—part of the more than six hundred million condoms distributed annually.[69] Prevention through education and condom distribution combined with treatment of approximately half of those already infected with HIV has shown conclusively that it is possible to curb the HIV/AIDS epidemic in developing countries. The World Bank had predicted that by 2000, 1.2 million Brazilians would be infected; instead, incidence has stabilized around 718,000 people—but more than one in five are unaware of their HIV status. The key challenge in combatting the disease is helping people understand their health condition.[70] In 2015 Brazil began to offer self-testing through pharmacies free of charge to help improve identification of HIV infected people.[71]

The struggle, however, has not been easy. Given rising costs for the next generation of antiretroviral drugs, it will be a challenge to sustain the coverage of antiretrovirals. Although many international health agencies have heralded Brazil's treatment program, it has also been the subject of ongoing controversy. The US government has launched legal proceedings against Brazil, claiming that the production of generic HIV drugs breaks international laws on patent production. In 2001, after months of debate, Brazil and the US-based pharmaceuticals came to an agreement, and the United States withdrew its patent complaint against Brazil. Tensions rose again a few years later when in 2005 Brazil pushed for the right to produce the more sophisticated AIDS drug Kaletra. Without the ability to produce a generic, Brazil would have spent an additional $259 million over six years to maintain patient access to antiretrovirals. A tough bargaining position nevertheless won. Brazil negotiated lower AIDS drug prices by threatening to break patents, without ever actually doing so. Its new strategy is to ally with other developing nations to push for lower-priced products.[72] It is bolstered by the ethical position that if Western governments are to commit themselves to reducing the AIDS epidemic and improving world public health, drug companies must take moral responsibility by providing affordable drugs to the less-developed world. The nature of AIDS prevention and treatment as a global public good provides a strong rationale for global action.

Violence has risen to become one of the most serious health problems in urban areas of the region. Violence manifests itself in different forms: political (state and nonstate), institutional (lynching, extrajudicial killings by security forces), economic (kidnapping, robbery, drug trafficking, car theft, small arms, trafficking in prostitutes, street theft), economic/social (maras or youth gangs, street children); and social (gender basis, child abuse, intergenerational, bar fights, road rage).[73] Latin America's crime rate is double the world average, taking a huge toll on the region's economic development and public faith in democracy.[74] Latin America's rate of twenty-four murders per 100,000 inhabitants is four times the world average.[75] The World Bank reports that every fifteen minutes, at least four people are victims of homicide in Latin America and the Caribbean and that in 2013, of the top fifty most violent cities in the world, forty-two were in the region.[76] The Inter-American Development Bank estimates that crime costs LAC between 2.41 and 3.55 percent of their GDPs—an amount equal to what they spend on

Home health agents bring basic services—and hope—to the very poor. *(Courtesy of David Mangurian and the Inter-American Development Bank)*

infrastructure.[77] Gangs proliferate in some Central American countries. The starkly high homicide rates in Honduras and El Salvador (60 and 103.3 per 100,000 in the 2015 population) are in counterpoint to countries such as Chile that are safer than most American cities. The cost of violence to El Salvador in 2015 was 6.1 percent of GDP; its homicide rate has gained momentum and surpassed Honduras, formerly known as the murder capital of the world. The IADB is even more pessimistic, estimating that the per capita GDP of the region would be 25 percent higher if the rates of violence were no worse than the world average.[78]

The explosion of violence sweeping the continent has complex causes. In Colombia and El Salvador it may be linked to historical conflicts over land. Rapid urbanization in the context of huge disparities between rich and poor may exacerbate social violence. Researchers at the World Bank find that stresses in early childhood can later lead to violently disruptive behavior. Traditional values practiced in the countryside are lost on the new generation of tough urban youth often lured by alcohol and drugs. Rising unemployment associated with globalization may also be a contributing factor. As police capabilities are overwhelmed and judicial systems choked, repression and brutality are more common than prevention and reform. Such violence exacts a high human and economic cost. One World Bank economist estimated that the net accumulation of human capital was cut in half because of the increase in crime and violence since the mid-1980s.[79]

Violence against women is prevalent. A study of select Latin American countries shows rates of ever-married women reporting spousal abuse of 44 percent in Colombia, 42 percent in Peru, and 30 percent in Nicaragua. Perhaps surprisingly, the highest rates of violence occur in moderately wealthy households, not as often assumed among the poorest.[80] Brazil's health system reports that 405 women a day needed medical care as victims of violence—and most women don't report for fear of reprisal.[81] Violence against women is a critical concern. In most cases, violence against women is not investigated further, which perpetuates its social acceptance. The United Nations defines violence against women as an act of gender violence that results or is likely to result in physical, sexual, or psychological harm or suffering to women. The Panos Institute reports that gender violence causes more death and disability among women ages fifteen to forty-four than cancer, malaria, traffic accidents, or war. The costs extend to families; children of abused women in Nicaragua drop out of school four years earlier and were one hundred times more likely to be hospitalized than children of nonabused women. A Costa Rican survey showed that 95 percent of pregnant girls age fifteen or younger were incest victims. According to one Honduran health worker, overburdened health care providers often don't have the time to talk to patients in diagnostic exams; many women will not discuss household violence unless directly asked. A PAHO study ties violence against women in the Americas to a macho culture that reinforces male control over wealth and decision making in the family.[82] LGBT people also face extreme degrees of discrimination that often lead to violence. Domestic violence remains a challenge for countries across the region.

Currently there is a large and widening treatment gap in **mental health care in Latin America**.[83] Mental health disorders comprise 24 percent of the burden of disease in the Americas, with depression being the principal component of that burden. Nearly 20 percent of children and adolescents suffer from disorders that require the support of or intervention by mental health care services, and those disorders lead to both social stigma and discrimination.[84] Mental illness is a leading cause of reduced productivity.[85] Health systems, however, are poorly equipped to gather information on mental health and substance abuse, develop and apply appropriate policies, strengthen services, and improve national legislation in order to enhance systems to prevent and control these problems. The slim portion of the budget attributed to mental health care can be attributed to the gap in treatment. Alcohol consumption at rates 50 percent higher than worldwide consumption creates a heavy disease burden, accounting for the fourth largest cause of death in men.[86] Key measures to respond to the mental health needs of the populations of the Americas are to integrate mental health into primary care, develop services in the community, and combat the stigma that mental disorders carry. Addressing the problem of alcohol will involve a focus on the availability of and access to alcohol and implementation and enforcement of these policies, including imposing taxes and putting in place public education campaigns.

As Latin American nations have experienced major transitions in health profiles, **occupational health concerns** have become a leading cause of morbidity among adults in the region. People spend more than a third of each day at work; conditions in the workplace clearly impact health. There are between twenty million and twenty-seven million work-related accidents annually in Latin American and the Caribbean, ninety thousand of which are fatal. Work with hazardous processes associated with international trade is particularly dangerous when workers cannot adequately read warning labels. Despite impacting more than two hundred million workers and their families, occupational safety and health have been largely ignored. The existing data underestimate the problem, and the institutional capacity to address concerns is weak. Heavy physical workloads, hazards such as noise or radiation, dangerous conditions, toxic chemicals, exposure to asbestos or coal dust, risk of cancer, social conditions, and exposure to viruses, fungi, and molds can damage workers' health. In the rural sector, acute pesticide poisoning is a major health problem. Workers do not wear appropriate protective clothing (perhaps because the heavy rubber is designed for colder climates) or follow safety directions. Miners suffer from falls, electrocution, lung disease, and neurological damage from exposure to chemicals such as mercury. Informal-sector employment, accounting for nearly 50 percent of the labor force in the region, increases health risks in that small firms, high turnover, absence of monitoring of conditions, and lack of insurance generate a higher incidence of health problems. Child labor is still widespread in the region, and children are more vulnerable to workplace risk. The fifty-six million women in the workforce face a dual burden: the stress of low-paying jobs and the double duty of their second workday in the evening at home. *Maquila* workers, primarily women, suffer from repetitive stress disorders on the musculoskeletal system. Latin America and the Caribbean's fatality rate in the workplace is approximately twice that of Canada's. This may even understate the data, as reporting in the informal sector is weak as well as the fact that in the formal sector insurance rates in the region are often tied to injuries. The economic cost of occupational health hazards is high; the International Labor Organization

(ILO) and WHO estimate the total burden to reach as much as 10 percent of GDP of developing countries, more than three times the estimated occupational health cost of the United States.[87] Despite the enormous burden of occupational health costs, extending regulation is problematic because of the need to create jobs and the weak institutional capacity for enforcement.

Finally, our list of modern disease must include traffic deaths—where Latin America ranks number one with the highest number of deaths from road traffic accidents. A lack of road safety, drunk driving and not using seat belts contributes to nearly 130,000 deaths, some six million injuries, and some form of disability for hundreds of thousands of people.[88] One study in the Americas of twelve countries showed that traffic accidents were the leading cause of death among boys and girls ages five to fourteen years and the leading cause for women and second leading cause for men between fifteen and forty-four years old. Latin America's narrow, poorly paved streets were simply not designed to accommodate the explosion of cars. As of 2013, El Salvador had the highest rate of deaths caused by transport injuries, at 33.32 per 100,000. Ecuador has the next highest rate, at 32.38 per 100,000. Nearly 3 percent of all deaths in Ecuador are due to pedestrian road injury. Forty percent of the unfortunate casualties in Mexico, Colombia, and Costa Rica were also on foot.[89] If you travel in Latin America, pedestrian beware!

HEALTH CARE SYSTEMS IN LATIN AMERICA

In addition to choices about the level of sophistication of health care, improvements in health require changes in systems of delivery. The health status of the people of Latin America is affected not only by extant diseases and each country's socioeconomic status but also by institutions and systems established to provide health services for the populations and the environments in which these institutions operate. The challenges to Latin American health care delivery systems are numerous and require a redefinition of the traditional health care system. Old or accumulated challenges include insufficient coverage of the population, poor technical quality, inadequate patient referral, and deficient management of institutions. New challenges to health delivery systems are composed of cost escalation, financial insecurity, and technological expansion in light of their opportunity costs in terms of PHC.

Rural health care poses particular challenges for 25 percent of the hemisphere's population. In some rural areas, health care can be a four- to eight-hour bus ride or a one- to two-hour walk away. Between 50 and 80 percent of all health expenditures go to hospitals located near urban centers. Inaccessible health facilities make prenatal and other types of preventive PHC particularly problematic. Shifting from hospital-based to community-based health systems can help direct resources toward the needs of the local population rather than urban patterns of demand. Although a hospital has the advantage of being a physically distinct unit in which health services can be coordinated under one roof, it can also be a center of power and influence that drains resources from community health systems. Major resources may be tied up in hospitals, equipment, and services that come at an opportunity cost to meeting people's PHC needs. Unless the hospital is integrated into a community health care system, when patients are discharged they may find little continuity of care and suffer from a fragmentation of health services.[90] Health care must extend into the community.

The organization of health care varies across the region. Although each Latin American country has a unique mixture of social security facilities, private practitioners, and government ministries responsible for health, generalizations can be made. Health care systems have two service dimensions: finance and delivery of service. Financing refers to how and by whom services are paid for. Delivery refers to the actual provision of services. Each factor can be provided either by the public or by the private sector. For example, financing could be public, through universal health insurance, but rely on the services of private practitioners. Alternatively, some financing—especially for the poor—might be public, with a mix of public hospitals and private providers. In Cuba, both financing and provision are public. The Costa Rican model is also largely public with nearly universal state coverage, although private-sector services are available. Paraguay and Argentina are closer to the US model, which is a mixture of private health insurance that includes out-of-pocket expenditures and public resources. The United States is a pure example of this model.

Moving from financing to delivery of health services, the most common structure in Latin America is a mixed system. Three main health sectors in Latin America are present: the social security institutes (SSI, or Cajas de Seguro Social)[91] for formal-sector employees, the private sector for those who can afford private insurance or those who are uninsured but choose to seek private services, and the MOH for the poor. The formal sector finances and provides health care services to its employees.

There are numerous problems with this common Latin American health care model. Because many institutions provide similar services to different client bases, there is unnecessary duplication of services, especially of costly high-tech items. Services are concentrated in urban areas. There are concerns of quality, especially for the lower classes who utilize the resource-poor MOH facilities. Rising health care costs have thrust the quality and efficiency debate into focus throughout the region. As they stand, funding, personnel, and management systems do not create incentives for efficiency. Doctors, for example, are typically paid a fixed salary irrespective of quality or efficiency of service.[92] Human capital in the sector is poor, as training and support are weak. Health care reflects broader social patterns in the region, defined by a high degree of class inequality. Better use of health resources will require a restructuring of the delivery systems in the region while tackling tough issues of social inequality.

Reforming Health Service Delivery: The Challenge to Policy

Health care policy is determined by a number of critical choices that a nation faces. How much should people pay for health care? How should the trade-off between high-quality, sophisticated treatment and increased access to basic health and nutrition be resolved? Should health services be provided by the public or the private sector? How should governments resolve the tension between hospital-based urban care and comprehensive rural coverage? What kind of health insurance schemes will meet society's goals? Policies to improve health care in Latin America include improving the choices that households face, transforming the pattern of public spending on health, and changing the structure of the health care market.

Latin American governments began addressing these issues in the mid-1990s. After the lost decade of development due to the debt crisis of the 1980s, a better economic climate and the pressures for more responsive government under democracy promoted reform. Increasing international momentum toward universal access to health accentuated the movement for change. Health is largely seen as a right in the region; the challenge is in articulating the entitlements that accompany that right. What services will be available to all regardless of their ability to pay? Without regard to labor or socioeconomic service, what can citizens expect in the quality and overage of their health care? How to finance a system where roughly half the population is in the informal sector and does not contribute to defined benefits schemes?

Reform efforts can be broken down into two categories: those fostering efficiency and those promoting equity through enhancing access. Some governments experimented with redesigning incentives to provide new payment and purchaser systems; others promoted hospital or clinic autonomy to make services more responsive to local conditions. There have been attempts to unify aspects of the three segmented sectors of health in the region, bringing the public and social security systems together to reduce duplication and take advantage of economies of scale. Accountability to decrease corruption is being improved by the creation of agencies that separate the purchase of medical supplies from the actual service provider.

Ideally, decentralization of services brings health care closer to the needs of the people. Decentralization involves the devolution of previously centralized responsibilities to the local level. In Chile, responsibility for health care was brought down to the municipal level; the budget for PHC and 50 percent of the health staff were transferred from the national health service to local governments. Chilean workers, with a mandatory 7 percent deduction from their paychecks, were given a choice of enrolling in either public (FONASA) or private (ISAPRES) health insurance plans.[93] To combat the marked inequality of services that evolved as a function of income in this dual system, Chile adopted a set of entitlements through Universal Access with Explicit Guarantees (AUGE) that now covers eighty priority conditions.[94] Costa Rica exhibits a deeper level of integration of the formal and non-covered sectors, insuring more than 93 percent of the population with employee health financing covering the gap left by those in the informal sector by 50 percent.[95] Costa Rica is therefore closer to a solidarity-based health system where access is blind to the contribution to financing. Colombia's decentralized contracting system also appears to be a viable model for reforming Latin American health care systems struggling to overcome limited MOH budgets and improve equity, participation, and intersectoral cooperation. Multinational companies such as Aetna and Cigna are entering the Latin American market as partners to local providers of private health insurance. Box 11.2 discusses reforms in Mexican health care in greater depth. Brazil's SUS (universal health system) is financed with general revenues that provide access to state-run health services; wealthier Brazilians supplement the public service set with

Box 11.2. Toward Universal Health Care in Mexico

MEGHAN HARWOOD

Azucena Mora Diaz has benefitted greatly from the beginning of health care reform efforts in Mexico. When her twin girls were born seven weeks early, she did not have to worry about how she would pay the expensive hospital bill with her husband's low-wage job in construction. Under the government insurance plan, SPSS, the girls were treated at the Women's Hospital nearby and received thorough follow-up care.

However, enormous gaps still remain, and as Ms. Mora stated herself, the standards completely fall at the local clinical level. "There is hardly any medicine there," she says. Local clinics are "just good for vaccinations." Lucila Rivera Diaz, for example, comes from one of the poorest regions in southwestern Mexico, in the state of Guerrero. When doctors suspected that her mother had liver cancer, she and her 13-month-old son were forced to pack up and travel to the neighboring state of Morelos for treatment. They have been living in the waiting room there for two weeks, sleeping on blankets outstretched over metal chairs.[a] While the system has made important strides as her girls came into the world, life cycle health remains wanting in Mexico.

In February 2015, the Mexican Treasury Secretary Juan Lopéz announced budget cuts of 10 billion pesos to the health care sector, putting on hold President Enrique Pena Nieto's 2012 campaign promise to pursue new investments in health infrastructure.[b] These budget cuts further delay the goal of achieving universal coverage set forth by 2004 health care legislation under President Vincente Fox. Secretary Lopez, reacting to criticism, cited pressing security issues as justification for the cuts. These delayed efforts initiated under President Fox included steps toward increasing the portability of health services, as well as unifying fragmented Mexican health institutions under a single resource pool to increase cost efficiency and universality of service quality.[c] The implementation lag points to the contentious politics in health care.

Why is there such a widespread global agreement on the benefit of universal health coverage—and yet slow implementation? The *Lancet* Commission on Global Health highlights anticipated gains including

- Improved productivity—healthier workers are more productive.
- Educational advances—healthier children are more likely to attend school, gain greater levels of cognitive capacity, and achieve higher education levels.
- Increased life expectancy—with incentives to save for retirement, national savings increases, boosting domestic investment.
- Demographic effects—although healthier populations bring falling infant mortality rates that temporarily increase the population, eventually family size shrinks as wealthier families invest more in fewer children, increasing the ratio of working-age people relative to dependents.[d]

THE MEXICAN HEALTH CARE SYSTEM: INEFFICIENCY IMPEDING GROWTH

Mexico's health system is an impediment to these growth-producing effects. Fragmented, it is divided between three major subsystems: the formal social security sector (IMSS); the private sector, which insures a small percentage of the population; and SPSS (the Social Protection System in Health). The IMSS is part of the social security scheme, which provides health insurance and pensions for salaried formal sector workers. SPSS, in contrast, was created in 2003 to provide services for all Mexicans not covered by the public health facility networks. Its central pillar is *Seguro Popular*, a publicly funded health insurance for 50 million Mexicans in informal sectors.[e] Enormous issues of inefficiency, of discrepancy in quality of care, and in fullness of coverage exist between these

continued

continued

two major systems. Life expectancy and infant mortality rates between wealthier communities and poorer communities (most likely to be insured within SPSS systems) are still glaring. Despite the creation of SPSS in 2003, out-of-pocket expenditures on health in Mexico remain the second worst amongst all OECD countries. More than 50% of total Mexican health expenditure is private; this is mostly burdensome for the uninsured or those with limited access to quality coverage.[f]

All three sectors have their own sources of funds, their own provider networks, and very little communication occurs across networks. Not only does this duplication lead to cost and resource inefficiency, but it also exacerbates the existing disparity in access to quality care across states. Largely due to the distribution of health resources, there were 312 doctors per 100,000 people in the Federal District in 2008, despite interventions there were only 94 in the more rural state of Chiapas.[g] In 485 municipalities in Mexico seven out of ten inhabitants speak an indigenous language; communications inhibit health provision in these poorest areas.[h] Highly segmented and underfunded, existing facilities in Mexico are poorly constructed, and are inadequately distributed geographically.

Despite these limitations, *Seguro Popular* has reduced the exposure to impoverishing health expenses to 8 percent of the population. The private health sector is heterogeneous in quality of care, size, scope, and more.[i] Good private care remains concentrated closest to wealthier populations, where the market is most effective. The lack of centralized planning and agency consolidation with the 2003 reform has failed to fix this problem of portability and access. A system of reimbursements to allow citizens to take their insurance to health providers of choice is one of the many policy prescriptions that have been presented as a potential solution to such disparities in quality.[j]

Health care reform is an essential step in addressing pressing productivity issues and social welfare in the region. However, tackling a universal health care system is a long process that requires a tremendous amount of systemic restructuring, as well as huge investments. Striking the balance between budget commitments at the state level to health care and other sectors is often controversial. The immediacy of such commitments in Mexico, however, is severe. Mexico suffers from an increasing burden of noncommunicable disease including diabetes and cardiovascular illness, which remain the main causes of death and disability in the country. These are preventable deficiencies in the health care system. In combination with persistent wealth disparity, inequality, and intense economic inefficiency in the health care sector, such deficits must be weighed in terms of their long-term costs.[k] Short-term investment in the convergence of health care subsystems, and in universalizing standards of care and resource pools, could be the key to unleash the long-term economic, social, and national benefit of increased national health.

a. Elisabeth Malkin, "Mexico's Universal Health Care Is Work in Progress," *The New York Times*, January 29, 2011: n. pag. *The New York Times*. Web. 11 May 2015.

b. Adriana Alatorre, "Anuncia Ssa recorte a inversiones." *Reforma* Feb. 2015: n. pag. *Reforma*. Web. 11 May 2015.

c. Maribel Coronel, "Tras elecciones, se espera reforma en salud." *El Economista*, Mar. 2015: n. pag. *El Economista*. Web. 11 May 2015.

d. The Lancet Commission on Investing in Health. "Global Health 2035: A World Converging within a Generation," *World Development Report* 382.9908 (2013): 1898–1955. *The Lancet*. Web. 11 May 2015.

e. OECD Review of Health Systems Mexico 2016, http://www.oecd.org/publications/oecd-reviews-of-health-systems-mexico-2016-9789264230491-en.htm.

f. M. E. Bonilla-Chacín and Nelly Aguilera, *The Mexican Social Protection System in Health*, 1.

g. Ibid., 14.

h. Pietro Dionisio, *Something Is Moving in Mexico! Steps towards Universal Health Coverage*, July 15, 2016, http://www.internationalhealthpolicies.org/something-is-moving-in-mexico-steps-towards-universal-health-coverage/.

i. Andrea Puig, José A. Pagán, and Rebeca Wong, "Assessing Quality across Health Care Subsystems in Mexico," *The Journal of Ambulatory Care Management* 32.2 (2009): 123-1-31. *US National Library of Medicine*. Web. 11 May 2015.

j. *Mexican Healthcare System; Challenges and Opportunities*. N.p.: ManattJones Global Strategies, LLC, 2015. Print.

k. World Bank 2013.

WORKS CITED

Alatorre, Adriana. "Anuncia Ssa recorte a inversiones." *Reforma* Feb. 2015: n. pag. *Reforma*. Web. 11 May 2015. <http://www.reforma.com/libre/acceso/acceso.htm?urlredirect=/aplicaciones/articulo/default.aspx?id=476047&impresion=1>.

Bajak, Aleszu. "Failures of Brazil's Universal Health Care Plan Offer Lessons for the US." *Global Post* Feb. 2014: n. pag. *Global Pulse*. Web. 11 May 2015. <http://www.globalpost.com/dispatches/globalpost-blogs/global-pulse/universal-health-care-brazil-obamacare>.

Bonilla-Chacín, M. E., and Nelly Aguilera. *The Mexican Social Protection System in Health*. Washington, D.C.: The World Bank, 2013. UNICO Studies Series 1. *The World Bank*. Web. 11 May 2015. <http://www-wds.worldbank.org/external/default/WDSContentServer/WDSP/IB/2013/02/13/000333037_20130213103933/Rendered/PDF/750080REPLACEM0ectionSystemin.

Coronel, Maribel. "Tras elecciones, se espera reforma en salud." *El Economista* Mar. 2015: n. pag. *El Economista*. Web. 11 May 2015. <http://eleconomista.com.mx/columnas/salud-negocios/2015/03/22/tras-elecciones-se-espera-reforma-salud>.

Jurberg, Claudia. "Flawed but Fair: Brazil's Health System Reaches Out to the Poor." *Bulletin of the World Health Organization* 86.4 (2008): 241–320. *World Health Organization*. Web. 11 May 2015. <http://www.who.int/bulletin/volumes/86/4/08-030408/en/>.

Lindelow, Magnus and Edson C. Araujo. "Universal Health Coverage for Inclusive and Sustainable Development: Country Summary Report for Brazil." World Bank Group Report, 2014. *The World Bank Group Health, Nutrition and Population Global Practice*. Web. 11 May 2015. <http://www-wds.worldbank.org/external/default/WDSContentServer/WDSP/IB/2014/10/08/000470435_20141008112629/Rendered/PDF/912140WP0UHC0C0Box385329B00PUBLIC0.pdf>.

The Lancet Commission on Investing in Health. "Global Health 2035: A World Converging within a Generation." *World Development Report* 382.9908 (2013): 1898–1955. The Lancet. Web. 11 May 2015. <http://www.thelancet.com/commissions/global-health-2035>.

Malkin, Elisabeth. "Mexico's Universal Health Care Is Work in Progress." *The New York Times* 29 Jan. 2011: n. pag. The New York Times. Web. 11 May 2015. <http://www.nytimes.com/2011/01/30/world/americas/30mexico.html?_r=0>.

Mexican Healthcare System; Challenges and Opportunities. N.p.: ManattJones Global Strategies, LLC, 2015. Print.

Perspectives on healthcare in Latin America. N.p.: McKinsey & Company, 2011. Latin American Healthcare. McKinsey Brazil. Web. 11 May 2015.

Puig, Andrea, José A. Pagán, and Rebeca Wong. "Assessing Quality across Health Care Subsystems in Mexico." *The Journal of Ambulatory Care Management* 32.2 (2009): 123-31. *US National Library of Medicine*. Web. 11 May 2015. <http://www.ncbi.nlm.nih.gov/pmc/articles/PMC3296558/>. <http://www.mckinsey.com.br/LatAm4/Data/Perspectives_on_Healthcare_in_Latin_America.pdf>.

2014 Global health care sector outlook. N.p.: Deloitte Global, 2014. *Deloitte*. Web. 16 Apr. 2015. <http://www2.deloitte.com/jo/en/pages/life-sciences-and-healthcare/articles/2014-global-health-care-outlook.html>.

private plans. Brazil prioritizes access to primary health care and protection against catastrophic illness. With the introduction of SUS, the national universal health care, infant and maternal mortality was cut in half and major public disease rates no longer pose national threats. The family health plan, ESF, covers the poor, providing incentive to utilize the services of the twenty-seven thousand Family Health teams active in 90 percent of Brazil's 5,565 municipalities. Health policy is brought to the local level with councils comprised of civil society, service providers, and public officials to address local priorities and promote accountability.[96] Public-private partnerships have facilitated improvements. Brazilian interventions are seen as successful with the number of people seeking public health up by 450 percent, medical consultations per capita up 70 percent, and the number of medical facilities expanded from twenty-two thousand establishments to seventy-five thousand.[97] However, like all progress toward universal and equity-based health, it is a work in progress. Long waits for services and high out-of-pocket expenses are common. The World Bank reports that 60 percent of cancer patients are diagnosed at a late stage and the wealthy continue to rely on private services. The Brazilian system illustrates the long road to quality and equitable services. Progress toward genuine universal coverage requires new mechanisms of financing for cash-strapped governments as well as stronger progress in the structural change to formalize labor markets and increase contributions to health.

Nonetheless, decentralization carries with it several risks. Some local health systems are deeply penetrated by clientelism and patronage.[98] The political will to implement health reform may vary by the commitment of governors and mayors and the technical capabilities of local service providers. Decentralization can perversely decrease equity and access to a poor state if finance does not follow the responsibility to deliver services. Small may not always be more efficient, particularly when economies of scale affect the purchasing of supplies or equipment. Nonetheless, decentralization need not be an all or nothing proposition. For example, the central government could retain the responsibility for purchasing commodities, saving through economies of scale on items such as contraceptives, while local entities manage personnel and services. Citizen participation in articulating local demands for health care have been quite effective in Peru. Under the Comunidades Locales de Administración de Salud (Local Health Community Administration) system, by the end of 1997 roughly 10 percent of PHC clinics were administered by city councils; by 2001 they had expanded to 19 percent, had produced some outstanding clinics, and worked better in less-poor urban settings than in rural.[99] Since 2005, Peru has further expanded SIS to reduce individual health expenses.[100] Table 11.5 synthesizes aspects of reform throughout the region.

Households are constrained by income and education in the choices they make about health care. Governments should consider pursuing policies that improve choices, particularly among the poor. Health policies to reach the poor include measures to empower users of health services, especially among the poorest in society. Rather than remain victims of a poor health system, changes to strengthen accountability to patients by providing information about services quality and rights can be provided along with channels for complaints to be heard. The design of public health systems should respond to the needs of the poor. For example, for many poor (and their families) the costs of a day at the public clinic include the

Table 11.5. Systematic Improvements in Universal Health Care

Country	Program	Goals	Description
Argentina	Plan Nacer	Improve health care access to uninsured pregnant women and children under six.	Publicly funded maternal and child health care that serves to provide basic health services as well as financially supporting health facilities. It uses results-based payments to generate enrollment.
Argentina	SUMAR	Expand Plan Nacer program and its results-based payment method for children age six to nineteen and women age twenty to sixty-four.	The success of Plan Nacer in changing the health structure encouraged the continuation of a larger-scale improved insurance program. Plan SUMAR uses the base of Plan Nacer to improve the public health system.
Brazil	SUS (Sistema Único, de Saúde, Unified Health System)	Reform disjointed health system to establish a tax-financed national system in which all Brazilians are entitled to care.	Brazil overhauled their public health care system as a means to meet the 1988 Constitution establishment of health care as a human right. This included restructuring the system and investing heavily in primary care.
Chile	AUGE (Acceso Universal con Garantías Explícitas; Universal Access with Explicit Guarantees)	Provide universal health care to all Chileans.	System of social health insurance comprised of two subsystems. Fonansa, the national health fund, covers three-quarters of the population; the remaining quarter is covered by Isapres, for-profit insurers that target the wealthy sector of the population.
Colombia	Contributory Regime and Subsidized Regime	Improve access to the right of health care through government-subsidized national health.	Implemented twenty years ago, these reforms were designed to improve access to health care across all demographics. They have made marked improvements, but now face question of future sustainability.
Costa Rica	Social Security of Costa Rica Health Insurance	Provide universal health coverage through national health insurance.	Costa Rica focused its universal health system on primary care, as well as public health interventions in order to prioritize preventative health measures.
Guatemala	PEC (Programa de Extensión de Cobertura, Expansion of Coverage Program)	Increase health care for people living in rural areas without access to Ministry of Health services.	The government of Guatemala aligned with NGOs to provide health and nutrition needs, especially among women and children in rural areas.
Mexico	SPSS (Sistema de Protección Social en Salud, Social Protection System in Health)	Provide health insurance to all Mexicans who do not have social security and improve primary and secondary treatment.	The largest component of SPSS, the PHI, provides subsidized insurance to approximately fifty-two million people who were otherwise uninsured.

wages foregone in long waits and the need to line up very early in the morning in order to be seen. Overall Latin Americans finance 45 percent of health needs out of pocket—a significant burden for the poor.[101] Improving accessibility and reducing other inconveniences will help the poor address their health care needs.[102]

Pro-poor health reform includes expanded investments in the link between education and health, particularly for girls. Girls in the region play important roles in the care of younger siblings. An example of public education is a radio program in Bolivia directed toward eight- to thirteen-year-old children providing lessons on food preparation, sanitation, diarrhea prevention, oral hydration, cholera, and immunizations to improve family health practices. Women are an important target group. The pattern of public spending might be oriented toward the financing of public health interventions and community health services that deliver the greatest improvements in health care per dollar spent rather than toward expensive investments in tertiary care for the wealthy. Some evidence from CCTs suggest improvements in height, weight, and immunization as a result of the conditionalities in cash transfer programs.[103] The use of health promoters—members of the community trained and practicing under a doctor's supervision—can extend the medical reach. Promoters engage in preventive medicine and health education as well as carry small medical kits to deal with wounds, infections, and simple medical problems such as diarrhea. As members of the community themselves, health promoters have the trust of their clients, travel to remote areas, and often help bridge the gap between modern medicine and traditional healing practices.

The direction of health policy should in part be shaped by the local demand for health care. The perceived need for medical care—generally determined by medical experts—may diverge from the demand for health care based on a community's assessment of its own health conditions and socioeconomic circumstances. Demand for health care might be influenced by cultural norms, traditional medical practices, income, and prices that include not only monetary fees paid for services but also the travel time and foregone income to seek care.[104] Perception of illness also varies across cultures. If an illness becomes a way of life for a community, fewer members might seek treatment than in a community in which the same disease is rare. Tourists, for example, rarely forget their malaria shots and pills or their diarrhea remedies; inhabitants in some tropic communities may simply find these diseases part of the natural cycle of life—and sometimes death. Education and literacy also condition the demand for health care. Sadly, what people don't know can kill them. Estimating local demand for health services is important to direct funds away from underutilized services and toward unmet needs. A process of health education at the community level can facilitate grassroots participation in the determination of the demand for health.

PAYING THE BILL FOR HEALTH

Who should pay for health services? Traditionally, public health services in Latin America have been paid for by central governments, although out-of-pocket expenses comprise up to 50 percent of health expenditures. Table 11.6 provides

Table 11.6. Health Resources, Access, and Coverage

	Human Resources per 10,000 Population			Hospital Beds per 1,000	National Health Expenditure (% of GDP)		Health Care by Trained Personnel (%) 2013		Immunization Coverage in Infants Under One Year Old (%) 2013			
	Physicians	Professional Nurses	Dentists		Public 2013	Private 2013	Prenatal	At Birth	DTP3	OPV3 (Polio)	BCG(TB)	Measles/ MMR
Mexico	16.0	25.1	1.00	1.56	3.23	3.01	97.5	96.0	99	99	99	99
Costa Rica	22.8	24.4	9.30	1.13	7.40	2.47	n/a	99.0	91	90	78	90
El Salvador	15.5	11.2	5.30	1.33	4.63	2.31	85.3	n/a	92	92	90	93
Guatemala	7.5	6.0	1.40	0.62	2.44	4.08	93.0	58.7	96	94	94	93
Honduras	10.0	3.8	0.25	0.67	4.28	4.44	97.0	83.0	88	88	89	93
Nicaragua	8.8	7.5	0.50	0.91	4.49	3.86	96.2	n/a	100	100	100	100
Panama	16.0	13.6	3.10	2.28	4.90	2.30	n/a	94.3	85	87	100	98
Cuba	75.0	79.2	13.70	5.24	9.60	0.62	100.0	99.9	100	98	100	100
Bolivia	8.9	5.1	0.82	1.12	4.75	1.31	83.4	74.5	80	79	87	84
Colombia	17.7	10.3	8.29	1.49	5.18	1.63	n/a	98.6	92	91	89	94
Ecuador	16.1	7.9	2.60	1.50	3.94	3.60	95.0	93.1	100	100	100	100
Peru	11.9	12.7	1.90	1.57	3.12	2.19	n/a	86.7	95	94	95	94
Venezuela	13.0	8.0	5.70	0.78	n/a	n/a	19.9	95.7	81	73	96	87
Brazil	16.0	7.1	5.50	2.24	4.66	5.01	96.0	99.0	94	97	100	100
Argentina	32.1	3.8	9.30	4.98	4.90	2.35	n/a	99.7	91	90	100	94
Chile	18.2	15.3	7.70	2.17	3.66	4.07	84.3	99.8	90	90	92	90
Paraguay	15.8	14.6	7.00	1.33	3.46	5.54	93.0	96.4	74	74	75	74
Uruguay	47.3	18.0	14.40	2.77	6.14	2.61	96.0	99.5	95	95	99	96
United States	26.0	111.4	6.20	2.86	8.05	9.05	98.6	99.3	94	93	n/a	91

Source: PAHO, Health Situation in the Americas Basic Indicators 2015.
Note: Data for Nicaragua taken from 2009 and data for Venezuela taken from 2006.

data on public and private spending as a percentage of GDP. Although definitions of what is included complicate cross-country comparisons, we see a wide range of public spending, from 7.40 percent of GDP in Costa Rica to 2.44 percent in Guatemala. The table also provides a broad indication of what the money is buying in terms of human resources—the doctors, nurses, and dentists per ten thousand people and the coverage of health care by trained personnel. Given fiscal constraints, some evidence suggests that even the poor can and should pay for at least a part of services rendered. The very poor can be given vouchers to cover expenses, but payment for service sets up greater accountability at the local level. In some areas, user fees have been introduced to stretch scarce public resources in the health field. Some research indicates that even the poor are willing to pay for health services if the introduction of fees is accompanied by an improvement in quality.[105] In cases such as El Salvador, where user fees have been instituted, evidence suggests that cost was an inconsequential factor in determining why rural residents did not seek health care. The additional income can be used to increase the stock and variety of effective drug treatments. In contrast to tax-funded "free" health services from the central government, payment at the local level establishes a direct relationship between quality of services delivered and fair compensation. It may encourage cost savings and more efficient delivery of health services.

Nevertheless, some medical experts on developing country health are wary of user fees, especially in very poor areas where barter practices and lack of cash income limits the ability to pay for health services. User fees can also be seen as a form of regressive tax by which the poor pay proportionately more of their income for health than the rich. Unfortunately, there may be few alternatives. With a fixed budget for public health, governments must make tough choices about the allocation of resources. Market-oriented reforms may be needed as a key element of system overhauls. Cost-effectiveness is a criteria that guides many decisions in the health care field.

In addition to user fees, some countries have experimented with the introduction or expansion of insurance schemes. Rather than pay out lump sums to hospitals to provide services, money can be transferred to the patients, creating demand-driven medical services. Colombia was a leader in this reform approach. Prior to the redesign of the Colombian health care system, one-sixth of those who fell ill did not seek medical care because they simply could not pay; other uninsured patients paid dearly out of pocket for services, driving them or their families further into poverty. Prior to reform, only 9 percent of the lowest income quintile and 21 percent of the second lowest group were insured against health problems, creating a huge problem of vulnerability to illness.[106] Colombia's goal was to provide greater access to health care by making it possible to pay for it. There was a widely held view in Colombian society that incorporation into this basic right—health—was critical in stemming social disintegration and building the legitimacy of the state. Under the reform, millions of Colombians became eligible for health insurance and newly increased health purchasing agencies. There were four main elements to reform. First, one had to pass an income test to become eligible for participation. Preference was given to children and single mothers. Second, traditional supply-side subsidies were then transformed into insurance premiums for the poor. Third, the insurance system for the poor was merged into a contributory regime for those working and able to make contributions. Nonetheless, there were two divisions within this unified system, one for the subsidized clients and another for the fund contributors. A 1 percent tax on the contribution plan helped finance the subsidized scheme. Finally, the insurance was designed to purchase services from both the public and private health care sectors.

The effects of the program are impressive. Insurance coverage in the first and second quintiles rose to 49 and 53 percent, respectively. Poverty was reduced. Pre-reform, 5 percent of those suffering an ambulatory shock were driven into poverty and 6 percent into indigence (deep poverty); hospitalization pushed 14 percent in poverty and 18 percent into deep poverty. Post-reform rates for an ambulatory shock reduced the fall into poverty caused by illness to 4.1 percent (poverty) and 3 percent (deep poverty); for hospitalization the economic costs was reduced to 3 percent (poverty) and 11 percent (deep poverty). The program also reduced the out-of-pocket expenses that the poor had to come up with by 50 to 60 percent. There was a 66 percent increase in child delivery assisted by a physician and a 49 percent increase in prenatal care. The program, however, has not been perfect. Despite the fact that its implementation was part of a national law that guaranteed the right to health care, Colombia has not had the resources to reach universal coverage. Furthermore, the insurance package in the subsidized scheme is not comparable to the coverage obtained by the contributory segment. There are, for example, limited benefits for disease prevention, birth, and basic services, and the quality of hospitals in the system is inferior.[107] Confronting significant political pushback, it has been difficult to transition out many traditional supply-side incentives. The contributory scheme has also been slow to incorporate the self-employed.

Other structural changes that were planned to complement insurance reform also lag. Competition is limited due to missing scale economies in small localities or in specialized services. The certification process of participating hospital partners has been slow as well. Some also worry about the sustainability of the program. The revision of the Colombian health care system was accompanied by an influx of resources that cannot be maintained over time. In the 1980s the Colombian government spent 1.2 percent of GDP on health. Between 1993 and 1996 commitments grew 21.6 percent a year, with public money reaching 3.6 percent of GDP in 1998 plus another 4.3 percent of GDP in private funds. In 2000, the total health care spending hovered at 8 percent. By 2013, it was down to 7 percent. Further improvements must be made through efficiency-enhancing measures without the commitment of additional resources. Despite these drawbacks, enhanced insurance schemes are an interesting approach to extending health benefits to the poor. Ecuador is proposing the implementation of a similar insurance scheme targeted at the first and second quartiles. Currently, more than two-thirds of the population has no contributory health insurance, and the public institutions and MOH face severe constraints in providing health care to nearly half the population.[108] Changing the rules of the game to enhance effective demand through insurance, although imperfect, can make a huge difference.

The market, however, is not enough. Market-based insurance schemes are not sufficient allocators of health services. Some services—for example, aerial spraying to reduce dengue-carrying mosquitoes—would simply not take place

Urban pollution—such as that created by epic traffic congestion—creates health hazards. (*iStock/alffoto*)

without government. Without proper state guidance and oversight, the market alone often fails to provide equity and, in many cases, does not yield the expected improvements in efficiency. The market for health services involves a complicated array of interconnected markets, including health care professionals, pharmaceuticals, medical equipment, and education. Market failures in health delivery bedevil sophisticated industrial economies.[109] Marketization of health care may also lead to a fragmentation of services.[110] In Chile, for example, as funding chased the quantity of services offered, quality suffered. Decentralization negatively affected the excellent preventive care that had traditionally characterized the Chilean system, in which funding was targeted to curative as opposed to preventive purposes.[111] Furthermore, as workers were given a choice between private and public plans, the healthier participants were drawn to the private sector; those unable to get coverage from risk-averse private insurers were left on the public rolls. Finally, marketization is unlikely to work for those most severely affected by the health crisis in Latin America: the poor, particularly the indigenous, outside the market economy.

The challenge for policy in Latin America is to achieve a workable balance between private-sector participation and public-sector control to address critical health challenges in the region. Given the merit-based nature of investment in health, its dimensions as a public good, and the unpredictable nature of consumption services, state involvement is necessary. Partnerships among governments, multilateral lending agencies, and the nongovernmental community represent the key to health-sector reform. Health interventions must accompany the life cycle, beginning with prenatal and early childhood and moving through care in old age. Health engages intersectoral coordination across the various aspects of education, housing, infrastructure, industry and environment that condition health outcomes. It is important to keep in mind that health care policies must be designed not only for nations but also for multiethnic communities within nations that may have differing health needs. Participation of communities with different traditional practices is critical in the design of health care policies.

Key Concepts

AIDS
epidemiological backlog
epidemiological
   transition
epidemiological backlog
global public good

Health for All (HFA)
mental health care
merit good
occupational health
   concerns

primary health care
   (PHC)
public good
universal health coverage
violence against women

Chapter Summary

Latin America's Health Profile: Unequal Access and Quality

- The health profile in Latin America shows suffering from a wide variety of health-related problems, many of which stem from the inequality of access to quality health care and the inability of overburdened governments to provide universal health care services.
- Health care provision and quality vary dramatically with socioeconomic and ethnic status. Those who can afford to pay for it receive excellent care from well-trained medical staff, while those who rely on government services must deal with overcrowded, underresourced, lower-quality services.

Indigenous Groups and Women

- Indigenous groups and women are hit especially hard by health problems in Latin America. Stunting, malnutrition, obesity, malaria and other serious diseases, birth complications, and infant mortality occur with higher frequency in indigenous groups and women than in other sectors of the population.
- Many women fail to receive proper health care during pregnancy, which has negative outcomes for the women and their children.

Policy Reform: Striking a Balance between the Private and Public Sectors

- Focusing on improving the education of citizens regarding health care can directly benefit a wide range of people, regardless of socioeconomic background. With many young girls being encouraged to stay home in order to learn how to take care of a family, it is vital to target girls in education initiatives to improve family health, which will ultimately improve public health.
- Many health care systems in Latin America are forced to make difficult choices regarding who they should target for improved health given limited budgets. Health care requires painful trade-offs.
- Inadequate health care institutions are major detriments to health performance in Latin America. Health care is most commonly delivered by a system made up of SSIs for formal-sector employees, private-sector providers, and an MOH for the poor.
- Policies to improve health care in Latin America should include increasing the health care choices made available to households, raising public financing to reflect local demand for health care, and striking a balance between the public and private sectors' roles in health care. Among solutions that have been used in Latin America are insurance schemes, which make health care affordable to the poor while increasing the accountability of health care providers.

Notes

1. UNDP in Latin America and the Caribbean, www.latinamerica.undp.org/content/rblac/en/home/regioninfo/.

2. Joan Nelson and Robert Kaufman, *The Political Economy of Health Sector Reforms: Cross National Comparisons*, Wilson Center update on the Americas May 2003, Creating Community series.

3. Eliza Barclay, *Mexican Migrant Communities May Be on Verge of HIV/AIDS Epidemic*, September 2005, Population Reference Bureau, www.prb.org/Template.cfm?Section=PRB&template=/ContentManagement/ContentDisplay.cfm&ContentID=13000.

4. Joan Nelson, "The Political of Health Sector Reform," *Crucial Needs, Weak Incentives: Social Sector Reform, Democratization, and Globalization in Latin America*, eds. Robert R. Kaufman and Joan M. Nelson (Washington, DC: Woodrow Wilson Center Press and Johns Hopkins University Press, 2004), 27.

5. Population Reference Bureau, Prb.org 2005 World Population Data Sheet.

6. *Unicef Child Survival Report Card*, 2004, www.unicef.org/progressforchildren/2004v1/latin-Caribbean.php, and Population Reference Bureau, 2005 World Population Data Sheet, Washington, DC.

7. Denisard Alves and Walter Belluzzo, "Child Health and Infant Mortality in Brazil," IADB Latin American Research Network Working Paper No. R-493, April 2005.

8. World Bank, "Government of Ecuador Program Information Document," Health Insurance Project, approved January 19, 2006.

9. Carlos Larrea, Pedro Montalvo, and Ana Ricaurt, "Child Malnutrition, Social Development and Health Services in the Andean Region," HEW 0509011, Economics Working Paper Archive EconWPA, 2005.

10. UNICEF, "Health Equity Report," www.unicef.org/lac/20161207_LACRO_APR_Informe_sobre_equidad_en_salud_EN_LR.pdf.

11. Larrea, Montalvo, and Ricaurt, "Child Malnutrition."

12. Roger Shrimpton and Claudia Rokx, *The Double Burden of Malnutrition: A Review of Global Evidence*, The World Bank November 2012, http://documents.worldbank.org/curated/en/905651468339879888/pdf/795250WP0Doubl00Box037737900PUBLIC0.pdf.

13. Patrícia Pelufo Silviera, André Krumel Portella, and Marcelo Zubaran Goldani, "Obesity in Latin America," *The Lancet* 366 (August 6, 2005).

14. UNICEF, "Health Equity Report 2016," September 6, 2016, www.unicef.org/.../20160906_UNICEF_APR_HealthEquityReport_SUMMAR....

15. FAO Regional Office for Latin America and the Caribbean, fao.org.

16. Maria Eugenia Bonilla-Chacin, *Prevention of Health Risk Factors in Latin America and the Caribbean: Governance of Five Multisectoral Efforts*, (Washington, DC: World Bank, 2014).

17. Shrimpton and Rokx, *The Double Burden of Malnutrition.*

18. Food and Agriculture Organization, "FAO in Latin America and the Caribbean," www.fao.org/americas/acerca-de/en/.

19. Jill Replogle, "Hunger on the rise in Central America," *The Lancet,* 363 (2004): 2056–2057 World Bank Indicators for new data.

20. FAO, *The State of Food Insecurity in the World*, 2005, fao.org.

21. Shrimpton and Rokx, *The Double Burden of Malnutrition.*

22. PAHO, *Strategic and Programmatic Orientations, 1995–1998* (Washington, DC: Pan American Health Organization, 1995), PAHO Official Document 269, www.paho.org.

23. Emerging diseases are new diseases such as Lyme's disease. Chronic diseases develop slowly and persist over a period of time and are generally related to lifestyle. Degenerative diseases involve decay of the structure or function of tissue.

24. "Latin American Indigenous People More Likely to Die from Malaria, Diarrhea and TB than their Counterparts," November 29, 2005, www.medicalnewstoday.com.

25. Erin Durlesser, Kerry Miller, and Olivia Perlmutt, "Malaria in Latin America: A Nutritional Problem," www.micronutrient.org/idpas/pdf/1961MalariaInLA.pdf.

26. CDC, "Areas at Risk for Zika," www.cdc.gov/zika/geo/ and www.who.int/emergencies/zika-virus/timeline/en/.

27. The Guardian, "World Health Organisation Declares Zika Virus Public Health Emergency," www.theguardian.com/world/2016/apr/13/zika-virusconfirmed-cause-microcephaly-birth-defect-cdc.

28. "Brazil Declares an End to Its Zika Health Emergency," www.theatlantic.com/news/archive/2017/05/brazil-ends-zika-emergency/526509/.

29. Olivia Brathwaite Dick, José L. San Martín, Romeo H. Montoya, Jorge del Diego, Betzana Zambrano, and Gustavo H. Dayan, "Review: The History of Dengue Outbreaks in the Americas," *The American Society of Tropical Medicine and Hygiene* 4 (2012): 584–593, doi: 10.4269/ajtmh.2012.11-0770.

30. "Dengue and Severe Dengue," *World Health Organization,* last modified March 2016, www.who.int/mediacentre/factsheets/fs117/en/.

31. "Chikungunya Virus," *Center for Disease Control and Prevention*, last modified August 3, 2015, www.cdc.gov/chikungunya/.

32. "Strategic Directions for Chagas Disease Research," www.who.int/tdr/diseases/chagas/direction.htm.

33. Marcela Valente, "Fighting Chagas Disease, Camera in Hand," IPS-Inter Press Service/Global Information Network, August 30, 2005.

34. UNICEF, *"Health Equity* Report 2016."

35. IADB, "Reproductive Rights," Technical Note No. 8, In Ana Langer and Gustavo Nigenda, *Sexual and Reproductive Health and Health Sector Report In Latin America and the Caribbean: Challenges and Opportunities*, November 2001, www.iadb.org.

36. Center for Population and Development Studies (CEPED, Paris), "Abortion in Latin America," www.ceped.org/cdrom/avortement_ameriquelatine_2007/en/chapitre1/page3.html.

37. UNICEF, *"Health Equity* Report 2016."

38. Mala Htun, *Life, Liberty and Family Values in Religious Pluralism, Democracy, and the Catholic Church in Latin America* (Notre Dame, IN: University of Notre Dame Press), 342. Retrieved from www.ebrary.com.

39. UNICEF, "*Health Equity* Report 2016."

40. Barbara Kwast, "Reeducation of Maternal and Peri-natal Mortality in Rural and Peri-urban Settings: What Works?," *European Journal of Obstetrics and Gynecology and Reproductive Biology* 609 (1996): 49.

41. Amy Packham, "Pregnancy Around The World: The Average Age Women Become First-Time Mothers Revealed," www.huffingtonpost.co.uk/2016/03/09/pregnancy-around-the-world-age-of-new-mums_n_9416064.html.

42. Sidney Choque Schuler and Ruth Choque Schuler, "Misinformation, Mistrust, and Mistreatment: Family Planning among Bolivian Market Women," *Studies in Family Planning* 25 (1994): 214.

43. Miriam Krawczyk, "Women in the Region: Major Changes," *CEPAL Review* 49 (April 1993).

44. "Racial and Ethnic Disparities in Health in Latin America and the Caribbean," Inter-American Development Bank, October 2007.

45. J. A. Casas, N. W. Dachs, and A. Bambas, "Health Disparities in Latin America and the Caribbean: The Role of Social and Economic Determinants," *Equity and Health: Views from the Pan American Sanitary Bureau*, Occasional Publication No. 8 (Washington, DC: PAHO, 2001), 37.

46. UNICEF, "*Health Equity* Report 2016."

47. Carolyn Stephens, Clive Nettleton, John Porter, Ruth Willis, and Stephanie Clark, "Indigenous People's Health—Why Are They Behind Everyone, Everywhere?" *The Lancet* 366 (July 2, 2005): 11.

48. Jessica Farber, "Political Upheaval in Brazil Threatens Future of Universal Healthcare System," Council on Hemispheric Affairs, August 12, 2016.

49. Gillette Hall and Harry Patrinos, "Indigenous Peoples, Poverty and Human Development in Latin America: 1994–2004," executive summary at web.worldbank.org; Gillette Hall and H. A. Patrinos, eds., *Indigenous Peoples, Poverty and Human Development in Latin America* (Houndsmill, Basingstoke, Hampshire: Palgrave Macmillan, 2005).

50. Gillette Hall and Harry Anthony Patrinos, "Latin America's Indigenous Peoples," *Finance and Development* 42(4) (December 2005).

51. PAHO, *Resolution V: Health of Indigenous Peoples*, Series HSS/SILOS, 34 (Washington, DC: PAHO, 1993), available at www.paho.org.

52. Anonymous, "Health of Indigenous Peoples," *Pan American Journal of Public Health* 2(25) (1997): 357–362.

53. Replogle, "Hunger on the Rise."

54. PAHO, "Report of the Working Group on PAHO in the 21st Century," August 24, 2005, CD 46/29, www.paho.org.

55. Antonio Giuffrida, William Savedoff, and Roberto Iunes, "Health and Poverty in Brazil: Estimation by Structural Equation Model with Latent Variables," March 2005, www.iadb.org/sds/publication/publication_4065_e.htm.

56. Visit PAHO's website at www.paho.org to read more about PAHO's goals and strategic plans.

57. PAHO, *Implementation of the Global Strategy: Health for All by the Year 2000*, Vol. 3 (Washington, DC.: PAHO, 1993), 10.

58. Also referred to as multisectoral cooperation or collaboration and the health-development link.

59. "Cost Information and Management Decision in a Brazilian Hospital," *World Development Report* (1993): 60.

60. World Bank, *Poverty Reduction and the World Bank*: *Progress in Fiscal 1996 and 1997*, available at www.worldbank.org.

61. Heidi Worley, "Chronic Diseases Beleaguer Developing Countries," *Population Reference Bureau*, prb.org, January 2006.

62. "Health in the Americas 2017," www.paho.org/salud-en-las-americas-2017/wp-content/uploads/2017/07/3.2.2.Figure3_ENG.png.

63. Cervical Cancer in Latin America and the Caribbean: The Problem and the Way to Solutions, *Cancer Epidemiology, Biomarkers & Prevention* 21(9) (September 2012): 1409–1413. doi: 10.1158/1055-9965.EPI-12-0147. Villa LL1. www.ncbi.nlm.nih.gov/pubmed/22956726.

64. UNAIDS "Prevention Gap Report 2016," www.unaids.org/sites/default/files/media_asset/2016-prevention-gap-report_en.pdf.

65. "HIV and AIDS in Latin America and the Caribbean, 2017 report, avert.org.

66. WHO, *Report on the Global HIV/AIDS Epidemic, June 1998* (Geneva: UNAIDS, 1998), available at www.who.int/emc-hiv.

67. Seth Amgott, spokesman for Oxfam, quoted by Barbara Crossette, "US Drops Case over AIDS Drugs in Brazil," *New York Times*, June 26, 2001.

68. This section was authored by Margaret Knight, Colby College graduating class of 2002.

69. "Ministry of Health Launches Campaign to Prevent STD and AIDS," www.aids.gov.br/en/noticia/2014/ministry-health-launches-campaign-prevent-std-and-aids.

70. Ibid.

71. UNAIDS "Prevention Gap Report."

72. Flavia Sekles, "Brazil's AIDS Policies Tightly Link Prevention and Treatment," Population Reference Bureau, March 2005, www.prb.org.

73. Caroline O. N. Moser and Cathy McIlwaine, "Latin American Urban Violence as a Development Concern: Towards a Framework for Violence Reduction," *World Development* 34(1) (January 2006): 89–112.

74. Testimony of Adolfo A. Franco, Assistant Administrator, Bureau for Latin America and the Caribbean, United States Agency for International Development, before the Committee on International Relations, U.S. House of Representatives, Subcommittee on the Western Hemisphere Wednesday, April 20, 2005, http://usinfo.state.gov/utils/printpage.html.

75. "The Costs of Latin American Crime," *The Economist,* February 25, 2017, www.economist.com/news/americas/21717439-many-governments-are-failing-their-most-basic-task-costs-latin-american-crime.

76. Laura Chioda, "Stop the Violence," World Bank Development Forum 2016, https://openknowledge.worldbank.org/bitstream/handle/10986/25920/210664ov.pdf, doi: 10.1596/978-1-4648-0664-3.

77. Laura Jaitman, "The Costs of Crime and Violence: New Evidence and Insights in Latin America and the Caribbean," 2017, https://publications.iadb.org/handle/11319/8133#sthash.8gecQSmp.dpuf.

78. "Out of the Underworld: Criminal Gangs in the Americas," *The Economist*, January 5, 2006, www.economist.com.

79. Robert L. Ayres, *Crime and Violence as Development Issues in Latin America* (Washington, DC: World Bank, 1998).

80. DHS Report, *Domestic Violence Threatens Health of Children with Lower Immunization Rates, Higher Mortality Rates, Poor Nutrition*, Press release September 9, 2004.

81. Mario Osava, "Violence against Black Women in Brazil on the Rise, Despite Better Laws," www.ipsnews.net/2016/11/violence-against-black-women-in-brazil-on-the-rise-despite-better-laws/.

82. Markjke Velzboer-Salcedo and Julie Novick, "Violence against Women in the Americas," *PAHO Perspectives in Health*, 5(2) (2000), available at www.paho.org.

83. Robert Kohn, Itzhak Levav, José Miguel Caldas de Almeida, Benjamín Vicente, Laura Andrade, Jorge Caraveo-Anduaga, Shekhar Saxena, and Benedetto Saraceno, *Revista Panamericana de Salud Pública/Pan American Journal of Public Health* 18(4–5) (October/November 2005): 229–240.

84. Mental Disorders in Latin America and the Caribbean Forecast to Increase," December 2005, www.medicalnewstoday.com/medicalnews.php?newsid=34832#.

85. "Poor Mental Health, an Obstacle to Development in Latin America," July 13, 2015, www.worldbank.org/en/news/feature/2015/07/13/bad-mental-health-obstacle-development-latin-america.

86. Hnin Hnin Pyne, Mariam Claeson, and Maria Correia, *Gender Dimensions of Alcohol Consumption and Alcohol-Related Problems in Latin America and the Caribbean* (Washington, DC: World Bank Publications, 2002).

87. William Savedoff, Antonio Giuffrida, and Roberto Iunes, "Economic and Health Effects of Occupational Hazards," IADB, Sustainable Development Department, June 2001, www.iadb.org.

88. World Bank, "Latin America: Time to Put a Stop to Road Deaths," May 10, 2013, www.worldbank.org/en/news/feature/2013/05/10/accidentes-trafico-carreteras-america-latina.

89. Health Data, www.healthdata.org/data-visualization/gbd-compare.

90. WHO, *Integration of Health Care Delivery: Report of a WHO Study Group*, WHO Technical Report Series 861 (Geneva: WHO, 1996), Table 5, "The Role of the Hospital in the District Health System."

91. It is important to remember that in most cases we are talking about more than one SSI. Often each public sector will have its own insurance fund and facilities, leading to unnecessary duplication within the sector not to mention across sectors.

92. Nelson and Kaufman, *The Political Economy of Health Sector Reforms.*

93. For an overview of the evolution of the Chilean health care system, see Jorge Jimenez de la Jara and Thomas J. Bossert, "Chile's Health Sector Reform: Lessons from Four Reform Periods," *Health Sector Reform in Developing Countries: Making Health Development Sustainable*, ed. Peter Berman (Cambridge, MA: Harvard University Press, 1995), 199–214.

94. Rifat Atun et al., "Health-System Reform and Universal Health Coverage in Latin America," *The Lancet*, 385(9974), (2015): 1230–1247.

95. Ibid.

96. Vera Coelho PhD and Alex Shankland, "Making the Right to Health a Reality for Brazil's Indigenous Peoples: Innovation, Decentralization and Equity, www.medicc.org/mediccreview/articles/mr_211.pdf .

97. WHO, "Fair but Flawed," *Bulletin of the World Health Organization* 86(4), April 2008, 241–320, www.who.int/bulletin/volumes/86/4/08-030408/en/.

98. Patricia Ramírez, "A Sweeping Health Reform: The Quest for Unification, Coverage and Efficiency in Colombia," eds. Kaufman and Nelson, *Crucial Needs, Weak Incentives*, (Baltimore, MD: Johns Hopkins University Press, 2004): 150.

99. Joan Nelson, "The Political of Health Sector Reform," in *Nelson and Kaufman, Crucial Needs, Weak Incentives,* citing L. C. Altobelli and J. Pancorvo, *Peru: Shared Administration Program and Local Health Administration Associations (CLAS)* (Washington, DC: World Bank and IESE, 2000).

100. World Bank Report No. 59218-PE, "Peru, Recurso Programmatic AAA–Phase IV: Improving Health Outcomes by Strengthening Users' Entitlements and Reinforcing Public Sector Management," February 4, 2011. http://siteresources.worldbank.org/INTLACREGTOPLABSOCPRO/Resources/PERURECURSOIV.pdf.

101. Daniel Titelman et al., "Universal Health Coverage in Latin American Countries: How to Improve Solidarity-Based Schemes," *The Lancet* 385(9975), (2015) 1359–1363.

102. Tania Dmytraczenko, Vijay Rao, and Lori Ashford, "Health Sector Reform: How It Affects Reproductive Health," Population Reference Bureau Policy Brief, June 2003.

103. Simone Cecchini et al., "Conditional Cash Transfers and Health in Latin America," *The Lancet* 385(9975), (2015) e32–e34.

104. D. R. Gwatkin, A. Wagstaff, and A. S. Yazbeck, eds, *Reaching the Poor with Health, Nutrition, and Population Services: What Works, What Doesn't, and Why* (Washington, DC: World Bank, 2005).

105. Harold Alderman and Victor Lavy, "Household Responses to Public Health Services: Cost and Quality Tradeoffs," *World Bank Research Observer* 11(1) (February 1996): 3–22.

106. Maria-Luisa Escobar, "Health Sector Reform in Colombia Development Outreach," Special Report, May 2005, World Bank Institute, www.worldbank.org.

107. Patricia Ramírez, "A Sweeping Health Reform: The Quest for Unification, Coverage and Efficiency in Colombia," in Kaufman and Nelson, *Crucial Needs, Weak Incentives*, 150.

108. World Bank, Ecuador Public Information Document, www.worldbank.org, 2006.

109. David Swafford, "A Healthy Trend: Health Care Reform in Latin America," *Latin Finance* 83 (December 1996).

110. William C. Hsiao, "Marketization—The Illusory Magic Pill," *Health Economics* 3 (1994): 351–357.

111. WHO, *Integration of Health Care Delivery.*

CHAPTER TWELVE

EDUCATION

The Source of Equitable, Sustainable Growth

Geography creates enormous challenges to inclusive education in the rural sector. *(iStock/Atelopus)*

Education is the key to promoting equitable, sustainable growth in Latin America. Education raises the level of human capital, making each person potentially more productive. Those with more education are less likely to fall into poverty; education can also open doors to social mobility. Upgrading basic skills as well as increasing the number of technologically sophisticated workers in an economy contributes to national productivity. A more informed citizenry is better able to participate in democratic decision making and to demand accountability to the people. A better-educated populace will make wiser decisions about health and family planning and can participate more fully in environmentally sustainable development practices.

The promise of education is alluring but the record in Latin America sadly falls far short of the potential. Although more children are in school in the region, learning lags behind Asia, North America, and Europe. Poorly educated work-forces are uncompetitive in the global labor market. Segments of the population are excluded from higher education by a primary and secondary school system that encourages repetition and dropping out rather than creating incentives toward completion. Public primary education has been emaciated as dollars are funneled into public university systems. Teachers are poorly trained and managed. Inadequate statistics provide little guidance or incentive for reform. Hard choices must be made between improving education at the preschool and primary levels, providing quality secondary education to promote competitiveness in a global economy, and promoting the expansion of tertiary education for the poor and middle classes. Education is a catalyst for equitable development. Yet paradoxically, unequal access to quality education in Latin America perpetuates **exclusion** and marginalization of the poor, rural citizens and the indigenous.

This chapter discusses the discouraging state of education in the region and assesses efforts and prospects for reform. Questions we will explore include the following:

- Why should a nation invest scarce resources in education?
- What is different about education as an economic sector? How do these characteristics impede the delivery of education as a good?
- What is the report card on education in Latin America?
- What policy interventions have been tried on the region?
- What innovations might catalyze improvements in the regional deficit in education?

INVESTING IN EDUCATION: THE MORAL AND ECONOMIC DIMENSIONS

Education as a right: Access to education is a fundamental human right embodied in international accords. The 1948 United Nations Declaration of Human Rights establishes this right to a free education as a foundation to improving quality of life and exercising freedom of thought. The 1990 UN World Conference on Education for All, assembled in Jomtien, Thailand, launched **Education for All** (**EFA**), a global program advocating that all people ought to be able to benefit from educational opportunities designed to meet basic learning needs. In 2000, the Dakar Framework for Action reaffirmed the international commitment to EFA, providing regionally specific goals. The six objectives for Latin America were to expand early childhood programs, ensure that all children, especially the vulnerable, have access to a good quality primary education, meet the learning needs of young people for life skills programs, improve adult literacy by 50 percent by 2015, promote gender parity in education by 2015 and focus on quality improvements through measurable learning outcomes.[1] Reinforced by the broader millennium development goals launched in 2000, these objectives were part of a global promise of opportunity for all.

As we will see, Latin America came closest of all developing regions in achieving these goals—but they simply are not enough. In the benchmarking meeting for 2015 in Dakar, stakeholders from around the world agreed that equitable, quality lifelong learning must reach the marginalized, quality learning outcomes need to become standard, opportunity should be extended beyond primary education and the cross-cutting nature of education should be emphasized. As the former UK Prime Minister Gordon Brown noted to the conference, "universal learning is a goal of goals, or a super goal;" without education we cannot unlock other development goals, such as employment opportunity, gender equality, environmental care and good health. UN Secretary-General Ban Ki-moon, in launching the **UN Education First Initiative**, heralded the seminal role of education in its power to transform lives, give people hope, confidence and dignity, and equip them with the tools to escape poverty.[2] The new focus on quality is at the center of the World Bank's education strategy, **Learning for All**; it not only targets young people going to school but also cautions that they learn relevant skills while there. From its declaration as a human right, through the campaigns for education, the challenge going forward is to meet the broadly shared goal that all children—boys and girls across the spectrum of race and ethnicities—not only have a right to a desk in school but also a reasonable expectation of quality learning while there. The sustainable development goals also provide policy guidance, indicating a broad vision of education tied to lifelong learning, including affordable technical and vocational education and training (TVET).

In addition to the view that education is a dimension of well-being in its own right, education features prominently in the policy discourse on improving growth, reducing inequality, and lowering poverty. Long-term economic growth improves with progress in students' learning levels.[3] Inequality of opportunity, squarely tied to education, determines between 20 and 50 percent of overall inequality. Education correlates with democratic political participation as well as health status.[4] Achieving secondary education is the best chance a person has to remain out of absolute poverty over the course of their lives. But the opportunities to achieve a secondary or a tertiary education are not equally distributed. Circumstances beyond an individual's control such as gender, race, and socioeconomic origin can impede those working equally hard for advancement. Indeed, as we'll see in the data below, this marginalization characterizes the Latin American experience.

The nature of education: The unique characteristics of education as an economic good also interfere with achieving educational goals. Education is a **merit good**, defined as when the social benefits of the good may exceed the private gains.

As a population is better-educated, positive **externalities** spillover to health, environmental sustainability, and economic productivity for society. But an individual cannot claim these shared benefits. Unable to gain from the social returns, the person may therefore underinvest in education. Demand for an education is further complicated by the **opaque nature of the good**. It is easy, for example, to tell when a car isn't working. In contrast, how do we observe poor quality in education? School systems might provide information through testing and publicize results, but these metrics are imperfect. In poor communities parents facing their own educational gaps may not be able to identify weak learning outcomes in their children. If one is functionally illiterate, it may be difficult to assess your child's reading level. Yet the reading-challenged parent makes decisions for the young child.

Some parents might choose to home school and others might have the resources to send a child to private school, but most parents entrust the delivery of education to the public school system. Does the system have the interests of the child at heart? For the majority, the public school acts as a monopoly in education; in many cases the supply of labor to this monopoly is heavily unionized, characterizing it as a bilateral monopoly. Whether privately or publicly schooled, the agent is the teacher in the classroom. In a **principal agent problem**, one party (the principal) contracts with another to undertake an activity (the agent) but cannot directly observe the extent to which the outcomes meet the contract's goal. As agents of learning, teachers have more information with respect to what is happening in the classroom than do parents or school administrators. When families cannot monitor all of the choices made by the teacher, **information asymmetries** exist. At the point of delivery of education, the service is highly discretionary; teachers decide what part of the curriculum to deliver. The service itself must be variable; in a single classroom teaching must be customized to various learning needs. It is also transaction intensive, the result of frequent repeated interactions between teachers and individual students.[5] The problem becomes how to design incentives such that the teachers act in the best interests of the child. It is possible to construct systems where the schools are made responsible for their results—but as we'll see this can become a thorny political problem.

Another issue thwarting progress in education is a coordination problem. Who decides upon the optimal outcomes in education? Is it better to improve literacy or to develop scientists? As educational demand in Latin America has been largely elite driven, how has the curriculum excluded the poor? What are the driving needs of industry, agriculture, and the social sector for workers? How are the different demands aggregated in society? A **coordination failure** exists when actions by one sector—education—depend on poorly articulated factors by another. Policy interventions might be indicated to bridge policy failures, better align incentives for agents to act on behalf of children, improve the transparency of outcomes in education, or invest longer years in the educational process. Latin America is rich in experimentation with new approaches to education. Unfortunately, interventions have not usually been accompanied by rigorous evaluation so we know frustratingly little about what works under various conditions. We'll turn to this policy mix shortly, but first we want to consider the record of educational achievement in Latin America.

LATIN AMERICA'S EDUCATIONAL REPORT CARD

"A" grades for putting kids in school: Latin America has made strong progress in making education a basic human right available to all. The map in figure 12.1 shows strong regional progress. In Latin America, the **net enrollment rate** at the primary level was 94 percent—a rate not far from the 96 percent in North America and Western Europe.[6] The net enrollment adjusts the number of students actually enrolled in a grade by the appropriate age cohort; net enrollment gives us a picture of an age cohort as it moves through the school system. **Gross enrollment ratios**

Figure 12.1. Years of Education in Latin America and the Caribbean

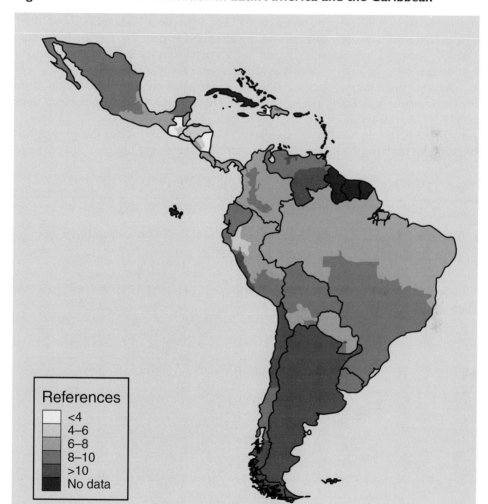

Source: Socio-Economic Database for Latin America and the Caribbean, CEDLAS and The World Bank, May 2013.

(GERs) are easier to estimate. In 2011 Latin America observed a gross enrollment ratio for nine-year-olds of 112 percent.[7] This is because ten- or eleven-year-olds, held back or late starters, were sitting in a classroom for nine-year-olds. In addition to strong primary school attendance, at this school level the Latin American region does well in terms of gender parity; both boys and girls are learning the basics. Reflecting the goals of EFA, the **Education for All Development Index (EDI)**, a composite of universal primary education, adult literacy, gender parity, and survival to grade five, shows that most countries are close to goals of an education for all.[8] We can see in table 12.1 that the region has achieved educational goals at high or medium development. This is good news; most kids are in primary school, opening a path for education. **Repetition rates** have fallen in most countries in the region. Repetition, being held back in a grade, wastes valuable teaching resources. Regionally, repetition fell from 12 to 8 percent between 2000 and 2010. The greatest drops were in Brazil, falling from 24 percent in 1999 to 18 percent in 2006; unfortunately rates have risen in Nicaragua from 5 to 11 percent over the last decade.[9]

Another encouraging factor is that the poor, rural kids and ethnic minorities are participating in schools at historic rates. While preschool attendance rates have increased overall by 21 percent over the past 20 years, they rose by 23 and 27 percent, respectively, among poor and rural children. The result is that almost half of poor and rural preschool children are receiving the early childhood investments

Table 12.1.   Education for Development Index, 2012

Rank	Country	EDI
High EDI: Have achieved or close to education for all (EFA) as a whole (0.95–1.00)		
28	Cuba	0.981
36	United States	0.975
40	Uruguay	0.969
42	Chile	0.969
49	Mexico	0.964
55	Venezuela, B. R.	0.956
Medium EDI: Intermediate position (0.80–0.94)		
67	Panama	0.938
72	Ecuador	0.924
74	Bolivia, P. S.	0.921
77	Peru	0.913
78	El Salvador	0.909
80	Colombia	0.902
82	Paraguay	0.892
85	Honduras	0.870
88	Guatemala	0.850
91	Guyana	0.877

Note: No data for Brazil, Argentina, Nicaragua in the 2015 Education for All Report.

in cognitive capacities for later learning. Secondary school enrollments increased 12 percent in the last 20 years; 15 percent more of the poor and 22 percent more rural children are now passing through this critical threshold. Where ethnic minorities were virtually excluded from schooling 20 years ago, now 70 percent attend primary and 50 percent attend secondary schools.[10] These more heterogeneous classrooms are encouraging but also create new teaching challenges.

Other good news comes in literacy rates; 91.4 percent of the region's population is literate. In the cohort from age 15 to 24—the group that best measures the outcomes from recent policies—literacy is nearly complete at 97.2 percent. Of course we need to interpret these numbers with caution; as in most of the world, literacy is self-reported. Furthermore, while it may mean that someone can sign their name, read signs, and make change, it doesn't assume a functional literacy in the workforce to comprehend a list of printed instructions needed for a good job in a factory.

Stalled Progression in Moving through Schools

Getting kids into primary school is a laudable first step, but it is far from sufficient. In half of the countries in Latin America, more than 16 percent of children who enroll in primary school will drop out before completion.[11] To self-insure against falling into poverty and to take advantage of returns in the global marketplace, a student needs the skill set developed in secondary schools. Chile, a regional leader in education along with Cuba, can now boast of 87 percent its population between 25 and 34 as having at least a secondary education; a further 27 percent has the benefit of completing tertiary education. The Chilean performance is comparable to the OECD benchmark. But these data, presented in table 12.2, are less flattering for Brazil and Mexico. In Mexico nearly two-thirds of the population doesn't hold a secondary certificate; in Brazil just a bit more than half have completed upper secondary education. If they existed, these data would be far more dismal for poorer countries in the region. Yet to be competitive in a global labor force that

Table 12.2.   Progression through School, 2010 (percentage of population)

	Below Upper Secondary, Ages 25–64	Upper Secondary, Ages 25–34	Upper Secondary–Postsecondary Nontertiary, Ages 25–34	Tertiary Education, Ages 25–34
Chile	29	87	45	27
Mexico	64	44	19	17
Brazil	59	53	30	11
OECD	26	80	44	30

Source: OECD Education Indicators at a Glance 2012, www.oecd.org/education/education-at-a-glance-19991487.htm.

has quadrupled in recent years, completion of secondary education is a critical threshold.

At Risk Kids Are in Danger of Dropping Out

The educational journey for Latin America's youth is a risky one, particularly if you are not wealthy. Table 12.3 shows the number of years of education by gender and income in the region. Latin Americans on average attend school for 8.2 years; this is a jump from 6 years in 2000.[12] Although we can see variation by country, girls receive about as much education as boys. The big gaps appear by income. In Bolivia, for example, if you are in the wealthy top quintile, you are likely to have eight more years of education compared to the student in the poorest strata. Venezuela and Chile do a bit better, but the rich and the poor are still separated by about five years of education. Education tends to perpetuate class differences in the region.

Table 12.3. Educational Inequality: Years of Schooling by Gender and Income Strata

| Country | Year | All | Gender | | Income Quintile | | | | | Inequality |
			Females	Males	Q1	Q2	Q3	Q4	Q5	Gap
Argentina	2009	11.0	11.2	10.8	8.4	9.4	10.3	11.5	13.6	5.2
Bolivia	2005	7.7	6.8	8.8	3.6	5.7	7.1	8.5	11.7	8.1
Brazil	2009	7.7	8	7.6	4.9	5.9	6.8	8.2	11.2	6.3
Chile	2009	11.0	10.9	11.1	8.9	9.6	10.2	11.3	13.7	4.8
Colombia	2006	7.9	7.9	7.9	5.3	5.5	6.6	8.1	12.0	6.7
Costa Rica	2009	8.7	8.8	8.6	5.8	6.7	7.3	9.0	12.7	7.0
Dom Rep.	2007	8.2	8.4	8.1	5.9	6.5	7.5	8.6	11.3	5.5
Ecuador	2009	8.7	8.7	9.0	6.3	6.8	7.7	9.0	12.2	5.9
El Salvador	2008	7.1	6.7	7.6	3.5	5	6.1	7.5	11.3	7.8
Guatemala	2006	4.8	4.3	5.4	1.4	2.3	3.4	5.1	9.0	7.7
Honduras	2009	5.9	5.9	5.7	3.4	3.6	4.7	6.3	9.6	6.2
Mexico	2008	8.4	8.1	8.7	5.3	6.7	7.5	8.9	12.0	6.8
Nicaragua	2005	5.8	5.8	5.8	2.7	3.8	5.0	6.2	9.4	6.8
Panama	2009	9.9	10.1	9.7	5.8	7.8	9.3	10.6	13.7	7.9
Paraguay	2009	8.3	8.1	8.4	5.3	6.1	7.7	9.1	11.4	6.1
Peru	2009	8.9	8.2	9.5	4.9	6.8	8.5	10.0	12.2	7.3
Uruguay	2009	9.4	9.7	9.1	6.7	7.5	8.6	10.1	13.0	6.3
Venezuela	2006	8.9	9.3	8.6	6.8	7.3	8.1	9.3	11.6	4.9
Average		8.2	8.2	8.4	5.3	6.3	7.4	8.7	11.8	6.5

Source: Guillermo Cruces, Caroline García Domench, and Leonardo Gasparini, "Inequality in Education" CEDLAS Working Paper 135, August 2012

Differentiation by class is driven by intersection with race, ethnicity, and geography. Those of indigenous origin continue to face educational marginalization. In Bolivia a speaker of Quechua aged seventeen to twenty-two accumulates four fewer years than Spanish speakers.[13] Mexicans who speak an indigenous language average over 1.5 years of school as compared to the national average of 8.4. Mexican living in the disadvantaged southern states such as Chiapas fall two years below the country average.[14] Rural areas with low population densities create barriers to education, especially for girls. Long journeys to attend school can be dangerous and costly. Ethnicity and social class intersect. Students from disadvantaged social groups are often taught in a language they struggle to understand and are compelled to follow a curriculum that is insensitive to cultural diversity. Being born into the lowest income group leads to marginalization as parents struggle to buy books, supplies, and uniforms or pay for transportation to schools. Malnutrition exacts a penalty equivalent to a full year of schooling. One can find nine million children under the age of five malnourished in Latin America. Poor nutrition goes hand in empty hand for the 32 million children under the age of six not enrolled in pre-primary education.[15]

Failing to Learn Is Failing Latin America's Future

Years in school measure *inputs* to education; they are a countable or quantitative metric for the time students are present in classrooms. Simply being in a school does not mean students are learning. Outcome measures capture the *quality* of education. By most tests, Latin American students are failing. Before looking at the dismal results, it is important to remember that standardized tests are controversial yardsticks for education; recall that since education is an opaque good, much of what goes on in a classroom in not directly observable. Comparing outcomes across cultures layers greater complexity. With these caveats, it is useful to look at a few benchmarks for learning outcomes in the Latin region. An internationally recognized test organized by the OECD is the *PISA* (*Programme for International Studies Achievement*), which assesses what fifteen-year-olds know. Administered every three years, it groups students from lowest (1) to highest (6).[16] Not all countries in the region participate; indeed the results would be even worse if the poorer Latin American countries were included. Across the three subject areas of reading, math, and science, between 30 and 80 percent of students performed at the lowest levels.[17] In reading tests, roughly half of the Latin American students failed to reach the minimally acceptable level; in OECD countries this figure is less than 20 percent.[18] This lowest level is associated with being at risk during the transition to work or further education; in Argentina, Brazil, Chile, Colombia, Mexico, and Uruguay (the participating countries in 2006) between 36 and 58 percent of students fell into this high-risk pool.[19] Latin American countries performed worse than their income levels would predict; outcomes in other poorer developing countries were better.[20] Only 3 percent of region's students scored in the top level; in

Mexico, Colombia, Panama, and Peru only 1 percent rose to the top. Less than 13 percent of Latin America students met the average OECD achievement level. Mexico's scores exhibited the greatest improvement over the last iteration; yet if one extrapolated this rate of improvement it would take twenty-four years to reach the rate Korea achieved in 2009.[21] Perhaps not surprisingly, scores were correlated to the teaching environments. Resource-poor public schools did far worse than elite private institutions.

Another international assessment is the *TIMSS* (*Trends in International Mathematics and Science Studies*). The high-scoring country in 2007 was South Korea; its scores were 1.6 to 1.8 times higher than those in Colombia and El Salvador. The performance of an average student in these Latin American countries was equivalent to the lowest 10 percent in higher performing countries. In a globally integrated economy, this puts Latin American youth at a huge disadvantage in the global job market. In the regionally based exam *SERCE* (*Segundo Estudio Regional Comparativo y Explicativo*), less than half of all third graders had more than very basic reading skills. Costa Ricans and Cubans were the exception to the low levels of primary literacy, with 85 percent performing above the benchmark.[22]

Latin America has taken the important first steps in getting more kids to school; it now must address the challenges these data underscore of providing a quality education for its students. Increasing the average number of years in school is an important first start—but it will not improve regional competitiveness unless this time in school is transformed into learning outcomes. Let's turn to consider policy initiatives in this sector critical to achieving human potential and economic development.

Policy Interventions: Improving Outcomes in Education

The goal of improving educational outcomes is broadly shared: families, firms, and communities all want better-educated students. Success, however, is complicated and largely elusive. There is no simple policy lever to motivate better reading, more agile math, and enhanced problem-solving skills. It is perhaps useful instead to think of education as a system with various points of entry and vulnerability. Figure 12.2 offers an adaption of the World Bank's Accountability Framework to help us visualize this system. In a system of strong accountability, the students and their families would pursue a "short route" and exercise client power, sending demand for a quality education to the schools. In its simplest form, this is the relationship between private schools and their client families. However, we know from our discussion of the principal agent problem, as information is asymmetric and hard to assess, that families most commonly contract through the state. (Private education is also costly!) Even in the case of private schools, families count on the state to provide a broad set of regulatory guidelines for educational outcomes. In the public schools, the state actively engages in the schooling flow. Families voice their demands for

Figure 12.2   The Accountability Framework

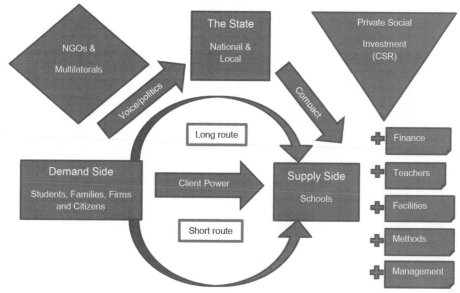

Source: Adapted by the author from Barbara Bruns, Deon Filmer, and Harry Anthony Patrinos, *Making Schools Work: New Evidence on Accountability Reforms* (World Bank, 2011).

education through political representatives, with society delivering a compact to the schools. In some cases, especially for those marginalized from political power, external actors such as NGOs or multilaterals might assist in empowering voice on the demand side or in providing strategies or best case practices for the state to consider in the design of the compact. These may have to do with structuring key inputs into education: financial resources, the role of teachers, the classroom environment, or the management of educational systems. The fundamental goal is to make schools accountable to their stakeholders. Let's consider these flows in turn.

The Demand Side: Empowering Students and their Families

Education systems evolve in response to constituent demand. If one believes that in their hearts parents want the best for their children, why don't families exercise client power to demand more? The sad state of educational outcomes in Latin America can be attributed to market and government failures to meet family demands. Markets work best with perfect information. Yet we noted above the opaque nature of education as a good; it is hard for a family to observe exactly what happens in a classroom or measure quality outcomes. Improving information flows can enhance accountability to students. National standards with transparent metrics allow families to judge one district against another. Systems of e-governance and citizen report cards can shine light on school performance. The formation of parent-teacher organizations and parent volunteer systems can also help articulate demands at the local level—particularly for parents who themselves may be functionally illiterate. In El Salvador, Guatemala, the Dominican Republic, Honduras, and Nicaragua, CERCA (Civic Engagement for Education Reform in Central America) empowers local school communities to gather information on the quality and conditions of teaching and learning in their schools. Students and their families learned to work together with teachers and schools to identify problems and establish goals for measurable results.[23] Even illiterate parents learned how to participate in their children's education.

Creating demand among historically marginalized groups is central to improving access to education and addressing inequality. The region has made healthy strides in increasing the enrollment of the poor, those living in remote rural areas, and children excluded for reasons of race or ethnicity. **Conditional cash transfers (CCTs)** have put more students in school. In addition to providing a mechanism to bring the poor out of poverty, CCTs are intended to decrease the opportunity costs of going to school. Programs such as Brazil's Bolsa Familia require an 85 percent attendance rate at school to receive the cash transfer. The program is designed to encourage students to stay in school because they will make more money there than from casual labor such as selling gum on the street corner. For the poor this addresses the problem that the opportunity costs of education—the time spent in school and not working—often outweigh the pressing need for families to have the income from their labor.

Some countries have chosen to enable families to demand better education by increasing their financial buying power. Educational **vouchers** are intended to allow students to choose the best schools. By permitting student mobility across the public and the private sectors, these systems are designed to encourage choice and increase competition on the part of the schools to attract the best students. In the Chilean case, however, subsides to increase the effective demand for good schools were also accompanied by the ability of schools to choose students. That is, a student had to be accepted into a choice school—so the choice was not exactly free. As a result, the deep socioeconomic inequality in the Chilean schooling system was replicated as schools receiving these subsidies tended to select students from the middle- and upper-income strata. With less complicated social needs, less-poor kids are easier to teach. A sorting process evolved where the very wealthy attend pricy elite private schools, the poor tend to cluster in underfunded municipal schools, and those in the middle who can afford to pay extra fees for books or facilities use vouchers to enroll in publicly subsidized private schools. Choice need not be accompanied by systemic creaming; the voucher system in Sweden, for example, prohibits schools from supply-side selection. The key is to be sure that the outcomes align with the intended effects of the intervention.

Supply Characteristics: Improving the Inputs into the Production of Education

Raising the quality of education in Latin America might be achieved by increasing the inputs into the educational system. As seen in table 12.4, Latin American nations spend 4.69 percent of GDP in education. As compared to some of the top spenders in Asia, this might appear low. However, there isn't a clear relationship between spending in education and quality outcomes. Spending on education in Latin America as measured in millions of constant dollars doubled from 1980 to 2008, yet outcomes did not improve commensurately.[24] When spending is correlated with performance on international tests, outcomes are all over the map. Some low-spending countries have quality indicators beyond what their GDPs suggest. Something else must be happening. Service delivery failures occur where inputs fail to produce effective improvements in quality education.

Table 12.4.   Public Expenditure on Education (% of GDP)

Country	2000	2011 or Most Recent
Argentina	4.6	5.8
Bolivia	5.5	6.9
Brazil	4.0	5.8
Chile	3.9	4.1
Colombia	3.5	4.4
Costa Rica	4.4	6.3
Cuba	7.7	12.9
Ecuador	1.3	4.4
El Salvador	2.5	3.4
Guatemala	3.0	3.0
Guyana	3.8	3.2
Mexico	4.9	5.3
Nicaragua	3.9	4.6
Panama	5.0	3.5
Paraguay	5.3	3.8
Peru	2.7	2.6
Dominican Republic	1.9	2.2
Uruguay	2.4	4.5
Venezuela	n/a	6.0
Average	3.91	4.69

Source: ECLAC Statistical Yearbook for Latin America 2014 Table 13.9.
Note: For countries with significant private provision, the percent underestimates the investment in education.

A logical place to focus policy efforts is on the performance of the teacher. Barbara Bruns has documented what many know intuitively: good teaching matters. Teacher quality is marred by weak mastery of academic content and poor classroom management. Bruns reports that unlike a good benchmark of 85 percent, teachers spend only 65 percent of class time on instruction—which adds up to about a full day of instruction per week.[25] Students with a strong teacher can progress with as much as an additional year of learning as compared to a mediocre one. Yet most school systems are not structured to improve teaching capacities. Although improving, poor countries and rural areas suffer from teacher training deficits. Early childhood education programs in particular suffer from a lack of professional training. Beyond training, teachers often do not face adequate incentives to improve performance. Think about the teacher who may invest long hours to help students prepare for exams. It may be intrinsically rewarding, but one's extra time might be better spent privately tutoring for cash. If that teacher is protected by union contracts, why work overtime for no financial rewards? When it is hard to fire someone, why show up for work at all? In a remote rural school, who would know? In contrast, randomized experiments have shown that financial incentives and monitoring of teachers can improve outcomes. Esther Duflo and colleagues have shown that when teachers were paid a bonus for improving performance and when their attendance was monitored using cameras, outcomes improved.[26] Not surprisingly, such policies are controversial. Addressing the power of unions and entrenched interests, Mexican President Enrique Peña Nieto has taken on teacher unions to promote accountability in schools. Mexico's high spending on education at 22 percent of public noncapital spending hasn't translated into significantly improved outcomes—in large part because it allocated nearly 94 percent of its education budget to teacher salaries and staff compensation (compared to a 64 percent OECD average) and the powerful unions have blocked innovative changes.[27] Accountability measures unfortunately did not permeate deep enough to promote a better environment for learning.

Teachers, of course, can't work miracles without complementary inputs. The facilities and classroom environment is also critical to raising outcomes. Poor school systems find it difficult to afford new books and destitute families struggle to provide supplies for their children. School facilities without basic sanitation infrastructure are off-putting to girls as they reach puberty. Rural schools are hard-pressed to equip students with science labs or to find the resources to adapt materials to make them relevant to the agricultural household. Mexico's Better Schools Program is heralded as an example of upgrading school facilities while building community engagement. Mexican law created organizations of social participation in education composed mostly of parents that helped diagnose the physical deficits in schools and participate in the refurbishing process with federal funding. Nationally 19,399 schools were identified as urgently needing repairs ranging from roofs and sanitation to creating twenty-first century teaching spaces. Benefitting from a transparent processing of bidding that engaged local contractors, programs created jobs. Creative projects included adaptation of solar technologies, rainwater recycling, waterless urinals, handwashing stations outside to reduce bullying, security fences in high violence areas, hydroponic gardens, and shade trees for physical education.[28] Investments such as this Better Schools Program in physical infrastructure may indeed deliver the best returns on the education dollar.[29]

Information and communications technology (ICT) can make a huge difference in secondary education especially for rural schools; distance learning can provide students with the exposure to a range of more advanced subjects in a multi-level single teacher classroom. Peru is a global leader in the one laptop per child program.[30] The Peruvian government resolved to confront the digital divide separating its students from international peers. In OECD countries 95 percent of fifteen-year-olds report having a computer at home; in Brazil and Mexico only half have such access and in Peru the ratio is far lower. Peru has aggressively introduced the XO computer, a laptop designed for kids in the developing world. It is durable, readable in sunlight, energy efficient, and has built-in wireless. Peru's goal is the introduction of one million laptops for its students. Randomized control trials conducted by outside investigators indicate that the program is improving cognitive skills among the recipient groups. The program, however, is still new and students were not all able to access the Internet. Nonetheless, the exposure to the training, word processing, games and e-books may have acted like a five- to six-month bonus in skill development. (Lamentably, the students didn't report more book reading.)[31] But distance learning is contingent upon access to computers and a broadband spectrum to carry image rich content. Here the role of the private sector might complement public-sector resources.[32]

One may need to think differently about the classroom schedule. Rural education poses significant obstacles for both families and schools. Flexibility is warranted in adapting schooling to the needs of rural children. In Colombia the multi-grade Escuela Nueva allows students to move through based on competencies rather than annual grade levels. For example, children who may have missed a key segment in mathematics due to harvest season can continue to develop that skill set upon their return rather than be held back to repeat a full grade. Stipends and priority for tenure for teachers in Ecuador have helped attract teachers to the remote areas. But teachers also need assistance in nontraditional classrooms. In Peru a teacher training program involved indigenous and nonindigenous experts to train bilingual teachers sensitive to cultural difference.[33] In Paraguay's little mathematicians program—called Tikichuela—audio lessons for preschoolers, delivered in both Guarani and Spanish, helped those most disadvantaged improve their math learning by about 10 percent. Teachers, 90 percent of whom felt unable to teach the topics in the preschool mathematics curriculum, received training in implementation. Peripheral schools that are chronically under resourced improved at nearly twice the rate of schools in strong networks, reducing the learning gap between rural and urban centers.[34]

Interventions on the supply and demand sides to promote accountability must be considered over the educational lifecycle. A child's education does not begin at grade one, nor is success defined by a secondary school diploma if the goal is education for life. Attention has been paid to increasing opportunities for **early childhood education**. Early childhood education has been shown to have a significant impact on the future learning trajectory of students. Without investments in early learning fundamentals, primary and secondary education bear less fruit.[35] Neurological pathways form early in life, beginning in the third gestational week. Prenatal and early childhood nutrition become key to learning capacities later in life. Environmental factors—strong parental interventions—or negative effects such as the stress of poverty interact with the biological to condition later educational outcomes. Developments in neuroscience indicate that early interaction shapes the brain structure through nutrition, attachment, and stimulation leading to increased wages, decreased violence, and improved health status. Despite the gains from intervention, evidence from cognitive tests during this period suggests a widening gap between children from high- and low-income families.[36]

Children also need to learn the soft skills—the socioemotional capacities that are key to many successful careers. During the first two years of life children learn to respond to others and develop trusting relationships as well as manage fear and aggression.[37] Some of the most cost-effective interventions to improve learning outcomes take place within families, coaching young parents to provide a nurturing environment. Despite the clear science that poor early childhood development (ECD) leads to cognitive delays that might place a student two years behind the cohort, the architecture of ECD in the region is shaky. Spending levels are too low and coordination among families, caregivers, and schools is weak. Where early childhood programs exist, the quality is poor—which can, according to Fiszbein, do more harm than good.[38] Parenting programs have been shown to improve IQs later in life. The NGO Supporting Child Caregivers, for example, is working with nurses in maternity hospitals in Peru and El Salvador to teach the caring interventions that will build the baby's executive functions including the ability to focus attention, make transitions, inhibit impulses, and plan toward future goals.[39]

After early childhood development, the second point of failure in education in Latin America is in the transition through high school. For most, the secondary degree is the terminal degree. Despite strong performance in primary attendance, youth deflect from educational pathways. Ninis—those neither in school nor in work—account for one in five youth between the ages of fifteen and twenty-four with devastating effects. Across the region twenty million youth miss the window of opportunity to enter the formal sector; once out of school and work for a year it is unlikely one will follow a pathway of formal employment. Instead, there is an increasing tendency for girls to become mothers at young ages and boys to resort to violence and gangs for social networks. Policy solutions vary. In El Salvador, where youth drop out early, larger payouts in CCTs extend the amount of full-time school. Merit scholarships, especially to vocational schools, can build skills development. Some programs create interventions to build the socioemotional skills demanded by formal-sector employers while also facilitating job search mechanisms for young entrants. Entra 21 (Latin America), led by the International Youth Foundation with support from multilaterals along with private-sector donors, provided short-term job training, soft skills development, internships, and job search assistance to youth ages sixteen to twenty-nine in twenty-two Latin American and Caribbean countries. Soft skills emphasized include teamwork, communication, conflict management, responsibility, ethics, time management, and self-awareness.

Six months after program completion, more than half of students were employed (92 percent in the formal sector), many had returned to school, and only 27 percent were neither studying nor working (compared to 66 percent at the beginning of the project). Programs can also build on frameworks within schools to keep youth in schools. The Ayrton Senna Institute—inspired by the dedication of the late race car driver—focuses on creating collaborative relationships with governments and the private sectors to develop skills and scale up creative lessons in educational policy.[40] Technical and vocational education and training (TVET) is critical to continue training. Half of human capital development comes after schooling.[41] With weak training programs within firms, 90 percent of learning is ad hoc learning by doing and peer instruction. More systematized training programs, including the articulation of socioemotional skills within firms, can help build success—and profits.

Education is geographically uneven, reflecting patterns of rural marginalization. Rural extension programs have expanded opportunities for children to continue in progression through secondary schooling. E-learning holds potential in the region, especially in addressing unequal access in the rural sector. It needs, however, broader accreditation and to be brought in line with job market demands.[42] School systems can benefit from institutional strengthening. There are varied experiments in school based management reforms to increase the autonomy of schools in making key decisions and controlling resources. Strong programs often involve families and corporate stakeholders. **Decentralization** is designed to empower local communities to identify their own needs. The curriculum for a coffee-growing area in Costa Rica may be quite different from the demands of students in San José hoping to enter the high-tech information and medical clusters in the capital city. Decentralization creates space from the requisites of bureaucratic central ministries of education to carve out a curriculum that will increase the local returns to education. But decentralization does have drawbacks. In some experiments, local control has meant increased reliance on local revenue sources. Although this is fine for students living in wealthy areas, poor regions become poorer. Desires for local control need to be balanced against improving nationwide outcomes in educational quality.

In addition to the need for technical training, policy interventions are indicated to bridge the gap between the skill sets developed in schools and those demanded by the labor market. The mismatch between education and jobs is challenging, particularly in light of the changing job landscape with globalization and technology. Students are incurring debt to train for yesterday's market; markets are failing to transmit the appropriate signals back to learners through the education system. Firms and educational systems appear to live in a parallel universe. **Private social investment** or the engagement of companies with schools to supplement resources can be productive. Beyond traditional philanthropy, there are opportunities for companies to partner with communities in improving local endowments. For example, Orsa, a Brazilian forestry company, has provided science-based programs in botany, teaching children to grow vegetable gardens. Not only do kids learn the science, but the irony that many poor rural families lack back nutrients is addressed.

Conclusion: Making Schooling Work

Creating opportunities for children from Latin America to achieve their own human potential and compete in the global marketplace involves not only empowering families to demand quality education but also augmenting the capacity for schools to deliver on their promise to society. This must be a whole of society effort. Schools cannot accomplish this in isolation from community and business stakeholders. Governments need to partner with NGOs as well as private enterprise to marshal the resources and the political will for change. Regional and global sharing of best practices, including randomized control experiments, are crucial in advancing our understanding of learning outcomes. Policy interventions must be tailored to local circumstances. It is important to understand, for example, where the central government is effective and when local control is best adapted for change. Matching reforms to local realities is key for success; controlled studies of policy interventions will help us understand what works and what does not.[43] Education is too important to leave to chance; kids' lives are literally at stake.

Key Concepts

conditional cash transfers (CCTs)
coordination failure
decentralization
early childhood education
Education for All (EFA)
Education for All Development Index (EDI)

exclusion
externalities
gross enrollment ratios (GERs)
information and communications technology (ICT)
information asymmetries
Learning for All

net enrollment rate
opaque nature of the good
principal agent problem
private social investment
repetition rates
UN Education First Initiative
vouchers

Chapter Summary

Education in Latin America: Deficits and Inequalities

- In comparison to other regions of the world, Latin America suffers from a severe education deficit.
- There is a marked education gap between socioeconomic groups. Those who can afford to send their children to private school benefit from a greater share of public educational expenditures along with higher-quality facilities and resources. The public school system is severely underfunded and deficient in resources and qualified teachers. As a result, poor children tend to have

weaker performance, higher dropout rates, and higher repetition rates than children with higher socioeconomic status.

Indigenous Difficulties

- Although Latin America has made progress on gender bias in education, these benefits do not broadly extend to indigenous communities. In addition to the gender bias still apparent among indigenous communities, language, cultural barriers, and high opportunity costs hinder indigenous groups from attending school.

Continuing Education

- Education should not be limited to younger students and formal classrooms. Adult education is an important aspect in reducing the education deficit in Latin America. Informal education programs that allow marginalized groups who are unable to attend school to define their own educational needs have proven to be effective measures in empowering these sectors of the population.

Education Reform: Increasing Both Quality and Access

- Reform should be both supply and demand oriented. On the supply side, measures should be taken to hold schools and teachers accountable for the quality of the education that is being provided. Teacher qualifications should be made more rigorous, and absence or poor performance from teachers and administrators should be punished.
- On the demand side, initiatives from private, nongovernmental, and public institutions should be implemented to encourage families and students to demand better access and a higher quality of education. Vouchers, scholarship programs, and CCTs are all ways in which governments and other institutions can encourage families to send their children to school and help cover the high opportunity costs incurred by education as well as involve communities in the decision-making process.

Notes

1. Unesco, *The Dakar Framework for Action*, April 2000, unesdoc.unesco.org.

2. Education for Global Development, World Bank Blog posted February 27, 2013, "The Global Education Imperative," http://blogs.worldbank.org/education/education-empowers-people-and-transforms-lives-says-secretary-general-ban-ki-moon.

3. Analyzing data on student performance on internationally benchmarked tests (such as PISA, TIMSS, and the Progress in International Reading Literacy Study [PIRLS]) from more than fifty countries over a 40-year period, Hanushek and Woessmann (2015, 2017) have demonstrated a tight correlation between average student learning levels and long-term economic growth. See Eric A. Hanushek and Ludger Woessmann, "The Economics of International Differences in Educational Achievement," in *Handbook of the Economics of Education*, Vol. 3, eds. Eric A. Hanushek, Stephen Machin, and Ludger Woessmann (Amsterdam: North Holland, 2011, 89–200). Also see Eric A. Hanushek, "The Value of Smarter Teachers: International Evidence on Teacher Cognitive Skills and Student Performance," National Bureau of Economic Research Working Paper, December 2017, www.nber.org.

4. Francisco H. G. Ferreira and Jérémie Gignoux, "The Measurement of Educational Inequality: Achievement and Opportunity," *The World Bank Economic Review,* February 20, 2013.

5. Barbara Bruns, Deon Filmer, and Harry Anthony Patrinos, *Making Schools Work: New Evidence on Accountability Reforms,* The World Bank, 2011, http://siteresources.worldbank.org/EDUCATION.

6. *Education for All Global Monitoring Report*, 2012, www.unesco.org.

7. UNESCO-UIS 2013. For the secondary level in 2011 we saw a GER of 90 percent while tertiary was 42 percent. The World Bank shows GER for primary in 2011 as 116 percent (WDI).

8. Unesco, Education for All Index found at /en.unesco.org/gem-report/education-all-development-index. The EDI is calculated by EDI = 1/4 (primary annual net enrollment rate) + 1/4 (adult literacy rate) + 1/4 (gender parity indexes of the primary and secondary gross enrolment ratios) + 1/4 (survival rate to grade 5). Data in Table 1 for Brazil and Chile are from the 2011 report. It is complicated to mix data years when presenting a ranking; it probably understates the position of the two countries as each made progress on educational benchmarks.

9. "Latin America and the Caribbean–Policies Yield Results but High Rates Persist in Some Countries," www.unesco.org/new/en/media-services/single-view/news/stumbling_blocks_to_universal_primary_education_repetition_rates_decline_but_dropout_rates_remain_high/.

10. María Soledad Bos, Marcelo Cabrol, and Carlos Rondón, "A New Context for Teachers in Latin America and the Caribbean," *Inter-American Development Bank Technical Notes*, No. IDB-TN-412, April 2012, http://idbdocs.iadb.org/wsdocs/getdocument.aspx?docnum=36887830.

11. Education for all Global Monitoring Report 2010, Latin America and the Caribbean Regional Overview, https://en.unesco.org/gem-report/sites/gem-report/files/LAC_en.PDF

12. UNESCO data.

13. UNESCO, EFA GMR 2010.

14. EFA GMR 2010.

15. Early Childhood Development," Columbia University's Center for Global Health and Development and the Earth Institute, http://cghed.ei.columbia.edu/?id=projects_ecd.

16. Alejandro J Ganimian and Alexandra Solano Rocha, "Measuring Up? How Did Latin America and the Caribbean Perform on the 2009 Programme for International Student Assessment (PISA)?," 2011, www.thedialogue.org/PublicationFiles/Preal_PISA_ENGLowres.pdf.

17. Ibid.

18. OECD and ECLAC, Latin American Economic Outlook 2012. Transforming the State for Development.

19. UNESCO, EFA GMR 2010.

20. Ganimian and Rocha, "Measuring Up?"

21. Marcelo Cabrol y Miguel Székely, Educación para la transformación editores Banco Interamericano de Desarrollo, 2012.

22. UNESCO, EFA GMR 2010.

23. Ana Florez Guio, Ray Chesterfield, and Carmen Siri, "The CERCA School Report Card: Communities Creating Education Quality," Implementation Manual, Academy for Educational Development, 2006.

24. Obviously the number of students also increased—but did not double in twenty years. Paul W. Glewwe, Eric A. Hanushek, Sarah D. Humpage, and Renato Ravina, "School Resources and Educational Outcomes in Developing Countries: A Review of the Literature from 1990 to 2010," NBER Working Papers 17554, National Bureau of Economic Research, Inc., 2011.

25. Barbara Bruns, and Javier Luque, *Great Teachers: How to Raise Student Learning in Latin America and the Caribbean* (Washington, DC: World Bank, 2015). doi:10.1596/978-1-4648-0151-8

26. Esther Duflo, Rema Hanna, and Stephen Ryan, "Incentives Work: Getting Teachers to Come to School," *American Economic Review* 102(4) (2012): 1241–1278.

27. Ana Canedo, "Mexico's Education Reform: What Went Wrong?" http://gppreview.com/2016/03/10/mexicos-education-reform-what-went-wrong/.

28. Alastair Blyth, Rodolfo Almeida, David Forrester, Ann Gorey, and Juan José Chávez Zepeda, "Upgrading School Buildings in Mexico with Social Participation," OECD, September 24, 2012.

29. Glewwe et al., "School Resources and Educational Outcomes in Developing Countries."

30. Julián P. Cristia et al., "Home Computers and Child Outcomes: Short-Term Impacts from a Randomized Experiment in Peru," Working Paper IDB-WP-304. Washington, DC, United States: InterAmerican Development Bank, 2012.

31. Ibid. and Diether W. Beuermann, Julian P. Christia, Yyannu Cruz-Aguayo, Santiago Cueto, and Ofer Malamud, Ofer, "Home Computers and Child Outcomes: Short-Term Impacts from a Randomized Experiment in Peru," NBER Working Paper No. 18818, February 2013

32. Beuermann et al., "Home Computers and Child Outcomes."

33. Regional Overview, Education for all Global Monitoring Report, 2010, p. 12.

34. The program was run in both rural and urban areas. Emma Näslund-Hadley, Hernández Juan Manuel Agramonte, Ernesto Martínez, and Caitlin Ludlow, "The Making of Little Mathematicians," IDB Briefly Noted: No. 20: September 2012, www.iadb.org.

35. Marcelo Cabrol y Miguel Székely, editores *Educación para la Transformacion*, Banco Interamericano de Desarrollo, 2012.

36. Claudio X. González Guajardo, "Would Expanding Preschool & Daycare Benefit Latin America?" InterAmerican dialogue Q&A, November 4, 2014.

37. S. Berlinski and N. Schady, "The Early Years: Child Well-Being and the Role of Public Policy," IDB, Development in the Americas, 2015.

38. Ariel Fiszbein, "Would Expanding Preschool & Daycare Benefit Latin America?," InterAmerican Dialogue Q&A, November 4, 2014.

39. SCC, https://supportingchildcaregivers.org/.

40. http://www.ayrton-senna.net.

41. Brassiola, CAF, Global Development Network Lima Peru 2016.

42. Federico Sucre, "Role of E-Learning in Higher Education in Latin America," April 12, 2016 PREAL Blog.

43. Ariel Fiszbein and YasuhikoMatsuda, "Matching Reforms to Institutional Realities: A Framework for Assessing Social Service Delivery Reform Strategies in Developing Countries," World Bank Policy Research Working Paper No. 6136. July 1, 2012, Available at SSRN: http://ssrn.com/abstract=2110097.

CHAPTER THIRTEEN

PROMOTING SUSTAINABLE ENVIRONMENTS IN LATIN AMERICA

The Amazon holds extraordinary environmental riches—but is threatened by development of roads and mineral exploration such as this petroleum camp. *(iStock/Atelopus)*

425

Addressing environmental challenges in Latin America is a central element of regional development. Environmental policy in Latin America engages complicated dimensions of industrial and agricultural policy, social inclusion, health, and foreign affairs in the region. A naïve North American might reduce environmental concerns in Latin America to deforestation and biodiversity loss. Although forest and natural resource management would also be on the mind of a Latin minister of the environment, as the most urbanized region in the world, questions of air pollution, sanitation, and waste disposal might rise to the top of the priority list. Creating opportunities for sustainable, inclusive development requires new approaches in both the industrial and agricultural sectors as well as new partnerships to address the pressures of poverty and inequality on ecosystems. Finally, the Minister of the environment would need to work closely with the Foreign Affairs ministry to address the global dimensions of environmental policy in the region.

This chapter focuses on the environmental aspects of economic developing in Latin America. After we analyze key characteristics of environmental challenges in the region, we explore some of the economic dimensions of environmental policy. We conclude by considering policy options to improve sustainability in Latin America and beyond. Key questions include:

- As one of the most urbanized regions in the world, how can Latin America minimize the externalities of air and water pollution along with solid waste management?
- Latin America is one of the most biologically diverse regions on the planet. How can this diversity be preserved in the face of competing demands on state budgets to address extreme poverty, promote health for all, and extend educational opportunities?
- Although the region's contributions to climate change are small compared to the global North, its capacity to reduce greenhouse emissions is high. Who should pay?
- When the damages from pollution are both local and global, how should responsibilities for cleanup be apportioned?
- Given limited government resources to mitigate climate change and adapt to its consequences, how can the private sector contribute to promoting sustainability?

ENVIRONMENTAL CHALLENGES IN LATIN AMERICA

Urbanization and City Living

Over 80 percent of Latin Americans live in cities—a demographic transition from rural to urban living that challenges urban sustainability.[1] Based on current trajectories, it is estimated that 90 percent of Latin America's population will live in large towns or cities by 2050.[2] This rapid growth of cities is a stark environmental challenge transforming the landscape and ecosystems. The mushrooming of urban spaces in Latin America has not kept pace with the ability to manage concentrated populations. The number of private vehicles has doubled in ten years, making gridlock and painfully long commutes the norm and exacerbating emissions with poor air quality. Although the region has 39 percent of global water resources, availability of clean water in major urban centers is problematic. Water crises are likely to become commonplace in the coming decades.[3] One in four Latin Americans lives in an informal settlement, creating a smelly challenge for sanitation. Industrial wastewater is largely discharged without prior treatment.[4] Although clean sanitation is seen as a human right and a cornerstone to a healthy society, only 20 percent of wastewater in the region is treated. Between 15 and 28 percent of wastewater goes to the sewers—explaining the horror many expressed over the filth in Guanabarra Bay during the Rio Olympics. Solid waste in urban regions has increased 65 percent since 1995; removal systems are largely private and relegated to the four hundred thousand desperately poor who pick garbage for a living. Recycling is weak, with only 2 percent of the region covered by formal programs.[5]

Globally, metropolitan living also contributes to 70 percent of the world's greenhouse gas emissions, and significantly impacts the local climate by creating urban heat islands that raise the overall temperature of cities in comparison to the surrounding countryside.[6] Additionally, urban areas are highly vulnerable to natural threats, including extreme weather such as earthquakes, tsunamis, and hurricanes. The prevalence of urbanization and city living in Latin America makes strategic, equitable, and environmentally sound urban planning and practices fundamental to ensuring an environmentally just and sustainable future.

As documented in table 13.1, pollution and contamination are two of the largest urban health risks. The Clean Air Institute in 2013 estimated that over one hundred million people in Latin America breathe air daily that exceeds the pollution levels deemed permissible by the World Health Organization. Perhaps this gives you a bit of a sense of the social damage from pollution.[7] As a result, approximately 35,000 deaths and the loss of an additional 276,000 life years occur annually due to air pollution in the region.[8] Air pollutants from fixed and mobile sources, volatile organic compounds (VOCs) and nitrogen oxides (NOx), react to increasing temperatures by forming ground ozone, particularly affecting children and older persons' health.[9]

Not all practices, however, are dismal. Santiago, Chile, has constructed a 28.5 km collector for wastewater. Along with Mexico City, it also has strong local regulation to control air pollution. Dubbed the valley of death in the 1990s, Cubatão Brazil has cut pollution levels by 90 percent.[10] By capturing methane from landfills and burning it into energy, São Paulo was able to cut carbon emissions by about eleven million tons, resulting in one of the largest methane harvesting initiatives in the world.[11] Carbon monoxide levels in Quito have dropped 30 percent since the city implemented a strict vehicle monitoring policy requiring private vehicles to pass annual emissions tests.[12]

Pollution is not, however, limited to the air. Pollution and waste seep into water supplies, causing gastrointestinal illness and other serious health concerns. The World Bank concluded in a 2012 report that 77 percent of Mexican

Figure 13.1.   Total Welfare Losses from Air Pollution

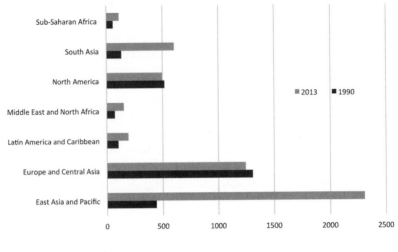

2011 US $ billions PPP adjusted

Source: The World Bank, The Cost of Air Pollution, 2016.

rivers are polluted to the extent that they pose a serious threat to human health.[13] This led Mexicans to spend as much as 10 percent of their incomes to purchase approximately 127 gallons of bottled water per person per year, the largest per capita rate in the world.[14] The water is not only used for drinking, but also for household cleaning, cooking, and even bathing.[15] Some see buying water as an unnecessary expense—and, as we noted in our health chapter, this leaves sugary drinks as an alternative for drinking when water quality is not trusted. Mexican officials believe there may be a negative perception problem preventing trust in local water, despite investments of approximately US$2.8 billion yearly since 1990 to improve water and sanitation. However, studies still indicate the highly polluted and sometimes dangerous nature of local water supplies; more changes will need to be implemented before perceptions will shift towards confidence in the local water supply.

Additional constraints arise from impeded access to local water. For example, 22 percent of households in Latin America must retrieve water by means of public taps, because water is not piped into their homes.[16] Despite these concerns, the proportion of the population with access to an improved source of drinking water has increased from 94 to 97 percent from 1990 to 2015 in urban areas, and from 63 to 84 percent in rural areas.[17] While not every family can turn on a spigot, improvements in community access and water quality are commendable. Data for improved sanitation and water access for 2012 can be found in table 13.1. Even though access has improved, the Intergovernmental Panel on Climate Change (IPCC) estimates that water access will become more exclusionary in the future, as 81 million Latin Americans in 2025 and 178 million in 2055 will experience water shortages.[18] Not surprisingly, the poor suffer most from unhealthy access to

Table 13.1.   Improvements in Sanitation and Water Source

Country	Improved Sanitation Facilities 2015		Improved Water Source 2015	
	(% of population with access) Rural	*(% of population with access)* Urban	*(% of population)* Rural	*(% of population)* Urban
Argentina	98	96	100	99
Belize	88	94	100	99
Bolivia	28	61	76	97
Brazil	52	88	87	100
Chile	91	100	93	100
Colombia	68	85	74	97
Costa Rica	92	95	92	100
Cuba	89	94	90	96
Dominican Republic	76	86	82	85
Ecuador	81	87	76	93
El Salvador	60	82	87	98
Guatemala	49	78	87	98
Haiti	19	34	48	65
Honduras	78	87	84	97
Jamaica	84	80	89	98
Mexico	75	88	92	97
Nicaragua	56	77	69	99
Panama	58	84	89	98
Paraguay	78	96	95	100
Peru	53	83	69	91
Puerto Rico	99	99	n/a	n/a
United States	100	100	98	99
Uruguay	93	97	94	100
Venezuela	70	98	78	95

Source: The World Bank, Data Indicators, http://data.worldbank.org/indicator, 2014.

clean water as they are unable to purchase the purifiers that have become standard in most wealthy homes.

Unfortunately, demand for water is increasing exponentially. Spurred by population growth and urbanization, industrial expansion, and greater irrigation needs, from 1990 to 2004 demands grew by 76 percent.[19] Merrill Lynch predicts global water demand will be 40 percent greater than supply by 2030.[20] There is a distributional element; the wealthy in Latin America consume ten times more water daily than the poor in the region (400 versus 40 liters per person per day).[21] Simultaneously, in cities such as Lima, as much as 30 percent of the drinking water supply is lost, indicating the inefficiency of certain water distribution systems. In contrast to waste, some cities have actually cut overall water consumption. Bogotá has reduced consumption by 20 percent by enforcing controls on water use, and

São Paulo has reduced water losses by controlling illicit water use and by investing in infrastructure.[22] Nonetheless, tensions remain and impeded access to drinkable water is not uncommon.

Even though cities are working to address water access concerns more fully, the reality of sanitation and waste services tells a different story. Generally, the majority of countries in the region still lack facilities to properly treat, dispose of, or recycle hazardous waste. In 2008, 45 percent of rural populations and 14 percent of the urban populations lacked improved sanitation facilities entirely, increasing health risk and rate of contamination.[23] As evidenced in box 13.1, the poorest of the poor often serve as informal recyclers—at great risk to their health. Wastewater treatment rates vary by country, from the immensely low 3 percent and 5 percent in El Salvador and Haiti, respectively, to 80 percent treatment in Chile.[24] Overall, waste management is a pressing concern, and the region must work to manage and monitor collection and processing more efficiently by means of safe disposal sites and the use of proper technological methods.[25]

BOX 13.1. PUBLIC-PRIVATE PARTNERSHIPS FOR SOCIAL GAINS: RECOGNIZING CARTONEROS IN BUENOS AIRES

During the 2001 crisis, which left nearly half the population unemployed, thousands of individuals saw opportunity in the six thousand tons of garbage that was sent to landfills, without formal recycling, every day in the greater metropolitan area of Buenos Aires.[a] Informal garbage and recyclables collectors, known as *cartoneros*, began to sort people's trash for recyclable material, which they would sell to private recycling plants. Because of the many opportunities for profit, collecting became a main source of income for cartoneros.

Cartoneros began to organize themselves into private and efficient cooperatives. Some were even able to buy trucks and open their own centers for sorting recycling. These centers, as in the case with El Ceibo Cartoneros, became homes for many struggling workers, and cooperatives formed strong ties and became families. Recognizing the value of the reliable and efficient services that these private cartonero cooperatives had provided to communities for over a decade, the city government of Buenos Aires in 2013 decided to form a partnership with these groups, assigning each cartonero co-op to a specific part of the city. In return, cartoneros would receive an official government salary of approximately US$700 per month, not including bonuses based on productivity.[b] Additionally, in 2014, in cooperation with these government recognized enterprises, the government would spend approximately US$8.5 million to install garbage and recycling dumpsters along the city and begin a campaign to educate communities about waste and recycling. In this way, the government saw an opportunity to formalize and privatize activity happening organically in the community. Looking forward, this initiative will reduce Buenos Aires' risk caused by improperly disposed of waste and pollution. Dumping has already gone down from six thousand to four thousand tons per day.

---

a. Ellis O'Neill, "Trash Piles Up in Buenos Aires: What's the Plan?," *The Christian Science Monitor* (October 2013), www.csmonitor.com/World/Americas/Latin-America-Monitor/2013/1008/Trash-piles-up-in-Buenos-Aires-What-s-the-plan, accessed June 4, 2014.
    b. Ibid.

Energy and Emissions

Economic growth, especially with its urban concentration, has pressured energy resources in the region. Like water, a good part of this problem is distribution and access given that the region is energy rich. Efficient energy services are vital to raising productivity in the Latin American economy and ensuring a sustainable future. This fact is especially clear when considering that energy consumption in the region has increased by 3 percent per year in the past decade, and that the World Bank estimates that the region's power consumption will double in the next 20 years, requiring an approximate US$430 billion in investment.[26] These demand increases are a result of strong economic activity, population growth, and shifts in the Latin America energy consumption culture, as tens of millions of new consumers move into the middle class. In Mexico alone in the next five years, the size of the middle class is expected to grow by approximately 30 percent. This increase in spending power drives a surge in demand for gasoline and diesel as private vehicles per capita grow with a corresponding decrease in the use of public transportation. In 2002, Mexico had 165 cars per 1,000 inhabitants. In less than a decade, by 2010, this had grown to 275—and is predicted to reach 491 by 2030.

In a vicious circle, climate change pumps up energy demand. Argentina experienced one of its most intense heat waves on record during the summer of 2013, causing a huge increase in the use of air conditioning. Brazil faced a similar situation in February 2014, which pushed electricity demand up to a record high of eighty-six gigawatts. This was a double whammy in a country that depends on dams for 80 percent of its electricity, because most water levels fell below capacity during this time. Some parts of the Iguazu Falls dam even dried up, making the meeting of energy demands even more challenging.[27] Overall, access in the region to electricity has improved steadily, reaching coverage rates in most urban regions of almost 100 percent, even though approximately 34 percent of the people in Latin America are still without electricity.[28] As those connected to the electrical grid acquire more devices to cool, heat, light, and connect, the pressure on the system will increase. The IDB report "Lights On?" forecasts that region-wide energy demand will be 80 percent higher than present levels—with inadequate supply and accompanying increases in emissions.[29]

Some reports, such as those of the World Energy Council, foresee a dim future in which "even in the best case, the growth of energy in [Latin America] will still be insufficient to meet the rising energy demand associated with economic growth."[30] This is also due partly to the fact that access to energy is very unequal. Infrastructure limitations often render safe and clean energy services exclusionary, especially for the urban poor. Many lower income families depend on illegal, possibly dangerous, or heavy polluting sources of energy. Nearly a quarter of the Latin American population, many of whom belong to the urban poor, rely on burning biomass, such as charcoal, wood and plant material, or animal waste, for heat and cooking, leading to high levels of air pollution. Approximately sixty-six million tons of firewood is burned annually for cooking and heating in the region.[31] Pollution reduction might be addressed by using improved cooking stoves, which may also help to lessen the blow of global climate change.[32]

As the fastest growing contributor of carbon emissions in Latin America, transportation is important in its energy equation. The 2012 United Nations Conference on Sustainable Development considered Latin American urban public transport to be generally "inefficient," failing to adequately address the transit needs of a large sector of the population, driving individuals who can afford it to choose private forms of transport.[33] Despite the widespread shortfalls in public transit, the shift to private transportation is not adopted equally across different socioeconomic groups. In cases like Mexico City, private transportation is used 8.6 times more by high-income households than low-income.[34]

It is important to emphasize the environmentally damaging nature of private motor transportation. Vehicle ownership in Latin America is expected to triple in the next 25 years, reaching more than 200 million vehicles by 2050.[35] With the fastest motorization rate in the world—over 4.5 percent a year—those sitting in polluting traffic for hours in urban centers can only expect it to get worse. Although only 18 percent of transportation in Mexico City is private, these trips account for 40.8 percent of CO_2 emissions; public transportation in contrast emits 25.9 percent of emissions and covers 82 percent of all daily transportation.[36] These statistics indicate that the high-income sector that chooses private methods of transportation is contributing substantially more to transportation related carbon emissions than the low-income sector. This underscores the importance of innovation in attractive, efficient, safe, rapid, and reliable forms of public or low-emissions transportation, motivating a reduction in overall transportation emissions.

Some cities have already begun new transportation initiatives. For example, since 2000, approximately 1.4 million passengers of Bogotá, Colombia, benefit daily from a TransMilenio rapid transit system that travels over 84 km of routes.[37] This TransMilenio system has contributed to an emissions reduction rate of 134,000 tons per year, motivating Colombia to begin transportation initiatives in seven other cities.[38] Bogotá's TransMilenio is regarded as the global gold standard for Bus Rapid Transport systems.[39] To facilitate emissions reductions in Buenos Aires, Argentina, a state-funded bicycle-sharing program, "Mejor en Bici," enables commuters to quickly borrow and return bikes in various points throughout the city, without charge. An account is guaranteed to all residents upon the presentation of one's resident identity and proof of address. Although it remains exclusionary for sectors of the population that lack either of these two requirements, and is only available in select districts such as Palermo, the chain is expanding due to popularity, and was already the method of transport for over five thousand individuals daily in April 2013, an immense increase from the one hundred commuters in 2010.[40]

Energy Mix

Despite innovation, energy for transportation nevertheless creates concern due to dependence on nonrenewable sources, such as petroleum. Latin America is currently home to approximately 10 percent of the world's total oil reserves and 9 percent of the world's oil-refining capacity, providing it with the second largest potential in the oil economy outside of the Middle East. Additionally, production of crude oil and liquefied natural gas, dominated primarily by Venezuela, Mexico, Ecuador, Bolivia, and Brazil, is estimated to increase from 9.4 million barrels/day in 2003 to 12 million barrels/day in 2030.[41] This dominance enables countries such as Venezuela to exert geopolitical influence and extract more rents from petroleum resources.[42] However, these profits and this power benefit only a select sector of the population, are inaccessible to large shares of the population, and are being depleted at unprecedented rates.

Generally, diesel engine plants, conventional steam, or gas turbine power plants do most power generation in Latin America, but the region also has immense potential in developing hydroelectric projects. Yet strong opposition from environmental, civil society, and indigenous groups inhibits many of these developments from being realized. Brazil and Chile have recently stalled the building of hydro-powered dams in the face of opposition and protests, due to human rights and environmental concerns. Consequentially, many Latin American economies are being driven to look elsewhere to meet their energy needs, such as by solar energy, wind, or biofuels. They are also setting goals to reduce consumption and emissions. Mexico aims to generate 35 percent of its electricity by means of renewable resources by 2024, according to its Law for the Use of Renewable Energies and Financing of Energy Transition. However, meeting this goal will be an incredible challenge, because Mexico has invested only 1 percent of total global investment in renewable energy, making it the lowest invested G20 country, demonstrating the complication of bridging the gap between theory and practice.[43] Chile is a regional leader in solar, aiming to have renewables provide 20 percent of its energy by 2025. Energy is a complicated sector. Large-scale provision of energy confronts problems in access in financing, regulatory hurdles, lack of interest in long-term consumer contracts, and variability in access to resources such as sun, wind, and water. Despite these difficulties, solar also has hidden benefits in a geography such as that in Chile with a large number of remote areas. In these isolated geographies, off-grid provision can be both environmentally and economically sustainable.[44]

Effects of Climate Change

Even in the face of shortfalls and inefficiencies, emissions in Latin America and the Caribbean make up only 3.9 percent of total global emissions of carbon dioxide, in comparison to the 23.8 percent produced by the United States.[45] Still, as shown in table 13.2, the rate of emissions per capita varies immensely by country, from 6.1 metric tons in Venezuela to 0.8 metric tons in Nicaragua and Paraguay. Despite their relatively low rate of contribution to global emissions, Latin America is expected to suffer disproportionately from global climate change's effects.

Climate change is predicted to bring radical changes to Latin America, with effects varying by subregion and scale. Latin America is highly vulnerable given its geography, climate, and socioeconomic condition as its sensitive natural assets. Four recognized hotspots include the mountain ecosystem in the Andes, bleaching and potential collapse of the Meso American coral reef, the wetlands and coastal system in the Gulf of Mexico, and the forest die-back in the Amazon. The IPCC estimates

Table 13.2. Energy and Emissions

Country	Access to Electricity 2012 (% of population)	CO_2 Emissions 2013 (kt)	CO_2 Emissions 2013 (metric tons per capita)	Methane Emissions 2012 (kt of CO_2 equivalent)	Electric Power Consumption 2013 (kWh per capita)	Energy Use 2013 (kg of oil equivalent per capita)	Fossil Fuels 2013 (% of total)
Argentina	99.8	189,819	4.5	88,476	3,093	1,895	88.9
Bolivia	90.5	19,703	1.9	23,231	705	786	85.1
Brazil	99.5	503,677	2.5	477,077	2,529	1,438	58.0
Chile	99.6	83,171	4.7	18,381	3,879	2,201	68.6
Colombia	97.0	89,625	1.9	67,979	1,177	669	75.8
Costa Rica	99.5	7,616	1.6	2,315	1,955	1,029	49.0
Cuba	100.0	39,340	3.5	8,560	1,425	1,031	87.3
Dominican Republic	98.0	22,072	2.1	6,861	1,517	731	86.4
Ecuador	97.2	43,527	2.8	15,786	1,333	980	89.8
El Salvador	93.7	6,359	1.0	3,032	915	693	45.8
Guatemala	78.5	13,597	0.9	6,877	555	768	32.7
Honduras	82.2	9,065	1.2	5,844	721	662	51.4
Nicaragua	77.9	4,569	0.8	6,492	598	595	39.6
Panama	90.9	10,363	2.7	3,378	2,038	1,057	75.4
Paraguay	98.2	4,972	0.8	16,246	1,473	764	33.6
Peru	91.2	57,154	1.9	19,321	1,270	708	76.5
Uruguay	99.5	7,603	2.2	19,549	2,985	1,351	52.9
Venezuela	100.0	185,532	6.1	58,199	3,245	2,271	88.4

Source: The World Bank, Data Indicators, http://data.worldbank.org/indicator, 2014, Climate Change in Latin America.

that related to warming alone, Latin America will experience a general increase in temperature of 2–6 °C. This temperature increase is foreseen to melt the lower-altitude glaciers in the Cordillera in the next decade, reducing water for agriculture and consumption in certain communities, signaling an increase in food prices.[46] Coastal cities had already experienced a rise in sea level of 2mm per year during the twentieth century, and many regions will face flooding and increased threat of storm damage in the future. Those impacted by extreme weather have already increased substantially, costing Latin America over US$40 billion in the past decade.

With 30 percent of its population in agriculture, Central America is one of the most exposed areas. Floods, hurricanes, landslides, and mudslides have increased approximately 7 percent a year since the 1970s. The projections with a temperature increase are dire: a 50 percent decline in the Caribbean fish catch; a 30 percent decline in cassava, bananas, sweet potatoes, and tomatoes by 2050; as well as more bleaching of coral reefs—perhaps leading to the collapse of the Mesoamerican coral reef home of hundreds of fish species, marine turtles, and sharks.[47] The United Nations Conference on Sustainable Development suggests that agricultural productivity might fall up to 50 percent by 2100 due to climate change consequences including changes in temperature, rainfall, carbon dioxide levels, pests, and diseases. Nevertheless, these estimates vary by region, indicating an 18 and 85 percent loss in agricultural production in Brazil and Mexico, respectively, which will lead to sharp increases in rural poverty, but a 5 percent increase in productivity in Argentina.[48] Precipitation is likely to fall between 7 and 22 percent in the Central American region and 22 percent in Brazil, and increase 25 percent in South East South America. Rising sea levels increase beach erosion, storm tides, impair freshwater supplies, leave smaller harvests from shorter seasons and drought, and frequently flood coastal settlements and damage the tourism industry.

Latin America is a hotspot for extreme weather. These disasters, including flooding, landslides, tropical storms such as hurricanes, droughts, heat waves, and earthquakes, have led to a devastating 240,000 extreme weather deaths in Latin America from 2005 to 2012.[49] The rate and distribution of fatalities and loss is subject not only to the severity of the extreme weather conditions. Weak infrastructure and socioeconomic status play a strong role, causing poor households to shoulder a disproportionate amount of the burden. Shoddy informal housing structures and poor investment in infrastructure, such as lack of storm drainage or solid waste disposal in informal housing sectors, can worsen flooding, lead to collapse or destruction of property, landslides, or loss of life, and increase the chances of illness and death by waterborne diseases such as diarrhea, cholera, typhoid, and meningitis. Malaria- and dengue-carrying mosquitoes can also breed in stagnant water, creating additional health concerns.[50] Flooding is especially concerning in the Paraguay River basin where population has grown rapidly, threatening the displacement of approximately one hundred thousand individuals.[51] As World Bank President Jim Kim has sagely noted, "We will never end poverty if we don't tackle climate change." It is clear that Latin America bears a larger cost from climate change as compared to its contribution in causing it. This also leads to limited options for regional mitigation as opposed to adaptation.

Without strong global action, there are limits to what the region can do to reduce emissions; constrained policy dollars are perhaps better targeted at adaptation measures. More on this shortly.

Biodiversity, Agriculture, and Degradation

In addition to urban challenges, climate change also has an immense impact on the region's agriculture, forestry, aquaculture, and overall biodiversity. Of the world's ten most biodiverse countries, five are in Latin America: Brazil, Colombia, Ecuador, Peru, and Mexico. Latin America is currently the most ecologically diverse region in the world, home to as much as 50 percent of the world's flora and fauna, the largest barrier reef in the Western Hemisphere, six megadiverse countries, and the most megadiverse area on the planet: the Amazon. This biodiversity is vital to the livelihood of communities. It possesses a great deal of economic, cultural, and social value and, on a global scale, helps to mitigate the effects of climate change.[52] The region has been dubbed a biodiversity superpower.[53]

Unfortunately, despite the value of the Latin American ecosystem, the region is experiencing devastating levels of environmental degradation. The first form of degradation is manifested in the form of deforestation. Deforestation has destroyed 45 percent of Mexico's and 85 percent of Paraguay's original forests since 1950.[54] In cases such as Paraguay, this lack of land protection is often spurred by governmental economic incentives to cooperate with large agribusinesses that clear lands in order to make way for soy or cattle. The Paraguayan government of Horatio Cartes continued the environmental pass given to agribusiness by passing Decree No. 453 of the Environmental Impact Evaluation in January 2014. This decree is in clear violation of the "Zero Deforestation Law" that prohibits deforestation in the eastern region of the country.[55] Decree 453 symbolically represents the state's alliance with agribusinesses, because it relieves landowners of the requirement to provide environmental impact reports for parcels less than five hundred hectares in the eastern region, and two thousand hectares in the western part of El Chaco. Environmentalists fear this will enable unregulated deforestation, completely nullifying the Zero Deforestation Law.

The consequences of this decree could be particularly severe, because deforestation in El Chaco is the highest rate in the world. Approximately 2,000 hectares are deforested per day, and 540,000 hectares were bulldozed in 2013.[56] Corruption and illegal logging can play a large role in deforestation. For example, the World Bank estimates that 80 percent of Peru's logging exports are harvested illegally with the help of bribery and counterfeit documentation.[57] However, the story of forestry is not completely grim. As table 13.3 demonstrates, some countries such as Chile and Cuba have increased forest as a percent of total land area in the past two decades by means of reforestation efforts, providing hope for the forestry and conservation dilemma.

Environmental degradation can also be the consequence of irresponsible practices in agriculture and aquaculture. Single crop farming exhausts the soil and leads to a reduction in crop yields, heavy pesticide use causes chemical contamination,

Table 13.3.   Forest as a Percent of Total Land by Decade

Country	1991	2001	2011
Argentina	12.6	11.5	10.7
Belize	69.1	64.9	60.6
Bolivia	57.7	55.2	52.5
Brazil	67.6	64.2	61.2
Chile	20.6	21.4	21.9
Colombia	56.3	55.3	54.4
Costa Rica	49.8	47.0	51.5
Cuba	19.5	23.2	27.3
Dominican Republic	40.8	40.8	40.8
Ecuador	49.2	46.9	38.9
El Salvador	18.0	15.8	13.6
Guatemala	43.8	38.8	33.6
Haiti	4.2	3.9	3.6
Honduras	71.2	56.1	45.3
Jamaica	31.8	31.4	31.1
Mexico	36.0	34.2	33.3
Nicaragua	36.9	31.1	25.3
Panama	50.4	45.2	43.6
Paraguay	52.8	48.3	43.8
Peru	54.7	54.0	53.0
Puerto Rico	34.4	53.3	63.2
United States	32.4	32.8	33.3
Uruguay	5.5	8.2	10.2
Venezuela	58.7	55.4	52.1

Source: The World Bank, Data Indicators, http://data.worldbank.org/indicator, 2014.

and livestock overgrazing reduces biodiversity. Similarly, aquaculture has grown at three times the world rate recently, providing 15 to 30 percent of the world supply of fish.[58] This expansion has caused high levels of degradation, due to actions such as the cutting of mangrove forests to open the area for shrimp ponds. This is particularly alarming, because mangroves act as barriers against extreme weather such as tsunamis.[59] Furthermore, 30 percent of Caribbean coral reefs have been destroyed or are at serious risk. It is estimated that, if current trends continue, an additional 20 percent will be lost in the next couple of decades.[60] The prevalence of these practices underscores the need for greater regulation and adherence to environmental laws regarding sound agricultural practices. Sharing of technology, know-how, and other resources to increase the technical capacity and knowledge base in developing regions will be vital to encouraging a sustainable agricultural environment.

Overall, it is important to emphasize that both the poor and nonpoor are responsible for environmental degradation. The poor may rely on clearing forests for income, or lack the means to invest in the environment by adopting environmentally sustainable practices with resource and financial demands. The case of Amazonian deforestation to pave the way for the Brazilian BR 163 highway provides an example of a situation in which the poor chose to invest in their immediate economic needs as opposed to environmental sustainability, demonstrating the importance of balancing growth and conservation. But environmental costs are glaring—so visible that one can see the road from the moon as a line of fires.[61] The BR 163 connects farms of Southern Brazil to overseas markets, providing farmers with greater opportunities for income and reducing travel costs substantially.[62] As a result, even though construction of the highway would undoubtedly contribute to environmental degradation in the region, the local population saw the project as necessary to promote their immediate and long-term economic needs. Dams to address water availability have also flooded hectares of rainforest; in the case of the Balbina Dam the flooded area is larger than the city of Buenos Aires.[63] Moving forward, it is important to keep in mind that both the poor and nonpoor need greater incentives to invest in the environment, whether through institutional or market-based initiatives.

This section characterized Latin America's paramount environmental challenges as urbanization, health, water, access to services, energy and emissions, climate change, and biodiversity degradation. Before turning to a possible policy mix, let's consider the nature of the environment as an economic good—why it is that sound environmental policy is both so necessary as well as so elusive.

THE ECONOMIC NATURE OF THE ENVIRONMENTAL PROBLEM IN LATIN AMERICA

The environment isn't like any other sector. Environmental policy is especially complex as it must take into account the notion of the environment as a global public good. We recall two dimensions of a public good: non-rival and non-excludable. When a good is classified as rival—such as the family popcorn bucket—when one person consumes there is less left for others. One nation's enjoyment of clean air does not come at the expense of another—hence it is a non-rival good. Obviously, one nation polluting the air or water creates negative externalities for others. If I can prevent or exclude one person from consuming the popcorn, I would create a willingness to pay or bargain for access to the goodie bucket. But if I am unable to exclude, free-riding behavior will likely ensue, where parties will continue to consume without restraint. The problem, of course, is exacerbated when the good in question is nonrenewable. In this situation, consumption by the present generation will make future generations less well-off. We also know that the consumption of a good can create negative externalities today—pollution—that may be imposed on society rather than cleaned up by the beneficiary. The environmental challenge becomes even more complicated when ecosystems extend over borders: what happens in one country spills over to another. Who then is responsible for promoting a clean environment?

Not all aspects of environmental management adhere strictly to the definition of a global public good. One of course can restrict access to a forest or a waterway; we also know that cutting down a tree takes away from the ability of another logger to bring it to market or a naturalist to enjoy unspoiled beauty. But the thorny aspects of the environment as a global public good raise questions about who pays for cleanup. Latin America's characteristic inequality deepens the complexity. The poor tend to suffer the most health consequences from exposure to dirty air and water; the wealthy may object to congestion and polluted beaches. Whose needs should be met and at what price? This prioritization process is of course essentially political. Sadly, governments have largely failed to address these market failures, compounding environmental damage.

One way to formalize this problem is through an enumeration of the costs of pollution versus cleanup. As shown in figure 13.2, we label the addition to social damages as pollution increases the **marginal social damage** curve (MSD). This represents the increase in health costs, the losses from depreciating biodiversity, and the general loss of well-being from living in an unsustainable environment. As pollution increases, no surprise, so does the MSD. Cleanup is captured by the **marginal abatement cost** (MAC) function. The slope of this curve suggests that when there is a lot of pollution (the right-hand side of the graph), there is much "low-hanging fruit" or easy steps to begin cleanup. When a society has very low pollution, cleaning up the last "stubborn" elements are likely to be more expensive, leading to higher marginal abatement costs. We can, awkwardly to some, label the intersection of the MSD and MAC as the point of "optimal pollution." It is optimal in the sense that the costs to clean up are equal to the social benefits (or avoiding the damage) of living in a polluted environment. The awkward element of course is when the optimal level for a given location may not coincide with the carrying capacity of an ecosystem into the future—or when the optimal level on one side of a border is untenable to citizens on the other side. A solution to addressing this mismatch of the optimal point with sustainability is to introduce technologies that might lower the cost of abatement or cleanup; we can graphically see this with the dotted line MAC_2. And if we are considering an aspect of environmental management such as climate change, we can think creatively about how people living in a wealthier part of the globe might have a willingness to pay for technologies and practices in a poorer region for the greater environmental good. But jumping to policy is getting ahead of our story. Let's first turn to understand the complex dimensions of sustainable environmental policy in Latin America.

The nature of environmental challenges in Latin America can lead us to think in terms of who is responsible for financing and facilitating sustainable environmental practices in Latin America. From a national perspective, some environmental challenges are the accompaniments of modernization—the externalities of pollution, congestion, and contamination that take place with economic growth. These negative externalities are often worse in the developing world because strong institutions to regulate and manage growth have not developed. Even when laws are on the books, governments often do not have the capacity for monitoring and enforcement—and powerful elites can subvert even the best intentions. Nonetheless, if environmental degradation is taking place as a result of market-based transactions, it is possible to introduce offsetting market mechanisms to force agents to internalize the social costs of production. If cars and dirty energy are central to the problem, user taxes can help. With a polluter pays principle, those driving cars or using inefficient energy sources can be assessed taxes that in turn are dedicated

Figure 13.2.   Optimal Pollution

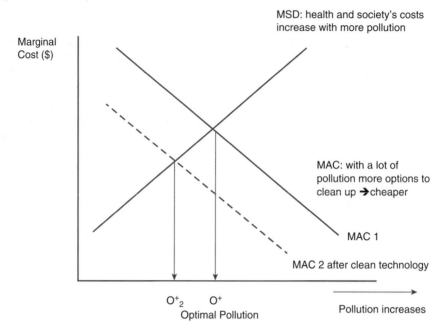

to social cleanup. Corporations, either voluntarily or through legal incentives, can provide resources through social responsibility practices.

But the complexity of the environmental problem in Latin America extends beyond what is commonly confronted in wealthier nations. With inadequate infrastructure and a lack of assets, poor people become agents of pollution. Urban pollution is intricately tied to the lack of public infrastructure for waste and water removal, especially for those in informal settlements. Rural deforestation is often a result of survival strategies in resource poor regions. In this sense, improving the environment is a central component of poverty reduction. States are working to address these basic infrastructure gaps—but acting alone is not enough when the externalities spill across borders. The degradation of Latin America's rich environmental resources creates global costs in terms of biodiversity and climate change mitigation. Encouraging Latin nations to adopt clean technologies, employ renewable energy, and avoid deforestation can contribute to international efforts to slow climate change. Returning back to the MAC curve above, it doesn't matter whether cleanup takes place in San José, Costa Rica, or San Jose, California—but if it is cheaper in Costa Rica, this makes most sense to stretch environmental investments. Avoiding damages and encouraging cheap abatement provide the urgent motivation for global cost-sharing in addressing this complex problem.

The environment is a critical point of entry to address the moral imperative of global development. Institutions such as the **Global Environmental Facility (GEF)** embedded within the World Bank work to encourage biodiversity conservation and sustainable use of resources, accelerate climate change mitigation, and protect water systems. The facility works as a co-financing mechanism alongside national partners to provide capital, information, technology, and institutional best practices to jump-start global sustainability.[64] No country can address its environmental agenda alone; global institutions can facilitate the achievement of sustainability goals. Some of the most important programs under the GEF circle back to the fundamentals of addressing poverty and asset deprivation as a cause of environmental damage.

EXPANDING OPPORTUNITIES: STATE AND MULTILATERAL INVESTMENTS IN SUSTAINABILITY

Environmental policy requires a multi-sectoral, multi stakeholder approach. In Latin America, one might break down environmental policies into those investments improving well-being for citizens today as well as those promoting sustainability, including global concerns, for the future. Investments today are critical in managing the environmental externalities of growth and the miseries of poverty. Governments across the region are struggling with the most cost-effective means of making their burgeoning cities livable, promoting clean air and water and introducing transportation and mobility systems that are sane and socially inclusive. Policy measures must traverse sectoral divides, embracing ministries of industry and agriculture, to promote environmental governance that is fair, transparent, and enforceable. Environmental policy at its core must be pro-poor, elevating the needs of its least well-off citizens to promote social well-being. But as the rich wield power, policy must be attentive to politics.

Strong environmental policy is premised on the ability to manage trade-offs and minimize costs to stakeholders. It is about the ability to balance the interests of agricultural and mining exporters with small-holders eking a living from depleted soil. It is about hard choices in what will be funded: new sanitation systems or renovated schools and hospitals? And it is about who pays. How can revenue be raised to promote sustainable development? The characteristic of the environment as a global public good presents opportunities in Latin America to reduce the tough trade-offs. The region, with its rich biodiversity and standing forests, can be seen as a powerful partner in addressing climate change. Let's turn to some of these options for sustainable development in the region.

Alternative Energy Investment and Innovation

Many states, institutions, and businesses are increasingly motivated to invest in and develop alternative energy systems in Latin America, due to growing market opportunities. The danger of dependence on nonrenewable resources, with their environmentally degrading and finite nature, is becoming a greater and more immediate concern, rapidly augmenting demand for alternatives. The emphasis on biofuels is particularly strong, although the region is also focusing on the development of solar, wind, and hydropower. Governments have even implemented laws, regulations, and incentives for biofuel production. In 2008, Brazil implemented legislation that required a blend of at least 2 percent biodiesel with diesel oil, and Argentina followed this example in 2010 by requiring a mandatory blend of 5 percent biodiesel with diesel oil.[65]

Alternative energy facilities, besides providing a substitute for nonrenewable resources, produce many additional positive externalities in the surrounding community. Alternative energy is incredibly labor intensive and creates numerous employment opportunities for both skilled and nonskilled workers in regions that might have otherwise lacked adequate and diverse formal employment options.

Although alternative energy has the potential to reduce dangerous emissions and create positive environmental and social externalities, its adoption is also very controversial. If the use of alternative energy is not responsible and strategic, incredibly harmful side effects will result. In fact, the negative externalities of the ethanol industry are already readily apparent. The quantity of corn required to produce ethanol generates shocks throughout the food system, spurring not only a rise in corn prices, but also in the prices of other grains that act as corn substitutes, such as wheat and rice.[66] In 2006, the price of tortilla flour in Mexico doubled, thanks to a doubling in US corn prices. This facilitated an immense crisis throughout Mexico, especially for Mexico's 107 million poor, who depend on tortillas as a staple.[67] Farmers who devote less and less space and time to planting other grains are mostly responsible for these increases, preferring to dedicate more land to lucrative corn production. In order to produce enough ethanol to fill a twenty-five gallon tank, over 450 pounds of corn, enough calories to feed a person for a year, must be processed, demonstrating why farm labor's focus on fuel, rather than food production, has particularly dangerous implications for global food security.[68] Biofuels have tied oil and food prices together, which will continue to force staple food prices to rise steadily.

Furthermore, irresponsible alternative production can lead to environmental devastation. Often it is more profitable for producers to resort to deforestation in order to acquire land for biofuels, and they may lack the proper incentives to choose a sustainable alternative. The release of carbon dioxide from such deforestation could cancel out any greenhouse gas benefits produced by the biofuels, proving the investment to be environmentally counterproductive.[69] Therefore, enforcement of environmental accountability in the alternative energy cycle is necessary, considering not just the production stage, but also the entire life cycle of production, transformation, and combustion.[70]

ADAPTATION, MITIGATION, AND RISK MANAGEMENT

The cost and severity of the impact of future shocks resulting from environmental degradation and climate change will depend on a country's capacity to reduce its vulnerability and increase its risk-management abilities. Latin American economies must consider the best adaptation and mitigation approaches to confront environmental challenges and reduce risk. Adaptation refers to risk-management actions that anticipate or compensate for the consequences of climate change and environmental degradation, whereas mitigation encompasses policies to lower emissions or diminish activity that contributes to climate change and degradation to lessen future impact.[71] Because Latin America contributes relatively little to global emissions, but will suffer intensely from the negative externalities, policymakers often suggest that the region focus primarily on adaptation as opposed to mitigation. But with the region's enormous capacity to contribute to abatement at a low cost, 94 percent of climate change financial resources in the region are invested in mitigation actions.[72]

Risk management is especially important to consider in urban contexts because 80 percent of disaster-related losses occur in cities. It is cost effective as it is approximately four times more expensive to reconstruct and repair damaged infrastructure than to implement risk reduction initiatives that could prevent damage from occurring.[73] While spending at both the national and multilateral level is currently directed at humanitarian aid after a disaster, it is more cost-effective to build resilience to prevent loss of life and property. The World Bank developed an Urban Risk Assessment (URA), integrating climate change and disaster risk management into urban planning to balance trade-offs among risk reduction, urban development, and poverty reduction.[74] For example, planners should consider hazard zones to better determine where development should or should not be allowed. This is crucial in preventing the creation of new housing, both formal and informal, in high-risk areas.[75]

Throughout Latin America, many impressive adaptation and mitigation strategies are being implemented. According to the World Bank, good programing to address climate change includes high-level coordination across multiple sectors, assessing vulnerability to climate risks and hazards, linking and leveraging investments, stakeholder engagement, learning and exchange, a role for the private sector and ownership in regional programs.[76] Over 114 million people in the region benefit from some sort of social protection **adaptation** program to boost the resilience of their communities, ideally reducing the future need for post-disaster humanitarian aid.[77] Sustainable and inclusive adaptation should focus on integrating settlement, infrastructure, equipment, and secure housing programs into poverty-reduction strategies with elements of prevention criteria and disaster control.[78] Policies might include water efficiency and food security measures, and incentives to promote resilience and climate-smart agriculture; they should be pro-poor as risks fall disproportionately on those without access to assets. It is estimated to cost 0.5 percent of the region's current GDP; these costs could be offset by taxes on carbon content of imports. The World Bank's Climate Investment Fund and other multilaterals can co-finance investments. For example, in Peru, an International Fund for Agricultural Development (IFAD) program is helping local communities to diversify their livelihoods, and in Nicaragua, coffee farmers are being trained in new production techniques to adapt to climate risks.[79] Coffee value chains create opportunities to promote high-quality beans and increased production for niche markets while also introducing preventative measures to anticipate agricultural changes and transition to low-emission economies.

Mitigation efforts are more prevalent and popular. They include initiatives such as Brazil's national greenhouse gas reduction target of 36 percent by 2020, which motivated a 39 percent decrease in greenhouse gas emissions between 2005 and 2010, and Ecuador's Yasuní-ITT initiative. This compensates landowners for untapped oil deposits in order to leave the resources untouched while protecting national parks and promoting renewable energy.[80] Embracing the importance of both adaptation and mitigation as part of a regional plan for disaster and risk management, all governments in the region have endorsed the Hyogo Framework for Action, the first international agreement that outlines the efforts necessary to strengthen institutional and legal capacity in order to coordinate and implement disaster risk reduction actions and adaptation to climate change.[81]

Despite the increase in these efforts, it is important to emphasize that many regions confront shortfalls in infrastructure and energy efficiency that act as obstacles to reducing risk.[82] Fragmentation in local governance and weak **institutional capacity** limit the delivery of basic services. Policies that appear feasible on paper fail in practice with weak monitoring, enforcement, or an insufficient understanding of stakeholder needs. Some find it hard to make the political case to invest in a threat that is not yet tangible or immediately visible—especially when the society has such striking needs in feeding and education the population.[83] As a result, when disaster does strike, often NGOs and community organizations, such as Red Cross, Oxfam, and Save the Children, have been responsible for crisis service delivery and emergency relief in the absence of strong formal institutions.[84] Paradoxically, the white knights of NGOs can weaken local democracy as citizens perceive their presence as evidence of weak and incapable local government. Multilateral institutions and regional forums can help convince governments to adopt a precautionary stance, strengthen institutional capacity, and cooperate with communities to determine case-specific risks and needs. For example, Condesan is an Andean regional organization that is working to overcome poverty through sustainable practices. It is affiliated with CAN (the Andean Community), regional universities such the Ecuadorean Polytechnic University, and NGOs including Conservation International. It has engaged in university partnerships such as with the University of Albany and the University of Seattle to develop sustainable forestry practices; through monitoring, dialogue, and knowledge creation, it is expanding its knowledge base in collaboration with residents.[85]

Insufficient funding for risk reduction and limited access to technology impedes the implementation of large-scale city-wide infrastructure investments, such as building a levee for flood protection, that could strengthen regions in the face of extreme weather. The funding gap increases dependence on international donors and multilateral development banks. In the absence of large-scale projects, small-scale investments in drainage, roads, health care services, and basic infrastructure are vital to building the resilience of communities, especially the urban poor. Overall, it is important to remember that risk reduction costs do not involve only physical investments, such as urban infrastructure and basic services, but also include investments in information systems, safety nets, and capacity building. Looking forward, public institutions might cooperate with the private sector, by means of public-private partnerships to address shortfalls in infrastructure and efficiency.

Expanding Opportunities: Market-Based Policy Initiatives

Investment by states, multilateral organizations, and NGOs are important to promote sustainability. But they are not enough. Environmental change is about altering people's incentives and behaviors. Some of these practices might be changed by rules (if enforceable), new technologies, or enhanced infrastructure, but this is not likely to be enough. **Market-based initiatives (MBIs)** are frequently considered as a complement to regulatory and state investment programs, incorporating a variety of strategies to engage different stakeholders and address diverse issues.

Market-based initiatives provide incentives to choose environmentally sustainable behavior. If greed is fomenting environmental degradation, what happens if it becomes more profitable to produce sustainability? If illegal logging is contributing to deforestation and lax laws have done little to restrict its growth, can loggers be paid more to harvest forests sustainably and engage in self-policing conservation behaviors? Market-based mechanisms can involve payments for environmental services, tax incentives, or other forms of compensation between parties.

For example, environmental income might be earned from the sale of carbon credits, payments by downstream users for conservation by upstream users of watersheds, rewards to forest landholders for conservation services, and the fares of ecotourists for participating in scenic and cultural beauty. The Clean Development Mechanism (CDM) is one of such market-based initiatives in which Annex 1 countries (those countries with emissions-reductions obligations under the Kyoto Protocol on Climate Change) can implement emissions reducing projects in non-Annex 1 countries (developing countries with no commitments under Kyoto) and gain Certified Emissions Reductions (CERs) for the cut in emissions that is achieved as a result of the project. The future of the CDM is a bit murky as countries look toward honoring promises under the Paris Agreement, but the flexibility of the mechanism to address climate change at its lowest cost point has attracted attention.[86]

Markets for environmental products and services are limited, because they may take time to develop credibility. Think about the conceptual parallels between a stock market and a market for carbon credits. In setting up the Brazilian Carbon Market, the two partners—the Brazilian Mercantile and Futures Exchange and the Brazilian Ministry of Development, Industry and Foreign Trade—need to construct the same kind of confidence-building elements that you can expect from an efficient stock exchange. That is, you aren't likely to plunk down cash for stock on someone's word. Instead, you would like a certified accounting of a business's track record and some assurance that there will be sufficient liquidity in the market should your portfolio preferences change. You would only invest in a market with clear and transparent rules to prevent insider trading and other corrupt practices. Carbon markets also need to develop these characteristics of certification, liquidity, and credibility—and this takes time. The question of credibility is central to the debate on avoided deforestation. Employing carbon mitigation strategies by paying agents not to log or cut timber for farming raises the challenge of guaranteeing that **additionality** as well as **verification** exist. That is, can it be shown that the trees wouldn't be left standing in any case, and how do you know if the forest remains intact for the specified period of time? Other caveats exist. Some market-based initiatives don't work as well with the poor due to informal employment, insecure property and resource tenure, high **transaction costs** related to working with myriad small service providers as opposed to several large interests, and little voice of the poor and marginalized in formation of the rules for a market based initiative. One size does not fit all in the case of market-based initiatives.

Despite these limitations, market-based initiatives hold promise. **Payments for Environmental Services (PES)** have been the focus of many recent studies in the region, attracting a great deal of attention for their role in sustainability efforts. The most popular definition of PES, crafted by Sven Wunder, explains PES as a "voluntary transaction where a well-defined environmental service is being 'bought' by an environmental service buyer from an environmental services provider, if and only if the provider secures environmental service provision."[87] Thus, PES embraces the notion that those who benefit from environmental services should pay for them and those that generate the services should be compensated for their efforts in providing them.[88] In other words, by pricing environmental services, PES acknowledges that environmental problems are linked to human incentives and capacity to make particular choices. In the same way, it accepts that if incentives are not changed, economic agents will focus on short-term direct returns and outlays, as opposed to the long-term social benefits and externalities.[89] Overall, PES initiatives are designed with the intent to function as "true markets" with prices based on supply and demand, with tangible buyers and sellers, and payments dependent on performance-based contracts. Box 13.2 provides an example of payment for environmental services in Mexico.

Payments tend to be directed at owners of low-productivity land; landowners of high-productivity land are less likely to participate in PES, because their opportunity cost is much greater. Most PES cases are user-financed, meaning the payments to service providers are dependent on service users, yet there are a variety of cases of government-funded PES initiatives, such as Costa Rica's 1997 PSA program, Brazil's 2008 *Bolsa Floresta,* Ecuador's 2008 *Socio Bosque*, and Mexico's 2003 PSA-H Program. Costa Rica is an eclectic mix of economics and regulatory measures, putting one million hectares under PES since 1997. Programs are contract based, favoring indigenous actors and areas with low socioeconomic status and smallholders with less than fifty hectares of property.[90] A key consideration to designing PES is equity: Who will benefit? Who might be negatively impacted?

Socio Bosque was developed by the Ecuadorian government in partnership with Conservation International to address what was at the time the highest deforestation rate in South America driven by agricultural expansion, illegal logging, and illegal mining. To address the simple fact that people will cut down trees if it generates benefit for them, the Ecuadorian PES pays landholders (individuals or communities) between US$30 per hectare per year up to fifty hectares, US$20 for the next fifty hectares, and US$10 for any additional hectares to conserve their land. Socio Bosque has signed nearly three thousand agreements protecting 1.4 million hectares and provided benefits to nearly two hundred thousand people.[91]

Drawbacks: Although PES can have an impact on poverty alleviation, such as the Mexican case, it can be dangerous to fall into the trap of seeing PES as primarily as a tool to achieve pro-poor social goals while ignoring its economic dimensions.

Box 13.2.   PES in Mexico: Can Market-Based Initiatives Embrace Social Goals?

In 2003, the Mexican state, under the administration of the Mexican National Forestry Commission (CONAFOR), implemented a national PES program, PSA-H, that contracted with rural landholders in zones of water scarcity and upstream from urban centers to conserve forest for hydrological services, carbon sequestration, biodiversity conservation, and improvement of agroforestry systems.[a] In 2006, the program joined with a second initiative, PSA-CABSA, which paid for biodiversity conservation through habitat restoration, creating the larger Proárbol program. As a part of this program, between 2003 and 2011, approximately US$490 million was distributed to participants in order to protect 5.2 percent of Mexico's total forest cover. Rather than merely creating markets, this PES program acts as a poverty reduction tool that targets marginalized communities by limiting participants to those who work four thousand hectares or less. Already between 2003 and 2005, approximately 78 percent of participants lived in municipalities with high or very high degrees of marginalization, and this factor was given a higher priority than environmental criteria. In fact, 61 percent of parcels were considered to have a low risk of deforestation, and 79 percent were in areas without problems of water scarcity.[b]

The lack of linkages between funding and the market for environmental services has attracted World Bank criticism, because it questions whether the programs have resulted in any additionality. This means that there has been little proof in the case of Mexican PES that landholders would have chosen to deforest their lands without the PES incentives. The World Bank promotes a PES model that focuses on generating valuable ecosystem services, and is therefore skeptical of deviation from the original project design in order to specifically address the needs of marginalized communities, rather than protect especially threatened areas. Nevertheless, 94 percent of Mexican PES participants chose to reinvest a large portion of their payments into forest management activities, regardless of whether they had been obligated to do so in their contract or not. So, even though much of the land might not have been under an immense degradation threat, payments encouraged more sustainable behavior and formed a positive relationship between consumers and providers of services, proving that working to find a balance between environment and equity is not impossible. One participant explained, "It is not just about sales and monetary gains, it is a new form of relationship: between the city and the countryside; industries and campesinos; developed countries and undeveloped countries; regions that are producers of waste and those that are producers of oxygen."[c]

---

a. Shapiro-Garza. "Contesting the Market-Based Nature."
b. C. Muñoz Piña, M. Rivera, A. Cisneros, and H. García, "Retos de la focalización del Programa de Pago por los Servicios Ambientales en México," *Revista Espanola de Estdios Agrosociales y Pesqueros*, 228(1) (2011): 87–113.
c. Shapiro-Garza, "Contesting the Market-Based Nature."

It is important to remember that PES is ultimately a market-based strategy. Its programs will not be sustainable unless service customers are satisfied with the product that they are paying for. Prioritizing poverty reduction over generating services might therefore inhibit the process in which customers receive their products, rendering the program less effective.

It is also important in evaluating the potential of payment for environmental services that the full **opportunity costs** of alternative activities be calculated. Although market-based mechanisms are appealing in that agreements are voluntary, and we can assume that people largely enter into contracts because they believe that doing so is good for them, sometimes asymmetries of information or power might lead to bad decisions. For example, if land values increase due to payments for environmental services, the poor will be pushed off the land by higher bidders. PES can also be seen as a commodification of the environment; some environmentalists object to the marketization of services that should be provided in the public domain. Therefore, launching a PES scheme raises a series of implementation issues. First, if a market-based mechanism is to be employed, a careful market analysis is in order. Is the market for the environmental services local or global in scope? Are buyers willing to pay enough to compensate providers for alternative uses of natural resources? Is the market reasonably efficient?

REDD: Reducing Emissions from Deforestation and Forest Degradation

REDD is a second market-based strategy that facilitates the conservation of Latin American biodiversity by making it more valuable to preserve forests than to cut them down. REDD makes this possible by assessing the financial value of forests, based on their role in carbon sequestration and storage, which play a large role in mitigating climate change.[92] Trees are particularly important in climate change mitigation, because they remove carbon dioxide from the atmosphere and convert it during photosynthesis to carbon, which they store in a process known as "carbon sequestration." In 2010, the Food and Agriculture Organization estimated that 104 gigatons were stored in Latin American forests.[93] Beyond degrading ecosystems, deforestation releases the carbon stored in wood, and is responsible for 70 percent of total carbon emissions in the region.[94] This is particularly alarming, because Latin America lost approximately 4.3 million hectares of forest per year between 2000 and 2005.[95]

In the REDD process, once this carbon value of particular forests is determined, developed countries pay developing countries to maintain their forests in order to prevent the release of more carbon. To expand the functions of REDD, the UN-REDD Program began the REDD+ Program in 2008 in collaboration with the Food and Agriculture Organization, the UN Development Program, and the United Nations Environment Program.[96] REDD+ expands on REDD by going beyond focusing on deforestation alone, and incorporates training on sustainable management of forests and enhancement of carbon stocks. REDD decision making, especially regarding budget allocation, is participative, and the United Nations has implemented measuring and monitoring systems to ensure that REDD conservation contracts are being upheld. REDD is an example of how international financing can move the MAC curve discussed above to a more sustainable level of pollution by decreasing costs of abatement. At the same time, it addresses the underlying poverty drivers contributing to deforestation in the first place. Guatemala has defined six REDD+ activities on a preliminary basis: incentives to improve carbon storage, incentives for the conservation of natural forests, incentives for small landowners, local communities and indigenous peoples, strengthening governability in forest regions, improved forest management and the promotion of competitiveness and legality in forest product value chains.[97]

REDD has faced many implementation issues. Like other PES programs, REDD-funded initiatives must verify that reductions are real and additional—that is they would not have happened without the program. Policy designers must be cognizant of leakages—reducing deforestation in one place not leading to increases in another location. It must tackle measuring, monitoring, and verifying emissions. Rights of smallholders must be secured, including the ability to access or enter preserves, withdraw resources, and make management decisions. NGO partnership is often crucial to promote the rights of the marginalized. In part due to these challenges, less than 10 percent of REDD+ funds were dispersed by 2011 due to lack of institutional capacity and the rigid nature of the program. Critics such as Anthony Hall are concerned about the dangers of a "one size fits all" approach; he reminds policymakers of the need to analyze the social dimensions of REDD. Hall underscores the need to focus on the limitations of a monetized incentive system and need for nonmonetary benefits, the diversity of populations, and the importance of horizontal and vertical connectivity among stakeholders.[98] Echoing ecotourism policy suggestions discussed below, Hall argues that REDD must provide benefits to the local community and engage them throughout the process.

Others criticize REDD as a cop out for developed countries to continue engaging in unsustainable practices. Although REDD alone will not meet global goals, paying developing countries to conserve their forests may discourage developed countries from reducing their own emissions. Overall, governance of forest resources and the equal distribution of benefits is vital within REDD policy, because if carbon rights are unenforced, objectives inconsistent or unclear, distribution of benefits unpredictable, or corruption prevalent, stakeholders will be deterred from participating in the program. Despite concerns with policy and implementation, both ecotourism and REDD provide greater market incentives to promote conservation, and create opportunities to encourage a step towards environmentally responsible behavior.

CSR and Green Jobs

It is important to provide market incentives for environmentally sustainable and conscious decision making for not only landowners, but also for businesses. Corporate engagement in socially responsible environmental behavior and the creation of environmentally conscious employment opportunities within their businesses, or "green jobs," represents a positive step in the direction towards reducing future risk and environmental damage. The *Financial Times* has praised Brazilian corporations such as Natura cosmetics and Vale mining for their sustainability efforts. Natura, seeking to expand its dominance in the market for sustainable goods, has set up partnerships with conservation NGOs, scientists, government agencies, farmers, and communities in some of Brazil's most remote areas. It works to ensure the production of sustainable body products, including acaí body oil and shampoo made from andiroba seeds, whose profits contribute to community development and conservation.[99] Similarly, recognizing the potentially devastating impact of its iron mining practices, and the nearly US$13 billion annual value of Amazon carbon sequestration, Vale has committed to conserving and protecting the 1.2 million hectares of rainforest surrounding its mines.[100] These corporations are motivated to adopt CSR practices, because they can have major effects on public perception of their products, boosting sales by improving their image.

NGOs, such as The Forest Trust (TFT), are also working, both by cooperation and pressure mechanisms, to encourage companies, including those with questionable environmental histories, to improve their CSR images by adopting more responsible practices. TFT, specifically, works as a mediator between Greenpeace and companies such as Nestlé, explaining Greenpeace's demands and helping businesses to translate these pressures into opportunities for sustainable and strategic operational response.[101] The World Wildlife Fund (WWF) and other organizations are also leading approval schemes to promote CSR. WWF hopes to encourage environmental CSR by offering WWF "Responsible" and "Sustainable" corporation labeling on products in exchange for evidence of environmentally conscious corporate projects and behavior.

Nonetheless, the WWF's approval scheme related to agribusinesses' "Sustainable" logo has caused concern, and has been considered green washing. In exchange for promising to reduce the four most serious negative impacts of their commodity crops by 70 percent, particular companies' products will be labeled WWF sustainable.[102] However, certification schemes often have low standards, inadequate monitoring, and no enforcement mechanisms, making it easier for irresponsible companies to greenwash their policies while continuing to behave in ways that endanger human health and the environment. As a result, NGOs such as Food First and Friends of the Earth have joined to sign a "Letter of Critical Opposition" to the WWF's creation of a Roundtable on Responsible Soy.[103] Thus, it is important to keep in mind that maintaining an appearance of CSR does not replace genuine commitment to environmental sustainability. Monitoring and enforcement mechanisms must be strengthened to verify the legitimacy and impact of corporate environmental practices.

Ecotourism: Preservation that Makes a Profit

Creation of value by means of conservation is especially strong in Latin America, due to the region's unique and abundantly diverse landscape. As a result, many actors in the region recognize that it is intrinsically valuable to preserve the ecosystem. Ecosystem conservation manifests itself in many ways throughout Latin America region. Regions are able to market natural biodiversity as a consumer good that can be purchased and experienced. Ecotourism has become a market activity that increases incentives to preserve Latin America's natural habitat and establish official protected areas. In 2002, the World Tourism Organization (UNWTO) created the Sustainable Tourism for Eradicating Poverty initiative, which has created technical assistance projects to promote ecotourism by distributing funds in order to protect areas for the "enjoyment of natural or cultural heritage."[104] Similarly, the Latin American Community–based Tourism Network (REDTURNS) has worked to make ecotourism more feasible for marginalized communities in biodiverse areas, and has created over three hundred community-based tourism destinations in thirteen countries, providing jobs for families that had been previously isolated from the market. By having a livelihood that depends on protecting their local ecosystems so as to attract tourists, landowners in ecotourism destinations are motivated to act in sustainable ways.[105]

Ecotourism schemes vary in design and effectiveness. It is important to emphasize that, for ecotourism to be equitable, it must be strategic and inclusive so that it benefits a variety of stakeholders and includes the local community throughout the process. For example, Mexico's Monarch Butterfly Biosphere Reserve, a World Heritage Site containing most of the over-wintering sites of the eastern population of the monarch butterfly, was heavily criticized because although indigenous land titles were preserved in establishing the reserve, forest-usage rights were taken away from indigenous communities that had depended on forestry for centuries. Without engaging indigenous communities in planning, the right was revoked without the creation of new opportunities for the maintenance of the people's livelihood. The Monarch Butterfly Reserve underscores the need to find a balance between meeting human needs versus protecting the local ecosystem, and demonstrates the importance of including communities in the ecotourism process.[106] Accounting for the socioeconomic dimensions of nature conservation is a lesson later appreciated by the Mexican government; it worked concert with Mexican and international donors to create local income generation and employment as alternatives to the illegal logging that took place for survival.[107]

In contrast, the Jeannette Kawas National Park in Honduras, home to 80 percent of Honduran birds and 60 percent of the country's plant life, was established in a more inclusive manner that considered, included, and benefitted the local community.[108] The planners encouraged the community to participate, and spoke with community leaders to determine local needs within thirteen communities surrounding the park. Leaders were included in decision making, possessed voting power, and cooperated with the private tourism sector. Profits generated by park tourism are considered a type of local revenue, and funds are distributed among the communities to be reinvested in further preservation and tourism development.[109] Comparing the nature of these two ecotourism ventures, it is important to recognize the need to make preservation a participatory and inclusive process.

CONCLUSION: LOW-HANGING FRUIT TOWARD HIGH HANGING AIMS

Addressing environmental sustainability in Latin America and in the world is the challenge of your lifetime. Policies will be subject to trial and error. We have centuries of experience in extraction and environmental degradation in the region; we have only been attentive to sustainability for a few decades. Environmental change is an intensely political process as it creates winner as losers. As the tragic history in the Amazon underscores, violence often accompanies transformative changes. But the difficulty of this process should not blind us to the opportunities. There is much low-hanging fruit in the region—changes that can promote wins for inclusive growth with sustainable outcomes. This is not to say that deeper, harder changes will follow. Instead, by implementing processes such as payment for environmental services on a national and global scale, people can become acclimated to negotiating the trade-offs in a sustainable future. Robert Zoellick, former World Bank President, once likened trade agreements to bike riding: once you stop you fall over and the trip ends badly. Perhaps environmental change is like learning to ride a tandem bike. The stakes for not addressing global public goods are calamitous. Countries need to learn to ride together; perhaps engagement at the level of low-hanging fruit can create pathways to sustainable change.

Key Concepts

adaptation
additionality
Global
    Environmental
    Facility (GEF)
institutional capacity

marginal abatement cost
    (MAC)
marginal social damage
    (MSD)
market-based initiatives
    (MBIs)

opportunity costs
payments for
    environmental
    services (PES)
transaction costs
verification

Chapter Summary

Environmental Challenges

- Latin America's most significant environmental challenges include urbanization, health, water, access to services, energy and emissions, climate change, and biodiversity degradation.
- Latin American cities have grown rapidly, outpacing the ability to manage populations. Urban areas are also highly vulnerable to natural threats. Pollution and contamination are two of the largest urban health risks, both directly, and indirectly by posing a threat to local water sources. Future water sources are predicted to become more exclusionary while demand for water increases exponentially. Sanitation and waste management are a pressing concern.
- Economic growth, especially with its urban concentration, has pressured resources in the region. Energy-efficient services are critical to increasing productivity in the region and ensuring a sustainable future. Transportation is the fastest growing contributor of carbon emissions in the region. Expanding public transportation is thus an important goal. Although the region has immense hydroelectric potential, strong opposition from environmental, civil society, and indigenous groups prevents many developments in this sector. Therefore, countries are looking to other forms of renewable energy.

- Latin America is expected to suffer disproportionately from climate change, with varying effects by subregion. The region is highly vulnerable due to its geography, climate, socioeconomic position, and sensitive natural assets. Available water is predicted to shrink and agricultural productivity is expected to fall; consequently food prices are expected to rise. Extreme weather patterns have already led to substantial damage costs, totaling US$40 billion in the past decade. The poor suffer the most from extreme weather due to weak infrastructure.
- Latin America is currently the most ecologically diverse region in the world, but climate change is set to have an immense impact on biodiversity in the region. Biodiversity is vital to communities; possesses economic, cultural, and social value; and helps mitigate the effects of climate change worldwide. In spite of the value biodiversity possesses, the region is experiencing severe environmental degradation. Deforestation, often in the pursuit of agribusiness, and irresponsible agriculture and aquaculture practices are contributing factors. Policymakers must balance the dual objectives of economic growth and conservation.

The Economic Nature of the Environmental Problem

- Environmental policy is especially complex because it must take into account the notion of the environment as a global public good. Public goods are nonrival and non-excludable. Exacerbating the problem, many environmental goods are also nonrenewable. Latin America's high level of inequality also increases the complexity of solutions required.
- The "optimal pollution level" (at the intersection of the marginal social damage curve and the marginal abatement cost function) represents the level where cleanup costs are equal to the benefits of a polluted environment. However, the optimal level may be above the sustainable level of pollution. New technologies can address this mismatch by lowering the cost of cleanup.
- There is urgent motivation for global cost-sharing to address the complex problem and overcome inadequate infrastructure and limited assets.

Opportunities to Address Climate Change and Environmental Problems

- Strong environmental policy requires a multisectoral, multistakeholder approach and the ability to manage trade-offs and minimize stakeholders' costs. Environmental policy must be also pro-poor, promoting social well-being. Policies can be broken down into investments improving current well-being and those that promote sustainability for the future.
- Alternative energy has the potential to reduce dangerous emissions and create positive environmental and social externalities; however, their adoption is controversial since side effects can be harmful. Therefore, greater enforcement of environmental accountability in the alternative energy cycle is necessary.

- The cost and severity of the impact of future environmental shocks depends on a country's capacity to reduce its vulnerability and increase its risk-management abilities. Latin American countries must consider the best adaption and mitigation approaches to reduce risk and impressive strategies are already in place. However, the region remains impeded by shortfalls in infrastructure and energy efficiency and insufficient funding. Public-private partnerships and multilateral institutions may play a role in addressing these shortfalls.
- Market-based initiatives (MBIs) provide incentives for people to choose environmentally sustainable behaviors and are a complement to regulatory and state investment programs. One such MBI in the region is Payments for Environmental Services (PES). MBIs require a careful market analysis.
- Corporate engagement in socially responsible behavior and the creation of environmentally conscious employment opportunities "green jobs" are important steps towards reducing future risk and environmental damage.
- There is great potential in the region to create value through conservation due to Latin America's rich biodiversity. However, ecotourism efforts must find a balance between meeting human needs and protecting the local ecosystem, and include local communities.
- Reducing Emissions from Deforestation and Forest Degradation (REDD) is another example of a market-based strategy that facilities the conservation of biodiversity by making it more valuable to preserve forests than to cut them down. Despite concerns with policy and implementation, ecotourism and REDD increase market incentives to promote conservation.

Notes

1. United Nations, *World Urbanization Prospects: 2014 Revision, Population Division*, Department of Economic and Social Affairs, United Nations, New York, 2015, http://esa.un.org/unpd/wup/.

2. Paulo A. Paranagua, "Latin America Struggles to Cope with Record Urban Growth," *The Guardian,* 2012, www.theguardian.com/world/2012/sep/11/latin-america-urbanisation-city-growth, accessed June 4, 2014.

3. Mariana Ceratti, *"Brazil may be the Owner of 20% of the World's Water Supply but it is still Very Thirsty,"* World Bank, August 5, 2016, *www.worldbank.org/en/.../2016/.../how-brazil-managing-water-resources-new-report-....*

4. Ibid.

5. UN-HABITAT State of Cities—Regional Reports Latin American & Caribbean, 2012. http://unhabitat.org/books/state-of-latin-american-and-caribbean-cities-2/.

6. The World Bank, "Climate Change with Green Innovation." September 25, 2013, www.worldbank.org/en/news/feature/2013/09/25/latin-america-climate-change-environment-green-innovation/.

7. Amanda Maxwell, "Air Quality in Latin America: High Levels of Pollution Require Strong Government Action," April 29, 2013, www.nrdc.org/experts/amanda-maxwell/air-quality-latin-america-high-levels-pollution-require-strong-government/.

8. United Nations Conference on Sustainable Development, *Sustainable Development 20 Years on from the Earth Summit*, The United Nations, 2012.

9. Eric Dickson, Judy L. Baker, Daniel Hoornweg, and Amita Tiwari, *Urban Risk Assessments: Understanding Disaster and Climate Risk in Cities*, Urban development series (Washington, DC: World Bank, 2012), http://documents.worldbank.org/curated/en/2012/06/16499064/urban-risk-assessments-understanding-disaster-climate-risk-cities.

10. How Brazil's "Valley of Death" Drastically Cut Pollution, *BBC News*, March 8, 2017, www.bbc.com/news/av/science.../how-brazil-s-valley-of-death-drastically-cut-pollutio...

11. Economist Intelligence Unit, "Latin America Green City Index: Assessing the Environmental Performance of Latin America's Major Cities," *Siemens*, 2010.

12. Ibid.

13. The World Bank, *Climate Change, Disaster Risk, and the Urban Poor* (Washington DC: The International Bank for Reconstruction and Development, 2012).

14. Elisabeth Malkin, "Bottled-Water Habit Keeps Tight Grip on Mexicans," *The New York Times,* 2012.

15. Ibid.

16. The United Nations Conference on Sustainable Development, *Sustainable Development 20 Years on.*

17. World Bank, Data Indicators, 2014, http://data.worldbank.org/indicator.

18. The United Nations Conference on Sustainable Development, *Sustainable Development 20 Years on.*

19. Ibid.

20. Merrill Lynch Global Research, www.ml.com/Publish/Content/application/pdf/GWMOL/MLWM_Transcript_looking-for-growth-and-a-better-future.pdf.

21. Sergio Bitar, "Why and How Latin America Should Think About the Future." 2016 Inter American Dialogue Report: Global Trends and the Future of Latin America, http://espas.eu/orbis/sites/default/files/generated/document/en/IAD10150-2016-Global-Trends-Report-08.29.16-FINAL-Sept.pdf, page 14.

22. Ibid.

23. Ibid.

24. Ibid.

25. The World Bank, Data Indicators, 2014, http://data.worldbank.org/indicator.

26. Salvador J Nunez, "3 Big Challenges for Latin America's Electricity Sector, 3 Big Strategies for a Successful Future," *The Huffington Post* (2014), www.huffingtonpost.com/jake-levine/3-big-challenges-for-lati_b_5276684.html [accessed June 4, 2014].

27. Ibid.

28. Roger Tissot, *Latin America's Energy Future*. Inter-American Dialogue, 2012.

29. InterAmerican Development Bank, Lights On? Energy Needs in Latin America and the Caribbean to 2040, www.19.iadb.org/intal/intalcdi/PE/2016/15969en.pdf.

30. Denée Reave, "Latin America Green News: Fracking in Chile, Environment and Elections in Costa Rica, Coastal Protection in Mexico," *National Resources Defense Council*, January 17, 2014.

31. Décui Luis Gazzoni, Ivan Azurdia, Gabrial Blanco, Claudia A. Estrada, and Isaias de Carvalho Macedo, *Sustainable Energy in Latin America and the Caribbean: Potential for the Future*, Rio de Janeiro: ICSU-LAC, 2010.

32. The World Bank, *Climate Change, Disaster Risk, and the Urban Poor.*

33. The United Nations Conference on Sustainable Development, *Sustainable Development 20 Years on.*

34. Jorgelina Hardoy and Patricia Romero Lankao, "Latin American Cities and Climate Change: Challenges and Options to Mitigation and Adaptation Responses," *Current Opinion in Environmental Sustainability* 3 (2011): 158–163.

35. Lisa Viscidi and Rebecca O'Connor, "The Energy of Transportation: A Focus on Latin American Urban Transportation, 2017" Ch 4 in Paul Isbell and Eloy Álvarez Pelegry (eds), *Energy & Transportation in the Atlantic Basin*. Jean Monnet Network on Atlantic Studies at Johns Hopkins, downloadable at /transatlanticrelations.org/publication/energy-transportation-atlantic-basin/.

36. Patricia Romero Lankao, "Are We Missing the Point?: Particularities of Urbanization, Sustainability and Carbon Emissions in Latin American Cities," *Environment and Urbanization* 19 (2007): 159–175.

37. The United Nations Conference on Sustainable Development, *Sustainable Development 20 Years on.*

38. Ibid.

39. Dario Hidalgo, "Why is TransMilenio Still So Special?" The City Fix, World Resources Institute, 5 August 2008, available at http://thecityfix.com/blog/why-is-transmilenio-still-so-special/.

40. BriAnne Illich, Interview with Lu Serrano, Buenos Aires, Argentina, April 30, 2013.

41. Gazzoni et al., *Sustainable Energy in Latin America and the Caribbean.*

42. Tissot, *Latin America's Energy Future.*

43. Reave, "Latin America Green News."

44. Claudio Agostini, Carlos Silva, and Shahriyar Nassirov, "Solar Energy in Chile," *ReVista* (Fall 2015): 42.

45. Sebastian Miller and John D. Smith, "A Big Job for Small Countries," *IADB* (January 9, 2013), accessed May 14, 2014.

46. IFAD, *Addressing Climate Change in Latin America and the Caribbean* (Rome, Italy: International Fund for Agricultural Development, 2011).

47. Hoda Baraka, Hoda, "The Realities of Climate Change in Latin America," 350.org. December 4, 2014, http://350.org/the-realities-of-climate-change-in-latin-america/.

48. Walter Leal Filho, Fátima Alves, Sandra Caeiro, and Ulisses M. Azeiteiro, *International Perspectives on Climate Change: Latin America and Beyond* (Springer, 2014).

49. The United Nations Conference on Sustainable Development, *Sustainable Development 20 Years On* and www.latinamerica.undp.org/content/rblac/en/home/ourwork/climate-and-disaster-resilience/overview.html.

50. The World Bank. *Climate Change, Disaster Risk, and the Urban Poor.*

51. Filho, Alves, Caeiro, and Azeiteiro, *International Perspectives.*

52. The United Nations Conference on Sustainable Development, *Sustainable Development 20 Years on.*

53. A. Bovarnick, F. Alpizar, and C. Schnell, eds., *The Importance of Biodiversity and Ecosystems in Economic Growth and Equity in Latin America and the Caribbean: An Economic Valuation of Ecosystems*, United Nations Development Programme, 2010, www.cbd.int.

54. IFAD, *Addressing Climate Change,* and Peter D. Richards. "Soy, Cotton and the Final Atlantic Forest Frontier," *The Professional Geographer* 63(3) (2011): 343–363.

55. Claudia Pompa, "Paraguay: Can the Deforestation Be Stopped?," *Latin America Bureau* (February 12, 2014), http://lab.org.uk/paraguay-can-the-deforestation-be-stopped, accessed February 28, 2014.

56. "Titular de la ARP Dice Que Deforestación En El Chaco Es Un 'Cuento Chino'" (January 30, 2014), http://ea.com.py/titular-de-la-arp-dice-que-deforestacion-en-el-chaco-es-un-cuento-chino/.

57. William Neuman and Andrea Zarate, "Corruption in Peru Aids Cutting of Rain Forest," *The New York Times*, October 18, 2013.

58. The United Nations Conference on Sustainable Development, *Sustainable Development 20 Years on.*

59. Ibid.

60. Ibid.

61. William F. Laurance, "Roads to Ruin," April 12, 2015, www.nytimes.com/2015/04/13/opinion/roads-to-ruin.html.

62. Indira A.R. Lakshmanan, "Amazon Highway Is Route to Strife in Brazil," *The Boston Globe*, 2005, published electronically December 27, 2005, www.boston.com/news/world/latinamerica/articles/2005/12/27/amazon_highway_is_route_to_strife_in_brazil/.

63. William F. Laurance, "Roads to Ruin."

64. Juha Uitto, "Evaluating the Environment as a Global Public Good," *Evaluation* 22(1) (2016): 18–115.

65. Gazzoni et al., *Sustainable Energy in Latin America and the Caribbean.*

66. Greg Meyer, "Ethanol: Logic of Circular Biofuel Trade Comes into Question," *The Financial Times,* May 16, 2013, accessed May 14, 2014, www.ft.com.

67. C. Ford Runge and Benjamin Senauer, "How Biofuels Could Starve the Poor." *Foreign*

Affairs (May/June 2007), www.foreignaffairs.com/articles/2007-05-01/how-biofuels-could-starve-poor, accessed May 31, 2018.

68. Ibid.

69. David Tilman, Robert Socolow, Jonathan A. Foley, Jason Hill, Eric Larson, Lee Lynd, Stephen Pacala, John Reilly, Tim Searchinger, Chris Somerville, and Robert Williams, *Beneficial Biofuels—The Food, Energy, and Environment Trilemma* (St. Paul, MN: University of Minnesota, 2009).

70. Ibid.

71. Omar Chisari, Sebastián Galiani, and Sebastián Miller, *Optimal Adaptation and Mitigation to Climate Change in Small Environmental Economies* (The Inter-American Development Bank, October 2013).

72. Joreglina Hardoy and Patricia Romero Lankao, "Latin American Cities and Climate Change: Challenges and Options to Mitigation and Adaptation Responses," *Current Opinion in Environmental Sustainability* 3 (2011): 158–163.

73. The United Nations Conference on Sustainable Development, *Sustainable Development 20 Years on.*

74. Dickson, Baker, Hoornweg, and Tiwari, *Urban Risk Assessments.*

75. The World Bank, *Climate Change, Disaster Risk, and the Urban Poor.*

76. Climate Investment Funds, "Key Lessons from the Pilot Program for Climate Resilience: Shaping Climate Resilience for Transformational Change," World Bank Group. July 2015, www.greengrowthknowledge.org/resource/key-lessons-pilot-program-climate-resilience.

77. The United Nations Conference on Sustainable Development, *Sustainable Development 20 Years on.*

78. http://repositorio.cepal.org/bitstream/handle/11362/39150/S1501174_en.pdf.

79. Filho, Alves, Caeiro, and Azeiteiro, *International Perspectives.*

80. Ibid.

81. Ibid.

82. Ibid.

83. Ibid.

84. The World Bank, *Climate Change, Disaster Risk, and the Urban Poor.*

85. Consorcio para el Desarollo Sostenible de la Ecorregion Andina (CONDESAN).

86. Thomas Forth, "Carbon Market Negotiations Should Exit Shallow Waters," *Carbon Mechanisms Review* (February–April 2017), www.climatefocus.com/sites/default/files/Where%20to%20now%20with%20the%20CDM.pdf.

87. Elizabeth Shapiro-Garza, "Contesting the Market-Based Nature of Mexico's National Payments for Ecosystem Services Programs: Four Sites of Articulation and Hybridization," *Geoforum* 46 (2013): 5–15.

88. Stefano Pagiola, *Using PES to Implement REDD* (Washington, DC: The World Bank, January 2011).

89. Maryanne Grieg-Gran, Ina Porras, and Sven Wunder, "How Can Market Mechanisms for Forest Environmental Services Help the Poor? Preliminary Lessons from Latin America," *World Development* 33(9) (September 2005): 1511–1527.

90. I. Porras, D. N. Barton, M. Miranda, and A. Chacón-Cascante, "Learning from 20 Years of Payments for Ecosystem Services in Costa Rica," International Institute for Environment and Development, London (2013).

91. Bruno Vander Velde, "To Fight Deforestation, One Country Changed the Equation," newstrust.org, November 24, 2015.

92. UN-REDD Programme, "Frequently Asked Questions," edited by UNDP and UNEP FAO, 2014.

93. United Nations Conference on Sustainable Development, *Sustainable Development 20 Years on.*

94. Indira A.R. Lakshmanan, "Amazon Highway Is Route to Strife in Brazil."

95. "Deforestation Rate 'Alarming', but Net Loss Slowing: FAO," first appearing in the *Agence France-Presse (AFP)*, November 14, 2005, reprinted at the World Business Council for Sustainable Development, www.wbcsd.org.

96. UN-REDD Programme, "Frequently Asked Questions."

97. ECLAC (Economic Commission for Latin America and the Caribbean), CAC (Central American Agricultural Council), COMISCA (Council of Ministers of Health of Central America), CCAD (Central American Commission for Environment and Development), COSEFIN (Council of Ministers of Finance/Treasury of Central America and Dominic Republic), SIECA (Secretariat of Central American Economic Integration), SICA (Central American Integration System), UKAID (United Kingdom Department of International Development) and DANIDA (Danish International Development Agency), "Climate Change in Central America," (2015), http://repositorio.cepal.org/bitstream/handle/11362/39150/S1501174_en.pdf.

98. Maria Digiano, "Anthony Hall: Forests and Climate Change: The Social Dimensions of Redd in Latin America," *Human Ecology* 41 (2013): 491–493.

99. Samantha Pearson, "No Trade-Off to Balance Growth and Conservation," *Financial Times,* November 28, 2011.

100. John Paul Rathbone. "Pristine Forest Is Finite Resource," *Financial Times*, November 29, 2011.

101. Scott Poynton, "Natural Capital: Thinking of the Environment as an Asset," edited by Duncan Gromko, February 11, 2014, http://naturalcapital1.blogspot.com/2014/02/interview-with-forest-trusts-scott.html.

102. Johathan Latham, "Way Beyond Greenwashing: Have Corporations Captured 'Big Conservation'?" (February 7, 2012), www.independentsciencenews.org/environment/way-beyond-greenwashing-have-multinationals-captured-big-conservation/.

103. Ibid.

104. David V Carruthers, *Environmental Justice in Latin America: Problems, Promise and Practice* (MIT Press, 2008).

105. United Nations Conference on Sustainable Development, *Sustainable Development 20 Years on.*

106. Carruthers, *Environmental Justice in Latin America.*

107. O. Vidal, J. López-García, and E. Rendón-Salinas, "Trends in Deforestation and Forest Degradation after a Decade of Monitoring in the Monarch Butterfly Biosphere Reserve in Mexico," *Conservation Biology*, 28(1) (2014): 177–186, http://doi.org/10.1111/cobi.12138.

108. Ibid.

109. Ibid.

Lessons (Not Quite) Learned

Cycles in Latin American Development

CHAPTER FOURTEEN

The old and the new combine to confront challenges of poverty, education, health, and environment in the region. *(Patrice Franko) Photo of a new mother's group at the Tani NGO clinic, Lima, Peru. (tallerdelosninos.org.pe).*

459

Nearing his seventy-second birthday, Colombian Nobel laureate Gabriel García Marquez (1927–2014) bought a newspaper company, *El Cambio*. He jokingly noted that after his 1982 Nobel Prize, no one would employ him as a journalist because he was too expensive. His reentry into journalism promoted a greater spirit of open press in his native country, a critical component of accountable government policy. Unfortunately, the magical realism of his novels finds stark parallels in contemporary life in Latin America, leaving much to report on. As he said in a *New York Times* interview describing his political activism as a writer, his engagement in critical issues was driven by the fact that "underdevelopment is total, integral, it affects every part of our lives."[1] Garcia Marquez's complex plots continue to characterize Latin American reality.

Many of the political obstacles to underdevelopment that concerned Marquez at the time of his award have changed. Most important, the region has gone from one dominated by repressive military regimes to one of open democracy. The economic model was radically altered from state-centered import substitution industrialization (ISI) to a market-driven approach, and a new hybrid model is now evolving. But political and economic openness have not yet fundamentally transformed the devastating landscape of underdevelopment in the region. Despite improvements, the cycle of poverty and oppression in Marquez's literature and his contemporary world remain a sad reminder of unresolved developmental challenges. Social protest and strikes mark the degree of dissatisfaction that many Latin Americans feel regarding the lack of improvement in their material lives. Only 14 percent in the region think economic performance is good or very good—and 40 percent rate the outcomes as bad and very bad. One in four Latin Americans has difficulty in securing basic nutrition; the Venezuelan humanitarian crisis distorts this regional average, with 72 percent finding it difficult to meet nutritional needs. Two out of three in the region are dissatisfied with the results of democracy.[2]

Such dismal views complicate the generation of confidence in the future of the region. At the turn of the century, social protest and strikes across Latin America registered the level of dissatisfaction with the neoliberal development model. Regional output contracted in the first half of 2002 by 2.5 percent, and financial conditions were extremely fragile. In 2004 and 2005, regional gross domestic product per capita grew by 4.3 percent and 2.8 percent, but the engines of growth varied. Many countries remain precariously dependent on the global commodity boom—rising, as in prior historical periods, with the explosion of growth in China or riding the tide of rising energy prices. Some continue to rely on the large US market and on the ability to serve as low-cost producers in an era of competing with even lower Asian wages.

As an example of the cycles of poverty, consider the challenges facing Honduras as it moved into the twenty-first century. Honduras, along with its Central American neighbors, was ravaged by Hurricane Mitch late in 1998. Decades of development were turned back by this powerful storm. Schools and hospitals were decimated, and the loss of life was staggering. Swelling rivers washed away homes, farms, and factories. Honduras lost export crops such as bananas, coffee, shrimp, and melons; its small farms have no arable soil left to grow sources of domestic sustenance, including rice and corn.

Honduras was terribly unlucky to be in the path of Mitch, but its own development path had made it more vulnerable to the destruction of the storm. Its fragile
ecosystem, weakened from overfarming, overlogging, and overpopulation, left
little resistance to wind and water. As noted by Edwin Mateo Molina, a Honduran
sociologist specializing in environmental issues for the Inter-American Development Bank (IADB), "Everyone realizes that the damage was magnified by the
misuse of resources. It will happen again, and will be even worse unless we look
for a way to use the land in a more responsible manner."[3] Climate change is accel-
erating the likelihood of natural destruction—and will likely take a devastating toll
on economic growth. IMF modeling suggests an outsized effect of climate change
on the global south.[4]

The news is not all bad. After decades of economic reform, Latin America
is more squarely on a sustainable development path. Decentralization has placed
more power in the hands of local governments. Women and indigenous groups
have achieved greater recognition in the design of development strategies, although
many tangible gains will accrue only over time. Environmental projects have
sprung up throughout the region to support sustainable practices. Macroeconomies
and current accounts are better balanced, and the region is integrating through
bilateral and regional accords. Cycles have persisted, but Latin America may have
reversed some of the practices promoting downward cycles and replaced them with
new directions in its unfolding development story.

A new pragmatism is emerging in the region, an approach to political economy
that respects fiscal constraints and embraces global markets but also recognizes
the need for investments in health, education, and infrastructure to promote a more
equitable, sustainable growth pattern. Pursuit of such a "policy of the possible" is
differentiating most economies in the region.[5] Governments elected on the recognition of the need for social investments are balancing these demands with the realities and rigors of fiscal restraint. In contrast, other governments are responding to
the popular demand for rapid change in the social sector—a reasonable response
to historical marginalization but fraught with difficulties of sustainability once
resource-based revenues peter out.

THE ECONOMIC LABORATORY OF LATIN AMERICA

Latin America has been a virtual economic laboratory to analyze imbalances across
the domestic and international sectors. Our study of ISI showed that its internal
focus grew from the dissatisfaction with the primary product export model in the
late 1880s and early 1900s. Despite comparable starts, it appeared that the region
was falling behind relative to Europe and North America. The surprising progress of Latin America under isolation during World War II from the international
economy led analysts to believe that international capitalism was a cause of the
underdevelopment of the region. According to the dependency theorists, powerful
industrial countries were draining Latin America of its wealth. Alliances between
elites in the center and the periphery perpetuated a model that privileged a few but
immiserated the masses. Patterns of asset distribution in large *latifundia* or estate

production determined by colonial decree were reproduced in industrial circles. Internal dynamism was lacking, with weak linkages between the export-oriented agricultural sector and the fragile and thin industrial sector. Technological prowess was building in the North, to the exclusion of the South. The perception was that the international economy was strangling dynamic domestic development.

To move beyond dependent development, ISI constructed the state as the defined agent of change. Employing planning tools and the aggressive arm of state-led firms, governments opened new sectors to industrial activity. A focus on linkages and breaking down bottlenecks of production led the state to target key sectors. High tariffs kept multinational firms at bay, unless special technological licensing agreements or local production were negotiated to provide critical inputs of production. Monetary policy was essentially passive, with central banking authorities accommodating the expansionist thrust of the model. An initial euphoria characterized the ability to promote development in the region. The ambitious plan to build Brasilia, moving it inland as a heartland capital to integrate diverse regions, was a symbol of the unbounded power of state energy. New light and heavy manufacturing sectors developed to meet the needs of domestic consumers. The labor movement strengthened as unions promoted workers' rights. Public utilities were expanded, providing electricity and telephone services throughout the region. Ambitious projects such as the trans-Amazonian highway and the Itaipu Dam were begun with financing from capital markets bullish on Latin America. Latin American nations were transforming their economic landscape.

Unraveling ISI

But signs of disequilibrium began to surface. Balance of payments accounts were pressured by the need to import costly intermediate machinery for final goods production. As import bills surged, the exchange rate bias worked against exports. The state's attempt to do too much too fast resulted in an inflationary tendency in the economy. Rapid change meant frequent supply shortages, and state-led megaprojects required high levels of public finance. Powerful firms and powerful unions passed cost increases around. It was not a total coincidence that as the economies began to twist and crack, militaries around the region were called by industrial elites to govern and maintain order and progress. Stability was threatened by an uneven and unbalanced development process.

Given highly unequal income distributions and a model that had promoted a new urban privileged class, it was risky to begin tinkering too much with the internal and external balance. Rapid structural change made the management of economic outcomes unpredictable. Populist policies to buy off labor and business without strong regard for external constraints dominated the region. Corruption was encouraged by the ability of agents within the state to control economic property rights. Many abused privileges for personal gain in protected state jobs. Quotas on foreign exchange or technology import licenses led to under-the-table payments to grease the economic wheels. Sadly but predictably, the poor were largely neglected, the rural sector was nearly abandoned, and the environment was devastated.

International price shocks dislodged the inward-looking system of ISI. Global interest-rate hikes to restrain worldwide inflation triggered a massive debt crisis across the region. Countries faced default in adjusting to high real interest rates after the artificial luxury of low to negative rates over several years. External constraints became overwhelming when the price of international capital rose. Consumption or imports for investment could no longer be cheaply financed and countries could not support living beyond their means. A radical reorientation of the development model was required.

NEOLIBERAL REFORMS

ISI was replaced by variants of the neoliberal model throughout the region. The state itself was delegitimized as the economic guardian. Instead, markets became the primary allocators of resources. State spending was slashed to maintain fiscal balance, and state firms were privatized to promote profit and efficiency as the way to provide goods and services in the market. Privatization created enormous profit potential, which enticed international capital back to the region. Tariff walls came tumbling down, exposing firms to competition in the international market. Openness to international competition rooted out inefficiencies in production and formerly protected firms scrambled to find new market niches. Nontraditional exports penetrated new markets. Agriculture and agroindustries got a boost from international demand. Cheaper imports from the global market provided consumers with new choices of goods at lower prices. Multinational firms established local production to meet the needs of consumers with real purchasing power for the first time in years. As countries looked outward and a democratic revolution swept the hemisphere, subregional integration efforts gained momentum. The external sector was again the engine of development.

Latin American nations once again became darlings of international capital. With inflation in retreat throughout the region and democratic governments installed in all nations except Cuba, stability encouraged investor confidence. Money flowed back to the region, this time through bond and stock markets rather than commercial bank lending. Foreign direct investment blossomed because multinationals were enthusiastic about long-term development prospects. Not every country, however, benefited equally. Larger countries attracted the bulk of capital, while smaller and poorer economies struggled. Pockets of violence developed in neglected zones. Nonetheless, the experiences of countries such as Costa Rica demonstrate that small countries that have invested in technology and workforce development can indeed succeed.

THE COMPELLING SOCIAL AND ENVIRONMENTAL AGENDA

Opening to the external economy also exposed weaknesses in the domestic political economy. Global attention to environmental and social issues promoted by new actors on the global stage, the nongovernmental organizations (NGOs), directed some attention to issues of sustainable development and labor standards. Protests on the negative social and environmental effects of International Monetary Fund (IMF) and World Bank types of conditionality packages led to a rethinking of the sustainability of short-term stabilization measures. Short-term export targets for the release of funds resulted in further deforestation; sweatshops started to spring up throughout the region as multinationals took advantage of cheaper, often female, labor. In response to international outcries, new units were set up in multilateral organizations to safeguard environmental concerns and promote the interests of the least advantaged in society. Greater attention was paid to issues of gender and ethnicity in development. Recognition of the economic and social contributions of women and indigenous peoples began to inform decision making. But institutional change is slow and incomplete, and the intermediate environmental and social costs have been high.

There was an extraordinary degree of financial dislocation in the process of rapid transformation from closed to open economies. Some governments have been better able to manage this process than others. Mistakes such as the Mexican management of the 1994 peso overvaluation were made, with devastating financial costs. Brazil weathered its 1998–1999 crisis after a bungled devaluation, fiscal imprudence, and political infighting that shook market confidence. The Argentine economy collapsed in 2001 under the weight of external debt that was unmatched by increases in international competitiveness. At the turn of the century, changing policies and outcomes challenged the ability of governments to maintain credibility with their citizens and with international investors. Citizens placed left-leaning politicians in Brazil, Argentina, Uruguay, Chile, Bolivia, and Venezuela to address the perceived social deficits—although the implementation of social policy in each country was strikingly different. Social protest gripped Ecuador, Argentina, and Guatemala. Pleasing one segment of society has sometimes come at a cost to another. Labor-market reform lagged for fear of upsetting domestic labor coalitions. Privatization often took place too rapidly, allowing some firms to be sold for less than market value. Appropriate regulatory measures were not always in place to protect consumer and environmental interests in the face of newly privatized monopolies. Finance ministers have had to manage not only money supplies but also extensive public relations efforts with the major brokerage houses around the world. Increasing transparency and credibility in policymaking has been critical to maintaining confidence in Latin American markets.

Latin America continues to operate as an economic laboratory. There is a wide degree of dispersion in the region, as policies adapt to popular pressures propelled by social media and weakly mediated by political parties. The first decade of the new millennium was marked by the rise of the pink tide—socially oriented governments such as the PT (Worker's Party) administrations of Lula and Dilma in Brazil or the Peronist Kirschers in Argentina; innovations such as CCTs helped engineer dramatic improvements in poverty and inequality. Many, however, have been replaced by market-driven policies such as those of Brazil's Temer and Argentina's Macri. Some socially committed governments such as Correa/Moreno in Ecuador or Morales in Bolivia have stood firm against the stinging backlash faced in other South American nations.

As of sending this book to print, the region is experiencing a sweeping set of elections in 2018—elections that are likely to change the political face of the region. Unlike the dominance of ISI or neoliberal policies in the 1980s and 1990s, policies in the next decades are more likely to speak pragmatically to four fundamental challenges: navigating macroeconomic stability in a globalized economy, promoting **productivity** and competitiveness, encouraging inclusive and sustainable growth, and deepening **institutional capacity** to weather the inevitable shocks for middle income countries in twenty-first century productive systems. The role of markets versus the guidance of the state is in tension as the region navigates global challenges.

ADDRESSING THE SOCIAL DEFICIT

At the same time that the economies have grappled with both the costs and the benefits of globalization, the Latin American state has struggled with how to do more with less. The accumulated social and environmental deficits are huge impediments to sustained future growth. Radical structural change shook up the system, energizing productive potential. Realizing this potential in the long run, however, is a function of enhancing investments in human capital. Health and education systems must be revamped. Latin America must contend with its epidemiological backlog, eradicating traditional diseases linked to poor living conditions and inadequate nutrition as well as making headway against the ills of modern society such as violence, AIDS, and heart disease. Quality improvements in the supply of educational services, including better teacher training, appropriate texts, and computer-based learning, are critical to compete in the global economy. Environmental decision making must be systematically incorporated at the local level because people themselves demand it. The complex host of environmental problems born of insufficient infrastructure and unmanaged economic expansion must be reconciled with communities' needs today and for the future.

Economic change can be disruptive, challenging stability. It can also threaten ruling elites if formulated to attend to the marginalized masses. Ironically, if policy does not include those most needy of government attention to raise living, health, and education standards to a level consistent with human dignity and self-empowerment, the development prospects will confront a human-capital deficit that is unsustainable in the modern global economy. Rising inequality exacerbates social tension as the marginalized make claims on the state for redress. State intervention in promoting human development is circumscribed by the domestic constraints of financing as well as by the role of the state as an institutional actor. Changing development problems require dynamic solutions.

THE CHALLENGE OF DEEP MICROECONOMIC REFORM

The decades of debt adjustment, hyperinflation, and currency crises from 1980 to 2000 scarred Latin American economies deeply. Historical memory of inflation and crisis leave less breathing room for expansionary economic policies. Although some countries such as Chile have stockpiled credibility, hints of inflationary finance quickly lower expectations and require oppressive interest rates. Those countries interested in attracting global capital must don the "golden straightjacket"—the mix of IMF-like policies formerly imposed by Washington institutions but now adopted voluntarily if reluctantly to create market confidence. Temporary market distortions are tolerated when credibility has been banked over time, allowing a greater degree of countercyclical policies. Although Chile may be able to pursue macroeconomic management more like that of mature economies, much of the region must overcompensate with austerity as payment for past excesses.

The region remains vulnerable to external forces and imbalances emerge as global markets ebb and flow. From 2002 to 2012—despite the global financial crisis—Latin America benefitted from the strong tailwinds of the China-driven commodity super cycle. High revenues from commodity-rich nations financed demands of a growing middle class for health and education. With low relative returns in North America and Western Europe, portfolio inflows combined with commodity payments to overvalue exchange rates. FDI flowed to growing markets, once again distorting industrial growth with the Dutch disease infection by commodities. The super cycle has now ended, reverting to low raw materials prices and higher financing costs. The tightening of global liquidity is pressuring emerging markets. Imbalances have emerged in highly leveraged economies limping alongside an anemic global economy. Adjustment is necessary to meet growing imbalances in financing growth; the lackluster performance of 2012–2017 is insufficient to meet the growing demands of middle-income Latin America. Low-growth scenarios push convergence with industrialized countries further into the future.[6]

Beyond adjustment on fiscal and current accounts, revitalizing growth requires deeper changes in how goods are produced and distributed. Weak microeconomic fundamentals undergird the contemporary macroeconomic malaise. Latin America missed opportunities to engage in deep structural change during its golden period of high growth. It is not surprising that the euphoria of the Latin American decade infected policymakers with a belief that rapid growth and poverty reduction were the new normal. Once again, nations were blindsided by the crash in natural resource–based growth. The truism that the only way to engage in sustained growth is through enhancing productivity is, well, true. To make people genuinely better off, people need access to the assets and complementary factors to produce more for the same quantity of inputs. Enhanced productivity will result in an increase in the standard of living—not paying more for less. We know that rather than rising efficiency and output per worker, the region has been beset by anemic rates of growth in productivity, expanding the distance between global competitors in the United States or in Asia. The contemporary challenge in Latin America is promoting productive transformation by stimulating quality investment and jobs—despite the adverse conditions that slow international growth and the automation-reducing technologies that replace labor. This is a tough structural challenge.

Adapting micro foundations to new challenges of labor-saving technologies and brutal competition is of course a task that all nations face in our globalized economy—but Latin Americans must catch up to the profound structural changes ignored during the last boom. The challenge is not just devising market interventions to stimulate growth; rather Latin American reform requires fundamental changes in both the shape of the market and the role of the state. Latin American economies are disproportionately dominated by the informal sector—an economic space where low productivity breeds as firms confront a variety of market and governance failures. Vicious cycles of low levels of growth are perpetuated by lack of access to to cheap capital, intrusive bureaucracies, corrupt agents, crumbling infrastructure, failing education systems, poor health delivery and threatening climate change. With roughly half of economic activity untaxed, governments cannot adequately provide the menu of public goods required to jump start healthier economies.

Latin America's slow growth and low productivity trajectory is colliding with rising social demands. Poverty was halved and a new middle class sprang up in the regional boom period. This demographic change creates new demands for improved housing, health, transportation, and environmental sustainability. Cash-strapped governments now find it difficult to meet these quite reasonable requests. Falling revenues complicate the fiscal picture, forcing unpopular spending cuts that restrict rather than expand the public services on offer. Political parties are largely weak and fragmented in the face of enormous social pressures. One observes similar tensions in more advanced economies as well from the losers in a globalized economy. A key difference, however, is the depth of relative poverty and the fragility of social support in developing regions. Latin America also faces more difficult political challenges than Asian countries such as China where free expression is curtailed. Discontent in overwhelmingly democratic Latin America is also stoked by the open flow of images across the world wide web, underscoring differences between haves and have nots. Latin America is falling behind and Latin Americans know it.

TOWARD PRODUCTIVE, SUSTAINABLE GROWTH

The challenge of productive transformation begins by deepening the institutional capacity for countries to deliver a growth-producing economic environment. Restructuring the corrupt practices that erode national institutions is a first step. Although massive corruption scandals clog Facebook feeds and newspaper front pages, one can be encouraged by the new tools of transparency and legal accountability recently adopted in the region. Cleaning up corrupt political and business practices expands the scope of the rule of law that encourages market confidence. It is not easy—but it leads to significant gains.

Changes can enlarge the options each society faces in allocating scarce resources as well as to promote economically and environmentally sustainable development. Far from easy, these reforms will profoundly shape the ways people interact within institutions. **Institutions** are the rules that shape the behavior of organizations and individuals. **Formal rules**, such as constitutions, laws, and regulations, or **informal rules**, such as values and norms, condition and are conditioned by the process of economic change.[7] Old or brittle institutions may collapse under the weight of new economic challenges. The private sector has demanded changes in the quality and efficiency of financial and public services and judicial reform as it now perceives competitiveness to hinge on strong social, financial, and legal institutions. Institutional reform may also promote changes in the way economic agents behave. Increased **transparency** in judicial systems, for example, will encourage accountability in business dealings and foster international confidence in economic transactions. Institutional reform poses significant political and technical challenges. Losers in the political systems must somehow be convinced that the long-run gains are worth the cost. It is clear that new models of institutional reform are difficult to implement in economies struggling with a range of unresolved social and economic issues. It is easier to address efficiency-enhancing mechanisms than it is to strengthen tools to redistribute assets and decrease inequality.

The development of positive, facilitating institutions in an era of austerity is in many ways a trickier task. A new social contract must be devised that places pragmatism over populism. Globalization has layered increased demands on complex systems poorly positioned to deliver public services. The tendency to overpromise and underdeliver was a hallmark of populist regimes of the 1980s and 1990s. Developing economies are characterized by coordination problems and other market failures unresolved by smoothly functioning institutions. Politics are polarized and fractured. Where shall we look for answers?

Where both markets and governments have both failed, perhaps together they can deliver stronger results. Public-private partnerships (PPPs) can serve to improve outcomes across a range of sectors to deliver a robust environment for growth. PPPs have been formally articulated in the infrastructure space by creating new legal vehicles to encourage private financing and delivery of large-scale projects. The PPP Knowledge Lab defines a PPP as "a long-term contract between a private party and a government entity, for providing a public asset or service, in which the private party bears significant risk and management responsibility, and remuneration is linked to performance."[8] PPPs transcend the political cycle to deliver predictable outcomes in public services. We can also think about more informal or ad hoc PPPs, where the private sector is provided incentives to deliver social value. Sometimes these incentives are born of the market: it may be good for profits to create both private and social value. In other contexts, as Geoffrey Heal suggests, private social investment may occur as a response to the failure of markets and governments to deliver adequate levels of goods and services.[9] Whether formal contracts or more flexible institutions such as local chambers of commerce or industry associations, leveraging the strengths of both public and private sectors is critical to advancing sustainable growth.

Yet with the exception of governments riding resource booms, states are not able to spend their way out of these challenges; the money just is not there. Instead, with diligent attention to the fiscal bottom line, states are attempting to create incentives for the market to pull some weight in the social arena. Public-private partnerships to improve delivery of health and educational services are being employed to reinvigorate moribund systems. Accountability for social services allows is encouraged through local ownership of projects. Local governments are partnering with businesses in communities that have a vested interest in the development of better-educated, healthier workforces and cleaner work environments. Nonetheless, the market is not a substitute for good policy or hard choices, particularly in the areas of public goods provision. It can complement good governance, but it cannot replace it.

THE BALANCING ACT OF THE STATE

In balancing between global demands and local needs, the tricky policy issue is deciding just how much government is enough. Most Latin American governments have historically overcommitted to deliver social goods—but failed to do so efficiently. The pendulum may have swung too far toward the market in light of the weakness of market institutions in guaranteeing property rights, overseeing competition policy, and promoting social welfare. Although public-private partnerships are useful to attend to unmet needs, the invisible hand of the market may not work its magic when economic agents are unable to make rational, self-interested decisions because they simply don't have the minimal level of social assets to invest in themselves. States must be vigilant in their attempts to promote incentives for the formation of a domestic economy oriented not necessarily toward short-term consumption but rather to long-term investments in social and environmental systems. Incentives must be structured to change time horizons to preserve choices in the future. Nonetheless, democracy makes this process problematic, as the electoral cycle is poorly matched to the long-term investments required by genuine, balanced development.[10]

In addition to political constraints, the economic feasibility of long-term decision making may be legitimately questioned. Orientation to the international arena drives countries to focus on short-term macroeconomic performance variables: prices, exchange rates, and fiscal and current account balances. The room to maneuver is extremely limited. Once international investors get a sniff of disequilibrium or social discontent, they quickly shift to another, more stable investment.

Development is not a process of harmonious equilibrium. Much like people, economies grow in fits and starts, taking new and unintended directions. Yet the costs today of short-term disequilibrium are loss of investor confidence and instantaneous capital flight. We may have arrived at a kind of twitter international economy with an attention span that is limited to 140 characters. Economic policymakers have to learn the tools of international marketing to sell information about the national product in the global marketplace. The message must be clear and consistent. But the message in Latin America won't be a pleasant one unless the roots of poor productivity are resolved. Unfortunately, short-term policymaking does not encourage the necessary social investments to reverse the plight of the poor, reduce inequality, and promote sustainable development. Latin America is precariously poised with one foot in the fast-moving international arena and the other stuck in a complicated web of unequal social relations that act as a drag on productivity and change. Economic policymaking in the region is a delicate art of selling pragmatic, often-muted responses to intense need. Given the historical record of preferencing elites, few politicians are up to the task of convincing electorates that incremental change over time will make the less-advantaged better off. Nonetheless, big social programs are only viable in booming resource economies—and only for as long as it is favored by the commodity lottery. Venezuela's descent into chaos has been caused in part by a refusal to adjust the social model to new global realities.[11] Sustainable growth can only be achieved by the hard micro reforms of investing in people and social capital to promote opportunity, unleashing the entrepreneurial energies fostering genuine competitiveness.

#youtoo

As the world has become more tightly integrated and the ability to make economic mistakes has become more circumscribed, there may be a stronger role warranted for multilateral institutions. But we have also witnessed in the United States and Europe a turn inward, away from global commitments. In a "me first" global economy, do you have a responsibility?

As a consumer of goods produced in the international economy, you too have a role in articulating your social preferences. Public attention is directed not only to governments; the international media and the Internet provide important devices to articulate demands for socially and environmentally sound production. In the least, it is hoped that by reading this book you have become more aware of the problems facing people in other parts of the world, are better able to interpret and contextualize the enormous challenges of development, and better prepared, should you so choose, to participate in this arena as a more informed manager, policymaker, activist, or consumer in the international economy.

Key Concepts

formal rules	institutions	stabilization
informal rules	productivity	transparency
institutional capacity		

Chapter Summary

- Cycles of development have persisted in Latin America, calling into question the resolution of internal and external constraints, the problem of stability in the face of change, the target of economic policy, the role of the state, and the tension between current needs and sustainable future development.
- The periods of primary product exports, import substitution development, and the neoliberal model have addressed these issues differently. The economic contradictions of one period cause the pendulum to swing to a different degree of openness and state intervention.

• Growth in a globalized economy characterized by increasing automation requires deep structural changes in micro foundations. In addition to strengthening institutions, investments are indicated to promote inclusive growth that facilitates a shift from a low productivity informal economy to more dynamic, high productivity growth.

N o t e s

1. Marlise Simons, "A Talk with Gabriel García Marquez," *New York Times,* December 5, 1982, sec. 7, p. 7, available at www.nytimes.com/books/97/06/15/reviews/marquez-talk.html and in the LEXIS-NEXIS database.

2. Latinobarómetro Informe, 2016, www.latinobarometro.org.

3. Dudley Althaus, "Deforestation Contributed to Tragedy by Mitch in Honduras, Experts Claim," *Houston Chronicle*, December 30, 1998, A1, as found in the LEXIS-NEXIS database.

4. IMF, Chapter 3, "The Effects of Weather Shocks on Economic Activity: How Can Low-Income Countries Cope?," *World Economic Outlook*, October 2017.

5. Javier Santiso, *Latin America's Political Economy of the Possible: Beyond Good Revolutionaries and Free-Marketeers,"* (Cambridge, MA: MIT Press, 2007).

6. IMF Regional Economic Outlook, "Latin America and the Caribbean: Stuck in Low Gear," October 13, 2017.

7. World Bank, *Beyond the Washington Consensus: Institutions Matter, Regional Brief* (Washington, DC: World Bank, 1998), available at www.worldbank.org.

8. https://pppknowledgelab.org.

9. Geoffrey M. Heal, *Corporate Social Responsibility – An Economic and Financial Framework* (December 2004). Available at SSRN: https://ssrn.com/abstract=642762 or http://dx.doi.org/10.2139/ssrn.642762.

10. Santiso, 2007.

11. Ricardo Hausmann, "D-Day Venezuela," Project Syndicate, January 2, 2018, www.project-syndicate.org/columnist/ricardo-hausmann.

Glossary

absorption Absorption is domestic consumption of goods both produced at home and imported from abroad. The IMF promoted the absorption approach, or the reduction of domestic utilization of resources to release them for export to earn hard currency to finance a country's debt.

active labor market policies (ALMPs) government programs such as training, apprenticeships, and vocational classes to help the unemployed find work.

adaptation A response to global warming and **climate change** to reduce the vulnerability of social and biological systems to relatively sudden **change**. Unlike mitigation, which addresses root causes, adaptation seeks to lower the risks of consequences from climate change.

additionality The verification that an intervention has had the intended effect compared to a baseline measure. For example, if a global organization paid a country to halt deforestation--but the country had no intention of cutting down trees in the first place--additionality would not be met.

agricultural extension programs Programs to introduce new agricultural practices to peasant farming communities.

AIDS Acquired Immunodeficiency Syndrome (AIDS) is a deadly condition caused by the human immunodeficiency virus (HIV), commonly spread through unprotected sexual activity or intravenous drug use. This global epidemic is a major cause of death in Latin America, particularly in Central America. The poor are disproportionately affected, with infection rates among the poor reaching over 50% in some nations.

ALBA (the Bolivarian Alternative of the Americas)—a regional trade association not allied with the United States, it has grown to include among Caribbean states Bolivia, Ecuador, and Nicaragua; Iran and Syria are observer countries. ALBA's developmentalist precepts of solidarity and state-driven trade stand in contrast to the open regional approaches of Peru and Colombia in the Pacific Alliance.

Austral Plan Argentina's Austral plan, named after the new currency put in place in 1985, was designed to combat inflation. The Austral plan was labeled as heterodox but also included some orthodox measures. To attack the inertial component of inflation, the administration declared a price freeze in June of 1985, froze wages, and implemented exchange-rate controls. These measures were taken to convince the population that prices would not increase, but the plan fell apart after people lost confidence in the ability of the government to manage the economy.

backward linkage   As industry A grows, demand for inputs to produce industry A's product will increase. This increase in demand can spur investment in a new industry B that will produce inputs for industry A. Central to the thought of A. O. Hirschman, investing in industries with strong backward linkages on the supply chain should promote growth.

Border Environment Cooperation Commission (BECC)   and the trinational Commission for Environmental Cooperation (CEC). To preserve, protect, and enhance human health and the environment of the US - Mexico border region, by strengthening cooperation among interested parties and supporting sustainable projects through a transparent binational process in close coordination with NADB, federal, state and local agencies, the private sector, and the general public.

bottom of the pyramid (BOP) marketing   BOP marketing provides products and services to low-income customers with packaging and payment plans tailored to those with limited budgets and often unpredictable income streams.

Bresser Plan   A follow-up to the Cruzado plan, the Brazilian use of heterodox policy to combat inflation in 1987. Wages were frozen, mini-devaluations were used to manage the exchange rate, and interest rates were targeted above the rate of inflation. Citizens were deputized as price inspectors. Despite initial success, shortages and external balance problems caused by excess consumer spending reignited inflation once again.

caciques   Spanish word for the landlords of large agricultural estates prevalent in the Latin American colonial period.

capital controls   Mechanisms such as licensing of foreign exchange used to limit imports or reduce capital flight, or taxation on short-term foreign investments to reduce the volatility of short-term capital flows.

capital flight   Large outflows of domestic capital into safer or more stable foreign banks and foreign stock markets to protect the value of that capital. This phenomenon is associated with countries suffering from severe inflation or the likelihood of devaluation. Individuals opt to invest abroad when they lose confidence in their country's currency.

Central American Common Market   Formed early in the 1960s, this attempt at integration among Central American countries to take advantage of economies of scale in production was set back in the 1970s and 1980s by political strife. The 1990s saw new commitment to strengthening the legal and institutional framework, joint actions to reduce debt, and cooperation on sectoral issues.

Chicago School   This free market school of thought, a precursor to the neoliberal model, advocated a hands-off role for the state. Adherents believe that the market and open international trade are the main engines behind development.

commodity lottery   A term used by Victor Bulmer-Thomas that describes the export-oriented pattern of the late 1800s, when most Latin American countries were dependent on one export good, such as nitrates in Chile, coffee in Brazil, and tin in Bolivia.

common market   A form of integration in which countries coordinate policy-making measures in such areas as agriculture and the social sector, along with establishing a common external tariff.

Community of Andean Nations (CAN)   Andean Community, Spanish Comunidad Andina (CAN), formerly (1969–97) Andean Group. South American organization founded to encourage industrial, agricultural, social, and trade cooperation. Formed in 1969 by the Cartagena Agreement, the group originally consisted of Bolivia, Colombia, Ecuador, Peru, and Chile; Venezuela joined in 1973 but withdrew in 2006, and Chile withdrew in 1977. Peru suspended its membership in 1992 but resumed it in 1997. CAN's headquarters are in Lima, Peru.

conditional cash transfers (CCTs)   In exchange for meeting health and education conditions such as vaccinations and 85 percent school attendance, families are given cash payments to offset the opportunity costs of children not working and provide incentives to keep kids in school.

corporate social responsibility (CSR)   A corporation's programs to assess and take responsibility for environmental and social wellbeing. CSR can build reputational capital, seek a license to operation, or be another form of advertising.

conditionality   A term associated with the prerequisites necessary for disbursal of IMF funds to developing countries. Countries seeking loans from the IMF must first implement tough stabilization policies such as a decrease in fiscal spending, tight monetary policy, and strict trade policies. Conditionality is strongly debated because it forces a government to contract its economy and imposes social costs.

Convertibility Plan   Introduced in 1991 in Argentina, this policy to combat inflation tied the Argentine peso to the US dollar and used a currency board to constrain monetary policy by law. The money supply could not increase unless there was a parallel increase in dollar reserves. Inflation was almost eliminated, but at a high cost in terms of recession and unemployment.

corruption   A complex and encompassing term, corruption is broadly defined as the abuse of power for private gain. Systemic corruption is pervasive across all levels of government in Latin America, damaging both national performance and public trust in institutions.

coordination failure   When actions of one sector depend on the actions of another sector, but the sectors do not coordinate, leading to an inefficient outcome.

cost-push elements   Certain conditions or external shocks such as food shortages or increasing oil prices that will fuel inflation through the interaction with powerful labor organizations or a concentrated industry structure. Rising costs are seen as pushing up prices.

Cruzado Plan   Based on a structuralist's diagnosis of inflation, the first Cruzado plan in Brazil, in 1986, focused on the inertial component of inflation and implemented heterodox measures by freezing prices, wages, and exchange rates. Brazilians were deputized as fiscais, or price inspectors, to police the price freeze in supermarkets and shopping malls. Indexation of contracts with less than one year's duration was prohibited. A new currency, the cruzado, was created at a value of 1,000 cruzeiros. After a devaluation, the cruzado was fixed at 13.84 cruzados to the dollar. A neglect of tough fiscal adjustments combined with passive monetary policy that accommodated domestic deficits resulted in the re-eruption of inflation.

customs union   A form of regional trade integration in which a common external tariff is established for the group.

debt-for-equity swap   A win-win method used by firms, banks, and indebted countries to reduce exposure to the debt crisis. A firm wishing to invest in a particular country would buy the country's debt at a discount from a bank through the secondary market. Owing the firm and not the bank, the country could pay the firm in local currency, as opposed to dollars, which the firm then used to buy local supplies and pay workers. Banks got risky loans off their books, countries were released from the need to earn hard currency to service the debt, and firms were repaid the full value of the loan bought at a discount. The plan was limited, however, by inflationary risk and the demand for equity investments.

debt-for-nature swap   An environmental twist on debt-for-equity swaps, in which international organizations buy a country's discounted debt from the secondary market. Debts are reduced or canceled in exchange for a country establishing nature preserves or otherwise protecting the environment. A financial commitment to long-term management of the parks, sometimes through a trust fund, was an important element of success.

debt sustainability   The ability of a country to meet its debt obligations without requiring debt relief, accumulating arrears or significantly compromising growth.

debt trap   When long-term projects are financed through short-term debt issues, countries may find themselves paying more in interest and principal than they are receiving in new money. Initially, the borrower is able to finance the project as well as pay the principal and interest with new lending each year. With each coming year, new lending available for investment dwindles because some of the money from new loans is used to pay the principal and interest on previous loans. The debt trap sets in when the new lending is not enough to pay for the principal and interest and the project is not yet generating significant returns to make up the difference.

decentralization   A devolution of governmental responsibilities from centralized bureaucracies to state and local levels. The ability to raise revenues is sometimes also moved to the local level, although systems of fiscal accountability need to be tightened to improve internal balance.

declining terms of trade   Terms of trade are the price of exports relative to the price of imports, mathematically expressed as Px/Pm, an index of export prices divided by an index of import prices. Declining terms of trade are reflected in a decrease in the ratio, meaning that the price of imports is increasing relative to the price of exports. Under these conditions, countries must export increasing amounts of their own goods (often agricultural goods or commodities) to pay for imports (more likely to be machinery and high-tech items).

demand-driven rural investment funds (DRIFs)   The allocation of central government funds to local governments or communities to promote local control of agricultural development. Certain eligibility requirements must be met, and beneficiaries must contribute to the cost of the projects, often through volunteer labor.

dependency theory   Despite different emphases by scholars, the central theme behind dependency is the proposition that a developing country's growth is constrained. Industrialized countries (the center) advance at the expense of the third world (the periphery), causing underdevelopment in the region through exploitation of cheap labor and extraction of resources. Underdevelopment was seen as linked to the relationship between the elite of Latin America and the center in their search for short-term profits as opposed to long-term growth.

development   The process of meeting the basic needs of the population and enhancing options for how economic resources will be allocated today and in the future to increase the choices citizens have in their daily lives.

discretionary   Something left up to the decision of the agent. In the case of education, what portions of a curriculum to teach or emphasize are at the teacher's discretion.

dualism   The simultaneous existence of modern and traditional economies, usually characterized by an expanding industrial sector and a large self-subsistence agricultural sector. Dualistic models tend to benefit the elite and marginalize the poor.

Dutch disease   Named after Holland's experience with natural gas, the term describes a country's inclination to concentrate its financial resources into a few profitable sectors. This behavior was prevalent throughout Latin American history with investments in oil and sugar, and it contributed to the unbalanced development of the region as other important sectors were ignored.

early childhood education   The education of young children before primary school, starting at infant age. Early childhood education has been shown to be crucial in determining future education and employment outcomes. Strong investment in early childhood education increases returns to investment in later education.

economic populism   Economic populism is patterned after the behavior of many charismatic Latin American leaders, such as Juan Perón in Argentina, whose programs were symbolically designed to attend to the needs of the poor. Industry was pacified with large subsidies. The welfare of future generations is sacrificed for the welfare of current generations through excessive current spending to satisfy pressure groups. In a desire to increase the standard of living today, this kind of behavior ignores external balance of payments constraints and large fiscal deficits, conditions that make inflation nearly inevitable.

economic union   A group of countries that have moved beyond a common market to embrace common sectoral policies. Common monetary policies and a common currency constitute an additional step toward an economic community. Mercosur is therefore an economic union, whereas the European Union has moved a step beyond.

Education for All (EFA)   A United Nations initiative advocating for adequate education that meets basic learning needs for all people.

Education for All Development Index (EDI)   An index that measures a nation's achievement of Education for All goals, based on universal primary education, adult literacy, gender parity, and survival to fifth grade. EDI numbers for Latin America show that most nations are close to achieving EFA.

ejidos   Land that had been held communally for centuries before the introduction of private property. This is the predominant form of peasant landholding in Mexico.

empowerment   The full participation of beneficiaries in their own development process.

enclaves   Industries, in isolation from the rest of the economy, that fail to spur domestic investment, employment, and income.

encomienda   Land received by conquistadors or other Spanish settlers from the Spanish Crown that was accompanied by the deeding of Indian labor to work this land.

Engel's Law   When the increase in the demand for agricultural goods is slower than an increase in income (that is, there is a low income elasticity of demand), exporters of agricultural goods lose ground to producers of manufactured goods. When a low income elasticity for agricultural products exists, this means that if individuals experience an increase in their income, they will not increase their consumption of food or commodities by the same proportion. There is, for example, only so much coffee or sugar one will consume, no matter the increase in income. Engel's Law was used by economists such as Raúl Prebisch to explain why the developing world, which tends to export agricultural commodities, experiences declining terms of trade.

epidemiological backlog   The simultaneous health challenge of addressing traditional diseases (such as cholera or dysentery tied to inadequate infrastructure and malnutrition) and the diseases of modern society (such as cancer and heart disease).

epidemiological transition   The transition from a focus on fighting traditional diseases such as cholera to a focus on more modern concerns such as heart disease.

equity   The access to equal opportunities within a nation. Although growth may increase inequality, models of growth with equity attempt to promote a more equal distribution of income. Equity also refers to ownership of capital—a very different use of the same term.

Exchange-rate-based stabilization programs   Address inflation by using the exchange rate as the main nominal anchor.

export pessimism   A term associated with the Prebisch-Singer thesis, stating that exports alone cannot be the engine of growth because of the effect of declining terms of trade.

externalities   A cost or a benefit that results from an activity or transaction that is imposed on parties outside the transaction. Pollution is a negative externality of production; reducing the spread of disease is a positive externality of education.

extreme poverty   Although levels vary by the local cost of living, those subsisting on roughly less than US$1 a day are considered to be living in extreme poverty. Moderate poverty is roughly US$2 per day, or between US$50 (World Bank benchmark) and US$60 a month (ECLAC level).

factor price equalization   As a country opens up to trade, the demand for its products, made with its most abundant (and cheap) factor, should in theory over time result in an increase in the price of this factor to world levels. Global factor prices should therefore become more uniform.

fazenda   Large feudal estates, similar to the *hacienda* in Spanish America, during the colonial period in Brazil.

financialization   Refers to the growth and strengthening of financial markets and institutions. Increasing financialization has interwoven global financial markets and increased the flows of capital across borders.

foreign direct investment (FDI)   Describes the investment by foreigners through ownership of equity shares or setting up production facilities within a country. The most common type of foreign direct investor is the multinational corporation.

formal rules   The constitutions, laws, and written regulations that structure economic activity and guarantee property rights.

forward linkage   The production of a good that is complementary to another industry may spur the development of that new sector; such development is called a forward linkage. As opposed to a backward linkage, which calls for the production of critical inputs, a forward linkage moves ahead in the production chain. Roadside restaurants might be a forward linkage to automobile production, whereas tires would be considered a backward linkage.

free trade area (FTA)   A form of regional integration in which trade restrictions are abolished between participating countries, but each country maintains an independent trade policy and separate tariff rates with the rest of the world.

gender gap   Differences between male and female ownership and access to agricultural assets.

Gini coefficient   A measure of income inequality that gauges the difference between a hypothetical society where income is perfectly equal and the actual income distribution. It is derived from the Lorenz curve. The higher the Gini coefficient, the more extensive is income inequality.

Global Competitiveness Index   This composite index attempts to capture the collection of factors, policies, and institutions that can determine the level of prosperity of an economy by weighting the quality of the macroeconomic environment, the state of public institutions, and the level of technological readiness in an economy.

Global Environmental Facility (GEF)   A global financing partner of 183 countries, international, civil society organizations, and the private sector to facilitate environmental change.

global public goods   Goods that transcend national boundaries, are difficult to exclude people from consuming, and the consumption by one does not diminish the good for another. A good example is clean air.

GMOs   Genetically modified organisms (GMOs) are crops that have been genetically altered to possess a more favorable trait, such as increased resistance to insects. GMOs typically cannot reproduce, so farmers must buy seeds every planting season. Agribusiness is largely dependent on GMOs, and the high cost of GMO seeds poses a barrier to entry to small farmers.

golden age of primary product exports   The period in Latin American history from the late 1800s to the early 1900s, when primary product exports boomed and contributed to the economic growth of the region.

gross enrollment ratio (GER)   A measure that shows the number of students enrolled at a particular grade level, as a ratio of students who qualify for that grade level.

growth   A simultaneous gradual increase in quantities such as GDP, population, savings, and wealth. If the benefits of growth are not widely shared, it may not be considered development.

hacienda   Large feudal estate in Spanish America.

headcount ratio   The headcount ratio (HCR) is the proportion of a population that exists, or lives, below the poverty line. The can be measured internationally (at $1.90) or by national standards of poverty.

Health for All (HFA)   is a WHO-sponsored universal health care initiative that promotes health as integral to development. It encourages increased access to water, sanitation, food, nutrition, mother and child care, family planning, immunization, and disease control, as well as other resources necessary for a healthy society. It emphasizes access to primary health care as a preventative health care strategy.

heart disease   A wide array of health conditions affecting the heart, ranging from high blood pressure to heart attack or stroke. Heart disease is extremely prevalent in Latin America, particularly among the poor, causing significantly more deaths than infectious diseases.

Heckscher-Ohlin theorem   A key theoretical construct in international trade that suggests that a country should trade the good that uses relatively intensively that country's most abundant factor.

heterodox policies   Monetary and fiscal policies grounded in the belief that one of the primary components of inflation is the inertia built into an economic chain, with wages increased in anticipation of future price increases, making inflation a self-fulfilling prophecy. Heterodox policies attempt to combat inflation by neutralizing expectations through price and wage freezes.

highly indebted poor country (HIPC) initiative   Through the HIPC initiative, nominal debt service relief of more than US$59 billion has been approved for twenty-nine countries, reducing their net present value of external debt by approximately two-thirds. Of these countries, nineteen have reached the completion point and have been granted unconditional debt service relief of more than US$37 billion.

Human Development Index (HDI)   The United Nations Human Development Report calculates the HDI as a composite of life expectancy at birth, educational attainment (measured by adult literacy and school enrollments), and income.

Human Opportunity Index (HOI)   Measures the degree to which exogenous circumstances such as family background predetermine outcomes. Running from zero to one hundred, a society enjoying nearly universal access to water, electricity, and sanitation as well as school enrollment and timely completion of the sixth grade would score closer to one hundred.

illiquidity   A condition in which cash flow does not match financial obligations. As opposed to insolvency, when an economic entity cannot and will not ever likely meet its obligations, illiquidity may be a temporary condition in which revenues do not cover costs of debt service. In the first stage of the debt crisis, countries were thought to have temporary liquidity problems; it was later seen that fundamental restructuring and debt relief were called for.

import substitution industrialization (ISI)   ISI was the dominant economic policy in Latin America during the 1950s, 1960s, and 1970s as a response to dependency and structuralist theories. It represented a shift away from the outward orientation of export promotion, to an inward-looking orientation. ISI was designed to replace imports with domestic production under the guiding hand of the state. Governments used activist industrial, fiscal, and monetary policy to achieve growth.

incomplete markets   Markets in developing countries may be incomplete in the sense that they do not efficiently convey price signals to buyers or sellers. This may be due to lack of information, a limited number of participants, or the market infrastructure. When markets do not adjust smoothly, transactions costs rise and economic activity is compromised. Neostructuralists and new institutionalists suggest a role for the state in supplementing economic activity where markets are incomplete.

indexation   Under a system of indexation, countries will revise wages and financial prices upward by taking into account expected as well as past inflation. When indexation occurs, countries have embraced inflation and it becomes a part of daily life. Because incomes are protected, the inflation is less painful.

inertial inflation   Implies that inflation is not driven solely by an increase in the money supply, but by expectations as well. As individuals anticipate inflation, they will demand higher wages or set prices accordingly, which will push prices upward.

inflationary expectations   The expectations of a society, based on past experience, of future rates of inflation. When they anticipate future price increases, economic actors demand higher wages or set prices higher to cover the inflation they expect in the future, making the expectations a self-fulfilling prophecy. Inflationary expectations are a large part of inertial inflation.

informal rules   Values and norms that condition and are conditioned by the process of economic change.

informal sector   Small-scale business operations such as selling goods on street corners or providing cleaning services in homes. The informal sector operates outside the official, taxed economy. It is characterized by a low capital-labor ratio, family-intensive production, and worker-owned means of production. The informal sector can be divided into three areas — microenterprise employment, own-account workers, and domestic service.

informality   The informal sector encompasses work that is not compliant with tax and labor laws. At the firm level, informality can mean being unregistered, evading taxes, or hiring self-employed contractors to avoid legal requirements of having actual employees. At the worker level, informality typically means unprotected labor, as informal workers are not covered by social insurance.

information and communications technology (ICT)   Telecommunications technology such as Internet, telephone, and audiovisual systems. Access to ICT introduces the option of distance learning, which is particularly important for increasing education access in rural sectors.

information asymmetries   When there is a difference in the information available to two agents in a decision-making process, negatively impacting an agent's ability to make an informed decision.

insecure property rights   When owners of property are not sure of their rights to use or dispose of their property. When institutions guaranteeing land titles are inefficient or nonexistent, farmers may underinvest in developing property because there is a good chance that the returns from efforts will be appropriated by another. Insecure property rights are an important cause of environmental damage, because economic actors may exploit land and natural resources now if they assume that they will not, or may not, continue to have access to these inputs in the future.

institutional capacity   The ability of governments, business, nongovernmental groups, and communities to plan and manage programs efficiently and effectively.

institutionalist tradition   A vision of development policy that accords a strong role for nonmarket institutions. Institutionalists assume that markets are not perfect; that people are not purely rational, self-interested maximizers; and that economic power rather than efficiency will shape outcomes. For institutionalists, access to and control over technology is an important ingredient of dynamic (or sluggish) growth.

institutions   Rules that shape the behavior of organizations and individuals engaged in economic activity.

involuntary lending   During the debt crisis, involuntary lending described the process of rolling over the principal and interest payments due on a loan into new (usually more expensive) loans to give countries breathing room to meet their financial obligations. It was believed that after their economies became more productive through the tough measures required by the IMF, these countries would then be able to pay off their debt. Banks preferred to package the interest and principal due into a new loan because it kept the loan in the "performing" category rather than having a past-due amount trigger a classification of this asset as nonperforming, and therefore worth less.

labor market distortions   Movements away from free labor markets, these include government intervention in setting wages, high costs of dismissal, high payroll taxes, and the contentious nature of labor-management relations.

land reform   Given unequal patterns of landholdings created by colonial patronage, some governments have attempted to redistribute land. These movements have been revolutionary at times, taking tracts of land from the rich and giving them to the poor, as well as progressive, where only land that has been idle or unproductive is reassigned to those who might use it more intensively.

latifundia   Feudal estates in Spanish Latin America, which stood in great contrast to the small parcels of land (known as *minifundias*) used by peasant farmers. The *latifundia* also served as a form of political, social, and economic organization and later contributed to a pattern of concentrated landholdings and power.

Learning for All   The World Bank's education strategy not only targets young people going to school but also cautions that they learn relevant skills while there.

logistics   is defined as the process for transporting inputs, goods, and services from the point of production to the final consumer. Several factors affect logistics, including transportation infrastructure and tracking and tracing systems. Poor logistics across the region are a major drag on regional competitiveness.

Lorenz curve   A graphical representation of income distribution. The population is sorted by income, usually deciles, and the percentage of income that each portion of the population holds is plotted. For example, in the Lorenz curve for Latin America, the first 20 percent of the population holds 2.5 percent of the income, and the first 40 percent a cumulative 8.6 percent. Altogether, the bottom 60 percent accounts for 19.6 percent of income, with the top 20 percent holding nearly two-thirds of the total.

mandamiento   A system by which communities, most often indigenous, were forced to provide workers for harvest when there were labor shortages, often under brutal working conditions.

marginal abatement cost   The cost to clean up a unit of pollution. When there is a lot of pollution, the easiest and cheapest alternatives can be chosen. As cleanup continues, the options become more expensive, leading to higher marginal abatement costs.

marginal social damage (MSD)   The increase in health costs, the losses from depreciating biodiversity, and the general loss of well-being from living in an unsustainable environment.

market-based initiatives Environmental policy instruments using markets, prices, taxes, or subsidies to provide incentives for polluters to address negative environmental externalities.

market failure Neoclassical economic theorists believe that when left on its own, the market will promote economic growth. When the market fails to promote growth, primarily because of information constraints or ineffective price signals, market failure occurs.

mental health care Health care services aimed at treating mental health disorders, which significantly burden Latin America. Mental health is highly stigmatized in the region, making it difficult to achieve adequate mental health care. Mental illness is the leading cause of reduced productivity, so providing effective mental health care is crucial for the region's development.

Mercosur The South American common market comprising Argentina, Brazil, Uruguay, Venezuela, and Paraguay as well as associate members Chile and Bolivia.

merit good Investment in public goods such as education and health that have benefits for society in general.

microcredit Banking services that reach down to the small-scale entrepreneur. Collateral for loans is often provided by an investment circle that guarantees repayment of members. Microlending makes investment over time possible for the poor, but some question whether, because of the amounts involved and the repayment structure, microcredit makes a significant difference in people's lives.

middle income trap (MIT) Refers to the challenge facing middle-income countries in the global value chain. These nations are too developed to have an advantage in low wages and cheap labor, but lack technology and efficiency to compete with highly developed nations in knowledge-intensive sectors.

minifundia The small parcels of land used for subsistence farming by Latin American peasants during the colonial period and whose remnants can still be seen today.

multidimensional poverty measures In addition to income measures, standardized metrics to assess well-being. The Human Development Index (HDI) uses metrics for life expectancy, mean years of schooling, and expected years of schooling in addition to per capita income.

net enrollment rate Net primary enrolment rate in primary education is the number of pupils of official primary school age who are enrolled in primary education as a percentage of the total children of the official school age population.

nontraditional agricultural exports (NTAEs) Policies such as agricultural extension training or preferential credit to promote goods that are not in the traditional export profile. By diversifying exports, countries are able to capture new markets and be less dependent on price swings in traditional commodities.

North American Free Trade Agreement (NAFTA) The Agreement was signed by the United States, Canada, and Mexico in 1994. It sought to reduce tariffs within a ten-year period, increase trade in the region, promote cross-border investment, and introduce environmental and labor standards across the region.

occupational health concerns   Health hazards originating from the workplace, such as heavy physical exertion or exposure to excessive noise, radiation, chemicals, viruses, or other toxins. Occupational health concerns are now the leading cause of health issues among adults in Latin America.

official flows   Official flows are comprised of Official Development Assistance (ODA) and Other Official Flows (OOF). ODAs refer to aid money distributed to poor countries with the goal of improving economic development. OOFs refer to aid money given without development as a primary goal. Official flows are typically distributed by developed nations, such as the United States, or multilateral organizations, such as the United Nations.

Olivera-Tanzi effect   The process by which inflation erodes the true value of tax receipts because of the time lag between assessment of tax liability and actual collection.

opaque nature of the good   When the characteristics of a good or service are not easily observable. For example, you know if a shoe has shoddy sewing; it is harder for a parent to observe the quality of education.

opportunity costs   The potential gain foregone from alternative A when alternative B is chosen.

overvalued exchange rates   Under a fixed exchange rate system, a rate is overvalued when inflation has eroded the true value of the money but a new par or official rate has not been established. For example, if inflation in country A is 25 percent a year higher than in country B and their currencies are fixed in terms of each other, the country experiencing inflation will have a currency that is 25 percent overvalued at the end of one year. Overvaluation of a currency is not sustainable because it encourages imports and discourages exports. If it is not corrected by contracting the economy, people will expect a devaluation, or adjustment in the currency price. As reserves to pay for the current account imbalance are drawn down, people will begin to vote with their feet, moving capital to currencies without the risk of devaluation.

Pacific Alliance (PA)   Chile, Colombia, Mexico and Peru signed the Pacific Alliance in 2012, aimed at increasing "the free circulation of goods, services, capital, and people," while also providing a unified platform for deeper integration with the Asia-Pacific region.

payments for environmental services (PES)   Ttransactions where a positive environmental service or cleanup activity is being paid for by another party, usually with confirmation that the service provision has met predetermined standards.

portfolio bonds   Short-term financial instruments held in emerging market portfolios that make a country vulnerable to quick movements of international capital flows.

poverty line   The minimum income required to purchase the goods necessary for subsistence. Although this varies by location, US$2 per day is the global benchmark for moderate poverty and US$1 a day for extreme poverty.

precarious employment   Employment in nonstandard sectors where employees lack many rights and protections such as insurance, benefits, or labor regulations. Women are particularly vulnerable to precarious employment.

preferential trade agreements (PTAs)   Trade agreements such as free trade arrangements or customs unions that promote economic activity within a region by favoring trading partners within that region over those outside it.

primary health care (PHC)   Health care that promotes basic sanitation and nutrition practices to increase people's control over improvements in their environment so as to maintain a decent quality of life and achieve human and social potential.

principal agent problem,   One party (the principal) contracts with another to undertake an activity (the agent) but cannot directly observe the extent to which the outcomes meet the contract's goal.

private social investment   Investment in the social sector by a private agent, often a corporation.

productivity   A measure of output in relation to inputs. Rising productivity is a key to economic growth.

provisioning   A response by banks to the debt crisis whereby they would set aside profits (before dividend payments) against risky loans so as to reduce their exposure to debt.

Real Plan   Introduced by Brazilian president Henrique Fernando Cardoso when he was minister of the economy, the Real Plan redenominated wages, prices, taxes, and the exchange rate in a new accounting unit called the urv. Later, a new currency, the real, was introduced. Contractionary monetary policies were undertaken. Unlike many previous attempts, the Real Plan proved to be successful, neutralizing inflationary expectations and curbing inflation.

regional integration   Regional integration is the matching of economic and other policies within a region. The simplest form of integration is a free trade area (FTA) covering goods, with lower (or no) tariffs on goods exchanged within the region. The next level would include an FTA with services and perhaps regulations in other areas such as the environment or social concerns. A customs union deepens the commitment with a common external tariff. A common market permits the movement of factors of production among member countries, and an economic union expands on this to cede sovereignty over commercial, fiscal, and monetary policy to a supranational authority. Regional integration may make the liberalization process politically palatable through playing on sentiments of reciprocity of neighbor markets, and it may improve the confidence of investors because policies of openness have been locked in by treaty.

remittances   Money sent back to families or communities in Latin America by those living abroad. Particularly in Central America, it is not uncommon for a head of household to support a family by working in the United States. Flows of remittances make up significant portions of GDP in some nations.

repartida   Monopoly control over mines and land in the New World was accorded through the encomienda system, which gave land rights to colonists, with a share of the output or repartida owed in return back to the home country.

repetition rates   The proportion of pupils from a grade cohort enrolled at a given school who study in the same grade in the following school year. When children are held back, this creates wasted teaching resources for the material that was learned.

rules of origin   The criteria needed to determine the national source of a product. Their importance is derived from the fact that duties and restrictions in several cases depend upon the source of imports.

secondary market   A market for a financial instrument that separates the initial debt issuer from the eventual lender. During the debt crisis, many banks were pessimistic about the ability of Latin American countries to repay loans. In particular, small- and medium-sized banks wanted to unload risky loans and offered them for resale below their face value in the secondary market. Larger banks (with a greater likelihood of being repaid) or multinational corporations interested in operating in a foreign market might choose to assume this credit risk at a discounted price. The larger bank or firm might, for example, pay 50 cents for a piece of paper saying that the borrowing country owed it a dollar. The greater the risk of default, the lower the secondary market price. Buyers of the debt could earn a substantial profit if a Latin American country paid off its debt in full, or in any proportion higher than what the debt was bought for.

seignorage   An increase in the money supply by the mere printing of more currency, usually for the purpose of financing government spending. A government can profit from such an operation because it results in inflation. The government then is able to repay its debts in currency that is worth less than the currency that was borrowed. The result of monetary expansion might be short-run expansion of output, but eventually the increase in money will mean only an increase in prices.

short- and long-term portfolio investments   In portfolio investments, foreign investors purchase assets such as stocks, bonds, and securities in nation's financial markets. These investments, particularly short-term ones, leave nations exposed to quick outflows of foreign capital, as well as speculation.

short-term money   This includes the "hot" capital flow of portfolio bonds and stocks that may be moved from country to country in an internationally linked global financial system with the stroke of a keyboard.

social entrepreneurship   Refers to organizations that cater to basic human needs that existing markets and institutions fail to satisfy. Combining the resourcefulness of traditional entrepreneurship with a mission of changing society, social entrepreneurship can create enormous social—and commercial—value.

sovereign guarantee   The backing of a national government (collateralized by national assets) in the extension of a loan.

Stolper-Samuelson effect   As the price of the more abundant (and cheaper) factor rises after an opening of trade, the owners of this factor — in the case of the developing countries, labor — will accrue the largest gain. Trade should therefore make owners of the cheapest factor better off.

structural adjustment programs   Often supported by the World Bank and the IMF, these programs are designed to address internal and external balance by decreasing domestic expenditure, enhancing revenue collection, promoting exports, and limiting luxury imports. These programs changed the shape or structure of economies from the inward-oriented import substitution model to an externally oriented export promotion program, simultaneously privatizing state industries, decreasing government expenditures, and encouraging inflows of foreign capital.

structuralists   Drawing on the work of the Economic Commission for Latin America (ECLA) under Raúl Prebisch, structuralists begin from the assumption that the underlying structure of developing economies differs from that of more industrialized nations. Macro policy for structuralists rests on the premise that relatively concentrated industrial elites can pass on price increases, resulting in inertial inflation. Structuralists tend to downplay the importance of fiscal balance in favor of an activist state policy to redress production bottlenecks. Structuralists and their intellectual descendants, the neostructuralists, have little faith in the ability of the market to generate spontaneous or equitable growth. Borrowing from dependency analysts, structuralists believe that the position of countries in the international system, especially their access to technology, limits possibilities for autonomous growth. Although neostructuralists appreciate the benefits of international trade and finance, they caution that states should intervene to mitigate the social and environmental costs of openness.

targeting   A method of allocating social expenditures by identifying and distributing funds to those most in need. Targeted policies have often replaced general programs such as price subsidies on tortillas or milk that could not distinguish between the needy and the well-off. An example of a targeted policy would be a food debit card that is replenished when a mother brings a child to a clinic for preventive health care.

technological change   The key to economic development, technological change allows for new combinations of capital and labor to create more efficient production.

theory of comparative advantage   This theory states that to maximize global output, each country should apply its resources to producing those goods that it can produce relatively most efficiently.

total factor productivity (TFP)   Total factor productivity refers to the effect of labor and capital on growth. TFP effectively measures an economy's technology and efficiency .

trade creation   A benefit of economic integration whereby a trade agreement leads to an increase in overall trade. An integration agreement has positive effects if trade creation exceeds trade diversion.

trade diversion   An effect of economic integration, when trade with a more efficient global producer is discontinued in favor of products from a regional trading partner.

transaction costs   Expenses incurred when producing or delivering a good or service. These might include communication charges, legal fees, informational, or search costs.

transnational corporations (TNCs)   Transnational corporations, also known as multinational corporations (MNCs) and transnational enterprises (TNEs), are firms with central offices located in one country but with operations abroad. Transnational corporations are the primary form of foreign direct investment. TNCs bring capital, expertise, and jobs but also may thwart the growth of local industries and have been accused of exploiting low-wage workers.

transparency   A policy principle that encourages governments to implement effective anticorruption laws and policies, promotes reform through international organizations, and raises public awareness of the business of governance.

UN Education First Initiative   The United Nations Secretary-General launched the five-year Global Education First Initiative (GEFI) in September 2012 to accelerate progress towards the Education for All goals and the education-related Millennium Development Goals.

universal health coverage   Guaranteed access to necessary health services for all peoples without risk of impoverishment or financial instability.

velocity of money   The amount of national output supported by the money supply; mathematically, it is expressed as GDP/M, or gross domestic product divided by the money supply. Velocity is higher when a small stock of money supports a higher level of output. The higher the velocity, the larger the effect of any increase in the money supply.

verification   Independent third-party quality assurance to assess the accuracy of data and veracity of commitments to environmental management. Verification is important in carbon markets to assess whether reductions claimed by one party were actually achieved.

violence against women   As defined by the United Nations, an act of gender violence that results or is likely to result in physical, sexual, or psychological harm or suffering to women.

vouchers   Government funding for a student at a school chosen by the student or the student's parents.

water rights   A critical element in agricultural policy. Access to water rights, if accrued on the basis of seniority or local power, often interferes with the efficient allocation of resources in an agricultural community.

Bibliography

"21 anos da morte de Margarida Alves." Movimento de Mulheras Camponeses. www.mmc-brasil.com.br.

"2030 Agenda for Sustainable Development." The United Nations Development Programme, 2015. www.latinamerica.undp.org.

Abdelal, Rawi. *The State*. Harvard Business School case #9-701-077. Boston: Harvard Business School, 2001.

Abramo, Laís, and María Elena Valenzuela. "Women's Labour Force Participation Rates in Latin America." *International Labour Review* 144(4) (2005): 369–399.

Acemoglu, Daron. "Root Causes: A Historical Approach to Assessing the Role of Institutions in Economic Development." *Finance & Development* (June 2003): 27–30.

Acemoglu, Daron, Simon Johnson, and James Robinson. "Institutions as the Fundamental Cause of Long-Run Growth." Chapter 6 in *Handbook of Economic Growth*, ed. Philippe Aghion and Steven Durlauf. Amsterdam: Elsevier, 2005.

Acevedo, Carlos, Deborah Barry, and Herman Rosa. "El Salvador's Agricultural Sector: Macroeconomic Policy, Agrarian Change and the Environment." *World Development* 23(12) (1995).

Action Plan for Universal and Quality Basic Education by the Year 2000, Summit of the Americas. Available online at www.summit-americas.org.

Adelman, Carol. "Aid and Comfort." Tech Central Station, August 21, 2002. www.globalissues.org.

Adelman, Irma, and Cynthia Taft Morris. "Development History and Its Implications for Development Theory." *World Development* 25(6) (June 1997): 841–840.

Adriance, Jim. "Living with the Land in Central America." *Grassroots Development* 19(1) (1995).

Agarwala, A. N., and S. P. Singh, eds. *The Economics of Underdevelopment*. New York: Oxford University Press, 1963.

Aggio, Carlos. "A Case Study on Debt Conversion, Spain and Argentina," May 2005. Background paper prepared for the Education for All Global Monitoring Report 2006, Literacy for Life, unesdoc.unesco.org.

Alaimo, Veronica, Mariano Bosch, David S. Kaplan, Carmen Pagés, and Laura Ripani. "Jobs for Growth." IDB, 2015.

"Alba Info: Information on the Bolivian Alliance." https://albainfo.org/what-is-the-alba/.

Alderman, Harold, and Victory Lavy. "Household Responses to Public Health Services: Cost and Quality Tradeoffs." *World Bank Research Observer* 11(1), February 1996: 3–22.

Alexander, Ruth. "Dollar Benchmark: The rise of the $1 a day statistic." *BBC news*, March 9, 2012.

Alfaro, Laura, and Eliza Hammel. "Latin American Multinationals." In *Latin America Competitiveness Report* (Geneva: World Economic Forum, April 2006).

Alix-Garcia, Jennifer, Alain de Janvry, and Elisabeth Sadoulet. "A Tale of Two Communities: Explaining Deforestation in Mexico." *World Development* 33(2) (February 2005): 219–235.

Allison, N. L., et al. "The Copenhagen Diagnosis: Updating the World on the Latest Climate Science," UNSW Climate Change Research Center, 2009: 11.

Althaus, Dudley. "Deforestation Contributed to Tragedy by Mitch in Honduras, Experts Claim." *Houston Chronicle*, December 30, 1998, A1, as found in the LEXIS-NEXIS database.

Alves, Denisard, and Walter Belluzzo. "Child Health and Infant Mortality in Brazil." IADB Latin American Research Network Working Paper No. R-493, April 2005.

Álvarez, Perla, Alicia Amarilla, Magui Balbuena, and Julia Franco. "ÑE'ê Roky." edited by CONAMURI, Boletin. Asuncion, March 2011.

Amann, Edmund, and Werner Baer. "Anchors Away: The Costs and Benefits of Brazil's Devaluation." *World Development* 31(6) (June 2003): 1033–1046.

"Amazon Suffers the Worst Drought in 50 Years." *LatinNews Daily*, October 19, 2005.

Amedo, Eduardo, José Márcio Camargo, Antônio Emílío S. Marques, and Cândido Gomes. "Fiscal Crisis and Asymmetries in the Education System in Brazil." In *Coping with Crisis: Austerity, Adjustment, and Human Resources*, ed. Joel Samoff. New York: UNESCO/ILO, 1994.

Ameur, Charles. *Agricultural Extension: A Step beyond the Next Step*. World Bank Technical Paper No. 247. Washington, D.C.: World Bank, 1994.

Amgott, Seth. Spokesman for Oxfam, quoted by Barbara Crossette, "US Drops Case over AIDS Drugs in Brazil." *New York Times*, June 26, 2001.

Analisis 365. "Gran Revés Para Monsanto En Venezuela: Por Ley Los Transgénicos No Entrarán Al País." *Revista Digital*, March 18, 2014.

Anayiotos, George, and Jaime de Piniés. "The Secondary Market and the International Debt Problem." *World Development* 18(2) (1990): 1655–1660.

Anderson, Sarah, and John Cavanagh. *The Rise of Corporate Global Power*. Institute for Policy Studies, December 2000.

Anderson, Sarah, and Karen Hansen-Kuhn. *America's Plan for the Americas*. Washington, D.C.: Alliance, February 2001.

Angel Gurría, José. "Capital Flows: The Mexico Case," in *Coping with Capital Surges: The Return of Finance to Latin America*, ed. Ricardo Ffrench-Davis and Stephany Griffith-Jones. Rienner, 1995: 189.

Aninat, Cristobal, Jose Miguel Benavente, Ignácio Briones, Nicolas Eyzaguirre, Patricio Navia, and Jocelyn Olivari. "The Political Economy of Productivity: The Case of Chile." IDB Working Papers No. 22, April 2010. www.papers.ssrn.com.

Aninat, Eduardo. "Growth and Stability in Latin America and the Caribbean: Challenges for the Epoch of Globalization." Lecture presented for the IMF in Port of Spain, May 26, 2000.

Anonymous. "Health of Indigenous Peoples." *Pan American Journal of Public Health* 2(25) (1997): 357–362.

Antle, John M., and Gregg Heidebrink. "Environment and Development: Theory and International Evidence." *Economic Development and Cultural Change* 43(3) (April 1995).

Araujo, Jorge, Ekaterina Vostroknutova, Konstantin M. Wacker, and Mateo Clavijo. "Understanding Latin America and the Caribbean's Income Gap." World Bank Report No. 97885-LAC, July 2015.

"Argentina, Brazil Agree on Regulating Bilateral Trade." *La Nacion—Argentina*, distributed by Latin America News Digest, February 2, 2006.

Argentina: Selected Issues and Statistical Annex. Report No. 00/160. Washington, D.C.: IMF, December 2000.

Argentina Business: The Portable Encyclopedia for Doing Business with Argentina. San Rafael, CA: World Trade Press, 1995.

"Argentina's New Struggle for Confidence and Growth." *The Economist*, November 18, 2000.

"Argentine Leader Races to Prop Economy." The Associated Press. *New York Times*, July 16, 2001.

Arriagada, Irma. "Unequal Participation by Women in the Working World." *CEPAL Review* 40 (April 1990): 83–98.

Ashman, Darcy. "Promoting Corporate Citizenship in the Global South." *Institute for Development Research* 16(3), 2000. www.jsi.com.idr.

Atun, Rifat, et al. "Health-System Reform and Universal Health Coverage in Latin America." *The Lancet* 385(9974), October 15, 2014: 1230–1247.

Audley, John, Sandra Polaski, Demetrios G. Papademetriou, and Scott Vaughan. "Jobs, Wages, and Household Income," in *NAFTA's Promise and Reality: Lessons from Mexico and the Hemisphere*. Carnegie Endowment Report, November 2003.

Authers, John. "Auther's Note." *Financial Times*, November 9, 2015.

———. "Mortgage Scheme Offers a Tiny Piece of Mexico." *Financial Times*, September 1, 2005: 212.

"Auto Industry Delivers Vote of Confidence in Brazil and Mercosur." *Latin American Weekly Report*, February 3, 1998.

Ayres, Robert L. *Crime and Violence as Development Issues in Latin America*. Washington, D.C.: World Bank, 1998.

Azevedo, Robert. "Why We Need a Global Trade Deal." *Americas Quarterly*, Summer 2015. www.americasquarterly.org.

Azzoni, Tales. "Latin America and Caribbean Nations Vow to Negotiate Price of AIDS Medication Together." *The Associated Press*, January 15, 2006.

Back, Aaron, Andrew Batson, and Bob Davis. "Early View on China's Currency Overhaul: Little Change." *World News*, July 16, 2010. www.wsj.com.

Bacon, Christopher. "Confronting the Coffee Crisis: Can Fair Trade, Organic, and Specialty Coffees Reduce Small-Scale Farmer Vulnerability in Northern Nicaragua?" *World Development* 33(3) (March 2005): 497–511.

Baer, Werner. "Changing Paradigms: Changing Interpretations of the Public Sector in Latin America's Economies." *Public Choice* 88 (1996): 365–379.

———. "Latin America and Europe in the Nineteenth Century: The Impact of an Unequal Relationship." In *Development and Underdevelopment in America*, ed. Walther Bernecker and Hans Werner Tobler. New York: Walter de Gruyter, 1993.

Baer, Werner, and Melissa Birch, eds. *Privatization in Latin America*. Westport, CT: Praeger, 1994.

Baer, Werner, and Annibal V. Villela. "Privatization and the Changing Role of the State in Brazil." In *Privatization in Latin America*, ed. Werner Baer and Melissa Birch. Westport, CT: Praeger, 1994.

Bahamondes, Miguel. "Poverty-Environment Patterns in a Growing Economy: Farming Communities in Arid Central Chile, 1991–99." *World Development* 31(11) (November 2003): 1947–1957.

Baker, Gerard. "Argentina Awakens US Pragmatism." *Financial Times*, August 7, 2001.

Balch, Oliver. "Growth in Ecotourism—Take the Green Road." Ethical Corporation Conferences, January 4, 2006. www.ethicalcorp.com.

Baldwin, Robert E. "Openness and Growth: What's the Empirical Relationship?" National Bureau of Economic Research Working Paper, No. 9578, March 2003.

Baraka, Hoda. "The Realities of Climate Change in Latin America." December 4, 2014. www.350.org.

Baran, Paul A. "On the Political Economy of Backwardness." *Manchester School* 20(1) (1952). Reprinted in *The Economics of Underdevelopment*, ed. A. N. Agarwala and S. P. Singh. New York: Oxford University Press, 1963; and *Political Economy of Development and Underdevelopment*, ed. Charles K. Wilber. New York: Random House, 1973.

Baranyi, Stephen, Carmen Diana Deere, and Manuel Morales. "Land & Development in Latin America, Openings for Research." North-South Institute and International Development Research Center. www.idrc.ca.

Barbier, Edward. "Agricultural Expansion, Resource Booms and Growth in Latin America." *World Development* 32(1) (January 2004): 139.

Barclay, Eliza. "Mexican Migrant Communities May Be on Verge of HIV/AIDS Epidemic." Population Reference Bureau, September 2005. www.prb.org.

Bardhan, Pranab. "Little, Big Two Ideas About Fighting Global Poverty." Bostonreview. net, May 20, 2013.

Barro, Robert J. "The Dollar Club: Why Countries Are So Keen to Join." *BusinessWeek*, December 11, 2000.

———. "From Seattle to Santiago, Let the Dollar Reign." *Hoover Digest* 3 (1999).

Bartlett, Christopher A., and Sumantra Ghoshal. "Going Global: Lessons from Late Movers." *Harvard Business Review* (March–April 2000).

Bastianensen, Johan. "Non-Conventional Rural Finance and the Crisis of Economic Institutions in Nicaragua." In *Sustainable Agriculture in Central America*, ed. Jan P. de Groot and Ruerd Ruben. New York: St. Martin's, 1997.

Bastos Lima, Marion. "Adjusting BioFuels Policies to Meet Social and Rural Development Needs: Analyzing the Experiences of Brazil, India, and Indonesia." International Policy Research Brief No. 40, March 1, 2013.

Bate, Peter. "Dollars for Everyone?" *IDB América* (May–June 1999).

———. "Education: The Gordian Knot." *IDB Today*. Online edition available at www.iadb. org/idbamerica.

Bauer, P., and B. Yamey. *The Economics of Underdeveloped Countries*. New York: Cambridge University Press, 1967.

Bell, David and Mary Shelman. "Note on Agriculture in Argentina." HBS case 9-515-069, December 2014.

Bellew, Rosemary T., and Elizabeth M. King. "Educating Women: Lessons from Experience." In *Women's Education in Developing Countries: Barriers, Benefits and Policies*, ed. Elizabeth M. King and Rosemary Bellew. Baltimore, MD: Johns Hopkins University Press, 1993.

Bellos, Alex. "Ronaldo's Fame Hasn't Hit Home." *Minneapolis Star Tribune*, July 10, 1998, C6.

Benavente, José Miguel, Gustavo Crespi, Jorge Katz, and Giovanni Stumpo. "Changes in the Industrial Development of Latin America." *CEPAL Review* 60 (December 1996).

Benavides, Enrique, and Gloriana Sojo. "Migration & Development in Central America: Perspectives for the Alliance for Prosperity." The Dialogue, January 14, 2016. www. thedialogue.org.

"The Benefits and Risks of Short-Term Borrowing." *Global Development Finance*. Washington, D.C.: World Bank, 2000.

Bennett, Bradley. "Plants and People of the Amazonian Rainforests: The Role of Ethnobotany in Sustainable Development." *BioScience* 42(8) (1992).

Benson, Todd. "Brazil's Big Stake in Cotton Likely to Become Bigger." *New York Times*, June 29, 2004.

Benvente, Jose Miguel, Gustavo Crespi, Jorge Katz, and Giovanni Stumpo. "Changes in the Industrial Development of Latin America." *CEPAL Review* 60, December 1996: 62.

Berdegue, Julio A., and Ricardo Fuentealba. "Latin America: The State of Smallholders in Agriculture." In *Conference on New Directions for Smallholder Agriculture*. Rome, IFAD HQ: IFAD, January 2011.

Berg, Andrew, and Eduardo Borensztein. "The Dollarization Debate." *Finance & Development* (March 2000).

———. "Full Dollarization—The Pros and Cons." *International Monetary Fund Economic Issue* 24 (December 2000).

Berger, *Marguerite. Microfinance: An Emerging Market within the Emerging Markets.* Draft. Washington, D.C.: IADB, 2000.

Bergsten, Fred C. "American Politics, Global Trade." *The Economist*, September 27, 1997.

Bernet, Thomas, Graham Thiele, and Thomas Zschocke. "Participatory Market Chain Approach (PMCA)." International Potato Center, 2006. cipotato.org.

Bernstein, H., ed. *Underdevelopment and Development*. Harmondsworth: Penguin, 1973.

Berry, Thomas. "The Dream of the Earth." Sierra Club Books, 1988.

———. "The Great Work: Our Way Into The Future." Bell Tower, 1999.

Berstein, Aarn. "Sweatshop Reform: How to Solve the Standoff." *BusinessWeek*, May 3, 1999.

Bertola, Luis, and Jeffrey Williamson. "Globalization in Latin America before 1940." NBER Working Paper, No. W9687, May 2003, 4.

Beuermann, Diether W., Julian P. Cristia, Yyannu Cruz-Aguayo, Santiago Cueto, and Ofer Malamud. "Home Computers and Child Outcomes: Short-Term Impacts from a Randomized Experiment." Peru Working Paper IDB-WP-304 InterAmerican Development Bank, January 2013.

Bhagwati, Jagdish. "Fast Track to Nowhere." *The Economist*, October 18, 1997.

———. "The FTAA Is *Not* Free Trade." In *Trade: Towards Open Regionalism*, Proceedings of the 1997 World Bank Conference on Development in Latin America and the Caribbean. Washington, D.C.: World Bank, 1998.

Biersteker, Thomas J. *Dealing with Debt*. Boulder, CO: Westview, 1993.

———. *Distortion or Development? Contending Perspectives on the Multinational Corporation*. Cambridge, MA: MIT Press, 1978.

Binswanger, Hans P., and Klaus Deininger. "Explaining Agricultural and Agrarian Policies in Developing Countries." *Journal of Economic Literature* 35, December 1997.

Birdsall, Nancy, and Augusto de la Torre. "Washington Contentious." Commission on Economic Reform in Unequal Latin American Societies, sponsored by the Carnegie Endowment for International Peace and the Inter-American Dialogue, 2001.

Birdsall, Nancy. "A Note on the Middle Class in Latin America." CGD Working Paper No. 303, 2012.

Birdsall, Nancy, and Carlos Lozada. "Prebish Reconsidered: Coping with External Shocks in Vulnerable Economies." *CEPAL Review* (October 2000).

———. "Recurring Themes in Latin American Economic Thought: From Prebisch to the Market and Back." In *Securing Stability and Growth in Latin America*, ed. Ricardo Hausmann and Helmut Reisen. Paris: OECD Publications, 1996.

Birdsall, Nancy, and John Nellis. "Winners and Losers: Assessing the Distributional Impact of Privatization." *World Development* 31(10) (October 2003): 1626–1643.

Birdsall, Nancy, and William Savedoff. "Cash on Delivery: A New Approach to Foreign Aid." Center for Global Development, March 16, 2010. www.cgdev.org.

Bitar, Sergio. "Migration on the Rise." Global Trends Report (2), (September 2016): 14. www.espas.eu.

Bitran, Eduardo, and Pablo Serra. "Regulation of Privatized Utilities: The Chilean Experience." *World Development* 26(6) (1998): 945–962.

Blackwood, D. L., and R. G. Lynch. "The Measurement of Inequality and Poverty." *World Development* 22(4) (1994): 567–578.

Blazquez, Jorge, and Javier Santiso. "Mexico: Is It an Ex-Emerging Market?" *Journal of Latin American Studies*, 36 (2004): 297–318.

Blomström, Magnus, and Ari Kokko. *Regional Integration and Foreign Direct Investment.* National Bureau of Economic Research Working Paper No. 6019. Cambridge, MA: National Bureau of Economic Research, 1997.

Blomström, Magnus, and Edward N. Wolff. "Multinational Corporations and Productivity Convergence in Mexico." In *Convergence of Productivity: Cross-National Studies and Historical Evidence*, ed. William Baumol, Richard R. Nelson, and Edward N. Wolff. New York: Oxford University Press, 1994.

Bloom, D., D. Canning, and J. Sevilla. "The Demographic Dividend: A New Perspective on the Economic Consequences of Population Change." 2003. www.policyproject.com.

Bloomberg Latin America. "Argentine Markets Climb after IMF, Banks Move to Shore Up Confidence." Retrieved July 14, 1999, from www.quote.bloomberg.com.

"Blooming Desert: Peru." *The Economist*, July 9, 2005.

Blowfield, Michael. "Corporate Social Responsibility: Reinventing the meaning of development?" *International Affairs* 81(3), 2005: 515–524.

Blumenstein, Rebecca. "GM to Build a Low-Priced Car in Brazil." *Wall Street Journal*, 19 March 1997.

Blustein, Paul. "Currencies in Crisis." *Washington Post*, February 7, 1999.

Blyth, Alastair, Rodolfo Almeida, David Forrester, Ann Gorey, and Juan José Chávez Zepeda. "Upgrading School Buildings in Mexico with Social Participation." OECD, 24 September 2012.

Bolio, Eduardo, Jaana Remes, Tomás Lajous, James Manyika, Eugenia Ramirez, and Morten Rossé. "A Tale of two Mexicos: Growth and Prosperity in a Two Speed Economy." McKinsey Global Institute, March 2014.

"Bolivia: Getting Kids Back in School." *IDB América* (November 1997): 14. Available at www.iadb.org.

Bolivarian Republic of Venezuela. "ECLAC: Venezuela Has Third-Lowest Poverty Rate in Latin America." Accessed January 13, 2012. http://venezuela-us.org.

Bondy, Krista, Dirk Mattern, and Jeremy Moon. "MNC Codes of Conduct: CSR or Corporate Governance?" International Centre for Corporate Social Responsibility, No. 40-2006 ICCSR Research Paper series ISSN 1479-5124.

Bonilla-Chacin, Maria Eugenia. "Prevention of Health Risk Factors in Latin America and the Caribbean: Governance of Five Multisectoral Efforts." World Bank, 2014.

Bonior, Congressman David. "I Told You So." *New York Times*, editorial, July 13, 1997.

Bordo, Michael, and Christopher Meisner. "Financial Crises 1880–1913: The Role of Foreign Currency Debt." In *Growth Institutions and Crises: Latin America from a Historical Perspective*, ed. Sebastian Edwards. Washington, D.C.: National Bureau of Economic Research, 2005.

Borenstein, E., J. De Gregorio, and J. W. Lee. "How Does Foreign Investment Affect Economic Growth?" *Journal of International Economics* 45 (1998): 115–135.

Bosch, Mariano, Ángel Melguizo, and Carmen Pagés. "Better Pensions, Better Jobs: Towards Universal Coverage in Latin America and the Caribbean." IDB, October 2013.

Bovarnick, Andrew, F. Alpizar, C. Schnell, eds. "The Importance of Biodiversity and Ecosystems in Economic Growth and Equity in Latin America and the Caribbean: An Economic Valuation of Ecosystems." United Nations Development Programme, 2010. www.cbd.int.

Bowman, Kirk, and Jesus Felipe. *Convergence, Catch Up, and the Future of Latin America* (Atlanta: Georgia Institute of Technology). Unpublished paper, October 17, 2000. Access at www.harvard.edu.

Bowman, Kirk S. "Should the Kuznets Effect Be Relied on to Induce Equalizing Growth?" *World Development* 25(1) (1997): 127–143.

Boyd, Stephanie. "A Natural Weapon for Preventing Malaria in the Peruvian Amazon." *Science from the Developing World*, January 19, 2001.

Bradford, Colin, Jr. "Future Policy Directions and Relevance." In *The Legacy of Raúl Prebisch*, ed. Enrique V. Iglesias. Washington, D.C.: IADB, 1994.

Braga, Carlos Alberto Primo. "Tropical Forests and Trade Policy: The Case of Indonesia and Brazil." In *International Trade and the Environment*, ed. Patrick Low. Washington, D.C.: World Bank, 1992.

Brainard, S. Lael, and David Riker. *Are U.S. Multinationals Exporting U.S. Jobs?* National Bureau of Economic Research Working Paper No. 5958. Cambridge, MA: National Bureau of Economic Research, 1997.

Brasher, Keith. "Earth-Friendly Elements, Mined Destructively." *The New York Times*, Dec. 26, 2009.

Brathwaite Dick, Olivia, José L. San Martín, Romeo H. Montoya, Jorge del Diego, Betzana Zambrano, and Gustavo H. Dayan. "Review: The History of Dengue Outbreaks in the Americas." *The American Society of Tropical Medicine and Hygiene* (4), 2012: 584–593. doi: 10.4269/ajtmh.2012.11-0770.

Braverman, Avishay, and J. Luis Guasch. "Administrative Failures in Government Credit Programs." In *The Economics of Rural Organization*, ed. Karla Hoff, Avishay Braverman, and Joseph Stiglitz. New York: Oxford University Press/World Bank, 1993.

"Brazil: Domestic Debt Dynamics and Implications." *ING Barings Emerging Markets Weekly Report*, March 5, 1999, 1–3.

"Brazil Boosts Border Surveillance as Bolivia Plans to Up Coca Production." *BBC Monitoring Latin America*, December 22, 2005.

"Brazil's Affluent Are Hurt by Crisis." *Washington Post*, January 25, 1999.

"Brazil's Iron King." *Financial Times*, June 29, 1998.

"Brazil's Neighbors Are Very Nervous." *BusinessWeek*, November 17, 1997.

Brenes, Esteban R., Arnoldo R. Camacho, Luciano Ciravegna, and Caleb A. Pichardo. "Strategy and Innovation in Emerging Economies after the End of the Commodity Boom—Insights from Latin America." *Journal of Business Research* 69(10), October 2016. www.sciencedirect.com.

Britan, Ricardo, and Keith McInnes. *The Demand for Health Care in Latin America*. Economic Development Institute Seminar Paper No. 46. Washington, D.C.: World Bank, 1993.

Britto, Tatiana. "Recent Trends in the Development Agenda of Latin America: An Analysis of Conditional Cash Transfers." Brazilian Ministry of Social Development, February 2005, tatib@brturbo.com.br.

Britton, John A., ed. *Molding the Hearts and Minds: Education, Communications and Social Change in Latin America*. Wilmington, DE: Scholarly Resources, 1994.

Brodzinsky, Sibylla. "Pulling Colombia's Coca by Hand." *Christian Science Monitor*, February 24, 2006, 7.

Brooke, James. "Home, Home on the Range, in Brazil's Heartland." *New York Times*, April 26, 1995.

Brookings Institution, World Bank, and IMF. *Emerging Market Economies Recover, but Debt Restructuring Problems Linger On*. News Release, 2001. www.brookings.edu.

Bruno Vander Velde, "To Fight Deforestation, One Country Changed the Equation." November 24, 2015. www.newstrust.org.

Brunori, Paolo, Francisco H. G. Ferreira, and Vito Peragine. "Inequality of Opportunity, Income Inequality and Economic Mobility: Some International Comparisons." Policy Research Working Paper No. 6304 The World Bank, January 2013.

Bruton, Henry. "Import Substitution." In *Handbook of Development Economics*, vol. 2, 3rd ed., ed. Hollis Chenery and T. N. Srivivasan. New York: Elsevier, 1996.

———. "A Reconsideration of Import Substitution." *Journal of Economic Literature* 36 (June 1998).

"Building the Post-2015 Development Agenda." The United Nations Development Programme, April 21, 2015. www.latinamerica.undp.org.

Bulmer-Thomas, Victor. "The Brazilian Devaluation: National Responses and International Consequences." *International Affairs* 75(4) (1999).

———. *The Economic History of Latin America since Independence*. New York: Cambridge University Press, 1994.

Buntin, John, and Christine Letts. *Accion International: Where Latin America Meets Brooklyn*. Cambridge, MA: John F. Kennedy School of Government, 1996.

Burbach, Roger, and Peter Rosset. "Chiapas and the Crisis of Mexican Agriculture." *Food First Policy Brief*, No. 1. San Francisco, CA: Institute for Food and Development, 1994.

Burki, Shahid Javed, and Sebastian Edwards. *Dismantling the Populist State*. Washington, D.C.: World Bank, 1996.

———. *Latin America after Mexico: Quickening the Pace*. Washington, D.C.: World Bank, 1996.

Burns, Bradford E., ed. *Latin America: Conflict and Creation: A Historical Reader*. Englewood Cliffs, NJ: Prentice Hall, 1992.

Burns, Tom. "Telefonica Moviles Expands Its Latin American Empire: Mexican Purchase Sharpens Interest Ahead of Listening." *Financial Times*, October 5, 2000.

Burrell, Jenna. "On the Overuse of Randomized Controlled Trials in the Aid Sector." Global Policy, October 30, 2012. www.globalpolicyjournal.com.

Busso, Matías, María Victoria Fazio, and Santiago Levy. "(In)Formal and (Un)Productive: The Productivity Costs of Excessive Informality in Mexico." IDB Working Paper Series No. IDB-WP-341, August 2012. www.services.iadb.org.

Buvinic, Mayra, and Andrew Morrison. "How Can We Measure Violence?" *Social Development* (July 2000).

———. *Women in Poverty: A New Global Underclass*. Washington, D.C: IADB, Women in Development, N WID-101, July 1998, p. 2. www.iadb.org.

Byrnes, H., and B. Spencer. "U.S. Must Aid Guatemala's Shift to Peace." *St. Louis Post-Dispatch*, December 20, 1996.

Caballero, Ricardo J. *Macroeconomic Volatility in Latin America: A View and Three Case Studies*. Working Paper 7782. Massachusetts: National Bureau of Economic Research, July 2000.

Cabrol, Marcelo, and Miguel Székely. "Educación para la Transformación." Banco Interamericano de Desarrollo, 2012.

"CAFTA Accord." *Oxford Analytica,* Latin America Daily Briefs, February 2, 2004.

"CAFTA's Missed Opportunities." *Bulletin of the Washington Office on Latin America*, March 2004.

Calcagno, Alfredo, Sandra Manuelito, and Gunilla Ryd. *Proyecciones Latinoamericanos 2000–2001*. Santiago: United Nations and ECLAC, January 2001.

Calderon, Ania. "On Finding the Right Bundles: Social Policy, Growth, and Equal Development: An Interview with Santiago Levy." *Journal of International Affairs* 66(2), Spring/Summer 2013.

Caldwell, Laura. "Swapping Debt to Preserve Nature." *Christian Science Monitor*, September 11, 1990.

Calo, Muriel, and Timothy A. Wise. "Revaluing Peasant Coffee Production: Organic and Fair Trade Markets in Mexico." Global Development and Environment Institute, Tufts University, October 2005.

Camargo, José Márcio. "Mercosur: Greater Protection Tends to Hurt Smaller Bloc Members." *Tendencias*, January 19, 2006.

Campbell, C. "The Assessment and Importance of Oil Depletion," in *The Final Energy Crisis, Pluto Press*, ed. A. McKillop, 2005

Campbell, C., and J. Laherrere. "The End of Cheap Oil," *Science,* June, 1998.

Campbell, Kurt M., Alexander T.J. Lennon, and Julianne Smith (Project Co-Directors), "The Age of Consequences: The Foreign Policy and National Security Implications of Global Climate Change." Washington, D.C., November 2007.

Camdessus, Michel. "The Private Sector in a Strengthened Global Financial System." Remarks at the International Monetary Conference, Philadelphia, June 8, 1999. Available at www.imf.org/external/speeches.

CAMTIC. "Cámara Castarvicense de Technología de Información y Comunicación." Projects web page, www.camtic.org.

"CANTV in 1994." *Harvard Business School Case Studies*, February 28, 1996.

"Capital Controversies." *The Economist*, May 23, 1998.

Cardoso, Eliana. "Brazil's Currency Crisis." In *Exchange Rate Politics in Latin America*, ed. Carol Wise and Riordan Roett, 70–92. Washington, D.C.: Brookings Institution Press, 2000.

Cardoso, Fernando Henrique. Interview on the occasion of the second anniversary of the Real Plan, as reported in FBIS-LAT-96-129 (Foreign Broadcast Information Services, Latin America), July 3, 1996. Originally appeared on the Rede Globo website, July 1, 1996.

Carnegie Endowment for International Peace. *Working Papers—Breaking the Labor-Trade Deadlock*, No. 17. Washington, D.C.: Inter-American Dialogue and the Carnegie Endowment for International Peace, February 2001.

Carnoy, Martin. "Structural Adjustment and the Changing Face of Education." *International Labor Review* 134(6) (1995): 653–673.

Carranza, Mario E. "Can Mercosur Survive? Domestic and International Constraints on Mercosur." *Latin American Politics and Society*, 2003.

Carruthers, David V. *Environmental Justice in Latin America: Problems, Promise and Practice*. MIT Press, 2008.

Cartaya, Vanessa F. "El Confuso mundo del sector informal." *Nueva Sociedad* 90 (July–August 1987): 81–84.

Carter, Michael, and Bradford Barham. "Level Playing Fields and Laissez Faire: Postliberal Development Strategy in Inegalitarian Agrarian Economies." *World Development* 24(7) (July 1996).

Carter, Michael, and Dina Mesbah. "State-Mandated and Market-Mediated Reform in Latin America." In *Including the Poor*, ed. Michael Lipton and Jacques van der Gaag. Baltimore, MD: Johns Hopkins University Press/World Bank, 1993.

Casas, J. A., N. W. Dachs, and A. Bambas. "Health Disparities in Latin America and the Caribbean: The Role of Social and Economic Determinants." Equity and Health: Views from the Pan American Sanitary Bureau, Occasional Publication No. 8, PAHO, 2001: 37.

Case, Brendan M. "Mexican Tariff on U.S. Beef Ignites Trade Dispute." *Dallas Morning News*, August 3, 1999.

Castañeda, Tarsicio. "Combating Poverty." In *Reforms in Education*. San Francisco, CA: International Center for Economic Growth, 1992.

Catán, Thomas. "Argentina Looks to $6bn IMF Injection." *Financial Times*, August 6, 2001.

Cavallo, Eduardo, and Tomás Serebrisky. "Saving for Development: How Latin America and the Caribbean Can Save More." Inter-American Development Bank, 2016.

Caves, Richard E. *Multinational Enterprise and Economic Analysis*, 2nd ed. Cambridge, UK: Cambridge University Press, 1996.

Cecchini, Simone, and Fábio Veras Soares. "Conditional Cash Transfers and Health in Latin America." *The Lancet* 385(9975), April 2015: e32 - e34.

Center for International Health Information. *Country Health Profile/Bolivia*. Arlington, Va.: Center for International Health Information, December 1996. Available at www.cihi.com.

Centers for Disease Control. "Areas at Risk for Zika." www.cdc.gov.

———. "Chikungunya Virus." Centers for Disease Control and Prevention, last modified August 3, 2015. www.cdc.gov/chikungunya/.

Central Intelligence Agency. *The World Fact Book*. Available at www.odci.gov/cia.

Cevallos, Diego. "Environment-Mexico: Toxic Waste, a Dirty Problem." Inter Press Service, August 11, 1995. Available on the LEXIS-NEXIS database.

———. "Foreign Corporations Backing Off." *Tierramérica*, March 16, 2006.

———. "Latin America: Farm Exports Grow, but Who Reaps the Harvest?" *IPS-Inter Press Service/Global Information Network*, November 8, 2005.

Cevellos Estarellas, Pablo. "La arquitectura institucional es clave para mejorar la calidad educative." *The Dialogue*, June 28, 2016. www.thedialogue.org.

Chaherli, Nabil, and John Nash. "America and the Caribbean: Harnessing Trade to Feed the World and Promote Development." World Bank, 2013.

Chami, Ralph, Connel Fullenkamp, and Samir Jahjah. "Are Immigrant Remittance Flows a Source of Capital for Development?" *IMF Staff Papers* 52(1) (2005).

Chant, Sylvia, and Nikki Craske. "Gender in Latin America." *Rutgers University Press*, 2003: 9.

Chauvin, Lucian. "With Money Sent from the US Peruvians Buy Homes." *Christian Science Monitor*, July 13, 2005, 14.

Chile Facts on Demand. (via fax: 1-888-821-2424, Doc. ID#260) as found at www.american.edu.

"China Ascendant: A Snapshot of Economic Performance." *Ideas* 6 (January–April 2005). www.iadb.org.

Chioda, Laura. "Stop the Violence in Latin America: A Look at Prevention from Cradle to Adulthood." World Bank Development Forum, 2016. doi: 10.1596/978-1-4648-0664-3.

Chipman, Andre. "U.S., Latin-American Oil Companies Build Alliance As Mideast Clout Fades." *Wall Street Journal*, March 9, 1998.

Chisari, Omar, Sebastián Galiani, and Sebastián Miller. "Optimal Adaptation and Mitigation to Climate Change in Small Environmental Economies." The Inter-American Development Bank, October 2013.

Choque Schulter, Sidney, and Ruth Choque Schulter. "Misinformation, Mistrust, and Mistreatment: Family Planning among Bolivian Market Women." *Studies in Family Planning* 25, 1994.

Chronic Poverty Research Center. "The Chronic Poverty Report 2004–5." Manchester: University of Manchester. www.chronicpoverty.org.

"Chronology of FTAA Process." Free Trade Area of the Americas.

Cifuentes, A., R. Krupnick, M. Ryan, and P. Toman. "Health Benefits of Reducing Air Pollution in Latin America." Society for Risk Analysis Annual Meeting 2004, lac@ing.puc.cl.

Cimoli, Mario, Giovanni Dosi, and Joseph E. Stiglitz. "Industrial Policy and Development: The Political Economy of Capabilities Accumulation." *Oxford Scholarship Online*, February 2010.

Cimoli, Mario, João Carlos Ferraz, and Annalisa Primi. "Science and Technology Policies in Open Economies: The Case of Latin America and the Caribbean." *Economic Commission for Latin America and the Caribbean*, Productive Development Series, No. 165 (Directors Office), October 2005. www.eclac.cl/.

"Citizen's Guide to Dollarization." Committee Documents Online—106th Congress. Senate Banking Committee, 2000. Available at www.banking.senate.gov.

Clements, Benedict. "The Real Plan, Poverty, and Income Distribution in Brazil." *Finance and Development* (September 1997).

Clendenning, Alan. "From Wine to Washing Machines, South American Trade Zone Faces New Challenges." *Associated Press*, February 15, 2006.

Cliché, Gilles. "Rural Women's Empowerment in Nonfarm Employment Issues for ICT Initiatives and Territorial Policies in Latin America. Accra." The United Nations, September 2011.

Coatsworth, John. "Notes on the Comparative Economic History of Latin America and the United States." In *Development and Underdevelopment in America*, ed. Walther Bernecker and Hans Werner Tobler. New York: Walter de Gruyter, 1993.

Coatsworth, John H., and Jeffrey G. Williamson. "Always Protectionist? Latin American Tariffs Independence to the Great Depression." *Journal of Latin American Studies* 36(2) (May 2004): 205–232.

Coelho, Nivaldo. "Ministry of Health Launches Campaign to Prevent STD and AIDS." *Carnival*, February 26, 2014. www.aids.gov.br.

Coelho PhD, Vera, and Alex Shankland. "Making the Right to Health a Reality for Brazil's Indigenous Peoples: Innovation, Decentralization and Equity." *MEDICC* 13(3), July 2011. www.medicc.org.

Coes, Donald V. *Macroeconomic Crises, Policies, and Growth in Brazil, 1964–90*. Washington, D.C.: World Bank, 1995.

Cohn, D'Vera, Ana Gonzalez-Barrera, and Danielle Cuddington. "Remittances to Latin America Recover—but Not to Mexico." *Pew Research Center*, November 15, 2013. www.pewhispanic.org.

Colclough, Christopher. "Education and the Market: Which Parts of the Neoliberal Solution Are Correct?" *World Development* 24(4) (1996): 589–610.

Colitt, Raymond. "Banking and Telecom Sectors Lead the Way: Brazil's New IT Markets." *Financial Times*, November 1, 2000.

"Coming Up Roses." *Latin American Economy & Business*, Intelligence Research Ltd., October 25, 2005.

Comision Económica Para América Latina. *Indicadores Económicos*. Santiago: Comision Económica Para América Latina, 1997.

"Commercial Debt Restructuring." *Global Development Finance*. Washington, D.C.: World Bank.

Commission on Development and Environment for Amazonia. *Amazonia without Myths*. Washington, D.C.: IADB, 1992.

"Competitiveness Is Vital." *Financial Times*, December 14, 2000.

Conamuri. "Karu Reko Sâ'ÿ: Tekoha / Soberanía Alimentaria: Tierra.". La Campana por la Soberania Alimentaria Video, October 14, 2013. www.youtube.com.

Conger, Lucy. "A Fourth Way? The Latin American Alternative to Neoliberalism." *Current History*, November 1998.

Constance, Paul. "A High Technology Incubator." *IDB América*, 1997. Available at www.iadb.org.

———. "Lousy Deal." *IDB América*, May–June 2000.

———. "The New Referees." *IDB América*, January–February 1998.

———. "A Seat at the Table: Union Leaders Urge IDB to Include Workers' Concerns in Reform Programs and Free Trade Negotiations." *IDB América*, April 1998. Available at www.iadb.org.

———. "A Smoother Road." *IDB América*, March 2006. www.iadb.org/idbamerica.

Constantine, Giles. "Mexico Rebrands Flagship Social Welfare Programme in Bid to Help Working Poor." *Eyes on Latin America*, September 26, 2014. www.eyeonlatinamerica. wordpress.com.

Contreras Murphy, Ellen. "La Selva and the Magnetic Pull of Markets: Organic Coffee-Growing in Mexico." *Grassroots Development* 19(1) (1995): 27–34.

Cooper, William H. "Free Trade Agreements: Impact on US Trade and Implications for US Trade Policy." Congressional Research Service Report RL31356, Washington, D.C., Library of Congress, December 6, 2005.

Corbo, Vittorio. "Economic Policies and Performance in Latin America." In *Economic Development: Handbook of Comparative Economic Policies*, ed. Enzo Grilli and Dominick Salvatore. Westport, CT: Greenwood, 1994.

Cornell University, INSEAD, and WIPO. "The Global Innovation Index 2016: Winning with Global Innovation." Ithaca, NY, Fontainebleau, and Geneva, 2016.

Cortés-Salas, Hernán, Ronnie de Camino, and Arnoldo Contreras. Readings of the *Workshop on Government Policy Reform for Forestry Conservation and Development in Latin America*, June 1–3, 1994. Washington, D.C.: Inter-American Institute for Cooperation on Agriculture, 1995.

"Cost-Cutting Takes a Private Road." *Euromoney*, September 1996.

"Cost Information and Management Decision in a Brazilian Hospital." In *World Development Report 1993*. New York: Oxford University Press/World Bank, 1993.

"The Costs of Latin American Crime." *The Economist*, February 25, 2017. www.economist.com.

Council on Foreign Relations. "Reforming Education in America." Study group on reforming education in Latin America, "The Second Wave of Reform," February–October 1996.

"Creating Jobs Is Main Headache." *Latin American Weekly Report*, January 5, 1999.

"Crime Could Drive Sony from Mexico." *Gazette*, May 10, 2000.

Cristia, Julian, Pablo Ibarraran, Santiago Cueto, Ana Santiago, and Eugenio Severin. "Technology and Child Development: Evidence from the One Laptop per Child Program." Research Department Publications 4764, Inter-American Development Bank, 2012.

Cruz, Antonio. "Poor Mental Health, an Obstacle to Development in Latin America." World Bank, July 13, 2015. www.worldbank.org.

Cuddington, John T. *Capital Flight: Estimates, Issues, and Explanations*. Princeton Studies in International Finance No. 58. Princeton, NJ: Princeton University Press, 1986.

Cuttler, Stephanie. "Valentine's Day Consumer Alert #2: Cut Flowers." *Calvert News*, January 31, 2006. www.calvert.com/news.

Cypher, James, and James Dietz, *The Process of Economic Development* (New York: Routledge, 1997), cited by Miguel D. Ramirez, "Foreign Direct Investment in Mexico and Chile: A Critical Appraisal," in *Foreign Direct Investment in Latin America*, ed. Werner Baer and William R. Miles. New York: The Hayworth Press, 2001.

Dadus, Uri, Dipak Dasgupta, and Dilip Ratha. "The Role of Short-Term Debt in Recent Crises." *Finance & Development*, December 2000.

Daly, Herman. *Beyond Growth*, Ch. 2 "Elements of Environmental Macroeconomics," Ch. 10 "Free Trade and Globalization vs. Environment and Community," and Ch. 11 "From Adjustment to Sustainable Development: The Obstacle of Free Trade." Beacon Press, 1996, pp. 143–170.

———."Ecological Economics: The Concept of Scale and Its Relation to Allocation, Distribution, and Uneconomic Growth," in *Ecological Economics and Sustainable Development: Selected Essays of Herman Daly*, Edward Elgar, 2007, pp. 82–103.

Davies, Paul J., Joanna Chung, and Kevin Allison. "Brazil Raises $1.5 Billion." *Financial Times*, September 20, 2005.

Davis, Bob. "Guatemala Logs Progress." *Wall Street Journal*, November 25, 2005, A9.

"Deal of the Year 2005: Core Transformation." *LatinFinance*, February 2006, 24.

"Debt Relief for Poor Countries (HIPC): What Has Been Achieved?—A Factsheet." *International Monetary Fund* (April 2001).

"Declaration and Action Plan for Latin American Economic Recovery." *UN Chronicle* 21(3) (March 1984): 13–17.

Deen, Thalif. "The Pros and Cons of Rising Oil Prices." *IPS Terraviva*, April 21, 2006.

Deere, Carmen Diana. "The Feminization of Agriculture: Economic Restructuring in Rural Latin America." UNRISD Occasional Paper No.1, February 2005.

Deere, Carmen Diana, and Magdalena Leon. "The Gender Asset Gap: Land in Latin America." *World Development* 31(6), June 2003: 925–947.

———. "Institutional Reform of Agriculture under Neoliberalism." *Latin American Research Review* 36(2) (2001).

de Ferranti, David, Guillermo Perry, Francisco H. G. Ferreira, and Michael Walton. *Inequality Latin America & the Caribbean: Breaking with History?* Washington, D.C.: World Bank, 2003.

De Gortari, Carlos Salinas, and Roberto Mangabeira Unger. "The Market Turn without Neoliberalism." *Challenge* 42(1) (January–February 1999).

Deininger, Klaus. *Land Policies for Growth and Poverty Reduction*. World Bank and Oxford University Press, 2003.

De Janvry, Alain, and Elisabeth Sadoulet. "Making Conditional Cash Transfer Programs More Efficient: Designing for Maximum Effect of Conditionality." *World Bank Economic Review* 20(1) (2006): 1–29. Available at www.wber.oxfordjournals.org.

———. "NAFTA and Mexico's Maize Producers." *World Development* 23(8), August 1995: 1349–1362.

———. *Rural Development in Latin America: Relinking Poverty Reduction to Growth."* In *Including the Poor*, ed. Michael Lipton and Jacques van der Gaag. Washington, D.C.: World Bank, 1993.

De la Torre, Augusto, Cristian Aedo, and Ian Walker. "Latin America and the Caribbean's Long-Term Growth: Made in China." World Bank, October 5, 2011. www.documents.worldbank.org.

De la Torre, Augusto, Federico Filippini, and Alain Ize. "The Commodity Cycle in Latin America: Mirages and Dilemmas." World Bank LAC Semiannual Report, April 2016. www.openknowledge.worldbank.org.

De la Torre, Augusto, and Sergio Schmulker. "Whither Latin American Capital Markets?" Working Paper, Office of the Chief Economist, The World Bank, October 2004.

De La Torre, Augusto, Alain Ize, and Sergio L. Schmukler. "LAC success put to test." World Bank, 2011. www.documents.worldbank.org.

Della Paolera, Gerardo, and Alan Taylor. *Finance and Development in an Emerging Market: Argentina in the Interwar Period*. National Bureau of Economic Research Working Paper Series No. 6236. Cambridge, MA: National Bureau of Economic Research, 1997.

Dellios, Hugh. "Storms Leave Guatemalans in Food Crisis." *Chicago Tribune*, November 18, 2005.

Delovitch, Emanuel, and Klas Ringskog. *Private Sector Participation in Water Supply and Sanitation in Latin America*. Washington, D.C.: World Bank, 1995.

Delph, Yvette M. "Health Priorities in Developing Countries." *Journal of Law, Medicine, & Ethics* 21(1) (1993).

Denes, Christian Andrew. "Bolsa Escola: Redefining Poverty and Development in Brazil." *International Education Journal* 4(2) (2003).

DePalma, Anthony. "Free Trade's Promise in Latin America; the Poor Survive It All. Even Boom Times." *New York Times*, June 24, 2001.

———. "Passing the Torch on a Chile Trade Deal." *New York Times*, January 7, 2001.

Derham, Michael Thomas. "A Less Uncertain World." *LatinFinance*, July 2005, 44.

De Schutter, Oliver. "The Transformative Potential of Agroecology." In *Food Movements Unite*, ed. Eric Holt-Gimenez. Food First Books, 2011: 223–237.

Desmarais, Annette. *La Via Campesina: Globalization and the Power of Peasants*. Fernwood Publishing, 2007: 32.

De Souza, Amaury. "Redressing Inequalities: Brazil's Social Agenda at Century's End." In *Brazil under Cardoso*, ed. Susan Kaufman Purcell and Riordan Roett. Boulder, CO: Rienner, 1997.

Devaux, Andre, Douglas Horton, and Miguel Ordinola. "Innovation to Value Native Potatoes' Biodiversity in Dynamic Markets: The Papa Andina Experience." International Potato Center, 2011.

Devlin, Robert, and Antoni Estevadeordal. "What's New in the New Regionalism in the Americas?" INTAL Working Paper No. 6, Inter-American Development Bank: Integration and Regional Programs Department, May 2001: 7–8.

Devlin, Robert, and Ricardo Ffrench-Davis. *Toward an Evaluation of Regional Integration in Latin America in the 1990s*. Working Paper No. 2. Buenos Aires: INTAL and ITD, 1998.

Devlin, Robert, Ricardo Ffrench-Davis, and Stephany Griffith-Jones. "Surges in Capital Flows and Development: An Overview of Policy Issues." In *Coping with Capital Surges*, ed. Ricardo Ffrench-Davis and Stephany Griffith-Jones. Boulder, CO: Rienner, 1995.

Dewees, Anthony, and Steven Klees. "Social Movements and the Transformation of National Policy: Street and Working Children in Brazil." *Comparative Education Review* 39(1) (1995).

DHS Report. "Domestic Violence Threatens Health of Children with Lower Immunization Rates, Higher Mortality Rates, Poor Nutrition." Press release, September 9, 2004.

Diáz Alejandro, Carlos. "International Markets for LDCs: The Old and the New." *American Economic Review*, May 1978: 254–269.

Diaz Bonilla, Eugenio, and Hector E. Schamis. *The Political Economy of Exchange Rate Policies in Argentina, 1950–1998*. Working Paper #R-379. IADB, April 1999.

Dickson, Eric, Judy L. Baker, Daniel Hoornweg, and Asmita Tiwari. "Urban Risk Assessments: Understanding Disaster and Climate Risk in Cities." World Bank. 2012 www.documents.worldbank.org.

Dietz, James L., and James H. Street, eds. *Latin America's Economic Development: Institutionalist and Structuralist Perspectives*. Boulder, CO: Rienner, 1987.

Digiano, Maria. "Anthony Hall: Forests and Climate Change: The Social Dimensions of Redd in Latin America." *Human Ecology* 41, (2013): 491–493.

"Digicel Haiti Revamps Mobile Money as 'Mon Cash.'" *TeleGeography*, August 18, 2015. www.telegeography.com.

Dijkstra, Geske. "The PRSP Approach and the Illusion of Improved Aid Effectiveness: Lessons from Bolivia, Honduras and Nicaragua." *Development Policy Review* 23(4): 443–464.

Dillin, John. "Crime Down, but Many Still Edgy." *Christian Science Monitor*, June 19, 2001.

Di Tella, R., and W. D. Savedoff. "Diagnosis Corruption." Washington, DC: Inter-American Development Bank, 2001.

Dixon, John. *The Urban Environmental Challenge in Latin America*. LATEN Dissemination Note No. 4, World Bank Latin America Technical Department, Environment Division. Washington, D.C.: World Bank, 1993.

Dixon, Thomas Homer. "The Upside of Down: Catastrophe, Creativity, Creativity and The Renewal Of Civilization." *Island Press*, 2006.

Dmytraczenko, Tania, Vijay Rao, and Lori Ashford. "Health Sector Reform: How It Affects Reproductive Health, Population." Reference Bureau Policy Brief, June 2003 www.prb.org.

Dollar, David, and Aart Kraay. "Growth Is Good for the Poor." *Journal of Economic Growth* 7(3) (2002): 195–225.

———. "Trade, Growth and Poverty." Development Research Group, the World Bank, June 2001. www.worldbank.org.

"Dollarization: Fad or Future for Latin America." IMF Economic Forum. Washington, D.C.: International Monetary Fund, June 24, 1999.

Donoso-Clark, Maria. "Rural Development." In *Ecuador: An Economic and Social Agenda in the Millennium World Bank*, ed. Marcelo Giugale, Jose Roberto Lopez-Calix, and Vicente Fretes-Cibils, 369–387. Washington, D.C.: World Bank, 2003.

Dore, Elizabeth. "One Step Forward, Two Steps Back: Gender and the State in the Long Nineteenth Century." In *Hidden Histories of Gender and the State in Latin America*, 1–32: Duke University Press, 2000.

Dornbusch, Rudiger. *Stabilization, Debt, and Reform: Policy Analysis for Developing Countries*. Englewood Cliffs, NJ: Prentice Hall, 1993.

Dornbusch, Rudiger, and Sebastian Edwards. "The Political Economy of Latin America." In *The Macroeconomics of Populism in Latin America* (A National Bureau of Economic Research Conference Report), ed. Rudiger Dornbusch and Sebastian Edwards. Chicago, IL: University of Chicago Press, 1991.

Dos Santos, Theodoro. "La crisis de la teoría del desarollo y las relaciones de dependencia en América Latina." *Boletin de CESO* 3 (1968). English translation in H. Bernstein, ed., *Underdevelopment and Development*. Harmondsworth: Penguin, 1973.

"Do We Not Bleed?" *Multinational Monitor* 26(1/2) (January–February 2005): 37–40.

Downie, Andrew, Whitney Eulich, and Andrew Rosati. "Chávez vs Lula: Two Distinct Approaches to Poverty Reduction in Latin America." *Christian Science Monitor* No. 08827729, March 7, 2013.

Drabek, Zdenek, and Warren Payne. "The Impact of Transparency on Foreign Direct Investment." IMF Staff Working Paper ERAD-99-02. Geneva: The World Trade Organization, 1999.

Druckerman, Pamela. "Argentina Wants to Speed or Boost Aid." *Wall Street Journal*, August 3, 2001.

———. "Argentine Bank Depositors Hold Reins of Nation's Fate. *Wall Street Journal*, July 17, 2001.

Druckerman, Pamela, Michael Phillips, Jonathan Karp, and Hugh Pope. "IMF Acts to Preempt Emerging-Market Crisis." *Wall Street Journal*, August 6, 2001.

Duflo, Esther, Rema Hanna, and Stephen Ryan. "Incentives Work: Getting Teachers to Come to School." *American Economic Review* 102 (4), 2012: 1241–1278.

Durlesser, Erin, Kerry Miller, and Olivia Perlmutt. "Malaria in Latin America: A Nutritional Problem." www.micronutrient.org.

Duryea, Suzanne, and Maria Eugenia Genoni. "Ethnicity, Race and Gender in Latin American Labor Markets." In *Social Inclusion and Economic Development in Latin America*, ed. Mayra Buvinic and Jacqueline Mazza. Washington, D.C.: Inter-American Development Bank, 2004.

Dyer, Geoff. "Brazil Markets Maintain Boost from IMF Deal." *Financial Times*, August 7, 2001.

———. "Brazil's Star Pupil Status Gets a Caning." *Financial Times*, August 5, 2001.

Eakin, Ken. "Monitoring and Evaluating Poverty Alleviation Programs in Peru. *Science from the Developing World*, September 4, 2001.

Earthtrends. "Environmental Information" database. www.earthtrends.org.

Eberlee, John. "Agenda Peru: Charting a Shared National Vision for the Future." *Science from the Developing World*, March 23, 2001.

Echavarría, Juan José. "Trade Flow in the Andean Countries: Unilateral Liberalization or Regional Preferences." In *Trade: Towards Open Regionalism*, Proceedings of the 1997 World Bank Conference on Development in Latin America and the Caribbean. Washington, D.C.: World Bank, 1998.

ECLAC. "Balance preliminar de las economías de América Latina y el Caribe." www.eclac.cl.

———. "Countries in the Region Should Invest 6.2% of Annual GDP to Satisfy Infrastructure Demands." ECLAC, October 2014. www.cepal.org.

———. "Economic Survey of Latin America and the Caribbean: Challenges to Sustainable Growth in a New External Context." ECLAC, 2014. www.cepal.org.

———. "Economic Survey of Latin America and the Caribbean." ECLAC, 2015. www.cepal.org.

———. "El nuevo patron de desarrollo de la agricultura en América Latina y el Caribe." *Outlook 2005, The New Pattern of Development of Agriculture in Latin America and the Caribbean*, September 2005.

———. "Financing and Management of Education in Latin America and the Caribbean." July 2004. www.eclac.org.

———. "Latin American and Asia: Productivity of Selected Ports 2008–2010." ECLAC, 2010–2011.

———. "Latin America and the Caribbean in the World Economy, 2005 Trends." Santiago, United Nations, 2005.

———. "Main Internet use in Latin America and the World." ECLAC, 2012.

———. "The Millennium Development Goals: A Latin American and Caribbean Perspective." Report Coordinated by José Luis Machinea, August 2005.

———. "The Pacific Alliance and its Economic Impact on Regional Trade." International Trade Series No. 128, 2016.

———. "Precarious Urban Conditions." Press release on study "Poverty and Precariousness in the Habitat of Latin America and the Caribbean Cities," January 18, 2005. www.eclac.org.

———. "Public Policies for the Development of Information Societies in Latin America and the Caribbean." June 2005. www.eclac.org.

———. "Social Panorama 2005." Press release, www.eclac.org.

———. "Structural Change for Equality: An Integrated Approach to Development." 2012. www.eclac.org.

———. "Worst Ever Coffee Crisis Hits Latin America," *Cepal News* 22(4), April 10, 2002.

ECLAC: Division of Production, Productivity and Management. "Public Policies for the Development of Information Societies in Latin America and the Caribbean." LC/W. 19 Junio, 2005. www.eclac.

ECLAC and IICA. "Survey of Agriculture in Latin America and the Caribbean." December 2001: 1990–2000. www.eclac.cl.

ECLAC, IICA, and FAO. "The Outlook for Agriculture and Rural Development in the Americas: A Perspective on Latin America and the Caribbean 2014." FAO, 2014. www.fao.org.

ECLAC/UNDP. *Financing for Sustainable Development in Latin America and the Caribbean.* Joint document prepared for the World Summit on Sustainable Development, August 2002.

Economic Commission for Latin America and the Caribbean. *Communique on the International Financial Crises.* September 15, 1998. Available at www.cepal.org.

———. "Data Characterizing Poverty." Social Panorama of Latin America, 2012. www.eclac.org.

———. *Economic Survey of Latin America and the Caribbean.* Santiago: ECLAC, various years. www.eclac.org.

———. *The Equity Gap: Latin America, the Caribbean, and the Social Summit.* Santiago: ECLAC, 1997.

———. *The Fiscal Covenant: Strengths, Weaknesses, Challenges.* Santiago: ECLAC, 1997.

———. *Foreign Investment in Latin America and the Caribbean, 2000,* table I.12, 65.

———. "Foreign Investment in Latin America and the Caribbean." ECLAC, June 2016.

———. *Indicadores Económicos.* Santiago: ECLAC, 1997.

———. "Latin American and the Caribbean in the World Economy: The Regional Trade Crisis: Assessment and Outlook." ECLAC, 2015: 61–77.

———. *Notes* N. 12, September 2000.

———. *Notes* N. 13, November 2000.

———. "The Pacific Alliance and Its Economic Impact on Regional Trade." International Trade Series No. 128.

———. *Panorama de la Insercion Internactional de América Latina y el Caribe, 1996.* Santiago: ECLAC, 1996.

———. *Policies to Improve Linkages with the Global Economy.* Santiago: ECLAC, 1995.

———. Preliminary Overview of the Economies of Latin America and the Caribbean, 1999. Santiago: United Nations and ECLAC, December 1999.

———. "Social Panorama of Latin America." ECLAC, March 2012. www.cepal.org.

———. *Statistical Yearbook for Latin American and the Caribbean, 1996.* Chile: ECLAC, 1996.

———. *Strengthening Development: The Interplay of Macro- and Microeconomics.* Santiago: ECLAC, 1996.

"Ecuador Drifts between Opportunity and Deadlock." *The Economist,* December 23, 2000.

"Ecuadorian 2004 Flower Exports at $314 M." *Latin America News Digest,* January 13, 2005.

Edwards, Sebastian. "Capital Flows into Latin America: A Stop-Go Story?" National Bureau of Economic Research Working Paper No. 6441. Cambridge, MA: National Bureau of Economic Research, 1998. Available at www.nber.org/papers/w6441.

———. *Crisis and Reform in Latin America: From Despair to Hope.* New York: Oxford University Press, 1995.

———. "The Mexican Peso Crisis: How Much Did We Know? When Did We Know It?" *World Economy* 21(1) (1998).

————. "The Opening of Latin America," in *Crisis and Reform in Latin America: From Despair to Hope.* New York: Oxford University Press, 1995.

————. "The Political Economy of Inflation and Stabilization in Developing Countries." *Economic Development and Cultural Change* 42(2) (January 1994): 235–266.

Edwards, Sebastian, and Daniel Lederman. "The Political Economy of Unilateral Trade Liberalization: The Case of Chile." National Bureau of Economic Research Working Paper No. 6510. Cambridge, MA: National Bureau of Economic Research, 1998. www.nber.org.

Edwards, Sebastian, and Nora Claudia Lustig, eds. *Labor Markets in Latin America: Combining Social Protection with Market Flexibility.* Washington, D.C.: Brookings Institution, 1997.

Eichengreen, Barry. "When to Dollarize." Presented for the ITAM Dollarization Project Meeting in Mexico City, December 3, 1999.

Eichengreen, Barry, and Ricardo Hausman. "Original Sin: The Road to Redemption." *NBER*, January 2005.

El-Ashry, Mohamed T. *Statement to the Fourth Session of the Conference of the Parties to the United Nations Framework Convention on Climate Change.* Buenos Aires, November 11, 1998. Washington, D.C.: Global Environment Facility, 1998.

"El Chaco Paraguayo Registra La Tasa De Deforestación Más Alta Del Planeta." *E'a,* January 22, 2014. www.ea.com.py.

Elliott, Kimberly Ann. "Trading Up: Labor Standards, Development and CAFTA." *CGD Brief* 3(2) (May 2004).

Ellison, Katherine. "Latin Summit's Focus: Education of Kids." *Miami Herald,* April 13, 1998, A1. Available at www.alca-cupula.org.

"El Hambre en Paraguay." *ABC Color,* October 18, 2013. www.abc.com.py.

"El Salvador." *FINCA.* www.finca.org.

"El Salvador Environmental Services Project." Project Appraisal Document, 1, April 22, 2005.

Elson, Anthony. "Dragon among the Iguanas." *IMF Magazine: Finance & Development* 51(4), December 2014.

"Emerging Economies to Lead Energy Growth to 2030 and Renewables to Out-Grow Oil, Says BP Analysis," January 19, 2011. www.bp.com.

"Emerging-Market Indicators." *The Economist,* November 4, 2000.

Emmott, Robin, "Bribery Costs Mexicans Up to 14% of Income." *Financial Times,* October 31, 2001.

Employment Policy Foundation. "Open Trade: The 'Fast Track' to Higher Living Standards." *Contemporary Issues in Employment and Workplace Policy* 111(10) (October 1997). Internet publication available at epfnet.org.

Energy Information Administration. *Petroleum Supply Annual, 1995.* Washington, D.C.: U.S. Department of Energy, 1995.

————. "World Proven Reserves of Oil and Natural Gas, Most Recent Estimates." Table posted January 18, 2006. www.eia.doe.gov.

"Energy in Latin America: Even Oil Is Growing Less Sacred." *The Economist,* June 1, 1996.

Engell, Alan. "Improving the Quality and Equity of Education in Chile: The Programa 900 Escuelas and the MECE-Basica." In *Implementing Policy Innovation in Latin America: Politics, Economics and Techniques,* ed. Antonio Silva. Washington, D.C.: IADB, 1996.

The Equity Gap—A Second Assessment. Prepared by ECLAC Secretariat for the Second Regional Conference. ECLAC, 2000.

Ernst, Christoph. "Trade Liberalization, Export Orientation and Employment in Argentina, Brazil and Mexico." Employment Strategy Papers 2005–15, International Labour Office, 2005.

Escobar, Maria Luisa. "Health Sector Reform in Colombia Development Outreach." World Bank Institute, World Bank Special Report, May 2005. www.worldbank.org.

Espindola, Ernesto, Arturo Leon, Rodrigo Martinez, and Alexander Schejtman. "Poverty, Hunger and Food Insecurity in Central America and Panama." *CEPAL Serie Políticas Sociales* 88 (May 2005): 28.

Esquivel, Gerardo, and Graciela Marquez. "Some Economic Effects of Closing the Economy: The Mexican Experience in the Mid-Twentieth Century." In *Capital Controls and Capital Flows in Emerging Economies: Policies, Practices and Consequences,* ed. Sebastian Edwards. NBER, 2005. Papers accessed at www.nber.org/books.

Estache, Antonio, and Danny Leipziger, "Utilities Privatization and the Poor: Lessons and Evidence from Latin America." *World Development* 29(7) (2001): 1181.

Estevadeordal, Antoni, and Kati Suominen. "Is All Well with the Spaghetti Bowl in the Americas?" *Economía* (Spring 2005): 63–103.

Estey, Daniel, Marc Levy, Tanja Srebotnjak, and Alexander de Sherbinin. "2006 Environmental Sustainability Index." New Haven, CT: Yale Center for Environmental Law and Policy. www.yale.edu.

Evans, Peter. *Dependent Development*. Princeton, NJ: Princeton University Press, 1979.

———. "The Eclipse of the State? Reflection on Stateness in an Era of Globalization." *World Politics* 50 (October 1997).

———, ed. "State-Society Synergy: Government and Social Capital in Development." *World Development* 24(6), special edition (June 1996).

Faiz, Asif, Surhid Gautam, and Emaad Burki. "Air Pollution from Motor Vehicles: Issues and Options for Latin American Countries." *The Science of the Total Environment* 169 (1995): 303–310.

Fajnzylber, Fernando. "Education and Changing Production Patterns with Social Equality." *CEPAL Review* 47 (August 1992).

Fanelli, José María, and Roberto Frenkel. "Macropolicies for the Transition from Stabilization to Growth." In *New Directions in Development Economics: Growth, Environmental Concerns, and Government in the 1990s,* ed. Mats Lundahl and Benno J. Ndulu. London: Routledge, 1996.

Fanelli, José Maria, and José Luis Machinea. "Capital Movements in Argentina." In *Coping with Capital Surges: The Return of Finance to Latin America,* ed. Ricardo Ffrench-Davis and Stephany Griffith-Jones. Boulder, CO: Rienner, 1995.

FAO. "Deforestation Rate 'Alarming,' but Net Loss Slowing." *Agence France-Presse,* November 14, 2005. Reprinted at the World Business Council for Sustainable Development. www.wbcsd.org.

———. "FAO and Brazil Prepare an International Conference." FAO Newsroom, November 24, 2005.

———. "FAO in Latin America and the Caribbean." www.fao.org.

———. "FAO Regional Review Executive Summary," www.fao.org.

———. "The State of Food Insecurity in the World 2005." www.fao.org.

———. "Trends and Challenges in Agriculture, Forestry and Fisheries in Latin America and the Caribbean." *FAO Regional Review Executive Summary,* July 2005.

Farber, Daniel. *Environment under Fire*. New York: Monthly Review Press, 1993.

Farber, Jessica. "Political Upheaval in Brazil Threatens Future of Universal Healthcare System." Council on Hemispheric Affairs, August 12, 2016.

Farrell, Diana, Jaana K. Remes, and Heiner Schulz. "The Truth about Foreign Direct Investment in Emerging Markets." *McKinsey Quarterly* 1 (2004).

"Fast Facts on Microenterpreneurship: International Year of the Microcredit 2005." www.yearofmicrocredit.org.

Faundez, M. Sebastian, Nanno Mulder, and Nicole Carpentier. "Productivity Growth in Latin American Manufacturing: What Role for International Trade Intensities?" MPRA Paper, University Library of Munich, Germany, 2011.

Fauriol, Georges A., and Sidney Weintraub. "The Century of the Americas: Dawn of a New Century." *Washington Quarterly* 24(2) (Spring 2001).

Fearnside, Philip M. "Conservation Policy in Brazilian Amazonia: Understanding the Dilemmas." *World Development* 31(5) (May 2003): 757.

———. "Deforestation in Brazilian Amazonia: The Effect of Population and Land Tenure." *Ambio* 22(8) (December 1993).

Federal Reserve Bank of Atlanta. "Imbalances in Latin American Fiscal Accounts: Why the United States Should Care." *EconSouth* 2(4) (2000).

Federal Reserve Bank of San Francisco. "U.S. Inflation Targeting: Pro and Con." *FRBSF Economic Letter*, May 29, 1998, 98–118.

Fernandes, Erick C.M, Soliman Ayat, Roberto Confalonieri, Marcello Donatelli, and Francesco Tubiello. "Climate Change and Agriculture in Latin America, 2020–2050: Projected Impacts and Response to Adaptation Strategies." World Bank, 2012. https://openknowledge.worldbank.org.

Fernández-Arias, Eduardo. "The New Wave of Capital Inflows: Sea Change or Tide?" Presented at the Annual Meeting of the Board of Governors, IADB and Inter-American Investment Corporation, March 26 2000.

Fernández-Arias, Eduardo, and Ricardo Hausmann. *Getting It Right: What to Reform in International Financial Markets.* Working Paper #428. Presented at the Tenth International Forum on Latin American Perspectives in Paris. IADB, November 1999.

———. *International Initiatives to Bring Stability to Financial Integration.* IADB, March 1999.

Fernández-Arias, Eduardo, and Sergio Rodríguez-Apolinar. "The Productivity Gap in Latin America: Lessons from 50 Years of Development." Inter-American Development Bank, May2016. www.publications.iadb.org.

———. *What's Wrong with International Financial Markets?* Working Paper #429. Presented at the Tenth International Forum on Latin American Perspectives in Paris. IADB, November 1999.

Ferreira, Francisco H. G., and Jérémie Gignoux. "The Measurement of Educational Inequality: Achievement and Opportunity." *World Bank Economic Review*, February 2013. doi: 10.1093/wber/lht004.

Ferreira, Francisco H. G., Julian Messina, Jamele Rigolini, Luis-Felipe Lopez-Calva, Maria Ana Lugo, Renos Vakis, Luis Felipe Lopez-Calva, and Renos Vakis. "Economic Mobility and the Rise of the Latin American Middle Class." World Bank, 2012.

Ffrench-Davis, Ricardo. Comment on L. Allan Winters, "Assessing Regional Integration." In *Trade: Towards Open Regionalism*, Proceedings of the 1997 World Bank Conference on Development in Latin America and the Caribbean. Washington, D.C.: World Bank, 1998.

———. "Policy Implications of the Tequila Effect." *Challenge*. March–April 1998.

Ffrench-Davis, Ricardo, Manuel Agosin, and Andras Uthoff. "Capital Movements, Export Strategy and Macroeconomic Stability in Chile." In *Coping with Capital Surges: The Return of Finance to Latin America*, ed. Ricardo Ffrench-Davis and Stephany Griffith-Jones. Boulder, CO: Rienner, 1995.

"Fifty Years On." *The Economist*, May 16, 1998, 22.

Filho, Leah, W. Alves, S. Caeiro, and U.M. Azeiteiro. "International Perspectives on Climate Change Latin America and Beyond." *Climate Change Management* (1) (2015).

"Financial Inclusion in Paraguay: New Mobile Money Regulation." *GMSA*, July 2014. www.gsma.com.

"Firms Now Pay Higher Gas Taxes to Bolivia." *Associated Press* LA PAZ, Bolivia, June 8, 2006. www.businessweek.com.

"The Fiscal Mire." *The Economist*, May 4, 1996.

Fisher, Stanley. "Reforming World Finance." *The Economist*, October 3–9, 1998. Reproduced at www.imf.org.

———. "Remarks to the Argentine Bankers Association." Presented at the 2001 Argentine Bankers Association Meeting. Buenos Aires: IMF, available at www.imf.org.

Fiszbein, A., and G. Psacharopoulos. *Income Inequality in Latin America: The Story of the Eighties*. Technical Department for Latin America Working Paper. Washington, D.C.: World Bank, 1995.

Fiszbein, Ariel, and Yasuhiko Matsuda. "Matching Reforms to Institutional Realities: A Framework for Assessing Social Service Delivery Reform Strategies in Developing Countries." World Bank Policy Research Working Paper No. 6136, July 1, 2012. www.ssrn.com.

Florez Guio, Ana, Ray Chesterfield, and Carmen Siri. "The CERCA School Report Card: Communities Creating Education Quality. Implementation Manual." Academy for Educational Development, 2006.

Foley, Michael. "Agenda for Mobilization: The Agrarian Question and Popular Mobilization in Contemporary Mexico." *Latin American Research Review* 26(2) (1991): 39–74.

Food and Agriculture Organization of the United Nations. *The State of Food and Agriculture*. Rome: Food and Agriculture Organization of the United Nations, 1994.

Fox, Tom. "Corporate Social Responsibility and Development: In Quest of an Agenda." *Development* 47 (3), 2004: 29–36.

Foxley, Alejandro. "Preface." In *The New Economic Model in Latin America and Its Impact on Income Distribution and Poverty*, ed. Victor Bulmer-Thomas. New York: St. Martin's, 1996.

Fraga, Arminio. "Monetary Policy during the Transition to a Floating Exchange Rate: Brazil's Recent Experience." *Finance & Development* 37(1) (March 2000).

Francis, David R. "Why Fighting Corruption Helps the Poor." *The Christian Science Monitor*, November 13, 2003.

Franco, Adolfo A. Assistant Administrator, Bureau for Latin America and the Caribbean, United States Agency for International Development. Testimony before the Committee on International Relations, U.S. House of Representatives, Subcommittee on the Western Hemisphere, April 20, 2005. www.usinfo.state.gov.

Frank, Andre Gundar. *Capitalism and Underdevelopment in Latin America*. New York: Monthly Review Press, 1967.

Free Trade Area of the Americas. "Free Trade Area of the Americas Declaration of Ministers Fifth Trade Ministerial Meeting." Canada: Free Trade Area of the Americas, November 4, 1999.

"Free Trade Area of the Americas Sixth Meeting of Ministers of Trade of the Hemisphere." Ministerial Declaration in Buenos Aires. Argentina: Free Trade Area of the Americas, April 7, 2001.

Freire, Paulo. *Pedagogy of the Oppressed*. New York: Seabury, 1970.

Freitas Jr, Gerson, and Jessica Brice. "World's Biggest Meat Producer Struggles with Bad Beef Allegations." *Bloomberg*, March 23, 2017. www.bloomberg.com.

"French Lyonnaise des Eaux Agrees to Close Unit in Bolivia." *Latin America News Digest*, March 28, 2006.

Freund, Caroline. "Streamlining Rules of Origin in NAFTA." Peterson Institute for International Economics, June 2017. www.piie.com.

Frias, Michael. "Linking International Remittance Flows to Financial Services: Tapping into the Latino Immigrant Market." *Supervisory Journal*, December 1, 2004.

Frieden, Jeffrey, and Ernesto Stein. *The Currency Game: Exchange Rate Politics in Latin America*. Washington, D.C.: Johns Hopkins University Press for the IADB, 2001.

Friedland, Jonathan. "Argentina's Tax Collector Names Names." *Wall Street Journal*, April 13, 1995.

———. "Their Success Earns Chileans a New Title: Ugly Pan-Americans." *Wall Street Journal*, October 3, 1996.

"From Marginality of the 1960's to the 'New Poverty' of Today." Latin American Research Review Forum. *LARR* 39(1) (February 2004).

"From Sandals to Suits." *The Economist*, February 1, 1997.

From Santiago to Quebec City—Report on the Achievements of the Inter-American System. Washington, D.C.: Summits of the Americas Information Network, Office of Summit Follow-up, March 2001. Available at www.summit-americas.org.

Frynas, Jedrzej George. "The False Developmental Promise of Corporate Social Responsibility: Evidence from Multinational Oil Companies." *International Affairs* 81(3), 2005: 581–598.

Fuentes, Federico. "Land Reform Battle Deepens." *Green Left Weekly*, New South Wales, Australia, October 12, 2005. www.worldpress.org.

Fuerbringer, Jonathan. "Economic Troubles Worsen in Argentina." *New York Times*, July 11, 2001.

———. "Trouble in Argentina May Help Other Emerging Markets." *New York Times*, July 15, 2001.

"Funds for Farmers Needed for Future." *Financial Times*, December 14, 2000.

Furtado, Celso. *Development and Underdevelopment*. Translated by Ricardo W. Agruar and Eric Charles Drysdale. Berkeley, CA: University of California Press, 1965.

Gabriel Palma, José. "Homogeneous Middles vs. Heterogeneous Tails, and the End of the 'Inverted-U': It's All About the Share of the Rich." *Development and Change* 42(1), January 2011: 87–153.

Gagné, Gilbert. "North American Free Trade, Canada, and the US Trade Remedies: An Assessment after Ten Years." *World Economics* 23(1) (January 2000).

Galal, Ahmed, Leroy Jones, Pankaj Tandon, and Ingo Vogelsang. "Divestiture: Questions and Answers." In *Welfare Consequences of Selling Public Enterprises*. Washington, D.C.: World Bank, 1994.

Gallagher, Kevin. "Trump Builds Walls, Xi Builds Bridges in LatAm." *Latin America Goes Global*, November 18, 2016. latinamericagoesglobal.org.

Gallagher, Kevin P., and Margaret Myers. "China-Latin America Finance Database." Washington: Inter-American Dialogue, 2016.

Gallup, John Luke, Alejandro Gaviria, and Eduardo Lora. *Is Geography Destiny?* Washington, D.C.: Inter-American Development Bank, 2003.

Ganimian, Alejandro J., and Solano Rocha. "Measuring Up? How Did Latin America and the Caribbean Perform on the 2009 Programme for International Student Assessment (PISA)?" *Partnership for Educational Revitalization in the Americas (PREAL)*, 2011.

García, María Isabel. "Forecast Bright for 'Clean' Agriculture." *Tierramérica*, July 24, 2001.

Garfield, Elsie, Maurizio Guadagni, and Daniel Moreau. "Colombia—Decentralization of Agricultural Extension Services." In *Agricultural Extension: Generic Challenges and Some Ingredients for Solutions*, ed. Gershon Feder, Anthony Willett, and Willem Zijp. Washington, D.C.: World Bank, 1999.

Gartlan, Kieran. "The Global Power of Brazilian Agribusiness." *The Economist* Intelligence Unit, November 2010.

Gasparini, Leonardo, and Nora Lustig. "The Rise and Fall of Income Inequality in Latin America." *Oxford Handbooks Online*, September 18, 2012.

"A Gathering Twilight." *The Economist*, July 14, 2001.

Gavin, Michael. "Hearing on Official Dollarization in Latin America." Presented to the Senate Banking Committee, July 15, 1999.

——. "Surviving Economic Surgery." *The IDB* (December 1996): 4–5.

Gavin, Michael, Ricardo Hausmann, Roberto Perotti, and Ernesto Talvi. *Managing Fiscal Policy in Latin America and the Caribbean: Volatility, Procyclicality, and Limited Creditworthiness*. IADB, Office of the Chief Economist Working Paper No. 326. Washington, D.C.: IADB, 1996.

Gazzoni, Décui Luis, Ivan Azurdia, Gabriel Blanco, Claudio A. Estrada, and Isais De Carvalho Macedo. "Sustainable Energy in Latin America and the Caribbean: Potential for the Future, Rio de Janeiro": ICSU-LAC (2010).

Gelbard, Alene H. *An Action Plan for Population, Development, and the Environment: Woodrow Wilson Center Spring 1996 Report*. Washington, D.C.: Woodrow Wilson Center, 1996.

Gereffi, Gary, and Peter Evans. "Transnational Corporations, Dependent Development, and State Policy in the Semiperiphery." *Latin American Research Review* 16(3) (1981): 31–64.

Giuffrida, Antonio, William Savedoff, and Roberto Iunes. "Health and Poverty in Brazil: Estimation by Structural Equation Model with Latent Variables." IADB Working Paper, March 2005. www.iadb.org.

Guiffrida, Antonio, et. al. "Racial and Ethnic Disparities in Health in Latin America and the Caribbean." Inter-American Development Bank, October 2007.

Glaister, Dan. "Emigrants Provide Lifeline." *The Guardian*, March 29, 2004.

Glewwe, Paul W., Eric A. Hanushek, Sarah D. Humpage, and Renato Ravina. "School Resources and Educational Outcomes in Developing Countries: A Review of the Literature from 1990 to 2010." NBER Working Papers 17554, National Bureau of Economic Research Inc., 2011.

Glewwe, Paul, and Michael Kremer. "Schools, Teachers and Education Outcomes in Developing Countries." CID Working Paper No. 122, prepared as second draft of chapter for *The Handbook on the Economics of Education* (Cambridge: Harvard University, September 2005).

Global Development Finance 2001, Washington, D.C.: World Bank Publications, 2001, 186, table A42.

Global Environmental Fund. "Participation Means Learning through Doing: GEF's Experience." In "Biodiversity Conservation and Sustainable Use," *GEF Lessons Notes*, July 12, 2001, 1–4. Available at ww.gefweb.org.

"Globalization and Education." ODI Briefing Paper, October 2005.

"Gloom over the River Plate." *The Economist*, July 14, 2001.

"Going Too Far in Support of Trade." *The Economist*, December 16, 2000.

Goldin, Ian A., and Kenneth Reinert. "Global Capital Flows and Development: A Survey." *Journal of International Trade and Economic Development* (2005): 9–11.

Goldstone, Jack. "The Population Bomb: The Four Megatrends That Will Change the World." *Foreign Affairs*, January/February 2010, pp. 31–43.

Gómez, Ricardo. "The Hall of Mirrors: The Internet in Latin America." *Current History* 99(634) (2000).

Gonzalez, David. "Gaining Dollars, Town Is Losing Its Folkways." *New York Times*, January 1, 2001.

Gonzalez, Elizabeth. "Weekly Chart: Latin America's Informal Economy." AS/COA, April 2015.

Gonzalez, Gustavo. "Microcredit Makes Strong Inroads in Latin America." Inter-Press News Service Agency, April 26, 2005. www.ipsnews.net.

Goodland, Robert, and Herman Daly. *Poverty Alleviation Is Essential for Environmental Sustainability*. World Bank, Environment Department, Divisional Working Paper 1993–42. Washington, D.C.: World Bank, 1993.

Gore, Albert. "The Inconvenient Truth." *Bloomsbury*, 2006.

Gori, Graham. "Mexicans Wait More for a Phone." *New York Times*, January 24, 2001.

———. "Mexico's Heavy Industries Threatened by Natural Gas Costs." *New York Times*, January 5, 2001.

Goulet, Denis. *The Cruel Choice: A New Concept in the Theory of Development*. New York: Atheneum, 1971.

Government Accountability Office. "Missed Deadline Prompts Efforts to Restart Stalled Hemispheric Trade Negotiations." *GAO Free Trade Area of the Americas*. GAO-05-166 Report to the Chairman, Committee on Finance, U.S. Senate, and to the Chairman, Committee on Ways and Means, House of Representatives, March 2005.

Graham, Carol. *Private Markets for Public Goods: Raising the Stakes for Economic Reform*. Washington, D.C.: Brookings Institution Press, 1998.

———. *Safety Nets, Politics, and the Poor: Transitions to Market Economies*. Washington, D.C.: Brookings Institution Press, 1994.

———. "Strengthening Institutional Capacity in Poor Countries," The Brookings Institution Policy Brief, No. 98, April 2002. www.brookings.edu.

Graham, Edward, M., and Erika Wada. *Domestic Reform, Trade and Investment Liberalisation, Financial Crisis, and Foreign Direct Investment into Mexico*. Washington, D.C.: Institute for International Economics, 2000.

"Green, As in Greenbacks." *The Economist*, February 1, 1997.

Greig, Alan, Michael Kimmel, and James Lang. *Men, Masculinities & Development: Broadening Our Work towards Gender Equality*. UNDP Gender in Development Monograph Series #10, May 2000.

Grieg-Gran, Maryanne, Ina Porras, and Sven Wunder. "How Can Market Mechanisms for Forest Environmental Services Help the Poor? Preliminary Lessons from Latin America." *World Development* 33(9), September 2005: 1511–1527.

Griffith-Jones, Stephany. "The Mexican Peso Crisis." *CEPAL Review* 60 (December 1996).

Grigoli, Francesco, Alexander Herman, and Klaus Schmidt-Hebbel. "Saving in Latin America and the Caribbean: Performance and Policies." International Monetary Fund Working Paper, May 2015. www.imf.org.

Grilli, Enzo, and Dominick Salvatore, eds. *Economic Development: Handbook of Comparative Economic Policies*. Westport, CT: Greenwood, 1994.

Grosh, Margaret E. *Administering Targeted Social Programs in Latin America*. Washington, D.C.: World Bank, 1994.

Gruley, Bryan, and Lucia Kassai. "Brazilian Meatpacker JBS Wranglers the U.S. Beef Industry: How a Brazilian Butcher Shop Became a $50 Billion Behemoth." *Bloomberg*, September 19, 2013. www.bloomberg.com.

Grynspan, Rebeca, and Luis F. López-Calva. "Multidimensional Poverty in Latin America: Concept, Measurement, and Policy." *The Oxford Handbook of Latin American Economics*, July 2011.

"Guadalajara Takes High-Tech Route." *Financial Times*, December 14, 2000.

The Guardian. "World Health Organisation Declares Zika Virus Public Health Emergency." *The Guardian*, April 2016. www.theguardian.com.

Guerguil, Marinte. "Some Thoughts on the Definition of the Informal Sector." *CEPAL Review* 35 (August 1988).

Guillaume, Agnes, and Susana Lerner. "Abortion in Latin America and the Caribbean." Center for Population Development, 2007. www.ceped.org.

Guivant, Julia. "Agrarian Change, Gender and Land Rights: A Brazilian Case Study." United Nations Research Institute for Social Development, PP SPD, June 14, 2003. www.unrisd.org.

Gunnarsson, C., and M. Lundahl. "The Good, The Bad, and the Wobbly." In *New Directions in Development Economics: Growth, Environmental Concerns, and Government in the 1990s*, ed. Mats Lundahl and Benno J. Ndulu. London: Routledge, 1996.

Gutierrez, Luish H., and Sanford Berg. "Telecommunications Liberalization and Regulatory Governance: Lessons from Latin America." *Telecommunications Policy* 24 (December 2000): 865–884.

Gwatkin, Davidson R., Adam Wagstaff, Abdo S. Yazbeck, eds. "Reaching the Poor with Health, Nutrition, and Population Services: What Works, What Doesn't, and Why." World Bank, 2005. www.openknowledge.worldbank.org.

Haass, Richard N., and Robert E. Litan. "Globalization and Its Discontents." *Foreign Affairs* 77(3) (1998).

Haber, Stephen. *How Latin America Fell Behind*. Stanford, CA: Stanford University Press, 1997.

Habitat for Humanity. "Affordable Housing Statistics." www.habitat.org.

———. "Causes of Inadequate Housing in Latin America and the Caribbean." povlibrary. worldbank.org.

Hall, Gillette, and Harry Patrinos. *Indigenous Peoples, Poverty and Human Development in Latin America: 1994–2004*. Hampshire, UK: Palgrave Macmillan, 2005. Executive summary at www.worldbank.org.

———. "Latin America's Indigenous Peoples." *Finance and Development* 42(4) (December 2005).

Hall, Susan E. A. "Conoco's Green Strategy." Harvard Business School Case #9-394-001, October 4, 1993.

Hallak, Juan Carlos, and James Levinsohn. "Fooling Ourselves: Evaluating the Globalization and Growth Debate." National Bureau of Economic Research Working Paper No. 10244, January 2004.

Hamilton, Roger. "Tourism's Green Frontier: How to Protect Nature and Make a Profit." *IDB América*, Inter-American Development Bank, January 2002. www.iadb.org.

Hammergren, Linn. "The Development Wars: Analyzing Foreign Assistance Impact and Policy." *Latin American Research Review* 34(2) (1999).

Hammond, Allen, William J Kramer, Rob Katz, Julia Tran, and Courtland Walker. "The Next 4 Billion: Market Size and Business Strategy at the Base of the Pyramid." World Resources Institute, 2007. pdf.wri.org

Hansen, James. "Storms of My Grandchildren." *Bloomsbury*, 2011.

Hanshaw, Margaret. "Venture Philanthropist." *Harvard Business Review* (July–August 2000).

Hanson, Simon. *Economic Development in Latin America*. Washington, D.C.: Inter-American Affairs Press, 1951.

Hardoy, Joreglina, and Patricia Romero Lankao. "Latin American Cities and Climate Change: Challenges and Options to Mitigation and Adaptation Responses." *Current Opinion in Environmental Sustainability* 3 (2011): 158–163.

Harris, Paul. "Chile's Copper: Surplus Spells Woe for Exporters." *Financial Times*, May 9, 2006.

Harriss, John, Janet Hunter, and Colin M. Lewis, "Introduction: Development and Significance of the NIE." In *The New Institutional Economics and Third World Development*, ed. John Harriss, Janet Hunter, and Colin M. Lewis. London: Routledge, 1995.

Harriss-White, Barbara. "Maps and Landscapes of Grain Markets in South Asia." In *The New Institutional Economics and Third World Development*, ed. John Harriss, Janet Hunter, and Colin M. Lewis. London: Routledge, 1996.

Hartshorn, Gary S. "Natural Forest Management by the Yanesha Forestry Cooperative in Peruvian Amazonia." In *Alternatives to Deforestation: Steps toward Sustainable Use of the Amazon Rain Forest*, ed. Anthony B. Anderson. New York: Columbia University Press, 1990.

"Harvesting Farming's Potential." *The Economist*, September 9, 2000.

"Harvesting Poverty: Napoleon's Bittersweet Legacy." *New York Times*, editorial, August 11, 2003. www.nytimes.com.

Harvey, David. *A Brief History of Neoliberalism*. New York: Oxford University Press, 2005.

Harvey, Hal, and Sonia Aggarwal. "The Costs of Delay," Climate Works Foundation, 2011.

Hasan Khan Mahmood. "Rural Poverty in Developing Countries—Implications for Public Policy." *IMF Economic Issues* 26 (March 2001).

Hausmann, Ricardo, and Helmut Reisen, eds. *Securing Stability and Growth in Latin America*. Paris: OECD Publications, 1996.

Hausmann, Ricardo, and Ernesto Stein. "Searching for the Right Budgetary Institution for a Volatile Region." In *Securing Stability and Growth in Latin America*, ed. Ricardo Hausmann and Helmut Reisen. Paris: OECD Publications, 1996.

"Heading Off Contagion." Editorial comment. *Financial Times*, August 7, 2001.

Heal, Geoffrey. "Corporate Social Responsibility: An Economic and Financial Framework." The Geneva Papers, 2005.

"Health Data." Institute for Health Metrics and Evaluation. www.healthdata.org.

Hecht, Susanna B., Susan Kandel, Ileana Gomes, Nelson Cuellar, and Herman Rosa. "Globalization, Forest Resurgence, and Environmental Politics in El Salvador." *World Development* 34(2) (February 2006): 308–323.

Heckman, James J., and Carmen Pages. "Working Paper 7773." NBER Working Paper Series, table 2, Summary of Existing Evidence on the Impact of Job Security in Latin America, June 2000: 15. www.nber.org.

Heinberg, Richard. *The Party's Over: Oil, War, And The Fate of Industrial Societies*. New York: Clearview, 2003.

Helleiner, Gerald K. "Toward a New Development Strategy." In *The Legacy of Raúl Prebisch*, ed. Enrique V. Iglesias. Washington, D.C.: IADB, 1994.

Hellinger, Daniel. "Understanding Venezuela's Crisis—Dutch Diseases, Money Doctors, and Magicians." *Latin American Perspectives* 27(1) (January 2000).

Helwege, Ann. "Poverty and Inequality in Latin America and the Caribbean." *CEPAL Review* 47 (August 1992).

———. "Poverty in Latin America: Back to the Abyss?" *Journal of Inter-American Studies and World Affairs* 37(3) (Fall 1995).

Hemispheric Social Alliance. *Alternatives for the Americas*. Prepared for the 2nd Peoples Summit of the Americas. Canada: Hemispheric Social Alliance, April 2001.

Henriot, Peter J. "Development Alternatives: Problems, Strategies, Values." In *The Political Economy of Development and Underdevelopment*, 2nd ed., ed. Charles K. Wilbert. New York: Random House, 1979.

Henriquez, P., and H. Li Pun (eds.). "Impactful Innovations: Lessons from Family Agriculture in Latin America and the Caribbean." Inter-American Development Bank: Inter-American Institute for Cooperation on Agriculture, 2014.

Hertsgaard, Mark. "Confronting the Climate Cranks." *The Nation,* January 20, 2011.

New York: *Hot: Living Through The Next Fifty Years On Earth.* Houghton Mifflin Harcourt, 2011.

Hey, Jeanne A. K., and Thomas Klak. "From Protectionism towards Neoliberalism: Ecuador across Four Administrations (1981–1996)." *Studies in Comparative International Development* (Fall 1999).

Hidalgo, Dario. "Why is TransMilenio Still So Special?" The City Fix, World Resources Institute, August 5, 2008. www.thecityfix.com.

"The Hidden Wealth of the Poor." Microcredit Survey, *The Economist*, November 3, 2005.

Higgins, B. *Economic Development: Problems, Principles, and Policies.* New York: Norton, 1968.

Hikino, Takashi, and Alice Amsden. "Staying Behind, Stumbling Back, Sneaking Up, Soaring Ahead: Late Industrialization in Historical Perspective." In *Convergence of Productivity: Cross-National Studies and Historical Evidence*, ed. William Baumol, Richard R. Nelson, and Edward N. Wolff. New York: Oxford University Press, 1994.

Hill, M. Anne, and Elizabeth M. King. "Women's Education in Developing Countries: An Over-view." In *Women's Education in Developing Countries: Barriers, Benefits, and Policies*, ed. M. Anne Hill and Elizabeth M. King. Baltimore, MD: Johns Hopkins University Press, 1993.

Hill, Nicole. "Lives Recycled in Argentina." *Christian Science Monitor*, January 25, 2006.

Hinds, Manuel E. "Hearing on Official Dollarization in Latin America." Presented to the Senate Banking Committee, July 15, 1999.

Hirata, Helena, and John Humphrey. "Workers' Response to Job Loss: Female and Male Industrial Workers in Brazil." *World Development* 19(6) (1991): 671–682.

"HIV and AIDS in Latin America and the Caribbean." Avert, last updated April 21, 2017. www.avert.org.

Hnin Pyne, Hnin, Mariam Claeson, and Maria Correia. "Gender Dimensions of Alcohol Consumption and Alcohol-Related Problems in Latin America and the Caribbean." World Bank Publications, 2002.

Ho, Vanessa. "How Technology is Transforming and Empowering Latin America One Person and Organization at a Time." *Microsoft News*, October 7, 2015. www.news.microsoft.com.

Hoff, Karla. "Designing Land Policies: An Overview." In *The Economics of Rural Organization*, ed. Karla Hoff, Avishay Braverman, and Joseph Stiglitz. New York: Oxford University Press/World Bank, 1993.

Hoff, Karla, Avishay Braverman, and Joseph Stiglitz. "Introduction." In *The Economics of Rural Organization*, ed. Karla Hoff, Avishay Braverman, and Joseph Stiglitz. New York: Oxford University Press/World Bank, 1993.

———, eds. *The Economics of Rural Organization.* New York: Oxford University Press/World Bank, 1993.

Holmes, Michael. "TDA Urges Mexico to Reconsider Beef Tariffs." *AM Cycle*, August 4, 1999.

Holmes, Rebecca, and Nicola Jones. "Rethinking Social Protection Using a Gender Lens." Overseas Development Institute Working Paper No. 320, October 2010.

Holm-Nielsen, Lauritz, Michael Crawford, and Alcyone Saliba. "Institutional and Entrepreneurial Leadership in the Brazilian Science and Technology Sector." World Bank Discussion Paper No. 325. Washington, D.C.: World Bank, 1996.

Holt-Gimenez, Eric. "Movimiento Campesino a Campesino: Linking Sustainable Agriculture and Social Change." *Food First Backgrounder*, Winter/Spring 2006.

Holt-Giménez, Eric, and Miguel A. Altieri. "Agroecology, Food Sovereignty, and the New Green Revolution." *Agroecology and Sustainable Food Systems* 37(1), 2013: 90–102.

"Hope for the No-Hopers." *The Economist*, December 23, 2000.

Hornbeck, J. F. "The U.S.-Chile Free Trade Agreement: Economic and Trade Policy Issues." Congressional Research Service Report RL31144, September 10, 2003. www.opencrs. cdt.org.

Hsiao, William C. "Marketization—The Illusory Magic Pill." *Health Economics* 3, 1994: 351–357.

Htun, Mala. *Life Liberty and Family Values in Religious Pluralism, Democracy, and the Catholic Church in Latin America*. Notre Dame, IN: University of Notre Dame Press, 2009. www.ebrary.com: 342.

Huber, Richard M., Jack Ruitenbeck, and Renaldo Serra De Motta. "Market-Based Instruments for Environmental Policy Making in Latin America and the Caribbean: Lessons Learned from Eleven Countries." World Bank Discussion Paper No. 381. Washington, D.C.: World Bank, 1998.

Hufbauer, Gary. *NAFTA in a Skeptical Age: The Way Forward*. Washington, D.C.: Institute for International Economics, 2000.

Hufbauer, Gary, and Diana Orejas. *NAFTA and the Environment: Lessons for Trade Policy*. Speech delivered at the International Policy Forum organized by the Bildner Center. Washington, D.C.: Institute for International Economics, February 28, 2001.

Hufbauer, Gary, and Jeffrey J. Schott. *NAFTA Revisited: Achievements and Challenges*. Washington, D.C.: Institute for International Economics, 2005.

Hufbauer, Gary Clyde, Cathleen Cimino, and Tyler Moran. "NAFTA at 20: Misleading Charges and Positive Achievements." Peterson Institute for International Economics, May 2014.

Hulme, David, and Andrew Shephard. "Conceptualizing Chronic Poverty." *World Development* 31(3) (March 2003): 403–423.

"Human Development Index." In *Human Development Report, 1997*, ed. United Nations Development Program. New York: Oxford University Press, 1997.

Human Development Sector Management Unit, Andean Country Management Unit, Latin America and the Caribbean Region. "Improving Health Outcomes by Strengthening Users' Entitlements and Reinforcing Public Sector Management." World Bank Report No. 59218-PE Peru Recurso Programmatic AAA–Phase IV, February 4, 2011. http:// siteresources.worldbank.org.

Hurtig, J., R. Montoya del Solar, and L. Frazier. "Gender's Place: Feminist Anthropologies of Latin America." New York: Palgrave Macmillan US, 2002.

ICT. "ICT Development Index 2016." ITU, 2016.

Idelovitch, Emanuel, and Klas Ringskog. *Private Sector Participation in Water Supply and Sanitation in Latin America*. Washington, D.C.: World Bank, 1995.

IFAD. "Addressing Climate Change in Latin America and the Caribbean." International Fund for Agricultural Development (November 2011).

———. "Born into Poverty—New Report Highlights the Harsh Inequalities Facing Latin America's Poor Rural People." IFAD, April 24, 2014. www.ifad.org.

———. "Rural Poverty Report Latin America." Rome, Italy, 2011.

"IFC: Making a Positive Difference for Sustainable Development." Washington, D.C.: The World Bank Group.

"If Not for NAFTA, When?" *The Economist*, October 28, 2000.

Iglesias, Enrique V. "The Search for a New Economic Consensus in Latin America." In *The Legacy of Raúl Prebisch*, ed. Enrique V. Iglesias. Washington, D.C.: IADB, 1994.

———, ed. *The Legacy of Raúl Prebisch*. Washington, D.C.: IADB, 1994.

Ignatius, David. "'Dollarization' in Latin America." *World News*, April 28, 1999, A26.

Illich, BriAnne. Anonymous Interview. Asuncion, January 14, 2014.

———. Interview with Diana Viveros. Personal Interview. Asuncion, January 22, 2014.

———. Interview with Hilaria Cruzabie. Personal Interview. Asuncion, January 14, 2014.

———. Interview with Lu Serrano. Buenos Aires, Argentina. April 30, 2013.

ILRF. "Codes of Conduct in the Cut-Flower Industry." Working Paper, September 2003. www.laborrights.org/projects/women.

"IMF Completes Brazil Fifth Review." IMF News Brief No. 00/33. Washington, D.C.: IMF, May 31, 2000.

"IMF Concludes Article IV Consultation with Argentina." Public Information Notice No. 00/84. Washington, D.C.: IMF, October 3, 2000.

"IMF Lending to Poor Countries—How Does the PRGF Differ from the ESAF?" Washington, D.C.: IMF, April 2001.

"IMF Managing Director Köhler Welcomes Argentine Senate Action." News Brief No. 01/67. Washington, D.C.: IMF, July 30, 2001.

"IMF Press Conference on Exchange Rate Regimes in an Increasingly Integrated World Economy." Washington, D.C.: IMF, April 14, 2000.

"The IMF's Poverty Reduction and Growth Facility (PRGF)—A Factsheet." *International Monetary Fund*, March 2001.

IMF Staff. "Financial Integration in Latin America." International Monetary Fund Staff Report, March 2016. www.imf.org.

"Indigenous Peoples, Poverty and Human Development in Latin America: 1994–2004." www.worldbank.org.

"Industry At a Glance," *World Oil Production*. www.worldoil.com.

Inter-American Development Bank. *Annual Report 2001*. www.iadb.org.

———. "Argentina—Country Paper."

———. "The Argentine Saga." *Latin American Economic Policies* 16 (4th Quarter 2001).

———. "Completion Point under the Heavily Indebted Poor Countries Initiative." www.iadb.org, March 8, 2004.

———. *Disaster Prevention Sector Facility*. Document GN-2085-5, March 2001.

———. *Economic and Social Progress in Latin America 1995 Report: Overcoming Volatility*. Washington, D.C.: IADB, 1995.

———. *Economic and Social Progress in Latin America 1996 Report: Making Social Services Work*. Washington, D.C.: IADB, 1996.

———. *Facing Up to Inequality in Latin America: Economic and Social Progress in Latin America, 1998–1999 Report*. Washington, D.C.: Johns Hopkins University Press/IADB, 1998.

———. *Group Support to the Microenterprise Sector (1990–2000)*. IADB, February 2001.

———. "The IDB and Micro, Small and Medium-Sized Enterprises." Small and Medium-Sized Enterprises Unit, IDB News. www.iadb.org.

———. *Intra-Hemispheric Exports by Integration Group*. July 12, 1997. Available at www.iadb.org.statistics/notaest.htm.

———. "Invisible Farmers." In *IDB Extra: Investing in Women*. Washington, D.C.: IADB, 1994.

———. "Is Growth Enough?" *Latin American Economic Policies* 14 (2nd Quarter 2001).

———. "Latin American and Caribbean Macroeconomic Report: Routes to Growth in a New Trade World." IADB, 51–52.

————. *Latin America after a Decade of Reforms: Economic and Social Progress, 1997 Report*. Washington, D.C.: Johns Hopkins University Press/IADB, 1997.

————. "The Millennium Development Goals in Latin America and the Caribbean: Progress, Priorities and IDB Support for Their Implementation." www.iadb.org, August 2005.

————. "Natural Disasters." Background papers, March 13, 2006. www.iadb.org.

————. "Reform Fatigue." IDEAS 3 (January–April 2004). www.iadb.org.

————. "Remittance Flows to Latin America and the Caribbean." www.iadb.org, 2004.

————. "Room for Development: Housing Markets in Latin America and the Caribbean." IBD Flagship Publication, April 2012.

————. "Reproductive Rights." Technical Notes No. 8, Ana Langer. *Sexual and Preproductive Health and Health Sector Report In Latin America and the Caribbean: Challenges and Opportunities*, November 2001. www.iadb.org.

————. "Saving for Development: How Latin America and the Caribbean Can Save More and Better." IADB report, 2016. www.iadb.org.

————. "Why Geography Matters." *Economic and Social Progress in Latin America* (2000): 21.

————. *Women in the Americas: Bridging the Gap*. Baltimore, MD: Johns Hopkins University Press, 1995.

International Assessment of Agricultural Knowledge Science and Technology for Development. "Agriculture at a Crossroads." IAASTD, 2009.

International Coffee Council. "Impact of the Coffee Crisis on Poverty in Producing Countries." ICC 89-5, Rev. September 1, 2003.

"International Cooperation At a Crossroads: Aid, Trade and Security in an Unequal World United Nations." United Nations Human Development Report 2005. www.undp.ord.

International Labor Organization. *World Employment Report 2001: The World Employment Report 2001; Life at Work in the Information Economy*. Geneva, Switzerland.

International Monetary Fund. *Bolivia—Interim Poverty Reduction Strategy Paper*. Prepared by the Bolivian Authorities.

————. "Cluster Report-Trade Integration in Latin America and the Caribbean." IMF Country Report No 17/66, March 2017.

————. *IMF Survey, 2005*. Available at www.imf.org.

————. "IMF Survey." *IMF* 34(2), July 18, 2005: 212. www.imf.org.

————. "International Financial Statistics, 1997." Washington, D.C.: IMF, 1997.

————. "Key Features of IMF Poverty Reduction and Growth Facility (PRGF) Supported Programs." Prepared by the Policy Development and Review Department, August 16, 2000.

————. "Trade Integration In Latin America and the Caribbean." IMF Country Report No. 17/66, March 2017.

————. "World Economic Outlook 2002." www.imf.org.

International Trade Administration, U.S. Department of Commerce. *U.S. Foreign Trade Highlights, 1995*. Washington, D.C.: U.S. Department of Commerce, 1995.

"Interview with Denise Cantarelli." *Cargill do Brasil*, 1 February 2007.

"Interview with Maria Christina Bao Nova." *Telefonica*, 1 February 2007.

"Interview with Silvia Morais." *Hedging Grifo*, 31 January 2007.

"In the Gap and Sweatshop Labor in El Salvador." NACLA Report on the Americas 29(4) (January–February 1996): 37.

"Involving the Private Sector and Preventing Financial Crises." *IMF Survey* 28(12) (June 21, 1999).

IPCC. "Climate Change 2007." The 4th Assessment Report, 2007. www.ipcc.ch.

————. "Fourth Assessment Report." 2007.

ISAAA. "Distribution of Biotech Crops by Country." International Service for the Acquisition of Agri-Biotech Applications, 2016. www.isaaa.org.

Isacson, Adam, and John Myers. "Plan Colombia's Drug Eradication Program Misses the Market." International Relations Center. www.americas.irc-online.org, July 18, 2005.

"It's Time to Bite the Bullet." *Euromoney*, September 1996.

Jaitman, Laura, et. al. "The Costs of Crime and Violence: New Evidence and Insights in Latin America and the Caribbean." IADB, February 2017. www.publications.iadb.org.

Jallade, Lucila, Eddy Lee, and Joel Samoff. "International Cooperation." In *Coping with Crisis: Austerity, Adjustment, and Human Resources*, ed. Joel Samoff. New York: UNESCO/ILO, 1994.

James, Canute. "Caribbean Banana Producers See Future in Organic Farming." *Financial Times*, November 13, 2001.

Jameson, Kenneth P. "Dollarization in Ecuador: A Post Keynesian Institutionalist Analysis." University of Utah Department of Economics Working Paper 2004–5.

————. "The Financial Sector in Latin American Restructuring." In *Privatization in Latin America*, ed. Werner Baer and Melissa Birch. Westport, CT: Praeger, 1994.

Jarque, Carlos. "Foreward." In *Escaping the Poverty Trap: Investing in Children in Latin America*, ed. Ricardo Morán. Washington, D.C.: Inter-American Development Bank, 2003.

Jenkins, Rhys. "Car Manufacture in East Asia and Latin America." *Cambridge Journal of Economics* (October 1995): 625–646.

————. "Globalization, Corporate Social Responsibility and Poverty." *International Affairs* 81(3), 2005: 525–540.

————. *Transnational Corporations and Industrial Transformation in Latin America*. New York: St. Martin's, 1984.

————. *Transnational Corporations and the Latin American Automobile Industry*. Pittsburgh: University of Pittsburgh Press, 1987.

Jessen, Anneke, et al. *Integration and Trade in the Americas*. Washington, D.C.: IADB, 1999.

Jewett, Dale. "Magna Touts Lower-Cost Navigational System." *Automotive News*, October 23, 2000.

Jimenez de la Jara, Jorge, and Thomas J. Bossert. "Chile's Health Sector Reform: Lessons from Four Reform Periods." In *Health Sector Reform in Developing Countries: Making Health Development Sustainable*, ed. Peter Berman. Cambridge, MA: Harvard University Press, 1995.

Johnson, Brian. *The Great Fire of Borneo: Report of a Visit to Kalimantan-Timur a Year Later, May 1994*. London: World Wildlife Fund, 1991.

Johnson, Ken. "Brazil and the Politics of Climate Change Negotiations." *Journal of Environment & Development* 10(2) (June 2001): 185.

Johnston, Jason Scott. "Corporate Social Responsibility Initiative Working Paper." Harvard University: John F. Kennedy School of Government, November 2005.

Jonakin, Jon. "The Interaction of Market Failure and Structural Adjustment in Producer Credit and Land Markets: The Case of Nicaragua." *Journal of Economic Issues* 31(2) (June 1997).

Jones, Geoffrey, and Ricardo Reisen de Pinho. "Natura: Global Beauty Made in Brazil." HBS Case, December 12, 2006.

Jordan, Miriam. "Remittances to Latin America Rose in 2014." *The Wall Street Journal*, February 25, 2015. www.wsj.com.

Juma, Calestous, and Lee Yee Cheon. "Innovation: Applying Knowledge in Development." UN Millennium Task Force on Science, Technology and Innovation, Belfer Center for Science and International Affairs, John F. Kennedy School of Government, 2005.

"Just Don't Call It Downsizing." *IADB América* (September–October 2000): 10–11.

Kadt, Emanuel de. "Thematic Lessons from the Case Studies." In *The Public-Private Mix in Social Services*, ed. Elaine Zuckerman and Emanuel de Kadt. Washington, D.C.: IADB, 1997.

Kahn, Joseph. "Congressional Leadership Agrees to Debt Relief for Poor Nations." *New York Times*, October 18, 2000.

Kaltenheuser, Skip. "Fitting Microcredit into a Macro Picture." *Christian Science Monitor*, February 5, 1997.

Kamil, Herman, and Jeremy Zook. "IMF's Western Hemisphere Department." Chapter 2 of the IMF's *2012 Selected Issues Paper for Mexico*, 2012. www.imf.org.

Kapstein, Ethan. "Global Rules for Global Finance." *Current History*, November 1998.

Karlan, Dean. "Interest Rate Elasticity and on the Impact of Microcredit." Presentation at Evidence on Innovations in Financial Capability Conference, Lima Peru, June 1, 2013.

Karp, Jonathan. "Brazilian Central Banker Plays It Cool." *Wall Street Journal*, July 18, 2001, A12.

Kate, Adriaan ten, and Robert Bruce Wallace. "Nominal and Effective Protection by Sector." In *Protection and Economic Development in Mexico*, ed. Adriaan ten Kate and Robert Bruce Wallace. Hampshire, UK: Gower, 1980.

Katz, Elizabeth G. "Gender and Trade within the Household: Observations from Rural Guatemala." *World Development* 23(2) (1995): 327–342.

Katz, Ian. "Snapping up South America." *BusinessWeek*, January 18, 1999.

Kaufmann, Daniel. "Corruption: The Facts." *Foreign Policy*, Summer 1997.

Kaufmann, Daniel and Aart Kraay. "Worldwide Governance Indicators (WGI)." World Bank Group (2010). www.info.worldbank.org.

Kaufman, Robert, and Joan Nelson. "The Political Challenges of Social Sector Reform." In *Crucial Needs, Weak Incentives: Social Sector Reform, Democratization, and Globalization in Latin America*, ed. Robert R. Kaufman and Joan M. Nelson. Washington, D.C.: Woodrow Wilson Center Press and Johns Hopkins University Press, 2004.

———. "The Political Economy of Health Sector Reforms: Cross National Comparisons." Wilson Center update on the *Americas Creating Community* series, May 2003.

Kay, Cristobal. "Rural Poverty Reduction Policies in Honduras, Nicaragua and Bolivia: Lessons from a Comparative Analysis." *European Journal of Development* 23(3), April 2011: 249–265.

Kay, Stephen J. "Privatizing Pensions: Prospects for the Latin American Reforms." *Journal of Interamerican Studies and World Affairs* 42(1) (Spring 2000).

Keen, Benjamin. *Latin American Civilization*, 3rd ed. Boston: Houghton Mifflin, 1974.

Kennedy, Steven. "A Global Partner For a Region on the Rise: The World Bank in Latin America and the Caribbean." The World Bank, 2010.

Kepp, Michael. "Refining Mining." *Latin Trade* (April 2002): 30.

Key, Cristóbal. "Rural Development and Agrarian Issues in Contemporary Latin America." In *Structural Adjustment and the Agricultural Sector in Latin America and the Caribbean*, ed. John Weeks. New York: St. Martin's, 1995.

"Key Indicators of the Labour Market (KILM)." International Labor Organization, 2005. www.ilo.org.

Keynan, Gabriel, Manuel Olin, and Ariel Dinar. "Cofinanced Public Extension in Nicaragua." *World Bank Research Observer* 12(2), August 1997.

"The Key Points of the FTAA Agenda." *Latin American Weekly Report*, WR-97-20, 1997.

"Kirchner Gets What He Came for in Brazil." *LatinNews Daily*, January 19, 2006.

Klare, Michael. *Blood and Oil*. New York: Henry Holt and Company, 2004.

———. *The Race for What's Let: The Global Scramble for The World's Last Resources*. Metropolitan, 2012.

———. *Resource Wars: The New Landscape of Global Conflict*. New York: Henry Holt, 2002

———. *Rising Powers, Shrinking Planet: The New Geopolitics of Energy*. New York: Henry Holt, 2009.

Kliksberg, Bernardo. "Public Administration in Latin America." *International Review of Administrative Sciences* 71(2) (2005): 325.

Klitgaard, Robert. "Subverting Corruption." *Finance & Development* (June 2000).

Knight, Alan. "Populism and Neo-Populism in Latin America, Especially Mexico." *Journal of Latin American Studies* 30 (1998): 223–248.

Koehler-Geib, Friederike, and Susana M Sanchez. "Costa Rica Five Years after CAFTA-DR: Assessing Early Results. Directions in Development—Trade." World Bank, 2015. openknowledge.worldbank.org.

"Köhler Says IMF Management to Recommend Accelerated Disbursement of US $1.2 Billion for Argentina." News Brief No. 01/17. Washington, D.C.: IMF, August 3, 2001.

"Köhler Says IMF Management to Recommend US $15 Billion Stand-By for Brazil." News Brief No. 01/72. Washington, D.C.: IMF, August 3, 2001.

Kohn, Robert, Itzhak Levav, José Miguel Caldas de Almeida, Vincente Benjamín, Laura Andrade, Jorge J. Caraveo-Anduaga, Shekhar Saxena, and Benedetto Saraceno. "Special issue of *On Mental Health*."*pyne Revista Panamericana de Salud Pública* 18(4–5) (October/November 2005): 229–240.

Kolb, Melina. "A Guide to Renegotiating NAFTA." Peterson Institute for International Economics, June 19, 2017. www.piie.com.

Koopman, Robert, William Powers, and Zhi Wang, et al. "Give Credit Where Credit is Due: Tracing Value Added in Global Production Chains." National Bureau of Economic Research, Working Paper 16426, September 2010.

Korczowski, Fernando, Thomas Pichon, Francisco Reyes, and Hiska Galeana. "PACTA: Rural Development in Honduras through Access to Land and the Development of Productive Enterprises." World Bank Brief No. 75, July 2005.

Krauss, Clifford. "Argentina's Austerity Plan Provokes Nationwide Strike." *New York Times*, July 20, 2001.

———. "Argentina to Hasten End of a Phone Monopoly." *New York Times*, March 11, 1998.

———. "Argentine with a Headache: The Economy." *New York Times*, July 18, 2001.

———. "Bolivia Wiping Out Coca, At a Price." *New York Times*, October 23, 2000.

———. "Economy Aide to the Rescue, As Argentina Fights Default." *New York Times*, March 30, 2001.

———. "Poll-Whipped and Pilloried, Chief Endures in Argentina." *New York Times*, July 8, 2001.

———. "When Even an Economic Miracle Isn't Enough." *New York Times*, July 12, 1998.

———. "Where the Coca Trade Withers, Tourism Sprouts." *New York Times*, November 2, 2000.

Krawczyk, Miriam. "Women in the Region: Major Changes." *CEPAL Review* 49 (April 1993).

Kroll, Luisa, and Allison Fass, eds. "Billionaires by Rank." Special Report. *Forbes* (2006). www.forbes.com.

Kronish, Rich, and Kenneth S. Mericle. "The Development of the Latin American Motor Vehicle Industry, 1900–1980: A Class Analysis." In *The Political Economy of the Latin*

American Motor Vehicle Industry, ed. Rich Kronish and Kenneth S. Mericle. Cambridge, MA: MIT Press, 1984.

Krueger, Anne O. *NAFTA's Effects: A Preliminary Assessment.* Oxford: Blackwell, 2000.

Krueger, Anne, Maurice Schiff, and Alberto Valdes. *Political Economy of Agricultural Pricing Policy.* Baltimore, MD: Johns Hopkins University Press, 1991.

Krugman, Paul. "A Latin Tragedy." *New York Times*, July 15, 2001.

———. "Other People's Money." *New York Times*, July 18, 2001.

Krugman, Paul R., and Maurice Obstfeld. *International Economics: Theory and Policy*, 3rd ed. New York: HarperCollins, 1994.

Kurlander, Lawrence T. "Newmont Mining: The Social License to Operate." University of Denver Colorado, October 2001. www.cudenver.edu.

Kuttner, Robert. "What Sank Asia? Money Sloshing around the World." *BusinessWeek*, July 27, 1998.

Kuznets, Simon. "Modern Economic Growth: Findings and Reflections." *American Economic Review* 63(3) (June 1973).

Kwast, Barbara. "Reeducation of Material and Peri-natal Mortality in Rural and Peri-urban Settings: What Works?" *European Journal of Obstetrics and Gynecology and Reproductive Biology* 609, 1996.

LaFraniere, Sharon. "Lead Poisoning in China: The Hidden Scourge," *The New York Times*, June 15, 2011.

Lains, Petro. "Before the Golden Age: Economic Growth in Mexico and Portugal, 1910–1950." In *Growth Institutions and Crises: Latin America from a Historical Perspective*, ed. Sebastian Edwards. Washington, D.C.: National Bureau of Economic Research, 2005.

Lakshmanan, Indira A.R. "Amazon Highway is Route to Strife in Brazil." *Boston Globe*, December 27, 2005.

Lall, Sanjaya. "Competitiveness Indices and Developing Countries: An Economic Evaluation of the Global Competitiveness Report." *World Development* 29(9) (September 2001): 1501–1525.

Lamb, James J. "The Third World and the Development Debate." *IDOC-North America*, January–February 1973.

"Land for the Landless." *The Economist*, April 13, 1996.

Lanjouw, Peter. "Nonfarm Employment and Poverty in Rural El Salvador." *World Development* 29 (3) (2001).

Lankao, Patricia Romero. "Are We Missing the Point?: Particularities of Urbanization, Sustainability and Carbon Emissions in Latin American Cities." *Environment and Urbanization* 19, po(2007): 159–175.

La Porta, Rafael, Florencio Lopez-de-Silanes, and Andrei Shleifer, 1999, as summarized in William Megginson and Jeffry M. Netter, "From State to Market: A Survey of Empirical Studies of Privatization," *Journal of Economic Literature* 39 (June 2001).

Lapper, Richard. "Policy under Pressure," *Financial Times*, October 6, 2002, weekend I.

———. "Workers Throw a Lifeline Home." *Financial Times*, March 29, 2004, 1.

Larner, Monica, and Ian Katz. "It's Ronaldo's World." *BusinessWeek*, June 22, 1998, 204.

Larraín, Felipe B., ed. *Capital Flows, Capital Controls and Currency.* Ann Arbor: University of Michigan Press, 2000.

Larraín, Felipe B., and Luis F. López-Calva, "Privatization: Fostering Economic Growth through Private Sector Development." Chapter 13 in *Economic Development in Central America, Vol. 2, Structural Reform.* Cambridge, MA: Harvard University Press, 2001, 68.

Larraín, Felipe B., Luis F. López-Calva, and Andrés Rodriguez-Clare. *Intel: A Case Study of Foreign Direct Investment in Central America*. CID Working Paper No. 58. Center for International Development at Harvard University. December 2000.

Larrea, Carlos, Pedro Montalvo, and Ana Ricaurte. "Child Malnutrition, Social Development and Health Services in the Andean Region." HEW 0509011, Economics Working Paper Archive, March 2004.

Larry Sawers, Income Distribution and Environmental Degradation in the Argentine Interior (pp. 3-33), *Latin America Research Review* 35(3) (2000).

Latham, Johnathan. "Way Beyond Greenwashing: Have Corporations Captured 'Big Conservation'?" *Independent Science News* (2012).

"Latin American Indigenous People More Likely to Die from Malaria, Diarrhea and TB than Their Counterparts." November 29, 2005. www.medicalnewstoday.com.

"Latin American Internet Users and Population Statistics 2016." Internet World Stats, December 2016.

"Latin America's Car Industry Revving Up." *The Economist*, April 27, 1996.

"Latin America Sees Progress." *Washington Times*, August 9, 2005. www.washingtontimes.com.

"Latin America's Export of Manufactured Goods." Special section of *Economic and Social Progress in Latin America 1992 Report*. Washington, D.C.: IADB, 1992.

Latin America Special Report. "Mercosur's Move towards Flexibility." https://www.latinnews.com/latin-american-monitoring-centre-country.html? November 2016.

"Latin America Struggles to Find Solutions to Megacity Woes." *Agence France Press*, June 2, 1992. Available on the LEXIS-NEXIS database.

Latin America Weekly Report. May 26, 1998.

Latin Watch. Banco Bilbao Vizcaya Agentaria, December 2000.

Lau, Lawrence J., Dean T. Jamison, Shucheng Liu, and Steven Rivkin. "Education and Economic Growth: Some Cross-Sectional Evidence." In *Education in Brazil*, ed. Nancy Birdsall and Richard H. Sabot. Washington, D.C.: IADB, 1996.

La Via Campesina. "Our Members." http://viacampesina.org/en/index.php.

———. "The Right to Produce and Access." viacampesina.org

Leahy, Joe. "Brazil Pensions Blamed for Curbing GDP." *The Financial Times*, March 6, 2012.

Lederman Daniel, William F. Maloney, and Luis Servén. "Lessons from NAFTA for Latin America and the Caribbean." Palo Alto, CA: Stanford University Press, 2004.

Leff, Nathaniel H. "Economic Development in Brazil." In *How Latin America Fell Behind*, ed. Stephen Haber, 1822–1913. Palo Alto, CA: Stanford University Press, 1997.

Lehmann, David, ed. *Agrarian Reform and Agrarian Reformism: Studies of Peru, Chile, China, and India*. London: Faber & Faber, 1974.

Lemoine, Maurice. "El Reino del Latifundio." *E'a*, January 21,2014. www.ea.com.py.

Lepziger, Danny, Claudio Frischtak, Homi J. Kharas, and John F. Normand. "Mercosur: Integration and Industrial Policy." *World Economy* 20(5) (1997).

Lewin, Bryan, Daniele Giovannucci, and Panayotis Varangis. "Coffee Markets: New Paradigms in Global Supply and Demand." World Bank, 2004.

Lewis, Colin M. "Industry in Latin America." In *Dependency and Development*, ed. Fernando Henrique Cardoso and Enzo Faletto, translated by Marjory Mattinglly Urguidi. Berkeley, CA: University of California Press, 1979.

Lewis, Paul. "Latin Americans Say Russian Default Is Hurting Their Economies." *New York Times*, October 6, 1998, A13. Online edition.

Lindsey, Brink. *Grounds for Complaint? Understanding the Coffee Crisis*. London: Adam Smith Institute, 2004. Available at www.adamsmith.org.

Lippert, John. "'Going Zunion' Is the Buzz at Magna Auto Parts Giant Pays Wages Half the Big Three's." *Toronto Star*, August 15, 1998.

Lizano, Eduardo, and José M. Salazar-Xirinach. "Central American Common Market and Hemispheric Free Trade." In *Integrating the Hemisphere, 1997: The Inter-American Dialogue*, ed. Ana Julia Jatar and Sidney Weintraub. Santa Fé de Bogotá, Colombia: Tercer Mundo, 1997.

Lizondo, S., et al. Chile: Selected Issues. IMF Country Report No. 01/120. Washington, D.C.: IMF, July 2001.

"Loan 'Club' Is a Useful Model." *Financial Times*, December 14, 2000.

Lomborg, Bjorn. "Smart Solutions to Climate Change: Comparing Costs and Benefits." Cambridge: Cambridge University Press, 2011.

Londoño, Juan Luis, and Miguel Székely. "Distributional Surprises after a Decade of Reforms: Latin America in the Nineties." Paper prepared for the annual meetings of the IADB. Barcelona, March 1997.

———. *Persistent Poverty and Excess Inequality: Latin America, 1970–1995*. Office of the Chief Economist. IADB Working Paper No. 357. Washington, D.C.: IADB, 1997.

López, Ramón. *Policy Instruments and Financing Mechanisms for the Sustainable Use of Forests in Latin America*. No. ENV-16. Washington, D.C.: IADB, 1996.

Lopez-Claros, Augusto. "Latin American Competitiveness Review 2006." World Economic Forum on Latin America, 2006.

Lora, Eduardo. "Should Latin America Fear China?" Inter-American Development Research Department Working Paper No. 531, May 2005. www.iadb.org.

Lora, Eduardo, and Felipe Barrera. "A Decade of Structural Reform in Latin America: Growth, Productivity, and Investment Are Not What They Used to Be." Document for discussion at the IADB Barcelona seminar, "Latin America after a Decade of Reform: What Next?" March 16, 1997.

Lora, Eduardo, Carmen Pagés, Ugo Panizza, and Ernesto Stein. *A Decade of Development Thinking*. Washington D.C.: Inter-American Development Bank Research Department, 2004, 26.

Lora, Eduardo, Ugo Panizza, and Myriam Quispe-Agnoli. "Reform Fatigue: Symptoms, Reasons, Implications." Paper presented at Rethinking Structural Reform in Latin America, Federal Reserve Bank of Atlanta, October 23, 2003.

Lorey, David E. "Education and the Challenges of Mexican Development." *Challenge* 38(2) (March–April 1995): 51–55.

Loser, Claudio M. "The Long Road to Financial Stability." *Finance and Development*, March 2000.

Loser, Claudio M., and Jesús Seade. *Second Review under the Stand-by Arrangement and Request for Augmentation*. Report No. 01/26. Washington, D.C.: IMF, January 2001.

———. *Staff Report for the 2000 Article IV Consultation, First Review under the Stand-By Arrangement, and Request for Modification of Performance Criteria*. Report No. 00/164. Washington, D.C.: IMF, December 2000.

Loungani, Prakash, and Philip Swagel. "Source of Inflation in Developing Countries." IMF Working Paper 01/198, Washington, D.C., International Monetary Fund, December 2001.

"Lousy Deal." *IDB América* (May–June 2000): 2.

Lovins, Amory. "Learning from Japan's Nuclear Disaster." *RMI Outlet*, March 19, 2011. www.commondreams.org.

Loyola, Gustavo. "Elusive Tax Reform: 'President Must Lead the Way.'" *UNICEF—InfoBrazil*, September 2001.

Luhnow, David, and John Lyons. "In Latin America, Rich-Poor Chasm Stifles Growth." *Wall Street Journal*, July 18, 2005, A1.

Lustig, Nora. *Coping with Austerity*. Washington, D.C.: Brookings Institution, 1995.

———. *NAFTA: Setting the Record Straight*. Brookings Policy Brief No. 20.

Lustig, Nora, and Ruthanne Deutsch. *The Inter-American Development Bank and Poverty Reduction: An Overview*. Washington, D.C.: IADB, 1998. Available at www.iadb.org.

MacCulloch, Christina. "Will She Make It? Guatemala Finds New Ways to Keep Girls in School." *IDB América* (April 1998): 4–7.

Macisaac, Donna. "Peru." In *Indigenous People and Poverty in Latin America*, ed. George Psacharopoulos and Harry Anthony Patrinos. Washington, D.C.: World Bank, 1994.

Maddison, Angus. "Economic and Social Conditions in Latin America, 1913–1950." In *Long-Term Trends in Latin American Economic Development*, ed. Miguel Urrutia. Washington, D.C.: IADB/Johns Hopkins University Press, 1991.

———. *Monitoring the World Economy, 1820–1992*. Washington, D.C.: OECD Publications and Information Center, 1995.

"Magna Auto Parts Boss on $33m a Year Roll." *Canadian Press Newswire*, April 10, 2000.

"Magna Forms Mexican Joint Venture." *Canada Newswire*, August 20, 1997.

"Magna International Inc.—Online Earnings Conference Call Notification." *Canada Newswire*, August 17, 2000.

Mahon, James E., Jr. "Was Latin America Too Rich to Prosper? Structural and Political Obstacles to Export-Led Industrial Growth." *Journal of Development Studies* 28(2) (1992).

"Making Money from Microcredit." *IDB América*, June 1998.

Malkin, Elisabeth. "Bottled-Water Habit Keeps Tight Grip on Mexicans." *The New York Times*. 2012.

Malpass, David. "Hearing on Official Dollarization in Emerging-Market Countries." Presented to the Senate Banking, Housing and Urban Affairs Committee, July 15, 1999.

Maltsoglou, Irini, and Aysen Tanyeri-Abur. "Transaction Costs, Institutions and Small-holder Market Integration: Potato Producers in Peru." ESA Working Paper No. 05-04, Agricultural and Development Economics Division, June 2005. www.fao.org.

Mandel-Campbell, Andrea. "I Bet the Ranch, and I Won—Absolutely." *BusinessWeek*, June 22, 1998, 64–65.

Mander, Benedict. "Darker Side to Argentina's Soya Success." *Financial Times*, June 7, 2006.

"The Man from Whom Miracles Hang." *The Economist*, October 28, 2000.

Mangurian, David. "Against the Odds: How a Seemingly Hopeless Energy Project Became a Model for Investors." *IDB América*, March 1998. Available at www.iadb.org.

Margolis, Mac. "Hat in Hand." *Newsweek*, October 12, 1998.

Márquez, Humberto. "Chávez to Further Strengthen Social Reform." *Inter Press Service*, August 31, 2002. www.americas.org.

Martinussen, John. *Society, State, and Market: A Guide to Competing Theories of Development*. London: Zed, 1997.

Masioli, Itelvina, and Paul Nicholson. "Seeing Like a Peasant: Voices from La Via Campesina." In *Food Sovereignty: Reconnecting Food, Nature and Community*. Oakland, CA: Food First, 2010: 35–37.

Mauro, Paulo. "The Persistence of Corruption and Slower Economic Growth." IMF Working Paper, 2002.

Maxwell, Amanda. "Air Quality in Latin America: High Levels of Pollution Require Strong Government Action." April 29, 2013.

Maxwell, Kenneth. "Latin America: Sustaining Economic & Political Reform—A Working Conference on the Underlying Realities." Conference Overview. New York: The Council on Foreign Relations, May 18, 2000.

Mayer-Serra, Carlos Elizondo. "Tax Reform under the Salinas Administration." In *The Changing Structure of Mexico*, ed. Laura Randall, Armonk, NY: Sharpe, 1996.

Mayorga, Román. *Closing the Gap*. IADB Working Paper SOC97-101. Washington, D.C.: IADB, 1997.

Mazza, Jacqueline. "Social Inclusion, Labor Markets and Human Capital." In *Social Inclusion and Economic Development in Latin America*, ed. Mayra Buvinic and Jacqueline Mazza, 188, table 10.3. Washington, D.C.: Inter-American Development Bank, 2004.

McCabe, Coco. "Turning on the Tap of 'People Power' in Guatemala." *Oxfam*, March 23, 2015.

McDonnell, Patrick, and Edwin Che. "Bush Exits Summit As Trade Talks End in Disagreement." *Los Angeles Times*, November 6, 2005.

McKee, Colin. "Realizing the Potential of the Internet in Latin America." Unpublished paper, Colby College, Waterville, Maine, 2001.

McKibben, Bill. "Crossing the Red Line." *The New York Review of Books*, 51(10) (2004).

McKinsey Global Institute. *Productivity: The Key to an Accelerated Development Path for Brazil 1998*. São Paulo: McKinsey, 1998.

McLarty, Thomas F. "Hemispheric Free Trade Is Still a National Priority." *Wall Street Journal*, May 26, 1995.

McQuerry, Elizabeth, Michael Chriszt, and Stephen Kay. "Patterns in Latin American Public Sector Accounts." Federal Reserve Bank of Atlanta, 2001. Available at www.frbatlanta.org.

Meadows, Donella H., Dennis Meadows, and Jorgen Randers. *The Limits to Growth*. New York: Signet Classics. 1972.

———. *Beyond the Limits*, London: Earthscan, 1992.

———. *Limits to Growth: The Thirty-Year*. White River Junction, Vt: Chelsea Green Publishing Company, 2004.

Meerman, Jacob. *Reforming Agriculture: The World Bank Goes to Market*. Washington, D.C.: World Bank, 1997.

Meier, Gerald M. *Leading Issues in Economic Development*, 6th ed. Oxford: Oxford University Press, 1995.

Meier, Gerald M., and Dudley Seers. *Pioneers in Development*. Oxford: Oxford University Press, 1984.

Mejido Costoya, Manuel. "Politics of Trade in Post-neoliberal Latin America: The Case of Bolivia." *Bulletin of Latin American Research* 30(1), 2011: 80–95.

Meller, Patricio. "IMF and World Bank Roles in the Latin America Foreign Debt Problem." In *The Latin American Development Debate: Neostructuralism, Neomonetarism, and Adjustment Processes*, ed. Patricio Meller. Boulder, CO: Westview, 1991.

"Memorandum of Economic Policies." International Monetary Fund. Public Information Notice No. 00/84. Washington, D.C.: IMF, 1999.

Mendez, Chico. *Fight for the Forest*. London: Latin American Bureau, 1990.

"Mental Disorders in Latin America and the Caribbean Forecast to Increase." December 12, 2005. www.medicalnewstoday.com.

Mercosur Consulting Group Limited. "Recent Developments Affecting the Mercosur Economic Integration Project." *Thunderbird International Business Review* 42(1) (January–February 2002): 1–7; www.mercosurconsulting.net.

"Mercosur Survey." *The Economist*, October 12, 1996.

"Mercusor Tribunal Rules on Paper Mills." *LatinNews Daily*, September 7, 2006.

Messina, Julian. "Presentation on the Rising Middle Class." Office of the Chief Economist. Latin America and the Caribbean Region, The World Bank, May 2013.

"Mexico City: A Topographical Error." *Environment* 36(2) (1994): 25–26.

"Mexico Domestic Sales Rise Sharply." *Reuters Financial Service*, June 4, 1997. U.S. Department of State, "Mexico FY 2000 Country Commercial Guide," July 1999.

"Mexico FY 2000 Country Commercial Guide." Washington, D.C.: U.S. Department of State.

Meyer, Greg. "Ethanol: Logic of Circular Biofuel Trade Comes into Question." *The Financial Times*, 2013.

Mezzera, Jaime. "Abundancia como efecto de la escasez. Oferta y demanda en el Mercado laboral urbano." *Nueva Sociedad* 90 (1997): 106–117.

Milesi, Orlando, and Marianela Jarroud. "Soil Degradation Threatens Nutrition in Latin America." *Inter-Press Service*, June 2016 www.ipsnews.net.

Mills, Frederick B., and William Camacaro. "Venezuela and the Battle against Transgenic Seeds." Council on Hemispheric Affairs, December 11, 2013. www.venezuelanalysis.com.

Miller, Eric. *Financial Services in the Trading System: Progress and Prospects*. Washington D.C.: IADB, 1999.

Miller, Sebastian, and John D. Smith. "A Big Job for Small Countries." IADB, January 9, 2013.

Miller, T. Christian, and Davan Maharau. "Coffee's Bitter Harvest." *Los Angeles Times*, October 7, 2002.

Milstein, Mark, Stuart Hart, and Bruno Sadinha. "Jari Celulose SA." Oikos sustainability case writing competition, 2003. www.oikos foundation.unisg.ch.

Mishkin, Frederick. "Understanding Financial Crises: A Developing Country Perspective." In *The Annual World Bank Conference Report on Development Economics, 1996*. Washington, D.C.: World Bank, 1997.

Mizala, Alejandra, Pilar Romaguera, and Carolina Ostoic. "Equity and Achievement in the Chilean School Choice System." Center for Applied Economics, Universidad de Chile, April 2005.

Moffett, Matt. "Deep in the Amazon, an Industrial Enclave Fights for Its Survival." *Wall Street Journal*, July 9, 1998.

Mogren, Arne, and Jesse Fahnestock, *A One Ton Future: A Guide to The Low-Carbon Century*. Varnamo, Sweden: Falth & Hassler, 2009.

Mokhiber, Russell, and Robert Weissman. "The Ten Worst Corporations of 2004." *Multinational Monitor* 25(12), multinationalmonitor.org.

Mol, Arthur. *Globalization and Environmental Reform*. Cambridge: MIT Press, 2001: 2.

Molano, Walter. *Financial Reverberations: The Latin American Banking System during the mid-1990s*. Working paper, SBC Warburg. April 1997.

Molinas Vega, José R., Ricardo Paes de Barros, Jaime Saavedra Chanduvi, Marcelo Giugale, Louise J. Cord, Carola Pessino, and Amer Hasan. "Do Our Children Have a Chance? A Human Opportunity Report for Latin America and the Caribbean." World Bank, 2012. www.openknowledge.worldbank.org.

Molyneux, Maxine. "Twentieth-Century State Formations in Latin America." In *Hidden Histories of Gender and the State in Latin America*. Durham, NC: Duke University Press, 2000: 44.

Monteiro, Viviane. "Fiscal Resolve Is Crucial to the Economy Says Finance Minister Palocci." *Noticias Financieras/Group de Diarios America InvestNews*, Brazil, September 13, 2005.

Moody-Stuart, Mark. *Putting Principles into Practice: The Ethical Challenge to Global Business*. Presented at the World Congress of the International Society of Business, Economics and Ethics in São Paolo, Brazil, July 19, 2000.

Mooney, Elizabeth. "South American Economic Crisis Hits Telecom Operators." *RCR Wireless News*, April 2002, 25.

Moore, Mick. "Toward a Useful Consensus." In *The Bank, the State, and Development: Dissecting the World Development Report, 1997. IDS Bulletin* 29(2), special issue (1998).

Moore, Molly. "Mayan Girls Make Fifth Grade History." *Washington Post*, June 20, 1996.

Morales, Juan Antonio, and Jeffrey Sachs. "Bolivia's Economic Crisis." In *Developing Country Debt and the World Economy*, ed. Jeffrey Sachs. Chicago, IL: University of Chicago Press, 1989.

Morán, Ricardo, Tarsicio Castaneda, and Enrique Aldaz-Carroll. "Family Background and Intergenerational Poverty in Latin America." In *Escaping the Poverty Trap: Investing in Children in Latin America*, ed. Ricardo Morán. Washington, D.C.: Inter-American Development Bank, 2003.

Morandé, Felipe G. "Savings in Chile: What Went Right?" *Journal of Development Economics* 57(1) (1998).

Morgan, Daniela Estrella. "Trade Developments in Latin America and the Caribbean." IMF, 2017.

Morris, Valerie, and Donald Van De Mark. "Magna Auto Parts Ceo." *Cable News Network Financial*, March 11, 1998.

Mortimore, Michael, Álvaro Calderón, Pablo Carvallo, and Márcia Tavares. "Foreign Investment in Latin America and the Caribbean." ECLAC Unit on Investment and Corporate Strategies. www.ec.as.org, May 2006.

Mosbacher, Robert, Chairman, Council of the Americas. "Trade Expansion within the Americas: A U.S. Business Perspective." Remarks at the Chile-United States Issues Round Table, Crown Plaza Hotel, Santiago, Chile, April 17, 1998. Available at 207.87.5.23/sr.html; accessed July 12, 1999.

Moseley, Paul, and David Hulme. "Microenterprise Finance: Is There a Conflict between Growth and Poverty Alleviation?" *World Development* 26(5) (1988): 783–790.

Moser, Caroline. "Gender Planning in the Third World: Meeting Practical and Strategic Gender Needs." *World Development* 17(11) (1989): 1799–1825.

Moser, Caroline O. N., and Cathy McIlwaine. "Latin American Urban Violence as a Development Concern: Towards a Framework for Violence Reduction." *World Development* 34(1) (January 2006): 89–112.

Moser, Titus. "MNCs and Sustainable Business Practice: The Case of the Colombian and Peruvian Petroleum Industries." *World Development* 29(2) (2001).

Motto, Carlos. "Presentation on Banco Real." *Fiesp Mostra*, August 2007.

"Mugged: Poverty in Your Cup." *Oxfam International*, 2002. www.maketradefair.com.

Mulligan, Mark. "Argentine Opposition Backs Government Austerity Package." *Financial Times*, July 18, 2001.

———. "Honeymoon Over for Cavallo." *Financial Times*, July 19, 2001.

———. "Protests Flare over Argentina Austerity Plan." *Financial Times*, July 18, 2001.

Munainghe, Mohran, and Wilfrido Cruz. *Economy Wide Policies and the Environment: Lessons from Experience*. Washington, D.C.: World Bank, 1995.

Muñoz Piña, C., M Rivera, A. Cisneros, and H. García. "Retos de la focalización del Programa de Pago por los Servicios Ambientales en México." *Revista Espanola de Estdios Agrosociales y Pesquero*. 228(1), (2011): 87–113.

Myers, William, ed. *Protecting Working Children*. London: Zed, 1991.

"NAFTA: Where's That Giant Sucking Sound?" *BusinessWeek*, July 7, 1997: 45.

"NAFTA Key Provisions." NAFTA Facts Document #3001.

Naik, Gautam. "Studies of the Amazon Rainforest Intensify Climate Change Debate." *Wall Street Journal*, October 20, 2005.

Naim, Moises. "Fads and Fashion in Economic Reforms: Washington Consensus or Washington Confusion?" *Foreign Policy Magazine*, October 26, 1999.

Nasar, Sylvia. "The Cure that Can Sometimes Kill the Patient." *New York Times*, July 19, 1998.

London: Nash, June. "Gender in Place and Culture." In *Gender's Place: Feminist Anthropologies of Latin America*, ed. Lessie Jo Frazier Rosario Montoya and Janise Hurtig. London: Palgrave Macmillan, 2002.

Näslund-Hadley, Emma, Juan Manuel Hernández Agramonte, Ernesto Martínez, and Caitlin Ludlow. "The Making of Little Mathematicians." IDB Briefly Noted: No. 20, September, 2012. www.iadb.org.

National Aeronautics and Space Administration. "Climate Change: How Do We Know?" NASA, July 28, 2011. climate.nasa.gov.

"National Trade Estimate Reports—1998 Country Report." Trade Compliance Center.

"National Trade Estimate 2000—Mexico." Trade Compliance Center.

Naughton-Treves, Lisa. "Deforestation and Carbon Emissions at Tropical Frontiers: A Case Study from the Peruvian Amazon." *World Development* 32(1) (January 2004): 173–190.

Nazmi, Nader. *Economic Policy and Stabilization in Latin America*. New York: Sharpe, 1996.

———. "The Internationalization of Capital in a Small and Vulnerable Economy: The Case of Ecuador." In *Foreign Direct Investment in Latin America,* ed. Werner Baer and William R. Miles. New York: Hayworth, 2001: 119–139

Nellis, John, Rachel Menzes, and Sarah Lucas. Latino barómetro poll 2001 and 2002, as cited in "Privatization in Latin America." *Center for Global Development Policy Brief* 3(1) (January 2004).

Nelson, Jane. "Corporate Citizenship in a Global Context." Corporate Social Responsibility Initiative Working Paper No. 13. Harvard University: John F. Kennedy School of Government, May 2005.

———. "Leveraging the Development Impact of Business in the Fight Against Global Poverty." CSRI Working Paper No. 22, April 2006.

Nelson, Joan. "The Political of Health Sector Reform." In *Crucial Needs, Weak Incentives: Social Sector Reform, Democratization, and Globalization in Latin America*, ed. Robert R. Kaufman and Joan M. Nelson. Washington, D.C.: Woodrow Wilson Center Press and Johns Hopkins University Press, 2004.

Nelson, Joan, and Robert Kaufman. "The Political Economy of Health Sector Reforms: Cross National Comparisons." Wilson Center update on the Americas May 2003, Creating Community series.

Nelson, Richard R. "Schumpeterian Competition." In *The Sources of Economic Growth*. Cambridge, MA: Harvard University Press, 1996.

Neuman, William, and Adrea Zarate. "Corruption in Peru Aids Cutting of Rain Forest." *The New York Times*, October 18, 2013 2013.

"The New Entrepreneurs: Preparing the Ground for Small Business." *IDB América* 1997. Available at www.iadb.org.

"New Era Dawns with Great Expectations." *Financial Times*, December 14, 2000.

Newfarmer, Richard S. *Profits, Progress, and Poverty*. South Bend, IN: University of Notre Dame Press, 1984.

"New Farms for Old." *The Economist*, January 10, 1998.

"A New Risk of Default." *Euromoney*, September 1996, 283.

"Nicaragua Expects $1.018 Billion Debt Write-Off." *Latin American News Digest*, October 21, 2005.

Nicoli, Marco. "5X5 = US$16 Billion in the Pockets of Migrants Sending Money Home." World Bank Blog, November 27, 2001. www.blogs.worldbank.org.

Nigenda, Gustavo, and Ana Langer. "Sexual and Reproductive Health and Health Sector Reform in Latin America and the Caribbean: Challenges and Opportunities." November 2001. www.iadb.org.

Noll, Roger G. *Telecommunications Reform in Developing Countries.* Working Paper 99–10. AEI-Brookings Joint Center for Regulator Studies, November 1999.

North, Douglass C. "The New Institutional Economics and Third World Development." In *The New Institutional Economics and Third World Development*, ed. John Harriss, Janet Hunter, and Colin M. Lewis. London: Routledge, 1995.

———. *Understanding the Process of Economic Change.* Princeton, NJ: Princeton University Press, 2005.

"The North American Free Trade Agreement Is Good for US Agricultural Trade." *World Food Chemical News*, July 23, 1997.

"North Is North and South Is South." *The Economist*, October 28, 2000.

Northoff, Erwin. "Cattle Ranching Is Encroaching on Forests in Latin America Causing Severe Environmental Degradation: FAO Model Predicts Land Use up to 2010," June 8, 2005. www.fao.org.

Nunez, Salvador J. "3 Big Challenges for Latin America's Electricity Sector, 3 Big Strategies for a Successful Future." *The Huffington Post*, 2014. www.huffingtonpost.com.

"Nuts in Brazil." *The Economist*, October 9, 1999.

Nygren, Anja. "Community-Based Forest Management within the Context of Institutional Decentralization in Honduras." *World Development* 33(4) (April 2005): 639–655.

O'Boyle, Brendan. "What Is CELAC?" American Society, January 27, 2015. www.as-coa.org.

"Obstacles to Business Development." *Latin American Economic Policies* 13(1) (2001).

Ocampo, José Antonio. "The Pending Agenda: A Decade of Light and Shadow." *ECLAC Notes* 20 (March 2001).

———. "Rethinking the Development Agenda." Presented at the American Economic Association Annual Meeting Panel "Toward a Post-Washington Consensus on Development and Security" in New Orleans, January 5, 2001.

———. "Towards a Global Solution." *ECLAC Notes* 1 (November 1998).

Odessey, Bruce. "U.S. Announces Completion of Free-Trade Agreement with Colombia." *Washington File*, February 27, 2006. www. usinfo.state.gov.

OECD. "Development Aid at a Glance: 3. America." 2016. www.oecd.org.

———. "Latin American Economic Outlook 2017." 2017. www.oecd.org.

———. "Tertiary Education Soars in Middle Income Countries." Press release No. 2005-120.

OECD/CAF/ECLAC *Latin American Economic Outlook (LEO) 2017: Youth, Skills and Entrepreneurship.* OECD Publishing, 2016.

OECD and ECLAC. *Latin American Economic Outlook 2012. Transforming the State for Development.* OECD Publishing, 2011.

"Of Cranes, Aid and Unintended Consequences." *The Economist*, October 5, 1996.

"Official Debt Restructuring." *Global Development Finance.* Washington, D.C.: World Bank.

Office of The United States Trade Representative. "Peru Trade Promotion Agreement." www.ustr.gov.

O'Grady, Mary Anastasia. "A Brazilian State Shows How to Reform Schools." *Wall Street Journal*, August 16, 1997.

———. "What Argentina Needs." *Wall Street Journal*, July 17, 2001.

"Oil Chief & Leading Candidate Breach Taboo on Privatisation of PDVSA." *Latin American Weekly Report*, WR-98-30, August 4, 1998.

Olpadwala, Porus, and William Goldsmith. "The Sustainability of Privilege: Reflection on the Environment, the Third World City and Poverty." *World Development* 20(4) (1992).

"On Valentine's Day, Cupid Is Dressed in Brown." *Canada NewsWire*, February 10, 2005.

O'Neill, Ellis. "Trash Piles up in Buenos Aires: What's the Plan?" *The Christian Science Monitor*, October 2013. www.csmonitor.com.

Ónis, Ziya, and Ahmet Faruk Aysan. "Neoliberal Globalisation, the Nation-State and Financial Crises in the Semi-Periphery: A Comparative Analysis." *Third World Quarterly* 21(1) (2000).

Organization for Economic Co-Operation and Development. "Poverty Rate." OECD Data. www.data.oecd.org.

Orozco, Manuel, and Julia Yansura. "Confronting the Challenges of Migration & Development." *The Dialogue*, January 13, 2016. www.thedialogue.org.

Orozco, Manuel, Laura Porras, and Julia Yansura. "The Continued Growth of Family Remittances to Latin America and the Caribbean." *The Inter-American Dialogue*, February 16, 2016. www.thedialogue.org

———. "RIO July 2015 Newsletter." *The Dialogue*, July 2015. www.thedialogue.org.

Orr, David. Earth in mind : on education, environment, and the human prospect" ... Washington, DC: Island Press, 2004.

Ortega, Emiliano. "Evolution of the Rural Dimension in Latin America and the Caribbean." *CEPAL Review* 47 (August 1992).

Ortega Goodspeed, Tamara. "Untangling the Soft Skills Conversation." *The Dialogue*, May 3, 2016. www.thedialogue.org.

Osorio, Nestor. "International Coffee Council: Impact of the Coffee Crisis on Poverty in Producing Countries." ICC 89-5, Rev. September 1, 2003. www.ico.org.

Osava, Mario. "Violence Against Black Women in Brazil on the Rise, Despite Better Laws." *Inter Press Service News Agency*, 2016. www.ipsnews.net.

Ostrovsky, Arkady. "Mexico Bucks Trend and Issues $1bn Bond." *Financial Times*, August 6, 2001.

Otteman, Scott. "Trade Policy Today." *Latin American Advisor*, July 2, 2001.

"Out of the Underworld: Criminal Gangs in the Americas." *The Economist On-line*, January 5, 2006.

Overhold, Catherine, and Margaret Saunders. *Policy Choices and Practical Problems in Health Economics: Cases from Latin America and the Caribbean. Economic Development Institute Resources Series*. Washington, D.C.: World Bank, 1996.

Oxford Analytica. "Latin America Daily Brief." Oxford Analytica, September 12, 2002. prodept@oxford-analytica.com.

———. "Problems with the Millennium Development Goals." *Latin America Daily Brief*, August 28, 2003.

———. "Sustainable Forestry." *Latin America Daily Brief* 23 (March 2006).

Ozório de Almeida, Anna Luiza, and João S. *Campari. Sustainable Settlement in the Brazilian Amazon*. Oxford: Oxford University Press.

Paarlberg, Robert L. "The Politics of Agricultural Resource Abuse." *Environment* 36(8) (October 1994).

Pacala, Steven, and Robert Socolow. "Stabilization Wedges: Solving the Climate with Current Technologies for the Next 50 Years." *Science* 305 (5686) (August 13, 2004): 968–972.

Pagiola, Stefano. "Using PES to Implement REDD." The World Bank, January 2011.

Pagiola, Stefano, Augustin Arcenas, and Gunars Platais. "Can Payments for Environmental Services Help Reduce Poverty? An Exploration of the Issues and the Evidence to Date from Latin America." *World Development* 33(2) (February 2005): 237–253.

PAHO. "Report of the Working Group on PAHO in the 21st Century," August 24, 2005, CD 46/29.

———. "Was 2005 the Year of Natural Disasters?" January 9, 2006. www.paho.org.

Palma, Gabriel. "Dependency: A Formal Theory of Underdevelopment or a Methodology for the Analysis of Concrete Situations of Underdevelopment?" *World Development* 6(7–8) (July–August 1979): 881–924.

Palmer, Ingrid. "Public Finance from a Gender Perspective." *World Development* 23(11) (1995).

Panagariya, Arvind. "The Free Trade Area of the Americas: Good for Latin America?" *World Economy* 19(5) (1996).

Pan American Health Organization. "Basic Indicators Data Base Educator." March 2006. www.paho.org.

———. "Cardiovascular Disease." www.paho.org.

———. *Implementation of the Global Strategy: Health for All by the Year 2000.* vol. 3. Washington, D.C.: PAHO, 1993.

———. "Mexico." *Health in the Americas,* vol. 2. Washington, D.C.: PAHO, 1998.

———. *PAHO Resolution V: Health of Indigenous Peoples.* Series HSS/SILOS, 34. Washington, D.C.: PAHO, 1993. Available at www.paho.org.

———. "Report of the Working Group on PAHO in the 21st Century." PAHO, August 24, 2005. CD 46/29. www.paho.org.

———. Strategic and Programmatic Orientations, 1995–1998. Presented at the Inter-American Meeting, Washington, D.C., April 25–27, 1995. www.paho.org.

"Panel Finds Mexican Antidumping Order Violates WTO Rules." Press Release, January 27, 2000. Office of the United States Trade Representative, WTO, Washington, D.C.

Panizza, Ugo. "Financial Contagion in Latin America: Measuring Morbidity." *Latin American Economic Policies* 6(1) (1999).

Panorama 2005. "El nuevo patron de desarrollo de la agricultura en america latina y el caribe," The New Pattern of Development of Agriculture in Latin America and the Caribbean, ECLAC, September 2005.

Pánuco-Laguette, Humberto, and Miguel Székely. "Income Distribution and Poverty in Mexico." In *The New Economic Model in Latin America and Its Impact on Income Distribution and Poverty,* ed. Victor Bulmer-Thomas. New York: St. Martin's, 1996.

Paranagua, Paulo A. "Latin America Struggles to Cope with Record Urban Growth." *The Guardian,* 2012. www.theguardian.com.

Parker, David, and Colin Kirkpatrick. "Privatization in Developing Countries: A Review of the Evidence and the Policy Lessons." *Journal of Development Studies* 41(4) (May 2005): 514.

Parry, Taryn Rounds. "Achieving Balance in Decentralization: A Case Study of Education Decentralization in Chile." *World Development* 25(2) (1997).

Partnership for Educational Revitalization in the Americas. *The Future at Stake: Report of the Task Force on Education, Equity and Economic Competitiveness in Latin America and the Caribbean.* Santiago: PREAL, in conjunction with the Inter-American Dialogue and CINDE, 1998. Available at www.preal.cl/index-i.htm.

———. *Quantity without Quality: A Report Card on Education in Latin America,* 2006. www.thedialogue.org.

Pastor, Robert A. *Lessons from the Old World for the New: The European Union and a Deeper, Wilder American Community.* HEL-Excerpts, May 5, 2000.

"Patience Runs Out in Bolivia." *The Economist,* April 21, 2001.

Patterson, Allen. "Debt for Nature Swaps and the Need for Alternatives." *Environment* 21 (December 1990): 5–32.

Peach, James T., and Richard V. Adkisson. "Enabling Myths and Mexico's Economic Crises (1976–1996)." *Journal of Economic Issues* 31(2), June 1997.

Pearson, Samantha. "No Trade-Off to Balance Growth and Conservation." *Financial Times*, 2011.

Pereira Leite, Sérgio. "International Capital Flows: A Challenge for the 21st Century." *Revista ILO*, July 1, 2001.

Perez-Aleman, Paola. "Learning, Adjustment and Economic Development: Transforming Firms, the State and Associations in Chile." *World Development* 28(1) (2000).

"The Permanent Crisis in Argentina." *Latin American Weekly Report* 24 (June 21, 2001).

Perry, Guillermo, and Ana Maria Herrera. *Public Finance, Stabilization, and Structural Reform in Latin America*. Washington, D.C.: Johns Hopkins University Press/IADB, 1994.

Peruzzotti, Enrique, and Catalina Smulovitz. "Enforcing the Rule of Law: Social Accountability in the New Latin American Democracies." Review by John M. Ackerman. *Latin American Politics and Society* 50(2), Summer, 2008: 192–194.

Peterson, Jim. "Commentary: Don't Buy into the Import Hype." *A Monthly Journal from the Lemhi Mountains*, September 2000.

Peterson, T.C., and M. O. Baringer. "State of the Climate in 2008." *Special Supplement to the Bulletin of the American Meteorological Society* 90(8), August 2009: 17–18.

Phillip, Michael. "South American Trade Pact Is under Fire." *Wall Street Journal*, October 23, 1996.

Picciotto, Robert. *Putting Institutional Economics to Work: From Participation to Governance*. World Bank Discussion Papers No. 304. Washington, D.C.: World Bank, 1995.

Picciotto, Robert, and Jock Anderson. "Reconsidering Agricultural Extension." *World Bank Research Observer* 12(2) (August 1997).

Pirog, Robert, and Stephen C. Stamos. "Energy Economics: Theory and Policy." Englewood Cliffs, NJ: Prentice-Hall, 1987, Ch. 1.

Pirages, Dennis. "Sustainability As an Evolving Process." *Futures* 26(2) (1994): 197–205.

Pleskovic, Boris, and Joseph E. Stiglitz, eds. *Annual World Bank Conference on Development Economics, 1997*. Washington, D.C.: World Bank, 1998.

Polaski, Sandra. "Jobs, Wages, and Household Income." Chap. 1 in John Audley, Sandra Polaski, Demetrios G. Papademetriou, and Scott Vaughan. "NAFTA's Promise and Reality: Lessons from Mexico." Carnegie Endowment Report, November 2003.

———. *Winners and Losers: Impact of the Doha Round on Developing Countries*. Washington, D.C.: Carnegie Endowment, 2006.

Pomareda, Carlos, and Frank Hartwitch. "Agricultural Innovation in Latin America: Understanding the Private Sector's Role." IFPRI Issue Brief No. 42, January 2006.

Pompa, Claudia. "Paraguay: Can the Deforestation Be Stopped?" Latin America Bureau, February 12, 2014. lab.org.uk.

Population Reference Bureau. "World Population Data Sheet 2005." www.prb.org.

Porras, I., D.N Barton, M. Miranda, and A. Chacón-Cascante. "Learning from 20 years of Payments for Ecosystem Services in Costa Rica." International Institute for Environment and Development, London, 2013.

Porritt, Jonathon. Capitalism: *As If the World Matters*. London: Earthscan, 2005.

———. *Capitalism: As If the World Matters, Part II: A Framework for Sustainable Capitalism*. London: Cromwell Press, 2007, Ch. 6–11, 14.

Porter, Michael E., Klaus Schwab, and Augusto Lopez-Claros. *The Global Competitiveness Report 2005–2006: Policies Underpinning Rising Prosperity*. New York: Oxford University Press, 2005.

Pou, Pedro. "Argentina's Structural Reforms of the 1990s." *Finance & Development* (March 2000).

"Poverty Reduction and the World Bank: Progress in Fiscal 1996 and 1997." World Bank, 1998. Available at www.worldbank.org.

"Poverty Reduction Strategy Papers and the HIPC Initiative." Statement of U.S. Treasury Secretary Lawrence H. Summers at the Joint Session of the International Monetary and Finance Committee and the Development Committee, Washington, D.C., September 24, 2000.

Powell, Robert. "Debt Relief for Poor Countries." *Finance & Development* (December 2000).

Powers, William. "Poor Little Rich Country." *New York Times*, June 11, 2005.

Poynton, Scott. "Natural Capital: Thinking of the Environment as an Asset." ed. Duncan Gromko, February 11, 2014. www.naturalcapital1.blogspot.com.

Prada, Paulo. "Low Cost Credit for Low-Cost Items." *The New York Times*, November 12, 2005. www.nytimes.com.

Prados de la Escosura, Leandro. "Colonial Independence and Economic Backwardness in Latin America." GEHN Working Paper Series, No. 10/05, February 2005. www.lse.ac.uk.

Prawda, Juan. "Educational Decentralization in Latin America: Lessons Learned." *International Journal of Educational Development* 13(3) (1993): 253–264.

Pribble, Jennifer. "Worlds Apart: Social Policy Regimes in Latin America." *Comparitive International Development* 46, 2011: 191–216.

"Prices Soar as Brazil's Flexfuel Cars Set the Pace." *Financial Times*, FT News Alerts, March 26, 2006.

"Pride before the Fall." *The Economist*, October 28, 2000.

"Privatization." *Euromoney*, September 1996.

PROCYMAF. 2000. Proyecto de conservación y manejo sostenable de recursos forestales en México. Informe y avance 1998–2000. Misión de avaluación de medio terino. SEMARNAP, Mexico; B. DeWalt, F. Olivera, and J. Betancourt Correa. *Mid-term Evaluation of the Mexico Community Forestry Projects*. Washington, D.C.: World Bank, 2000.

"Profits and Poverty." *The Economist* 372(8389), August 19, 2004.

"Progress in Privatization." *Global Development Finance*. Washington, D.C.: World Bank, 2001.

Psacharopoulos, George, and Harry Anthony Patrinos, eds. *Indigenous People and Poverty in Latin America*. Washington, D.C.: World Bank, 1994.

Psacharopoulos, George, Carlos Rojas, and Eduardo Velez. "Achieving Evaluation of Colombia's Escuela Nueva: Is Multigrade the Answer?" *Comparative Education Review* 37(3) (1993).

Psacharopoulos, George, et al. *Poverty and Income Distribution in Latin America: The Story of the 1980s*. World Bank Technical Paper No. 351. Washington, D.C.: World Bank, 1997.

Puder, Don. "U.S. Bill Would Country-of-Origin Labeling for Beef." *Times-News*, April 17, 2000.

Puryear, Jeffrey M. "Education in Latin America: Problems and Challenges." Presented to the Council of Foreign Relations, February 24, 1996, for the Latin American Program Study Group, "Educational Reform in Latin America," New York. Available at www.preal.cl/index-i.htm.

———. "Quantity without Quality: A Report Card on Education in Latin America." PowerPoint Presentation at Education in Latin America, IDB Social Development Week, October 2005.

"Putting 'Missed' Chances Behind." *Financial Times*, December 14, 2000.

Rajapatirana, Sarath. *Trade Policies in Latin America and the Caribbean: Priorities, Progress, and Prospects.* San Francisco, CA: International Center for Economic Growth, 1997.

Ramírez, Patricia. "A Sweeping Health Reform: The Quest for Unification, Coverage and Efficiency in Colombia." In *Crucial Needs, Weak Incentives: Social Sector Reform, Democratization, and Globalization in Latin America.* ed. Robert R. Kaufman and Joan M. Nelson. Washington, D.C.: Woodrow Wilson Center Press and Johns Hopkins University Press, 2004.

Ramos, Joseph. "Poverty and Inequality in Latin America: A Neostructuralist Perspective." *Journal of Inter-American Studies and World Affairs* 38(2–3) (Summer–Fall 1996).

Randall, Laura, ed. *Changing Structure of Mexico: Political, Social and Economic Prospects.* Armonk, NY: Sharpe, 1996.

Rapoza, Kenneth. "Brazil Senator Maggi Joins Forbes Billionaire List." *Forbes*, April 10, 2014. www.forbes.com.

"Rate of Growth Moves Up a Gear." *Financial Times*, December 14, 2000.

Rathbone, John Paul. "Mexico and Nafta at 20. Why it went wrong for one of 'Tres Amigos.'" *FT editorial*, Feb 18, 2014. www.ft.com.

Rathbone, John Paul. "Pristine Forest Is Finite Resource." Financial Times. (November 29, 2011).

Rawlings, Laura B. "A New Approach to Social Assistance: Latin America's Experience with Conditional Cash Transfer Programs." *International Social Security Review* 58(2–3) (2005).

Reardon, Thomas. "Rural Nonfarm Employment and Incomes in Latin America: Overview and Policy Implications." *World Development* 29(3) (2001).

Reave, Denée. "Latin America Green News: Fracking in Chile, Environment and Elections in Costa Rica, Coastal Protection in Mexico." National Resources Defense Council, January 17, 2014.

Redclift, Michael. "The Environment and Structural Adjustment: Lessons for Policy Intervention." In *Structural Adjustment and the Agricultural Sector in Latin America and the Caribbean*, ed. John Weeks. New York: St. Martin's, 1995.

Redlener, Irwin. "Program on Child Well-Being and Resilience." Early Childhood Development Columbia University's Center for Global Health and Development and the Earth Institute, October 29, 2013. blogs.ei.columbia.edu.

The Reform of the Mexican Health Care System. OECD Economic Surveys: Mexico. Paris: OECD, 1998.

"Regional Overview of Foreign Investment in Latin America and the Caribbean." Chapter I of the *2000 Report on Foreign Investment in Latin American and the Caribbean.* ECLAC, United Nations, April 18, 2001.

"The Regulation of Foreign Capital Flows in Chile." Report by Innovative Experiences. Available at www.undp.org.

Reilly, Lopez, and G. Cortizas. "Imm Obliga a Identificar Transgenicos." *Eco Portal*, January 9, 2014. www.ecoportal.net.

Reimers, Fernando. "Educacion para todos en América Latina en el Siglo XXIL. Los desafíos de la estabilización, el ajuste y los mandatos de Jomtien." Paper presented at UNESCO workshop, Peru, December 1990.

———. "The Impact of Economic Stabilization and Adjustment on Education in Latin America." *Comparative Education* 35(2) (May 1991).

Rennhack, Robert. "Banking Supervision." *Finance & Development* (March 2000): 27.

Replogle, Jill. "Hunger on the Rise in Central America." *The Lancet* 363(19) (June 2004): 2056. www.thelancet.com.

Report on the Binational Commission, International Studies Association meetings, Washington, D.C., February 20, 1999.

"Responsible Regionalism." *The Economist*, December 2, 2000.

"Revolution Ends, Change Begins." *The Economist*, October 28, 2000.

Ribe, Helena, David A Robalino, and Ian Walker. "From Right to Reality: Incentives, Labor Markets, and the Challenge of Universal Social Protection in Latin America and the Caribbean." World Bank, 2012.

Rich, Jennifer L. "Compressed Data: Brazilians Think Basic to Bridge the Digital Divide." *New York Times*, February 12, 2001.

Richards, Michael. "Alternative Approaches and Problems in Protected Area Management and Forest Conservation in Honduras." In *Sustainable Agriculture in Central America*, ed. Jan P. de Groot and Ruerd Ruben. New York: St. Martin's, 1997.

Richards, Peter D. "Soy, Cotton and the Final Atlantic Forest Frontier." *The Professional Geographer* 63(3), (2011): 343–363.

"Rich Is Rich and Poor Is Poor." *The Economist*, October 28, 2000.

RICYT. "El Estado de la Ciencia. Principales Indicadores de Ciencia y Tecnología Iberoamericanos / InterAmericanos 2004." The Network on Science and Technology Indicators, Ibero-American and Inter-American. www.ricyt.edu.ar.

Riggirozzi, Pi´a. "Social Policy in Post-Neo-liberal Latin America: The cases of Argentina, Venezuela and Bolivia Development." *Development* 53(1), 2010: 70–76. doi:10.1057/dev.2009.96.

Rivoli, Pietra. *The Travels of a T-Shirt in the Global Economy*. Hoboken, NJ: John Wiley and Sons, 2005.

Rizvi, Haider. "Biodiversity: Brazil's Lula Lashes Out at Rich Nations." *IPS Terraviva*, March 28, 2006.

Roberts, Paul. "The End of Oil." Boston, MA: Houghton and Mifflin, 2004.

Robeyns, Ingrid. "The Capability Approach." *The Stanford Encyclopedia of Philosophy*, Summer 2011. plato.stanford.edu.

Rocca, Francis X. "Pope Francis Calls for Judicial Transparency in Front of Audience that Includes Paraguay's president." *The Wall Street Journal*, July 11, 2015. www.wsj.com.

Rodriguez-Clare, Andres. *Innovation and Technology Adoption in Central America*. Inter-American Development Bank Research Department, Working Paper Series 525, July 2005.

Rodriguez-Garcia, Rosalia, and Ann Goldman, eds. *The Health-Development Link*. Washington, D.C.: PAHO, 1994.

Rodriguez-Mendoz, Miguel. "The Andean Group's Integration Strategy." In *Integrating the Hemisphere, 1997: The Inter-American Dialogue*, ed. Ana Julia Jatar and Sidney Weintraub. Santafé de Bogotá, Colombia: Tercer Mundo, 1997.

Rodriguez Salvez, Daniel. "Access for Latin American and Caribbean Agrifood Products to International Markets." *Communica*, January–July 2010.

Rodrik, Dani. "The Global Governance of Trade as If Development Really Mattered." United Nations Development Programme, October 2001. www.undp.org.

———. "Growth and Poverty Reduction: What Are the Real Questions?" *Finance & Development* (August 2000). ksghome.harvard.edu.

———. "Institutions for High-Quality Growth: What They Are and How to Acquire Them." *International Monetary Fund 1999*. Available at www.imf.org.

———. "King Kong Meets Godzilla: The World Bank and the East Asian Miracle." CEPR Discussion Paper No. 944. London: Centre for Economic Policy Research, 1994.

———. "Why Do More Open Economies Have Bigger Governments?" *Journal of Political Economy* 16(5) (1998).

Rodrik, Dani, and Arvind Subramanian. "The Primacy of Institutions (and What This Does and Does Not Mean)." *Finance and Development* (June 2003): 32.

Rohloff, Greg. "Beef Processor IBP Inc. Agrees to Buyout by Investment Bank." *Amarillo Daily News*, October 5, 2000.

Rohter, Larry. "Brazilians Uneasy Despite Help by I.M.F." *New York Times*, August 6, 2001.

———. "Bush and Brazil Chief Have Politics, If Not Trade, to Discuss." *New York Times*, March 30, 2001.

———. "Crisis Whipsaws Brazilian Workers." *New York Times*, January 16, 1999. Online edition.

———. "Ecuadorian President Imposes Sweeping Austerity Measures." *New York Times*, March 21, 1999.

———. "For Brazil's College-Bound, a Brutal Test of Mettle." *New York Times*, December 29, 2000.

———. "Loggers, Scorning the Law, Ravage the Amazon." *New York Times*, October 16, 2005.

———. "U.S. Aid to Colombia Worries Hemisphere's Defense Leaders." *New York Times*, October 18, 2000.

———. "Where Darwin Mused, Strife over Ecosystem." *New York Times*, December 27, 2000.

———. "With a Big Boost from Sugar Cane, Brazil is Satisfying Its Fuel Needs." *New York Times*, April 10, 2006.

Rohter, Larry, and Elizabeth Johnson. "Brazil Deforestation: Pioneer Loggers Suffer a Setback." *FT News Alerts*, October 7, 2005. www.ft.com.

Rojas, Eduardo. *The IDB in Low-Cost Housing the First Three Decades*. Strategic Planning and Operational Policy Department, February 1995.

Rojas, Patricia. "IDB Welcomes Creation of Brazilian Carbon Market." *IDB América*, April 2, 2006. www.iadb.org.

Rojas-Suarez, Liliana. "Financial Inclusion in Latin America: Facts and Obstacles." Center for Global Development Working Paper No. 439, October 20, 2016. www.cgdev.org.

———. "Dollarization in Latin America." Presented to the Hearing on Official Dollarization in Latin America for the Senate Banking Committee, July 15, 1999.

Rojas-Suarez, Liliana, and Steven R. Weisbrod. "Building Stability in Latin American Financial Markets." In *Securing Stability and Growth in Latin America*, ed. Ricardo Hausmann and Helmut Reisen. Paris: OECD Publications, 1996.

Roldán, Jorge. Interview. *IDB Extra*, June 14, 1998. Online edition.

Romero, Simon. "Where the Risk Is Riskier Yet." *New York Times*, December 16, 1999.

Rosegrant, Susan. *Banana Wars: Challenges to the European Union's Banana Regime*. Kennedy School of Government Case Program, 1999 Abstract.

Rosenthal, Gert. "Development Thinking and Policies: The Way Ahead." *CEPAL Review* 60 (December 1996).

———. "On Poverty and Inequality in Latin America." *Journal of Inter-American Studies and World Affairs* 38(2–3) (Summer–Fall 1996).

Ross, Jen. "Brazil's Disappearing Jungle." *Toronto Star*, August 6, 2005.

Rothkopf, David J. "Rising Above the Moment." *New Democrat* (September/October 1997).

Ruete, Marina. "Financing for Agriculture: How to Boost Opportunities in Developing Countries." International Institute for Sustainable Development Brief #3, September 2015. IISD.org.

Runge, C. Ford, and Benjamin Senauer. "How Biofuels Could Starve the Poor." *Foreign Affairs* (2007).

"Rural Poverty Remains Strong in Latin America in Spite of Agriculture Boom." *Merco Press*, November 8, 2010. www.en.mercopress.com.

Russell, Clifford S., and Philip T. Powell. *Choosing Environmental Policy Tools: Theoretical Cautions and Practical Considerations*. No. ENV-102. Washington, D.C.: IADB, June 1996.

Ryan, John. "The Shrinking Forest." *NACLA Report on the Americas* 25(2) (September 1991).

Saavedra, Jaime, and Omar S. Arias. "Stuck in a Rut." *Finance and Development* 42(4) (December 2005).

Sachs, Jeffrey D. "Common Wealth: The Economics for a Crowded Planet." London: The Penguin Press, 2008.

———. *The End of Poverty*. New York: Penguin, 2005, 253–254.

———. *Tropical Underdevelopment*. CID Working Paper No. 57. Cambridge, MA: Harvard University Press, December 2000.

Sachs, Jeffery and Joaquin Vial. "Can Latin America Compete?" *Latin American Competitiveness Report*. New York: Oxford University Press, 2002.

Sachs, Jeffrey, and Alvaro Zini. "Brazilian Inflation and the Plano Real." *World Economy* 19(1) (January 1996).

Sachs, Wolfgang, ed. *The Development Dictionary: A Guide to Knowledge As Power*. London: Zed, 1992.

"Safeguarding against Crisis: The Near-Term Agenda." In *Global Development Finance*. Washington, D.C.: World Bank, 2000.

Salzinger, Leslie. "Making Fantasies Real—Producing Women and Men on the Maquila Shop Floor." *NACLA Report on the Americas* 34(5) (March/April 2001).

"The Samba and the Tango." *The Economist*, February 24, 1996.

Samor, Geraldo. "Brazil's Petrobras Self-Reliant or Pliant?" *Wall Street Journal*, April 21, 2006, A7.

Sampaio Malan, Pedro, and Arminio Fraga Neto. *Brazil—Memorandum of Economic Policies*. Washington, D.C.: IMF, April 20, 2000.

Sampson, Anthony. *The Seven Sisters: The Great Oil Companies And The World They Made*. London: Hodder and Stoughton, 1975.

Samuelson, Robert J. "Dollarization—a Black Hole." *Washington Post*, May 12, 1999, A27.

Sánchez, M., R. Corona, L. F. Herrera, and O. Ochoa. "A Comparison of Privatization Experiences: Chile, Mexico, Colombia, and Argentina." In *Privatization in Latin America*, ed. M. Sánchez and R. Corona. Baltimore, MD: Johns Hopkins University Press, 1994.

Sanchez, Ricardo, and Gordon Wilmsmeier. "Bridging Infrastructural Gaps in Central America: Prospects and Potential for Maritime Transport." ECLAC, Series CEPAL, Recursos Naturales e Infraestructura, No. 97, September 2005.

Santiso, Javier. *Latin America's Political Economy of the Possible*. Cambridge, MA: MIT Press, 2006.

———. "Political Sluggishness and Economic Speed: A Latin American Perspective." *Social Science Information* 39(2) (2000).

Savedoff, William, Antonio Giuffrida, and Roberto Iunes. "Economic and Health Effects of Occupational Hazards." IADB, Sustainable Development Department, June 2001.

Sawers, Larry. "Nontraditional or New Traditional Exports." *Latin American Research Review* 40(3) (October 2005): 1.

Sawyer, Suzana. "Indigenous Initiatives and Petroleum Politics in the Ecuadorian Amazon." *Cultural Survival* (Spring 1996).

Schaefer, Elizabeth, and Chris Rasmussen. "Jobs Supported by Export Destination 2014." International Trade Administration: Department of Commerce, June 18, 2015. www.trade.gov.

Schatan, Claudia. "Lessons from the Mexican Environmental Experience: First Results from NAFTA." In *The Environment and International Trade Negotiations: Developing Country Stakes*, ed. Diana Tussie. St. Martin's in association with International Development Research Center, 2000.

Schemo, Diana Jean. "The ABC's of Doing Business in Brazil." *New York Times*, July 16, 1998. Online edition.

———. "Brazil Farmers Feel Squeezed by Tobacco Companies." *New York Times*, April 6, 1998. Online edition.

———. "Brazilians Fret As Economic Threat Moves Closer." *New York Times*, September 20, 1998. Online edition.

———. "Ecuadorians Want Texaco to Clear Toxic Residue." *New York Times*, January 31, 1998.

———. "A Latin Bloc Asks U.S. and Europe to Ease Trade Barriers." *New York Times*, February 23, 1999. Online edition.

Scherr, Sara J., Andy White, and David Kaimowitz. "Making Markets Work for Forest Communities." *Forest Trends*. Washington, D.C., 2002.

Sciaudone, Christiana, and David Biller. "A New York Pizza Man's Brazil Nightmare and the Mess It Exposed." Brazil Institute, July 7, 2015. www.bloomberg.org.

Schiesel, Seth. "Brazil Sells Most of State Phone Utility." *New York Times*, July 30, 1998, D1.

Schiff, Maurice, and Alberto Valdes. "The Plundering of Agriculture in Developing Countries." 1994 draft paper. www.worldbank.org.

Schmitz, Hubert, and José Cassiolato. *Hi-Tech for Industrial Development: Lessons from the Brazilian Experience in Electronics and Automation*. London: Routledge, 1992.

Schneider, Mycle, Antony Froggatt, and Steve Thomas. "Nuclear Power in a Post-Fukushima World." The Worldwatch Institute, July 1, 2011.

Schneider, Stephen, Armin Rosencranz, and John O. Niles, eds. *Climate Change Policy: A Survey*. Washington, D.C.: Island Press, 2002.

Schott, Jeffrey J. "NAFTA: An Interim Report." In *Trade: Towards Open Regionalism*, Proceedings of the 1997 World Bank Conference on Development in Latin America and the Caribbean. Washington, D.C.: World Bank 1998.

———. "NAFTA: An Interim Report." Data from Lustig's comment .125.

Searcey, Dionne, and David Lubnow. "Verizon Pulls Out of Latin America." *Wall Street Journal*, April 4, 2006, A18.

Sedelnik, Lisa. "CANTV: Inside the IPO." *Latin Finance* 83 (1997): 43–46.

Seers, Dudley. "What Are We Trying to Measure?" *Journal of Development Studies* (April 1972).

Sekles, Flavia. "Brazil's AIDS Policies Tightly Link Prevention and Treatment." March 2005. www.prb.org.

SELA. "Current Trends in Migrants' Remittances in Latin America and the Caribbean." Caracas, Venezuela, November 2003. www.sela.org.

Seligson, Mitchell. "The Measurement and Impact of Corruption Victimization: Survey Evidence from Latin America." *World Development* 34(2), February 2006: 381–404.

Sen, Amartya. "The Concept of Development." In *Handbook of Development Economics*, Vol. 1. Netherlands: North-Holland, 1988.

Senser, Robert A. "Corporate Social Responsibility: A Fledgling Movement Faces a Crucial Test." *Dissent Winter*, 2007: 77–82.

Serant, Claire. "Sony Will Play Solectron—Sale of Two Plants May Fling Open Japan's Doors." *Electronic Buyers News*, October 23, 2000.

Shah, Fared, David Zilberman, and Ujjayant Chakravorty. "Water Rights Doctrines and Technology Adoption." In *The Economics of Rural Organization*, ed. Karla Hoff, Avishay Braverman, and Joseph Stiglitz. New York: Oxford University Press/World Bank, 1993.

Shapiro, Helen. Engines of Growth: The State and Transnational Auto Companies in Brazil. Cambridge, UK: Cambridge University Press, 1994.

———. *Mexico: Escaping the Debt Crisis*. Harvard Business School Case. Boston: Harvard Business School, 1991.

———. *North American Free Trade Agreement: Free for Whom?* Harvard Business School case #5-792-059. Boston: Harvard Business School, 1993.

Shapiro-Garza, Elizabeth. "Contesting the Market-Based Nature of Mexico's National Payments for Ecosystem Services Programs: Four Sites of Articulation and Hybridization." *Geoforum* 46, (2013): 5–15.

"Share the Love with Flower Workers." Pesticide Action Network Updates Service (PANUPS), February 7, 2006.

Shatz, Howard, "Expanding Foreign Direct Investment in the Andean Countries." CID Working Paper No. 64. Cambridge, MA: Center for International Development at Harvard University, March 2001.

Sheahan, John, and Enrique Iglesias. "Kinds and Causes of Inequality in Latin America." In *Beyond Trade-Offs: Market Reform and Equitable Growth in Latin America*, ed. Nancy Birdsall, Carol Graham, and Richard Sabot. Washington, D.C.: Brookings Institution Press/IADB, 1998.

Shifter, Michael, and Cameron Combs. "The Politics of Poverty: South America's Conditional Cash Transfers." *World Politics Review*, May 14, 2013.

Shinkai, Naoko. *Does Stolper-Samuelson Theorem Explain the Movement in Wages? The Linkage between Trade and Wages in Latin American Countries*. Working Paper #436. Washington, D.C.: IADB, November 2000.

Shore, Keane. *Harvard Economist Calls for New Approach to International Development*. IRDC Report, August 9, 2001.

Shoumatoff, Alex. *The World Is Burning*. Boston: Little, Brown, 1990.

Shrimpton, Roger, and Claudia Rokx. "The Double Burden of Malnutrition: A Review of Global Evidence." The World Bank, November 2012. www.documents.worldbank.org.

Sillars, Les. "A Bull Market for Beef and Pork: Investment in Western Meat Processing Continues to Surge." *Alberta Report*, April 14, 1997.

Silviera, Patrícia Pelufo, André Krumel Portella, and Marcelo Zubaran Goldani. "Obesity in Latin America." *The Lancet* 366 (August 6, 2005).

Simons, Marlise. "A Talk with Gabriel García Marquez." *New York Times*, December 5, 1982, sec. 7, p. 7. Available at www.nytimes.com/books/97/06/15/reviews/marquez-talk.html and in the LEXIS-NEXIS database.

Sims, Calvin. "Peruvians Climb onto the Web." *New York Times*, May 27, 1996.

Singh, Anoop, Agneés Belaisch, Charles Collyns, Paula DeMasi, Reva Krieger, Guy Meredith, and Robert Renhack. "Stabilization and Reform in Latin America: A MacroeconomicPerspective on the Experience since the Early 1990's." International Monetary Fund, Occasional Paper No. 238, February 2005.

Skidmore, Thomas E. "Brazil's Persistent Income Inequality." *Latin American Politics and Society* 46(2) (2004): 133–150.

"Skills Gap May Be Biggest Trade Barrier." *Journal of Commerce*, April 20, 1998. Online edition. Available at www.alca-cupula.org.

"Slicing the Cake: What Is the Relationship between Inequality and Economic Growth?" *The Economist*, October 19, 1996.

"The Slow Road to Reform." *The Economist*, December 2, 2000.

Smith, Geri. "Slim's New World." *Business Week* (International edition), February 2000.

Smith, James F. "Mexican Beef Growers Decry Duties on U.S. As Too Low." *Los Angeles Times*, August 4, 1999.

Sokoloff, Kenneth. "Inequality and the Evolution of Institutions of Taxation: Evidence from the Economic History of the Americas." In *Growth Institutions and Crises: Latin*

America from a Historical Perspective, ed. Sebastian Edwards. Washington, D.C.: National Bureau of Economic Research, 2005.

Sola, Lourdes, Christopher Garman, and Moises S. Marques. *Central Reform and Overcoming the Moral Hazard Problem: The Case of Brazil*. Paper Presented for the XXII International Latin American Studies Association Congress, 2000.

Soledad Bos, María, Marcelo Cabrol, and Carlos Rondón. "A New Context for Teachers in Latin America and the Caribbean." *Inter-American Development Bank Technical Notes* No. IDB-TN-412, April 2012. www.idbdocs.iadb.org.

"Some Mutual Funds Go Back Full Throttle to Emerging Markets." *Wall Street Journal*, November 12, 1996.

"Something for a Refresco." *The Economist*, October 28, 2000.

Soto, Alonso. "UPDATE 1—Brazil, Argentina push for closer trade with Mexico in Trump era." *CNBC*, February 7, 2017. www.cnbc.com.

"South Africa's Moral Victory," *The Lancet* 357(28), April 2001.

Spar, Debora. *Regarding NAFTA*. Harvard Business School Case #5-798-122. Boston: Harvard Business School, 1998.

Speth, James Gustave. "Modern Capitalism: Out of Control." Chapter 2 in *The Bridge at the Edge of the World: Capitalism, the Environment, and Crossing from Crisis to Sustainability*. New Haven, CT: Yale University Press, 2008.

———. "Red Sky at Morning." Chapter 7 in *Globalization and the Environment*. New Haven, CT: Yale University Press, 2004: 140–147.

Sprague, Courtnay. *Debt Restructuring under the Brady Plan*. Harvard Business School case #9-796-130. Boston: Harvard Business School, 1998.

"The Sputtering Spark from South America's Car Industry." *The Economist*, April 15, 1995.

Stahl, Karin. "Anti-Poverty Programs: Making Structural Adjustment More Palatable." *NACLA Report on the Americas* 29(6) (May–June 1995).

Stallings, Barbara, and Wilson Peres. *Growth, Employment, and Equity: The Impact of the Economic Reforms in Latin America and the Caribbean*. Summary. ECLAC, Spring 2000.

Stampini, Marco, and Leopoldo Tornarolli. "The Growth of Conditional Cash Transfers In Latin America And The Caribbean: Did They Go Too Far?" IDB Policy Brief No. IDB-PB-185, November 2012.

"State of the World 2011: Innovations That Nourish The Planet," The Worldwatch Institute, 2011.

Stauder, Monique. "Colombian Cocaine Runs through It." *Christian Science Monitor*, June 13, 2001.

Steele, Diane. "Guatemala." In *Indigenous People and Poverty in Latin America*, ed. George Psacharopoulos and Harry Anthony Patrinos. Washington, D.C.: World Bank, 1994.

Stein, Elizabeth. *Regarding NAFTA*. Harvard Business School Case #9-797-013. Boston: Harvard Business School, 1998.

Stein, Ernesto, Ernesto Talvi, and Alejandro Grisanti. *Institutional Arrangements and Fiscal Performance: The Latin American Experience*. National Bureau of Economic Research Working Paper No. 6358. Cambridge, MA: National Bureau of Economic Research, 1998.

Stenfeld, Jacob. "Development and Foreign Investment: Lessons Learned from Mexican Banking." Carnegie Papers No. 47, Carnegie Endowment for International Peace, July 2004.

Stephens, Carolyn, Clive Nettleton, John Porter, Ruth Willis, and Stephanie Clark. "Indigenous People's Health—Why Are They Behind Everyone, Everywhere?" *The Lancet* 366 (July 2, 2005): 11. www.thelancet.com.

Stern, Nicholas. *The Global Deal: Climate Change and the Creation of a New Prosperity*. Philadelphia: PublicAffairs USA, 2009.

————. "The Economics of Climate Change: The Stern Review." Cambridge, UK, 2007.

Stewart, Alastair. "Brazil's Impeachment Brings Maggi to Ag Ministry." *DTN Progressive Farmer*, May 12, 2016. www.dtnpf.com.

Stewart, Frances. *Adjustment and Poverty: Options and Choices*. London: Routledge, 1995.

Stiglitz, Joseph. *Globalization and Its Discontents*. New York, Norton, 2002: 214.

————. "More Instruments and Broader Goals: Moving toward the Post-Washington Consensus." The 1998 WIDER Annual Lecture. The World Bank Group, Washington, D.C.: 1998.

————. "Post–Washington Consensus." Initiative for Policy Dialogue, Working Paper Series, Columbia University, 2005.

————. "The Role of Government in Economic Development." In *Annual World Bank Conference on Development Economics 1996*. Washington, D.C.: World Bank, 1997.

"Stopping the Rot in Public Life." *The Economist*, September 16, 2000.

Strahan, Spencer, and Adrian Wood. "Making the Financial Sector Work for the Poor." *Journal of Development Studies* 41(4) (May 2005): 657–675.

Streeten, Paul. "A Basic Needs Approach to Economic Development." In *Directions in Economic Development*, ed. Kenneth P. Jameson and Charles K. Wilber. Notre Dame, IN: University of Notre Dame Press, 1979.

————. "From Growth to Basic Needs." In *Latin America's Economic Development: Institutionalist and Structuralist Perspectives*, ed. James L. Dietz and James H. Street. Boulder, CO: Rienner, 1987.

Strong, Maurice. "Where on Earth Are We Going?" *Texere*, 2001: 26.

Sturzenegger, Federico A. "Description of a Populist Experience: Argentina, 1973–1976." In *The Macroeconomics of Populism in Latin America*, ed. Rudiger Dornbusch and Sebastian Edwards. Chicago, IL: University of Chicago Press, 1991.

Sucre, Federico. "Role of E-Learning in Higher Education in Latin America." PREAL Blog, Apr 12 2016.

Sullivan, Mark P. "Panama: Political and Economic Conditions and U.S. Relation." Congressional Research Service Report RL30981, February 15, 2006. www.opencrs.cdt.org.

"Summing Up by the Chairman of the IMF Executive Board Enhanced Initiative for Heavily Indebted Poor Countries (HIPC) and Poverty Reduction Strategy Papers (PRSP)—Progress Reports and Review of Implementation." Executive Board Meeting of September 5, 2000. Washington, D.C.: IMF, September 11, 2000.

"The Summiteers Go to School." *The Economist*, April 25, 1998, 37–38.

Sunkel, Osvaldo. Development from Within: Toward a Neostructuralist Approach for Latin America. Boulder, CO: Rienner, 1993.

Suro, Roberto. "Remittances Senders and Receivers: Tracking Transnational Channels." Joint Report of the MIF and the Pew Hispanic Center, Washington, D.C., November 24, 2003.

Swafford, David. "A Healthy Trend: Health Care Reform in Latin America." *Latin Finance* 83 (December 1996).

Swinton, Scott M., Germán Escobar, and Thomas Reardon. "Poverty and Environment in Latin America: Concepts, Evidence and Policy Implications." *World Development* 31(11) (November 2003): 1865.

Sylos Labini, Paolo. "The Classical Roots of Development Theory." In *Economic Development: Handbook of Comparative Economic Policies*, ed. Enzo Grilli and Dominick Salvatore. Westport, CT: Greenwood, 1994.

"A System That Needs Some Simplifying." *Financial Times*, December 14, 2000.

Székely, Miguel. *The 1990s in Latin America: Another Decade of Persistent Inequality, but with Somewhat Lower Poverty.* Working Paper No. 454. IADB, June 2001.

Székely, Miguel, Nora Lustig, Martin Cumpa, and José Antonio Mejía. *Do We Know How Much Poverty There Is?* Working Paper 437. IADB, December 2000.

Tanzi, Vito. "Fiscal Federalism and Decentralization: A Review of Some Efficiency and Macroeconomic Aspects." Paper presented at the World Bank Conference on Development Economics, World Bank, May 1995. As summarized by *The Economist*, June 3, 1995.

Tanzi, Vito, and Howell Zee. *Tax Policy for Developing Countries.* Washington, D.C.: IMF, 2001.

Tardanico, Richard, and Rafael Menjívar Larraín. "Restructuring, Employment, and Social Inequality: Comparative Urban Latin American Patterns." In *Global Restructuring, Employment, and Social Inequality in Urban Latin America*, ed. Richard Tardanico and Rafael Menjívar Larraín. Miami, FL: University of Miami North-South Center Press, 1997.

"A Taxing Problem." *The Economist*, June 3, 1995.

Taylor, Alan. *Argentina and the World Capital Market: Saving, Investment and International Capital Mobility in the Twentieth Century.* National Bureau of Economic Research Working Paper No. 6302. Cambridge, MA: National Bureau of Economic Research, 1997.

———. "Foreign Capital in Latin America in the Nineteenth and Twentieth Centuries." NBER Working Paper No. W9580, March 2003.

———. "On the Costs of Inward-Looking Development: Price Distortions, Growth and Divergence in Latin America." *Journal of Economic History* 58(1) (March 1998).

Taylor, Jerry. "The Challenge of Sustainable Development." *Regulation* 17(1) (1994): 35–50.

Taylor, Lance, and Ute Piper. *Reconciling Economic Reform and Sustainable Human Development: Social Consequences of Neo-Liberalism.* UNDP Discussion Paper Series. New York: United Nations Development Programme, 1996.

"A Teacher's Lot." *The IDB*, May 1996.

Teichman, Judith. "Policy Networks and Policy Reform in Mexico: Technocrats, the World Bank and the Private Sector." Paper presented to the Congress of the Latin American Studies Association, March 16, 2000.

"Telebras Sold for US$19.lB." *Latin American Weekly Report*, August 4, 1998.

Templeman, John. "Is Europe Elbowing the U.S. Out of South America?" *BusinessWeek*, August 4, 1997, 56.

Tendler, Judith. *Good Government in the Tropics.* Baltimore, MD: Johns Hopkins University Press, 1997.

"Tequila Freeways." *The Economist*, December 16, 1996.

Thatcher, Peter S. "The Role of the United Nations." In *The International Politics of the Environment: Actors, Interests, and Institutions*, ed. Andrew Hurrell and Benedict Kingsbury. Oxford, UK: Clarendon, 1992.

Thomas, Vinod. "Why Quality Matters." *The Economist*, October 7, 2000.

Thompson, Ginger. "At Home, Mexico Mistreats Its Farmhands." *New York Times*, May 6, 2001.

———. "Chasing Mexico's Dream into Squalor." *New York Times*, February 11, 2001.

———. "In Guatemalan Town Buried by Mud, Unyielding Hope for a Little Girl." *New York Times*, October 9, 2005.

Thomson, Adam. "US Latin American Trade Policy under Scrutiny As FTAA Fall Off Summit." *Financial Times*, November 7, 2005.

Thorp, Rosemary. "Import Substitution: A Good Idea in Principle." In *Latin America and the World Economy: Dependency and Beyond*, ed. Richard J. Salvucci. Lexington, MA: Heath, 1996.

———. *Progress, Poverty, and Exclusion: An Economic History of Latin America in the 20th Century*. Baltimore, MD: Johns Hopkins University Press/IADB, 1998.

Thorpe, Andy. "Sustainable Agriculture in Latin America." In *Sustainable Agriculture in Central America*, ed. Jan P. de Groot and Ruerd Ruben. New York: St. Martin's, 1997.

Thrupp, Lori Ann. *Bittersweet Harvests for Global Supermarkets: Challenges in Latin America's Agricultural Export Boom*. Washington, D.C.: World Resources Institute, 1995.

"'Til Debt Do Us Part." *The Economist*, February 28, 1987.

Tilman, David, Robert Socolow, Jonathan A Foley, Jason Hill, Eric Larson, Lee Lynd, Stephen Pacala, John Reilly, Tim Searchinger, Chris Somerville, and Robert Williams. "Beneficial Biofuels—the Food, Energy, and Environment Trilemma." University of Minnesota, 2009.

Tissot, Roger. "Latin America's Energy Future." *Inter-American Dialogue*, 2012.

Titelman, Daniel, et al. "Universal Health Coverage in Latin American Countries: How to Improve Solidarity-Based Schemes." *The Lancet* 385(9975), October 2014:1359–1363.

"Titular De La Arp Dice Que Deforestación En El Chaco Es Un 'Cuento Chino.'". *E'a*, January 30, 2014. www.ea.com.py.

Todaro, Michael P. Economic Development. 5th ed. White Plains, NY: Longham, 1994.

Tokman, Victor E. "Jobs and Solidarity: Challenges for Post-Adjustment in Latin America." In *Economic and Social Development in the XXI Century, Proceedings of the 1997 IADB Conference*, ed. Louis Emmerij. Available at www.iadb.org.

Tokman, Viktor. *Beyond Regulation: The Informal Economy in Latin America*. Boulder, CO: Rienner, 1992.

———. "Policies for a Heterogeneous Informal Sector." *World Development* 17(7) (1989): 1067–1076.

Toman, Michael A. "Economics and 'Sustainability': Balancing the Trade-offs and Imperatives." *Land Economics* 70(4) (November 1994): 399–413.

Toomy, Gerry. "Combining Environmental Protection and Poverty Alleviation in Colombia." *Science from the Developing World*, August 7, 2001.

Torres, Carlos A. *Education and Social Change in Latin America*. Albert Park, Australia: James Nicolas, 1997.

Torres, Carlos Alberto, and Adriana Puiggrós. "The State and Public Education in Latin America." *Comparative Education Review* 39(1) (1995).

"Trade in the Americas." *The Economist*, April 21, 2001.

Transparency International. "Global Corruption Reports." Transparency International, 2001. www.transparency.org.

———. "Corruption Perceptions Index 2014: Results." Transparency International, 2014. www.transparency.org.

———. "Integrity Pacts in Public Procurement: An Implementation Guide." Transparency International, April 15, 2014.

Trebat, Thomas. *Brazil's State-Owned Enterprises: A Case Study of the State As Entrepreneur*. New York: Cambridge University Press, 1983.

Tricks, Henry. "Electronic Expansion for Cemex." *Financial Times*, December 13, 2000.

Trivelli, Carolina, Javier Alvarado, and Francisco Galarza. *Increasing Indebtedness, Institutional Change and Credit Contracts in Peru*. IADB, Office of the Chief Economist. Working Paper #R-378. Washington, D.C.: IADB, 1999.

"Trouble Brewing." *The Economist*, March 10, 2001.

Tucker, Mary Evelyn. *Worldly Wonder: Religions Enter Their Ecological Phase*. Chicago: Open Court, 2003.

Tullio, G., and M. Ronci. "Brazilian Inflation from 1980 to 1993: Causes Consequences and Dynamics." *Journal of Latin American Studies* 28 (October 1996): 635–666.

Tussie, Diana. *The Multilateral Development Banks, Vol. 4, The Inter-American Development Bank*. Ottawa: North-South Institute, 1995.

Tussie, Diana, and Cintia Quiliconi. "The Current Trade Context." HDR Publications, Background Papers, 2005. Available at hdr.undp.org/publications/.

Tussie, Diana, and María Fernanda Tuozzo. "Multilateral Development Banks and Civil Society Participation in Latin America." Presented to Facultad Latinoamericana de Ciencias Sociales for the LASA Conference, March 2000.

"21 anos da morte de Margarida Alves." Movimento de Mulheras Camponeses. www.mmc-brasil.com.

Twomey, Michael J. Multinational Corporations and the North American Free Trade Agreement. Westport, CT: Praeger, 1993.

Uitto, Juha. "Evaluating the Environment as a Global Public Good." *Evaluation* 22(1), (2016): 18–115.

UNDP. "About Latin America and the Caribbean." UNDP in Latin America and the Caribbean. www.latinamerica.undp.org.

———. "Climate and Disaster Resistance: Overview." UNDP in Latin America and the Caribbean. www.latinamerica.undp.org.

———. "Human Development Data (1990–2015)." UNDP. www.hdr.undp.org.

UNESCO. "The Dakar Framework for Action." UNESCO, April 2000. unesdoc.unesco.org.

———. "Education for All, Literacy for Life 2005." Education for all Global Monitoring Report. www.unesco.org.

———. "Education for all Global Monitoring Report 2010. Annex." United Nations Educational, Scientific and Cultural Organization, 2010. www.unesco.org.

———. "Educational Panorama 2005: Progressing Toward the Goals." Regional Education Indicators Project, Summit of the Americas, November 2005. www.unesco.cl.

———. "Latin America and the Caribbean—Policies Yield Results but High Rates Persist in Some Countries." UNESCO. www.unesco.org.

"Unfinished Business." *The Economist*, March 2, 1996.

United Nations. "AIDS Epidemic in Latin America: Fact Sheet." www.unaids.org.

———. Human Development Report 2005. Human Development Indicators. hdr.undp.org.

———. "A Latin American and Caribbean Perspective." United Nations Development Programme, Millennium Development Goals, August 2005, 232.

———. "Millennium Development Goals: A Latin American and Caribbean Perspective." www.unesco.org, August 2005.

———. "Prevention Gap Report." UNAIDS, 2016. www.unaids.org.

——— "State of the World Population 2003." www.unfpa.org.

———. *Unicef Child Survival Report Card, Progress for Children, 2004, Vol. 1*. www.unicef.org.

———. "United Nations Framework Convention on Climate Change." www.unfccc.org.

———. "World Economic and Social Survey 2005: Financing for Development." www.un.org.

———. *World Investment Report 1994*. New York: United Nations, 1994.

The United Nations Children's Fund. "Health Equity Report 2016." UNICEF and Tulane University, November 2016. www.unicef.org.

The United Nations Conference on Sustainable Development. "Sustainable Development 20 Years on from the Earth Summit." The United Nations, 2012.

United Nations Development Programme. *Human Development Report, 1997*. New York: Oxford University Press.

United Nations General Assembly, *Report of the World Commission on Environment and Development: Our Common Future*, 1987.

United Nations Office for Drug Control and Crime Prevention. *World Drug Report 2000*. New York: Oxford University Press, 2000, Annex 1. www.odccp.org/pdf/world_drug_report2000/report_2001-01-22_1.pdf.

UN-REDD Programme. "Frequently Asked Questions." edited by UNDP and UNEP. FAO, 2014.

"U.S. and Mexican Labor Secretaries Sign Consultation Agreements." *PR News*wire, May 22, 2000.

U.S. Department of State. *1996 Country Reports on Economic Policy and Trade Practices*. January 1997. Available at www.state.gov/www/issues/trade_reports/latin_america99/costarica96.html and www.state.gov/www/issues/economic/trade_reports/latin_america96/panama96.html.

U.S. Trade Representative "Mexico." Foreign Trade Barriers. 2000 National Trade Estimate Report. www.ustr.gov.

Valcarel, Juan Manuel. "Calling Someone in Argentina: Dial M for Monopoly." *Wall Street Journal*, August 16, 1996.

Valdivia, Martin. "Peru: Is Identifying the Poor the Main Problem?" In *Reaching the Poor with Health, Nutrition and Population Services*, ed. Wagstaff A. Gwatkin and A. S. Yazbeck. Washington, D.C.: World Bank, 2005.

Valente, Marcela. "Argentina: The Environmental Costs of Biofuel." *IPS Terraviva Online*, April 21, 2006.

———. "Fighting Chagas Disease, Camera in Hand." *IPS Terraviva Online*, August 30, 2005.

———. "Latin America: End to Subsidies Would Not End Rural Poverty." I*PS Terraviva Online*, December 5, 2005.

Van der Hoeven, Rolph, and Gyorgy Sziraczi. *Lesson from Privatization*. Geneva: International Labour Office, 1997.

Vandermeer, John, and Ivette Perfecto. *Breakfast of Biodiversity: The Truth about Rain Forest Destruction*. Oakland, CA: Institute for Food and Development Policy, 1995.

Van Zyl, Johan, et al. (1995), cited in Binswanger and Deininger. "Explaining Agricultural and Agrarian Policies in Developing Countries." *Journal of Economic Literature* 35(4), March 11, 1997.

Varo, Vicente. "Argentine Stocks Rebound on Budget Cut Accord." *Financial Times*, July 17, 2001.

Veiga, Petro da Motta. "Mercosur: In Search of a New Agenda." *The Challenges of a Project in Crisis*. INTAL-ITD, July 2004. www.iadb.org.

Velzboer-Salcedo, Markjke, and Julie Novick. "Violence against Women in the Americas," *PAHO Perspectives in Health* 5(2) (2000). www.paho.org.

"Venezuela: Accession Will Not Affect Mercosur's Economy." *LatinNews Daily*, January 26, 2006.

"Venezuela: Blitz of Ranch and Industrial Plant Seizures." *Latin American Weekly Report*, September 13, 2005.

"Venezuela on Wrong Path: Seizing Assets of Resource Firms Will Scare Off Foreign Investment." *Calgary Herald* (Alberta), April 10, 2006, A14.

"Venezuela Quits Andean Trade Bloc." *BBC News*, April 20, 2006. news.bbc.co.uk

"Venezuela's Chaotic Land Reform," *The Economist* 374(8409) (January 15, 2005): 34.

Vera-Vassallo, Alejandro C. "Foreign Investment and Competitive Development in Latin America and the Caribbean." *CEPAL Review* 60 (December 1996).

Verhovek, Sam Howe. "Pollution Problems Fester South of the Border." *New York Times*, July 4, 1998. Online edition.

Vetter, Stephen G. "The Business of Grassroots Development." *Grassroots Development* 19(2) (1995): 2–12.

Villa, L. L. "Cervical Cancer in Latin America and the Caribbean: the Problem and the Way to Solutions." *Cancer Epidemiol Biomarkers* (9), September 21, 2012: 1409–13. doi: 10.1158/1055-9965.EPI-12-0147.

Villarreal, M. Angeles. "Mexico's Free Trade Agreement." Congressional Research Service, April 25, 2017. www.fas.org.

Villarreal, M. Angeles. "Trade Integration in the Americas." Congressional Research Service Report RL33162, November 22, 2005. Washington D.C.: Library of Congress. www.opencrs.cdt.org.

Vives, Antonio. *Private Infrastructure: Ten Commandments for Sustainability*. The IADB, Sustainable Development Department, February 1997. www.iadb.org.

Vogel, Thomas T., Jr. "Venezuela Privatization Proves Paltry." *Wall Street Journal*, July 17, 1996.

Vosti, Stephen A., Evaldo Munoz Braz, Chantal Line Carpentier, Marcus D'Olveira, and Julie Witcover. "Rights to Forest Products, Deforestation and Smallholder Income: Evidence from the Western Brazilian Amazon." *World Development* 31(11) (November 2003): 1889–1901.

Wacziarg, Romain, and Karen Horn Welch. *Trade Liberalization and Growth: New Evidence*. National Bureau of Economic Research Working Paper 10152, December 2003.

Wade, Robert. "The Asian Crisis and the Global Economy: Causes, Consequences and Cure." *Current History*, November 1998.

Wallace, Robert Bruce. "Policies of Protection in Mexico." In *Protection and Economic Development in Mexico*, ed. Adriaan ten Kate and Robert Bruce Wallace. Hampshire, UK: Gower, 1980.

Walsh, Sharon. "Tyson Foods to Buy Competitor Hudson; Rival Had Been Hit by Massive Beef Recall." *Washington Post*, September 5, 1997.

Wampler, Brian, and Mike Touchton. "Brazil Let Its Citizens Make Decisions about City Budgets. Here's What Happened." *Washington Post*, January 2014.

Warburg Dillon Read. "The Impact of the Asian Crisis on Latin America." Fax newsletter, July 14, 1998, 2.

———. *The Latin American Adviser*. Fax newsletter, February 1998.

———. *The Latin American Adviser*. Fax newsletter, July 9, 1998.

Warburton, Eve. "A Right, a Need, or an Economic Good? Debating our Relationship to Water," News from the Columbia Earth Institute Water Center blog, June 6, 2011.

Warts, Tom. "Protection and Private Foreign Investment." In *Protection and Economic Development in Mexico*, ed. Adriaan ten Kate and Robert Bruce Wallace. Hampshire, UK: Gower, 1980.

"Water Works in Buenos Aires." *The Economist*, February 24, 1996.

Weeks, John. "Macroeconomic Adjustment." As noted in *Economic and Social Progress in Latin America 1992 Report*, special section, "Latin America's Export of Manufactured Goods." Washington, D.C.: IADB, 1992.

———. "The Manufacturing Sector in Latin America and the New Economic Model." In *The New Economic Model in Latin America and Its Impact on Income Distribution and Poverty*, ed. Victor Bulmer-Thomas. New York: St. Martin's, 1996.

Weersma-Haworth, Teresa S. "Export Processing Free Zones as Export Strategy." In *Latin America's New Insertion in the World Economy*, ed. Ruud Buitelaar and Pitou Van Dijck. New York: St. Martin's, 1996.

Weforum, Bain & Company, and World Bank. "Enabling Trade: Valuing Growth Opportunities 2013." World Economic Forum, 2013. www3.weforum.org.

Weinberg, Bill. *War on the Land: Ecology and Politics in Central America*. Atlantic Highlands, NJ: Zed, 1991.

Weiner, Tim. "Terrific News in Mexico City: Air Is Sometimes Breathable." *New York Times*, January 5, 2001.

Weintraub, Sidney. "Ideological Generalizations about Financial Rescue Packages." *Issues in International Political Economy*, No. 15. Washington, D.C.: CSIS, 2004.

———. "In the Debate about NAFTA, Just the Facts, Please." *Wall Street Journal*, June 20, 1997, A19.

Welch, John. "The New Face of Latin America: Financial Flows, Markets, and Institutions in the 1990s." *Journal of Latin American Studies* 25 (1993): 1–24.

Werther Jr., William B., and David Chandler. "Strategic Corporate Social Responsibility as Global Brand Insurance." *Business Horizons* 48 (2005): 317–324.

"Western Union Launches a New Product Called Quick Pay." *Metropole Haiti*, July 9, 2015. www.metropolehaiti.com.

"Western Union and Sogexpress Innovate: Remittances to Fund Renewable Energy in Haiti." *Investor Relations*, July 23, 2015. www.ir.westernunion.com.

Weston Phippen, J. "Brazil Declares an End to its Zika Emergency." *The Atlantic*, May 12, 2017. www.theatlantic.com.

Weyland, Kurt. *The Politics of Market Reform in Fragile Democracies*. Princeton, NJ: Princeton University Press, 2002.

Weymouth, Stephen, and Richard Feinberg. "National Competitiveness in Comparative Perspective: Evidence from Latin America." *Latin American Politics and Society* 53(3), Fall 2011: 141–159.

Wheeler, David, *Racing to the Bottom? Foreign Investment and Air Pollution in Developing Countries*. Washington, D.C.: World Bank, Environmental Division.

White, Allen T. "Venezuela's Organic Law: Regulating Pollution in an Industrializing Country." *Environment* 33(7) (September 1991).

"Why Corporate Governance." IFC. www.ifc.org.

Wiggins, Steve. "Agriculture and Rural Development Reconsidered." IFAD 2016: 36.

Wiggins, Steve, Johann Kirsten, and Luis Llambí. "The Future of Small Farms." *World Development* 38(10), October 2010: 1341–1348.

Wigley, T. M. L., and D. S. Schimal, eds. *The Carbon Cycle*. Cambridge, UK: Cambridge University Press, 2000: 258–276.

Wilber, Charles K. *The Political Economy of Development and Underdevelopment*. New York: Random House, 1973.

Wilber, Charles K., and Steven Francis. "The Methodological Basis of Hirschman's Development Economics: Pattern Modeling vs. General Laws." *World Development* 14(2), special issue (February 1986): 181–191.

Williams, Frances, and Michael Mann. "Delay Threat to US and EU Banana Deal." *Financial Times*, August 1, 2000.

Williamson, John. *Dollarization Does Not Make Sense Everywhere*. Institute for International Economics, 2001. Available at www.iie.com.

———. "What Should the Bank Think about the Washington Consensus?" Institute for International Economics paper prepared as a background to the World Bank's 2000 World Development Report. July 1999. www.iie.com.

———. "What Washington Means by Policy Reform." In *Latin American Adjustment: How Much Has Happened?*, ed. J. Williamson. Washington, D.C.: Institute for International Economics, 1990.

Willis, Eliza, Christopher da C. B. Garman, and Stephan Haggard. "The Politics of Decentralization in Latin America." *Latin American Research Review* 43(1) (1999).

Wills, Rick. "Mexico Beef Dispute." *New York Times*, August 3, 1999.

Winters, L. Allan. "Assessing Regional Integration." In *Trade: Towards Open Regionalism*, Proceedings of the 1997 World Bank Conference on Development in Latin America and the Caribbean. Washington, D.C.: World Bank, 1998.

Wise, Carol. "Latin America and the State-Market Debate: Beyond Stylized Facts." Paper presented to the Latin American Studies Association, March 16, 2000.

Wolfensohn, James D. *Building an Equitable World—Address to the Board of Governors*. Prague: The World Bank Group, September 26, 2000.

———. Remarks to the Board of Governors of the World Bank Group, October 1, 1996. Available at the LEXIS-NEXIS database.

Wolff, Laurence. "Educational Assessments in Latin America: Current Progress and Future Challenges." *Partnership for Educational Revitalization in the Americas*. June 1998. Online publication, available at www.preal.cl.

Wolff, Laurence, Juan Carlos Navarro, and Pablo González. *Private Education and Public Policy in Latin America*. Washington, D.C.: PREAL, 2005.

Wolff, Laurence, Ernesto Schiefelbeing, and Jorge Valenzuela. *Improving the Quality of Primary Education in Latin America and the Caribbean: Toward the 21st Century*. Washington, D.C.: World Bank, 1994.

Wood, Bill, and Harry Anthony Patrinos. "Urban Bolivia." In *Indigenous People and Poverty in Latin America*, ed. George Psacharopoulos and Harry Anthony Patrinos. Washington, D.C.: World Bank, 1994.

Woodruff, David, Ian Katz, and Keith Naughton. "VW's Factory of the Future." *BusinessWeek*, October 7, 1996.

World Bank. "Agricultural Insurance in Latin America—Developing the Market." International Finance Corporation Report No. 61963, 2010. www.ifc.org.

———. "Agricultural Price Distortions, Inequality, and Poverty." World Bank, 2010.

———. "Agriculture in Nicaragua: Promoting Competitiveness and Stimulating Broad-Based Growth." World Bank, 2003.

———. "Beyond the Washington Consensus: Institutions Matter. Regional Brief." World Bank, 1998. Available at www.worldbank.org.

———. "Challenges & Opportunities for Gender Equality in Latin America and the Caribbean." World Bank, 2003. www.worldbank.org.

———. *Climate Change, Disaster Risk, and the Urban Poor*. Washington, D.C.: The International Bank for Reconstruction and Development (2012).

———. "The Costs of Corruption." World Bank, April 2004. www.web.worldbank.org.

———. "Data Indicators." World Bank, 2014. http://data.worldbank.org/indicator.

———. "Doing Business 2017." World Bank, October 25, 2016.

———. *Economic Growth and Returns to Work*. Washington, D.C.: World Bank, 1995.

———. "Ecuador—Public Enterprise Reform and Privatization Technical Assistance Project." World Bank, June 1999.

———. "Ecuador Public Information Document." World Bank, 2006. www.worldbank.org.

———. "Education Program Objectives." www.worldbank.org.

———. *Energy Efficiency and Conservation in the Developing World: The World Bank's Role*. Washington, D.C.: World Bank, 1993.

———. *Environment and Development in Latin America and the Caribbean: The Role of the World Bank*. Washington, D.C.: World Bank, 1996.

———. "Fighting Poverty in Latin America and the Caribbean." The World Bank Group, September 2000.

———. *Global Development Finance 1997*. Washington, D.C.: World Bank, 1997.

———. *Global Development Finance 1998*. Washington, D.C.: World Bank, 1998.

———. *Global Development Finance 1999*. Washington, D.C.: World Bank, 1999.

———. *Global Development Finance 2004*. Washington, D.C.: World Bank, 2004.

———. "Global Economic Prospects 2005: Trade, Regionalism and Development." World Bank Annual Report 2005. www.worldbank.org.

———. "Global Harnessing Cyclical Gains for Development." Global Development Finance 2004, World Bank, Washington, D.C.

———. "Government of Ecuador Program Information Document, Health Insurance Project, Approved." January 19, 2006. www.worldbank.org.

———. "Guatemala Improves Maternal-Infant Health and Nutrition." World Bank, August 7, 2014. www.worldbank.org.

———. "Guatemala—Infrastructure, Privatization, Technical Assistance Loan." World Bank, April 1997.

———. *IFC: Making a Positive Difference for Sustainable Development.* Issue Brief. Washington, D.C.: The World Bank Group.

———. "Inequality in Latin America and the Caribbean: Breaking with History." Draft publication, October 2003.

———. *Labor and Economic Reforms in Latin America and the Caribbean: Regional Perspectives on World Development Report.* Washington, D.C.: World Bank, 1995.

———. "Latin America: Facing Climate Change with Green Innovation." World Bank, September 25, 2013. www.worldbank.org.

———. "Latin America: Time to Put a Stop to Road Deaths." World Bank, May 10, 2013. www.worldbank.org.

———. "Lessons from NAFTA for Latin America and Caribbean." World Bank, 2003.

———. "Measuring Poverty." World Bank, 2018. www.web.worldbank.org.

———. *Meeting the Infrastructure Challenge in Latin America and the Caribbean.* Washington, D.C.: World Bank, 1995.

———. "Mexico—Municipal Development in Rural Areas Project." July 2002. www.worldbank.org.

———. "Mexico: Schools without Leaks." World Bank external news, August 29, 2005. www.worldbank.org.

———. "A Model from Mexico for the World." World Bank, November 19, 2014.

———. Other Financial Mechanisms: Debt-for-Nature Swaps and Social Funds. Available at www.worldbank.org.

———. "Poverty & Equality Data FAQs." World Bank, September 30, 2015. www.web.worldbank.org.

———. "Poverty Reduction and the World Bank: Progress in Fiscal 1996 and 1997." www.worldbank.org.

———. *Privatization Principles and Practice.* IFC Lessons of Experience Series. Washington, D.C.: World Bank, 1995.

———. "Reaching the Rural Poor: A Rural Development Strategy for the Latin American and Caribbean Region." Box A4.1, Public/Private Partnerships in Research and Extension Projects, 2002.

———. "Remittances to Latin America Grow, but Mexico Bucks the Trend Faced with the US Slowdown." World Bank, October 8, 2013. www.worldbank.org.

———. *Rural Development: From Vision to Action.* Environmentally and Socially Sustainable Development Studies and Monographs Series No. 12. Washington, D.C.: World Bank, 1997.

———. *Rural Poverty Alleviation in Brazil: Toward an Integrated Strategy.* Washington, D.C.: World Bank, 2003.

———. "Shifting Gears to Accelerate Shared Prosperity in Latin America and the Caribbean." World Bank, June 2013. www.worldbank.org.

———. "Tariff Rate, Applied, Weighted Mean, All Products." http://data.worldbank.org/indicator/TM.TAX.MRCH.WM.AR.ZS

———. *Ten Things You Never Knew about the World Bank*. Issue Brief. Washington, D.C.: The World Bank Group.

———. *Trade: Towards Open Regionalism*. Proceedings of the 1997 World Bank Conference on Development in Latin America and the Caribbean. Washington, D.C.: World Bank, 1998.

———. *Update on Implementation of HIPC Debt Relief Programs and Poverty Reduction Strategy Papers*. Press Conference. Washington, D.C.: The World Bank Group, April 23, 2001.

———. "WDI Poverty Figures." World Bank.

———. *World Debt Tables*. Washington, D.C. World Bank, various years. "World Bank and the IMF Agree on Debt Relief for Poor Countries."

———. *World Development Indicators, 1997*. Washington, D.C.: World Bank 1997.

———. *World Development Report 1988/9*. New York: Oxford University Press/World Bank, 1989.

———. *World Development Report 1992*. New York: Oxford University Press/World Bank, 1992.

———. *World Development Report 1994*. New York: Oxford University Press/World Bank, 1994.

———. *World Development Report 1995*. New York: Oxford University Press/World Bank, 1995.

World Bank Poverty Net. "Too Much or Too Little Water Can Spell Disaster in the World's Poorest Nations." World Bank, March 17, 2006. www.worldbank.org.

World Bank Staff and IMF Staff. *100 Percent Debt Cancellation? A Response from the IMF and the World Bank*. Washington, D.C.: IMF, July 2001.

World Commission on Environment and Development. *Our Common Future*. Oxford: Oxford University Press, 1987.

World Health Organization. "Denge and Severe Dengue." World Health Organization, last modified March 2016. www.who.int.

———. "Fair but Flawed: Brazil's Health System Reaches out to the Poor." *Bulletin of World Health Organization* 86(4), April 2008: 241–320. www.who.int.

———. "The History of Zika Virus." WHO. www.who.int.

———. *Integration of Health Care Delivery: Report of a WHO Study Group*. WHO Technical Report Series 861. Geneva: World Health Organization, 1996.

———. "Preventing Chronic Diseases: A Vital Investment 2005." www.who.org.

———. "Report on the Global HIV/AIDS Epidemic, June 1998."1 Geneva: UNAIDS, 1998. Available at www.who.int/emc-hiv.

———. "Strategic Direction for Chagas Disease Research." www.who.org.

World Press Review. "Brazil's Amazon Rainforest Twice As Deforested As Estimated." October 21, 2005, newsbureau@worldbank.org.

World Resources Institute. *World Resources: A Guide to the Global Environment 1996–7*. New York: Oxford University Press, 1997.

———. *World Resources, 1994–5*. New York: Oxford University Press, 1995.

World Trade Organization. "Trade Facilitation." WTO Committee Meeting, May 16, 2017. www.wto.org.

———. "Trade in Value Added and Global Value Chains." Data from WTO Statistics.

———. "World Merchandise Trade in 1996 by Region and Leading Trader." *International Trade*, July 30, 1997. www.wto.org.

"World Water Day: Latin America Leads in Water Management but Inequalities in Access Remain." *The World Bank Economic Review*, March 22, 2013. www.worldbank.org.

Worley, Heidi. "Chronic Diseases Beleaguer Developing Countries." Population Reference Bureau, January 2006.

Wrobel, Paulo. "A Free Trade Area of the Americas in 2005?" *International Affairs* 74(3) (1998).

"WTO Adopts Panel Findings against Mexican Measure on High-Fructose Corn Syrup." Press Release. Office of the United States Trade Representative. Washington, D.C.: World Trade Organization, February 28, 2000. www.iadb.org.

Yeager, Timothy. "Encomienda or Slavery? The Spanish Crown's Choice of Labor Organization in Sixteenth-Century Spanish America." *Journal of Economic History* 55(4) (December 1995).

Yergin, Daniel. *The Prize: The Epic Quest for Oil, Money, and Power*. New York: Simon and Schuster, 1991.

Young, Kate. *Planning Development with Women: Making a World of Difference*. New York: St. Martin's, 1993.

Zadek, Simon. "The Logic of Collaborative Governance: Corporate Responsibility, Accountability and the Social Contract." Corporate Social Responsibility Initiative Working Paper No. 17. Harvard University: John F. Kennedy School of Government, January 2006.

Zbinden, Simon, and David Lee. "Paying for Environmental Services: An Analysis of Participation in Costa Rica's PSA Program." *World Development* 33(2) (February 2005): 255–272.

Zibechi, Raúl. "Paraguay: Women at the Center of Resistance." *CETRI*, January 10, 2014.

Zimbalist, Andrew. "Costa Rica." In *Struggle against Dependence: Nontraditional Export Growth in Central America and the Caribbean*, ed. Eva Paus. Boulder, CO: Westview, 1988.

Zoninsein, Jonas. *The Economic Case for Combating Racial and Ethnic Exclusion in Latin America and Caribbean Countries*. Research Report. Washington, D.C.: IADB, May 2001.

Zuckerman, Laurence. "In South America Car Makers See One Big Showroom." *New York Times*, April 25, 1997.

Index

Note: Page numbers in *italics* refer to pages where tables, boxes, and figures appear.